Weaving New Worlds

Weaving New Worlds

SOUTHEASTERN CHEROKEE WOMEN

AND THEIR BASKETRY

by Sarah H. Hill

The University of North Carolina Press

CHAPEL HILL AND LONDON

The paper in this book meets the guidelines for permanence and durability
of the Committee on Production Guidelines for Book Longevity
of the Council on Library Resources.

Library of Congress Cataloging-in-Publication Data

Hill, Sarah H.
    Weaving new worlds : Southeastern Cherokee women and their
basketry / by Sarah H. Hill
        p.   cm.
    Includes bibliographical references (p.   ) and index.
    ISBN 0-8078-2345-7 (cloth : alk. paper). — ISBN 0-8078-4650-3
(pbk. : alk. paper)
    1. Cherokee women.   2. Cherokee baskets.   3. Cherokee Indians—
History.   4. Human ecology—Southern States—History.   I. Title.
E99.C5H68   1997
746.41′2′0899755—DC21   96-47882
                                                                    CIP

Publication of this work was aided by a generous grant
from the Z. Smith Reynolds Foundation.

01   00   99   98   97   5   4   3   2   1

In Memory of Ben

Contents

Acknowledgments
xi

Introduction
xv

Prologue
1

Chapter 1. Rivercane
35

Chapter 2. White Oak
110

Chapter 3. Honeysuckle
185

Chapter 4. Red Maple
254

Epilogue
314

Notes
327

Bibliography
373

Index
405

Maps

✤ ✤ ✤

1. Cherokee Lands, 1720

xxiv

2. Cherokee Settlements, 1720–1730

68

3. Cherokee Land Losses, 1721–1819

75

4. Cherokee Settlements in
Western North Carolina after Removal

138

5. Cherokee Lands and
the Great Smoky Mountains National Park, 1990

277

Acknowledgments

Writing this book has been like weaving a basket. Gathering and preparing the material has taken time; the creativity and experience of others, past and present, have been invaluable. When I expressed my intent to write a history of Southeastern Cherokee women, teacher and friend Allen Tullos encouraged and inspired me. He also gave me the telephone number of Rayna Green, who suggested basketry as an avenue for research. To each I am profoundly grateful.

Jim Roark and Brad Shore advised and nudged me in early stages, and their questions remained as signposts long after our work together. Colleagues who generously lent ears, eyes, and minds along the way include Gretchen Maclachlan, Andy Ambrose, Rose Cannon, Dale Rosengarten, Suzanne Marshall, Margaret Brown, Kent Leslie, Susan McGrath, Amanda Gable, Tim Bookout, Saralyn Chestnut, and Laverne Byas-Smith. Many Cherokee scholars have influenced and helped me. Among them, I am particularly indebted to Tom Hatley, Theda Perdue, Ray Fogelson, John Finger, and the late John Witthoft.

To locate materials, I called and visited numerous institutions where I found knowledgeable staff members who responded to repeated requests. For their assistance with documents and artifacts in various government repositories I express special appreciation to Gayle Peters and Maryann Hawkins of the East Point Federal Records Center, Tim Wehrcamp of the National Archives, Deborah Wood and Felicia Pickering of the National Museum of Natural History, Nancy Rosoff of the National Museum of the American Indian, and Kitty Manscill of the Great Smoky Mountains National Park Archives.

While negotiating the intricacies of university holdings, particular help came from William R. Erwin Jr. in the Special Collections Department of Duke University's Perkins Library, the staff of Hampton University Museum and Archives, the staff of the North Carolina and Southern Historical Collections of the University of North Carolina at Chapel Hill, and George Frizzell in Western Carolina University's Special Collections Library.

Utilizing state collections required special assistance, and I owe thanks to the Georgia Department of Archives and History, the Historical Society of Pennsylvania, the New York State Museum, Martha Battle of the North Carolina Museum of History, the North Carolina Department of Cultural Resources, the Oklahoma Historical Society, and the Archives and Manuscript Division of the Tennessee State Library.

For guidance in locating particular resources I am grateful to Joan Greene at the Museum of the Cherokee Indian, Richard Starbuck of the Moravian Archives in Salem, North Carolina, Vernon Nelson of the Moravian Archives in Bethlehem, Pennsylvania, Susan Drydopple of the Moravian Historical Society, Daniel McPike of the Gilcrease Museum, Sara Irwin of the Philbrook Museum, John Aubrey and Helen Tanner of the Newberry Library, and Martin Leavitt of the American Philosophical Society.

Locating, researching, and photographing baskets woven by Cherokee women has indebted me to Jonathan King of the British Museum, Laila Williamson of the American Museum of Natural History, Joyce Herrold of the Denver Museum of Natural History, Susan Otto and Dawn Scher Thomae of the Milwaukee Public Museum, Nina Cummings of the Field Museum of Natural History, Julie Droke of the Oklahoma University Museum of Natural History, Lucy Fowler Williams of the University of Pennsylvania Museum of Archaeology and Anthropology, Jefferson Chapman of the University of Tennessee's Frank H. McClung Museum, Beverlye Hancock at Wake Forest University's Museum of Anthropology, Lisa Blalock of the Philbrook Museum of Art, Martha Hill of Yale University's Peabody Museum of Anthropology, Frankie Mewborn and Jeff Stancill of the Chief Vann House Historic Site, Tom Underwood of the Medicine Man Gift Shop, Pat Hall of the New Echota Historic Site, and Bill Morphew and Marion Ingram of Robbinsville. Photographers Ron Ruehl of Significance Communications, William F. Hull of the Atlanta Historical Society, and William K. Sacco of Yale University's Peabody Museum traveled many miles with cumbersome equipment to photograph baskets at my request. Their labor has made a singular contribution to this publication.

Many members of the Eastern Band of Cherokee Indians have contributed generously and courteously to my understanding of their history, landscapes, and traditions of basketry. Foremost are the basketweavers, including the late Dora Bigmeat, Eva Bigwitch, Rowena Bradley, Annie French, Emmaline Garrett, Dinah George, Lucy Ben George, Louise Goings, Annie James, Bessie Long, Betty Lossiah, Lucille Lossiah, Mattie Panther, Martha Lossiah Ross, Emily Smith, Amanda Smoker, Dolly Taylor, Emma Taylor, Joyce Taylor, Shirley Taylor, Martha Wachacha, Mary Wade, the late Alice Walkingstick, Elsie Watty, Agnes Welch, Carol Welch, Dinah Wolfe, and Eva Wolfe. I express my deep appreciation for their help, in equal measure with great respect for their weaving.

On Qualla Boundary and in the community of Snowbird I have benefited from the kindness of Lucille Beck, Ken Blankenship, Mollie Blankenship, Jackie Bradley, Mary Bradley, Reva Bradley, Robert and Jean Bushyhead, Lois Calonaheskie, the late Edna Chickalilly, Mary and G. B. Chiltoskey, Jim Cooper, Myrtle Cooper, Betty DuPree, Buddy Guess, Helen Houser, Gene Jackson, Marie Junaluska, Posey Long, Driver Pheasant, the late Mary Jo Plott, Robin Swayney, and the late Maggie Wachacha.

It has been a pleasure to work with the University of North Carolina Press, where David Perry has been both shepherd and friend and Mary Caviness has combined meticulous editing with sensitive reading. Jeff McMichael of the Georgia State University Cartography Laboratory undertook the painstaking task of preparing the maps. My research was supported in part by a fellowship at the Newberry Library, whose incomparable resources enriched my thinking.

Throughout the course of this study Penny Smith has stood beside me, lending invaluable assistance and support, advice and insight, and a sense of joy in the undertaking. From the beginning she understood the importance of a book about women and their work. She read every draft, explored every map, and examined every photograph. The bibliography is a product of her careful hand and diligent review. When I wanted to investigate trade paths, logging roads, or river channels, Penny was ready with hiking boots and compasses. She delighted equally in archival discoveries and conceptual connections. No challenge diminished her commitment to the project or confidence in my ability. It is an honor to thank her for giving new meaning and power to the blessing of friendship.

To my husband, Harvey, and my children Harvey, Carrie, Roby, and Betsy I express that special gratitude reserved for families of scholars. As all who have preceded me on this path know well, a book becomes a part of the family, requiring time and demanding attention, and perhaps most of all, continually distracting the author. Harvey has shared his life and love with uncommon equilibrium and generosity. There is no one like him.

Introduction

The early spring morning was crisp and clear as I drove into Soco Valley of the Qualla Boundary in western North Carolina to visit Rowena Bradley (b. 1922).[1] One of the best known Cherokee basketweavers, Rowena Bradley speaks often of her mother, who was perhaps the most skilled weaver of her generation. Nancy George Bradley (*Tahtahyeh*) excelled at rivercane basketry, including the intricate and difficult technique known as doubleweave. She also worked with white oak and honeysuckle, sometimes by choice but often by necessity. Rowena Bradley explains that acquiring material for baskets has long been a problem. "You know, at times, she couldn't get cane."[2] Once *Tahtahyeh* even made a few baskets of bamboo. A man from the neighboring town of Bryson, six miles west, "put up a craft shop" and brought her some bamboo. He was curious about the material and the weaver. Rowena Bradley smiles with the memory. "He wanted to know if she could make a basket out of it. Well, she did, but she dyed it just like she does the rivercane."[3]

A craft shop owner from the heart of the Boundary keeps one of Nancy Bradley's bamboo baskets in his extensive private collection. He considers it one of his most valuable acquisitions because of the unusual material and because it was made by Nancy Bradley. "She was the best," he recalls. "Her work was exquisite." Rowena Bradley thinks he bought the basket from the Bryson trader who commissioned it. Over the years, several shop owners have become basket collectors, buying from weavers, customers, and other dealers. Traders are well known to weavers, for they have often been reliable customers.

Nancy Bradley's mother, Mary Dobson (b. ca. 1857) was also an outstanding weaver who worked with rivercane and white oak. She was one of the few weavers able to make white oak baskets with the difficult technique of doubleweave. In the early twentieth century, New York ethnologists came to western North Carolina and purchased some of Dobson's baskets. Subsequent scholars added the work of her daughter to museum collections. Neither woman ever spoke English, yet both expanded their markets well beyond the Qualla Boundary to different regions and urban centers like New York and Washington. Rowena Bradley is the third generation of known weavers in the family, and she sells to collectors throughout the country. Her specialization is rivercane, including doubleweave.

The youngest of eight children, Rowena Bradley lived at home with her parents, Nancy and Henry Bradley, until they died. As a child, she learned to weave by watching her mother. Today she readily recognizes her mother's work in photographs. The subtle and intricate patterns Rowena Bradley weaves are often those her mother used. "A lot of designs I learned from my mother," she says. "I just remember them." She never knew her grandmother nor saw any of her baskets. When I told her about the museums that own her grandmother's work, Rowena Bradley said quietly, "I sure would like to see a picture of one of her baskets."[4] The basket seems to be a representation of her grandmother.

Thinking about the women of these three generations, Mary Dobson, Nancy George Bradley, and Rowena Bradley, I crossed the narrow wooden bridge over Wright's Creek and drove up the steep gravel road to the Bradley house. Built on a cleared knoll, the red brick house sits on the lot in such a way that if you turn slightly to the left, all you can see are the high forested ridges of the surrounding mountains—Jenkins's Divide, Dobson Ridge, Rattlesnake Mountain, Owl Knob, and Thomas Peak. When the trees are in leaf from May through September, you might think there are no houses for miles. The wooded landscape absorbs the sight and sound of almost everything.

That spring morning, Rowena Bradley was sitting in a kitchen chair at the edge of her front yard. Dogs slept fitfully nearby, a cat stared from the window, and hens pecked nervously at the ground. Looking out toward the mountains as she wove a rivercane basket, Rowena Bradley followed with her fingers a pattern that lives in her memory. Occasionally selecting a cane split from a bucket half-filled with water, she wove quickly, scarcely pausing to examine her work. She knew without looking how the pattern would develop in the basket. She has woven rivercane baskets most of her life. The pattern she was weaving is sometimes called "Flowing Water," but the name has no meaning to Rowena Bradley. "Well now," she says, "I'll tell you just like I've told everybody else. My mother never had no names or no meaning to her designs. She just made them. And that's the way I do."[5]

Mary Bradley, who is named for her great-grandmother, emerged from the house, preceded by her four-year-old son, George. Pulling up a chair to sit next to her mother, she held in her arms an infant daughter, Savetta Rowena. Called Yoda by close family members, Savetta Rowena has inherited the names of her Cherokee maternal grandmother and her Mexican paternal grandmother. She was beginning the second week of her life.

Three descending generations, Rowena Bradley, Mary Bradley, and Savetta Rowena Bradley, represent patterns of life as they are formed and transformed. Of the many memories from visits to the Qualla Boundary, this scene remains the most evocative, powerfully fusing and confusing. Three Cherokees, the oldest with braids down to her waist, the youngest in a pink terry cloth playsuit, sit together in front of the home they share in the mountains of western North Carolina. One weaves a basket of rivercane splits that have been dyed with the roots of wildflowers and trees, making patterns learned from her mother. One gently rocks the new baby she holds in her arms. Past, present, and future intertwine.

Among Cherokees, women have been the primary makers and users of baskets. The story of Cherokee basketry and the story of Cherokee women are like a doublewoven basket, interwoven, inseparable, and complex. The stories encompass strands of the past and present, and represent transformations in lives, minds, and landscapes.

For centuries, baskets have been part of Cherokee ceremony, work, and trade. They have been part of Cherokee life and legend. Made from materials gathered from local landscapes, they evoke the world in which their makers live and move and work. Over a period of more than 250 years, Cherokees developed four major basketry traditions, each based on a different material—rivercane, white oak, honeysuckle, and maple. The incorporation of new materials has occurred in the context of lived experience, ecological processes, social conditions, economic circumstances, and historical eras. Each basket is both an individual and a collective expression of these complex processes.

My goal has been to apprehend and comprehend baskets and weavers of baskets in order to illuminate the history of Cherokee women. I have relied on different kinds of sources for the task—written records, woven records, and spoken records. Historical records offer glimpses of women and the worlds they lived in and helped shape. Written documents reveal details about baskets, their materials, decoration, form, functions, use, cost, and value. Baskets themselves have provided perspectives about varying landscapes, economies, and concepts. Conversations with contemporary weavers and buyers of baskets have enriched the more conventional sources. Together, the three kinds of sources disclose transformations in Cherokee worlds.

Basketry is a whole tradition. It includes landscapes where weavers collect materials, the social environment of basket production and use, and the cultural complex that encompasses the past as well as the present. Baskets provide a way to examine Cherokee history because of their antiquity, persistence, and importance among Cherokees. Baskets and changes in traditions of basketry serve as metaphors for historical transformations in subsistence practices, rituals and beliefs, exchange networks, social conditions, and ecological systems.

In these pages, basket materials correspond to chronological periods. The rivercane period extends from the earliest contact with Europeans until the removal, encompassing the era when Cherokees depended most on cane as a basket source. Prior to removal, Cherokee society appears as an integrated whole, richly textured and densely interwoven. Women played complex roles in the matrilineal, matrilocal society that depended on agriculture, gathering, and hunting. They made and used rivercane baskets for daily subsistence activities, for exchange, and for ceremonies and rituals. The invasion of Europeans and subsequent epidemics, wars, and land cessions began to unravel Cherokee society. Women's lives, roles, and environments changed, and in turn, women added different forms to their most enduring tradition. They did not abandon rivercane. Rather, they added to it different customs of weaving and ways of living.

The white oak period begins with removal. Nineteenth-century Cherokees fully incorporated white oak into conventions of rivercane basketry as they recast settlement patterns, subsistence customs, and social systems on the mountainous land that became the reservation. White oak basketry is a European American tradition that includes men as well as women. Among Cherokees, gender roles blurred as men joined women as farmers and weavers of baskets. Access to rivercane, and to all that it had meant, became increasingly limited. By the end of the nineteenth century, white oak baskets were as much an index of change as rivercane baskets had been signifiers of continuity.

The honeysuckle period develops around the turn of the twentieth century, when new federal policies aimed to assimilate Native Americans through formal education, industrial training, and the eradication of native languages and customs. The determination to "solve the Indian problem" by destroying indigenous cultures was accompanied by a growing interest in Native American societies and artifacts. Influenced by the British Arts and Crafts movement, craft revivalists intervened in indigenous cultures to redirect the production of handwork in economically depressed areas. The logging industry turned southward and reshaped Southeastern ecosystems and economies. In this strange combination of genocide and preservation, eroding land and a longing for traditional lifeways, weavers began to make baskets of Japanese honeysuckle vine. This inclusion of a nonindigenous material for baskets and a completely new technique of weaving signifies larger transformations in culture and consciousness and in landscapes where weavers gathered materials. Changing basket forms represent changing concepts.

Baskets, once sturdy, resilient utilitarian wares, became light and colorful decorative items. Weavers did not relinquish rivercane or white oak basketry. Rather, they incorporated a third material and developed a new tradition.

The red maple period includes the New Deal for Indians, a program implemented by the Roosevelt administration and Indian commissioner John Collier, and it follows the development of Cherokee dependence on tourism that has continued through the last decade of the twentieth century. In this era, federal policies trumpeted respect for Native American culture while encouraging those who lived on economically depressed reservations to market themselves as tourist attractions. Cherokees capitalized on their history in order to attract tourists whose images of Indians often were shaped by Hollywood films. Whites leased reservation land parcels to build motor courts and craft shops, employing Cherokees as maids, cooks, or clerks. The Great Smoky Mountains National Park opened adjacent to the Boundary, and a handful of artisans organized a cooperative to market their work year-round. In keeping with changing markets and concepts, baskets in all four materials became highly ornamented market commodities. What had appeared in rivercane as a continuous and internally constructed field gradually became in maple an elaborate design that was externally applied. Reviewed historically, changes in basketry can thus be seen as transformations in culture, landscapes, and consciousness. The inclusion of new materials from the removal to the present testifies to deep levels of social and ecological change. The retention of old materials suggests the persistence of certain values, customs, and concepts.

Baskets have both meaning and reason. The meaning of Cherokee basketry, evident in legend, custom, and history, relates to the role and work of women as the source of food and life, as providers and sustainers for their families. The reason for basketry in the twentieth century is primarily economic. Contemporary women weave beautiful baskets in order to survive in a chronically depressed economy. The examination of basket materials, forms, and functions brings into relief historical processes and illuminates the interrelationships of material objects and the society that produces them. It deepens the significance of basketry as representative of internalized patterns of life and work, of landscapes and tradition. The study raises questions about ecology, technology, economy, and cultural politics. It brings to the foreground the lives and work of women.

Well-known difficulties abound in researching women, Native Americans, and material culture. The direct evidence, Cherokee baskets, is quite variable. Few baskets have survived from the eighteenth century. Perhaps a dozen remain from the early nineteenth century, before removal. These beautiful and intricate containers are subtle and invaluable records of women as shapers of their landscapes through repeated exploitation of certain vegetation. They document women's technological skill and inherited wisdom. They inscribe a text that is essentially Cherokee and specifically female. Toward the end of the nineteenth century, basket collectors discovered the Cherokees, and accordingly, from the turn of that century to the present, many baskets of rivercane, white oak, and honeysuckle can be found in collections in Oklahoma, New York, Pennsylvania, Wisconsin, Illinois, Colorado, Washington, D.C., Tennessee, and North Carolina.

Written records present other challenges. Early documents give relatively full accounts of some aspects of Native American lives. Eighteenth- and early-nineteenth-century naturalists like John Lawson, Mark Catesby, William Bartram, and André and F. A. Michaux left meticulous details about what they found interesting. Their descriptions of Native American physical environments provide essential contextual information. And traders who lived among Cherokees in the eighteenth century left lively records with their impressions of daily life and long-held customs.

As the nineteenth century began, however, those most often involved in recording the Cherokee world were those most committed to changing it—missionaries, teachers, and government officials. The nature of evidence begins to shift in two directions, each becoming more explicitly paternalistic. Records of missionaries and schoolteachers detail rapid rates of change in Cherokee society. Eager to convince the federal government that Cherokees were fast becoming "civilized," these cultural interveners emphasized what mimicked most closely the society of whites. Their documents are permeated with reports of intermarriage with whites, of literacy, of the acquisition of domestic arts such as spinning and weaving, the adoption of Christianity, ownership of black slaves, facility with the English language, and the abandonment of hunting or "the chase."

The reports are not inaccurate. At the geographical margins of the Cherokee Nation, cultural expressions actually were changing rapidly. Cherokees who interacted most with whites appeared to become most like them. Those who lived closer to one another and to other Southeastern Indians, however, tended to retain and reinforce customs and beliefs.[6] Few records describe Cherokees who lived in the mountainous interior of the Southeast, where whites chose not to settle. The missionary and agency reports we have for this period leave an incomplete picture.

The second primary source of information about preremoval Cherokees is government documents. These, however, are most concerned with politics. They focus on organized resistance to the ongoing policy of Indian removal, giving little information about women and almost none about their transforming work in ecosystems.

Following removal, approximately 1,000 Cherokees remained in western North Carolina. The fullest records of their daily lives are store accounts kept by their white business agent, William H. Thomas. Thousands of pages record the purchases of women and men, and document the importance of bartered labor in their cash-poor economies. Contrary to widely shared assumptions, baskets seldom appear in store accounts or inventories, suggesting that women established a household-to-household system of exchange using their most utilitarian wares.

At the end of the nineteenth century, the federal government pursued its national reservation policy and a new interest developed in Native American culture. As reformers worked for the assimilation of Indians into white society, ethnologists and museum representatives began to collect artifacts and information from Native American tribes.

In 1888, James Mooney inaugurated a century of anthropological fieldwork with the Eastern Band of Cherokees. For the last hundred years, scholars and students have gathered myths and medical formulas, photographed dances and ball games, interpreted social systems and subsistence practices. Some Cherokees say that whites tried to get rid of them throughout most of their history, but now, they joke, whites cannot seem to get enough of them. The Tribal Council of the Eastern Band, however, passed an ordinance requiring all researchers to obtain council permission to conduct studies on the Qualla Boundary.

Anthropological reports provide much useful information about particular aspects of Cherokee life. Mooney's priceless collection of myths and medical formulas, although fragmentary, suggests a culture that had been fully integrated, densely interwoven, and highly structured. Frank Speck came from the University of Pennsylvania for field work in 1913, 1922, 1928–31, and 1934–35 and published the first examination of Southeastern Cherokee baskets. John Witthoft's subsequent research on economic botany has been particularly illuminating for this study. Missing from most reports, however, is information about women. Even Speck's basket publication refers only once to women, when he identifies baskets as "receptacles . . . particularly required by women."[7]

The richest information has come directly from women. Interviews with Cherokee weavers over the course of this study have been invaluable, and their kindness has made the journey immeasurably richer. In talking with them, I heard repeatedly that they weave baskets in order to make money, pay bills, help their families, support themselves, and raise children. I also heard about baskets that didn't "look right" and had to be redone, about "rough" baskets and "fine" baskets, about colors that didn't "look good," and about baskets that were, or were not, "well-made." A deep current of concepts about basketry underlies and nourishes such expressions. Some weavers said that they feel lonely when they have sold all their baskets, and others commented that they think of their mothers when they weave. Many like to weave at night, when it's quiet and they feel peaceful. For some, basketry resonates with deeper meaning; for others, basketry is an economic enterprise. Almost all remember the first basket they ever made and sold, usually for less than a dollar.

Without fail, they tell me that they recognize their own work and that of their mothers and sisters and daughters wherever they see it, in photographs, in shops, and in homes, even after periods of up to thirty years. Louise Goings says that "everybody has their own way of making stuff."[8] "Their own way" includes details such as basket shapes, split widths, organization of colors, and varieties of ornamentation like rim bindings and curls. There is also something ineffable about their work that basketmakers can't define. In the long run, as one explains, "even my own baskets, I know, they're not two made alike."[9]

In a basket, there is both something very personal and something related to a collective consciousness. Contemporary weaver Agnes Welch says that she makes a basket the way she does because "that's how it is supposed to look."[10] My effort in this work has been to bring together the multiple strands that underlie the consciousness of "how it is supposed to look," and by so doing to come closer to an understanding of these remarkable women and transformations in their worlds.

Weaving New Worlds

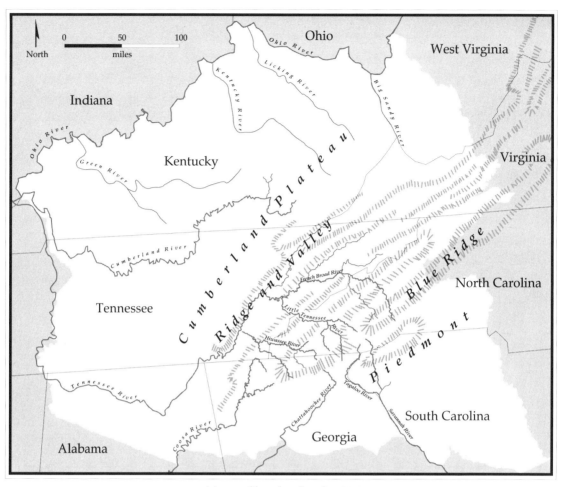

Map 1. Cherokee Lands, 1720

Prologue

How the World Was Made
[As Told by Swimmer and John Ax]

The earth is a great island floating in a sea of water, and suspended at each of the four cardinal points by a cord hanging down from the sky vault, which is of solid rock. When the world grows old and worn out, the people will die and the cords will break and let the earth sink down into the ocean, and all will be water again. The Indians are afraid of this.

When all was water, the animals were above in *Galun-lati*, beyond the arch; but it was very much crowded and they were wanting more room. They wondered what was below the water, and at last *Da-yuni-si*, Beaver's Grandchild, the little Water-beetle, offered to go and see if it could learn. It darted in every direction over the surface of the water, but could find no firm place to rest. Then it dived to the bottom and came up with some soft mud, which began to grow and spread on every side until it became the island which we call the earth. It was afterwards fastened to the sky with four cords, but no one remembers who did this.

At first the earth was flat and very soft and wet. The animals were anxious to get down and sent out different birds to see if it was yet dry, but they found no place to alight and came back again to *Galun-lati*. At last it seemed to be time, and they sent out the Buzzard and told him to go and make ready for them. This was the Great Buzzard, the father of all the buzzards we see now. He flew all over the earth, low down near the ground, and it was still soft. When he reached the Cherokee country, he was very tired, and his wings began to flap and strike the ground, and wherever they struck the earth there was a valley, and where they turned up again there was a mountain. When the animals above saw this, they were afraid that the whole world would be mountainous, so they called him back, but the Cherokee country remains full of mountains to this day.[1]

In the mountains of western North Carolina in 1888, Cherokee elders Swimmer (*Ayun-ini*) and John Ax (*Itagu-nabi*) recounted for anthropologist James Mooney a fragment of their ancient story of creation. The story recalls a troubled time when the world they knew had grown too crowded and all creatures felt concerned, apprehensive, even fearful. Crowded times meant worn-out fields and diminishing game, shrinking forests and fewer plants, and inadequate valleys for sowing and meadows for gathering. It was a time when camps and towns of enemies seemed too close and resources seemed too few. Everyone felt a need to move, but there was no place left to go.

Then, one of the smallest among them performed the task that was most natural, and so was best. Dropping from the sky vault like an infant from its mother's womb, the Grandchild crossed from one world to another, from the firmament that was home through the primordial sea of mystery to the depths of the vast, dark waters beneath everything, to find new soil that could be a new home. The tiny Grandchild brought from the watery deep such a meager and formless piece of land that some were surely skeptical that it could ever be enough. But then, like tended crops and nurtured children, the piece of earth transformed, spreading across the sea until it grew large enough to support all those who watched anxiously from a distance. They saw mountains arching so high they could have been shaped only by the sweeping wings of one unafraid of death, the great healer, the Buzzard. They saw narrow valleys slicing between mountains like furrows in cornfields. The island looked like the whole world to them. It became the Cherokee homeland.

Following the creation of the island home, one who was never named wove cords so strong they could hold all the world in place. They dropped from the sky like umbilical cords, lifelines that fastened the homeland at four corners, tied it to the sky vault, and held it secure. Like a basket, the Cherokee earth was supported by woven strands that connected it to another world, a place beyond sight and touch, where the past and ancestral beings dwelled. Back beyond the edge of their collective memory, weaving held together the world of Cherokee people. Weaving secured their world for so long that no one could remember how it began or who wove the first strands. When the weaving gives way, according to the Cherokee story of creation, they will die as a people and the world they know will disappear.

Water and Mountains: *ama, katu-si*

Water in the Southern Appalachians seeps and drips, runs and falls from streams, creeks, and rivers, backtracking upon itself to twice and thrice water every physiographic zone. It has invited and encouraged human settlement since as early as 10,000 B.C. Ancestors of the Cherokee people chose for their settlement areas the rivers and tributaries of the Southern Appalachians, where all forms of waterways flow. Scores of rivers, streams, creeks, falls, cascades, shoals, pools, and swamps create bottomlands, floodplains, and rich alluvial valleys, enhancing soil productivity, encouraging generation and growth, inviting game.

To Cherokees, among all spiritual forces none was more important than water, the river *Yunwi Gunahita*, the Long Person. Going to water (*amo-hi atsv-sdi*) was an activity and ritual that preceded or followed every important event. Going to water brought purification and rebirth. Regularly during pregnancy, following the birth of a child, and after monthly menses, women went to water to begin new life. Mothers took newborn infants to water to invest them with purifying strength. Before competitive games and before and after warfare, men went to water for purification and protection. The sick or wounded went to water to heal and cleanse their spirits. Cherokees who returned from captivity went to water before reentering society. At each new moon, families went to water to maintain spiritual health. Entire towns and villages went to water before agricultural harvests. By going to water, Cherokees experienced renewal and regeneration, and preparation for the future. Their relationship to water was ancient and spiritual, involving attitudes toward lovers and enemies, families and priests, toward processes of birth, death, illness, and healing, toward fortune in games, hunting, love, and war. All converged at the water.[2]

Cherokees believed running water was a pathway to another world. A fragment of their origin myth imparts ancient beliefs about an alternative cosmos beneath flowing water:

> There is another world under this, and it is like ours in everything—animals, plants, and people—save that the seasons are different. The streams that come down from the mountains are the trails by which we reach this underworld, and the springs at their heads are the doorways by which we enter it, but to do this one must fast and go to water and have one of the underworld people for a guide. We know that the seasons in the underworld are different from ours, because the water in the springs is always warmer in winter and cooler in summer than the outer air.[3]

Running water and flowing streams were sacred, magical, and powerful. They were sources of purification, prophesy, and healing. They were sites of other worlds and other beings.[4]

Among Cherokees, women were the bearers of water. They went daily to streams, creeks, and rivers that flowed in and around their settlements to fill gourds and pitchers with water to carry back to their homes. Transporting water was so profoundly a part of women's domain that "it was considered disgraceful for men or boys to be seen carrying water."[5] With water, women transformed raw food into cooked food, vegetation into medicines and dyes, and natural elements into domestic goods. In the hands and households of women, water became a powerful agent of change.

Waterways in Cherokee settlement areas flow from massive mountains forming the eastern and western flanks of the Southern Appalachian chain. The Blue Ridge Mountains (*Sahkanaga*: Great Blue Hills) form the southeastern rim. Standing more than 3,000 feet high, the Blue Ridge also includes three peaks of nearly 6,000 feet. Fifty miles west, the Unaka Mountains (*Une-ga*: White) form the southwestern arc of the Southern Appalachians. A series of ridges, the Unakas contain some of the highest peaks in eastern North America, including the Great Smokies, the most massive range in the entire Appalachian system. A virtual wall of mountain seventy miles long, the Smokies contain sixteen peaks higher than 6,000 feet.[6]

Linking the Unakas and Blue Ridge, a series of immense cross ridges rises above both. Out of the Black Mountains, the peak called Mount Mitchell soars to 6,684 feet, the highest summit in eastern North America. The Unakas, Blue Ridge, and their cross ranges contain more than forty peaks above 6,000 feet, eighty peaks from 5,000 to 6,000 feet, and hundreds more from 4,000 to 5,000 feet. One after another, mountains rise and swell like waves in an endless sea. The Southern Appalachians, the Cherokee homeland, comprise the greatest mass of mountains east of the Mississippi River.[7]

Cherokees settled in three physiographic provinces along valley waterways between mountains. By the early 1700s, one group of settlements lay in the Piedmont Plateau at the base of the Blue Ridge Mountains. From the mountain's crest, water flows east to the Atlantic Ocean or west to the Mississippi-Gulf drainage. The Keowee (*Kuwa-hi*: Mulberry Place) and Tugalu (*Dugilu*: perhaps indicating a place where a stream forks) run east to the Savannah River, while the Chattahoochee follows a westward course to the Gulf of Mexico. The Cherokee settlements called *E-ladi* (Level Ground; Low) and known to early English settlers as the Lower Towns lay on the headwaters of the Chattahoochee and Savannah Rivers.

Two groups of settlements clustered in the Blue Ridge province on the far side of the Blue Ridge crest. Landforms there differ from those in the Piedmont. From the crest's inner rim, streams and rivers twist both north and south through a maze of mountains before draining into tributaries of the Tennessee River, once called the

Cherokee River. The waterways drop precipitously from high elevations, cutting narrow valleys through forested ridges. In the valleys between the Blue Ridge and Unakas, Cherokees concentrated their Middle Towns. The Middle Towns (*Kitubwa*: the name of a major Cherokee settlement) scattered along two nearly parallel rivers, the Little Tennessee (*Tanasee*: the meaning is lost) and the Tuckasegee (*Tsiksitsi, Tuksi-tsi*: Traveling Terrapin?).

River valleys in the cross ridges provided homesites for the Valley Towns. Southeast of the cross ridge called Snowbird, the Valley River (*Gunahi-ta*: the Long One) threads south and west, then drains into the upper Hiwassee River (*Ayuhwa-si*: a savannah). The Valley Towns lay along the broad floodplains of the Valley and Hiwassee Rivers in the southern Blue Ridge province.

Northwest of the Snowbirds, the fourth group of Cherokee settlements followed the Little Tennessee and Hiwassee Rivers and tributaries across the Unakas. These Overhill Towns (*Otali*: mountain) lay near the base of the Unakas in the gently rolling terrain of the southern Ridge and Valley province.

Trails connecting the four settlement areas led through mountain passes cut by waterways and compressed by geological shifts over eons of time. The Appalachians are the oldest chain of mountains in the world and have been weathering for more than 200 million years. As the region has been repeatedly uplifted, folded, and tilted, the massive landforms have eroded considerably. As a result, mountains may be precipitous, studded with rocky outcrops, and covered with dense vegetation. In a few areas, treeless meadows called balds (*u-dawagun-ta*) stand in bold relief on mountain summits. Along the Blue Ridge, vertical rock faces reveal where ridges have been weakened by water until they crumbled into adjacent ravines.

Temperatures in the high mountains are ten to fifteen degrees cooler than those in surrounding coves and valleys. Winter snowfall ranges from four to forty-seven inches in different latitudes and exposures. Ice and snow may remain on northern mountain faces until late spring, keeping the ground laden with moisture.[8] Winter rain seeps into rock crevices, then freezes and expands, fracturing the rocks and adding to continual disintegration of the mountains. As mountains erode, countless creeks, streams, and rivers carry detritus down to lower elevations. Rocks and boulders strew the landscape, making travel difficult and slow.

In the spring of 1775, naturalist William Bartram punctuated his travel diary with allusions to the rocky trails of the Southern Appalachians. Following the path from the Lower Towns across the Oconee Mountain (*Ukwu-ni*: the meaning is lost) toward the Overhills, Bartram noted "the winding rough road carrying me over rocky hills." He guided his horse over boulders "through which the glittering brook . . . ran rapidly down, dashing and roaring over high rocky steps." Stumbling on, he finally "gained the top of an elevated rocky ridge . . . as the rough rocky road led me, close by . . . a large rapid brook, which . . . pouring down rocky precipices, glided off." The trail Bartram followed "down a steep rocky hill" was "very troublesome." It was, he protested, "incommoded with shattered fragments of the mountains."[9]

In contrast to Europeans, Cherokees assigned spiritual significance to shattered mountains around them. They incorporated into legend the story of *Nun-yunu-wi* (I am Clothed with Rock), the Stone Man who was a great shaman (*ada-webi*) and terrifying cannibal. With skin of solid rock, *Nun-yunu-wi* created fear and dread as he stalked the mountains in search of victims. Finally overwhelmed by the taboo power of seven menstruating women, the prostrate *Nun-yunu-wi* was stabbed by a medicine man with seven stakes of a sourwood tree. That night, Cherokees covered his body with logs and set them ablaze. As the flames grew intensely hot, the cannibal sang to his captors ritual songs for good hunting and imparted secret plant knowledge for successful healing. When daylight broke and all was quiet, Cherokees gathered from his ashes red *wa-di* (paint; *Ani-Wa-di*: Paint Clan) and a magic divining crystal (*Ulunsu-ti*).[10]

A fearful counterpart to *Nun-yunu-wi* was a female monster, *U-tlun-ta* (He or She has it, Sharp; Spearfinger), who assumed different forms to entrap humans and extract their livers with her long forefinger. *U-tlun-ta's* skin was so stony that she was also called *Nun-yunu-wi*. She exercised special power over rock, lifting boulders and smashing them to pieces with a sweep of her craggy hand.[11]

According to Cherokees, *U-tlun-ta* once began to build a rock bridge from the Hiwassee River to Whiteside Mountain in the Blue Ridge so that she could readily cross the landscape searching for victims. Lightning struck before she could complete the bridge, however, scattering rock fragments all over the ridge, "where the pieces can still be seen by people who go there."[12] The sheer Blue Ridge scarp called Whiteside Mountain (*Sa-nigila-ki*: the Place Where They Took It Out) stands near the rocky trails where Bartram and his horse stumbled repeatedly. The rockiness so troublesome to Bartram signified to Cherokees the awesome powers that lay around them.

Behind the legendary tales and reflections of power lay matters of practicality, for rocks also provided material for tools that enabled women and men to survive and transform the world. Women made certain kinds of rocks into knives, scrapers, awls, and drills to fashion clothing from skins, feathers, and bark. Women and men shaped stone into axes and hoes to cut trees for housing and clear fields for planting. Women used stone knives and scrapers to prepare rivercane and bark for weaving into baskets and mats. They selected certain rocks for household hearths and others for boiling stones. They gathered grinding and pounding stones to process foods or to crush hulls, bark, and roots for dye and medicine. Invested with tradition and meaning, stones and rocks of Cherokee settlement areas became practical goods in women's tool kits.

From the Piedmont province across the mountains to the Ridge and Valley, altitudes vary from 50 to 6,000 feet above sea level, with extraordinarily diverse environments in between. Growing seasons in the valleys average between 170 and 200 days, perhaps three weeks longer than those in the mountains. Rapid changes in topography and climate necessitate different planting times in areas less than fifty miles apart. Rainfall ranges from 20 to perhaps 100 inches a year in the high peaks of the Southern Appalachians, which are among the wettest places in North America.[13] Highland rain and heavy dew from low-lying clouds provide water for an immense array of trees, shrubs, vines, mosses, ferns, and other vegetation. In turn, dense vegetation filters the flowing waters and leaves them rich in nutrients.

Ancestors of the Cherokees migrating from the Northeast hundreds or perhaps thousands of years ago found in the Southern Appalachians a generally moderate temperature, distinct seasons, fertile soil, and abundant vegetation and wildlife. As they established their settlements along mountain waterways, Cherokees claimed adjacent lands for hunting. Their territory ultimately exceeded 124,000 square miles, with northern limits from the Kanawha River west to the Ohio and southern limits from the Wateree and Santee west to the Savannah and Chattahoochee Rivers.[14] In their entire settlement area, Cherokees lived amid an astonishing array of flora and fauna from at least 1400 A.D. until their forced removal in the mid-nineteenth century.

Trees: *tlu-gv-i*

In the early 1700s, Southern Appalachian trees formed a forest so varied and beautiful that English surveyor William DeBrahm called it "the American Canaan." His words prophesied the philosophy of Europeans who spilled down and through the Southern Appalachian valleys for the next two centuries. Providence, they believed, ordained American forests for European occupation and development. "This country," DeBrahm mused, "seems longing for the hands of industry to receive its hidden treasures, which nature has been collecting and toiling since the beginning, ready to deliver them up."[15] The "longing" lay in European hearts and minds, not in the country. The "hands of industry" DeBrahm envisioned were European, not Native American. From the beginning, Cherokee land and resources formed the core of the "hidden treasures" Europeans sought. And Cherokees, "collecting and toiling," were never ready "to deliver them up."

It is little wonder Europeans like DeBrahm coveted the Cherokee homeland. The Southern Appalachians contain the greatest number of tree species in North America, and more than in the whole of Europe. They prosper in forests from the Piedmont Plateau to the western Ridge and Valley and on all the lofty ridges in between. More than 125 species develop according to varied elevation, exposure, soil, rainfall, ground water, disturbance, and seed viability. Different forest communities grade into one another, confounding simple classification even in relatively small geographic areas.[16]

In general, mixed deciduous forests spread across the Cherokee homelands and hunting grounds. Natural forces and Native Americans burned and cleared these forests for generations. Each disturbance, whether natural or human, recast landscapes and altered forest compositions. The trees that grow back first and fastest after clearing are pines, which predominate until sun-tolerant oaks such as white, black, chestnut, and red take hold. Depending on elevation, exposure, and land use, the succession may take more than a century.[17] Maturing forests become shadier and cooler, which encourages more than forty-five other species, including three different hickories, sweet gum, poplar, sycamore, red maple, and magnolia. With increasing shade, dense understories of dogwood, redbud, witch hazel, and rhododendron develop.

Cherokees continually modified forests in their home- and hunting lands. They cleared acres of woodland for villages and agricultural fields. When they sought "fresh planting land," they simultaneously took advantage of the successional vegetation that followed in fallowing fields. In old fields (ka-lage-si) up to 3,500 feet, persimmon (tsa-lu-li: pucker mouth) pioneered and provided sweet autumn fruit for Cherokees, songbirds, and foraging game like deer, bear, raccoon, rabbit, turkey, and possum. Women collected persimmons to dry and store or to seed, pound, and knead into cakes. From "pissimmons," according to eighteenth-century Scottish trader James Adair, they made "very pleasant bread, barbicuing it in the woods." Such storing, processing, and feeding activities disseminated seeds that rooted in the spring to begin new forestation. Although often the first tree species to colonize open spaces, persimmon was soon joined by red cedar, red mulberry, and sassafras.[18]

At elevations up to 2,000 feet, red mulberry (ku-wa) produced large sweet fruits in the late spring and summer. Cherokees as well as numerous birds and mammals consumed mulberries and seasonally dispersed their seeds across wide areas. Invading Spaniards of the mid-1500s found "very large mulberry trees" in Cherokee settlement areas. More than two centuries later, Bartram identified red mulberry as one of the "vast variety of wild or native vegetables" women collected for food.[19] Cherokees called a mountain pass in the Middle Towns, one of their major rivers, and their principal settlement in the Lower Towns by the name Keowee, an indication of the importance of mulberry trees in their landscape and economy.

Women found multiple uses for red mulberry. In addition to relying on the fruit for food, they wove the bark into floor and wall coverings. In 1715, a group of women made "a large carpet" of mulberry bark for Queen Anne and "twelve small ones for her Counsellours."[20] Such "very handsome" carpets, wrote Adair, were painted with "images of those birds and beasts they are acquainted with" or depictions "of themselves, acting in their social, and marital stations."[21] Women also made the inner bark of mulberry into clothing. They wore soft "petticoats" of mulberry bark woven "like basket work."[22] In 1724, English naturalist Mark Catesby sent Sir Hans Sloane, his London patron, "an Indian apron made of the bark of wild mulberry." Such aprons, Catesby condescended, were the "only mechanick arts worth noting" among Indians, although he acknowledged the appeal of "a kind of basket they make with split cane."[23] Every apron and every basket documented and revealed how women lived in and shaped the world around them.

Along forest margins (and in coves of lower elevations), black walnut trees appear with yellow poplar, hickory, black locust, various oaks, eastern hemlock, basswood, and sweet birch. At higher elevations, black walnut grades into white walnut, or butternut, which has a similar growing habit. Like old fields, forest margins encourage particular kinds of vegetation that played complex roles in Cherokee ecosystems. Nut-bearing trees, for example, grow best and produce most in open or edge habitats. Hickory trees yield eight times more nuts in clearings than under closed canopies. Equally intolerant of shade, walnut trees inhibit competition from surrounding vegetation by secreting a toxic chemical called juglone that impedes growth in plants near its root zone. Hickory and walnut sites naturally remain relatively open, which facilitates greater nut production.[24] In turn, humans and animals who utilized nut trees helped maintain clearings and redistribute seeds to colonize new areas.

Women encouraged nut- and fruit-bearing trees near their settlements. By repeatedly gathering certain kinds of vegetation, they shaped landscapes and sustained resources for food, medicines, clothing, tools, and dyes. Spanish invaders found walnut trees "growing about over the country, without planting or pruning, of the size and luxuriance they would have were they cultivated in orchards."

Bartram's more sensitive observations suggest that such luxuriance was not accidental. Finding nut trees in deserted Indian towns, he recognized that they "thrive
better, and are more fruitful, in cultivated plantations" than in the wild.[25] Village
clearings provided suitable habitats for nut-bearing trees.

Autumn in deciduous forests signaled special responsibilities for women, who
"gathered in incredible quantities of Nuts and Acorns." Extremely high in fat and
crude protein, hickory nuts (so-hi) comprised a major part of Cherokee diet. From
September (Dulu-stinee: Nut Month) through December (U-ski-ya: Snow Month),
women carried baskets to the woods to "gather a number of hiccory-nuts." After
pounding them in mortars, they sifted the nuts in baskets to separate meats from
hulls. "When they are fine enough," wrote Adair, the nutmeats were mixed "with
cold water in a clay bason" for nourishing "hiccory milk" (ganu gwala-sti), a bever-
age Bartram considered "as sweet and rich as fresh cream."[26] Hickory trees produced food for Cherokees as well as numerous species of animals and birds, and
they maintained their wide distribution by adapting to varied soils, climates, and
exposures, by discouraging competing vegetation, and by prolific sprouting after
cuts or fires.[27]

Sweet, edible walnuts (se-di) also contributed to all Southern Appalachian diet.
Women collected walnuts, placed them on nutting stones in baskets, then ham-
mered them with stones to extract meat, oil (tsade-ka-i), and milk. Their "most excellent kind of food" was a combination of corn grits and "the meat of hickory or
black walnuts." Admiring Europeans thought the nuts "render this kind of food a
real luxury." Women also exploited walnut's medicinal qualities, peeling out the inner bark of trees and roots (ha-wi-na-ti-tla u-hya-la-tu; u-na-ste-ti) to pound and boil
for cathartics. And from earliest memory, they taught their daughters to dig walnut roots, strip off the outer bark, and crush the stems in huge pots of boiling water to make dye that stained baskets a rich dark brown or black.[28]

At one time, the American chestnut dominated the Blue Ridge and Ridge and
Valley provinces. Growing at elevations up to 4,000 feet, chestnut trees comprised
from one-quarter to one-half of some forest communities. Immense trees reached
heights of more than 120 feet, with circumferences greater than 7 feet. Autumn
carpets of fallen chestnuts blackened the earth and attracted bear, deer, raccoon,
squirrels, wild turkeys, and mice. Foragers grew so fat from the nuts they could
scarcely escape hunters. In the 1700s, women traded chestnuts (ti-li) by the bushel
basket to white settlers and relied on the nuts and chestnut bread (gadu ti-li) as winter staples.[29]

On sunny, dry exposures of deciduous forests, four types of pine predominate:
shortleaf, Virginia, pitch, and table mountain, growing alongside scarlet and chest-

nut oak. Secondary deciduous trees include hickories, basswood, sweet gum, honey locust, tupelo, red maple, sassafras, and serviceberry. Black, chestnut, and red oak gradually prevail, and white oak (*tala*) can reach its greatest height of 150 feet and live up to 600 years. Often a reliable source of nuts, a fertile white oak tree may produce as many as 10,000 acorns in a good year. More than 180 kinds of birds and mammals rely on acorn mast, including humans, deer, bear, wild turkey, quail, squirrels, mice, chipmunks, raccoon, blue jays, and red-headed woodpeckers. So many species scavenge acorns that they may destroy virtually the entire crop.[30] Continually competing with animals and birds, women gathered, dried, hulled, and pounded acorns (*ku-le*) for bread flour or oil.[31]

Forests become denser as proximity to water increases and exposure to wind and sun diminishes. In a few areas, old-growth forests retained immense stands of poplar, sycamore, tupelo, locust, birch, magnolia, hickory, silverbell, sourwood, and sugar maple. In such forests, more than thirty species of huge trees share dominance, forming a canopy that nearly blocks sunlight from underlying thickets of shrubs. Deep shadows on forest floors encourage 375 native mosses, 250 kinds of lichens, and 60 species of ferns that grow from organic remains.[32] Sheltered in coves where they are nourished by moist soil and protected from desiccating wind and cold, deciduous hardwoods and evergreen hemlocks reach enormous proportions. Poplars, basswood, hemlocks, silverbell, buckeyes, ash, birch, beech, red oak, black cherry, magnolia, and sugar maple have all attained record sizes and ages in cove hardwood forests. Many trees may live more than 500 years, and poplars can attain their maximum height of 190 feet, the tallest of all North American deciduous trees, with circumferences as great as 30 feet. In the optimum growing conditions of coves, the circumference of the sugar maple reaches 13 feet, while that of birches is 14 feet, and buckeye, 16 feet; hemlock, the most shade-tolerant of all species, grows to a maximum circumference of 20 feet.[33]

At elevations above 4,000 feet, close-growing conifers predominate, including red spruce and Frazer fir, whose deep green, fragrant needles on thick boughs form a dense and dark canopy. High elevations also include a few northern hardwoods such as yellow birch, beech, red oak, black cherry, and two types of maple, striped and sugar. Where sufficient sunlight filters through, an understory of rhododendron, scarlet elder, blueberry, gooseberry, and bush honeysuckle develops.[34] At the edges of spruce-fir forests, heath or grassy balds occur on exposed ridges.

The Southern Appalachians were never glaciated. Northern ice sheets drove and scattered before them plants and seeds that took cover in the mountains, evolving in relative isolation after the last glacial sheets retreated. Relics of glacial scattering remained as small islands of tundra vegetation on high peaks. The spruce-fir forests represent the southernmost extension of northern boreal forests that survived the ice ages by retreating southward to warmer environments. In warming trends following each ice age, boreal forests drew back to the north, leaving spruce-fir communities behind only in cold temperatures of the highest elevations.[35]

With such a richness of trees, it is little wonder Cherokees found so many uses for them. Food, clothing, shelter, tools, medicine, weapons, and ceremonial wares all came from surrounding woodlands. Continually reshaping landscapes to exploit vegetation, Cherokees carefully wove concepts about flora into patterns of belief and behavior. Economically important trees became legendary and powerful. In the beginning, elders disclosed, animals and plants were told to watch and keep awake for seven nights. When *Ta-gwadihi* (Catawba Killer) recounted the story, neither he nor anyone else recalled who gave the command. What remained certain was that most could not follow it. By the seventh night none but "the cedar, the pine, the spruce, the holly, and the laurel were awake." These five were rewarded for their steadfastness, and "to them it was given always to be green and to be the greatest for medicine."[36]

Cherokees venerated seven kinds of trees, which they related to seven matrilineal clans in an annual cycle of rituals. The seven-day celebration for the First New Moon of Spring included fasting, going to water, distributing medicinal roots, consulting the *Ulunsu-ti*, hunting, dancing, sacrificing meat, and kindling a fresh town house fire.[37]

To make sacred fire (*tsila-galun-kwe-ti-yu*) in the spring, clan representatives gathered wood from the eastern sides of seven trees, peeled off the outer bark, and placed the wood in a circle on the central altar of the town house. The woods included white oak, black oak, water oak, black jack, bass wood, chestnut, and white pine. Once the fire ignited, women carried burning coals to start fresh fires in their homes.[38] The town house fire "never goes out," wrote British trader Alexander Longe in 1725; it burned continuously in each town until it was ceremonially extinguished and rebuilt. Neither embers nor ash could be removed from the fire, nor pipes lit there. Cherokees offered supplications to the fire, whose smoke was "always in readiness to convey the petition on high."[39] The source of heat, light, and smoke rising to the Upper World, wood for the town house fire carried singular significance.

Fires built for fall celebrations required different kinds of wood. The Festival of Propitiation and Purification (*Ah-tawh-hung-nah*) commemorated and renewed the relationship between earth dwellers and the creator. Perhaps the most solemn of the seven festivals, it included rituals to purify, heal, and cleanse the bodies and spirits of all. Before dawn on the seventh ritual day, firemakers ceremonially prepared a fresh town house fire of black jack, locust, post oak, sycamore, red bud, plum, and red oak.[40] The fire burned under an immense pot of water in which the priest submerged seven medicine plants "fastened into a cane basket, expressly fashioned for this purpose." The medicine spiritually purified Cherokees and defended them from illness and contagion. Medicinal plants included the legendary cedar and white pine, along with hemlock, mistletoe, evergreen brier, heartleaf, and ginseng.[41]

Cherokees believed that "every Tree, Shrub and Herb, down even to the Grasses and Mosses, agreed to furnish a cure for some one of the diseases."[42] Vegetation was more than a resource. It was an ally in the continual war against disease. To avert or cure illness, Cherokees needed to become familiar with all plants, recognize their properties, and understand their healing potential. They had to discern from the spirit of the plant the medicine it provided. Supernatural powers assisted them, for the death chants of Stone Man taught them about medicines, formulas, and the use of vegetation.

Specialists in each generation disclosed the secret words of formulas to novices, initiating them in proper use of trees and plants. Whether they made sacred drink from the "beloved" yaupon, poultices from buckeye and dogwood, or tea from sassafras, sweetgum, white oak, or the powerful and cherished ginseng (a-tali-guli: it climbs the mountain), Cherokees knew each plant offered something special. Each was gathered with ritual. Both women and men, selected as children to be trained by clan relatives, became medical practitioners. Most specialized in particular kinds of problems, utilizing certain skills and knowledge. Some became experts in the mysteries of love, others in finding lost objects, and many became healers. Physician-priests, inadequately identified in English accounts as conjurors, combined knowledge, training, experience, and ritual. In addition to the specialists, most individuals knew a variety of herbal remedies as a matter of practicality. Their "great knowledge of specific virtues in simples," Adair acknowledged, was "instigated by nature and quickened by experience."[43]

Through their daily work, women learned much about the location and properties of vegetation. They assumed responsibility for gathering foods and collecting wood for daily household fires. They moved regularly and knowledgeably through the world of plants and trees. Moreover, a profound mythological association existed between women and medicine. It was the natural power of women that overwhelmed the feared *Nun-yunu-wi*. Embedded in Cherokee belief lay the notion that the taboo power of women's blood (*wo-di*)—a negative force—could overcome the greatest medicine.[44]

Cherokees ceremonially connected women with medicine. When epidemics threatened, seven clan women danced "with a slow step . . . round the fire in single file, followed by all the other women, and then by the girls, forming a large circle."[45] As though encircling their island home to recreate it, townswomen joined together to subdue through ritual the unseen causes of tribal distress.

Women also danced during the Great New Moon of Autumn Feast (*Nung-tah-tay-quah*), which was held when autumn leaves began to fall into Appalachian waterways. As leaves imparted healing powers to the water, women danced seven times in "a slow step in a circle round the fire."[46] During the subsequent Propitiation Ceremony of *Ah-tawh-hung-nah*, seven women led all the women and girls in a ritual dance. On the first and fourth nights they danced single file around the fire the entire night, "forming large circles within circles."[47] Women, wood, medicine, and healing all interwove in ritual to express and implore power.

Plants and Vines: *ga-nu-lv-hi*

Beneath Appalachian trees, microhabitats encourage an enormous variety of ground vegetation. In late winter, a profusion of plants bursts forth to obtain sunlight before the leaf canopy appears. Contributing food, medicines, and vegetable dyes to Cherokees, early bloomers include bloodroot, spring beauty, hepatica, and violets. In April (*Tsi law-nee*: Flower Month), additional varieties such as columbine, trout lily, trillium, iris, phacelia, and geranium signal lengthening days and warming earth. More than 200 species of wildflowers grow in the Southern Appalachian spring, and at higher altitudes the blooming season extends well into summer months.[48] Women gathered dozens of kinds of spring greens for potherbs and dug the roots of many more for medicines, foods, and dyes.[49]

Different kinds of plants and vines colonized open spaces. Old fields sprouted wild grapes "in great variety and abundance," their seeds deposited by scavenging birds and mammals. Women gathered "large quantities of grapes," tied them in bunches, and hung them from roofs to dry. During winter, they boiled the grapes, "strained them through a cane sieve," and combined the juice with cornmeal for "a very delicious dish." Huckleberry, blackberry, raspberry, and strawberry vines also spread profusely through old fields. When Bartram rode through such clearings he found strawberries so lush they stained his horses' hooves bright red.[50]

According to Cherokee belief, strawberries (*a-nv*) came from the sun (*Une-lanun-hi*: Great Apportioner) to lure a woman back to her husband after a quarrel. The berries so powerfully evoked memories of her beloved that the woman gathered them up for him. The Cherokee festival year began in *Anoyi* (Strawberry Moon), when fruits began to ripen. Soon afterward, women took baskets to old fields to harvest berries that were "larger," wrote Adair, "than I have seen in any part of the world."[51] Near Keowee Lower Town, Bartram once happened upon "companies of young, innocent Cherokee virgins" filling baskets with wild strawberries. Accompanied by a local trader, he made his way forward to pursue "an innocent frolic with this gay assembly of hamadryades." A few "decently advanced to meet us," he recounted, and "presented their little baskets" of fresh berries, "merrily telling us their fruit was ripe and sound."[52]

Maypop, angelica, chenopodium, and wild potato also volunteered in clearings, this last giving name to one of the seven hereditary clans (*Ani-Go-tage-wi*: Wild Potato Clan). Sumac (*kalogwa*) was another pioneer, flowering in summer months and fruiting in the fall. Birds flocked to the berries, but women were their constant competitors. They gathered sumac berries to dye baskets or to grind into powder for their hair "to preserve its perfect blackness." Bartram claimed to have seen "quantities of this red powder in their houses."[53]

Pokeweed (*tsa-hytika*) is a rapid colonizer that represents the symbiosis in Cherokee ecosystems. An indigenous perennial, poke competes poorly with other vegetation because its seedlings are easily overwhelmed and overgrown. The plant's evolutionary response to its initial disadvantage is efficient seed dispersal and germination. When pokeweed stalks begin to die in late fall, the lush, mature berries remain attached to their purple stems and attract migratory birds who eat the fruit and disperse the seeds. Only seeds that have been scarified in digestive tracts will germinate. Scarified seeds can remain dormant for as long as fifty years and will sprout quickly when the ground where they lie is disturbed by flooding, erosion, or alluvial deposition. Human disturbances such as clearing, burning, or planting also encourage germination.[54] Poke thus recurred in areas where Cherokees lived, ate, gardened, farmed, and worked. Women harvested young poke greens for food and gathered fall berries for medicine and dye.

The Cherokee homeland "abounds with the best herbage, on the richer parts of the hills and mountains," exclaimed Adair, "and a great variety of valuable herbs is promiscuously scattered on the lower lands." With abundant and useful plants prospering in the fertile soil around them, Cherokees lived in a "magnificent landscape," which Bartram considered "infinitely varied, and without bound."[55]

Some plant species in the Cherokee homeland confirm that several million years ago the forests of Asia and North America belonged to the same temperate zone and formed a continuous belt of homogeneous flora that extended across North America and Eurasia. Many plants and trees of eastern North America grow 5,000 miles away in eastern Asia, but nowhere else in the world. Native to the two continents that are now so distant are forty-eight genera of plants and fourteen species of trees, including hickories, magnolias, tupelos, catalpas, witch hazel, sassafras, and tulip poplar. As a result of the ancient relationship and climatic histories of the two regions, plants native to Japan and China readily transplant and adapt to eastern North America.[56]

The antiquity of Southeastern forests marks ecological process and dynamism rather than stasis. The very richness of the soils indicates the birth, growth, and death of millions of trees, plants, and animals over eons of time. Natural disturbances such as fires, floods, earthquakes, diseases, storms, droughts, landslides, and temperature fluctuations have shaped the land and its vegetation. So too have Cherokees and other Native Americans who cultivated soil and encouraged certain plants as early as the late Archaic Period (3,000–900 B.C.).

Fire was their primary means of landscaping. Indians relied on fire to clear forests, promote vegetation, and surround and flush game. Repeated firing converted woodland to grassland, maintaining forest margins with special plant communities. In 1728, smoke from Indian fires that filled the air and drifted for miles prompted Virginian William Byrd to complain that "the Atmosphere was so smoaky all around us, that the Mountains were again growing invisible." Byrd knew who was responsible for the poor visibility. "This happen'd not from the Hazyness of the Sky, but by the firing of the Woods by the Indians." DeBrahm realized that "the burning of grass and underwood in the forests is an ancient custom of the Indians." He thought "they practiced it in order to allure the deer upon the new grass." Few Europeans recognized the importance of successional vegetation that followed firing. More interested in men's war and hunting than women's farming and gardening, they seldom acknowledged that firing also facilitated women's responsibilities.[57]

No fixed, unadulterated wilderness has ever existed in the Southern Appalachians. Birds and mammals consume and destroy vegetation in seasonal struggles to survive. Every hunting camp or night's shelter, every meal or browse or battle tramples herbs, seedlings, and shrubs. Natural disasters burn, flood, parch, overturn, and destroy acres of trees and plants. Where one kind of vegetation prospered and died, another might colonize, preventing soil erosion and attracting new species. For centuries, Native Americans fired and cleared, harvested and reseeded, planted and gathered in every woodland and grassland near their settlements. Southern Appalachian forests have always been living and dying simultaneously, always changing as life forms compete for sun, water, shelter, and nutrients.

Four-Toed Forest Dwellers: *nvh-gi dikanasa-dv inagehi*

In the 1700s, over sixty species of wild mammals inhabited Cherokee settlement areas. Along with the "incredible number of buffaloes, bears, deer, panthers, wolves, foxes, raccoon, and opossums" identified by the English lieutenant Henry

Timberlake in 1761, there were flying, gray, and ground squirrels, skunk, mink, woodchuck, mice, rabbit, beaver, otter, wildcat, porcupine, and elk.[58] Men hunted such animals to supply meat and clothing for their families and to acquire community prestige.

Reports of men's hunting activities—isolation, preparation of weapons, purification, special rituals and particular formulas, as well as their dramatic firing of woods, tracking and killing animals and, increasingly, trading their pelts—have all but eclipsed the intensive involvement of women with animals.

When they accompanied men on hunts or when men hunted near their settlements, women retrieved the skinned carcasses and carried them back to camps and villages. They butchered the meat, then prepared it for storage or consumption by smoking, barbecuing, or boiling it in soups and stews. Perhaps most time-consuming of all, women prepared skins by stripping them of hair and fur, stretching them on racks, and tanning them with animal brain until they became soft and supple enough for the next task—making them into clothing, bedding, blankets, moccasins, ties, containers, and headpieces. Before Cherokee horses became commonplace in the mid-1700s, women also joined men as burdeners, carrying pelts for the deerskin trade.[59] Although men dominated the hunt for animals and the mystique surrounding it, women were responsible for much of what happened afterward.

Hunting was central to Cherokee concepts of manhood. John Stuart reported to the Board of Trade in 1764 that "the whole business of an Indians life is war and hunting."[60] Like many European reporters, Stuart referred only to men, but his summary of their activities bore some accuracy. War and hunting were certainly two principal activities of Indian males. Around these two endeavors they established elaborate rituals and regulations.

Warfare and hunting took place primarily in fall and early winter, when game was fat and pelts dense, when rutting bucks came into the open and warriors from enemy tribes left their settlements lightly defended. During warfare and hunting, men abstained from sexual relations, believing that any contact with women would overwhelm the power imparted by medicine men. On war paths, they were forbidden even to speak of women.[61] The acceleration of the deerskin trade in the eighteenth century drastically altered not only the economy, but beliefs, gender roles, and ecosystems as well.

In contrast to Europeans, Cherokees posited no essential difference between humans and animals. Like humans, animals lived in towns with councils and chiefs, wars, ball games, and dances. Animals and humans both went to the Darkening Land (*Usunhi-yi*) after death, coexisting in afterlife as they had in the time of genesis.

Joined in reciprocating relationships, each held certain powers over the other. The power of hunters to kill animals counterbalanced the power of animals to cause disease. Appropriate behavior toward animals was literally a matter of life and death.

Elders recounted how disease originated when animals felt crowded and abused by humans. Resentful and angry, animals "decided to begin war" by sending disease to punish humans for hunting. Disease became to humans what hunting was to game, a cause of death and reduced population. Saved only by the willingness of plants to offer themselves as medicines, Cherokees believed overhunting would cause immediate retaliation by animal spirits.[62] Men hunted with prudence, offering intercessory prayers prior to and following every hunt.

Buffalo (*yansa*) migrated into the Southeast from the Great Plains, following food resources. As Cherokees engaged in long cycles of clearing, cultivation, and abandonment of fields, they created grassy meadows that enticed grazers like buffalo. In turn, grazing animals kept grasses short, maintaining open areas for particular vegetation that then attracted other wildlife. Moving nearly continuously during feeding, buffalo extended grasslands by dispersing seeds caught in their shaggy coats and deposited in their excrement.

The availability of buffalo must have transformed Cherokee life. By the 1700s, buffalo provided food, clothing, bedding, war paraphernalia, utensils, and musical instruments. According to Adair, women "continually wear a beaded string round their legs, made of buffalo hair" as ornamentation and to prevent misfortune, thus weaving together concepts of beauty and medico-magic. In winter, "they wrap[ped] themselves in the softened skin of buffalo calves" with "the shagged wool inward." Alexander Longe wrote that one of the "great many dances to divert their king" honored the buffalo. Warriors made quivers of buffalo hide and shields of buffalo crania, and war chiefs wore bracelets and headbands of buffalo skin. Men blew through buffalo horn trumpets and crafted horns into spoons and scapula into hoes. Women prepared the nourishing meat, spun hair for thread, and dressed calfskins for the special bedding of infant girls. Giant buffalo roamed through Cherokee myths, and *Yansa-i* (Buffalo Place) identified a site where a legendary buffalo lived underwater.[63]

Next to humans, wolves (*wa-hya*) were the foremost predators in Southeastern ecosystems and the totem identity of a Cherokee clan (*Ani-Wahya*: Wolf Clan). Wolves pruned animal communities of young, old, weak, and sick members, which helped maintain healthy herds and relieved pressure on plant populations. Wolves greatly reduced small game predation of agricultural fields and gardens, for in their absence, animals like rodents and rabbits reproduced rapidly. After feeding, wolves abandoned carrion that then fed scavengers like foxes, eagles, ravens, and buzzards. Decaying wastes from wolf kills fertilized soil and replenished nutrients.[64] Wolves affected virtually the entire Southeastern food chain.

The most important Cherokee game animal was white-tail deer (*ahwi*), which gave name to one of the seven clans (*Ani-Kawi*: Deer Clan). Deer frequent forest edges and continually alter forest composition by feeding on succulent foliage during spring and early summer, on woody leaves and shoots in late summer, and on forest mast in autumn and winter. Dependent on shrubby growth for cover, they restrict their range to sheltered areas of lower elevations in winter months. Among Cherokees, extensive hunting coincided with deer concentrations in relatively small, predictable locales.

Cherokees utilized virtually all parts of the deer, which comprised as much as half the meat in their diet. Payment for tribal obligations could be made in deerskins. Women and men made deer sinews into string and made entrails into bow strings and thread. They worked antler and bone into tools, musical instruments, and beads. Women boiled antlers and hooves for glue and converted small bones into needles and awls. They tanned hides with deer brains, then fashioned the leather into clothing or bedding, moccasins or hairpieces, bags or belts. For dances, they fastened rattles on "white-drest deerskin" tied onto their legs.[65]

During special ceremonies and at annual celebrations, the priest sat on one deerskin, which was painted or chalked white, and rested his feet on another. To assemble a general council, the "beloved man" (*uku*) raised over the town house a deerskin painted white with red spots. At the ceremony of the First New Moon of Spring, the priest performed special rituals with buck, doe, and fawn skins prepared by women.[66] Ceremonial feasts always included ritual sacrifice of deer tongue. The priest "cuts a piece of it and throws it in the midst of the fire," according to Longe, then "cuts 4 other pieces and throws one north the other south the other east and the other west." After the ritual offering, he passed the remainder of meat "through the flame of the fire and then [gave] it to the women to dress for the priest and all others that pleases to eat of it."[67] Important in myth, exchange, food, clothing, and ceremony, the deer was one of the most valuable animals in the Cherokee universe and culture of women.

Black bear (*yanu, yona*) also held a place of honor. The largest omnivore in the Southern Appalachians, black bear dwell in deep forests whose dense understories protect their young. The primarily solitary adults mate in early summer, and subsequent pregnancy coincides with the time of greatest abundance of food resources in late summer and fall. "The she-bear," wrote Adair, "takes an old hollow tree for her yeaning winter-house, and chuses to have the door above" to protect her cubs. Males make winter beds in "solitary thickets" by breaking "a great many branches of trees" for the bottom and adding "the green tops of large canes."[68] In January of alternate years, sows give birth to one or two cubs, who remain with their mother for a year. Never in a true state of hibernation, a black bear sleeps intermittently through two months of Southern Appalachian winter.

With a home range of ten to fifteen square miles, black bear attain greatest population density in deciduous forests where food resources are abundant and varied. When they emerge from winter sleep, the voracious feeders rip up young spring plants and trees for their leaves and overturn fallen logs to root out insects, grubs, small rodents, or carrion. During late spring and summer they devour wild fruits, and as fall signals the onset of food depletion, bears spend up to twenty hours a day eating. They claw their way up trees of every size, break off branches and descend rapidly to eat the fallen fruits and nuts. Along with deer, black bear profoundly reduce forest seeds, redistributing them through excrement that fertilizes wide areas of forest.[69]

Believed to have been human at one time, black bear populated Cherokee legend. Their town houses were said to be under four mountains in the Smokies, and the great bear chief lived in the one called *Kuwa-hi*.[70] Bear oil was a favorite food among both Europeans and Cherokees, particularly after the animals fattened on "Acorns, Chestnuts and Chinkapins, Wild-Hony and Wild Grapes."[71] Women fried the oil, "mixing plenty of sassafras and wild cinnamon with it over the fire," and stored it "in large earthen jars, covered in the ground." The oil was delicious, claimed Adair, and also "nutritive to hair."[72] Women oiled their hair with bear fat as a mark of beauty, and both women and men greased their bodies with it to ward off insects. Bear claws, teeth, and bone became tools and jewelry in the hands of artisans. Women also processed the skins for clothing, bedding, and blankets; and they spun the coarse black hair into thread.[73]

While Cherokees relied on deer and bear for the widest variety of uses, they utilized numerous other mammals for subsistence, ceremony, and economy. Women spun thread from the hair of opossum (*sikhwa*) and dyed their pelts red and yellow for ceremonial crowns. They decorated deerskin moccasins with dyed porcupine quills. Medical practitioners invoked various animals in formulas to prevent specific ailments. For example, they petitioned wolf, fox, deer, rabbit, and opossum to prevent frostbite because these animals seemed impervious to cold. Foxes and wolves provided headdresses and ritual costumes for warriors. Cherokees hung the scent pouches of skunks over household doors to ward off contagion. Social dances honored and imitated groundhog, beaver, skunk, bear, buffalo, and raccoon.

Elders recounted animal stories at night around a fire in the winter hothouse (*osi*). They considered the Four-toed Ones to be instructive and humorous but treated them with cautious respect because of their power.[74]

Flyers: *anina bilidabi*

While a rich variety of mammals browsed, hunted, and nested in Cherokee settlement areas, hundreds of species of birds roosted in trees and shrubbery, some passing through on fall and spring migrations, many remaining through spring and summer breeding seasons, and others living in the area year-round. "The American woods swarm with a surprizing variety of beautiful wild fowl," exclaimed Adair, while Timberlake identified "turkeys, geese, ducks of several kinds, partridges, pheasants, and an infinity of other birds" in the Overhills. Martin Schneider, a Moravian missionary, was startled by the noisy honking and swirling of wild geese and swans who "flew about me in great numbers" as he tried to sleep one cold winter night near the French Broad River.[75] Cherokees claimed a totemic relationship with birds, identifying one of their seven matrilineal clans as the Bird Clan (*Ani-Tsiskwa*).

Eagles, ravens, crows, buzzards, geese, crane, ducks, grouse, swallows, blue herons, wild turkeys, hawks, woodpeckers, owls, osprey, partridges, cuckoos, and doves populated Cherokee settlements areas, shaping ecosystems by nesting and feeding, transporting foods, and fertilizing soil. Passenger pigeons (*wo-yi*) by the millions flew through forests in the late fall, bleaching the ground white with their dung. Astonished by one such flight, William Byrd reported that "the Flocks of these Birds of Passage are so amazingly great, sometimes, that they darken the Sky." Even at rest, migrating pigeons overwhelmed the landscape, lighting "in such Numbers on the Larger Limbs of the Mulberry-Trees and Oaks as to break them down."[76]

Birds redistributed nuts, acorns, and seeds, culled fish, amphibians, and reptiles, and became food for omnivores. Those birds that preyed on insects protected forest and fruit trees by devouring crickets, weevils, beetles, borers, and larvae. Their continual feeding also limited insect destruction of garden and field crops. Raptors like screech owls (*wa-bubu*), hoot owls (*u-guku*), and hawks (*tawodi*) reduced crop predation by small mammals such as moles, mice, snakes, toads, rabbits, and squirrels.[77]

Cherokees watched birds carefully for indications of changing weather. Something in "the temperature of their bodies" or "the moistness of air felt in their quills" might predict showers in a dry season. At the sound of quacking ducks or croaking ravens, weather prophets would assure their communities of imminent rain. Birds so accurately forecast diurnal rounds that Adair identified them as "the feathered kalender." Birds' "sufficient knowledge of the seasons" cast them as harbingers of impending spring or fall, time to plant or gather, hunt or harvest.[78]

Ascribing spiritual power to feathers (*tsu-lunu-hi*), Cherokees plucked and preserved them for ceremonies and rituals. In certain ceremonies, special assistants fanned the priest with turkey feather wands. The priest presiding over the Green Corn Festival "rises up with a white wing in his hand and commands silence."[79] When a "beloved woman" prepared medicine for the Chilhowee "physic dance" in the Overhills, she "took out the wing of a swan, and after flourishing it over the pot stood fixed for near a minute" as she offered prayers.[80] Feathers served as emblems of office and at the same time as intercessors poised midway between humans and their creator. Those individuals who carried feathers—both women and men—exerted authority and assumed responsibility. Each clan wore "feathers of different colors attached to their ears." Warriors and ballplayers tied their hair with dyed feathers from the eagle, raven, mountain hawk, sparrow hawk, long tail hawk, chicken hawk, or goose, hoping to become imbued with swiftness, keen vision, and cunning. Particularly skilled scouts wore raven or owl skins, and outstanding warriors were honored with the name Raven (*Ka-lu-na*), the "second war-title."[81]

Women made bird soup (*u-ka-mu*) and cooked their eggs (*tsu-way-tsi*), though Cherokees never ate "birds of prey or birds of night" who consumed the blood of animals. As food preparers, women assumed a particular moral authority by maintaining dietary prohibitions. When traders brought them "unlawful" food like hawks, they "earnestly refused" to cook them "for fear of contracting pollution."[82] In the Cherokee worldview, impurity led to disease and even death. By monitoring what foods they processed and served, women safeguarded community morality and health.

"They esteem pigeons," according to Adair, "only as they are salutary food, and they kill the turtle-dove" (*gu-le disgoh-nihi*), whose onomatopoeic name was given to little girls. Using blowguns made of cane and darts of thistle down, children hunted an "infinity" of birds, "which they seldom miss[ed]." Whenever women prepared meat, they "put some of whatever they cooked on the fire for sacrifice." They usually offered "a little of the best" meat from deer or bear or buffalo, but birds necessitated a slightly different sacrifice. Women selected one from the assorted carcasses, "plucked off the feathers, took out the entrails and then put the whole bird on the fire."[83]

Wild turkey (*gv-na*) was the largest and most common bird in Cherokee settlement areas, providing food, ornamentation, tools, and clothing. Although turkeys ate fruit of virtually every deciduous tree, Adair claimed that "they live on the small red acorns and grow so fat in March, that they cannot fly farther than three or four hundred yards," thus facilitating their own capture. Their appetite for dogwood berries both reduced and dispersed communities of dogwood, whose hard, dense wood provided Cherokees with tools and handles.[84] Medical practitioners made ritual scratchers (*kanuga*) and medicine tubes with turkey bone. Women wove soft turkey breast feathers into elaborate blankets, cloaks, and short gowns that were "pleasant to wear and beautiful" as well as extremely warm. They strung turkey bone beads around their necks "in such manner that the breast was frequently nearly covered with beads."[85]

Cherokees considered the eagle (*awa-hili*) sacred, a great shaman, and a symbol of peace. They exchanged eagle feathers to signify friendship. Timberlake reported that eagle feathers were so important "they sometimes are given with wampum in their treaties, and none of their warlike ceremonies can be performed without them." In the fall or winter, designated warriors hunted eagles for the Eagle Tail Dance, which was performed to welcome visitors, celebrate victory, and recount exploits of war. The raptor's power was so formidable that eagle hunting was prohibited in spring and summer for fear of precipitating early frost. Unauthorized eagle hunting caused nightmares and illness, endangering the entire community.[86]

Fish: *u-tsu-ti*

Southeastern waterways teemed with fish, including bass, trout, mullet, perch, carp, gar, pike, eel, sturgeon, redhorse, drum, walleye, sculpin, lampreys, suckers, and catfish. They furnished food for Cherokees as well as animals like mink, otter, muskrat, bear, and raccoon, and numerous birds and reptiles. In the Holston River, Timberlake found "fish sporting in prodigious quantities, which we might have taken with ease."[87] The Tennessee River supported so many kinds and numbers of mussels—the densest assemblage in the world—that one section was called Mussel Shoals (*Takana-yi*: Mussel Place), a name later corrupted to Muscle Shoals.

In the 1700s, women and men fished cooperatively, usually in summer months and always with baskets. Men swam into icy waterways with woven handnets (*dasu-du-di*) to net fish. Women watching at the shore scooped the water with baskets to trap those that swarmed from the nets. Other times, men thrashed fish downstream into creels, from which "it is no difficult matter to take them with baskets." Cherokees living on narrow waterways dammed up streams, then scattered the surfaces with crushed buckeyes or walnut roots to stun the fish. As fish floated to the surface, women and children waded into the water with winnowing baskets to collect them. They "barbecue the largest," which traders like Adair appreciated, "for they prove very wholesome food to us, who frequently use them."[88]

Frogs, Turtles, Snakes: *wa-lo-si, dak-si, inada*

At water's edge, on forest floors, or in grassy fields, nesting and feeding areas abounded for reptiles and amphibians. Lizards, frogs, turtles, more than two dozen kinds of salamanders, and an equal number of snake species populated Cherokee settlement areas.[89] Important in ecosystems as food and feeders, they appeared in myths, songs, medicine formulas, dances, and often as giants in folktales. For sacred dances, beloved women wore leg rattles made from the shells of box turtle. The yellow lines segmenting the shells evoked the division of Cherokee society into separate clans. As the women danced, pebbles clattered rhythmically inside the shells, making a sound like snakes' rattles or falling rain.

Water creatures were profoundly associated with rain, an element necessary for life as well as being potentially destructive. Such tension existed in much of the Cherokee world, where events, elements, creatures, and humans could be forces for good or ill, success or defeat. Cherokees thus honored and also palliated powers in their midst with carefully constructed behavioral systems that encompassed foodways, warfare, ceremony, hunting, relationships, names, clothing, and even ornamentation.

As water bearers for villages and households, women were closely associated with herpetofauna. A Seneca captive once recounted his dramatic experience of the connection between women and snakes. He appeared before two women "who had the power to decide what should be done with him." Each bore on her lips the tattoo of two snakes in profile. When the women opened their mouths to speak, the snakes appeared to be opening theirs to strike.[90] The power of life and the threat of death belonged to women, and these powers were signified by serpents.

On an Overhills tour in 1797, Louis-Philippe saw in the Toqua Town House three octagonal shields painted with figures of "the snake, the tortoise, and the lizard," symbols, he thought, of "the Tcherokee tribes."[91] Timberlake reported that he heard of a conjuror who subdued an enormous serpent and removed from his forehead a brilliant jewel. The conjuror hid the stone from everyone except two women, who steadfastly guarded the secret.[92] Middle Town Cherokees told stories of "some bright old inhabitants, or rattlesnakes, of a more enormous size than is mentioned in history." Their mesmerizing power was so great, wrote Adair, that "no living creature moves within reach of their sight, but they can draw it to them."

Each serpent bore in his head "a large carbuncle" that sullied and repelled the sun's rays.[93]

The *Uk-tena* was the "great snake, as large around as a tree trunk, with horns on its head and a bright blazing crest like a diamond on its forehead." The marvelous creature was once a man, transformed into a mythical monster in order to kill the sun (*Nunda Igehi*: Dwelling in the Day). When he failed, other creatures banished the furious *Uk-tena*. Some like him, Cherokees said, remained behind, stalking deep woods and dark waters of the mountains in a ceaseless search for victims.[94] The crystal on the *Uk-tena's* forehead was called *Ulunsu-ti* (transparent), like the *Ulunsu-ti* gathered from the ashes of *Nun-yunu-wi*.

Once, elders said, a Shawano warrior killed the *Uk-tena* by shooting an arrow through its heart. Poisonous blood "poured from the *Uk-tena's* wound and down the slope in a dark stream" into a trench the warrior had dug. Later, they said, the trench of blood became a lake, "and in this water the women used to dye the cane splits for their baskets."[95]

How the World Was Made
[Ayasta's Conclusion]

Men came after the animals and plants. At first there were only a brother and sister until he struck her with a fish and told her to multiply, and so it was. In seven days a child was born to her, and thereafter another, and they increased very fast until there was a danger that the world could not keep them. Then it was made that a woman should have only one child in a year, and it has been so ever since.[96]

In 1888, when *Ayasta* (Spoiler) was well past the middle years of her long life, she disclosed to Mooney a portion of the Cherokee creation story. *Ayasta's* contribution is unique, for it is the only narrative Mooney recorded that accounts for the origin of humans. In light of Cherokee social systems that honored and reinforced the generative and regenerative power of women, this is appropriately a woman's story.

Ayasta's short account begins with the order of creation, a sequence that places animals and plants in the world first and humans after. The pattern underlying the story winds back to the creation of an island home for animals who felt crowded and sought another place to live. It weaves a background for the Origin of Disease and Medicine, which came about when "the poor animals found themselves beginning to be cramped for room."[97] In story after story, the notion of more people and fewer resources threads through and beneath the consciousness of Cherokee spinners of tales.

The first two humans in this new world are siblings, sister and brother. No other woman, no other man, no other relationship exists, and the sibling relationship between sister and brother is thus positioned as primary and singularly important. They are enough to form a clan.

The brother initiates reproduction. He is the one to act, to speak, to strike. He wants to create a social order, wants to reproduce something of himself, someone of themselves. Yet, as a man he cannot bear children and as a brother he cannot conceive them with the only woman in the world. The prohibition against incest is never stated, but implied, it becomes part of the natural order. The incest prohibition is revealed only by its marvelous circumvention. In order to procreate and still avoid incest, the brother inseminates his sister with a fish. At the same time, he creates a social order with his words. "He told her to multiply," *Ayasta* explained, and a new world came into being. Words spin out along with the fish; he speaks and strikes, and she responds. The brother assumes a leading role in his sister's life and in the lives of her children, who are their children.

If the beginning of the myth fragment belongs to the brother, the remainder is surely the sister's, for she is the life bringer, the source of children and the future. In response to her brother's fish/touch and his words/speech, she gives birth again and again. But then the deep, recurring fear wells up, the fear that the world itself, suspended from the sky by woven cords, will collapse, will be unable to keep them nourished, safe, productive. Resources will fail. To avoid the final danger, to avoid overwhelming the world, women thereafter spaced the births of their children.

Ayasta's fragment discloses that the closest relationship in the Cherokee universe was that of sister and brother, the people of one clan, the source of all children. The story prohibits incest among clan siblings. It assigns men the responsibility for their sisters' children. It positions women in the center of the kinship system. It reveals women's control of reproduction, their freedom to choose how many children to bear and when to bear them. It explains that children trace descent from mothers because only her blood flows in their veins. Fathers are nowhere to be seen or heard or felt; only a mother and her brother and the phallic, asexual fish.

The story profoundly implies the kinship of all people, yet it undercuts familial bonds by revealing the pervasive anxiety that within a clan or nation the number of kin might strain resources common to them all. The spoken fear suggests an unspoken one—a deep ambivalence about women's reproductive power, perceived as wholly necessary and at the same time as potentially threatening to the balance carefully maintained by each family in the Cherokee world. As it turned out, it was not the swelling numbers of clan relatives who imperiled Cherokee resources, but the waves of European Americans that wanted them.

Clans (*hstahlv-i*: You and I Originate; *anata-yun-wi*: Relationship)

"The Cherokee Nation," wrote Moravian missionaries, "is divided into tribes, but they are not called *Tribes* here, but *Clans* or *Families*."[98] Clans embraced the entire population, weaving patterns of relationships and responsibilities into the fabric of kinship. Every individual belonged to a family that extended beyond households, through settlements, and across the nation. From the most remote house in the Overhills to the far boundaries of the Lower Towns, every Paint or Deer or Wolf could find kin. The network extended to several thousand people in the four settlement areas.[99]

Clan identity came from the mother "without any respect to the father," and neither time nor distance diminished it. "Someone who is so descended," suggested missionaries, "no matter how many years back," need only reveal that a "grandmother or great-grandmother" was Cherokee to assume a place in her clan. The mother's clan identity took precedence over all other ancestry, even for one who had "lost himself" among white people, or whose fathers and grandfathers were white.[100] Identity and a complex of clan possessions, which ranged from land and insignia to customs and prayers, descended from mothers.

Language encoded clan relationships and responsibilities. Baffled missionaries complained that "all close relationships are identified with one noun, as for example father, step-father, father's brother, mother's brother, and more than one degree of close relationship are all called *Father*." Equally frustrating was that "all the female relatives are called *Mother* and similarly the relatives of the grand-parents are all called grand-father and grand-mother."[101] It appeared to despairing missionaries that children could not identify their biological parents. The Cherokee language actually identified clan position so precisely that anyone "could tell you without hesitating what degree of relationship exists between himself and any other individual of the same clan." Specific terms distinguished mothers, their parents and siblings, older and younger brothers, and sisters and their children. A special term identified maternal uncles (*ak-du-tsi*). Blood brothers were signified by the word *dani-taga* ("standing so close as to form one"). Each relationship prescribed certain kinds of behavior and varied responsibilities.[102]

One House: *sita-nela*

Reciprocal hospitality was a paramount clan responsibility. Cherokees have an "advantage over us," wrote Englishman William Fyffe to his brother, "in their mutual love not only in the same family but throughout the Nation."[103] Although clan affiliations did not guarantee love, Fyffe was on the right track. Clan relations were extensive, expressive, and mutual. When Cherokees traveled to another settlement, "they enquire for a house of their own tribe [clan]," wrote Adair, where "they are kindly received, though they never saw the persons before." Visitors to the homes of clan relatives "eat, drink, and regale themselves with as much freedom, as at their own tables."[104]

Women stood at the heart of hospitality. They grew, harvested, gathered, prepared, and served foods for guests in households they owned. Each meal and every visit reinforced the strands of relationships and responsibilities that bound Cherokees to one another. The common thread throughout was the identity and work of women.

Revenge: *tsu-tsa-si*

Along with hospitality, clan relatives shared an obligation to avenge the deaths of clan members. Clan revenge "is rigorously insisted on by the Relations of the deceased," explained John Stuart in 1764, and "a Near relation only can carry out the execution." Women led the "Near relations" who demanded vengeance. As mothers, it was their right and responsibility. Singing and dancing, they celebrated the capture of prisoners and joined in torturing them at the stake. Their participation helped retaliate for the deaths of relatives and guaranteed the repose of their spirits.[105]

Clan revenge assured surviving Cherokees of exact compensation for the loss of kin. The custom led warriors and relatives on warpaths to enemy camps and villages for prisoners, scalps, or lives. Stuart reported that when warriors, who were "generally Relations to the people killed," sought revenge, they were "careful to kill the same Number which they lost." One life for one life, or ten for ten, the goal was to replace the losses in each family rather than to exterminate an enemy.

The phrase "near Relations" recurs throughout Stuart's careful explanation of Cherokee retribution, subtly weaving women into the politics of war. Clan members sat together in town house meetings to make decisions that affected the entire polity, such as declarations of peace or war.[106]

"Many of the Indian women" also served as warriors, becoming "as famous in war" as the legendary Amazons, each earning the title of "war woman." Some accompanied men on warpaths "to take care of the Camp, Fire, Provisions, etc." They too became war women and assumed the right to claim prisoners as slaves, adopt them as kin, or condemn them to death "with a wave of a swan's wing." War women sat with chiefs and male warriors in council and spoke with singular authority. Older war women who could no longer go to battle "but [had] distinguished themselves in their younger days," wrote Timberlake, "[had] the title of Beloved." Beloved and war women participated in peace treaties, sealing their personal pledges with gifts of tobacco, pipes, cloth, beads, and other symbolic goods.[107]

Young *Nane-hi* (Nancy) of Chota accompanied her husband, Kingfisher, to the 1750s battle of Taliwa against the Creeks, where she accrued particular honor. When Kingfisher fell mortally wounded, Nancy took his place. Following the Cherokee victory, she became *Ghi-gau* (Greatly Beloved Woman), an authority at council meetings and treaty conferences for the next fifty-six years. While Nancy Ward became the most famous woman warrior among European Americans, others acquired honor among Cherokees. Battles of the Revolutionary period included several war women, such as *Cuhtahlatah* (Wild Hemp?), who led Cherokee warriors to victory after her husband fell. She later participated in the victorious war dance in the town house, "carrying her gun and tomahawk."[108]

Returning warriors offered captives or scalps to women, "each family getting an offer" to compensate for "the number they've lost in the war." Positioned to save or destroy hostages, women assumed heroic dimensions among frightened prisoners. Captured in battle, English surgeon David Menzies was appalled by a chief's "nauseous" mother sitting "squat on the ground with bear's cub in her lap." She looked him over briefly before muttering his "rejection and destruction." Had she found him pleasing, the chief's mother might have adopted Menzies as a member of her family and clan. "By these adoptions," Fyffe explained, they "endeavor to supply their Losses by the wars."[109]

My Daughter: *akwetsi*

Special bonds tied women to female children. Maternal grandmothers or the oldest female relations named infant girls. Honorific names might be passed on to some, while affectionate characterizations—"the Pretty Girl, the kind Girl, the lovely Girl, the Dance Leader or the Climber of Trees"—were given to others. Alexander Longe reported that when a girl was born "all the female relations looks on the child to be their proper daughter." Women's collective responsibilities began at the moment of a child's birth, for if the mother died, "any of the woman's relations that gives milk will take the child and give it suck." When women took in clan children, they made "no distinction betwixt that child and their own proper children." Among Cherokees, there were no "improper" children. All belonged to a clan.[110]

My Sister's Son: *u-kiwina*

Men assumed other kinds of responsibilities for clan children. Elder brothers trained and educated their sisters' sons. "You know such and such boys in the town that are my near relation," a priest explained patiently, "I am now alearning them all sorts of doctoring for when I die they'll be in my place." Clan specializations and customs moved through time and across generations, tying Cherokees of the present to those of the past and future. "When they are old and perhaps dead," the priest continued, "their relations are in their place." Their "place" might be in the priesthood or war council, the domains of medicine or prophecy or leadership, or the intricacies of dance or song or even weaving or potting. A "certain family," wrote Longe, "always hold[s]" the priesthood, and no one else could "minister in that affair." Every clan possessed its own distinct body of magic, formulas, dances, and symbols.[111]

My Wife, My Husband: *akwatalu, uhyei*

Deeply embedded in the clan system lay its most important and enduring function, the regulation of marriage. Members of one clan were forbidden to marry one another. Those of the Wolf Clan sought partners beyond Wolf, Paint Clan beyond Paint, Deer beyond Deer. To do otherwise was incestuous, and the penalty was death. Few social transgressions carried such a severe penalty. Incest, which threatened the stability of the matrilineage, was the most abhorrent crime. Marriages formed alliances among clans, guaranteeing their survival. Marriage within clans diminished potential alliances and strained resources.

In the early 1700s, incest prohibitions were firmly in place and deeply internalized. Men "will in no wise marry with a woman of their own family [clan]," cautioned Longe, "counting them their proper sisters." When the British trader spoke of Christian marriage uniting wife and husband as one, the priest retorted that becoming "one flesh" with a woman meant he would be "married to his own mother or sister." Clans, not marriage, united Cherokees for life. "Our wives is nothing to us but mere strangers," the priest advised, "therefore we cannot be one flesh as you say." Those of one flesh were sister and brother, mother and child, never wife and husband. Marriage partners were "mere strangers" and wives were "nothing akin" to their husbands.[112]

Cherokees interested in marriage "goes and visits one another and promises to each other." They notified "the ould people" of their commitment, and if all agreed, the "young man" cut a "kording of wood" to lay at his beloved's door. She signified her acceptance by making a fire with the wood and "giving him vitoles to eate." The marriage was thus confirmed, and the woman became a wife (*usda-yv-hv-sgi*: the one who cooks for me). Their families publicly reenacted the ritual, joining clan to clan. The man's kin from "fare and nere" brought a vast quantity of wood to the woman, and her "relations prepared for them a grate feast."[113] The locus of marriage lay in a woman's willingness to accept responsibility for food and fire and a man's willingness to provide game. If the marriage proved unsuccessful, the couple parted "with as little concern as if they had never known one the other." A priest made clear to Longe that they "had better be asondor than together" if they could not live in harmony.[114]

Within the constraints of the clan system, women exercised considerable autonomy and sexual freedom. They entered liaisons with colonial traders, surveyors, and soldiers as well as with their own tribesmen. Some took partners for love and life, others changed marriage partners with ease and frequency, and none suffered punishment for divorce or adultery.

Women's sexual freedom titillated Europeans, who reported it throughout the eighteenth century. Stressing the erotic aspects of women's behavior, their reports neglected restraints urged by tribal elders. At Green Corn festivals, priests gave "sharp and prolix" lectures to women, admonishing them to observe "the marriage law." They ardently reproved the "vicious way" of young men "running after other men's wives and debauching them." Priests attributed epidemics to divine anger over the "adulterous intercourses of their young married people" and their "unlawful copulation in the night dews."[115] Reports of such reproaches reveal common occurrences, but also social sanctions. Priests publicly warned that violations of sexual constraints threatened tribal harmony, community health, and agricultural harvests. They blamed famine, war, and disease on clan members' failure to heed their warnings.

Though William Bartram joined other Europeans in sly allusions to women's sexual activities, he added an important observation about the role of elders. As he and his host approached the "young, innocent Cherokee virgins" who were filling their baskets with strawberries, the lusty men were nearly thwarted by "some envious matrons" serving as "guardians." Clan mothers monitored the behavior of those in their care and imparted to young women sexual codes of conduct that Europeans never recorded. Among Cherokees, women and men enjoyed sexual freedom, which was tempered—as other freedoms were—with concern for the maintenance of societal well-being.[116]

Sexual sanctions were strictest for menstruating women, who were considered extraordinarily powerful and dangerous. They isolated themselves in special "lunar retreats" where the negative force of their blood would not overwhelm medicine, spoil crops, or incapacitate warriors. Before reentering society, they went to water. Similar rules applied to postpartum women, who "keep retired" until their blood ceased to flow. They abstained from any contact with men, crops, or weapons. Sexual intercourse while bleeding was sternly prohibited.[117]

Adultery was the freedom that set Cherokee women and society completely apart. Adair complained that married women "plant their brows with horns as oft as they please." Unlike women of "all civilized or savage nations," they did so "without fear of punishment." Women's sexual liaisons beyond marital households struck Adair as such a profound expression of power that he declared the entire nation was "under petticoat-government." Wives never failed "to execute their authority," he protested, "when their fancy directs them to a more agreeable choice." Authority, governance, and power were European constructs of women's sexual autonomy. In such a "wanton female government," Adair was little surprised that marriages were often "of a short duration."[118]

Women's autonomy was born of social and economic security. Marriage customs, residence patterns, and social structures all protected women and children and enhanced their rights. After marriage, a woman usually remained in her home village and continued to live in her family compound. Her household might contain her mother, sisters, and aunts, along with her new husband. She owned her house and garden and, through the matrilineage, controlled clan fields as well. Whereas men moved away from home and even from their villages after marriage, women remained in their households and towns of origin. Close to their families and fields, they retained access to economic and social resources. "The wives generally have separate property," explained Timberlake, "that no inconveniency may arise from death or separation."[119]

Economic security derived from the matrilineage, allowing women to participate independently in nearly every kind of trade. Throughout the eighteenth century, they followed trails to neighboring houses or tribes, to European settlements or garrisons, carrying slaves, food, and crafted goods such as baskets and beadwork to obtain items they wanted or needed. For example, in 1716, "Indian Peggy" appeared before the Commissioners of Trade with a "French Man" purchased by her brother and given to her. The man had come dearly, costing her brother "a Gun, a white Duffeld Match Coat, two broad Cloth Match Coats, a Cutlash, and some Powder and Paint." Peggy was willing to exchange her hostage for the gun, and "the Value of the Rest of the Goods might be paid her in Strouds." When the commissioners paid her, she turned in her captive.[120] In a single transaction recorded in the Charles Town Journals of Trade, it is evident that the interlacing systems of clan obligations, blood revenge, and economics empowered women.

Through her lineage, Peggy had obtained something—a Frenchman—to exchange. Whatever debt her brother owed was forgiven, and Peggy moved outside the household and beyond her village to pursue another kind of exchange. Her payment in guns and strouds suggests that she would continue dealing in men's worlds with men's wares. Through such intricate processes, the matrilineage provided women with bartering power as well as goods.

The matrilineage also protected women who chose to trade outside the parameters of current political expediency. When British soldiers garrisoned at Ft. Loudon in 1761 ran low on provisions, they depended on Cherokee women to bring them food. Headman *Willinawaw*, according to Timberlake, angrily threatened the women with death for supplying the enemy. Secure in the custom of clan revenge, the women laughed at the headman and retorted that "their relations would make his death atone for theirs."[121] *Willinawaw* withdrew, knowing that any injury he caused would be returned in kind. Relations and revenge were inextricable, and enhanced the autonomy of every woman and man.

Women-centered households, the strong matrilineage, and weak marriage bonds facilitated the custom of polygyny. "The corrupt Cheerake," bristled Adair, "marry both mother and daughter at once." When related women married the same man, they reduced potential male competition for household and agricultural resources. They shared responsibilities for children, farming, gardening, and gathering. Polygyny also solved the problem of finding suitable partners when women outnumbered men, as they did during eras of warfare. Not all households were polygynous, and the occurrence most likely varied from one settlement to another and one decade to the next. The Cherokee term for a man who married sisters (*ukinali*: friends), however, indicates a custom based on something more than male eroticism or authority.[122]

As long as women retained control of their resources and lived in female-centered households, they could support their descendants. When marriage partners separated, wrote Timberlake, "the children go with, and are provided for, by the mother."[123] Women's ability to support their children and themselves emerged from a densely woven social fabric. Matrilineal ownership of land gave women access to foods, whether grown or gathered, served or sold. Matrilocal residence patterns facilitated sharing of responsibilities and resources. Nucleated settlements maintained and reinforced household connections. It is little wonder Alexander Longe thought "the women Rules the Roost and weres the brichess."[124] They appeared to be little dependent on their husbands.

The world made for and by Cherokees in the 1700s was a land of abundant resources where women worked long and hard to gather and process foods, fashion clothing, and make household goods. It was an arena where women might act as healers and warriors as well as wives and mothers, where they acknowledged kinship with brothers and children more than with husbands of short or long term. In this realm, women took charge of special dances, certain kinds of exchange, and hospitality. They loaded pelts or baskets or chestnuts on their backs and walked to European or other native settlements to engage in trade. They commanded the deaths of some prisoners and adopted others as family members. They went to war and to peace, tortured captives and healed the injured.

They taught young girls how to be Cherokee women. Training took place in homes where girls watched female relatives make meals, baskets, pottery, beadwork, and clothing. Teaching by example, showing girls how to be mothers and sisters, daughters and wives, storytellers and traders, was part of every relationship. It occurred in household gardens and clan fields where young girls gradually learned about plants and crops, seeds and seasons, formulas and weather. Becoming a Cherokee woman meant weaving together knowledge from and of the past with experiences and resources of the present. With every decade of the 1700s came a change in knowledge, experiences, and resources. With every decade, women transformed and were transformed, weaving new worlds from old.

CHAPTER 1

Rivercane

The First Fire
[As Told by Swimmer and John Ax]

In the beginning there was no fire, and the world was cold, until the Thunders (*Ani-Hyun-tikwala-ski*), who lived up in *Galun-lati* sent their lightning and put fire into the bottom of a hollow sycamore tree which grew on an island. The animals knew it was there, because they could see the smoke coming out at the top, but they could not get to it on account of the water, so they held a council to decide what to do.

Every animal that could fly or swim was anxious to go after the fire. The Raven offered, and because he was so large and strong they thought he could surely do the work, so he was sent first. He flew high and far across the water and alighted on the sycamore tree, but while he was wondering what to do next, the heat scorched all his feathers black, and he was frightened and came back without the fire. The little Screech-owl (*Wa-huhu*) volunteered to go, and reached the place safely, but while he was looking down into the hollow tree a blast of hot air came up and nearly burned out his eyes. He managed to fly home as best he could, but it was a long time before he could see well, and his eyes are red to this day. Then the Hooting Owl (*U-guku*) and the Horned Owl (*Tsikili*) went, but by the time they got to the hollow tree the fire was burning so fiercely that the smoke nearly blinded them, and the ashes carried up by the wind made white rings about their eyes. They had to go home again without the fire, but with all their rubbing they were never able to get rid of the white rings.

Now no more of the birds would venture, and so the little *Uksu-hi* snake, the black racer, said he would go through the water and bring back some fire. He swam across to the island and crawled through the grass to the tree, and went in by a small hole at the bottom. The heat and smoke were too much for him, too, and after dodging about blindly over the hot ashes until he was almost on fire himself he managed by good luck to get out again at the same hole, but his body had been scorched black, and he has ever since had the habit of darting and doubling on his track as if trying to escape from close quarters. He came back, and the great blacksnake, *Gule-gi*, "the Climber," offered to go for the fire. He swam over to the island and climbed up the tree on the outside, as the blacksnake always does, but when he put his head down into the hole the smoke choked him so that he fell into the burning stump, and before he could climb out again he was as black as the *Uksu-hi*.

Now they held another council, for there was still no fire, and the world was cold, but birds, snakes, and four-footed animals, all had some excuse for not going, because they were all afraid to venture near the burning sycamore, until at last *Kanane-ski Amai-yehi* (the Water Spider) said she would go. This is not the water spider that looks like a mosquito, but the other one, with black downy hair and red stripes on her body. She can run on top of the water or dive to the bottom, so there would be no trouble to get over to the island, but the question was, How could she bring back the fire? "I'll manage that," said the Water Spider; so she spun a thread from her body and wove it into a *tusti* bowl, which she fastened on her back. Then she crossed over to the island and through the grass to where the fire was still burning. She put one little coal of fire into her bowl, and came back with it, and ever since we have had fire, and the Water Spider still keeps her *tusti* bowl.[1]

Swimmer and John Ax described for James Mooney what the world was like in the beginning. It was an unimaginable time, an incomprehensible place, a world without fire, and so, a world eternally cold. In this cold, dark world, nothing could grow, there could be no fall harvest, nor spring planting, nor summer blooming. No fruits could ripen on bushes or vines, no nuts could fall from autumn trees, no roots could fill with nutritious starch. There was nothing to gather and little to eat.

The blast of lightning split the sky as the animals watched anxiously to see where it struck. Like a messenger from another world, smoke revealed where the fire began. But the cold and frightened creatures were separated from the gift of fire by a world of water. As they always did when faced with a problem that affected them all, they held a council, each taking a turn to speak. Many volunteered to go. Some known for their strength and size tried first, and as they failed the fire transformed them forever. Others famous for cunning and daring ventured out to the wonderful tree and returned black as the night around them, choking, dazed, half blind, and empty-handed.

The last to offer to bring the fire was so small that everyone seemed surprised, skeptical, perhaps even hopeless, perhaps resigned to the cold and the dark and the endless hunger. But then, as easily as though the little one were born for this work, she brought forth from her body all that was necessary to assure their survival. From the remarkable material, a part of herself, she wove a container, carrying it almost as part of her body across the water to the tree, then put into the container just a single burning coal, and that was enough. Across the dark and cold water, the container cradled their future like a mother carries a child. The little one had woven a miracle. Weaving, it seemed, was her very nature.

In the deep consciousness of Cherokee people, the weaving of a woman enabled them to survive. The First Fire and the life-saving, life-bringing weaving of the spider carried such meaning that twice each year Cherokees reenacted the legendary acquisition of fire. At festivals of the First New Moon of Spring and the Great New Moon of Autumn, women carried coals from new town house fires to start fresh fires in their homes. The seasonal first fire in the town house and in individual homes signified the beginning of new life, mythologically and literally borne by women.

The story denotes the importance of fire to Cherokees and of heat and light to all living things. It associates forest fires with thunder, explains characteristics of familiar creatures, and evokes similarities between animal and human worlds. It connects women and fire and assigns to women the responsibility for regeneration and maintenance of household fire, of life itself. And finally, the story of the First Fire signifies the long and deep association of Cherokee women with the weaving of containers.

Baskets, Mats: *talu-tsa, a-yehstu-ti*

For more than a thousand years, women wove an astonishing array of baskets and mats for scores of uses. They made them for exchange with friends, neighbors, and strangers, for food gathering, processing, serving, and storage, and to utilize in ceremonies and rituals. They kept ceremonial objects and medicinal goods in baskets. They covered ceremonial grounds, seats, floors, and walls with mats. They concealed and protected household items and community valuables in baskets. Basketry was central to women's activities and to Cherokee society.

Early European writers consistently identified basketry with women, "the chief, if not the only manufacturers."[2] Women were the primary users of woven goods and so were also the customary weavers. The association of women with basketry

Rivercane doubleweave basket and its lid (?), dyed red and black with poke (?) and walnut. Governor Francis Nicholson of South Carolina carried these to London in 1725. [basket, l: 48 cm, w: 20 cm; lid, l: 47 cm, w: 19.5 cm]. Copyright British Museum.

is one of the most enduring aspects of Cherokee culture. Woven goods—baskets and mats—document what women did, when, and how. They illuminate the work of women who transformed the environments that produced materials for basketry. They point to women's roles in ceremonial, subsistence, and exchange systems. As objects created and utilized by women, baskets and mats conserved and conveyed their concepts, ideas, experience, and expertise. They asserted women's cultural identity and reflected their values.

Before the removal, the material women used most often for basketry was rivercane (*i-hya*). Cane once grew along virtually every kind of Southeastern waterway. Great stands lined rivers, banked streams and creeks, and radiated from swamps, bogs, and lakes. They sometimes grew so dense that neither the ground beneath nor the horizon beyond them could be seen. The tall evergreen stalks attracted the attention of most European travelers whether they came by foot, horse, or boat.

In 1673, as Abraham Wood trekked toward Cherokee country from the Virginia colony, he saw "many slashes upon ye heads of small runs." All along the waterways, "the slashes are full of very great canes." At the northwest margins of Cherokee lands, Father Marquette descended the Ohio River where he "began to see cane, or very large reeds, on the banks of the river." Like beacons "of a very beautiful green," stalks stood "crowned with long, narrow, pointed leaves." The French explorer for souls and pelts was startled by the density of canebreaks. Stalks were "so thick-set," he exclaimed, "that the wild cattle [buffalo] find it very difficult to make their way through them."[3]

When William Byrd blazed the dividing line between Virginia and Carolina in the fall of 1728, he hacked through "a Forest of Tall canes, that grow more than a furlong [220 yards] in depth." The stumbling and slashing surveyor complained that "it cost us abundance of time and Labour to cut a Passage thro' them wide enough for our baggage." Repeatedly drenched by rain, Byrd concluded that the "thick" canebreaks were "the best guard that can be of the riverbank." Were it not for the plants whose "roots lace together so firmly," the banks might be "wash't away by the frequent Inundations" that watered the Southeast.[4] Rivercane literally held together Southeastern soil.

Southwest of Cherokee lands, William Bartram came across "perhaps the most extensive Canebreak that is to be seen on the face of the whole earth." Stalks were "ten or twelve feet in height," growing so close that "there is no penetrating them" without cutting a road.[5] Botanist François André Michaux found cane in the woods of Kentucky "from three to four inches diameter" and "seven or eight feet high." Father James Gravier discovered cane stalks along the Mississippi River that "were not over seven or eight feet high on the sides of the hills, but are twenty, thirty, or forty feet high in the wood."[6]

Byrd speculated that the northeastern limits of cane's distribution was "38 Degrees of Latitude," near the border of the Ohio River. In the following century, André Michaux confirmed his calculation. "This grass," he wrote, appeared in the "southern and maritime portion of Virginia" as well as "in the Carolinas, in the Floridas, and in lower Louisiana."[7] The upper regions where cane could grow corresponded with the northern boundaries of Cherokee hunting lands.

Just as it flourished in most of the Southeast, cane lined the waterways threading through Cherokee settlements. In 1724, naturalist Mark Catesby found Piedmont rivers "covered with spacious tracts of cane." In the late 1700s, Benjamin Hawkins followed a line of old settlements along the Chattahoochee, Tallulah, Chattooga, Etowah, and Hiwassee Rivers. The creeks, he noted repeatedly, were "abounding," "rich," and "well stored with cane."[8] Throughout the Southeast, cane was the water's companion. Spreading across landscapes where women and men lived and worked, hunted and warred, gathered and traded, cane provided raw material for everything from house walls and hair ornaments to game sticks and musical instruments.

Rivercane doubleweave mat, undyed (prehistoric) [l: 198 cm, w: 102 cm].
National Anthropological Archives, Smithsonian Institution.

Toys, weapons, tools, and beds were made of cane. When crops failed and famine came, Cherokees made flour from cane. Before going to battle, warriors purified themselves with cane and root tea.[9] Cane played a part in most Cherokee activities, whether ceremonial or utilitarian.

Baskets (*talu-tsa*) and mats (*a-yehstv-ti*) represent women's most frequent, complex, and significant use of rivercane. Cane mats covered house benches and beds, decorated interior walls, served as ceremonial rugs, and wrapped the bodies of the dead. "With this material these Indians make neat and well-woven mats," wrote a Spanish invader. "And by throwing four, five, or six of them on top of each other, they fashion a roof which is useful as well as beautiful." The Spaniard seemed surprised at the skill of the weavers. "Neither sun nor water," he marveled, could "penetrate" the beautiful and dense mats.[10]

Cane baskets were also serviceable, handsome, and considerably more numerous than mats. The number of hours women spent harvesting cane, preparing it, and weaving it into containers for everyday use or celebrations, for gifts or trade, or for themselves or their families or their neighbors can hardly be imagined. The amount of time a young girl might spend during her childhood watching her mother or grandmothers or aunts make splits and dyes for useful containers with intricate patterns remains inestimable. Generation after generation, women turned cane stalks into containers. The tradition of weaving rivercane baskets reaches back beyond the edge of memory, tying women of the present to those of the distant past. From contemporary women who continue to make baskets of cane, we learn how it is done and contemplate how it might have been done centuries ago.

Preparing Material

Cane is green year-round and can be harvested at any time. Since spring and summer are periods of rapid growth, fall and winter are the best seasons for gathering.[11] Women cut hundreds of long cane stalks and immerse them in streams to keep them fresh. If the stalks dry out, they become too brittle to work with. Weavers leave them in running water until they have time to prepare the splits, a task that requires a sharp knife, several days, and hard work.

Before Europeans introduced metal tools, Indians made knives of flint, obsidian, shell, bone, and cane. All were adequate for preparing cane even though it is extremely tough and fibrous. A weaver uses the knife only to initiate a cut and guide the subsequent splitting down the length of the stalk. She pulls the stalk apart as she directs the cut. Metal knives are not necessary, but they unquestionably facilitate the process. The widespread adoption of metal tools in the 1700s made cane preparation faster and easier.

Cane is the most challenging of all materials used by contemporary Cherokee weavers, in part because of the demanding preparation. Making splits is the most difficult part of basketry and is often the last stage learned. No basket material is simple to work, but proficiency in cane basketry identifies the most accomplished weavers. Most began developing their skills as young children, playing with scraps on hand from their mother's bundles of splits. As novices acquire patience along with technique, they gradually learn to prepare their own material.

The weaver trims the leaves from each stalk, smooths the rough joints, and then splits the stalk in half once and once again, making four or even eight sticks of approximately the same size. Experts can split a stalk in less than five minutes. They coordinate two simultaneous movements, a rapid upward flick of the knife in the center of the stalk and the motion of pulling the halves apart. Weavers never look away from the stalk they are preparing. The task requires patience, practice, and a feel for the material. One careless motion will pull the split across the grain and break it.

To thin the quartered sticks, the weaver repeatedly inserts the knife under the cane's outer cortex and then pulls the core back as she guides the cut with her knife. She works down the length of the stick, detaching the interior core until only the exterior of the cane remains as a thin, pliable split. Around her feet, long segments of discarded cores pile up, filling the air with a fresh, pungent odor. The work continues hour after hour, the rhythmic strokes of the weaver's hands keeping time with the sounds of splitting cane.

She finally extends each thin split across her lap, with the interior facing up. With one hand she presses the edge of the knife blade onto the split, using her other hand to pull the split up and out from under the knife again and again. The edge fibers and the inner pith curl up and fall away with each motion. She scrapes until no trace remains of the interior and no fibers spin out from the edges.

After hours of work, the weaver has "taken out" all the splits from the cane stalks. She rolls them into circular bundles, secures the bundles with ties, and begins the process of dyeing. Near each weaver's home, a large iron pot of water sits on a hearth of river rocks or metal andirons. Stoking the fire under the pot until the water simmers, she immerses roots, bark, hulls, berries, or leaves by the handful to make natural dyes that endure for decades or even centuries.

Vegetation for dyes include ripe berries of pokeweed (*tsayatika*) for pale red, oak galls (*atagu*) for rich red, anjelica leaves (*wane-kita*) for green, bark and roots of sumac (*kwalaga*) for brown, and yellow root (*daloni-ge unaste-tsi*) for yellow. Through the long, complex development of Cherokee basketry, weavers have undoubtedly experimented with many indigenous and introduced plants for basketry materials. Any berry or nut or root that stained the fingers gathering them must have been potential dye.

From earliest memory, however, Cherokee weavers have chosen red, dark brown, and black hues for basketry. Black comes from hulls, roots, or bark of butternut or white walnut (*ko-hi*), brown from hulls, roots, leaves, or bark of black walnut (*se-di*), and red from roots of the bloodroot plant (*gigage unaste-tsi*). Material from black and white walnut trees can be gathered any time of year, then dried and stored for later use. Though all parts of the tree can be used, the roots supply the most intense colors. Bloodroot is an early spring forb that thrives in the soil of deciduous forests. The fragile blossom that appears in early March is followed by deeply scalloped, blue-green leaves that grow through the summer. The orange-red dye comes from small rhizomes attached to multiple underground stems. The roots must be dug before the plant dies back in early autumn, for it leaves no sign of where it has grown.[12] Weavers can dry and bury roots to store over fall and winter, but mold will cause rapid decay. In modern times, some weavers preserve bags of roots in their freezers.

Each color requires a separate pot of simmering water, which may account for the limited number of colors on baskets. To speed the dyeing and set the color, weavers might add a mordant. Before commercial additives became widely available, mordants came from ashes, urine, or alum. Without mordants, splits take at least one full day to absorb brown or black walnut dyes. Red dye from bloodroot sets in a few hours. Weavers submerge the coils of splits into the simmering dye, weighing them down with rocks or heavy roots. Some cover the pots, and all check them periodically to replenish the water and stoke the fire. Dyeing requires a watchful eye and plenty of time.

When splits are a satisfactory color, the weaver removes the bundles, rinses them, and puts them aside to dry. Once the demanding process of preparation is complete, she can wait indefinitely to weave the splits. The capability to use splits weeks or months after preparation gives the basketweaver greater control of her time. She can stop midway through a basket, attend to other responsibilities, and return to it later. When other tasks permit time for basketry, she dampens the splits to restore their pliability and soften their razor-sharp edges.

Building Baskets

The weaver visualizes the completed basket. Even before she reaches for the first split, she knows the size, shape, and form of the container and how many splits she will need. Every decision she makes draws on personal experience and on collective traditions of weaving. Each decision must take into account the amount of available material. One stalk of cane produces four to eight splits that are less than a half inch wide, nearly translucent, and completely flexible. A medium-size single-weave rivercane basket may require fifty to seventy-five splits. The number varies with the length of the stalk, width of the splits, and the size, shape, and density of the container.

Over time, certain features, such as shape, handles, rims, lids, binding, split size, and color, have come to characterize Cherokee rivercane basketry. The basket bases are square or rectangular because cane is woven on a grid. The bodies are gently rounded or completely circular. Prior to removal, Cherokees made handles with fabric or thong rather than carved wood. They pushed a narrow strap through the basket sides and knotted each end of the strap on the inner sides. Lids did not attach to the baskets. A separate lid fitting tightly over the sides could be removed and used as an additional basket. Splits for baskets or mats might be less than a quarter inch wide and were woven with the shiny cane surface turned to the outside. Rims were splits of cane bound on with narrow strips of cane or hickory.

Cane patterns are made by varying the twill weave and dyeing the splits. By changing the number of vertical splits crossed by each horizontal split and by alternating splits of different colors, a weaver can produce an almost unlimited number of angular designs. Each pattern is numerically based and has to be memorized, which means that continual counting is required for each design. The complexity and distinctive character of cane patterns suggest that at one time they belonged to their creators and were passed down from mother to daughter. Many weavers would have seen them, but none could readily reproduce them.

As clearly as seals on documents or signatures on letters, such characteristics of form identified Cherokee baskets. In 1754, a group of warriors from "Great Terraqua" (Tellico) in the Overhills followed enemy tracks to a "Mush Basket" that had been taken from a canoe and abandoned. "Knowing it to be of Cherokee make," the warriors pursued and killed the thieves. The basket was not made by a woman of Tellico but of neighboring Tannassee.[13] Yet, the attributes of size, shape, weave, dye, and pattern were so distinctively Cherokee that the warriors readily identified it as one of their own.

One of the oldest and most difficult traditions in basketry is a technique called doubleweave. A doubleweave basket is actually two complete baskets, one woven inside the other, with a common rim. The weaver begins with the base of the first, or interior, basket, placing the shiny outer surface of the splits facing up. She weaves obliquely up all four sides to the rim, bends the splits outward, and then continues weaving obliquely down the sides of the second, or external, basket. She finishes on a diagonal at the base of the outside basket. The result is a strong, flexible, double-layered basket with the glossy side of the splits showing on both the interior and exterior. Since the inner and outer baskets join only at the rim, a skilled weaver can put different patterns on the inside and outside.

Doubleweaves are the most durable of baskets, and cane is the most durable basket material. Like the *tusti* bowl of *Kanane-ski Amai-yehi*, woven rivercane naturally resists damage by water or fire. The tough, glossy cortex of cane makes it nearly impervious to the elements.

In 1982, a fire on the Cherokee reservation completely burned a row of buildings, including a shop whose front window displayed a rivercane doubleweave storage basket and lid. Winter rain and snow gradually covered the ashes. Several months passed before shop owner Tom Underwood poked through the debris scattered at the site and discovered the cane basket. It was burned, soaked, and crushed, lying under a collapsed table at the rear of the shop where it had been blown by a blast of water from the firefighters' hoses. Underwood extracted the basket and carried it home, cleaned it with abrasive solvents over a period of several months, and gradually reconstructed it. He subsequently brought the container to his new shop and put it on a shelf for display. With colors still strong, the designs intact, and the shape restored, it stands as remarkable testimony to the durability of rivercane doubleweave baskets.

Rivercane doubleweave basket with lid, dyed with walnut and bloodroot. Made by Rowena Bradley in 1982, the basket and lid survived a fire, water damage, compression, and harsh cleaning solvents. Private collection. Photograph by Sarah H. Hill.

The hard, glossy finish so characteristic of cane derives from silica, a component of every grass from cane to corn. Silica encrusts and permeates cane's outer sheath, providing a hard covering that is perhaps ten times more resistant to breaking or tearing than woods of the same weight.[14] Silicic hardening begins when cane tissues stop elongating, a process that takes about three years. While stems are growing, their internodes fill with water and silica in solution. The water gradually transpires to the developing foliage, leaving behind small particles of hydrous silica in the form of a cottony residue.[15] It appears as white tufts in the nodes and is familiar to anyone who has ever split a cane stalk. After about three years of growth, cane has become good basket material.

Ceremonial Baskets

Our understanding of the development of rivercane basketry among Cherokees and their predecessors is fragmentary because so little has been preserved in archaeological sites. Like all textiles, woven rivercane yields to the vagaries of Southeastern climate. Over long periods of time, alternating or simultaneous cold, moisture, heat, and aridity gradually destroy fibrous materials. Recovering complete baskets from centuries-old Southeastern sites is virtually impossible.

Rivercane doubleweave fragment, dyed
with walnut (Mississippian Period?).
Museum of the Cherokee Indian,
Cherokee, N.C.
Photograph by Sarah H. Hill.

Even in the poorly preserved archaeological record, however, occasional fragments of basketry have been recovered because they were protected by contact
with certain minerals. Fragments of woven rivercane that have been preserved by
copper salts are found on sites that date to the Mississippian Period (A.D. 900–
1500). They document centuries of technological sophistication and periods of
complex ritualism.

Along river valleys of the Tennessee, Arkansas, and Mississippi, woven rivercane
cradled and shielded copper headdresses, breastplates, axes, and jewelry in burials
of high-ranking individuals. The surviving fragments represent baskets and mats
manufactured specifically as ceremonial containers, affirming that Mississippian ancestors of Cherokees associated rivercane baskets with sacred and powerful objects,
events, and people.

Even older fragments of cane basketry have been recovered from settlement areas along the Tennessee River. These small, broken pieces date to the Late Woodland Period (A.D. 600–900), indicating that Cherokee precursors made rivercane
mats and baskets more than a thousand years ago.[16] By the time Europeans invaded
their settlement areas, highly skilled weavers regularly created rivercane baskets
and mats for ceremony, utility, and trade. Of the three kinds, the most elusive are
ceremonial.

Before the removal, Moravian missionary Daniel Butrick learned that the home
of each Cherokee priest or conjuror contained a private area no one but he was allowed to enter. There, "in a cane basket, curiously wrought," the priest kept his
revered instruments of prophecy—conjuring beads, grains, and the *Ulunsu-ti*. Cane
baskets safeguarded the crystal and at the same time protected household members from its formidable power. Cherokees considered the crystal to be so powerful that when a priest died, they buried it with him. If it was not buried, the force
of the *Ulunsu-ti* could cause the death of every member of the priest's household.[17]

Large doubleweave cane baskets held ceremonial clothing that signified spiritual

Rivercane doubleweave basket with lid, dyed with walnut. M. R. Harrington purchased this small basket for fifty cents from Nancy Goingsnake in the summer of 1908. [l: 21 cm, w: 10.2 cm, h: 9.5 cm]. Courtesy of the National Museum of the American Indian, Smithsonian Institution, no. 1/9150. Photograph by Pamela Dewey.

and sacred authority. Following a special rite of consecration, the initiate (*u-ku*) placed his elaborate costume "in a double cane basket having a lid."[18] Whether for ritualistic objects or ceremonial clothing, rivercane doubleweaves were associated with powerful and sacred objects, heavy clothing, or fragile beads. Containing venerable goods and concealing mythological elements, they signified—and perhaps even legitimized—power. We cannot be sure of their appearance, but they may have resembled the container called *ti-hyah-theli* (the narrow one). The oblong lidded doubleweaves could secure shells or feathers, needles or awls, objects of the most common utility or those of particular reverence.[19]

Cherokees also wove cane baskets and mats for festival use. During the Propitiation Festival (*Ah-tawh-hung-nah*), the priest sat in a special seat covered with white deerskin, "and a cane matting was expressly prepared for the occasion to receive his feet." In ceremonies to consecrate a new leader, the candidate was carried to a white chair in the town house and "the ground under his feet was spread with a mattress of cane."[20] Practicality and meaning interlaced as woven cane, perhaps covered with emblems of clan or family, community or status, ceremony or season, simultaneously protected and connected the priest and the earth beneath his feet.

During the Propitiation Festival, medicinal woods "were fastened into a cane basket, expressly fashioned for the purpose." The priest submerged the basket in a cauldron of boiling water, where it remained for several days. After all the townspeople took a portion of the medicine, the "sacred basket" was removed from the water and stored in the treasure house.[21] Woven cane could withstand the heat and water. And the weight and density of cane baskets made them suitable for holding medicine bundles while letting water flow through and around them. Just as *Kananeski Amai-yehi*'s container held life-bringing fire, special cane baskets secured life-saving medicine.

Baskets also contained food during special ceremonies to honor corn, the basic staple of Cherokee subsistence. The New Green Corn Festival (*Selu Tsu-istigi-sti-yi*) celebrated its initial ripening, and the Ripe Corn Festival (*Tu-nakah-ni*) its subsequent fruition. During corn festivals, townspeople covered "all the seats of the beloved square with new mattresses, made out of the fine splinters of long canes."[22] Fresh mats for the town's ceremonial arena suggest a symbolic renewal of collective households, a ritual rebirth of the town to accompany the harvest of new foods for the coming year.

The turning point of the Ripe Corn Festival was the kindling of ceremonial fire and the sacrifice of harvest foods. As the assistant priest proclaimed that fresh fire blazed in the town house, he called for "an old beloved woman to pull a basket-full of the new-ripened fruits, and bring them to the beloved square."[23] Emblematic of the future of the entire community, the container of food was the gift of women. As the water spider carried her container of fire and as women bore their children, the beloved woman carried a basket of food, representing clan mothers in the ceremonial blessing of regeneration.

During corn festivals, women participated in the selection, preparation, and presentation of over sixty courses of sanctified foods.[24] To begin the feasts, they brought "to the outside of the sacred square" a great variety that included "all those good things, with which the divine fire has blessed them in the new year."[25] They placed the food on the town house square, "the meat in large earthen pans and the bread and fruit in baskets." Everyone gathered for the harvest they had eagerly awaited during the weeks of planting and tending fields, warding off predators, scanning the skies, and importuning priests for good weather. A good harvest provided for them all in the long nights and cold weeks that lay ahead. They must have gathered with relief and hunger as they "sat around each pan and basket in a circular manner."[26]

Storing ritual paraphernalia, holding sacred medicines, bearing harvest foods, serving ceremonial feasts, covering shared and sacred ground, woven rivercane expressed and partook of profound mysteries and rhythms of life. Different kinds of baskets and mats served different functions that imparted meaning to them. They also signified the lives, labor, concepts, customs, and beliefs of those who wove and used them.

Domestic Baskets

Ritual use of cane connects women to elaborate cycles of belief. Through their weaving, women both assumed and enacted ceremonial roles. The domestic counterparts of ceremonial basketry document the lives and work of women in the household as well as in subsistence activities, the heart of Cherokee society.

In each household, women kept carrying baskets for harvesting crops and collecting wild foods. Large storage containers held clothing or dried foods through the winter, and smaller ones kept jewelry, personal items, or seeds for the next planting season. Women relied on woven winnowers, sifters, and sieves to process vegetables, fruits, nuts, and roots. They fished, cooked, prepared medicine or dye, and served food with baskets. The relationship between women and baskets was so intrinsic that Cherokees inquired about the sex of newborns by asking if they were "sifters" or "bows."[27]

The carrying, pack, back, or burden basket (*iti*) was as much as three feet high with a square base and a circular, flaring rim. A tumpline, or sling, encircled the basket neck and crossed the bearer's shoulders, suspending the basket on her back. With both hands free and the weight of "burdens" distributed evenly on their backs, women gathered firewood, wild foods, and crops. "My mama's grandmaw," recalled Alice Walkingstick (1903–95), "used to tie it on . . . and put it on her back, carrying it when she goes to the corn fields to get the corn off the stalks."[28] Pack baskets could hold about three bushels. When women distributed "a certain proportional quantity of each kind of the new fruits" to the priest, they measured the amount "in the same large portable back-baskets, wherein they carried home the ripened fruits."[29] As they carried pack baskets of food on their backs, women reenacted the work of *Kanane-ski Amai-yehi*.

The most common baskets were those made to process vegetables, nuts, tubers, and fruit and to prepare bread, soup, gruel, stew, mush, gravy, pudding, dumplings,

Rivercane singleweave storage basket (preremoval) [l: 35.5 cm, w: 34.5 cm, h: 26.3 cm].
Reprint from Duggan and Riggs, *Studies in Cherokee Basketry*.
The Frank H. McClung Museum, The University of Tennessee, Knoxville.

cake, and beverages. Sifting, winnowing, and sieving baskets resembled one another in form but differed in size. Shallow and flat, they varied in size from two inches square to three feet square. Their durable weave distributed weight and pressure evenly across the surface of the basket, facilitating women's tasks and prolonging basket life.

Winnowing baskets (*saga-i*: flat) were the largest. Tightly woven and as much as three feet across with convex sides a half foot deep, winnowing baskets enabled women to separate corn particles, sort beans, and mix dough. Weavers sometimes reversed the splits in the basket base so that the shiny cane exterior lay faceup. The smooth base created a slick surface that did not absorb moisture or snag food particles. And the texture of the reversed splits in the base contrasted with those in the sides, creating a subtle design. In their most ordinary wares, women thus interlaced aesthetics and utility.

Every day, women prepared corn meal by combining sifted ashes and corn kernels in a pot of boiling water. After the skin loosened from the kernels, they

Rivercane winnowing basket, dyed with walnut. Ethnologist M. R. Harrington purchased this old winnower from Lucina Swayney in 1908. [l: 38 cm, w: 38 cm, h: 14 cm]. American Museum of Natural History. Photograph by William K. Sacco.

scooped out the corn with a woven sieve and carried it to a nearby stream to rinse off the skin and ashes.[30] Women poured the damp, skinned corn into a mortar (*ka-no-na*), which had been carefully shaped from a tree stump left standing near the house. They pulverized the corn with a large pounder (*tes-taki nun-yu, a-ta-lu*) carved from hickory. The pestle and mortar signaled the presence of women, and corn-pounding drummed the rhythms of their daily work throughout the settlement. After pounding the damp kernels, women scooped them into winnowing baskets. They gently shook the winnowers until coarser food fragments fell to the bottom. Skimming off the chaff, they removed the lightest particles and then poured the remaining pieces back into the mortar to repound them into fine flour.[31] With daily use, the sides of the winnower spread farther apart, accommodating the work-worn hands of its maker. The durability of the cane and the strength of the weave enabled women to continue using winnowing baskets until the corners gave way and the rims unraveled.

With tightly woven bases, winnowers held foods that were coarse or fine, dry or damp, processed or unprocessed. Like other baskets, they served multiple purposes. "They had many kinds of bread to bake," wrote Butrick, and "they had many ways of baking bread." Women shaped loaves in a "large, shallow basket" by spreading dough across its base and covering it with long, broad leaves of the cucumber

Rivercane sieve, dyed with bloodroot. The basket was purchased from Katy Cochran
in 1908 by M. R. Harrington. [l: 20 cm, w: 20 cm, h: 12 cm].
American Museum of Natural History. Photograph by William K. Sacco.

magnolia tree. "Then the basket was turned bottom upwards on the hot clay or
stone hearth, and taken off," leaving the dough to bake on the leaves. By shaping
the dough in baskets, "they would make loaves as large as they pleased."[32]

Women relied on sieves of "different sizes, curiously made with the coarser or
finer cane-splinters" for various tasks.[33] They used them to sift wood ashes, seed
fruit, screen nuts, strain oils, sort and rinse foods, infuse herbs, and refine grains.
Sieves enabled women to "produce as fine Flour as any Miller." But Moravian missionary Martin Schneider found the time involved a distinct problem. "The richer
people," he confided to his diary, sifted corn "thro'a fine sieve of Reed . . . but they
can scarce prepare as much in a forenoon as they consume the rest of the day."[34]
Brother Martin may have been right. Cornmeal was the base for so many dishes
that pounding and sifting must have occupied many hours of a woman's day.

Larger sieves (*ka-ti-ta, ti-di-a*) measured approximately eight inches across and
five inches deep, with checkerweave bases for leaching corn and sorting meal. The
smallest sieves (*gu-gu-sti, ha-i yolugiski*) ranged from three to five inches across and
one to four inches deep, with extremely narrow splits and tightly woven sides.
Made to scoop cornmeal and strain parched corn (*gahawi-sita*), the small baskets

Mollie Runningwolfe Sequoyah of Big Cove pounding corn in a wooden mortar with a wooden pestle (1936). Photograph, Great Smoky Mountains National Park.

Rivercane food basket with splits reversed in the base, undyed. The basket was purchased by M. R. Harrington from Lucy Hornbuckle in 1908. Food baskets were also used for the popular butterbean game. [l: 16.5 cm, w: 16 cm, h: 7 cm].
American Museum of Natural History. Photograph by William K. Sacco.

were profoundly associated with the role of women as sources of generation and regeneration. The sieve represented "a sacred container which holds the meal of life," a basket that never emptied completely.[35] These small, unassuming baskets simultaneously evoked and honored food and women, the potential and promise of life itself.

Women's ingenuity with food and baskets made a favorable impression on Europeans. "It is surprising to see," Scottish trader James Adair asserted, "the great variety of dishes they make out of wild flesh, corn, beans, peas, potatoes, pompions, dried fruits, herbs, and roots." Baskets were the tools that enabled women to "diversify their courses, as much as the English, or perhaps the French cooks." One admirer thought "the Indian women are, evidently, among the best cooks in the world."[36]

Serving food to family and guests required still different baskets. Although women also made and used pottery containers, baskets became common serving vessels. They "are frequently used by the *Indians* for the purposes that bowls and

Rivercane doubleweave trade basket and lid, dyed with walnut (ca. late 1700–1838) [l: 39.2 cm, w: 5.2 cm, h: 17.5 cm]. The Frank H. McClung Museum, The University of Tennessee, Knoxville. Photograph by W. Miles Wright.

dishes are put to," Catesby pointed out, since "many of them are so closely wrought they will hold water." Scores of "small flat baskets, made of split canes" lined the ground when Henry Timberlake arrived in Overhill Chota. They were filled with "venison, bear, and buffalo, . . . likewise potatoes, pumpkins, homminy, boiled corn, beans, and pease."[37]

Trade Baskets

While ceremonial baskets connect women to ritual power, and utilitarian containers point to their varied subsistence activities, trade basketry illuminates the little-known world where women made and marketed their work. Expressing both individual concepts and shared customs, trade baskets directly linked makers to buyers from different places. They extended women's social, political, and economic relationships beyond their own communities, transcending boundaries of race, gender, economics, geography, and class.

Enjoying an unparalleled reputation for weaving, women developed trade networks that reached to the shores of the colonies. As a result, even those who did not know them often knew something of their work. "A great way up in the Country," wrote John Lawson in 1709, "both Baskets and Mats are made of split Reeds, which are only the outward shining part of the Cane."[38] Lawson's travels never took him beyond the Lower Piedmont, but he knew about cane basketry. And women farther inland knew about trade.

At the time Lawson was writing about the new world he had discovered, various colonial governments were maneuvering for economic hegemony. Taking many forms and occurring in various arenas, trade was the economic linchpin securing Anglo-Indian relationships at every level. While governors and proprietors struggled with the havoc caused by unscrupulous and abusive traders, wealthy planters and merchants employed their own representatives to seek out native villages and establish private trade relations. Indians also initiated their own exchange systems, coming steadily to English, French, German, and Spanish households or communities for vermilion, "duffeld" blankets in red, white, or "blew," strouds, guns, ammunition, salt, metal tools, and rum. They brought with them slaves, pelts, foods, and crafted goods. Women's baskets became their best-known trade item. Traveling to English communities, Cherokee women "sold baskets to the Planters" when Cherokee men "came amongst them to dispose of their Deerskins, Furs, and other Commodities."[39]

In the 1700s, deerskin was the major commodity sought by Europeans and supplied by Native Americans. Through most of the century, deerskin trade dominated economic relationships between the two cultures. Its importance has left in deep shadows other commodities, including women's baskets.[40] Occasional references to Cherokee baskets and mats, however, make plain the high regard both cultures held for the weaving of women. European travelers, traders, merchants, soldiers, and surveyors all were buyers of baskets.

In 1715, the Charles Town (Charleston) government organized control of Indian trade in the Carolina colony by establishing a public monopoly under the direction of a board of commissioners. In turn, the board reported to the Commons House of Assembly, which established government trade centers in three locations. For a time, Cherokees traveled to the Congarees, Winyah Bay, and Savannah Town to exchange their goods for money or wares imported from England. Illegal private trade also persisted, and unlicensed traders moved stealthily in and out of native settlements to avoid the penalties and punishments set by trade regulators. Commons, and the commissioners, became increasingly vigilant in their efforts to monopolize trade.

When Cherokees resisted traveling to the English trading houses, the commissioners appointed Colonel Theophilus Hastings as the first "Public Factor and Trader to the Charikees" and directed him to their settlements. The autumn following his 1716 appointment, Hastings prepared a list of nearly a dozen "Matters" for the commissioners to consider. He asked "that Leave be given him to purchase a few Baskets" to bestow on friends. Hastings had been the Cherokee factor for only three months, but baskets had caught his eye and interest. He also requested money for "Provisions" and "Expences while in Charles Town." The commissioners sent his petition to Commons, which promptly resolved that "no Expences be allowed the said Hastings . . . nor Anything allowed him to buy Baskets" or anything else from the Cherokees for his personal use.[41]

Hastings appeared in person before the board to insist on "Leave to purchase Baskets and such Trifles as Chestnuts, etc."[42] Women had quickly found their way to the trader's store in their settlements and rapidly established their own networks and relationships. Baskets appeared sufficiently important for the trader to know he needed special permission to purchase them. And they must have been expensive.

Recognizing the commissioners' resistance to private trade, Hastings assured them the items would come "out of the Cargo" he purchased from Cherokees. The board no longer needed the advice of Commons to decide "in the Negative." The commissioners asserted that "a private Trade in Baskets, etc." would "infringe the trade, and be a President [sic]" to others.[43] It seems a terse exchange, one revealing more than the board's determination to regulate trade and traders. Baskets carried the potential to create a separate market beyond the commissioners' control. Europeans held them in high regard, and they were part of the regular "Cargo" traders brought down to the public store.

At the instruction of Commons, the commissioners resolved that "all Baskets" Hastings purchased were to be "for and on the Account of the Publick, only." Thereafter, pack horses and burdeners came staggering down from Cherokee settlements loaded with "Indian Baskets" and "parcels of skins" to be delivered to the public store. In turn, the storekeeper sold them to the general public and other merchants. Women's baskets thus followed far-flung routes from their settlements to traders, then to colonial stores, and on to European countries and other colonial territories.[44]

Cherokees expected prompt payment for baskets and complained to the highest authorities if they felt cheated. In 1716, two Lower Town warriors reported to the board that the commander of the Edisto garrison was a thief. Captain John Jones not only walked off with pelts, one charged, he wanted "three painted baskets" as well. Another vowed that Jones took a basket and "promised him a Shirt, but cheated him likewise." Two days later an indignant chief appeared, protesting that Jones had "cheated his people" of skins and baskets. Jones denied the charge, but the commissioners made "full Amends" for the affront.[45]

Private trade continued, and women's baskets circulated among the European elite. "The baskets made by the more southern Indians," reported Catesby, "are exceedingly neat and strong, and is one of their masterpieces in mechanicks." Compact, sturdy, and technically complex, the baskets also appealed to a European sense of aesthetics. They were "beautifully dyed in black and red with various figures." While the young naturalist admired food containers—those so tightly woven they served as plates and bowls—he also drew on his personal experience to identify the baskets most useful "to the *English* inhabitants." The "commodious" rivercane traveling cases were so sturdy, he claimed, they "will keep out wet as well as any made of leather."[46]

Later in the century, Adair described the containers so admired for "their domestic usefulness, beauty, and skilful variety." Made of "large swamp canes" divided into "long, thin, narrow splinters," they were doublewoven with so much skill that "both the inside and the outside are covered with a beautiful variety of pleasing figures." He considered them "the handsomest clothes baskets I ever saw." According to Adair, women made nests "of eight or ten baskets, contained within each other," four or five baskets with lids or eight to ten separate baskets, depending on the needs and perceptions of the buyer. Although the nests varied in size, he continued, women "usually" made "the outside basket about a foot deep," a foot and a half wide, and "almost a yard long." It is little wonder the wealthy colonists paid for them with gold pieces.[47]

Women's baskets appeared in the households and among the belongings of the powerful, positioned, and wealthy. In the early summer of 1725, Sir Francis Nicholson, the first royal governor of the Carolina colony, made his final voyage to London and took with him a rivercane doubleweave basket and lid.[48] Sometime during the remaining three years of Nicholson's life, the baskets became part of the extensive collections of his influential colleague, Sir Hans Sloane. Court physician, naturalist, and president of the Royal Society of London, Sloane was an avid collector. As he neared his own death in 1753, Sloane notified Parliament that he wished to establish a public museum. The British government agreed to purchase his collections, and around them developed the British Museum. Nicholson's doubleweave baskets are among his other artifacts, with a catalog notation indicating that "they will keep anything in them from being wetted by rain."[49]

As the oldest surviving Cherokee baskets, the two containers housed in the British Museum are rich documents that convey information about Cherokee women of the early eighteenth century. Each basket is nearly two feet long, six inches wide, and four inches deep, with convex sides. The splits are less than a quarter inch wide. The weaver used dark brown and red dyes to enhance several complex designs. The source of the brown hues is not identified, but Sloane's catalog entry claims the red is from *Solanum magnum Virginianum racemosum rubrum*, or great red Virginia nightshade.[50] In 1753, according to the new Linnaean classification system, great red Virginia nightshade became known as *Phytolacca americana* or pokeweed.[51]

Patterns cover the surfaces of both containers, preserving concepts and symbols valued by women of the early 1700s. Horizontal rows of rectangles, triangles, and bars appear to be superimposed on alternating diagonal bands of dark brown, red, and natural splits. Designs on the exteriors differ from each other and from those on the interiors. The narrow splits, the size of the containers, their shape, and the number and complexity of the patterns indicate that they are the creation of a weaver of uncommon skill, a woman of unusual technological sophistication. Nicholson's baskets exemplify the kinds of linkages women established with their basketry. Exchange occurred at the highest levels, from the most accomplished Cherokee women to the most prominent European men.

While the value of other goods rose and fell in the first half of the eighteenth century, women's baskets retained singular popularity. In his comprehensive report on Southeastern Indians, Charleston merchant Edmund Atkin identified Cherokees as "the most ingenious Indians," choosing as proof "their Baskets and Carpets." Men in positions of colonial authority continued to select baskets to bestow on friends and sponsors. In 1759, Captain Paul Demere sent word to Governor Lyttelton that he was sending him "a Nest of Indian Basketts" from the Overhills.[52]

Yet, Adair's comments signal a midcentury change in attitudes among colonists toward the basketry of Cherokee women. "Formerly," he claimed, their baskets were "highly esteemed" in South Carolina. His words do not indicate that the skill of weavers had diminished, but rather, the regard of colonists had. Hostilities between the European Americans and Cherokees escalated in the second half of the eighteenth century, culminating in the Cherokee destruction of Ft. Loudon in 1760 and retaliatory devastation of Cherokee settlements. One of the many casualties of war was women's basketry trade with gentry. When Adair said that Charlestonians "formerly" held Cherokee baskets in high regard, he did not have to add that colonists had formerly esteemed Cherokees as well. Baskets subtly represented Cherokees and their status among Europeans.

Women continued to weave baskets to establish networks with other Native Americans, to convey something of themselves and their intentions. For example, in 1779, two women who accompanied a peace party to the Delawares presented "small baskets made of cane" to the leaders of the nation they had always called their grandfather.[53] In such presentations, women's baskets become signifiers of their desire for alliance and peace, woven emblems of the heart and mind of the Cherokee people.

Rivercane: *i-hya*

The continual use of rivercane for basketry indicates that women transformed their environment and shaped their landscapes. Gathering basket materials was not a matter of simple extraction; it was part of women's interactive system of exploiting and replenishing resources. Certain materials that were suitable for basketry prospered in Cherokee ecosystems, and women directly and indirectly enhanced their growing conditions.

Some botanists recognize three species of rivercane: *Arundinaria tecta*, which grows in the moist and sandy soils of the Coastal Plain, and *Arundinaria gigantea* and *macrosperma*, which commonly appear inland and at higher elevations up to 2,800 feet. Variations in the size and height of cane stalks derive from soil fertility, age, and certain conditions of generation and regeneration.[54]

Cane is a disturbance-driven plant that spreads primarily by its heavy underground stems or rhizomes rather than by its capricious seeding habit. Fire and flood are the two primary sources of regenerative disturbance. When either occurs, cane stalks and leaves die, but the underground rhizomes, where nutrients are stored, are not affected. Cane thrives when disturbance clears out accumulated litter and competing vegetation, creating room for its dense root system to expand and send up new shoots. In the nutritious soil matrix derived from flooding or fire, cane stalks regenerate and grow as much as one and a half inches in twenty-four hours.[55]

Although stalks vary in height, denser stands are evidence of recent flood or fire disturbance followed by intensive new growth. From the banks of the largest rivers in the Piedmont, Catesby saw "vast thickets of Cane, being of a much larger stature than those before-mentioned, they being between twenty and thirty feet high, growing so close they are hardly penetrable but by Bears, Panthers, Wildcats, and the like." His description suggests that fire or flood disturbance had taken place three to ten years earlier.[56]

In the absence of enriching fire and flood, canebrakes reach maturity in about ten years. Stalks then begin to decline in vigor and gradually die. In contrast to the rapid regrowth that follows disturbance, undisturbed regeneration may take as long as several decades.[57] In Cherokee settlement areas, undisturbed cane was exceptional because of the frequent natural floods and fires that occurred and the people's own steady contribution to the transformation of landscapes.

Floods recharged nitrogen and phosphorous in soil depleted of nutrients by corn agriculture, greatly enriching the land where women farmed, gardened, and gathered.[58] They also invigorated and regenerated cane stands that extended beyond town boundaries.[59] Rivers and creeks where Cherokees lived, wrote Adair, "have a quick descent; they seldom overflow their banks," although he reported that "a heavy rain" that "falls on a deep snow" inevitably caused flooding.[60]

Fires sparked by lightning recast landscapes and also enhanced complex, interrelated systems of belief and behavior. Cherokees recalled the power of lightning in the story of the First Fire, when so many animals were permanently transformed in its presence. Their myth isolated lightning in a tree on a remote island, recapitulating their strict avoidance of struck trees. They "will not approach within 50 paces" of trees hit by lightning, claimed Alexander Longe, because "the ground is dreadful where it falls." Cherokees correctly assessed the power of lightning, for it does electrically charge the ground around trees, killing or causing mutations in surrounding vegetation for a distance of thirty feet.[61]

Heavy storms accompanied by rolling thunder and flashing lightning occurred in Cherokee settlement areas an average of sixty-eight days a year, usually during spring and summer months when masses of warm and cold air collided. The "almost-daily showers of rain" Bartram endured on his way to Keowee were "frequently attended with tremendous thunder." Near the "ruins of the ancient famous town of Sticoe," he marveled at a storm "armed with terrors of thunder and fiery shafts of lightning."[62] Struck trees, cleared brush, and burned cane stands must have followed many such storms.

Human-set fires also reshaped the environment. Cherokees fired woods and grasslands in fall and winter as part of farming, gardening, gathering, and hunting strategies. They fired to clear underbrush, release nutrients to the soil, create and maintain fields and forest edges, encourage specific kinds of vegetation, enhance nesting sites, and drive game. Women assumed some responsibility for fire maintenance by "setting fire to the grass in the woods." Without fires, Southeastern forests would replace grasslands within a period of five years, and cane stands would gradually die.[63] Firing maintained cane vigor and ensured its regeneration. Two years after burning, cane stands recover fully.[64]

Cutting cane also stimulated its regeneration by creating openings for the spread of new stems. Selective cutting of stalks for baskets is an effective way to prune stands. One cane stalk produces four to eight basket splits, and one small storage basket requires seventy-five splits of cane, or eighteen to twenty stalks. Since most households contained at least three baskets just for food processing, a settlement of a hundred households might harvest several thousand stalks of cane for food basketry, and many more for storage, ceremonial, and trade basketry. The importance of basketry to women's work and to Cherokee society changed the appearance of landscapes wherever they lived.

The same kinds of activities that maintained the health of cane stands encouraged vegetation for black, brown, and red dyes. Since black and white walnut trees grow best in clearings or along forest edges, Cherokee settlements provided suitable habitats for the trees while assuring their inhabitants access to necessary foods, medicines, and brown and black dyes. Clearings and old fields encouraged pokeweed, whose fall berries produced a pale red dye. Molding leaves in deciduous woodlands hosted bloodroot for early-spring and summer gathering of red dye.

Each basket or dye provides shape and texture to the work of women, documenting their dynamic interaction with the world around them. Every basket is a piece of woven history. Fragments recovered from archaeological sites, the few baskets that have survived from the early days of trade with Europeans, and written references to Cherokee basketry attest to women's repeated selection of rivercane for splits and of black walnut, butternut, bloodroot, and poke berries for dyes. Rivercane baskets and mats represent traditions, customs, techniques, ideas, and values passed from one generation to the next over centuries. Just as rivercane represents the ecology of Southeastern Cherokees in the 1700s, rivercane basketry evokes and expresses the culture of Southeastern Cherokee women, up until the time of removal.

How They Came on This Maine
[As Told to Alexander Longe]

We belonged to another Land far distant from here, and the people Increased and multiplied so fast that the land Could not hold Them so that they were forced to separate and travel To look out for another country[.] They travelled so far that they came to a country that was so cold that it was insufferable. Yet going still on they Came to mountains of snow and Ice. The priests held a council to pass these mountains; and that they believed that there was warmer weather on the other side of those mountains because it lay nearer to the sun setting which was believed by the whole assembly. We were forced to make Raccitts to put on our feet old and young; and being all loaded with provisions and fat lightwood, we pressed on our Journey and at last found ourselves so far gone over these mountains Till we lost the sight of the sun and went through darkness for a good space, and then pursued the sun again and going on we came to a country that could be inhabited and there we multiplied so much that we overspread all this maine. We brought all manner of grains with us as corn and peas, pumpkin and muskmellon and watermelon. As for all sorts of wild fruits we found here naturally growing. As we were on our Journey over these mountains, we lost a vast quantity of our people by the unseasonable Cold and darkness that we went through. When we Came on this maine first we were All of one language; but the pride and ambition of some of Our leading men that caused a Civil war amongst the Tribes. They separated from one and the other and the language was Corrupted. Moreover, we are told by our ancestors That when we first came on this land that the priests And beloved men was writing but not on paper as you Do but on white deer skin and on the shoulder bones of buffalo for several years but the proudness of the Young people being so great that they would not obey the priests nor learning but let their minds Run After hunting of wild Beasts, that the writing was Quite lost and could not be Recovered again.[65]

In 1725, the British trader Alexander Longe attempted to reinstate himself in the good graces of the colonial government in Charles Town by providing an account of "the ways and maners of the Indians called Charikees." His initial seventy-five-page account has disappeared, but from his postscript to it, we learn something of the eighteenth-century ceremonies, beliefs, and collective memory of Cherokees, including the story of their migration into the Southeast.

The story recounts a strain on resources so severe that the land could no longer support the people. A time of such trouble and tension underlay the great myth of the origin of the world. Just as creatures in the primal era left *Galun-ladi* because they felt crowded and fearful, ancestral Cherokees journeyed into the unknown because there were too many people and not enough land. Land, the literal and metaphorical ground of support and conflict, was always the issue. From their earliest memories Cherokees needed land, enough for towns and villages, for fields and gardens, enough to hold them safe from enemies and secure from hunger. And so they set out, camping in clans and trusting their priests to lead them to a new place, a land of enough.

There must have been many on the journey who worried, and some who grieved, for this narrative of migration is also a story of separation. A few stayed behind, while others began a long journey to the south and west to find a country closer to the sun (*nv-da*), to the place it rested in the west (*wudeligv-i*). Those on the ancient journey struggled to survive the withering cold of a hostile environment, an insufferable region with mountains of ice, a time of great darkness in spirit and body. Many died. Yet they pressed on, attempting to pursue the sun and follow the counsel of their priests who believed, and surely prayed, that warmer weather and better land lay beyond the vast and frozen darkness. The cold and the dark were ever their adversaries.

All were borne up on their journey by the ingenuity of those who could weave, for weavers were able to make "raccitts to put on our feet, old and young," providing the pilgrims with shoes to carry them over the snow. The *Ani-yunwiya*, the Real People, came at last to a land of enough, where wild fruits flourished in rich soil and deep forests offered abundant shelter. The new world they found offered land to settle and a place to rest, room to build and grow, to hunt and gather, to sow and harvest. They found land enough to spread over and across as far as they could see or hear, as far as they could walk in the length of several days.

Like most migration stories, this one told of the past and foretold a future. Portending the devastation occasioned by the deerskin trade, the tale reveals a divergence between tribal traditions and new ways, a rift between generations, dissension among leaders, and, finally, a tear that rent them all. Communication faltered, their common language diffused, many kinds of knowledge disappeared, and harmony disintegrated. Like a morality play, the migration story warned the people of the peril of tribal discord and affirmed the importance of tradition to their survival.

During the eighteenth century, town priests drew on their knowledge of tribal traditions and archaic language to recite the migration story at the annual Green Corn Festival. Gradually, however, the ancient narrative with its portents and lessons was all but forgotten.[66]

The Real People: *Ani-yunwiya*

Relative to other Southeastern native populations, Cherokees were late arrivals to the region, migrating at least several hundred—and perhaps more than a thousand—years ago into the Southern Appalachians. Linguistically related to the Iroquois, Cherokees presumably broke away from the Northeastern concentration of tribes, migrated southward, and finally settled along the headwaters of the Savannah, Little Tennessee, and Hiwassee Rivers. When Spanish invaded the Southeast in the sixteenth century, seeking gold and slaves, those who became known as Cherokees lived in compact towns with extensive fields and sufficient stored foods to supply the conquistadors who assaulted their villages, raped women, murdered men, captured slaves, and demanded tribute.[67]

The spring of 1540 brought a singularly ruthless expedition into the Southeastern mountains. Led by Hernando de Soto, an army of 500 Christians, as they called themselves, marched and rode through Indian settlements from coastal plains to the mountainous interior, burning alive those who would not reveal routes to adjacent towns. The barbaric invaders were breathtakingly distinctive. Their ranks included two races—one white, one black—previously unknown to Southeastern Indians. Nearly half of de Soto's men rode horses, a species that had vanished from the North American continent thousands of years earlier. Equally unfamiliar were pigs that accompanied the army and multiplied from thirteen to some seven hundred during the three-year invasion.[68] With the first Spanish footfall, rooting hog, and trampling horse, the transformation of Southeastern ecosystems began to accelerate.

Of all the aliens who arrived in the next few decades, none were more lethal than the unseen microbes hidden in clothing and fur, on bodies and in goods. Diseases that preceded the Spanish inland and surpassed them in devastation left native villages empty and silent. Borne by Europeans who pressed relentlessly upon coastal regions, disease traveled silently and quickly over trading paths and through tribes, overwhelming natives, bewildering healers and priests, and killing untold thousands.[69] Those on the coast died first, paying with their lives for the trade goods offered by Europeans. Those who lived inland and in the mountains suffered in direct proportion to their contact with Europeans and with their own neighbors who traded with those called Christians. The destruction of coastal societies brought Cherokees into greater proximity to Europeans and opened clearings in the middle ground between them, the ground occupied by traders.

In several mountain villages, de Soto's army encountered Indians who were likely Cherokees, though the Spaniards did not refer to them as such. These "very domestic people," according to a disdainful narrator, "subsisted on the roots of plants they dig there in the wilds and on the animals they destroy there with their arrows."[70] Indian food was not a matter of idle interest. Spaniards lacked adequate provisions to support their invasions and exacted supplies for themselves and their livestock from every village they penetrated. To comply with their demands, Indians of one mountain settlement offered 700 turkeys, another village provided 300 dogs, and at a third, "twenty men came out from the town on the road, each laden with a basket of mulberries."[71] Every basket represented the women who remained hidden in the households, every berry their work of gathering summer fruits in old fields.

Scribes of de Soto's expedition exulted in the abundance of foods they found, the trees laden with mulberries and persimmons, the stands of walnut trees so luxuriant they appeared cultivated.[72] These were trees of Piedmont forest edges, land where women and men cleared and burned, gathered and harvested, shaping the landscape in continual acquisition of resources for food, medicines, dyes, and clothing.

As Spaniards pushed forward, the forests they so admired betrayed them. Woods concealed the escape of their most prestigious captive, the Cacica of Cofitachequi, whose aunt ruled the province. When the Cacica fled, she took three black slaves of the Spaniards and her rivercane box filled with "very precious" pearls.[73] Her prestige and power surpassed that of most native women. Other details, however, tie her to those of subsequent generations. This ruling woman who chose her sexual partners represents the "wanton" and authoritative women who were so disturbing to later Europeans. And her rivercane box of valuables materially connects her to makers and users of ritual baskets and containers for items of special power.

Twenty-seven years later, Spanish militia attempted to gain dominion over the interior. The Juan Pardo expeditions of approximately 250 men and horses encountered numerous chiefs, both women and men, as they crossed and recrossed inland ranges. Some were undoubtedly Cherokees, identified in the Pardo accounts not by personal names but by the names of their towns and villages that later became familiar as Cherokee sites—Xenaca (Senneca) and Atuqui (Taucoe), Quetua (Kattewa; Kitu-hwa), Nequase (Naquassee), and Estate (Estatoe). Chiefs who called on Pardo received knives, wedges "like chisels," axes, conch shells, enameled buttons, and green and red pieces of taffeta.[74] Such gifts were as useful and appealing to women as to men. In exchange, native rulers gave Pardo corn and declarations of obedience.

Like their predecessors, Pardo's chroniclers repeatedly praised the fertility of the land, "a very good land where great harvests of all sorts can be made." In a three-day sojourn over a mountain range the Spaniards found "many grapes, many chestnut trees, many nuts, [and] quantities of other fruits." Numerous "flat lowlands" held fertile soil. "Such a rich land," one wrote, "I don't know how to extoll it."[75]

Pardo also saw among those subsequently known as Cherokees a man who "went among the Indian women, wearing an apron as they did." The startled Spaniard summoned his interpreters and "many soldiers" to ask the local chief about him. The man was his brother, the chief explained, and was not "a man for war." With neither elaboration nor scorn for the scribe to record, the chief said his brother "went about in that manner like a woman," doing "all that is given to a woman to do."[76] It is a slender thread of history suggesting that among Cherokees, as among many native peoples, gender and labor interwove to create identity.

Pardo's legions failed to gain dominion and retreated to their coastal missions to win what souls and wars they could. These early European contacts left a trail of sorrow behind them, evident in mass burials, deserted villages, and vanished tribes. Other kinds of legacies recast landscapes where Spaniards had walked or only wished to. Some of the fruits they brought into the region spread so rapidly that by the time Alexander Longe sought his refuge among Cherokees, their priests believed they had brought such foods with them on their long and difficult emigration into the Southeast.

While Cherokees and other survivors of the early Spanish encounters rebuilt their communities, another wave of Europeans was arriving, this one from the shores of the British Isles. By the time the English established Charles Town in 1670 and British traders took up residence in their towns and villages, Cherokees lived in the Lower, Middle, Valley, and Overhill settlement areas.[77] Three speech dialects, Lower, Kittuwah, and Upper, were the most obvious indication that groups of Cherokees had separated many generations earlier. Regardless of dialect differences between them, however, they shared a common root that differentiated them from their neighbors. As Iroquoian speakers they were exceptional in the Southeast, which was generally populated with speakers of Muskhogean and Siouian languages. Cherokees were in no sense isolated, however, for trading paths on land and water connected their towns and villages with one another, with those of other Native Americans, and ultimately with European settlements.

In 1715, when the urge for dominion goaded them to enumerate Southeastern natives, representatives of the English government estimated that 2,100 Cherokees lived in 11 Lower Towns and 2,760 more lived on the far side of the mountains in 19 Overhill Towns. The colonial government calculated that an additional 6,350 Cherokees lived in 30 Middle settlements.[78] The total number of Cherokees estimated by the English in 1715 was 11,210.

The figures tell a story of immense loss. Two generations earlier, Cherokees were the most populous tribe in the Southeast, numbering between 30 and 35 thousand women, men, and children. In 1697, European smallpox devastated them. Whole families and entire towns died, horrified and bewildered by the scourge. The epidemic probably destroyed one-half to three-quarters of the population, an assessment comparable to epidemic deaths among other Native American populations.[79] The wreckage provides stark testimony to the result of the contact between whites and Cherokees, and Cherokees and other Indians. Trade, intermarriage, and even war became sources and means of contagion. Every town was vulnerable. Every trail led to changing worlds.

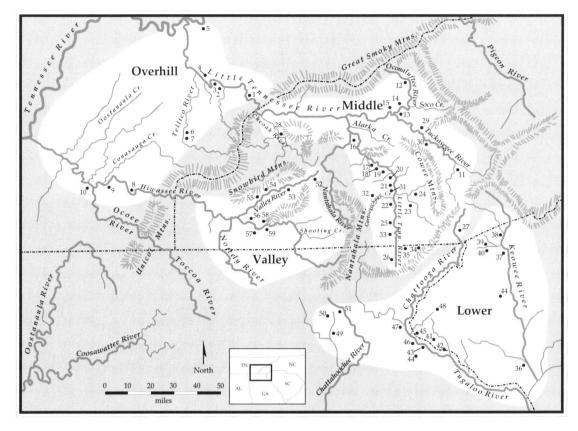

Map 2. Cherokee Settlements, 1720–1730

KEY TO TOWNS

Overhill Towns
1 Tallassee
2 Settico
3 Chota
4 Tennassee
5 Watoga Old Town
6 Great Telliguo
7 Chatuga
8 Great Hiwassee
9 Amoye
10 Chestoe

Middle Towns
11 Tuckaseegee
12 Tuckoreche
13 Sticoe
14 Newni
15 Kattewa
16 Nunhale
17 Coweche
18 Cowee
19 Jore

20 Watoga
21 Naquassee
22 Echoe
23 Erachy
24 Ellijay
25 Nunra
26 Stecoe
27 Chattoogie
28 Cheowe
29 Connutra
30 Cunnawishee
31 Tunanutte
32 Cutagochi
33 Tuchanto
34 Tuckaretchi
35 Old Estatoe

Lower Towns
36 Senneca
37 Kewohe
38 Cheowe
39 Tomassee

40 Oconne
41 Toxaway
42 Chauga
43 Togalu
44 Taucoe
45 Noyowe
46 Estatoe
47 Tarrurah
48 Echy
49 Nauguche
50 Chotte
51 Sukehi

Valley Towns
52 Tamatle
53 Nayowee
54 Little Telliquo
55 Connusse
56 Iwasse
57 Quanasse
58 Tasetche
59 Cuttacoche

Towns: *gatu-gi*

The size of Cherokee towns varied, but during the eighteenth century, they consisted of at least three elements—residential dwellings, ceremonial centers, and agricultural fields, both common and familial. Towns lay in bottomlands following the contours of the land. Where river valleys narrowed, villages extended across both sides of the waterways and clustered at the bases of hills. As little as two or three miles separated most villages, enough distance to disperse settlers and fields, and enough proximity to facilitate communication, exchange, and mutual aid.

Wherever they settled, Cherokees transformed the land to establish and maintain their settlements. They felled hundreds of thousands of trees for housing and ceremonial centers. They eliminated vegetation for as much as two miles to clear and prepare ground for farming and gardening. In many areas they depleted the surrounding woodland to build defensive palisades for settlements and town houses.

The Place Where I Stay: *akwenasu*

The number of houses in each town ranged from as few as twelve to more than one hundred. Each residence included separate summer and winter houses made from local trees, saplings, bark, clay, cane, and grass. To build a house, "the whole town" joined forces, according to Adair, often assisted by "the nearest of their tribe [clan] in neighboring towns." In one day, they could complete the construction of a house.[80]

For rectangular summer houses, which were considerably larger than winter dwellings, they barked and cut locust, sassafras, white oak, hickory, pine, chestnut, and poplar trees. They made house frames, rafters, roofs, eaves, bindings, and doors from tree trunks, bark, and saplings. Summer houses in the Overhills were "no more than sixteen feet in breadth" and perhaps "sixty to seventy feet in length." In mountainous settlements with narrower floodplains, smaller summer houses were more common.[81]

Virtually every part of a tree went into house construction. Builders outlined residential structures with large trees or "thick posts" set deep in the ground, Timberlake wrote, and "between each of these posts is placed a smaller one." They laid "narrow boards" across the width of the house to form a roof. Walls were "wattled with twigs like a basket" and then made smooth and fireproof with a layer of plaster. Lower Town Cherokees finished their homes with "a clay white as lime which is found in this country," while Overhills settlers made plaster from crushed shells. Even the English had to admit that "the houses are remarkably neat." The hardened finish was durable, insular, and attractive. To DeBrahm's practiced eye, the subtle hues of the finishes had the "splendor of unpolished silver."[82] These residential buildings, whose walls were woven together like baskets, belonged to the women.

Inside the summer houses, two transverse partitions created "three apartments" that "communicate with each other by inside doors."[83] One room contained a stone-lined pit for fire, whose smoke curled out a hole in the roof. "Some of these houses are two story high, tolerably pretty and capacious," offered Timberlake, although he found them "very inconvenient for want of chimneys." He objected to the single "small hole" that seldom released all the "smoak" that caused him to feel wretched.[84]

Smoke from homes signaled women's activities, for women were the makers of household fires (a-tsila), tending them as diligently as *Kanane-ski Amai-yehi* had cared for the fire she carried on her back. Houses were like baskets, containers of fire made and preserved by females. To maintain household fires, women walked each day to ever-receding forests to gather wood. The sound of an ax was rare, Adair wrote, "if we except the women chopping firewood for daily use."[85]

Small storehouses made of logs and chinked with mud rose from the ground behind each house. A ladder of saplings led to a low door, the only opening in the storehouse. Like the homes shared by daughters and mothers, these corn cribs (*unwada-li*) belonged to the women. They climbed up to the storehouses daily to deposit or retrieve corn and beans. "Their corn-houses," recorded DeBrahm, "are raised up upon four posts, four and some five feet high from the Ground" with floors of "round Poles, on which the Corn-worms cannot lodge, but fall through."[86] Predatory animals could not reach the stored foods, and the round poles, often stalks of rivercane, resisted fire, water, and insects.

Household furnishings and utensils also came from forest resources. "Their stools they cut out of poplar wood," Adair explained, and "chests are made of clapboards." They carved rhododendron branches into spoons and ladles used to serve and eat from pottery bowls.[87] Women's domestic wares, Timberlake wrote, were "proofs of their ingenuity," particularly the "excellent vessels" they made of red or white clay, their tanned deerskins, and their "basket-work."[88]

Hot House: *osi*

For each family, a winter hot house (*osi*) stood opposite the summer house. Fewer trees, but of a larger size, went into the construction of these small, circular buildings. Builders first sank into the ground several "strong forked posts." Above the posts "they tie very securely large pieces of the heart of white oak" interwoven "from top to bottom." Adair reported that inside the circle of posts, the builders

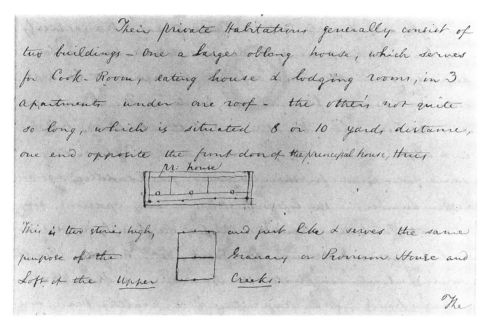

Their private Habitations generally consist of two buildings – One a large oblong house, which serves for Cook-Room, eating house & lodging rooms, in 3 apartments under one roof – the other not quite so long, which is situated 8 or 10 yards distance, one end opposite the front door of the principal house, this

pr. house

This is two stories high, and just like & serves the same purpose of the_ Granary or Provision House and Loft of the_ Upper _Creeks._

The

John Howard Payne copied William Bartram's drawing of a Cherokee house and hot house. Bartram based his drawing on Cherokee homes he saw during his 1775 visit to the Cherokees. The Historical Society of Pennsylvania.

formed a rectangle with four large pine trunks sunk "very deep in the ground," then laid on top of them "a number of heavy logs" to construct a conical roof. "Above this huge pile" they put "a number of long dry poles," weaving them tightly together with split saplings. They covered the entire roof with six or seven inches of "tough clay, well mixt with withered grass." The final insulation was thatch made of "the longest sort of dry grass, that their land produces."[89]

Cane benches , which were "raised on four forks of timber of proper height" and tied with "fine white oak splinters," lined the interior walls. Mats "made of long cane splinters" covered the benches. For warmth, there were skins of "buffalos, panthers, bears, elks, and deer," which women had dressed until they were "soft as velvet." When the miserable Timberlake retreated from ceremonies in the Chota Town House to a bench in a hot house, he found it so sweltering that he "could not endure the weight of my own blanket."[90]

In the center of each hot house, "some of the women make a large fire of dried wood, with which they chiefly provide themselves." The fire burned all day and night in winter. A long cane lay by every bench, and as the flames diminished, a single sweep of the cane pushed aside the ashes, and the fire blazed up again.[91] Smoke rose through the hole in the roof, replicating smoke from the First Fire on a far-off island. Children and elders spent cold winter days in the hot houses, and everyone gathered there at night. In the *osi*, elders told stories of the creation of the world and morality tales of the animals, and in turn, children learned their tribal traditions.

Town House: *te-ka-la-wi-u-a*

A large, circular, ceremonial center stood in the middle of all but the smallest towns. Construction of town houses was a community enterprise that cleared more vegetation from settlement areas. The buildings, where religious, social, and secular transactions took place, were central to Cherokee life. Men congregated there to smoke and discuss war and politics or receive Europeans who came to negotiate issues of state and faith. Townspeople gathered there for sacred ceremonies and social dances.

Built on a cleared and level square of ground, often on the summit of an ancient mound, the huge, windowless rotunda was covered with earth and thatch, giving it "all the appearance of a small mountain at a little distance."[92] Enormous trees went into the construction of ceremonial centers, which had heavy, dense, conical roofs. Smoke curled continuously skyward through the center hole, confirming for townspeople that the sacred fire still burned inside.

At Cowee Middle Town, builders sank into the ground a large circle of "posts or trunks of trees about six feet high at equal distances," then set within them another circle of "very large and strong pillars, about twelve feet high," and finally, within that circle, set yet a "third range of stronger and higher pillars." In the center they raised up the tallest, sturdiest post "which forms the pinnacle of the building." Rafters of forest woods lay between the posts, "strengthened and bound by cross beams and laths." Builders layered bark across the top "to exclude the rain," then covered the bark with dirt and thatch.[93]

European visitors entering town houses for the first time were struck first with numbing darkness. Passing through the narrow entry door, Timberlake wound and turned through a mazelike passage until he reached at last a great, open arena with raised rows of cane benches against the walls. "It was so dark," he wrote of the Overhills Settico Town House, "that nothing was perceptible till a fresh supply of canes were brought" for fire and light. As his eyes grew accustomed to the dim and smoky atmosphere, the surprised Englishman discovered around him "about five hundred faces."[94]

Bartram found benches in the Cowee Town House covered with "mats or carpets, very curiously made of thin splits of Ash or Oak." In most town houses, how-

ever, the benches attached to the walls were covered with mats made of rivercane, like those at Chota. Clan members sat together on benches along each of
the seven sides of the town house. Special seats were reserved for chiefs and
important guests, and all benches faced the center, where the hearth lay and the
fire burned.[95]

Townhouses "are very hot," complained missionary William Richardson from
Chota, exasperated and frightened by nearly everything he found in the Overhills,
"and here they sit and smoke and dance sometimes all night." In those January
weeks Richardson remained in the Mother Town, Cherokees were busy preparing
"physicks which they say will drive away all their disorders." It was time for the *Ah-
tawh-hung-nah* Festival, and Cherokees undoubtedly danced all night for several
nights, and enacted certain rituals. The missionary, however, chose not to record
"the ceremony of it."[96]

Town houses included storage areas, either inside or beyond the rotunda, where
"their consecrated vessels" were stored.[97] When women brought "some of each
sort" of the newly ripened "fruits of the season" for Green Corn feasts, they deposited them in the ceremonial storehouse. Harvest baskets thus joined the ranks
of "consecrated vessels." Similarly, for *Ah-tawh-hung-nah*, the sacred rivercane basket with medicinal woods was "stored in the treasure house" adjacent to the town
house.[98] The special place also held important secular materials. William Fyffe explained that "the wampum or other presents" that accompanied treaties were deposited "in their Court House," underscoring the collective ownership of documents recording "the History of their Treaties."[99]

Weapons were generally prohibited in town houses, for the centers were places
of communication rather than conflict, arenas in which society joined physically
and psychologically for negotiation, decision making, performance, recreation,
and ritual. Weapons were reminders of unsettling times and unsettled scores and
symbols of imbalance and disharmony. The great rotunda was the heart of each
town just as the household was the heart of each family. Cherokees sought harmony and balance in their personal and communal hearts. When they returned
from captivity, women and men were "keept four day's and Nights in the Town
House."[100] Thus returned to the core of the settlement, they once again became
fully Cherokee.

In addition to the substantial number of trees cut for residential and ceremonial
structures, Cherokees often surrounded their towns and town houses with palisades made from hundreds of saplings. In 1673, English trader and explorer James
Needham arrived in an Overhill town that was defended by "trees of two foot
over, pitched on end, twelve foot high" and topped by "scaffolds placed with

parrapits."[101] Fifty years later, Indian agent George Chicken encouraged the Lower Town people of Tugalu and Keowee to repair their aging palisades. In Chagey, he found that "round their town house is built a very Substantial Fort" and a "slight fortification" surrounded the town as well. Perhaps the most imposing palisades outlined Old Estatoe Middle Town, which was "very well fortifyed all round with Punchins." The town house was also "enforted," and a dry moat beyond the palisade was "stuck full of light wood Spikes." At Great Tellico and Chatuga Overhill Towns, the ceremonial centers were "both enforted."[102]

For palisades, summer and winter residences, corn cribs, town houses, moats, and other structures, Cherokees cut an immense number of trees and saplings, cane stalks and grass thatch, adding bark from trees, soil and clay from the ground, and even shells from the waterways. Town construction transformed the environment and created new landscapes with terraces, fields, and clearings that crisscrossed waterways like patchwork. With each new settlement, nearby woodland resources dwindled.

In 1760, Rich Dudgeon reported to his British superiors that soldiers garrisoned on the Keowee River were "often distressed for Fewell, which is nearly a mile from them." And across the river, women in the old and populous Lower Town of Keowee walked farther and farther to cut wood for daily fires. That same year, Timberlake saw the elderly mother of Chief Ostenaco regularly carry "200 weight of wood on her back near a couple of miles" to her Overhills home.[103]

Cleared landscapes characterized settled areas all over the Cherokee nation. Bartram claimed women were "obliged to undergo a great deal of labour" caring for their homes and families in fall and winter. Such work included cutting wood, "which they toat on their backs or heads a great distance, especially those of ancient large towns, where the commons and old fields extend some miles to the woodland."[104] Open valleys and plains soon replaced forests wherever Cherokees settled.

Diminishing Worlds

As Cherokees extended woodland margins in the eighteenth century, the outer limits of their nation gradually shrank inward under increasing pressure from white settlers, colonial American policies, and war with other tribes. Between 1721 and 1755, Cherokees ceded more than 11,000 square miles to South Carolina. They abandoned other parts of their nation to escape epidemics. Disease struck nearly every generation, devastating towns and villages and reshaping populations. Smallpox swept away Cherokees in 1738, 1760, and 1784. The epidemic of 1738 killed thousands, causing survivors to abandon settlements along the Chattooga, Tugaloo, and Chattahoochee Rivers.[105]

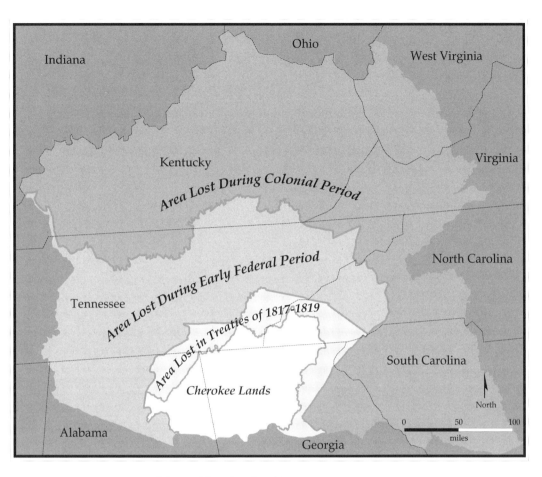

Map 3. Cherokee Land Losses, 1721–1819

In these same decades, warfare with neighboring Indians expanded from small raiding parties for prisoners and scalps to consolidated attacks with (or against) Europeans on whole villages and entire tribes. Hostilities against Creeks exhausted Cherokees at their southwestern borders, while continual war with Northern tribes threatened them from the Northeast. Frontier warfare between European Americans and Cherokees terrorized the borders of each before escalating to punitive invasions of all Cherokee and numerous white settlements. Generations of Cherokees who lived between 1760 and 1790 knew war well, witnessing the destruction of their towns more than a half-dozen times. Their lands absorbed the blood of both sexes, all ages, and every Southeastern race and nation.

In 1761, soldiers' diaries recorded the appearance of land long turned for towns and fields. Captain Christopher French carefully noted the clearings around and between towns in all four settlement areas, describing them in similar terms. Echoy Middle Town stood "in a large plain," and two miles away an open road led to

Tasse, also "on a plain." A few miles down another "open road," French reached Neucasse "situated in a plain." He found the great Middle Town of Kittuwah in "a large plain" on the Tuckasegee River. He crossed "a small plain" to Tuckareetchih, "very pleasantly situated in the largest plain we had found inhabited." In the Valley Towns, a "very good road" led to Natali and on to the town of Hiwassee, which stood "on a plain." [106]

Christopher French's attention to the clearings around Cherokee settlements was not idle curiosity. He participated in James Grant's expedition to lay waste to the towns in order to punish Cherokees for destroying the English garrison at Ft. Loudon in the Overhills. Every clearing offered the soldiers better views of enemy towns. Each road facilitated their approach. They marched from March 20 until July 9, 1761, with wagons, horses, 700 cattle, and nearly 1,000 men. Europeans called the invasions the Cherokee War, a series of conflicts that recast the worlds of all participants. Cherokees sued for peace in the fall of that year. [107] The damage to their towns and fields was well recorded by officers like Christopher French. The impact it had on the surrounding environment can only be imagined.

In 1777, following the third destruction of their settlements, Lower Town Cherokees ceded their Piedmont lands east of the Blue Ridge. From 1755 to 1777, treaties with colonies, and then states, reduced Cherokee holdings by some 57,000 square miles. [108] Whole towns withdrew to the mountainous Middle Town region, and others moved farther down the Little Tennessee. Old palisades, homes, hot houses, corn houses, and town houses rotted into the ground, useless in the rapidly changing world. Grass and scrub began to grow where fields and gardens once flourished.

Where Cherokees remained, the exploitation of local resources intensified. When Moravian missionary Martin Schneider arrived in the Overhills in 1783, he estimated that the distance between Sitiko and Chota was eight miles, "the half of which is cleared at least a Mile broad, as far as the even land goes." As a result of land clearing, "there is but little Wood between the above mentioned Towns." Landscapes were similar from town to town. "In this manner," Schneider wrote, "lie within 20 miles 9 Towns of the upper Cherokees." [109]

The Origin of Game and Corn
Selu and Kana-ti
[As Told by Swimmer and John Ax]

Long years ago, soon after the world was made, a hunter and his wife lived at Pilot Knob with their only child, a little boy. The father's name was *Kana-ti* (The Lucky Hunter), and his wife was called *Selu* (Corn). No matter when

Kana-ti went into the wood, he never failed to bring back a load of game, which his wife would cut up and prepare, washing the blood from the meat in the river near the house. The little boy used to play down by the river every day, and one morning the old people thought they heard laughing and talking in the bushes as though there were two children there. When the boy came home at night his parents asked him who had been playing with him all day. "He comes out of the water," said the boy, "and he calls himself my elder brother. He says his mother was cruel to him and threw him in the river." Then they knew that the strange boy had sprung from the blood of the game which *Selu* had washed off at the river's edge.[110]

Those who gave James Mooney this story said that it was so sacred that "in the old days" only priests could tell it, and any who wished to hear had to fast and go to water.[111] It is a story of miraculous origins, of the birth of all that sustained the people. It recalls the genesis, when hunting was simple, predictable, easy. The father knew where the game was. He never failed, winter or summer, in darkness or light. One wife, one child, one woodland, and control of the game—it was an ideal world.

The story is, in part, a cautionary tale about the power of blood. The mother is called the cruel one, for she cuts and slices and tears and cooks, discarding living matter, blood, into the flowing water. Shed blood with care, the story warns, for blood is life itself. Death and birth wind around each other, creating a pattern from woman's labor. Life emerges from her cast off blood, taking form, shape, identity. An elder brother springs from the blood of game. The story makes plain that humans and animals are kin, that game is the firstborn who is also miraculously reborn and transformed in water and blood at the hands of woman. As elder brother, game assumes eternal responsibility to provide meat and skins for younger brother, the Cherokee people.

The narrative continues, weaving words of secret power. *Kana-ti* and *Selu* adopted the Wild Boy, who soon led his brother in world-shaping mischief. Warnings abound. Adopted members, new relationships, elder brothers, undisciplined young men, kinship with game, all pushed out the boundaries of the world. The alliance between brothers made it easy, even inevitable, to disobey the father, to change forever the life of the Lucky Hunter.

The boys released all the four-toed ones and flyers that *Kana-ti* had secured in a cave, and his easy hunting ended in a single curious moment. *Kana-ti* had been able to catch each animal or bird that darted forth as he uncovered the opening to the secret place, but the boys changed all that. The air and forests soon filled with game, and men thereafter had to struggle to hunt, had to discover magic formulas to lure elusive and cunning game. Hunters would come to know failure and hunger and need. Luck ran out with the game.

Having recast the lives and labor of game and men, the boys returned to make mischief with the work of women:

> When the boys got home again they were very tired and hungry and asked their mother for something to eat. "There is no meat," said Selu, "but wait a little while and I'll get you something." So she took a basket and started out to the storehouse. This storehouse was built upon poles high up from the ground, to keep it out of the reach of animals, and there was a ladder to climb up by, and one door, but no other opening. Every day when Selu got ready to cook the dinner she would go out to the storehouse with a basket and bring it back full of corn and beans.[112]

When men were absent or game was scarce, everyone depended on foods that women harvested and stored. The myth recounts what everyone knew, the life-sustaining work of women. As elders sat at night in the *osi* telling stories of origins, they evoked familiar images of women, baskets, and food, of mothers emerging, of women filling containers with corn and beans day after day in every season of every settlement. On dark winter nights, surrounded by smoke from the central hearth fire, elders intertwined the commonplace and mysterious, daily bread and secret knowledge, all in a story about the power of women.

> The boys had never been inside the storehouse, so wondered where all the corn and beans could come from, as the house was not a very large one; so as soon as Selu went out of the door the Wild Boy said to his brother, "Let's go and see what she does." They ran around and climbed up at the back of the storehouse and pulled out a piece of clay from between the logs, so that they could look in. There they saw Selu standing in the middle of the room with a basket in front of her on the floor. Leaning over the basket, she rubbed her stomach -so- and the basket was half full of corn. Then she rubbed under her armpits -so- and the basket was full to the top with beans. The boys looked at each other and said, "This will never do; our mother is a witch. If we eat any of that it will poison us. We must kill her."[113]

Mystery and magic permeate the myth. *Selu's* marvelous body brought food, actually was food, and from one container to another, from body to basket, the fertility of woman guaranteed a future. The sight struck fear in her wild and innocent, curious and frightened children. They knew about power so terrible that it bent toward evil rather than good, the power feared above all else, the force called witchcraft. It came disguised to entrap the unsuspecting, came in the form of old women or men or scavengers or birds.[114] In all memory, those suspected of witchcraft were put to instant death, for they lived by taking life from others.

And so the boys decided to kill their mother; and the narrative weaves more magic, for *Selu* knew and understood their plans. Before she died, she gave her murderous children careful instructions about how to produce abundant corn when she was no longer there. Then came her death, and with it their life. "They killed her with their clubs, and cut off her head."[115] No mourning, no remorse, no struggle, just apparent death and dismemberment in a parent's death and dismemberment. As she directed them, the boys dragged her body around a cleared area, and wherever her blood dripped onto the ground, corn sprung up. She had advised them to clear a large area, but the boys cleared only seven small spots, establishing forever the custom of farming in seven places. And though she told them to drag her body seven times across the clearing, they did so only twice. From that moment, Cherokees could harvest only two times each season.

The children took their mother's severed head and put it on the roof of their house. It was a strange and wonderful kind of re-membering, for she thus became forever a part of their household. They turned her face toward the west, the direction where defeat and death lay waiting. "Look for your husband that way," they told her, turning her sightless eyes to the darkening distance where the hunter had run out of luck.

The great myth of *Selu* evokes multiple images of women as sources of knowledge, food, and life. Words and concepts weave back and forth—rivers and birth, children and death, storehouses and bodies, blood and crops, prophecy and regeneration—interlacing notions of women and power. Just as women provided children for the social order, *Selu's* body and blood produced food for her children. Death, birth, and life cycle around each other, transformed by time. "Wait a little while," *Selu* told her hungry sons, "and I will get you something."[116] All of it was mysterious, and it was *Selu* who brought to her sons knowledge of agriculture, understanding of death, recognition of cycles, and respect for blood. Men learned to prepare the ground, women to produce the corn. And the mother became, finally and literally, the head of the household, placed there by her own children. Directly associated with *Selu*, with women performing their most fundamental tasks and assuming powerful responsibilities, was the basket that the first great mother carried with her each day.

In ceremonies and social systems, Cherokees associated women with generativity and with foods harvested, prepared, served, and stored in baskets. The association was most profound with corn, the foundation of their subsistence. Corn and women signified fertility and the future. "A female," according to Payne, "is held in special honor, and identified with Indian Corn, or Maize. Most of the all night dances refer in some way to her."[117]

At the two annual corn festivals, women reenacted the work of *Selu* by bringing baskets of food to the town square for the community to share. Each night of the festivals, seven women sang and danced, the sound of their rattles like falling rain and the drops of *Selu*'s blood. In times of drought, petitions were offered to the Woman of the East who had promised "to answer them with rain in plenty." When rain came, the "whole town united in a solemn dance of thanksgiving."[118] The festivals and dances ritually expressed beliefs about the sacred, about order in the world. Through ceremony, music, and dance, the community acknowledged and reinforced the literal and metaphorical role of women as the source of agricultural bounty, the source of life itself.

Gardens: *a-wi-sv-di-yi*

Women maintained household gardens in clearings "pretty close to" their dwellings, sowing "a variety of large and small beans, peas, and the smaller sort of Indian corn" that ripened in two months. By starting their gardens in early spring, they harvested "an earlier supply" of vegetables than those available from "their distant plantations," the common fields of the town.[119] Whether for "the first small corn" or varieties planted later in the season, women followed the same methods. They dug holes "about two inches distant" from one another, placed in each hole seven grains of corn, then covered them "with clay in the form of a small hill." The straight rows lay about three feet apart, and in between, women planted "pumpkins, watermelons, marsh-mallows, sunflowers, and sundry sorts of beans and peas."[120]

Timberlake gave little credit to their farming skill. He considered the Overhills soil to be "so remarkably fertile" that they had only to do "a little stirring with a hoe" to grow "vast quantities of pease, beans, potatoes, cabbage, Indian corn, pompions, melons, and tobacco."[121] If women did not appear to be laboring hard, it was likely because they labored wisely. They balanced soil ecology by intercropping complementary plants like protein-rich beans, which fix nitrogen at their roots in the soil, and carbohydrate-rich corn, which depletes nitrogen.[122] Intercropping also enabled climbing vegetation like beans to support itself on the stalks of tall vegetation like corn. The appearance was distinctly un-European. Europeans considered Cherokee gardens messy and their methods inferior. They "choak up the field," complained Adair, "in their desire for *multum in parvo*."[123]

By the time Adair recorded their gardening practices, Cherokee women had incorporated several European and African foods that were most useful, least time-consuming, and most comparable to their traditional crops. Old and new plants grew side by side, indicating women's willingness to adopt different customs and fit them into existing lifeways.

For several centuries, corn, beans, pumpkins, sunflowers, and squash had been mainstays of Cherokee agriculture. Watermelons were another matter. Spanish colonists brought African watermelons to the Southeast in the 1500s, and the fruits spread so rapidly through native societies that many came to believe they were indigenous. The old priest told Alexander Longe that his people had brought "pomkin and muskemilon and watermilon" on their ancient migration into the Southeast.[124] Botanically and ecologically similar to cucurbits already in cultivation, watermelon required little tending and no new farm practices. Plants even germinated spontaneously from abundant seeds. Like indigenous melons, the import became a popular dietary supplement for Cherokees and a familiar sight to Europeans. In the fall of 1756, Old Hop and his wife presented English captain Raymond Demere with bread and "Water Mellons" when he arrived in the Overhills to begin construction of the Ft. Loudon garrison. The presentation of such preferred foods was a singular expression of hospitality and alliance.[125]

When eighteenth-century women adopted sweet potatoes, a Spanish import from the Caribbean, the starchy tuber quickly became important in Cherokee diet.[126] Growing fast and spreading prolifically, sweet potato ripened underground where it remained safe from warfare's destruction of crops. It could be planted well before the last frost and harvested after its surface leaves had died.[127] While enemies slashed and burned other vegetation, sweet potatoes continued to ripen. Like corn, beans, and pumpkins, the nutritious tubers could be dried and stored for winter use.

In January of 1742, a young French captive named Antoine Bonnefoy was taken to Overhill Chota and fed "all that the women had brought from the village, bread of different sorts, sagamite [corn porridge], buffalo meat, bear meat, rabbit, sweet potatoes, and graumons."[128] Each vegetable Bonnefoy ate represented a part of women's culture—spring and summer gardens, hours of food processing, and a variety of baskets.

Women also incorporated new fruits, adding imported peach and apple trees to the native vegetation they encouraged near their homes. Introduced by Spaniards, peach trees made their way to Cherokee settlements by the late 1500s. Like watermelon, they were often considered indigenous because of their wide distribution and long history in the region. Peach trees reproduce spontaneously, bearing fruit within five years after seed germination. Readily colonizing open and disturbed areas, they grew near mulberry and plum trees in old fields as well as around houses. They required minimal care and fit well in existing systems of horticulture. Peaches (*khwa-na*) were prepared like persimmons, either "pounded" and mixed with flour for "great loaves" of bread, barbecued and dried for winter storage, or "seethed" to flavor soups and drinks.[129]

Gardens and their produce belonged to women. They delineated each garden plot's boundaries with "narrow strips or borders of grass." In May (*Ana-sku-tee*: Planting Month), Bartram carefully guided his horse along the margins of garden after garden, "being careful to do no injury to the young plants." The "little plantations" in Watoga appeared "all before me and on every side," he wrote, sprouting "young Corn, Beans, etc." Gardens spread from the dwellings to the town house, edging the trail and occupying every available spot of fertile ground.[130] A similar sight must have greeted visitors to every settlement during Planting Month.

Fields: *ga-gesi*

In the spring, women walked "a considerable distance from the town" to sow fields of "pompions, and different sorts of melons." They chose to plant when days were longer and warmer and predators might bypass their fields in favor of other succulent foods. By May, "the wild fruit is so ripe," wrote Adair, "as to draw off the birds from picking up the grain." After planting time, old women guarded outfields from high scaffolds that overlooked "this favorite part of their vegetable possessions." If hungry animals or birds approached, the sentries frightened them away "with their screetches." It was dangerous work, for human predators came first to such far-flung fields and "sometimes kills them in this strict watch duty."[131] Long past the age of farming, older women continued to share responsibility for food, even endangering their lives to do so.

Community fields of corn, beans, and other staples stretched two to four miles beyond the towns. In addition to small, early corn, Cherokees raised a "yellow and flinty" variety called "hommony-corn" with red, blue, white, or yellow kernels that were smooth and hard, and a large, "very white and soft grain" for "bread corn."[132] The diversity and sequential planting of staple foods offered a slender margin of defense against crop failures and pest invasions. At the very least, seeds from limited crops could be harvested and stored for the following year.

Town priests allotted land to each clan in proportion to their numbers and need. In May, the entire town joined together to plant under the direction of a chosen leader. They began "fellowshiply on one End," continuing across each field "till they have finished all." As they worked, "one of their old orators cheers them on with jests and humorous old tales, and sings some of their most agreeable wild tunes." Drumming and singing, joking and calling, elders urged on planters while reinforcing town customs and community solidarity. Everyone, including chiefs, joined in the labor. Though disdainful Europeans usually described them solely as hunters and warriors, men—brothers—also prepared community fields clan by clan, as *Selu* had instructed.[133] Landholdings remained centered in the matrilineage, cared for by male as well as female members.

While Longe professed regret that Cherokees were not Christians, he found them "short of nothing else" including "loving and assisting one and other and Especially those that are in want." Community fields underlay the capacity and obligation to help those in need. Sharing land and labor, "there is no respecting of persons amongst the poorer sort." Farming was a great leveler of social distinctions. Community lands meant community crops so that "thire vitols" could be "comen to all people."[134] Portions from every clan's field went into the "publick Granery," a resource "to repair to in case of necessity." Since every family contributed, each could claim an allotment if their own food "falls short, or is destroyed by accidents or otherwise." The public storehouse also made it possible to offer hospitality to "armies, travelers, or sojourners," as well as neighboring towns.[135]

When fields "became impoverished," town members left them "with one consent" and found "a fresh spot" to clear and sow.[136] Old fields then became an important component of a settlement's changing resources. Fallowing fields were gradually colonized by useful weeds like poke and by fleshy fruits such as strawberries, maypops, sumac, plums, and persimmon. Over time, pioneering shrubs and tree seedlings transformed old fields into patches of secondary growth. Such scrub communities supplied food, medicine, and dye to gatherers and attracted a variety of animals and birds for hunters. Bartram journeyed through five miles of such fields "now under grass, but which appeared to have been planted the last season." Soil in Cowee old fields, Bartram reported, looked "exceedingly fertile, loose, black, deep, and fat," a promising matrix for colonizing vegetation.[137]

Women's agriculture was not a closed system, although it was a generally successful one. Farming skill and fertile soil produced an "abundance of corn, beans, and vegetables" unless disasters intervened; but forces of nature frequently injured or destroyed even the most carefully tended fields.[138] Floods, droughts, or crop failures were reported several times a decade throughout the eighteenth century, and surely many "hungary times" went unrecorded in smaller settlements that lay beyond the pen of Europeans.[139] The specter of famine hovered over Southeastern fields, and farmers of all races and both sexes regularly watched the skies and felt the soil with anxiety.

Long memories of early frosts, harsh winters, spring floods, and summer droughts contributed to a rich complex of religious beliefs and social behaviors. Townswomen enacted secret rituals to avert disaster; for example, they disrobed every full moon "at the dead of night" to circle "entirely around the field of corn." They sang "thanks and prayers in a series of devotional chaunts" to *Selu* while they tended corn and weeded fields. When drought came, women from each clan fasted while men brought deerskins and meat to the priest. The priest then prayed to the creator moon and sun, shaking a terrapin shell filled with pebbles to summon thunder and rain. To avert cold, priests built fire of seven special woods and sacrificed to the Woman of the East a terrapin shell filled with old tobacco. In ritual speeches at Green Corn festivals, priests urged strict adherence to customs and prohibitions in order to maintain harmony in the universe, health in the community, and abundance in the harvests. All these aspects of life were intertwined. Such formal admonitions Alexander Longe "heard very often" at the Feast of First Fruits.[140]

Livestock: *u-lv-nida*

Throughout the eighteenth century, women continued to make adaptations that recast their economies as well as their landscapes. They gradually accepted European livestock and assumed responsibility for animal husbandry. Since domesticated animals destroyed gardens and fields, women accepted them only when they devised ways to control and use them.

Absent from the North American continent since the Pleistocene, horses were reintroduced by sixteenth-century Spanish invaders. Every European mission, settlement, survey, and *entrada* included horses, and virtually every European trader who entered a Cherokee town did so on horseback. In the second decade of the eighteenth century, Lower Town Cherokees still objected to traders' horses "continually amongst their corn"; but eventually, all began to use them for hunting and to carry pelts to European settlements.[141] Horses were essential to the rapid growth of the deerskin trade, facilitating the geographic expansion of hunting and the delivery of hundreds of thousands of pelts. There is good reason Cherokees called the animals *sa-gwa-li* (there is a pack on him).

By the mid-1700s, Cherokees owned "a prodigious number" of horses. Women tethered horses with bark ropes and built fences to protect their gardens. They fastened "stakes in the ground" that supported "a couple of long, split hiccory or white oak saplings at a proper distance." Even so, the animals might "creep through these enclosures" to graze on young spring vegetables. Angry women warned them that greed would turn their hearts and "spoil them." When horses returned again and again, however, women were likely to "strike a tomahawk" into their sides.[142]

Hogs were more numerous and certainly more destructive to vegetation. From the earliest days of English settlement, Cherokees objected to crop depredation by hogs, but women and children raised them "for the ugly white people." To safe-guard crops, they confined hogs "in convenient penns" from early spring planting until fall harvest. They fed them "chiefly on long pursley, and other wholesome weeds," setting them loose in fall and winter to eat rivercane and forest mast. The rich diet made "Indian bacon" firmer and "better tasted" than any Adair found in "the English settlements."[143]

As overhunting diminished game, pigs became a primary meat source and trade item. "Droves of hogs" were "brought up and driven out" of Cherokee settlements to markets in Charleston and Augusta. Like garden fences, pigpens became part of changing landscapes that signaled the expansion of women's economy. By 1761, Timberlake found "a numerous breed of horses, as also hogs" in the Overhills.[144] Women retained responsibility for hog raising until the end of the century.

Through most of the 1700s, Cherokees rejected "wasting their time in fencing and childishly confining their improvements, as if the crop would eat itself." Rais-ing cattle required fencing fields, and Cherokees resisted "white man's buffalo" more than any other livestock. "Some of the natives are grown fond of horned cattle," wrote Adair, "but most decline them because their fields are not regularly fenced."[145] Women could fence their gardens and pen their pigs, but building bar-ricades around agricultural fields was another matter.

English garrisons inevitably kept cattle, although Cherokees killed them if they wandered beyond the forts and near corn fields. When Captain Raymond Demere found that "the Cattle are all gone astray" from Ft. Prince George in 1756, he must have known what news would follow. "The Man that has the Care of the Cattle" soon reported that "the Indians had killed some of them and all Probability would kill more." Cherokees at nearby Keowee apparently ate the garrison's livestock, but the next year their Overhills kin simply ran the creatures off.[146] Resistance to cattle husbandry continued as long as the matrilineages controlled the fields and women remained the primary agriculturalists.

Trade: *dana-liska*

Women's management of foods gave them a measure of autonomy in a world where the availability of provisions could be uncertain. Whether conferring gifts or trading produce, they established networks within and between towns and across boundaries of race and nation. When Raymond Demere stopped in Ft. Prince George before proceeding to the Overhills in 1756, "the Ladies of the Towns" pre-sented him "with a great Number of Cakes of Bread of their own make and green Peas and Squashes." It must have been an impressive display as "every Woman" brought "something of this Kind in a Basket," setting them before him. Their gardens should have been flourishing by June, but Demere knew that "Provisions are now scarcer amongst them than ever was known."[147] Although they may have been hard to come by, baskets of food established a relationship between Cherokee women and Demere that led to future trade.

The role of women in providing "Necessarys" was so firmly established that it influenced Demere's decision of exactly where to erect Ft. Loudon. As construction neared completion, he reported to Governor Lyttleton that the garrison had taken on the "Appearance of a Market" as they came "by land and Water with eatables" to sell. Dependence on women's provisions ultimately put Demere at a disadvantage. Facing dwindling supplies and rising hostility that winter, he "was obliged to pay very dear for Corn" purchased from "an Indian Wench."[148]

Enemies "Encamped among the Corn": The Destruction of Cherokee Settlements

Raymond Demere's experiences with bountiful gifts and costly purchases of women's food signaled changing worlds for Cherokees and Europeans alike from the middle until the final decade of the 1700s. Increasing tensions erupted into the Cherokee Wars of 1759–61, with attendant murders of members of all ages, three races, and both sexes, the loss of livestock, and destruction of thousands of acres of women's crops. Diaries of British soldiers reveal that Cherokee fields and storehouses of foods, those "astonishing magazines of corn," invariably impressed even those who came to destroy them.[149] After burning the Lower Town of Keowee in 1760, Lieutenant Colonel James Grant confided to Governor William Bull that "their knowledge of agriculture would surprise you." Annihilation of homes, crops, and storehouses, which unraveled the fabric of Cherokee society, became integral to European war policies. Under the command of Archibald Montgomery in 1760, Grant's expedition burned the Lower Towns and fields of Estatoe, Toxaway, Qualatche, and Conasatche.[150]

Following Montgomery's march and the subsequent murder of Cherokee hostages at Ft. Prince George, Cherokees destroyed the British garrison at Ft. Loudon. Grant led another invasion of the settlements, with even greater devastation. In the summer of 1761, the militia marched for a month from one town and field to the next, laying waste to all the Lower and most of the Middle Towns. Stecoa "was destroy'd as the other," recorded Captain French, and Echoe "we tore to pieces and set Fire to." The mournful dirge continued through "two new settled Villages call'd

Neowee and Canuga," a "place call'd Watogui," and on to Ayoree, Burning Town, Coweetchee, Cowee, Tessantih, Allijoy, Ussanah, Nickassee, Estatoe, and Tucka-reechee. In every town, troops "pull'd up all the Corn, cut down the Fruit Trees, and burn'd the Houses."[151]

The peace that followed did not hold for an entire generation. In the Revolutionary period, seven major European American offenses devastated Cherokee settlements, and once again, diaries of those who destroyed the thirty-six towns recall the most about them. Arthur Faerie, a soldier who accompanied Andrew Williamson's forces in the summer of 1776 as they burned the Valley Towns, conjectured that the "smallest of these" had more than "200 acres of corn, besides crops of potatoes, peas, and beans." Cornfields along the Hiwassee River towns covered "better than nine hundred acres," and all were burned to the ground. In Burning Town, troops "encamped among the corn," destroying everything they could not eat or carry away. The militia hacked to pieces and set fire to "all vegetables belonging to our Heathen enemies." The task was "no small undertaking, they being so plentifully supplied." Troops that laid waste to the Overhills found deserted towns from which Cherokees had fled in such haste they left "horses, cattle, hogs, fowls, and even dogs." The loss of crops and livestock meant hunger or even starvation. It is little wonder "Provisions" the following year were "very scarce amongst the Indians."[152]

"Our Cry is All for Peace": The Words of Women

At the 1781 Treaty of Long Island, beloved woman Nancy Ward claimed her authority to admonish the warriors to cease fighting. "We are your mothers, you are our sons," she reminded them. "Our cry is all for peace." She had known war, death, and destruction. "This peace must last for Ever," she cautioned the assembly. Speaking as a mother, Ward then rhetorically adopted the white soldiers. "Let your women's sons be ours," she offered, "and let our sons be yours." To make sure her intent was conveyed to white women, she asked the soldiers to "let your women hear our words."[153]

While most whites and Cherokees remained at peace following the Long Island Treaty, border hostilities continued to terrorize settlements of each along the Tennessee River. Participating in treaty deliberations, women spoke out again and again for peace. In 1785, the first treaty between the new American government and the Cherokees was signed at Hopewell. The war woman of Chota announced that she was "fond of hearing that there is a peace." To signify amity, she offered a pipe and tobacco to the treaty commissioners "to smoke in friendship." She said pointedly to the American delegates, "I hope you have now taken us by the hand in real friendship." She had "seen much trouble during the late war" and hoped Cherokees and whites "shall have no more disturbance." Her role as mother grounded her speech. Though she had "born and raised up warriors," the war woman looked to a future when she might "bear children who will grow up and people our nation." Children rather than warriors, life rather than death, regeneration rather than vengeance—these were her wishes. She presented her talk "from the young warriors I have raised in my town, as well as myself."[154]

Two years later, *Katteuka*, a beloved woman of Chota, sent Pennsylvania governor Benjamin Franklin a letter describing a meeting she had attended. *Katteuka* informed him that she had "this day" filled pipes with tobacco "that they smoked in piece, and I am in hopes the smoake has reached up to the skies above." Addressing Franklin as "Brother," *Katteuka* voiced her hope that "you have a beloved woman amongst you who will help to put her Children Right if they do wrong." She pledged to do the same with her own warriors. "I am glad in my heart," she proclaimed, "that I am the mother of men" who can and will pledge peace. "Woman Does not pull Children out of Trees or Stumps nor out of old Logs," she reminded Franklin, "but out of their Bodies, so that they ought to mind what a woman says." As the source of generation and regeneration, women commanded special authority. She closed her letter by thanking Franklin for his gifts to her and for "the kind usage you gave to my son."[155]

At a 1789 conference on the French Broad River, a beloved woman again invoked maternal authority to call for peace from her "sons and warriors." The last to address the treaty commissioners, she spoke plainly: "I hope my warriors will all remember they sprung from a woman." Like crops in a field, warriors came from and were nurtured by women. As *Selu* commanded her children to remember her always, the beloved woman admonished the warriors to remember their mothers. Desiring that "the children of the white and the red might be raised in peace," she pledged to "keep my feet on top of" the bloody hatchet "buried deep under ground."[156]

Rising up from the destruction of their food and fields, the voices of beloved women united in a call for peace. "This peace must last forever," Ward had said at Long Island. "My children shall keep the path clear and white," *Katteuka* pledged to Benjamin Franklin.[157] How "pleasing" it was that "the bloody hatchet is buried deep in the ground" so that children could be "raised in our land," acknowledged another. In the context of desolation and promise, past sorrow and present hope,

President George Washington proposed a program to civilize the Cherokees and teach them to farm.

How the World Was Remade

Treaty on the Bank of the Holston River Between the President of the United States of America and the Chiefs and Warriors of the Cherokee Nation, July 2, 1791

Article 1.: There shall be perpetual peace and friendship between all the citizens of the United States of America and all the individuals composing the whole Cherokee Nation of Indians.

Article 7.: The United States solemnly guarantee to the Cherokee Nation all their lands not hereby ceded. . . .

Article 14.: That the Cherokee Nation may be led to a greater degree of civilization, and to become herdsmen and cultivators, instead of remaining in a state of hunters, the United States will from time to time furnish gratuitously the said Nation with useful implements of husbandry, and further to assist the said Nation in so desirable a pursuit, and at the same time to establish a certain mode of communication, the United States will send such, and so many persons to reside in said Nation as they may judge proper. . . .[158]

At base, the federal government's civilization program aimed to acquire Indian lands. In order "to counteract" the Indians' policy of "refusing absolutely all further sales" of their territory, the government resolved "to encourage them to abandon hunting" in favor of animal husbandry, agriculture, and "domestic manufactures." Men who lived by hunting needed more land than herdsmen and farmers. Their "extensive forests" would "become useless" to them once they fenced and raised domesticated animals, once they gave up the chase to pursue mules and plows.[159] Animal husbandry and farming were the activities of civilized men. The transposition of men from hunting to husbandry and farming included a corollary for women—moving them from tilling the soil and harvesting crops to spinning yarn and weaving cloth.

Gifts of spinning wheels, looms, plows, grains, and livestock became the means of redefining Indian culture and the route to acquiring lands. Federal agents came to live among the Indians, followed soon after by missionaries who were ultimately subsidized by the government. All sought to civilize the Cherokees, which included converting them to Christianity and promoting private rather than collective land ownership. Civilization meant the abandonment of towns and the dissolution of traditional gender roles. Christianity included the rejection of medical practitioners and of ceremonies that expressed beliefs about how the world was made, about the first fire, and about the origin of game and corn.

It was a breathtaking—really a lifetaking—policy, a "gift" whose acceptance meant change of the most fundamental elements of culture—belief, subsistence, settlement, and the very ways women and men defined their genders and roles and their responsibilities to themselves, their kin, and their communities. The alternative to civilization and Christianity, which became evident by the early 1800s, was removal.

Scattered Houses on Treeless Plains: Changing Landscapes

When government agents and missionaries moved onto Cherokee lands in the 1790s, they found the countryside vastly different from that which greeted Europeans in the early part of the century. In 1799, Moravian brothers Abraham Steiner and Frederic de Schweinitz rode "through broken country" to Hiwassee Town, where "several houses" lay scattered "in a great treeless plain." To reach Big Tellico, which was "very compact and thickly settled" in 1725, they passed a "beautiful plain, entirely clear of woods" with widely dispersed homesteads. "The houses were scattered" throughout the valleys and across the ridges "so that a large town may be several miles long and broad." In places "a few houses are close together, at some distance there are a few more, further off only isolated houses, without any order or plan."[160]

Only five houses remained "scattered in the plain" at Chota, which earlier was said to have contained "upward of one hundred and ten houses," and at Toka, all but two "were so far away that we could not see them."[161] Peach, apple, and plum trees that once surrounded households dropped rotting fruit years after Cherokees fled from burning towns in the Revolutionary period. In places, the imported trees were virtually the only signs that homes and hearths once clustered there. In 1809, Major John Norton found settlements extending "forty or fifty miles" along the Conasauga River, with houses built "wherever the fertility of the soil or convenience of the situation invites."[162]

Missing from the landscape was the plant so closely associated with women in one of their most fundamental responsibilities—rivercane. Livestock had eradicated "vast thickets of cane" that had been "scarcely penetrable" in the early part of the century. Europeans found rivercane an abundant and free source of forage that enabled them to maintain the animals on which they were so dependent for food and trade. "The spacious tracts of cane," wrote Catesby in 1724, "are a great benefit particularly to Indian Traders." By midcentury, the destruction of cane was well underway in Cherokee settlements, where traders kept "flocks of an hundred, and a hundred and fifty excellent horses" because the cane provided them "hearty food" year round. "Formerly," wrote Adair of the Cherokee landscapes, "such places abounded with great brakes of winter-cane."[163]

Horses and cattle ravaged cane stands. They stripped the leaves and macerated the stalks, then killed them "by breaking the body of the plant while browsing on the tops of the stalks." Hogs caused far greater damage as they scoured the earth to gouge out nutritious roots. "Whenever the Hogs come," complained Byrd in the 1730s, "they destroy them in a Short time, by ploughing up their Roots, of which, unluckily, they are very fond." In 1802, botanist F. A. Michaux observed that "in proportion as new plantations are formed, these canes in a few years disappear." Settlers began to clear cane for agricultural fields and set hogs loose in the stands for the express purpose of eliminating the native grass.[164]

The destruction of cane also derived from the European practice of firing woods in early spring to "reveal the new green grass to the cattle and other stock."[165] Whereas Cherokees fired vegetation in the fall and winter when plants lay dormant, Europeans fired as spring began, taking advantage of the nutrient elevation in fresh growth. Since young cane is especially sensitive, burned cane stands must be protected in the months following fire.[166] Spring firing, repeated grazing of new growth, and root disruption gradually eliminated the great Southeastern stands of cane. By the end of the eighteenth century, the destruction of canebrakes became a mark of civilized settlement.

Killing Five and Wounding More Than Twenty: Diminishing Game

The world made by, for, and with Cherokees changed in other ways during the 1700s. Some kinds of game, buffalo and elk especially, completely disappeared and others, like wolf, mountain lion, and fox, were greatly diminished. "The buffaloes are now become scarce," Adair wrote in the mid-1700s, "as the thoughtless and wasteful Indians used to kill great numbers of them, only for the tongues and marrow bones, leaving the rest of the carcases to the wild beasts."[167]

European behavior was equally destructive, their weapons more efficient, their hunting crueler. In a 1722 journey down the Mississippi, Diron D'Artaguette recorded the exploits of the ten men in his boat. "We saw a buffalo crossing [the river]," he wrote. "We overtook it in the middle of the river and hitched our boat to it for more than a quarter of a league, after which we killed it. We took only the tongue." The eager travelers then found another opportunity. "About noon we landed to go after a herd of more than a hundred buffaloes, both bulls and cows, of which we killed five and wounded more than twenty. We cut out only the tongues."[168]

Such hunting and sporting exterminated Southeastern buffalo. The "animal productions," wrote Bartram in 1775, "have been affrighted away since the invasion of the Europeans. The buffalo (*urus*) once so very numerous, is not at this day to be seen in this part of the country." The naturalist also noted the disappearance of elk (*ahwi egwa*: great deer) from the lowlands. "There are but few elks, and those only in the Appalachian mountains." Both species foraged on Southeastern prairies, which vanished as settlers eliminated wild grazers and converted grassland to farmland. Only an occasional prairie plant remained to suggest how much the landscape had changed as buffalo and elk disappeared.[169]

Europeans hunted for food, money, security, and glory. Southern history and folklore abound with stories of expeditions by whites bent on conquering the wilderness and its inhabitants. For example, Tennessee historian Philip Hamer reported that in 1780, a single group of hunters killed 105 bear, 75 buffalo, and 87 deer in 5 days.[170] For some, hunting protected their settlements and fed their families. For others, chasing and killing took on a ritualistic nature bound up with notions of dominance and masculinity.

The assault on Southeastern ecosystems was not limited to the activities of individual hunters. Governments developed systematic programs to exterminate indigenous species that endangered the vulnerable livestock of white settlers. Colonial and then state governments offered bounties for predator carcasses including those of wolves, foxes, mountain lions, and panthers. Wolves commanded the deepest fear and highest rewards, for they terrorized all European settlements. Howling and hunting at night, wolf packs dragged off and consumed calves, colts, lambs, goats, pigs, and chickens, who huddled squalling and helpless in their enclosures.

By 1700, Virginians had passed an "Act for Destroying Wolves" that required Indians to deliver wolves' heads in return for their right to remain in the colony. North Carolina's 1748 "Act for Destroying Vermin in This Province" established a reward of ten shillings for a head or the scalp and ears of panthers or wolves. About the same time, Salem Moravians encouraged their neighbors to pay premiums for wolf scalps. In the early 1800s, the government of Carroll County, Tennessee, made a blanket offer of three dollars per wolf scalp. David Crockett, "the gentle-man from the canebrakes" of Tennessee, claimed he financed his legislative cam-paign with bounties from wolf scalps.[171] The bounties encouraged massacres by those who were frightened, defiant, poor, or prosperous in order to eliminate in-digenous species.

Other predators disappeared as well, as nesting sites dwindled along with food sources. In the early 1800s, bald eagles vanished from remaining Cherokee settle-ment areas. The "eagles have mostly deserted the boundaries of civilization," noted one white observer in the 1830s, although "some eagle feathers are preserved" by Cherokees for ceremonial use.[172]

"Originating From Religious Institutions": Forgotten Ceremonies

In worlds that were rapidly transforming, ceremonies turned and shifted, modified and decreased to accommodate changing needs and different people. The annual festivals once celebrated in every town house gradually coalesced into one Green Corn Feast that incorporated features of the other rites.[173] Some Cherokees re-membered the lengthy festivals of their childhoods, when priests offered impas-sioned incantations in a language long forgotten. One mused to John Norton that he "could clearly comprehend" only one phrase in the priest's invocation. "We are emigrating into a strange country," he understood the priests say, "and now move our encampments." The ancient migration story with portents and admonitions about customs and behavior had become a vague memory of strange words. Green Corn festivals diminished into occasions for "mutual congratulation and rejoicing that the crops have so far ripened."[174] Though he recalled that the festival "origi-nated from a religious institution," the middle-aged Cherokee to whom Norton spoke did not mention any sacred admonition to honor the work of *Selu*.

Town houses still held sacred fire, although the wood they burned varied from town to town and time to time. Some might be made with "black jack, locust, post oak, sycamore, red bud, plum and red oak." The imported peach joined indigenous woods in ceremonial fires built to implore warm weather. The annual ritual of puri-fication disappeared, although many Cherokees held a "Physick Dance" when "some very mortal sickness is feared." Purifying woods for medicine included "cedar, white pine, hemlock, mistletoe, evergreen brier, heart leaf, and ginseng," though other vegetation might suffice as well. Regardless of changes taking place across and within the Nation, the deep association between women, woods, and medi-cine persisted. In 1818, Charles Hicks claimed the medicine dance "belongs to the women in particular."[175]

"Half Cherokees and Quarter-Bloods": Changing Populations

Human inhabitants of the Cherokee world changed as well. The American population increased by 35 percent between 1775 and 1800, and competition for land intensified greatly. Lacking money, the Continental Congress and individual states paid Revolutionary veterans with land grants. As a result, many who had fought against Cherokees in the Revolutionary period found themselves afterward in possession of their land. The Piedmont woods of the Carolinas were cleared as restless settlers pressed toward the receding borders of the Cherokee nation. By 1800, more than 300,000 whites had moved into the states of Kentucky and Tennessee, which recently had been carved out of Cherokee land cessions.[176]

By the 1790s, the Cherokee nation included a substantial number of offspring of mixed parentage, particularly children and grandchildren of Cherokee women and white men. Many soldiers and virtually every trader entered alliances with Cherokee women, leaving English-speaking descendants who occupied the broad middle ground between two distinct cultures. Civilization proponents usually referred to them as "half Cherokees," "half-breeds," and "half" or "quarter-bloods" and relied on them for everything from interpreting sermons to negotiating boundary disputes. The matrilineage identified them as Cherokees, though they might bear names like Timberlake and Adair, or Scott, Ward, Ross, and Vann. Living in two worlds conceptually if not physically, such women and men bridged the divide between Cherokee and white. From 1791 until the removal, descendants of mixed marriages increasingly assumed positions of leadership and influence and contributed to the brilliant effort to avoid removal.

By 1825, nearly 3,000 Cherokees of mixed ancestry lived in the Southeast, 60 with African forbearers.[177] Intermarriage with European or African men produced children whose sources of authority increasingly lay beyond the clan system. Intermarriage with European or African women produced children with no clan identity at all. Cherokees of mixed ancestry were well represented on the National Council, which was established in 1827 and explicitly modeled on the American form of government. Those with white parentage also comprised the majority of students educated in missionary schools, a high percentage of converts to Christianity, and virtually all the members of the developing economic upper class.[178] Such Cherokees diverged from clan systems by race, language, and residence, and increasingly by education, wealth, and subsistence. To accommodate their changing population, the Cherokee Nation adopted specific aspects of the American legal system.

"Conforming More and More": Signs of the Civilization Program

In the first quarter of the nineteenth century, Cherokees formulated, then codified, laws comparable to those of whites who were their neighbors, supporters, converters, or detractors. Laws served as written signs of civilization and the abandonment of Cherokee traditions. "The decrees and laws of their council," wrote Brother Abraham Steiner to Rev. John Heckewelder, "conform more and more to the customs and laws of the United States."[179]

Proponents of the civilization program considered clan revenge "savage and barbarous" and urged its abolition. During the 1700s, horrified whites watched the Cherokee system of justice punish innocent settlers for crimes committed by their neighbors. To Cherokees, clan revenge assured everyone of restitution and assigned collective responsibility for individual behavior. They believed that a clan—like a village, a house, and even a basket—was only as strong as its weakest member, and so each person attended closely to the behavior of clan kin. However, no compromise existed between white and Cherokee interpretations of justice. In 1810, leaders of the seven clans officially ended the custom of clan revenge.[180] Words rather than blood formed the basis of the new Cherokee legal order.

The abolition of clan revenge struck at the heart of social systems by removing from the matrilineage its responsibility for regulating behavior. By 1820, Cherokees had established a new form of government, appointed a Lighthorse Guard, codified laws, and established a court system. Their government conformed to that of America while it established for the Cherokees a single institution to negotiate with the federal government about land cessions, road building, mission development, river access, and pressures for removal. Whether as sincere converts or as skeptical participants determined to avoid removal, Cherokees who embraced the civilization program decried old vengeance customs as "vestiges of ignorance and barbarism."[181]

Although the termination of clan responsibility for the maintenance of order undermined the matrilineage, inheritance remained centered in the mother's clan. In 1806, however, President Thomas Jefferson encouraged a delegation of Cherokee chiefs to devise new laws of inheritance. "When a man has enclosed and improved his farm, builds a good house on it and raised plentiful stocks of animals," Jefferson declared, "he will wish when he dies that these things shall go to his wife and children, whom he loves more than he does his other relations." Private property formed the cornerstone of American liberty, and its inheritance promoted individual wealth. The president instructed the chiefs how best to express their regard for their wives and children: "You will," he asserted, "find it necessary to establish laws for this."[182]

Two years later, the first law passed by the Cherokee National Council gave "protection to children as heirs of their father's property."[183] The blow struck directly at the matrilineage and instantly enhanced the rights of clanless men—whites who married Cherokee women. Children could inherit farms or fields, horses or hogs, ferries or inns, slaves or mills from white fathers who made alliances in the Cherokee Nation. In November of 1825, the council passed a law acknowledging the rights of children of Cherokee fathers and white mothers "as equal to" children descended from Cherokee mothers.[184] Since children of white mothers inherited no clan identity, the new law severed clan membership from economic inheritance.

Like other changes occurring across the Cherokee Nation, the new laws were more complex than they appear. Did they signal a partial or complete break from Cherokee custom, or did they signify partial or complete accommodation to white standards in order to protect Cherokee rights? No single or simple interpretation can encompass the minds and hearts of approximately 14,000 Cherokees living from the Tennessee River in northern Alabama to Deep Creek in the mountains of western North Carolina. Laws directly affecting women, however, reveal some interesting continuities.

"The Law Is in Favor of Females": Women and Property

The council left intact the inheritance rights of women, and Cherokee leader John Ridge pointed out that "property belonging to the wife is not exclusively at the control and disposal of the husband." While hoping to convince his readers that Cherokees were becoming as civilized as whites, Ridge acknowledged that women all over the Nation retained "exclusive and distinct control" of their own property. "The law is in favor of females in this respect," regardless of education, affluence, or kin, he admitted. The Cherokee custom of protecting married women's property rights differed entirely from English and American law, which accorded all property rights to husbands.[185]

Polygyny also remained "very much in vogue." Ridge acknowledged that the National Council failed in its initial attempt to abolish the custom since "nearly all of our legislature" would be affected. In the 1820s, it was "very common for a man to marry a mother and her daughter at the same time and raise a numerous family from both of them." Missionaries from the Georgia line to the North Carolina Valley Towns besieged supervisors for advice about men with multiple wives and a conflicting interest in Christian conversion.[186] The council finally banned polygamy in 1825. It established no penalty for infractions and ignored existing polygynous alliances.

Similarly, the council never prohibited adultery. Norton reported that Creeks beat adulterers senseless and cut off their ears, but "the Cherokees have no such punishment for adultery." Husbands scarcely took notice of their wives' infidelity, he claimed in 1809, though they might seek another wife.[187] So doing, of course, was also consistent with polygyny.

Marriage partners continued to separate with such ease and frequency that Moravian missionaries like the Gambolds began to refer to Cherokee women by their family names. "Many an Indian woman," they wrote in 1810, "because of the frequent changing of husbands, would get together a really long catalogue of names." One complication of such alliances was that "the same name could easily be common to a whole string of women." The Gambolds chose to go along with "the customs of the country," calling women by their original names.[188]

Family Order and Civil Wars: Changing Authority

The importance of clans as regulators of marriage sanctions apparently waned in the decade before removal. In 1783, the prohibition against intraclan marriage was the one social law Brother Martin Schneider could discover among Cherokees. He confessed that "of their Family Order I could only learn so much, that children of one Family dare not marry each other."[189] In 1810, Gambold claimed that intraclan marriage "would be something unheard of." Less than a decade later, however, the *Missionary Herald* reported that the prohibition "is invaded with impunity."[190]

Although women retained control of their own property, occasionally entered polygynous marriages, and were never punished for adultery, their domestic authority declined as European patriarchal traditions spread. In contrast to her predecessor's reputed position of power, a midcentury woman was likely to find that her husband "treats his wife as an equal." In Fyffe's view, no woman "pretended to lord it over the Husband who is absolute in his own family." Tacit acknowledgement of the husband's authority, he claimed, prevented "civil wars."[191] Following his 1775 visit, Bartram declared that he "never saw nor heard of an instance of an Indian beating his wife." In return, wives were "discrete, modest, loving, faithful, and affectionate to their husbands." Great distance separates Longe's 1725 assertion that irate wives might "beat their husbands to that height that they kill them outright" and Bartram's judgment a half century later that husbands refrained from abusing their wives. Bartram's description of Cherokee marriage perfectly inverts Longe's, marking a shift in domestic authority.[192]

"Made By the Hands of Indians": Women and Trade

In 1795, as part of its Indian trading policy, the federal government established a factory in the old Overhills town of Tellico. The purpose of government factories was to drive independent traders out of business and gain control of Indian lands through debt. In 1803, President Jefferson wrote to Governor William Henry Harrison "an unofficial and private" letter describing the "extensive policy respecting the Indians." In order to promote a "disposition" to cede their lands, he wrote, "we shall push our trading uses, and be glad to see the good and influential individuals among them run into debt." As their debts mounted, "they become willing to lop them off by a cession of land."[193]

In 1798, Louis-Philippe found the Tellico store "always well stocked" with a supply of game, eggs, and fruits. When he visited in the early spring, women were bringing in strawberries to sell at "ninepence the gallon." The following winter, Steiner and de Schweinitz recorded that "Cherokees supply the local garrison with butter, eggs and fruit, chiefly apples." These goods were the province of women, documenting that they continued to trade and that they included new kinds of foods in their economy.[194]

As in the early 1700s, women left their towns and farms to seek markets, but the government's elimination of local traders made it necessary for them to travel greater distances. At Pine Log in 1796, Benjamin Hawkins met a woman who had just returned from "the settlements" in Augusta to sell "a bushel and a half of chestnuts" she had carried "on her back," doubtless in a pack basket. The trip took seventeen days. And near the old town of Stecoah, two women on horseback passed Hawkins "driving ten very fat cattle to the station for a market."[195] Their destination was likely Charleston. If the government store at Tellico could not accommodate native exchange, either in terms of stocked shelves or purchasing power, women took their business elsewhere.

Restricting trade to the Tellico factory also enhanced private exchange. Since every neighbor and every visitor represented a potential market, women often kept food or crafted goods on hand to sell. Making his rounds through the Nation, Hawkins more than once stopped to buy "some corn of the women" or "provisions for the road" before proceeding on his travels.[196] In the village of Pine Log, women presented some items that gave them particular pride: "a sample of their ingenuity in the manufacture of baskets and sifters, out of cane." The agent acknowledged the skill of the weavers: "The dies of the splits were good, and workmanship not surpassed in the United States by white people."[197] It was the highest compliment Hawkins could offer.

In the early 1800s, the Moravian Springplace Mission became a locus of private exchange. Cherokees often came by the mission not for religious instruction but "when they have something to sell." Meticulous records left by missionaries reveal how extensive the networks became. "The beads, binding, pocket mirrors, some scarves, some sewing needles and some thread," wrote Brother Gambold, "have been given to the Indians in exchange for meat, some baskets, etc., instead of money." [198] Beads and binding, needles and thread, all were goods utilized by women who came with baskets to the Springplace Mission.

By 1810, a wealthy woman who lived near Springplace became one of the mission's most faithful supporters and a reliable source of trade baskets. Peggy Scott represents many of the crosscurrents that existed in Cherokee society in the early nineteenth century. Born August 20, 1783, to a Cherokee mother and Scottish father, Scott became the third wife of James Vann, a chief who was also of mixed parentage. One of Vann's other wives was Scott's sister, who no longer lived with him. [199] Following her conversion to Christianity in the summer of 1810, Scott began sending baskets to friends of the Gambolds in Salem, North Carolina, and Nazareth, Pennsylvania. In September, she forwarded "a little basket constructed more or less like Moses' little 'ark' on the Nile River" as a "remembrance" to a child in Salem. The next month, she sent six baskets in one "large black package." Around the edges of three of them, she had sewn strips of cloth containing pieces of paper. Each paper requested that the baskets "may be accepted." The three remaining baskets, according to Gambold, Scott had "secured by trading beads of coral." The same mailing carried yet another "little basket" holding a pipe and a collection of seeds. "The only thing remarkable about the pipe and the baskets," Gambold concluded, "is that they were made by the hands of the Indians." [200]

Four Springplace baskets have survived to the present. [201] Two of them indicate the persistence of the oldest Cherokee basketry customs—the use of cane and doubleweave technique, in addition to the particular selection of dyes, forms, and linear patterns. The other two are completely different in material, form, technique, and function.

The rectangular basket has traditional dark brown dye that enhances the patterns. The form is long and narrow, like storage containers for personal valuables. Its doubleweave is comparable to baskets made throughout the 1700s and traded to prominent and wealthy patrons. Demonstrating an extraordinary continuity of design, the square and cross pattern also appears on an eighteenth-century basket and on several containers made just prior to removal. And the triangular pattern occurs on one of the baskets Governor Nicholson carried to London in 1725. Across a century of dislocation, epidemics, war, and a 75 percent reduction

Rivercane doubleweave trade basket, dyed with walnut,
from the Moravian Mission to the Cherokees at Springplace (ca. early 1800s)
[l: 20 cm, w: 10 cm, h: 9.5 cm]. Photograph courtesy of the Peabody Museum
of Natural History, Yale University, YPM 14688.

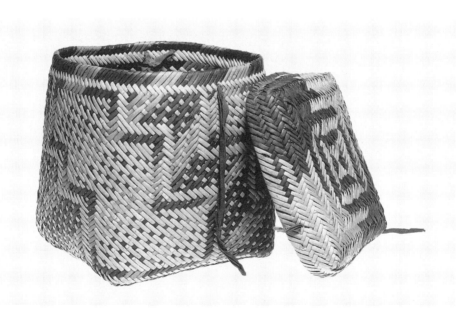

Rivercane doubleweave trade basket and lid, dyed with bloodroot and walnut,
from the Moravian Mission to the Cherokees at Springplace (ca. early 1800s) [basket,
l: 17 cm,w: 17 cm, h: 19 cm; lid, l: 16.5 cm, w: 16 cm, h: 3.5 cm]. Photograph courtesy
of the Peabody Museum of Natural History, Yale University, YPM 14689.

Rivercane doubleweave trade basket, dyed with walnut. East Tennessean Sophia Moody Pack purchased this clothes basket with the square and cross pattern from a Cherokee neighbor during the removal period. [l: 47.2 cm, w: 48.7 cm, h: 29.5 cm]. Museum of the Cherokee Indian, Cherokee, N.C. Reprint from Duggan and Riggs, *Studies in Cherokee Basketry.* The Frank H. McClung Museum, The University of Tennessee, Knoxville.

in land, women retained the knowledge and skill that produced the same forms, techniques, colors, and designs. The rectangular basket records the preservation of technological expertise and of symbols meaningful to generations of women.

The cubicle basket is dyed red and black, hues similar to those obtained from walnut and bloodroot. The fabric strap handles characterize early basketry. The distinctive patterns on the lid and base tell yet another story. Elaborately woven inside and out on a continuous field of cane, the intricate designs do not appear on any other known Cherokee baskets. They are unique to the Springplace cane basket and lid. The designs raise questions about possible ownership of patterns and knowledge. Some designs may have been widely known and shared. Others may have belonged to a particular weaver, family, clan, or settlement, or signified certain customs, concepts, events, stories, or status. As worlds changed in the 1700s, certain patterns on baskets disappeared, vanishing as well from families, customs, communities, and landscapes.

Rivercane doubleweave basket, dyed with walnut and bloodroot (preremoval)
[l: 30.5 cm, w: 30.5 cm, h: 30.5 cm]. Designs on the interior differ from those
on the exterior. Wake Forest University Museum of Anthropology.
Photograph by Doug Reinhardt.

Rivercane doubleweave basket in a square and cross pattern, dyed with walnut
(preremoval) [l: 20.3 cm, w: 20.3 cm, h: 20.3 cm]. Wake Forest University Museum
of Anthropology. Photograph by Doug Reinhardt.

Vine basket with lid, undyed, from the Moravian Mission to the Cherokees at Springplace (ca. early 1800s) [basket, d: 15.3 cm, h: 9 cm; lid, d: 16.6 cm, h: 0.6 cm]. Photograph courtesy of the Peabody Museum of Natural History, Yale University, YPM 146786.

As some conventions faded, however, others emerged in the minds and hands of women. The two other Springplace baskets resemble each other but differ entirely from all other Cherokee baskets of the period. The material is a smooth and round vine that has aged to a light tan. In contrast to the rectangular bases of cane baskets, the vine containers have round bases and bodies. Rather than the usual twill or plaited weave, the vine baskets are like wicker, with flexible splits laced around sturdy frames. No color ornaments the containers. Interlaced vines rather than fabric straps form handles. The baskets are light, delicate, and fragile. They could neither protect valuables nor process foods. They could not carry anything heavy, bulky, hot, or damp. The containers would disintegrate in water and incinerate in fire. They appear to be fanciful items of exchange, made for household decoration

Vine basket, undyed, from the Moravian Mission to the Cherokees at Springplace
(ca. early 1800s) [d: 17.2 cm, h: 11.4 cm]. Photograph courtesy of the Peabody
Museum of Natural History, Yale University, YPM 146786.

rather than for labor or storage. The little vine containers represent changing customs, new trading partners, and different concepts about how baskets should look and what they should do.

The Springplace baskets were presentations, much like those of food or dances or other baskets offered by earlier women to visiting Europeans. "Made by the hands of Indians," each container initiated relationships and established alliances between women, cultures, belief systems, and nations. Collectively, they bore more than messages from one Moravian community to another. They contained the intention and wishes of their makers to signify their culture in all its dimensions of change and continuity to those living beyond the boundaries of their world. As a collection of disparate baskets, they capture a moment and an era of complexity, when past and present interwove. They represent not one but two civilizations—the Cherokee and the European.

"The Great Industry of Cherokee Women": Changing Economies

In 1799, *Kulsathee* told missionaries that when "it became necessary" for Cherokees to "live as do the white people," he did not believe it would be possible. Nevertheless, he had built a "weaving house" and anticipated acquiring a loom. His daughter had already become proficient with carding combs and spinning wheels.[202]

Following the inauguration of the civilization program, women expanded their farming economy to raise cotton, their first crop that produced neither food nor medicine nor dye. In his 1796 trip through the Nation, Benjamin Hawkins was gratified that the women of Pine Log "had made some cotton, and would make more and follow the instructions of the agent and advise [*sic*] of the President." By 1805, Agent Return J. Meigs believed that "raising cotton, spinning and weaving is carried on in almost every part of the nation." Wherever cotton production occurred, "it is done totally by the females."[203]

Other visitors also reported favorably on the progress of the civilization program among women. In the broad river valleys of the Oostanaula and Tennessee, Norton discovered over and over "women who were busily employed in spinning cotton on the large wheel." The "great industry of Cherokee women enabled them to make cloth, not only in sufficient quantities for their own families, but to trade with the Creeks or Muscogui in exchange for cattle."[204] Like foods, medicines, and baskets, cotton became a part of women's economy, good for trade as well as home use.

The civilization proponents marked with enthusiasm that there were 1,572 spinning wheels for 6,279 women in 1809. By 1835, there were 8,322 females of all ages in the Nation, and 3,129 of them—more than a third—were identified as spinners.[205] Some women were unquestionably coming closer to approximating the behavior of their white counterparts.

"Eating Up the Cane": Animal Husbandry

Spinning and weaving became a code to communicate women's progress in assimilating white cultural norms. The number of stock animals and plows served the same function for men. By 1801, Agent Hawkins felt gratified by Cherokee progress toward civilization. The "acquirement of individual property" along with stock raising and domestic manufactures "seems to have taken a strong hold." He felt confident that Cherokees soon "will accommodate their white neighbors with lands on reasonable terms."[206]

Adoption of livestock signaled a completely different relationship between Cherokees and their land. Owning domestic animals affected crops, fences, fields, housing, labor, tools, roads, and trade. Livestock needed to be fed and housed and protected. Animals' explicit dependence on their owners conflicted with traditional beliefs, gender roles, and modes of subsistence. "The bouflow are our cows, the Deare our sheep, and the Bare our hogs," the priest told Longe in 1725.[207] Each wild animal had a special role and place in Cherokee ecosystems.

By the mid-1700s, however, horses and hogs had become part of their ecosystems, and by the early 1800s, domestic animal bones filled their refuse pits "in prodigious quantities." In 1809, Return J. Meigs enumerated more than 6,000 horses and nearly 20,000 "swine" among 12,395 Cherokees. In 1828, the *Cherokee Phoenix* reported that more than 7,000 horses belonged to a population of approximately 15,000; the number of pigs had increased to more than 38,000.[208]

The adoption of cattle, resisted until the end of the 1700s, marked significant change. Demanding the most intensive labor, cattle husbandry also required women to fence their agricultural fields. By 1796, the women of Etowah raised "hogs, some Cattle, and a great many poultry." Less than two decades later, Norton found "droves" of cattle at Oostanaula and Hiwassee, and he lost his way near Chickamauga because of the numerous cattle paths crisscrossing the trail. Meigs enumerated more than 19,000 head of cattle, found in all but four small settlements. The numbers increased slowly until 1828, when Cherokees owned more than 22,000 cattle.[209]

By the 1800s, animal husbandry seemed a viable alternative and occasional supplement to hunting, for game was scarce, land limited, and settlers plentiful. Like their white neighbors, Cherokees sent cattle to feed in the canebreaks and even moved their households to accommodate the needs of livestock. People who once lived in Willstown, Norton noticed, had scattered to "where the cane, yet abounding, enables them to raise cattle with less labour than here where it has been eat up."[210]

"The Relinquishment of Their Towns": Changing Settlement Patterns

The incorporation of European traditions of agriculture encouraged dispersed settlement. "They do not . . . dwell compactly, as formerly they did," a missionary proudly reported in 1818. "Since agriculture has been introduced among them, they have broken up."[211] But agriculture itself, once part of the fabric binding them together, did not pull Cherokees apart. What "broke them up" was the changing world of European American customs embodied in the civilization program.

Towns with land collectively owned and women at the heart of inheritance represented barbaric customs to proponents of the civilization program. The Reverend Jedediah Morse was gratified to report to the U.S. government in 1822 that "only the most indigent and degraded continue to live in towns." The government continued "to employ all its influence to wean them" from town centers. Just four years later, prominent Cherokee spokesman Elias Boudinot pointed with pride at the progress Cherokees were making. "The rise of these people," he told a New England congregation, "may be traced as far back as the relinquishment of their towns."[212]

The gradual breakup of settlements reduced the number of female-centered homes and clan compounds, separated clan families, and diminished women's autonomy. By 1826, John Ridge claimed the population was "dispersed over the countryside on separate farms," preferring to "govern their own individual plantations." Ridge's report, like Boudinot's, was calculated to impress policy makers. In truth, the dispersal occurred in areas closest to white settlements, while those "that live yet together in the Valley Towns" of North Carolina continued community life until removal.[213]

Men who devoted their lives to the civilization of Cherokees marked change in terms of private farms and use of plows, but the lines cannot be drawn so readily. Adoption of white customs was sporadic, uneven, unpredictable, and often deceiving. Rather than expanding their houses as their white neighbors did, for example, Cherokees might build several small houses on their farmsteads. And even though they adopted livestock, they seldom built barns.[214] While much about their landscapes and lives appeared indistinguishable from those of whites, their customs did not entirely disappear in the embrace of the agents of civilization.

The houses themselves suggested the coexistence of old and new conventions. Homes made with upright poles and central hearths stood near cabins of horizontal logs with fireplaces at one end and "chimneys fixed on the outside." At Hiwassee in 1799, *Kulsathee*'s small dwelling was "built of hewn logs; is neatly floored, has a walled fireplace, and everything looks neat and clean." Between Hiwassee and the new town of Wachovee, Betsy Martin's house "of hewn logs, well chinked and covered on the inside with white clay" stood near a dwelling "built only of poles, not boarded, with nothing inside but fire and people."[215]

As the eighteenth century turned into the nineteenth, housing styles varied from simple cabins to elaborate plantations, indicating increasing disparity in wealth. "The great majority" built log houses with wood "put up rough as they came from the forest" and roofed with wide strips of bark held down by poles. Others hewed logs for more spacious dwellings, and some faced the logs with "common boards" in the manner of prosperous whites. Along the new public roads that brought traffic and money through the Nation, affluent Cherokees (like James Vann) built "elegant houses of brick or painted board." By 1830, missionary Samuel Worcester reported that Cherokee housing ranged "from an elegant painted or brick mansion, down to a very mean log cabin."[216] The homogeneity that once characterized residential structures disappeared. Housing became an expression of individuality rather than community.

Interior furnishings also varied from one household to the next. In Hiwassee, *Kulsatbee* filled his house with furniture such as "chairs, tables, feather-bed with bed-stead, several trunks, presses, kitchen and table utensils and dishes and a large mir-ror." Betsy Martin's house included "two bedsteads with bedding, woven chairs, a table of walnut-wood and a closet with tin and china ware." But in a nearby home, missionaries Steiner and de Schweinitz ate "boiled sweet potatoes in a vessel on the floor" while their guide filled his tobacco pouch with sumac leaves that were drying on the roof. In his 1809 sojourn through the Nation, John Norton was en-tertained by Cherokees playing fiddles as often as by those playing traditional ball games.[217] Change and continuity interwove in every region and life.

Hot houses—those ubiquitous models of *Kanane-ski Amai-yebi*'s container of fire—remained common. Hawkins found the "old people and many of the women and children" of Etowah sleeping in hot houses in the winter of 1796. He assumed the tradition persisted because people were "unprovided with blankets and winter cloathing." Hawkins may have been right. When Norton toured the Nation in 1809, he thought hot houses were "getting much out of use."[218] In those same weeks, however, young *Itagu-nubi* was spending long winter nights around a hot house fire learning the stories of creation. And when he was an old man called John Ax, he related some of them to anthropologist James Mooney.

"The Land Was Given to Us": The Pleas of the Women

Differences in settlements, housing, furnishings, livestock, governance, and even baskets represented more than different tastes, varied resources, diverse skills, and changing bloodlines. They grew out of and were part of larger transformations. Each kind of change forged a new system of living as Cherokees faced the greatest challenge and threat to their existence. In 1802, President Jefferson signed a com-pact with the state of Georgia agreeing to extinguish all Indian land title in the state. For the next three decades, pressure for land cessions and removal intensified in an ironic lockstep with increasing signs of the success of the civilization program.

In response to the rising clamor for their land and removal, women spoke passionately and forcefully for their right to remain in their homeland. Peggy Scott wrote "a gentleman at the seat of government" to describe "our neighboring white people." With the exception of the Springplace missionaries, she wrote, whites "seem to aim at our destruction." She asked for support in her people's resistance to removal. The land that lay between Cherokees and their oppressors, Scott wrote, "is as dear to us as our own lives."[219]

On May 2, 1817, beloved woman Nancy Ward gave her last talk and strongest admonition to the National Council at Amovey. By then another treaty had been proposed, the tenth between Cherokees and the federal government, and the twentieth between Cherokees and whites since the arrival of Europeans in the Southeast. The Treaty of 1817 proposed to exchange all Cherokee lands for property beyond the Mississippi River. Ward addressed the council members as her children. "We have raised all of you on the land which we now have," she said. "The land was given to us by the Great Spirit above as our common right, to raise our children upon, and to make support for our rising generations."[220]

Once again, land was the issue. The woven cords supporting the earth seemed to be fraying. By repeated sales, the island home of the Cherokees had become "circumscribed to a small tract." The portents of the legends cast dark shadows over the soil. "We do not wish to go over to an unknown country," Ward stated emphatically. Separating women from their land was nearly inconceivable. To agree to such a move, she admonished the council, "would be like destroying your mothers." Like generations before her—war women, beloved women, and anonymous women—Ward spoke from her authority as a mother, the receiver and transmitter of clan identity and custom. "I have a great many grandchildren," she pointed out, "and I wish them to do well on our land."[221] The time had come again for women to weave new worlds.

CHAPTER 2

White Oak

❖ ❖ ❖

Ko-hi's Basket

One day in the late 1800s, Josiah Axe (b. ca. 1868) walked from his Wolftown home to the community of Whittier on the Tuckasegee River. According to his son Posey Long, Axe went "looking for a wife and brought home a basket instead."[1]

In the living room of their modern wood-frame house, which stands immediately in front of the log cabin where Axe raised his family, Posey and his wife, Bessie Catolster Long (b. 1917), discussed how to translate into English the name of the woman who made the basket. "We were thinking," Bessie Long says, "she could be called the way it's said, *Ko-hi*. Carol. *Ko-hi*. I think it's Carol in English. I asked Emmaline. She's older than I am, Emmaline Cucumber, I was asking her and she didn't know what they called her because they didn't talk English back then. I think, if it had been me, I'd have called it Carol, *Ko-hi*, like you carry something."[2]

Speaking to each other in Cherokee and responding to me in English, Bessie and Posey Long continuously cross cultural and temporal boundaries in language and in lifeways. The Longs have lived in the same place on Laurel Branch in Wolftown since they married in 1938. Some years ago, Posey Long moved his father's cabin to his own homesite, restored it, and placed it directly behind his modern house.

Laurel Branch is a tributary of Soco Creek. The branch, according to Posey Long, "starts down here at Santa Claus Land and ends up at that big mountain. There's a spring, a good spring."[3] Laurel Branch gets its name from "the laurel, because it was the whole laurel all up to the mountain here on down." For years, the branch and its associated road have gone by the name "Long Branch," after a family that lived "up yonder." Thinking about the new name, and perhaps other transformations as well, Posey and Bessie Long agree with each other that "everything changes." "That's the Long Branch," he points out. "It doesn't make much difference, but the real name is Laurel Branch."

White oak handle basket with ribbed double lid, dyed with walnut (ca. 1839–99). Made by *Ko-hi*. Photograph by Sarah H. Hill.

The Longs still use the old Josiah Axe cabin behind their house. By walking just a few steps from her back door, Bessie Long can go into the cabin to cook on the fireplace the kinds of food she and her husband grew up eating—bean bread, chestnut bread, pumpkin bread. "We eat that bread sometimes," she says with a smile. Many older Cherokees prefer traditional foods from their childhoods, the breads and soups and stews made with corn, beans, chestnuts, sweet potatoes, or pumpkins, even though contemporary doctors disapprove of them.

Bessie Long is a skilled basketweaver. When she was about eight years old, she learned from her mother and sister how to make white oak baskets "just for use, like carrying something in it, like shopping basket, market basket." In those days, women like Sally Ann Saddle Catolster made baskets to barter with rather than sell. "She didn't sell them on money," Long recalls. "She went to take them over to Waynesville or Sylva somewhere or just around Shoal Creek, just anywhere where white people lived. She just traded for groceries like potatoes and beans, just whatever they got to give, just trade in like that." Waynesville, Sylva, Shoal Creek—the list of places where women traded baskets is a litany sounded all over the reservation. While the names change from one township to another, the common refrain is "anywhere white people lived."

Sally Catolster, Eve Catolster, and Ettie Hill (1907). Churchill Collection. Courtesy of the National Museum of the American Indian, Smithsonian Institution, no. 26832.

Sitting in a chair on the old cabin porch, Bessie Long prepares white oak splits for baskets. She scrapes the oak with a knife so strong she calls it "Sampson." Her husband made the knife from a file, working in his blacksmith shop beside the cabin. "He makes the tools himself," she says quietly. "He's got all kinds of tools, you know, he makes him a corn meal beater, that big old block, a corn pounder." Posey Long's skills as a carver and metalworker have supplied their household needs for nearly sixty years.

Most days, the Longs stay home attending to various tasks. Her specialty is weaving white oak baskets, made to order, and his is carving ball sticks like those used in the traditional ball game.[4] His ball sticks, carefully carved of hickory and netted with buckskin or bark, have won many prizes at Cherokee Fall Festivals. On Sundays, the Longs visit different churches to sing hymns in Cherokee and shaped notes (or sacred harp). During most of their marriage they have cultivated a big garden, but now "we just do very little what we can nowadays. We're getting old." None of their children live with them, and they no longer need to raise much food.

Bessie and Posey Long keep Josiah Axe's basket in their home, bringing it out for visitors, both Cherokee and white, who come to see it. Most try to buy it. In 1989, a prosperous Cherokee man offered them more than one hundred dollars for the old basket. Posey Long laughs about the offers. "I'm not going to sell it," he jokes. "I'm going to go with it."

Josiah Axe paid twenty-five cents for the unusual basket and hung it from a peg in his cabin. Gesturing toward the old home, Posey Long remembers where his father "just kept it. . . . We used that old house right there. He had that basket on there, and he just had his shaving stuff in there, that's all." Throughout the nineteenth century Cherokees and whites relied on woven containers to hold all manner of things such as food, clothes, medicines, sewing goods, firewood, utensils, documents, tools, dyes, and basket splits. While few homes in western North Carolina had closets, cabinets, or drawers, virtually all contained baskets. They hung from pegs and nails in ceilings and walls. They sat on cabin roofs, porch stoops, and interior floors. They lay outside on the ground beside corn pounders and fishing poles.

The Longs believe Josiah Axe's basket is between 100 and 150 years old. If that is the case, it was made sometime between 1839 and 1889, an era of significant changes among Southeastern Cherokees. Combining features of baskets traditionally made by whites with characteristics of Cherokee baskets, the container documents the increasing interaction between two cultures. Its unusual form and function are indicative of the North Carolina Cherokees' changing social systems, subsistence practices, lifeways, and concepts following removal. Conceived and woven by one woman, the basket expresses subtly a personal experience of changing worlds. Representative of other containers, it reveals women's participation in change, not as passive observers but as active transformers of old conventions, as creators of new customs.

Cherokees were unquestionably familiar with white oak baskets well before the nineteenth century. Any woman or man who passed a white settler's farm, a Christian mission or school, or a trade store run by whites surely saw oak baskets. White oak basketry flourished in Europe long before the first white man or woman ever set foot on Southeastern soil. European immigrants to the Cherokee world brought white oak containers with them along with expertise in oak technology. Whites who settled in Southern Appalachian valleys used oak for everyday needs. They cut and carved, whittled and hewed everything—from wagon wheels and musical instruments to cabin roofs and burial coffins—from white oak trees of every size. Perhaps for more than anything else, European settlers used white oak for baskets.[5] Stiff and rigid compared to pliant rivercane containers, white oak baskets are extremely tough and enduringly strong.

White farmers made small white oak baskets to gather eggs, fruit, herbs, nuts, seeds, wool, and feathers. Suspending the containers from the crooks of their arms, they picked corn, beans, and potatoes, or cotton, wheat, and tobacco. They used them to carry feed to pigs, chickens, and turkeys and fodder to horses, cows, oxen, and mules. They put clothes to be washed, mended, or worn in oak hampers. They also stored material for clothing—yarn, wool, cotton, linsey, scraps, ribbons, dyes, buttons, thread, hooks and eyes—in oak hampers.[6] In their need for and use of baskets, whites did not differ from Cherokees at all. Their concepts of how baskets should look, how they should be made, and who should make them, however, differed completely.

The traditions Europeans brought with them did not include doubleweaving, dyed splits, linear patterns, detached lids, or twill work. Cherokee baskets did not include carved handles, attached lids, or whittled foundations. But the most important difference between the two traditions was that European basketry did not include rivercane and Cherokee basketry did not include white oak. Regardless of the abundance of other materials or their familiarity with the potential of other materials for baskets, Cherokees continued to rely on rivercane for their primary basket material until the removal.

Even though Cherokees and whites lived in increasing proximity and traded with each other for two centuries before removal, no evidence indicates that Cherokee weavers fully incorporated white oak into their basketry traditions prior to the nineteenth century. They certainly possessed the technology and skill; and the material was widely available. They cut white oak for other purposes such as house and roof construction, and they even made white oak "splinters" to lash roof beams together.[7] Yet, with one important exception, no documents refer to their use of white oak for basketry. In his 1775 sojourn to Cowee, Bartram saw town house "sophas . . . covered with mats or carpets, very curiously made of thin splints of Ash or Oak, woven or plaited together."[8]

While Cowee weavers made mats of oak or ash, Europeans found other Cherokees continuing to use rivercane for basketry until removal.[9] As Cherokees were driven from their homes at gunpoint, they left behind baskets made of cane in houses, cabins, fields, and gardens. Traveling in sorrowful exile following the infamous Treaty of New Echota, weary fugitives carried their belongings in rivercane

Rivercane doubleweave basket, dyed with walnut (preremoval)
[l: 16 cm, w: 16 cm, h: 10 cm]. Chief Vann House, Chatsworth, Georgia.
Photograph by William F. Hull.

baskets, a few of which have survived as eloquent reminders of earlier times and worlds. After removal, Cherokees from households ranging from those of a few possessions to those with livestock, spinning wheels, looms, cotton cards, and plows filed spoilation claims seeking compensation for their losses. Their inventories included cane baskets of every size and sort.[10]

Nathaniel Fish of Taloney claimed five cane riddles, *Culsatehee* of Cheowa listed two cane fanners, one cane riddle, and one cane sifter, and Running Wolf of Red Hill claimed one cane back basket. Anna of Chickamauga itemized three cane sieves and two cane riddles.[11] Thousands of lists include the simplest notations such as "cane baskets, large cane baskets, small cane baskets, double cane baskets, single cane baskets," leaving no hint as to exact size or use, age or complexity. On many inventories the basket material is not identified. When it is, however, the material is inevitably rivercane. The persistence of cane basketry until removal underscores the extraordinary resilience of women's culture and values, even in the face of disastrous social upheaval. The incorporation of white oak following removal indicates profound change.

Rivercane basket, dyed with walnut and bloodroot (preremoval)
[l: 24 cm, w: 24 cm, h: 47 cm]. Baskets found in Cherokees' abandoned homes
following removal illustrate the skill of Cherokee weavers
and evoke the harshness of their abrupt expulsion.
Chief Vann House, Chatsworth, Georgia. Photograph by William F. Hull.

Rivercane doubleweave basket, dyed with walnut and bloodroot (preremoval) [d: 39.4 cm, h: 18.4 cm]. During the forced removal from their homeland, many Cherokees carried their belongings in rivercane storage baskets to their new homes in the West. Oklahoma Museum of Natural History, University of Oklahoma.

White Oak: *ta-la*

White oak (*quercus alba*) is one of thirty-seven oaks that reach tree size and are indigenous to the Southeast. Readily identified by the light color of the fissured bark that suggests its name, the white oak ranges in maximum height from eighty to one hundred feet, and in diameter from three to four feet. Early spring brings bright green, unevenly lobed leaves as long as nine inches, accompanied by male and female flowers. The long, drooping catkins of the male flower dust the wind with yellow pollen, while sessile female flowers hold tightly to tree stems and form acorn cups. Fertile trees begin to produce acorns when they are between twenty and twenty-five years old. When the slightly bitter acorns fall to the ground, they root almost immediately.[12]

Fire has encouraged the dominance of oaks in upland forests. Oaks tend to survive burns and will sprout prolifically afterward where other species fail. With thick bark, they resist serious fire damage and seldom rot after fire scarring. Like other early- to midsuccessional forest species, they prosper when competing vegetation is cleared away. Oak acorns germinate rapidly, a characteristic that enhances their potential to sprout in seedbeds created by fire. Rapid rooting makes them hardier and more adaptable to the dry conditions that follow fire clearing. Damaged sprouts may die back, but they can resprout again and again, even years after rooting.[13]

Widely distributed in the Southern Appalachians up to 4,000 feet, white oak was one of the "vegetable productions" Bartram found on the "extremely well timbered" slopes of the Oconee Mountains as well as on the higher, colder elevations of the Cowees. In the early 1800s, F. André Michaux considered Appalachian white oak common "in every exposure, and in every soil which is not extremely dry or subjected to long inundations." Removal soldiers reported forests of white oak and chestnut along the Nantahala and Hiwassee Rivers. A decade after removal, botanist Asa Gray made his way to western North Carolina and described "steep or precipitous" mountains that were "heavily timbered, chiefly with chestnut, white oak, the tulip tree, the cucumber tree, and sometimes the sugar maple." Gray found them so frequently "that it is for the most part unnecessary to distinguish particular localities."[14]

Oaks provided shelter and mast for a variety of indigenous animals and birds, contributing to the rich diversity of faunal life. Acorns (*ku-le*) sustained bear, deer, squirrels, raccoon, turkeys, ducks, woodpeckers, and blue jays. The abundance of acorn mast greatly facilitated the introduction and survival of pigs and hogs. Beginning in the early 1900s, acorn mast also fed European wild boars, which escaped from a North Carolina resort and in increasing numbers became a serious threat to indigenous vegetation. Disease and the high degree of acorn predation counterbalances the abundance of acorn production. Animals, birds, and humans reduce mast by about 80 percent.[15]

Archaeological evidence indicates that acorns were important in human diet as early as the Woodland Period (900 B.C.–900 A.D.). Relatively high in carbohydrates and low in protein and fat, acorns satisfied the same nutritional needs as corn. Following the full-scale adoption of corn agriculture in the Mississippian Period (A.D. 900–1500), acorns diminished in dietary importance but remained valuable in times of food shortages. Cherokee women strained baskets of acorns with water to leech out the tannin, boiled them to extract oil, and ground them for flour when corn was scarce.[16]

White Oak Baskets: *talu-tsa ta-la*

The adoption of a custom so deeply associated with European culture expressed and grew out of changes in collective consciousness regarding basketry. From conceptualization to completion, white oak and cane basketry differ in important ways.

Eva Bradley of Big Cove hunting for white oak for baskets (1955). North Carolina
Collection, University of North Carolina Library at Chapel Hill.

The initial step, gathering the material, takes place on mountain slopes rather than at water's edge. To find good material, Cherokees look for straight young saplings that are free of blemishes, knots, or side shoots. Sometimes they run their hands along the bark to try to detect the qualities of the concealed wood, searching for "slick" trees that are the right age. They may pass by many saplings before finding one that is the right size, shape, and texture. Some say white oak growing on north slopes is best. Others warn that no one can work white oak that is cut during a full moon. Saplings harvested in the spring and summer when the sap is rising are easier to work with than fall and winter wood. The selection process once included walking over several acres of woods, looking, touching, and testing. Few basketweavers today, however, have the luxury of waiting for the best season, attending to changing lunar cycles, or searching acres of woodland.

To find good white oak, "I always chipped a little chip out, test it," recalls Emma Squirrel Taylor (b. 1920), a highly skilled weaver from Birdtown. By cutting a wedge from near the base of the tree, watching the way it comes out, then testing it by pulling it apart, weavers can tell if the grain is straight and the tree sufficiently supple to work into splits. Pliant wedges mean more splits. "If it was soft, and breaks up," Taylor explains, "then the grains would be, you know, where you could get two splits out of one grain. And that's the way."[17]

Cutting out a chip kills the sapling, so among contemporary weavers who harvest their own materials, some refuse to wound a tree. Yet, by not testing the wood, they may end up with wood they cannot use for baskets. For white oak weavers, life on a restricted land base produces constant tension between preserving resources and harvesting material. The continuing loss of woodlands makes the problem acute.

The weaver selects a sapling, then fells it with an ax. Cutting trees for dugout canoes, town houses, corn pounders, ball sticks, dance masks, or their numerous weapons, utensils, furniture, and housing material was traditionally the work of men. Weaving splits into baskets was the work of women. Yet, for more than a century, both women and men have cut white oak trees and have woven white oak splits into baskets. In contrast to cane basketry, white oak basketry was never identified exclusively with women. The association of white oak basketry with men as well as women indexes profound change. It indicates the diffusion of gender roles, values, and identities and points to the increasing interactions of Cherokees with white culture, where white oak basketry originated and where men dominated in private as well as public spheres. Once the province of women, basketry became common to their husbands and fathers, brothers and sons. For the first time, the work that had long signified the community and culture of women became part of the male domain.

Emma Squirrel Taylor, basketweaver from Birdtown, carries a white oak sapling she has cut to make basket splits (1974). Photograph courtesy of the Indian Arts and Crafts Board.

Contemporary Cherokees remember that their mothers and fathers both made white oak baskets. "My daddy, he got the white oaks for my mother," one recalls, "and he was the one, you know, after she married him, he was the one made the baskets." To accommodate their needs, sons learned to weave alongside daughters, and in turn, men taught women. The daughter of two weavers continues, "his mother made baskets and he learned from her." Having learned from his mother, he then taught his wife. "So he was the one made the baskets and he showed mom how to make them."[18] The same story could be told again and again.

To make one large basket or several small ones, a weaver needs more than one sapling. From contemporary weavers, we begin to get a sense of how many times they had to shoulder their axes and walk the mountains to find enough wood to make a work basket for home or a few baskets for trade. Bessie Long went once a week to get white oak for baskets. Accompanied by a relative, she walked up the mountainside above Laurel Branch. They "just got about four and then we'd split it up and divide it. It don't make much. . . . If they're good ones, we'd get about two baskets, about a small one."[19] A sapling three to six feet long and four to six inches in circumference is heavy and cumbersome. Dragging two of them down the steep slopes is all one person can manage. If they are good, two saplings produce eight sticks or two to four baskets.

"Really, the first part of it is going out into the woods to get your material," comments Taylor, "because you can't be a basketmaker if you can't learn how to take your material out on your own."[20] Among older weavers, their identity as basketmakers has long been tied to the ability to get their own material and to their knowledge gained from a deep understanding of woodlands. "You have to start with where the white oak comes from," says Bessie Long.[21] To be a white oak weaver, you have to start in the woods.

While the cut sapling is fresh, the weaver strips off the outer bark, then "busts up" the core. That is, she splits the core in half with a mallet and wedge, then quarters it the same way. If she hits the wedge right, the wood breaks smoothly into sticks, or slabs of equal size. Getting multiple splits from one slab means separating the light early wood formed in the spring from the denser late wood that grows in the summer. It requires skill gained by lifelong practice. If she misses, the wood breaks across the grain, producing uneven sticks and a few that are useless. "You have to get them the same width," explains Shirley Taylor (b. 1946) from her Birdtown home, "or your basket will be lopsided."[22] Weavers look for grain lines in the early wood. "See, this is the grain part right there, and it's soft," Emma Taylor points out. When a weaver as experienced as Emma Taylor describes it, the task sounds deceptively simple. "So you come back and you hit it right in the middle, right through there, and it'll give you two splits."[23]

Henry Bradley of Big Cove cutting white oak for basket splits (1955). North Carolina
Collection, University of North Carolina Library at Chapel Hill.

To "take the splits out," which Shirley Taylor explains means "making them to where you can work with them,"[24] weavers separate the wood along the annual growth rings. Some prefer splits of sapwood, the lighter part of the tree closest to the bark. Others also work with heartwood, the darker, denser wood of the interior. Variations in the size of the growth rings indicate changing patterns of weather. In dry years, trees grow slowly and form narrow growth rings that are difficult to pull apart. Abundant rain results in wide growth rings whose coarser wood is hard to work. With so many variables, taking out splits requires expertise, concentration, and sensitivity to the material. The work never becomes automatic.

Sitting and turning the knife blade down toward her lap, the weaver repeatedly scrapes the splits until they are thin, flexible, and uniform. Slender, fragrant white oak peelings cling to her clothing and curl up on the ground around her. She cuts the splits into different widths with scissors or a knife, then trims and smooths the edges. Work baskets have uniformly wide and thick splits, while fancier trade baskets have splits of different widths, which, woven together, create a design.

Before the splits dry out, weavers prepare the dyes. White oak is more porous than cane and absorbs dye faster. Nonetheless, the process takes at least a day, and dying techniques vary greatly. Some weavers make black dye from the bark of walnut roots, as *Ko-hi* did. The roots "will dye a darker shade than any part of the walnut tree," a deep shade preferred for centuries by Cherokee weavers. Ultimately, however, taking the bark from the root kills the tree. "I guess the only time we ever use bark and the roots," says Louise Goings (b. 1947), "is when somebody's removing a walnut tree from near their garden." Since "walnut trees causes the vegetables in the garden not to grow,"[25] farmers and gardeners on limited land may need to eliminate them. The benefit to weavers is temporary, however, since the number of walnut trees steadily declines.

Other weavers favor the lighter brown or even gray shades that come from different parts of the trees. "In the summertime," Goings says, "we use the leaves from the tree, and then in fall we can use the green nuts, crush them up."[26] After hulls turn brown, they can be stored for winter dyes. Among contemporary weavers and surely among those of the past, some rely on the same dyes as their mothers did, while others experiment with different colors and sources. "We used to try out all kinds of bark on them," recalls Bessie Long.[27]

The dyes used varied from season to season, settlement to settlement, weaver to weaver. Sumac, poke, angelica, and oak galls have all made their way into dye pots, along with flowers, berries, roots, and leaves of hundreds of unrecorded plants. Yellowroot (*daloni-ge na-ste-tsi*) was popular in the early part of the twentieth century but has generally lost favor. "I might have used the yellowroot once in a

Helen Bradley, basketweaver from Big Cove, making white oak splits (1955). North Carolina Collection, University of North Carolina Library at Chapel Hill.

Agnes Welch, white oak basketweaver from Big Cove, checks her dye pot (1990).
Photograph by Sarah H. Hill.

while," says Goings, "[but] I just don't like yellow." Bessie Long laughs and puts it another way. "Yellow root's kinda not look too good to me. It's yellow."[28]

Weavers may use soda, alum, or copper as as a mordant. Some remember that their mothers added old iron froes, ax heads, or nails to walnut dye pots. All recognize that different kinds of containers affect the dye in various ways. Bloodroot, Goings explains, "dyes different shades of orange depending on what kind of metal your pot is."[29] While one believes "aluminum pots don't dye too good," another relies on "a pot of white enamel" to get good color from bloodroot and "an old pot that's got this old teflon lining"[30] for walnut.

Whatever containers or materials they select, weavers dye all the splits at one time because "you can dye splits one day and the next day dye again, and you never get the same color." Shirley Taylor says that "you about know what baskets you're going to make" before you start, then "dye enough for that many." The reason is simple. "You usually can't mix your browns together."[31] Contemporary weavers will re-dye all the splits rather than combine splits dyed at different times.

Like cane, prepared white oak splits last season after season. Martha Lossiah Ross (b. 1931), an accomplished weaver from Big Cove, keeps on hand a box full of splits and handles she "worked up" more than a decade ago. She still plans to make them into baskets. Many children have grown up familiar with the sight of dyed and trimmed splits lying in bundles on the kitchen floor or table. Many began their own work by playing with old splits carefully made by their mothers and fathers, sisters and brothers.

Techniques for weaving patterns differ in cane and white oak basketry. Cane splits are the same width and thickness. White oak splits can be any width or thickness. Cane patterns are made with contrasting weave called twill. White oak patterns are made by contrasting the size and color of splits. Cane weavers can make an almost infinite number and size of geometric patterns with dyed splits and twill weave. In contrast, white oak weavers rely on color, as *Ko-hi* did, and on the use of wide and narrow splits in a simple plait.

When they fully incorporated white oak into earlier basketry customs, Cherokee weavers expanded their repertoire of forms and techniques. In addition to varying the ways they made patterns, they began to add handles and lids. And whereas earlier baskets had square or rectangular bases, those made after removal included round bases with ovoid and globular bodies. *Ko-hi*'s basket includes a number of traits borrowed from whites after removal.

Ko-hi's basket has a carved handle. Europeans traditionally carved wooden handles for baskets, but Cherokees did not. They carried large baskets with tumplines. For smaller baskets, Cherokees used flexible handles of thong or cord. Once they fully incorporated white oak, however, weavers began carving wooden handles for baskets. The term "carrying basket" (*talu-tsa ko-hi-nu-s-ti*) became part of Cherokee terminology as carved handles became part of container technology. The addition of carved handles stands as a material divide, marking a shift to smaller baskets and different tasks, and to changing economies and roles.

The strength of a white oak basket is tied closely to the strength of its handle and the way it is attached to the basket. Nineteenth-century weavers made dense handles that interlocked under the basket to provide greater support. "They had, they call them, you know, these handles, these interlock handles," one weaver recalls of her grandparents' baskets.[32] With interlock handles, carrying baskets could bear greater loads for longer periods of time. The handles were so durable they

A Cherokee woman demonstrates for a visiting ethnologist how she suspends her white oak burden basket from a tumpline. Photograph by M. R. Harrington (1908). Courtesy of the National Museum of the American Indian, Smithsonian Institution, no. 2733.

often outlasted the baskets they carried and so rigid they seldom yielded to the stresses that reshaped containers over time.

Men and women became handle carvers as well as basketweavers. Bessie Long's father "made all kinds of, like, handles" for baskets "and just almost everything." Handle baskets meant farm chores, the daily labor of every household member. They were "just carrying baskets, carrying the corn, go feed the pig and the chicken, go get the corn." For others, handle baskets indicated household work, "picking up wood chips, you know, them little chips" for household fires.[33] Whoever made the containers or handles and however they were used, baskets continued to be associated with essential tasks.

Along with a carved handle, *Ko-hi's* basket has an attached lid, a feature Cherokees did not include in their baskets prior to the nineteenth century. Earlier weavers secured lids by tying them onto their baskets. Detachable lids could be removed and used as separate baskets. "You take the whole lid off," Bessie Long explains, "you could use that for a tray."[34]

Ko-hi not only attached the lid to her basket, she also made the lid with an entirely different technology known as rib work. A technique brought to the Southeast by white immigrants, rib work produces a distinctive basket form. In contrast to the flat surface of a split basket, the surface of a rib basket is actually ribbed, or corrugated, a texture produced by weaving splits over and under rounded rods. Cherokees may have begun to carve handles and attach lids when they incorporated the European convention of rib basketry.

To make a rib basket (*talu-tsa de-ga-nu-li-dsi-yi*: basket, ribs it has, there), the weaver carves two relatively wide and dense pieces of white oak, tapers their ends, and binds them together to make two intersecting hoops that form a frame. She then whittles ribs in graduating lengths to outline the basket body and prepares very narrow splits for weaving the ribs together. By changing the shape of the frame and the lengths of the ribs, the weaver creates different forms. Rib baskets can have square, round, or bilobed bases and square, ovoid, or flat-sided bodies. The same technique of framing rods and interlacing splits produces flat lids, like the one *Ko-hi* attached to her basket.

Ko-hi's ribbed lid indicates that by the second half of the nineteenth century, Cherokees had adopted the rib basketry of their white neighbors. Sturdy and varied, rib baskets index changing subsistence and social systems, as clan and community agriculture in large villages gave way to family farming and animal husbandry in small settlements of nuclear households. Clan fields receded into memories shaped by the loss of land and merging subsistence roles. Large burden baskets, so closely associated with women, gradually disappeared, and rib baskets made by men and women became the most common harvesting containers. Spreading her

White oak rib basket woven by *Ayasta* but left unfinished to show technique (1913)
[l: 16.5 cm, w: 14 cm, h: 9 cm to rim]. Catalog No. 281407,
Department of Anthropology, Smithsonian Institution.

White oak rib basket, undyed (ca. 1910–21) [l: 47.5 cm, w: 32 cm, H: 23 cm to rim].
American Museum of Natural History. Photograph by William K. Sacco.

hands apart, Alice Walkingstick recalled that her father "used to make rib baskets that big . . . with a handle" to carry food to livestock and gather vegetables from the household garden.[35]

While some rib baskets became identified with particular tasks—egg, pie, and market baskets—others were known by their distinctive shapes—gizzard, melon, and fanny baskets. Mallets, wedges, scissors, and nails joined axes and knives in the weaver's tool kit. Whittling became as important as scraping to complete a basket. Technologies, forms, and materials long noted but never adopted gradually became part of the lives of nineteenth-century Cherokees.

The distinction between white oak and cane basketry encompasses different gender associations, the location and nature of material, the methods and tools of harvesting, the density and width of splits, the carved ribs and handles, the weaving techniques, the kinds of patterns, and the combination of elements in each container. Extending from gender roles to kinds of environments, the differences indicate deep systemic change.

Most profoundly, *Ko-hi*'s basket signifies increasing interaction between Cherokees and whites, for the basket is a hybrid of expressions of both cultures. The material, the ribs, attached lid, rounded base, and carved handle derived from old European customs. The reliance on dyed splits and the particular pattern—a woven chain design—characterized traditional Cherokee basketry. But *Ko-hi*'s basket represents more than intensive contact and blended customs from two cultures. It also demonstrates Cherokee proficiency in developing and expressing entirely new concepts. The pedestal base, double lid, and decorative bands are innovations. The attached ribbed lid on a conventional basket is unique. None of these traits appeared in the traditional basketry of whites or Cherokees. And the technique of attaching the lid—inserting its stems into small holes burned into the handle with a heated nail—originated in the nineteenth century and became a hallmark of Cherokee rib basketry. "That's the way they put the lids on them," Bessie Long remembers, "they'll put lids on them but they made holes on the handles."[36]

Perhaps the most eloquent statement *Ko-hi*'s basket makes is a personal one. The container, which interlaces Cherokee and white forms, overlays convention with innovation and tells a story of a woman who lived through, absorbed, and responded to many kinds of change. Like other Cherokee women in western North Carolina, *Ko-hi* was literally and metaphorically weaving new worlds.

North Carolina Cherokees

Prior to removal, Cherokees signed a series of treaties that contracted their territorial holdings, confined their population, and erased their towns from the map.

White oak rib basket with burned holes for lid attachment (ca. 1913) [l: 16.5 cm, w: 14 cm, h: 9 cm to rim]. Catalog No. E281409, Department of Anthropology. Smithsonian Institution.

Between the end of the American Revolution and 1819, the margins of the Cherokee Nation steadily shrank from all sides. Of all the agreements to sell or cede land, few were more momentous than the Treaty of 1817, which was amended in 1819. It was the first treaty that contained provisions for removal.

In exchange for tracts on the Arkansas River occupied by tribal members who had already emigrated, Southeastern Cherokees relinquished 6,959 square miles of land. Nearly five million acres that included the sites of countless settlements and sacred grounds merged silently into the states of North Carolina, Tennessee, Georgia, and Alabama. Almost all the old Middle and Overhill towns disappeared under furrows plowed and roads laid by white settlers. Tribal land along the Tuckasegee and Oconaluftee Rivers, everything east and north of the Little Tennessee, and all settlements east of the Nantahala Mountains became part of North Carolina. Long eager for the removal of Cherokees and the acquisition of their territory, North Carolina discovered that the fastest way to attract white settlement was to sell the newly acquired lands at public auction. The prices ranged from five cents to a few dollars an acre.[37]

Second and third generation North Carolinians, Virginians, and Pennsylvanians borrowed money and bought land that spread from the young town of Asheville on the French Broad River west to the river valleys of the Tuckasegee, Oconaluftee, and Little Tennessee. They settled along the Great War Road, which was forged by General Rutherford in his 1776 destruction of the Middle Towns. Along that pathway of retribution, the communities of Canton, Waynesville, Webster, and Sylva developed on lands ceded in 1817–19. Enterprising whites opened trade stores to attract their own kind to Iolee, Savannah, and Caney Forks, and to Shoal, Soco, Cartoogechay, and Scott's Creeks. The state set aside 400 acres of ceded land west of the Cowee Mountains for the new town of Franklin, which was built on the site of *Nikwasi*. Cherokees shared memories and legends of the sacred *Nikwasi* mound, in whose center their perpetual fire burned and the immortal *Nunnehi* (Dwellers Everywhere) lived. It was, some said, the largest Indian mound in North Carolina.[38]

Following the 1817–19 treaties, many Cherokees who lived on lands in the old Middle and Overhill Towns dispersed. Some moved south and west into the shrinking confines of the Cherokee Nation. A few thousand emigrated to the Arkansas River settlements.[39] And some along the Oconaluftee and Tuckasegee Rivers took advantage of a particular treaty clause that set them permanently apart. Forty-nine Cherokee families in North Carolina, including several headed by women, accepted a provision of the 1817–19 treaties that enabled them to become state citizens. Each family assumed possession of an individual tract of land called a life estate, which consisted of 640 acres or one square mile. By becoming citizen Indians, they were guaranteed the right to remain in the Southeast and to live on their own private landholdings under the protection of North Carolina.[40]

The single restriction on life estates was requested by a Cherokee woman, Ruth Phillips. She asked that any man who took a life estate "not have the power of selling the land during his lifetime, so as to deprive the wife and children of the same." Like countless women whose voices are more felt than heard in the corridors of history, Phillips believed that "worthless white men might come in and marry Cherokee women, to take reservations and then sell." When such opportunists sold their life estates, their Cherokee families would be left with nothing.[41] Phillips found support in an unlikely corner. General Andrew Jackson, who subsequently presided over the Indian Removal Act as president, drew up the treaty and acceded to her request. He included a clause prohibiting the heads of families from selling life estates. He also stipulated that when the (male) head of a household died, the life estate reverted to his widow and children.[42]

Many Cherokees took life estates in the Oconaluftee River valleys near an old settlement called Qualla, or Quallatown. Some say the name Quallatown honored *Kwa-li*, a woman who lived in the area. Gradually, the story goes, people came to refer to the settlement as *Kwa-lun-yi*, Kwali's place, or Kwalitown, a term ultimately corrupted to Quallatown. The name was in common use in the 1830s when Baptist missionary Evan Jones met "two candidates from Qualai" who came to his Valley Town mission to learn about Christianity. Their mountain town, according to Jones, consisted of "about three hundred persons."[43] In 1838, as most Cherokees were forced into exile, Qualla became a primary settlement of those who eluded removal and subsequently became known as the Eastern Band of Cherokees.

The Oconaluftee River descends from a high gap in the Smoky Mountains. As it cuts its way down the steep mountainside, numerous creeks from an eastern ridge add their cold waters to its rapid flow. Cherokees lived "beside the water" (*egwa-nul-ti*) in the deep and narrow valleys cut by flowing streams. By the late 1700s, whites had corrupted *egwa-nul-ti* to Oconaluftee and the word came to identify the river flowing through Quallatown. From their association with the river, Qualla Cherokees were also collectively identified as Lufty Indians.[44]

Long regarded as the most conservative members of the Nation, preremoval Cherokees from mountain settlements were considerably less accessible to white encroachment than their kin in the broad river valleys of Georgia, Alabama, and Tennessee. Even Christian missionaries who had labored for decades in the Nation continued to discover towns like Qualla hidden between mountain passes. In December of 1829, Evan Jones made his first visit to *Egwanee* (Beside the River; perhaps the Nantahala settlement whose name was later corrupted to Acquone), "a small town about thirty miles in the mountains," where his sermon marked "the first time the gospel has ever sounded in this dreary place." While Cherokees in the lower part of the Nation were entering their second generation of Christianity, the missionary call had yet to sound in some of the mountain settlements of western North Carolina.[45]

The proximity of whites carved a sure passage for the kinds of change they called civilization. Variously encouraging Cherokees to adopt Christianity, English literacy, a market economy, private landholdings, plantation agriculture, black slavery, monogamy, stock raising, fence building, loom weaving—in short, any and all attributes of their own societies—whites also began urging Cherokees to migrate west, where they could continue to live as hunters. In the western North Carolina mountains, however, such advocates carried little influence.

In 1835, few of the 3,644 Cherokees in North Carolina married whites or descended from a white parent or grandparent. Living well beyond the toll roads, ferries, hostelries, taverns, missions, and schools that increasingly connected their kin with whites, mountain Cherokees retained more of their customs and lifeways. Most lived in small settlements with less arable land. They incorporated fewer implements of husbandry and owned fewer looms, spinning wheels, plows, and livestock.[46] Observing their customs, an 1835 census taker complained that they "do not appear to be progressing in the art of civilization as much as those in the heart of the Nation."[47]

Contours of the land and quality of the soil shaped the settlements and influenced the lifeways of their occupants. Farm size, crops, livestock, tools, labor, and marketing all were affected by the amount of land that could be cultivated. Cherokees in Georgia, Alabama, and Tennessee settled primarily in the Ridge and Valley province, where undulating terrain accommodated large farms and fertile soils produced surplus crops. Cherokees in these alluvial lowlands, particularly those with white ancestry, encouraged the construction of roads and ferries, the building of inns and mills, and the acquisition of English literacy and private property. Such changes expedited marketing and enhanced individual wealth.[48]

In 1835, North Carolina Cherokees owned half as many farms and less than a quarter of the arable land of their Georgia kin. They owned a tenth as many slaves as Tennessee Cherokees and harvested about a third as much corn per farm as Alabama Cherokees.[49] Differences in agricultural assets, methods, produce, and surplus translated into different relationships to the market. In 1835, most mountain Cherokees practiced subsistence farming and rarely engaged in a market economy. They ate what they grew, accumulated small surpluses, and sold little produce and other goods. They relied on barter more than cash, exchanging commodities and services with neighbors. Although their lives, labor, lands, and goods distinguished them from their kin, their race and nationality did not. Following the fraudulent Treaty of New Echota, most North Carolina Cherokees were exiled to the West.

Georgia led the removal charge. In 1830, the state extended its civil and criminal laws over the Cherokee Nation, nullified existing Cherokee laws, prohibited the right to public assembly, and authorized a survey of all Indian lands in order to dispose of them in a lottery. In stunning disregard for treaty obligations, Georgia systematically oppressed Cherokees, finally prohibiting them from bringing lawsuits against whites or testifying against whites in court.[50] As a result, Georgia Cherokees had no recourse through law, that institution so often proclaimed as the ultimate defense of individual rights in civilized nations.

Cherokees in Tennessee and Alabama, including those on life estates, fared little better than their Georgia kin. Most lost their lands and goods to whites through intimidation, fraud, or theft. State authorities refused to intercede or protect the dispossessed.[51] Thus, in three of the four states where Cherokees took life estates, the provision securing their property was ignored. The clause insuring land to their widows and children was meaningless.

North Carolina Cherokees found themselves in a unique situation. Following the 1817–19 treaties, state authorities assumed possession of ceded lands and initiated a survey. Lax record keeping and distant courthouses, however, complicated their work. Deeds were filed weeks, months, and even years after land was sold, and tracts were sold and resold before their deeds were recorded. Moreover, since life estates were granted by the federal government, they should have been exempt from state surveys. White speculators and settlers who purchased life estates discovered that the state had no record of the titles. By 1824, property disputes ended up in the state Supreme Court. In the 1824 decision of *Euchella v. Welch*, the court ruled in favor of Cherokee landholders.[52]

The decision upheld Cherokee ownership of property granted by the federal government, even though the state had subsequently sold the same land to whites. Following the court decision, Congress allocated money to the state for the purchase of all Cherokee tracts.[53] Some Cherokee citizens then moved into the Cherokee Nation or onto mountain lands the state considered too worthless to survey. Others retained their life estates and North Carolina citizenship. Four years after *Euchella v. Welch*, approximately sixty citizen families were living in the Quallatown area along the Oconaluftee River and its tributaries. Their private landholdings lay about fifty miles outside the boundaries of the Cherokee Nation. During removal, these few Indians who had "acquired the right to remain on the Oconeelufty" were carefully excluded from the disastrous roundup, incarceration, and expulsion.[54]

In 1835, the federal government ordered a Cherokee census in anticipation of removal. Nathaniel Smith, the North Carolina enrolling agent, found in Macon and Haywood Counties 233 Cherokees "who have left their families [in the Cherokee Nation] and settled among the whites."[55] Agent Smith had it backward, of course, for it was the whites who had settled among the Cherokees. And some, like the Qualla, or Lufty, Indians, had become state citizens. Yet, Smith's comment reveals the common presumption that whites held first claim to the land. It also indicates that state citizenship did not really distinguish Qualla Cherokees from others in the minds of many whites.

While citizen Cherokees watched with apprehension, their kin in the Nation struggled to avoid removal. When a handful of Cherokees signed the Treaty of New Echota in violation of the laws of their Nation, they delivered all remaining Southeastern Cherokee lands to the United States and committed the entire Nation to removal. Under the leadership of Principal Chief John Ross, Cherokees all across the Nation signed petitions protesting the treaty, its terms, and its signers. More than 3,000 in the North Carolina portion of the Nation added their names to memorials sent to Congress asking for redress.[56]

Protests and legal briefs led nowhere. Greed, racism, ethnocentricity, paternalism, and that arrogant and proprietary notion called manifest destiny lay too deeply embedded in the dispassionate word "removal." The federal government, the states of Georgia, Tennessee, Alabama, and North Carolina, and hundreds of thousands of whites were determined to expel the Cherokees.

Although they were no longer members of the Nation, citizen Cherokees in North Carolina could not be sure they were exempt from removal. They had good reason for concern. Gold had been discovered along various waterways on their land. Federal agents enumerated their communities in terms of "warriors" and characterized them as a potential "useful auxiliary" to any Cherokees in the Nation who might resist removal. Anxious to secure their rights and determined to receive compensation for the final sale of the Nation's lands, they turned to various white lawyers to represent their claims in Washington. William H. Thomas of Stecoa Old Fields, near Whittier, was one such agent.[57]

Giant Leeches and Going Snakes

When Josiah Axe walked to Whittier and back home again, he followed a route worn deep in Cherokee history and memory. Whittier was established in the 1880s near the site of Stecoa (*U-tsu-ti-gwa*: Big Fish Place), one of fifteen Middle Towns destroyed in 1761 by Grant's army of 2,800 British soldiers. Fifteen years after Grant's invasion, the rebuilt and resettled town was the first of thirty-six Middle and Valley Towns ravaged by Rutherford's Revolutionary War army. Once again resettled, Stecoa was among the Tuckasegee River sites swallowed up by North Carolina in the treaties of 1817–19.[58]

Three white brothers named Enloe purchased the tract in the Cherokee land auction of 1820 and subsequently used it to pay a debt they owed to William Holland

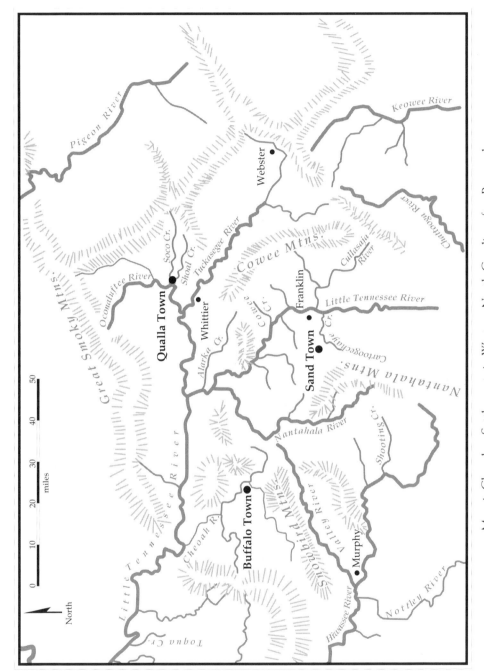

Map 4. Cherokee Settlements in Western North Carolina after Removal

Thomas. Pleased with the property and its view of the Tuckasegee River, Thomas expanded the small farmhouse that had been built where the Stecoa Town House once stood. Years later, he recalled hearing that Stecoa villagers had interred the bodies of their deceased chiefs in the earth beneath the town house. He assumed that accounted for the numerous bones, potsherds, and arrow points unearthed by laborers who constructed his cellar. Thomas named his 1,500-acre farm Stecoa Old Fields and lived there approximately thirty years.[59]

Born February 5, 1805, on Raccoon Creek of the Pigeon River, Thomas and his widowed mother moved to an Oconaluftee tract she had acquired following the treaties of 1817–19. At the age of thirteen, Thomas began working as a clerk in Felix Walker's store on Soco Creek (*Sagwa-hi*: One Place), an Oconaluftee tributary. The story of William Thomas interweaves with that of North Carolina Cherokees from that moment on.[60]

As a clerk, Thomas became acquainted with many Cherokees who frequented the store to exchange hides and labor for cloth and tools. He learned to speak Cherokee and write in the syllabary that had been created in 1821 by *Sikwa-yi* (Sequoyah). Among his Cherokee patrons, Thomas counted as a friend the great peace chief Yonaguska (*Yanugun-ski*: the Bear is Drowning Him; Drowning Bear). Yonaguska had sold his life estate on the Tuckasegee River and moved to the north prong of Soco Creek. He and his daughter *Katal-sta* (Lending; Lending It) soon became steady customers at the Thomas trading post.[61]

In 1831, as gold prospectors swarmed over Cherokee lands equipped with picks, armed with rifles, and nearly mad with greed, Yonaguska and fifty-nine other Qualla Cherokees retained Thomas as their attorney and agent. They were joined by 192 families evicted from their homes in every part of western North Carolina by white zealots. By the time of removal, the federal government also relied on Thomas as its agent to negotiate with the Cherokees he represented. Thomas continued to acquire powers of attorney from additional Cherokees for the next several years.[62]

Brilliant, determined, and restless, Thomas developed broad interests that matched his varied skills. By 1860, he was one of the largest slaveholders in western North Carolina. He owned more than 150,000 acres of land and raised and sold livestock. Politics commanded a considerable amount of his devotion, and from 1848 to 1862 he represented his district in the state legislature, where his zeal for internal improvements helped develop turnpikes and railroads. When he failed to get elected to the Confederate Congress, Thomas turned instead to the Confederate Army, and for three years commanded a home guard that was served in part by

400 Cherokees he recruited. Financial reversals and declining health during the war led to his bankruptcy and hospitalization. By the end of his life he had lost his wife, his fortune, and his mind, dying at the age of eighty-eight in the Western Insane Asylum in Morganton, North Carolina. More than anything else in his long and active life, Thomas is remembered for his constant and troubled political representation of those he called his dear friends, the North Carolina Cherokees.[63]

A shrewd businessman, Thomas opened seven trade stores between 1822 and 1837. He followed the politics of Cherokee removal closely and took advantage of the economic opportunities generated by state and federal policies. It was obvious that the government would need garrisons, roads, and supplies for the 7,000 troops coming into the Cherokee Nation. Only the most cynical could have anticipated how much the Cherokees ultimately required, but Thomas surely recognized that they would need mediators, translators, and finally, legal representation.

When the old Felix Walker store went bankrupt, Thomas started his own trading post near the junction of Soco Creek and the Oconaluftee. For several years, his store records identified the area as Indiantown and usually carried separate accounts for Cherokee customers.[64] The trading post later became known as the Quallatown Store and remained one of Thomas's more successful ventures until the Civil War. Cherokees, whites, and a few blacks bought, borrowed, bartered, and sold goods and labor at the Thomas store. The "small wooden building with a porch" became a nexus of interaction between three races and cultures.[65]

The Indiantown trading post placed Thomas in the heart of Cherokee settlements and history. At the Soco Town House, Middle Town Cherokees had spurned Shawnee chief *Tecumseh*'s entreaty to join the 1812 revolt against the Americans.[66] Many who traded at Thomas's store had listened to the plea, debated, and finally rejected it. The following year, they joined American forces under Andrew Jackson to crush the Creek Red Stick revolt. It was often said that *Tsunu-labunski* (Junaluska: He Tries but Fails) of Cheoah had saved Jackson's life in the final battle at Horseshoe Bend. The warrior had cause to regret his heroism, however. "If I had known that Jackson would drive us from our homes," he later said, "I would have killed him that day at the Horseshoe."[67]

Thomas established a second store with a tannery at the head of Scott's Creek near Webster, a town that had been developed on the site of an Indian mound from which curious whites collected artifacts. Webster was adjacent to the ancient settlement of *Tuksi-yi* (Terrapin Place?), which was destroyed in 1781 by Captain John Sevier of Tennessee. Cherokees reoccupied the site until the treaties of 1817–19. A rock formation in the shape of a corn crib had once towered over Scott's Creek. After a lightning strike scattered the rocks, Cherokees referred to the place as

Un-wada-tsu-gilasv (Where the Storehouse Was Taken Off). The name, as it had turned out, was like a prophecy. And in 1851, the town became the seat of Jackson County, named to honor the architect of Cherokee removal.[68]

Thomas built five more stores near the removal garrisons and stockades where Cherokees were imprisoned before beginning their long forced march to the west. Four of his five removal stores were located in the North Carolina portion of the Cherokee Nation. One trading post stood near Ft. Butler at the juncture of the Valley and Hiwassee Rivers in the area of present-day Murphy. Known to Cherokees as *Tlanusi-yi* (Leech Place), Murphy was established in 1836 on tribal land taken by the Treaty of New Echota. *Tlanusi-yi* designated a great chasm in the waters of the Valley River where a giant leech dwelled. His immense body created boiling waterspouts that swept bystanders into the rushing stream. A woman who once went fishing there, Cherokees said, nearly lost her baby to the leech. She had placed the infant on a ledge by the water while she fished. But when she saw the waters begin to surge and churn, she quickly snatched up her child from certain death.[69]

Three miles south of *Tlanusi-yi*, Thomas built another store at Nottely (*I-nadu-li*: Going Snake Place). Close to the Georgia line, the settlement lay along the Nottely River where it flowed into the Hiwassee. A swirling gulf in the waters of the Nottely revealed to Cherokees the second dwelling place of the *Tlanu-si*. Gathering at night in the town house or around fires in their own hot houses, they listened to stories of the giant leech in the river and the unpredictable *Nunnehi* in surrounding forests, and cautioned each other about the forces of destruction and beguilement that lay in wait. The landscape held other evidence of valor and death, for in rocky cliffs above the Hiwassee lay the bones of warriors long since dead, covered by rock cairns.[70]

Northeast of *Tlanusi-yi* and *I-nadu-li*, Thomas established a third removal store near Ft. Montgomery on the Cheoah River (*Tsiyo-hi*: Otter Place), a tributary of the Little Tennessee. The new garrison was built on the ballground where warriors once played games to win honor and prestige, conjurors prayed and prophesied, and women danced to weaken the opposing ball teams.[71] *Tsiyo-hi* "is fenced in by almost impassable mountains," wrote Butrick in 1825, "but contains a beautiful tract of land sufficient to support a great number of inhabitants." The tall and rugged Snowbird, Unicoi, and Cheoah Mountains surrounding *Tsiyo-hi* included barren summits called balds (*uga-wagun-ta*). Cherokees identified two of them as *Sehwate-yi* (Hornet Place) for the giant hornet who was believed to sun himself on the treeless crowns.[72] They watched the mountains for swarming hornets who could capture their children and thereby steal their future. Nearly 500 Cherokees who still belonged to the Nation lived in five towns along the Cheoah and its tributaries.

"These dear people," according to Butrick, "are in general full Cherokees and igno-rant of the English language." One of their larger settlements, called *Yunsa-i* (Buf-falo Town), stood near the mythical dwelling of a giant underwater buffalo. By the time of removal, some said, the *yunsa* had migrated to another secluded home.[73]

Thomas established his fourth removal store near the Ft. Delaney stockade at Valley Town (*Gu-nahitun-yi*: Long Place). More than 600 Cherokees lived in the broad plains of the Valley River and its tributaries.[74] Cherokees believed a giant lizard with a gleaming throat and rough scales sunned himself on the high, barren rocks (*Diya-hali-yi*: Lizard Place) facing the valley. From his overlook the lizard could see the valley floor with an ancient mound that had once been part of a town house. The *Nunnehi* had tried to carry the town house across the sky, they said, but part of it had fallen into the valley.[75] The mound remained a silent and perpetual reminder of the possible destruction of ceremonial centers and disappearance of native builders.

By locating his stores near removal stockades, Thomas took advantage of two aspects of the Cherokees' eviction. The government needed immediate supplies for the garrisoned troops, which he could provide. And Thomas needed roads, which the government ultimately would have to build in order to round up and evacuate the Cherokees. For merchants like Thomas, road construction promised expanding populations and increasing commerce. The rugged mountains and countless water-ways of western North Carolina had long proven formidable obstacles to road con-struction. In turn, the scarcity of roads had continued to limit white settlement.

As part of the government survey of the Cherokee Nation in North Carolina, Captain W. G. Williams reported to his superiors that the only state road in west-ern North Carolina ran west from Franklin to Athens, Tennessee. Williams's de-scription of the route so familiar to Cherokees and challenging to removal armies reveals how rugged the terrain appeared. The state road climbed up "the steep eastern side of the Nantahala ridge," he wrote, before descending nearly 3,000 feet to the Nantahala River. Leading away from the river, it crossed several creeks be-fore making another ascent to a pass in the Snowbird Mountains, a range so exten-sive Williams named it "the Long Ridge." Slicing through that narrow pass, the "great State Road" stumbled down "a very rugged and precipitous hillside" to the Valley River, whose broad plains provided welcome relief to travelers, farmers, merchants, and soldiers. Following Valley River eighteen miles, the state road then traced the Hiwassee and crossed three more creeks before finally surmounting a pass in the great Unaka Mountains.[76] The contours of the land illustrated why "a few white families only have been able to gain a footing in this country." Williams could claim that literally and figuratively "the Indians have resisted all inroads."[77]

In addition to the state road, Williams reported, "many trails cross the country in several directions," creating patterns on landscapes. They were the paths of least resistance made by game animals, roaming livestock, and Cherokees visiting neighboring settlements. Footpaths followed alongside every stream "whose banks were not too steep." In a few places, however, the banks rose straight up from the water and forced trail blazers to higher ground. A path beside the Nantahala climbed "along dangerous rocky precipices of tremendous height."[78] In the 1820s, a frightened missionary followed that trail "with trembling steps sometimes crawling on my hands and feet afraid to look to the right or left." When he lifted his head, he was "alarmed again and again by mountains above mountains rising to an astonishing height."[79] An entrepreneur like Thomas did well to locate his stores where the forces of the federal government could muster the manpower and money to build thoroughfares.

While removal armies surveyed and opened roads in the mountains surrounding Cherokees along the Nantahala, Cheoah, and Valley Rivers, white settlers and merchants were gradually recasting the lands east of the Nation's boundary. No matter what the reason—economics, politics, faith, or dispossession—the construction and extension of mountain roads signaled white settlement, expanding markets, and increasing interaction between whites and Cherokees.

As early as the 1830s, Thomas's efforts to develop roadways from Tennessee to the Carolinas included Cherokee women and men as laborers. Until that decade of astonishing change, a single wagon road led to Quallatown. It struggled north and west out of Waynesville across the Balsam Mountains and through Soco Gap, then followed Soco Creek to the Oconaluftee, where Thomas opened his store. Thomas wanted to connect the wagon road to a steep and rugged trail from Tennessee that crossed the Smokies at Indian Gap, then snaked down the mountain along the Oconaluftee south to Soco Creek. Narrow and rocky, steep and slippery, the trail was useful only to the hardiest.

Thomas turned his attention to converting the trail into a turnpike that would bring commerce and cash to Quallatown. As dozens of white and Cherokee men (and a few blacks) worked on the "Smoky Mountain Turnpike," Thomas and his associates recorded in a ledger "the names of the Squass that Done the Cooking." Scores of women earned twenty-five cents a day for feeding the road workers, who were paid the same amount. Salla and Nancy, Winna and Nakah, Jinnah and Cata, some of them wives and a few of them daughters or "girls," prepared hundreds of heads of cabbage and bushels of turnips and pumpkins Thomas purchased from white settlers. When Robert Collins became toll keeper of the turnpike, he paid nearly seventy "Squaws" for their help on the road "Heading towards Tennessee."[80]

From the 1830s until the Civil War, virtually every surviving store account contains the names of Cherokees who settled debts by "work on the road." Completed roads connected people and places, but even in the earliest stages of construction, they served as avenues of exchange. Cash, labor, goods, and ideas moved from one community to another as Cherokees and whites attempted to make and maintain roads. Day after day, year after year they moved rocks, cut trees, dug roots, filled holes, and forded streams with logs and planks. The task was not easy nor ever really completed. Their efforts continued throughout the nineteenth century, bringing people and customs together.

Settlers, farmers, merchants, and governments shared the goal of transforming footpaths to roadways. For nearly a decade after the 1820 auction of Cherokee lands, whites had spilled down trails on foot or horse, with wagons or no possessions at all, to make their mark, their fortune, or their way. When the flow of settlers slowed in the 1830s, the North Carolina General Assembly reduced the price of land to attract more purchasers. Eager immigrants enlarged trails to facilitate more settlement. In the 1820s a wagon road was forged from Quallatown southeast to Webster along the old Tuckasegee River trail.[81]

Merchants like Thomas relied on state roads, turnpikes, and wagon byways to access suppliers on the far side of the Smokies. And from the other side of that mountain wall, Tennessee stock drovers plunged through every kind of clearing to herd the thousands of hogs, cattle, horses, and fowl that rooted and trampled their way to Carolina markets in summer and fall months. With these few roads and multiple trails, western North Carolina became an increasingly active region of commerce and tourism that connected different races and cultures.

Inaccessible Mountains and Delightful Scenery

Although they required roads for Cherokee deportation, removal soldiers recognized that trailways might also provide routes of resistance. Anticipating a revolt that never occurred, the officers surveyed every trail and cabin in the North Carolina portion of the Cherokee Nation. Since the dense Carolina forests offered sanctuary where escapees might conceal themselves, military reports included comments on the complex environment. Captain Williams, for example, gave detailed accounts of the Cherokee landscapes. Most waterways, he wrote, wore "a skirting of laurel" that spread rapidly into "extensive thickets." Rising above the laurel, mountains were "clothed with woods to their summits." Forests remained "generally very open" because of the "fires which the Indians continually make" to clear underbrush. Williams knew the woodlands were the Cherokees' allies, for "many kinds of oak" along with "hickory, walnut, chestnut, and gums" produced mast that could and did nourish escapees during the summer and autumn of removal.[82]

While removal officers acknowledged the forests could jeopardize their task, other kinds of government agents saw Cherokee landscapes in more promising terms. The 1835 census taker reported that nearly 2,000 acres along the Cheoah River were "fit for cultivation." The waterways held even greater riches. "There is more gold in this creek than in any part of the Cherokee Nation," he exulted, surprised that the Cheoah had never been tested by whites. Valley River floodplains, which were two miles broad, included "10,000 acres of land of very superior quality," while the river "abounds with iron ore." Near Tomatla, indications of old mining operations fueled continual speculation that sixteenth-century Spanish invaders had found the gold they so desperately sought.[83]

South of the Valley River, even the most "poor and mountainous" land along the Hiwassee offered "valuable sites for machinery" and abounded in "excellent beds of iron ore of superior quality." It was that other mineral, however, that captivated everyone's interest. "Gold has been found in this river and all its tributary streams that have been examined," the census taker exclaimed. For the more aesthetic, the "mountain scenery" ranged from "delightful" to "very grand."[84] Cherokees along the Valley, Tomatley, and Hiwassee Rivers, and Shooting, Peach Tree, and Tusquitta Creeks—more than a thousand in all—might have read their collective doom in the margins of the 1835 census. Reports of their land and mineral assets surely inspired interest, hope, and greed among observant, hungry whites.

Beyond the Nation's boundaries, luxuriant woodlands comprised the landscapes' most distinguishing features. The highest mountain of the Smokies, wrote Thomas, "is covered with a dense forest of walnut, mulberry, hickory, poplar, dogwood, elm, ash, chestnut, sugar maple, white pine, spruce pine, fir, and cedar trees." Beneath the forest canopy "an undergrowth of laurel, ivy, and the sweet shrub" lay interlaced in a barricade that few could penetrate. The mountains, Thomas overstated, were "almost inaccessible to any persons except Indians and a few Whites who have become acquainted with the passes in the Mountain by hunting and attending to stock."[85] The mountains may have seemed intimidating, but they were never inaccessible to whites. The changes apparent in *Ko-hi*'s basket tell us as much.

For North Carolina Cherokees, the forced removal began June 8, 1838. After herding them into stockades, removal armies drove grieving exiles along the new roads leading to Tennessee and Georgia. After the removal, increasing numbers of settlers followed those roads into the old Cherokee homeland. Welcoming white settlement, the North Carolina legislature organized a county in the area and named it Cherokee. It was a cruel and ironic memorial to those so despised and so recently displaced.[86] The dimension of loss occasioned by the removal period is incomprehensible. Family and friends, customs and prayers, stories and songs, rituals and celebrations, patterns of life and ways of thought—even words and meanings and nuances—staggered across mountains and disappeared down trails before the bayonets and guns of the U.S. Army. Women and children proved particularly vulnerable during the tortuous process. Census rolls from 1840 toll the dirge of women's removal deaths. Caty's grandmother, *Culasteh's* sister, Jesse's grandmother and sister, Wilson's aunt, *Wilnota's* mother, *Inoque's* wife, George's mother and wife, *Cheah-cun-eskih's* wife and three children—a few recorded names and relationships represent unknown thousands who took to their graves generations of knowledge and wisdom.[87] Every town, settlement, clan, and family was bereaved as the strands binding them together and to the land were broken. The miracle is that some remained and endured, utilizing their wonderful familiarity with forests and streams around them, interweaving new skills and old customs, creating new worlds.

"It is but natural to suppose," theorized W. G. Williams, "that the love of home is a paramount sentiment with the Indian," a feeling the removal officer attributed to a "limited range of ideas" and "superstitious veneration" of ancestral burials.[88] Perhaps lacking such roots of his own, Williams could not understand that home was in the mountains that shielded families from removal troops and fields in which women tended crops as rhythmically as they bore children. Home was the forests providing food, medicine, shelter, and tools for their daily lives and concealing the bones of their mothers and fathers for eternity. It was the waterways where mythical animals held councils and priests conducted sacred rituals. Home was memory and hope. Home was where they lived. Home was theirs.

Years earlier, *Ghi-ghau* (Greatly Beloved Woman) Nancy Ward had informed the National Council convened at Amovey that the women she represented "thought it their duty as mothers to address their beloved chiefs and headmen." The women's message was plain. "Your mothers, your sisters ask and beg of you," she admonished, "not to part with any more of our lands." Words written on papers had already taken too much. If the men would "keep your hands off of paper talks," she reasoned, "it would be impossible to remove us all, for as soon as one child is raised we have others in our arms." Between 1840 and 1844, the women of Quallatown gave birth to 166 babies, increasing the population of the settlement by an aggregate of 113. "Listen to the talk of your sisters," Nancy Ward had commanded, "for it is our country." The Cherokees of western North Carolina intended to stay there.[89]

New Settlements and New Neighbors

Following removal, approximately 1,000 Cherokees remained in North Carolina. Fewer than one-third of them were citizen Indians who had never moved. The remainder included escapees from stockades, fugitives from all parts of the Nation who had hidden in mountain caves and forests, and a few who returned from earlier emigrations west. In addition, a hundred or so Nantahala Cherokees received federal consent to stay because their leaders assisted William Thomas and government officers in the capture and execution of a family who killed two removal soldiers.[90]

Several hundred refugees settled in Quallatown, more than doubling the population of the Oconaluftee valleys. Another 400 or so spread out along the Cheoah, Valley, and Hiwassee Rivers. A few went to old settlements like Cartoogechaye, Deep Creek, Alarka, Turtle Town, Tusquitta, Peach Town, and Acquona. In addition to the North Carolina Cherokees, several hundred more eluded removal in the adjacent states of Georgia, Alabama, and Tennessee.[91]

Wherever they lived, Cherokees shared a common history of dispossession, dislocation, and dismemberment. Their individual histories, however, varied considerably. They came from settlements in different parts of the Nation, from Tennessee, Alabama, Georgia, and, occasionally, from Arkansas and beyond. Even those from towns and villages in North Carolina had lived in diverse settings and conditions, as the agents of civilization so often noted. Reweaving broken strands was not simple. The story of North Carolina Cherokees after removal is as complex as *Ko-hi's* basket. It is a story of change and continuity, tradition and innovation woven together in a new world populated with different cultures. A common thread is their increasing interaction with whites, the dominant culture wherever Cherokees lived. And, in general, the behavior and attitudes of whites was characterized by increasing paternalism. Whites continued to focus on the "civilization" of Cherokees, and they intensified their focus throughout the century.

With the powers of attorney for many Cherokees, William Thomas subsidized their money with his own and began purchasing land for them along the Oconaluftee, Tuckasegee, Valley, Nantahala, and Cheoah Rivers. Some tracts, like those along the Valley, Nantahala, and Cheoah, lay on lands just ceded and scarcely vacated. Parcels along the Tuckasegee and Oconaluftee had been included in the cessions of 1817–19 but had long been occupied by citizen Cherokees and white settlers.

A hundred or so Cherokees returned to Cartoogechaye Creek, just six miles from Franklin and the sacred *Nikwasee* mound, resettling land that William Siler bought following the 1817–19 treaties. It is known that at least one Cartooge-chaye native had successfully avoided removal. *Oos-kel-lo-kih* (Hogbite) was in his nineties when the removal armies arrived and left without him. He carried in his memories the destruction of most of his family and Nation. As a young warrior he had joined the fight against Rutherford's Revolutionary armies in Waya Gap (*wa-hya*: wolf), the high and wooded passageway that led from Cartoogechaye west across the Nantahalas to the Nantahala River. When the battle ended, astonished soldiers discovered the dead body of a woman warrior. *Oos-kel-lo-kih*, her warrior son, survived their attack.[92] With dimming memories of valor and resistance, he remained at Cartoogechaye until he was more than a century old.

When Siler admitted the fugitives to their former homesite, they built cabins along Muskrat Brook where sandy soil gave rise to their identity as Sand Town (*No-hu-yi*: Sand Place) Indians. A swinging bridge across the creek connected the Sand Town community with the Silers.[93] The paths and customs of Cherokees and whites often intersected, and the exchange of goods and concepts became apparent in material ways.

In 1852, visiting essayist Alexis and his companions "took the liberty of entering all the houses we came to," dwellings that appeared from the outside to be very similar. "They live in log cabins," he wrote, "with no windows, and a door just large enough to enter." Cabin interiors, however, indicated differential prosperity and interwoven customs. *Yonah-cunna-heet* (Long Bear) and his wife *A-lee* kept "cups, sau-cers, plates, knives, forks, and other things" stored in a wall cupboard. A "brightly polished rifle" hung above the door, and the roof joists held a bow and arrows along with a cane blowgun and "well thistled arrows." Traditional weapons coex-isted with contemporary ceramics and furniture, and hunting continued to provide meat for food, fat for oil, and pelts for exchange. Brightly colored calicos could now be obtained from nearby trade stores in the growing settlements of Franklin and Ft. Montgomery.[94]

Alexis saw additional signs of tradition interlaced with change. Several Chero-kees, he wrote, "have imitated the whites" by building "a kitchen and smoke house" apart from their homes. Although kitchens and smokehouses may have been imi-tative, multiple structures had long been common on native homesteads. The out-buildings provided a sanctuary for Sand Town women, who took their children and quickly retreated there "whenever a stranger goes to call on them."[95] Domes-tic structures, in other words, remained part of women's domain. Whether build-ings were in the domain of women or men, however, whites like Alexis increas-ingly seemed to enter Cherokee households with impunity in order to satisfy their intellectual curiosity.

Subsistence practices also intertwined old and new. A garden patch "on which they grow corn, beans and potatoes" surrounded each dwelling. Nearby mountainsides provided forage for "a few hogs and cattle . . . kept by the rich." *Yonah-cunna-heet*, according to Siler family lore, was "a good farmer" who raised grain on a hillside above Muskrat Brook. The cornfield was known to everyone as the "*A-lee* field," however.[96] Long Bear may have been the farmer, but the field of corn was still identified with the woman, the mother, *A-lee*.

Alexis also described the town house, "where they dance, hold court, and preach." The building was polygonal and covered "with old boards and brush." Inside, benches around the sides faced "a fire built in the middle." Dancers wearing "terrapin-shells fastened below the knee" encircled the fire and sang in unison. The preaching likely belonged to *Yonah-cunna-heet*, who used an English testament and sang hymns in Cherokee.[97] Town houses and hymns, central fires and old boards, terrapin shells and English testaments were woven together, writing a complex story of new worlds.

About the time Alexis took his liberties in Sand Town, Chief *Chu-tah-so-tih* (James Woodpecker) purchased from the Silers 200 acres of land on both sides of the creek, which he later supplemented with land bought from other whites. His daughter, *A-lee*, acquired more than 100 adjacent acres. Every transaction recorded in deed books must have occurred alongside many more, for the Siler children grew up speaking Cherokee, and when *Chu-tah-so-tih* and his wife *Cun-sta-tee* died, the Silers buried them in the graveyard of the local Episcopal church.[98] Households of increasing interaction and overlapping belief systems were avenues of change, pathways where baskets of white oak and ribs easily joined those of cane and doubleweave.

Across the Nantahalas, Cherokees resettled the Cheoah valley along Buffalo, Snowbird, and Little Snowbird Creeks. Some, like Nancy Bullet and Tom Bear Paw, came from the Valley River, where Indians and whites were "living neighbors" before removal. Others like *Tel-tlua-gih* had lived at Judge Felix Axley's farm near Murphy. And still others, like Lowen and *Teyoet-lih* brought their families from Hanging Dog Creek, where removal surveys had noted "there are no white persons." Nearby Slick Rock had concealed many Cheoah men during removal while women courageously crossed the mountains into Tennessee to trade pelts and goods for food and clothes. The valley settlement of these diverse families became identified collectively as Buffalo, and later, as Cheoah.[99]

Whites who moved into the Cheoah valley traded labor and goods with Cherokee neighbors. From household to household, baskets were among the items commonly exchanged. One of the earliest white settlers of the valley received two

Rivercane doubleweave storage basket from Cheoah, dyed with walnut and bloodroot (ca. 1840). Private collection. Photograph by Ron Ruehl.

Rivercane doubleweave storage basket from Cheoah, dyed with walnut (ca. 1840). Following removal, whites who moved into settlements like Cheoah traded with their Cherokee neighbors for baskets. Private collection. Photograph by Ron Ruehl.

baskets from Cherokee women in the 1840s. The small rivercane storage baskets, doublewoven in twill and dyed with bloodroot and walnut, testify to the persistence of cane basketry as an expression of women's culture, a survivor of the most profound shock of Cherokee history. The baskets also demonstrate how rapidly women established exchange networks when removal armies had disappeared down their new roads.

Custom married change among weavers of baskets. Following removal, weavers continued to make some baskets for their own domestic use and others to sell or barter. The manufacture of baskets for ceremonial use disappeared. Of the three functions of baskets seen prior to the nineteenth century—utilitarian, trade, and ceremonial—only two remained visible after 1838, testifying eloquently to deep levels of cultural dislocation.

After removal, baskets became increasingly important to family economies. Near Knoxville in the winter of 1842, Drury Armstrong encountered along the Tennessee River "an encampment of Cherokee Indians, in number ten. Found them making cane baskets." The diarist leaves little information about the group, but it seems likely they were family members working together. Did they live nearby in an enclave that escaped removal? Or did they load up their wares from a North Carolina settlement and walk across the mountains on the trails to Tennessee? Little is certain other than the reason they were there. Armstrong remarks that they "had on hand and up for sale perhaps 100 baskets."[100] His diary entry marks the first documentation of collective basket production. In the hungry times after removal, basketry became a cottage industry that included men as well as women. And basket trade took place between households and settlements more than between weavers and traders. But, regardless of their widespread use as currency, baskets seldom appear in surviving store records or inventories.

About the same time Armstrong discovered the encampment of basketweavers, another east Tennessean, Sophia Moody Pack, purchased from a Cherokee neighbor a large rivercane doubleweave clothes hamper. The weaver's use of cane, doubleweave technique, and walnut dyes and the hamper's shape, form, and geometric patterns characterize traditional basketry. The container documents values that women continued to share through the removal period, and the transmission of certain kinds of knowledge across place and time. The basket ties weavers of the past to those of the present and future. The same pattern appears on three earlier baskets: a rivercane basket made in the previous century, the Springplace basket of the early 1800s, and a basket carried west during removal.

Although stores were not centers of basket exchange, they served multiple other purposes. William Thomas's Ft. Montgomery store and post office became a meeting ground for the three cultures of Cheoah valley. Account books from the 1850s reveal the kinds of interactions that gradually recast the societies of those who lived there. William Thomas and Samuel Sherrill's black slaves bought and sold merchandise on their owners' accounts. Whites like smithy William Adams, miller John Hyde, and Reverend R. Deaver were among more than one hundred whites purchasing everything from wool hats and tin plates to cows and coffee pots. In 1852, nearly 100 Cherokees also kept active accounts.[101] Men came to the store more often than women, and Cherokee women came more frequently than white or black women. All three races shopped in every season and for similar items. The transactions indicate a degree of trust, at least rudimentary common language, and comparable needs and interests.

Women who kept accounts apparently made clothing for their entire families. Over the course of a single year they purchased, usually on credit, hundreds of yards of shirting, stripes, checks, prints, and muslins. Some bought vesting, and others purchased velvet. Their sewing baskets held much from the store—a pair of scissors, a paper of needles, "thimbols," buttons, pins, ribbon, patterns, hooks and eyes, and spools and skeins of thread. Women like *Charlotta* and *Cut-clo-clena* purchased silk and cotton handkerchiefs several times a year, usually two at a time. In December, they took home dress shawls and hats, and *Charlotta* included marbles, a brass bucket, and a "looking glass."[102]

Blankets from the store in green, red, or "blew" warmed many Cheoah Cherokees in the winter of 1852. Sam Owl's wife *Woleyohah* purchased a brass candle stand to brighten their cabin. Some Cherokees may have lacked housewares, but over a period of four years, records indicate that women bought numerous kitchen utensils such as frying pans, skillets, salt cellars, tin cups, coffee pots, pitchers, "tea kittles," plates, knives and forks, and "boles."[103] Such accounts indicate a continuing decline of pottery making, once an important task of women. At the same time, the records suggest the persistence of conventional men's work—the cutting and carving and whittling of furniture. No one, white or Cherokee, purchased furniture of any kind. And no records indicate that anyone, white, black, or Cherokee, bought or sold baskets at the store.

The variety of tools that women and men purchased traces an outline of how they lived. Axes, saws, and knives of every sort and size transformed wood into cabins and whatever furnishings they contained, including beds and baskets. Spades, shovels, and hoes turned the earth for planting or extracting roots. Gun-locks, powder, flints, lead, and fishhooks confirm the continuing importance of game. Whites sometimes paid on their accounts with apples, but no Cherokees did. The almost complete absence of foods on store accounts indicates a successful subsistence based on farming, gardening, gathering, and trade—activities that encouraged basket production.[104]

Livestock played a small role in Cherokee commerce, for some owned cattle and paid on their accounts with cowhides or butter. *Charlotta* must have kept a horse, for once she bought a curry comb. Similarly, Old Grass purchased a saddle, a horse collar, and a sidesaddle for his wife.[105] Few others traded livestock or related items through the store. And although the store purchased enormous quantities of pork in amounts ranging from a few to a few thousand pounds, none came from Cherokees nor were purchased by them.

The store also served as a bank and clearinghouse where Cherokees and whites hired and paid each other with credit or cash. Through the trading post, Cherokee and white men alike found work ferrying goods across the mountains to other settlements or even to places as far as Tennessee. In the fall of 1852, Cockerham Farm "pad Chuny Luskey per halling," although by that year the hero of the Creek War was an old man, granted state citizenship after he walked back from the Cherokee Nation in the west. Joseph Wiggins received credit for "halling cross mountains" and David Henessa's account included "545 lbs. butter and sang halling cross the mountains to Athens."[106] The records reveal that negotiations, credit, and exchange went from Cherokees to whites and vice versa. *Tiyohih* paid George Deaver "for work" and was himself reimbursed "for driving hogs." William Thomas paid Cherokee Edward Welch one dollar a day for "3 days interpreting at Ft. Montgomery." Even the exchanges that render Cherokees anonymous—as when Samuel Sherrill or M. Le Brittain "paid Indians" or "the farm" paid "Indins for making road round the pon"—verify the kinds and amount of interaction between cultures.[107]

Another kind of connection between Cherokees and whites emerges in census data. The 1851 Buffalo Town census includes the name of Robert Love, a "mixed" grandson in the household of Nancy *Kata-tihi*. All other family members are recorded as Indian, with distinctive Cherokee names. What seemed rare in Buffalo was commonplace in other areas. Among the hundred or so Cherokees who lived along the Valley River, more than half descended from mixed marriages. Some, like Thomas's translator Edward Welch, descended from and married whites. At least three-quarters of the Cherokees living along the Hiwassee descended from a white parent or grandparent.[108]

Like their kin along the Valley and Hiwassee, those few Cherokees who returned to Alarka, Stecoa, and Tomatla found themselves in racial and cultural minorities. The century's events had completely reversed the ratio of Cherokees to whites. Nearly seventy-five years earlier, between Stecoa and Tomatla, William Bartram had taken his pleasure in the "sylvan scene of primitive innocence," the sight of Cherokee women gathering strawberries in baskets.[109] No such scene was ever recorded again.

Approximately fifty miles east of Cheoah, Thomas purchased several thousand acres of land around Quallatown, where hundreds of Cherokees dispersed into contiguous townships that were sufficiently autonomous to support their own councils, clerks, chiefs, and judges.[110] The townships were not isolated, however. Cherokees visited, played, danced, prayed, worked, healed, and traded from one settlement to another, and with neighboring whites.

Five townships bore names of hereditary clans. Two of them, Paint Town (*Ani-Wodi-hi*) and Wolf Town (*Ani-Wahya-hi*), lay in the Soco valley along Soco Creek and its tributaries. Eleven miles long and a half mile wide, the valley had attracted white settlers for decades. By the end of removal, the Sherrill, Jenkins, and Enloe families along with the Andersons, Welches, Gillespeys, Fullbrights, Hydes, and many others were longtime neighbors, and often landlords and employers, of nearly 500 Cherokees. A creekside mill, built on land that one James Janes sold to Thomas in 1840, provided occasional jobs and attracted business from three cultures. At least one Soco family, the Saunders, descended from a Cherokee mother and a black father.[111]

Soco Cherokees lived closest to the single road that led into Qualla and to the Thomas store. Regardless of the increasing presence and dominance of whites in the valley, however, Soco Cherokees maintained a distinct autonomy. Long Blanket and Yonaguska were among several Cherokees who purchased their own Soco tracts from Abraham and Asaph Enloe, thereby attaining an independence from Thomas and all whites that set them apart. Yonaguska was perhaps the only North Carolina Cherokee who owned a slave, Cudjo.[112]

Other kinds of autonomy survived elsewhere in the valley. *Ah-nee-cheh* and *Salo-la* (Squirrel) were blacksmiths who made and repaired tools for whites and Cherokees. Charley was a Methodist preacher, and Jefferson and Charley Hornbuckle were translators for Thomas and virtually every federal agent who negotiated with Cherokees. And somewhere along the tributaries of Soco Creek, two figures were growing into adulthood, learning about healing and magic, and spinning the world into existence as they told stories of its creation to those around them. *Ayasta* (Spoiler), barely an adolescent when the removal armies came and left, lived in Wolf Town. *Ayun-ini* (Swimmer), a young child during removal, lived in Paint Town.

Faith and education paved a crossroad where Cherokees and whites could share concepts and knowledge. In 1840, the Holston Methodist Conference appointed the Reverend Ulrich B. Keener as a circuit rider for the region. Until midcentury,

Keener preached to Cherokees and whites of every persuasion. Cherokees helped build a cabin for the Keener family adjacent to one of their own homesteads in Soco valley. The cabin served as the local schoolhouse, where Keener and his daughter taught about ninety Cherokees, both adults and children. Less than a decade after Keener's arrival, medicine man and Wolf Town clerk *Ino-li* (Blackfox) also received a Methodist license to preach. By 1858, the Echota Methodist Church claimed 172 Cherokee members from three different townships.[113]

Ino-li's integration of his own traditions with Christianity, like that of *Yonah-cunna-heet* and numerous others, represents merging customs. To Cherokees, Indian and Christian belief systems were both approaches to and expressions of the sacred. Cherokees could easily be Christians and also medicine men and women. Adopting aspects of white culture did not mean they were no longer Cherokee or needed to abandon all Cherokee customs. Their approach to faith was like *Ko-hi's* basket— an intermingling of Cherokee, white, and something entirely new—a collective and an individual expression.

At the western end of Qualla, Bird Town (*Tsiskwa-hi*) lay along the Oconaluftee to its junction with the Tuckasegee. One of the oldest settlements along the river, Bird Town was located closest to white communities developing along the Tuckasegee. Just five miles beyond Bird Town, whites established the town of Charleston on the site of the great Mother Town of *Kitu-hwa*, building trade stores, boarding houses, and farmsteads on the old Bear Springs. Like the Soco valley, the bottomlands of Bird Town attracted white and black settlers who lived and moved and married among Cherokees. An 1851 census records the name of fourteen-year-old *Na-kih* as the daughter of *Kul-lo-nos-kih* and "a negro man here with the Indians."[114] In keeping with the tradition of matrilineal descent, the child was recognized as Cherokee. The following year, Baptist preacher Richard Evans of Tennessee became pastor of the Bird Town church. He served for two years, preaching through a translator and converting 60 of the 100 Cherokee members. The Bird Town Baptist church paid Evans a slightly higher salary than the ten or fifteen dollars a year offered by his white pastorates at the towns of Lufty and Shoal Creek.[115]

Qualla Cherokees settled in at least two more townships with clan names, though neither maps nor census takers recorded their existence. Until midcentury, Thomas's records refer to Pretty Woman Town (*Ani-Gila-hi*) and Deer Town (*Ani-Ahwi-hi*). Each provided homes for about fifty families, somewhat fewer than did the other townships.[116]

In addition to the five towns identified with clans, two more settlements existed. Yellow Hill (*Ela Wo-di:* Painted Ground) developed on the Oconaluftee River at Arneechee Ford, and an older community called Raven (*Kho-lanun-yi*) remained on

Raven's Fork north of the Oconaluftee valley. Many Cherokees hid from removal troops in the densely wooded mountains above Raven, where they were protected and assisted by a white family named Lufty. Raven never appeared in census records, and Yellow Hill appeared only after the Civil War. Over time, Raven became known as Big Cove, and Yellow Hill, finally, as Cherokee.[117]

Whites settled in and around both communities. In 1839, Mt. Zion Baptist Church was built "a few hundred yards from the Arneechee ford" with the support of Dr. John Mingus, the Robert Collins family, the John Becks, and the Samuel Conners. The following year, Mt. Zion preachers baptized Cherokee Tom Conot and "received" his wife, Nelly.[118] Higher up in the mountains, Raven Cherokees encountered whites in quite a different way. Located closest to the Indian Gap trail to Tennessee, Raven became an entryway for restless whites looking for land and opportunities throughout the century.

The federal government had distributed much of these conquered lands to white soldiers and speculators. Joseph Dobson, a member of Moore's Revolutionary expedition, received one of the first land grants on the Oconaluftee, "including the forks of said creek." Felix Walker, son of another expeditionary soldier and William Thomas's early employer, received a grant of nearly 3,000 acres along the Oconaluftee and Raven's Fork. Andrew Welch obtained forty acres, including "an Indian camp," south of "Felix Walker's upper Big Survey." In the fall of 1812, John Fergus sold to John Mingus 200 acres on both sides of the river, "including a long bottom known by the name of the Big Cove." The largest tract by far was the Cathcart Survey, a 1795 grant of several thousand acres extending from the top of Big Cove south across Rattlesnake Mountain past Soco Creek to the Plott Balsams.[119] Thomas purchased land parcels from many such speculators and settlers.

Like the Ft. Montgomery records, Quallatown store accounts document interactions between Native, European, and African Americans as employers and laborers, debtors and creditors, suppliers and buyers. The records indicate the mobility of Cherokees who walked down hundreds of trails covering as many miles to work or purchase or sell. And they reveal the changing fortunes of those engaged in the expanding networks of commerce and culture.

Thomas generally kept separate records for Cherokee accounts, many of which have not survived. Immediately after removal, however, a Quallatown store clerk filled half a ledger book with the names of more than 200 Cherokee women and men who came from more than a dozen settlements to get some of the things they needed to begin new lives. They walked to the trading post from Cheoah and Nantahala, from Valley River and Peach Town, Tusquitta and Acquona, Deep Creek and Turtle Town, and even "The Nation." The ledger recorded their purchases and payments for nearly a year.[120]

Cherokees' circumstances differed from place to place and person to person. Some lived on land owned by whites or even on white farmsteads, perhaps as laborers. For example, *Amacutta* lived at Cockerham Farm, Jinny at the Tekins's, *Chootlew* and *Nalowah* at the Hayes's place, and *Cunnatiska* at the Andrews's. Others apparently lived independently and relatively well, paying for purchases with cash and, occasionally, with gold.[121] They used additional kinds of currency on a seasonal basis. Beginning in the late summer and continuing through November, Cherokees brought in ginseng, receiving credit of about eight cents a pound for the medicinal. The same season, bear skins brought fifty cents and deer pelts even less. Those who lived on established farms paid with corn or potatoes, which were both valued at fifty cents a bushel for buyers as well as sellers.[122]

Clothing was an immediate and continuing need for them all, and women and men bought many hundreds of yards of cloth, from shirting and stripes to "flannell," checks, and gingham. Purchases of madder, copperas, and indigo suggested that dye pots for clothes stood alongside those for adding color to basket splits. The volume of fabric and the scissors, needles, dyes, thread, and buttons purchased in 1840 represent untold hours of labor for women who made the dresses, coats, pants, vests, aprons, shawls, suits, and shirts for themselves and their families or even for trade.

The Quallatown store also sold new and used clothes, and customers took home old pants, vests, and coats in addition to new hunting shirts, socks, and shoes. Nearly every purchase included combs, differentiated as fine or wooden or side, or the most common, tuck combs. Numerous women and men purchased beads at one dollar a bunch or by the strand for slightly less. As in Cheoah, cotton and silk handkerchiefs were common purchases.[123] But the extent to which the handkerchiefs, cloth, or clothing were for personal use or for paying local medicine women and men can only be imagined.[124]

The importance of agriculture and hunting can be gleaned from records of tool purchases. Cherokees bought axes and tomahawks to cut trees and saplings, mattocks to break hard ground and grub stumps, and plows and hoes to plant fields and gardens. During summer months, they brought hoes and axes to the store for sharpening, or axes and plows to have the steel set. Virtually every customer bought, repaired, or improved farm tools in 1840. No one purchased guns, but almost everyone got something related to them—gunlocks, flints, small shot, and, recorded over and over in every account, powder and lead. Fishhooks went by the dozen. The success of the hunt for meat and fish that year can be found in the quantities of salt purchased by the quart, gallon, and bushel.

As in Cheoah, the trading post became a place where labor was registered as payment on accounts to the extent that stores served as banks keeping record of virtually every kind of business transaction. Prosperous settlers hired Cherokees to cut boards and make fence rails by the thousands, permanently altering landscapes and forest composition. In the early 1840s, the Sherrill Farm, Enloe Farm, Thomas's Stecoa farm, and the Quallatown Store gave store credit to at least a dozen men for making from 100 to 300 rails each. One notation stated simply that Bird Town Indians "made 4,800 boards instead of 5,000." It was with good reason that agent Thomas decided in 1850 to post a sign prohibiting anyone from "entering the Indian boundary for the purpose of cutting saw logs."[125] Whites and Cherokees who lived there were already cutting extensively.

Changing seasons brought certain jobs that were dutifully registered on store accounts. Corn shucking and fodder pulling took place in winter months on every farm. Summer was the time for roadwork, or for plowing, hoeing, or grubbing fields. Even whites who owned slaves hired Cherokees to harvest fall crops and to cut wood all year.[126] Men worked on and in saw- and gristmills, Thomas's shoe shop and tanyard, and private homes. They repaired fences, drove oxen, daubed houses, hauled rocks, and salted cattle. Every month of every decade until the Civil War, Cherokees from all the townships entered systems of debits and credits with neighbors and merchants, changing the shape and face and heart of their communities, and changing themselves.

Another source of change came into the valleys immediately after removal. In 1840, South Carolina Catawbas sold the last of their lands and began moving to the Qualla townships by twos and threes, then by the score. By 1848, virtually the entire population of one hundred Catawbas lived among the Cherokees.[127] Some intermarried, and all influenced Qualla life. Nancy George, Old Polla, Salla, Mary Redhead, Susan Kegg, Salla Harris, and Rosa Ayers were among the numerous Catawba women who left their names in store records, along with their special knowledge in traditions of pottery and basketry. One of the great Catawba potters, Sallie, married an Owl (*Wa-huhu*) and remained in Qualla the rest of her life. Polly married a Sanders and doublewove her dual heritage in rivercane baskets.[128]

By 1850, Qualla supported several stores. From his trading post, Samuel P. Sherrill kept separate accounts for whites, slaves, Cherokees, and his ginseng trade. J. W. Bird, B. H. Cathey, and W. A. Enloe ran general stores. Four years later, four more businesses were operating in the community: N. Blackburn's, Dickey and Tabor, Fisher and Bryson, and Parks and Co.[129] The expanding market engaged

Rivercane basket with lid, undyed. Purchased from Polly Sanders in 1908, this basket has a carefully cut hole in the base that suggests a medicinal or ceremonial function. [l: 24.2 cm, w: 12.7 cm, h: 14 cm]. Courtesy of the National Museum of the American Indian, Smithsonian Institution, no. 1/9149. Photograph by Pamela Dewey.

whites, blacks, Cherokees, and Catawbas in networks of buying, bartering, selling, and trading. They were four distinctive societies, four splits, woven together to hold a new world in place.

"Many Frauds and Faithless Agents": Census Takers and Cherokee Resistance

Ten years after removal, Congress authorized a census of all Cherokees who had been living in North Carolina when the Treaty of New Echota was ratified in 1836. The purpose was to distribute the funds originally designated for their removal. At the same time, the federal government still hoped to persuade them to emigrate. Persistent pressure on North Carolina Cherokees to relinquish their land greatly enhanced the authority of men like Thomas, who continued to serve as their agent until the end of the Civil War. In that first decade after removal, he was not the only agent, though he may well have been the best.

Indian Office clerk John C. Mullay left the Washington Indian Office in September of 1848 to canvass the mountains and enroll Cherokees. He worked in the town houses of each settlement to gather the names of those who had eluded the army's wide nets. As Mullay wrote out the census lists, "frequently until a late hour at night," Cherokees gathered, "amusing themselves at a short distance from my work-table in the mazes and circles of their wild and grotesque dances." It was fall (*U-la-ga-ba-sti*), a season that encompassed Nut Month (*Du-lu-sti-nee*), Harvest Month (*Duna Na-dee*), and Big Trading Month (*Nu-da-na E-gwa*). Two decades earlier, autumn summoned hundreds of clan members to town houses for community rituals directed by hereditary priests, but Mullay saw no such sacred drama. Surrounded by Cherokees "almost wholly ignorant of our language," the agent wrote out their names as they danced and sang in diminishing celebrations of harvest.[130]

Cherokees living along Valley River refused to identify themselves, expecting armies to return soon after. Writing to the secretary of war, they explained that their caution grew out of "the many frauds which have heretofore been practiced upon us by faithless agents."[131] It was a profound expression of distrust and the lasting legacy of removal.

Mullay's was not the first federal census of Cherokees and certainly not the last. By the time of removal, however, federal enrollment carried a deadly undertow. The persons accepted by agents as Cherokees received federal money, and those disputed as Cherokees did not. A nearly obsessive preoccupation with the biological fiction called "race" had infected Indian policy since the civilization program. Federal agents asked and recorded the quantum of "Cherokee blood" of each person, setting up a tension that has persisted for more than a century. A more divisive and destructive policy for Native Americans can hardly be imagined.

"Household Employments and a Knowledge of Agriculture": Reports of Cherokee Industry

The enrolling agent reported favorably on the Cherokees. Although their circling dances seemed wild to him, their subsistence patterns made perfect sense. Men appeared to be responsible for farming, and women for household matters. So much about the Cherokee world had changed in the removal period. Repeated land cessions and the relocation of families eroded town and clan structures. Populations were drastically reduced, and townships were small. The land base was restricted, and its ownership was often uncertain. As families of origin moved apart, women no longer held clan fields in common and no longer assumed responsibility for clan production of agriculture.

Mullay wrote the Indian Office that North Carolina Cherokees were "advancing encouragingly in the acquirement of a knowledge of agriculture as well as . . . in spinning, weaving, etc." It remained to New England journalist Charles Lanman to elaborate on their advancement. Following his 1848 visit to Qualla, where Thomas proved a gracious host, Lanman wrote that "the men labor in the fields, and their wives are devoted entirely to household employments."[132] Thomas later claimed he provided farming tools and livestock to the men and "supplied the females with cards, wheels, and looms" so they could make their own clothing. Such products, he stated flatly, "laid the foundation of the subsequent improvements which those Indians have made."[133]

Although the amount of fabric purchased through his stores belies Thomas's claim that women relied on his cards, wheels, and looms for clothing, the appearance of livestock in Cherokee landscapes is undeniable. By 1850, Qualla Cherokees owned more than 1,000 stock animals, nearly half of which were hogs. Ten years later, the number of hogs, horses, and cows increased while the total number of animals declined. Cherokees owned about one-quarter as many sheep in 1860 as they had ten years earlier.[134] By then, the civilization of women could no longer be marked by their attachment to spinning wheels and weaving looms.

The uneven distribution of livestock among Qualla Cherokees gives credence to the comments of essayist Alexis, who claimed that among Sand Town Cherokees, "the rich" owned animals. In 1850, translator Jefferson Hornbuckle kept three horses, two cows, one ox, ten sheep, and six hogs. *Nicea*, whose name is listed next on the census and who owned the same size farm, had no livestock at all. Ten years later, Wolf Town clerk *Ino-li* kept two horses, five cows, four oxen, and twenty hogs, while his neighbor *Aroneach* (or *Ah-nee-cheh*) owned four hogs and no other livestock. In 1860, almost all the Qualla Cherokees kept "swine," and a few owned as many as forty.[135] Differential prosperity, animal husbandry, and men in agricultural fields all signaled diversifying systems among Cherokees.

"A Tidy Wife and Several Children": Transformations in Households

Subsistence roles changed along with residence patterns. Matrilocal residence no longer bound Cherokees to one another in an orderly pattern. Once an intrinsic part of matrilineal inheritance and clan agriculture, matrilocal residence diminished in importance after removal. Wives and husbands established their own households apart from the woman's family of origin. By midcentury, visitors to Cherokee settlements found households that appeared similar to those of whites and blacks, with a husband, a "tidy wife, and several children." Mothers, sisters, and married daughters usually lived in separate homes.[136] Even households that included mothers did not resemble the matrilocal residences that once characterized Cherokee society.

As clan members dispersed and couples moved into nuclear households, polygyny also disappeared. Although *Walliz*, Little *Suaga*, and Yonaguska each had two wives, postremoval census rolls generally do not indicate the presence of multiple wives. In 1843, Cherokees "passed an ordinance prohibiting polygamy," according to a friend of Thomas's, "and have required those having a plurality of wives to confine themselves to one."[137] The ordinance may have been intended to impress policy makers, but Cherokees seldom abandoned what functioned well for them. When wives shared land ownership and farm responsibilities with marriage partners rather than clan relatives, polygyny became ineffective. Moreover, since it was a lightning rod for whites eager for complete removal, its public renunciation seemed wise.

Traditions of matrilineal land inheritance also declined. During the years that William Thomas purchased property for Cherokees and retained the titles in his own name, matrilineal inheritance effectively ceased. Varying and intricate property arrangements followed the treaties of 1817–19, removal, and Thomas's land purchases. Removal had dismembered families, clans, and residential groups. In such contexts, the transformation of landholding and inheritance patterns occurred easily. Like their white and black neighbors, North Carolina Cherokees increasingly lived in nuclear households on small farms passed down from fathers, as well as mothers, to their children.

In 1859, Cherokees met in Wolf Town to record new regulations for marriage and landholding. Council clerk *Ino-li* noted that couples were to obtain marriage certificates, select preachers and clerks for the ceremonies, and inscribe "in the thick book that they are married." Marriage records would henceforth also identify residences "so that both cohabitants will know that they and their children will live upon their own property."[138] By connecting land to marriage and registering them both in township records, Cherokees acknowledged husbands and wives as joint owners of property, which their children inherited from them.

Change of another sort appeared in the new marriage regulations. "This rule," wrote *Ino-li*, "is for the marrying of the Cherokees" and not for blacks. "If one of the couple is black," the ordinance stated, "they are not to be married." How or why was marriage with blacks a problem? The mandate adds the explanation that "it would be improper to have to separate them." But who would "have to" separate them? No comment was recorded about existing mixed marriages or offspring from them. Perhaps encouraged by Thomas and others enmeshed in politics beyond the Qualla boundaries, perhaps evolving racism of their own, or perhaps documenting existing bias, Cherokees officially prohibited marriage with blacks. The law also placed emphasis on one gender. It stated flatly that "a black man is not to be given a paper."[139] The regulation thus specifically restricted the longstanding sexual freedom of Cherokee women.

Regardless of changes in social systems, the vitality of the matrilineage persisted in some ways. Clan identity continued to govern marriage choices, and memories of the severe punishment for intraclan marriage remained vivid among the transmitters of myths and customs. As late as the end of the century, John Ax (*Itagunahi*) recalled that "marriage into the same gens [clan] was punishable by death."[140] Children continued to identify themselves as members of their mother's lineage and to learn their exact relationship to others in the same lineage.

In their own households, women retained domestic authority in ways expressed in stories passed from one generation to the next. Elders told of the wonderful work of *Kanane-ski Amai-yehi* and *Selu*. They talked about the Sun—the source of light and heat—a female who visited her daughter each day. They related stories of mothers who instructed their daughters about acceptable mates and drove away lazy suitors. Children heard of animals trying desperately to find wives and of angry wives humiliating their husbands, leaving them, or expelling them from their homes.[141] Common and familiar stories portrayed women as powerful and authoritative, especially in households.

In some families, sisters and brothers continued training children in the intricacies of clan ritual, dances, lore, and medicine. *Ayasta* and her brother began early to instruct and prepare her son, Will West Long, to become one of the great modern medicine men.[142] Widespread knowledge of the Sequoyan syllabary helped such healers record and retain formulas across many generations, reinforcing traditions developed in the matrilineage. At the same time, use of Christian hymnals and testaments published in Sequoyan before removal encouraged the spread of Christianity. Clan customs and Christianity, medico-magical procedures and literacy interlaced in the Cherokees' new world.

"Pilgrim Dances and Trifling Wages": Entertaining White Visitors

At midcentury, every aspect of life that recalled the past simultaneously acknowledged the present. In each settlement, a circular or polygonal town house built of logs served as the center for council meetings and social gatherings. Cane benches, however, no longer lined the walls to provide seating, and cane mats woven by townswomen no longer hung in the town house, lay on the benches, or ceremonially covered the grounds. In 1848, the town house on Soco Creek contained "but one short bench intended for the great men of the nation."[143]

On occasions when the fire blazed in the center, Cherokees danced around it for reasons that were not accessible to whites. "The dances were of the common Indian sort," Lanman wrote, except for one he thought "particularly fantastic . . . called the Pilgrim Dance." The Northeastern visitor believed the dance represented "their hospitality toward all strangers who visited them from distant lands," and ironically, he was correct. The False Face or Booger Dance among all Native Americans signaled their hostility toward invaders.[144]

Towns continued to compete in ball games, and rival conjurors vied for victory as earnestly as the athletes. The night before a game, seven women still danced ceremonially, and players went to water before and after the contest for ritual purification. Under the influence of Thomas, however, the games at Qualla took some interesting turns. "They are not allowed to wager their property on the games, as of old," recorded Lanman, "unless it be some trifle in the way of a woollen belt or cotton handkerchief." Only Thomas could have portrayed himself as having authority to "allow" Cherokees to wager or not, either "trifles" or goods of unknown significance. Whatever the circumstances of the prohibition, its effect was to make a favorable impression on the visiting journalist. Lanman was "greatly pleased" with the women's behavior as they placed their bets with "bashfulness and yet complete confidence."[145]

Lanman attended a ball game on Soco Creek that "was gotten up especially for my edification." The use of the traditional and significant game to entertain or educate whites was entirely new. Missionaries had long abhorred virtually every aspect of ball games and considered attendance at them sufficient grounds for church expulsion. Resentful whites cited the games as examples of practices that were "disgusting to civilized Society and calculated to corrupt our youth." Lanman, however, represented a different attitude, an intellectual curiosity about "the manly game" he thoroughly enjoyed. Another innovation attended the edifying games. Thomas paid the ballplayers for their participation.[146]

"A Suffering and Bleeding Country": The Civil War on Cherokee Lands

The Civil War brought a new wave of misery to the Cherokees. Hundreds of men enrolled under Thomas to serve in a home guard, and western North Carolina became the site of skirmishes and raids that depleted the countryside of natural and cultivated resources. Farm, store, tanyard, mill, and odd jobs vanished, and few could purchase the blackberries and chestnuts, peaches and corn, deerskins and ginseng Cherokees customarily bartered even from those fortunate enough to acquire them.

Battles were fought in Charleston adjacent to Bird Town, on Deep Creek where many Cherokees lived before and after removal, and in Murphy at the junction of the Valley and Hiwassee Rivers. Skirmishes and raids crossed the gap at Soco and pocked the long valley. Disease rolled through encampments, and Cherokee soldiers died of mumps and measles as often as battle wounds. "Today I am not well," one soldier wrote home to *Ino-li*, "but I am alive." Many of his comrades were not so fortunate. Five died shortly after they encamped at Strawberry Plains, and others were "very sick." Sickness also afflicted those at home, for *Tse-ghisini* wrote to ask "how those quite a few sick at home are getting along."[147]

When crops failed in 1863, the counties of western North Carolina were reduced to a "suffering and bleeding country." Even "the best of our citizens," wrote Margaret Love of Quallatown to Governor Vance, "are not able to get provisions." Clergymen cautioned their mourning congregations that they could offer no help. In the spring of 1864, Cherokee women and children were living "on weeds and the bark of trees." To feed their children, Love wrote, many women "have gone to the South in search of bread."[148] Those who remained at home planted their crops with hoes made of gun barrels.[149]

The war ended for Thomas and the Cherokees in May 1865, and survivors who returned to Qualla brought smallpox with them. More than a hundred Cherokees died, fifteen in a single month from Wolf Town. Those who wished to leave Jackson County to "trade . . . some baskets . . . for clothing, old dresses, and goods" with whites in Haywood County had to carry a pass from F. B. Sherrill certifying that they "have not had the small pox and have kept away from where it was."[150]

Thomas went bankrupt and insane and spent most of the remainder of his life in an institution. Anguished that Cherokees could no longer rely on his guidance, he wrote in telling confusion that they were like "bees without a king." Intermittently lucid, he occasionally emerged from the hospital to testify in court cases brought to resolve Cherokee land issues. He died in May 1893 at the age of eighty-eight. By then, Cherokees had centralized their government, incorporated as the Eastern Band of Cherokee Indians, and gained title to their tribal lands.[151]

"Noble Forests": Cherokee Landscapes

As the troubling nineteenth century neared its end, Cherokee landscapes once again attracted the attention of New England missionaries, botanists, and naturalists. The ruggedness of the Southern Appalachians protected a variety of flora and fauna that finally proved irresistible to collectors and explorers. In May of 1885, Harvard zoologist William Brewster came to the mountains on a pursuit of rare birds and left a journal that offers glimpses of environments near Qualla.

Riding by carriage from Asheville, Brewster described the countryside as "rolling and varied," with "ridges, either wooded or under cultivation, sloping steeply down to narrow valleys." He looked across deep vales between the Cowees and Balsams where oak and chestnut trees dominated the forests "with a few scrubby hard pines." Land under the canopy seemed "rather fertile, the soil clay of a deep blood-red color." The pastures and fields that crisscrossed the valleys marked crop rotation by white settlers. From time to time and place to place, he saw "occasional fields of clover in full bloom."[152] The zoologist delighted in his Appalachian surroundings. Untouched by the lumbering industry yet to come, trees of "gigantic proportions" marked the trail between the towns of Franklin and Highlands. Ascending the steep slopes of the Cowees, he rode through "noble forests of oak, chestnut, black walnut, and tulip trees." Dense understories of rhododendron banked the rivers, but ground beneath the deciduous forests was clear, having been burnt annually by whites "to improve the cattle ranges which extend over all these mountains."[153]

Nearby stood Whiteside Mountain, *Sa-nikila-ki*, the eastern terminus of the great rock bridge made by the dreadful Spearfinger. As Brewster's carriage lurched toward Whiteside, he passed through "a superb rhododendron swamp" with plants arching above him to "a height of twenty-five feet." Above the rhododendron towered "a forest of superb hemlocks" seventy to eighty feet tall. The climax stand covered thousands of acres around Whiteside Mountain.[154] "The scenery was simply superb" to Brewster. On the landscape cast by fired woods and ranging stock, "many of the oaks and tulip trees exceeded five feet in diameter," and the ground under them lay "perfectly open."[155] About ten miles away stood the town of Sylva, where Sally Ann Saddle Catolster traded baskets for food from whites. The town of Whittier, where Josiah Axe found a basket instead of a wife, lay about ten miles to the northwest.

William Brewster represents the probing and presumptuous spirit of inquiry that brought so many restless souls into Cherokee settlements. Leaving his laboratory and classroom in New England, he came to the Southern Appalachians to collect birds. In less than one week, as he recorded meticulously, he shot dozens of different species, including birds who were courting, pairing, mating, incubating, feeding young, or about to lay. Between Asheville and Black Mountain he "shot . . . a pair with eight young. I killed all but two of the entire number but failed to find them."[156] In order to assemble collections to study and exhibit in a distant world, such men participated in the colonization or destruction of countless indigenous populations. Unmindful of parallels between his pursuit of birds and earlier hunts for game, Brewster noted the scarcity of animals in the area. "That of mammals," he wrote with disappointment, "we saw nothing besides the two Squirrels[,] but I found the track of a large buck . . . and my guide pointed out the footprint of a small bear." Where deer, bear, panthers, wildcat, wolves, and foxes once abounded, "half-wild mountain cattle" bolted awkwardly away, their tinkling bells startling smaller game into hiding.[157]

Over the decades of successive crises that marked the nineteenth century, much had changed in Cherokee landscapes. For those who wanted to make baskets of cane, gathering the material took several days and covered many miles. No cane could be found around Qualla at all, so women had to walk to South Carolina to collect the stalks and carry them home to prepare. Whites continued to settle every valley, and fertile lands that could no longer be left fallow became impoverished. An 1882 visitor asserted that the entire Soco valley was "worn out by bad farming." Far up in the mountains above the Oconaluftee, a white man claiming Cherokee ancestry trapped the only remaining colony of bald eagles and penned them up to sell. Since the buyer never appeared, the eagles died in their chicken-wire cages. In the final decade of the century, someone recorded shooting the last passenger pigeon in North Carolina.[158]

Coming to Qualla

When Rebecca Harding Davis left her Philadelphia home to spend the summer of 1874 at an Asheville resort, she followed a friend's admonition to "see Qualla—see Qualla!" Getting there was no simple task. The road from Asheville to Qualla was "little traveled and scarcely practicable—a slippery cartway cut halfway up the precipice, and never repaired since it was built." Guided from the town of Webster by the "shrewd, intelligent man" who had begun the road, Davis and her party passed through landscapes of lost opportunities and futile hopes. A deserted mica mine, an abandoned sawmill, and vacant cabins "fallen to the ground" left evidence that whites "had failed in gaining here" whatever it was they sought.[159] In every hamlet and household beyond Asheville, Davis confirmed her notion that the in-habitants of the Southern Appalachians—white, black, and Cherokee—were poor and ignorant.

The visitors entered Qualla on mules through a "succession of ravines . . . and high wooded hills." The land was "well watered, the soil rich and black with veg-etable mould," indicating that an abundance of vegetation remained on the hill-sides. Like Alexis before them, Davis and her party looked for Cherokee house-holds, but could hardly find them. It appeared that cabins and even cornfields were "back in the densest thickets, avoiding sunny, wholesome exposures." Secluded cabins prompted more than one white visitor to think "the Indians have no towns"; but the truth was, settlements fit the contours of the land, and unseen trails connected every household.[160]

"The first hut we entered," Davis wrote, "was a fair type of the majority of them." *Oo-tla-no-teh* and his wife, *Lan-zi*, lived on Soco Creek in a dirt-floored, one-room cabin with no windows and a single door. Sitting around an iron pot at the fireplace where *Lan-zi* heated corn and beans, the couple ate with wooden spoons carved from rhododendron or hickory or tulip. Furnishings were limited to "a stool" and "a bedstead with some straw," although Davis saw in the corner a blowgun with a thistled dart, which was used to bring down squirrels and birds from surrounding trees. Lack of education, Davis believed, created poverty and isolation: "Shut out from the world of knowledge and action," *Lan-zi* was "left to live like an animal."[161]

Davis confirmed her connection between prosperity and education as she entered other households where she found Cherokees literate in the Sequoyan syllabary whose "small degree of education told in clean floors and neat flannel dresses." Shelves on their walls held "half a dozen cups and saucers of white stoneware, kept for show in beautiful glistening condition." Educated Cherokees owned trunks packed with "dress-suits of cloth and bright woolen stuffs," including "a high hat for the men and hoop-skirts for the women." *Ino-li*, "an intelligent old man of sixty," made the best impression. His Wolf Town cabin was filled with furniture, a carpet covered the floor, and shelves held books in Cherokee and English. Outside, the beegums and livestock on his property indicated his diverse interests, skills, and industry. The only thing "his people" wanted "of the white men," wrote Davis, was schools.[162]

In fields behind the cabins on Soco, Davis "found the men always at work busily hoeing their corn." At long last, Cherokee men had become farmers. Chief Sowenosgeh (*Sawanu-gi*: Flying Squirrel) was "hard at work digging, as were his two sons." His wife, who was a "daughter of the great Yonaguska," also attended to a field of corn "with a majestic air of command."[163] In a studied observation of one family at work, Davis captured a moment that had grown out of a century of reform. Women and men shared responsibilities for agriculture, just as they did for basketry. And still, in either field, women might justifiably carry "an air of command."

During her visit, Davis and her friends were guided by Wilowisteh, "a bright-faced lad of nineteen" who served as "a medium of communication between his people and the whites."[164] He too, according to Davis, yearned for education and suggested that a few tribal members go north for training so they could "bring their people up to be like whites." An inspired Davis returned home to publish several articles about the Cherokees and to raise the question soon taken up by reformers all across the nation. "What can be done for them?" she asked. What can be done for the Indians? While reformers like Davis considered what could be done for them, Native Americans found themselves in a position to assist other interested whites. Davis's bright-faced guide, Will West Long, continued to translate for countless visitors who came to see Qualla and the Cherokees. And he brought one of them, anthropologist James Mooney, to meet his mother, *Ayasta*, and to learn a few things from her.

"Coarse Baskets to Trade"

By the 1880s, when Bessie Long's mother was periodically walking to Shoal Creek, Sylva, and Waynesville to trade baskets, Cherokees obtained "the necessaries of life by making baskets of reeds and wooden splits." During her visit to Qualla, Rebecca Davis stayed with a white family who often exchanged goods with Cherokees. Several Cherokees "came down the mountain," she reported, "with coarse baskets to trade for a bit of pork." Coarse baskets meant work baskets, containers necessary to every household, made and traded by women and men. In those same years, Susan Ned of Big Cove (b. ca. 1858) made white oak rib baskets, bundled them up in a sheet, and took them "to white people's houses to trade for what she needed, like meat." Language was no barrier to the communication of trade. Susan Ned "couldn't even speak English."[165]

Basketry connected women and men, white and Cherokee, prosperous and impoverished. So many reports of basket trade come from the literate, well-born, and articulate that other kinds of buyers may be forgotten too readily. Many whites who lived near Cherokees were neither wealthy nor educated. But every neighbor was a potential resource for whites, blacks, and Cherokees alike; what one family might have outgrown or overplanted, another could readily use. When Davis and her companions took refuge from a sudden storm near Qualla, they found themselves in the dogtrot cabin of a poor white family. On the exterior, the "log walls gaped open," and the interior was papered over with newspapers and magazines. Yarn, peppers, herbs, and "Indian baskets filled with the family clothing" hung from the ceiling. Polly Leduc lived in the cabin with her husband and baby, so isolated that she commented, "it's two months since I've seen the face of woman, white or red."[166] Yet, the baskets hanging from the ceiling testify to the presence of networks that connected Cherokees and their neighbors.

"The Indian Day is Nearly Spent"

By the 1880s, other visitors who were interested in coarse baskets began to call on the Cherokees. Anthropologists and ethnologists made their way to the reservation

Rivercane sifter (ca. 1881) [l: 28 cm, w: 28 cm, h: 15.5 cm]. The faded red and brown hues may have come from aniline dyes. Catalog No. E063063, Department of Anthropology, Smithsonian Institution.

to collect artifacts and, gradually, traditions and memories. A sense of urgency pervaded their work, for nearly all believed the "Indian day is nearly spent."[167] In the face of continuing annihilation of Native American cultures, ethnologists undertook to survey, map, and document the remaining tribes of America.[168]

In 1881, Dr. Edward Palmer, a physician and collector of botanical specimens, visited Qualla and purchased the Smithsonian's first assemblage of Southeastern Cherokee baskets from the Council House at Yellow Hill. He obtained seven containers that are representative of those used in households at the end of the century and point to some of the ways women, and men, were weaving new worlds. Cane and white oak, dyed and plain, twilled and plaited, with cloth and carved handles, for sieves and storage, the baskets combine the oldest traditions with the more recent innovations in material, form, and function.

The old cane sieve Palmer bought was the most common container in Cherokee homes of the nineteenth century. Similarly, the two berry baskets made of cane and dyed with walnut and bloodroot are indicative of the continuing importance of gathered foods in the Cherokee diet. "The larger," according to the museum catalog, "will hold about a half bushel, the smaller about a gallon." The newness of

Rivercane berry-gathering basket, dyed with bloodroot (ca. 1881) [l: 24.2 cm, w: 24.2 cm, h: 19 cm]. The old fabric strap handle indicates that carved handles had not yet become universal among Cherokee weavers. Catalog No. 063076, Department of Anthropology, Smithsonian Institution.

one gathering basket underscores the age of the second, which even has a downy feather still stuck in the splits to reveal that eggs were gathered as often as berries. The "general storage" container has the narrow neck and rim that characterized Cherokee food storage baskets. It is so well worn that it could have come from the peg of a porch any place on the reservation.[169]

The three remaining baskets of white oak are equally representative. One is a worn fishing basket with the customary constricted neck to confine fish and open-weave base to drain out water. Fishing baskets were so common that most Cherokee porches wore "a fringe of the queer upright baskets of splits, like a narrow jar, in which they carry fish."[170] Palmer also bought a seed storage basket, tightly woven with thick splits to protect seeds between harvest and the next planting season. His final purchase was a small, rectangular handle "basket for general use," whose

Rivercane berry basket, dyed with walnut (ca. 1881) [l: 17.8 cm, w: 17.8 cm, h: 11.4 cm].
Catalog No. E063075, Department of Anthroplogy, Smithsonian Institution.

pokeberry dye has almost faded away entirely. Women increasingly used such containers for personal belongings; in the twentieth century, they became known as purse baskets.

Palmer's collection allows us to glimpse the minds and memories of weavers in a single moment toward the end of the nineteenth century. The cane baskets are all rimmed with cane and bound with hickory, a characteristic that was considered a hallmark of Cherokee weaving. Two have fabric handles knotted through the sides, like those made before removal. By the beginning of the twentieth century, fabric handles were obsolete and carved white oak handles gripped baskets of every size and shape. At least one container is a hybrid, like *Ko-hi's* basket. Its function—to store seeds—was traditional, as is the twill weave. But the material is white oak.

The Palmer collection documents a subsistence still based on farming, gardening, and gathering. It records the coexistence and interweaving of white, black, and Cherokee basketry traditions. It testifies to the continuing role of exchange. And it reveals a new market—the world of antiquarians and ethnologists, who perfectly inverted the century of reform by expressing greater interest in custom than change.

Rivercane storage basket with fabric strap handle, dyed with walnut (ca. 1881)
[l: 15.2 cm, w: 15.2 cm, h: 20.3 cm]. Catalog No. E063074,
Department of Anthropology, Smithsonian Institution.

White oak fish basket, undyed (ca. 1881) [l: 12.7 cm, w: 12.7 cm, h: 26.7 cm].
Fish baskets were commonplace among Cherokees, who caught native trout
from the numerous streams in their settlements. Catalog No. E63072,
Department of Anthropology, Smithsonian Institution.

White oak basket for storing seeds, undyed
(ca. 1881) [l: 15.2 cm, w: 15.2 cm,
h: 20.3 cm]. Cherokee weavers continued
to use their customary twill weave even
on white oak baskets. Catalog No. 063073,
Department of Anthropology,
Smithsonian Institution.

White oak basket for general use (ca. 1881) [l: 12.7 cm, w: 20.3 cm, h: 10.2 cm].
The carved handle that originally was on this basket has broken off.
Catalog No. 063077, Department of Anthropology, Smithsonian Institution.

Six years after Palmer's visit, James Mooney went to the reservation as the Smith-sonian's first field-trained ethnologist and began his long, fruitful study of Chero-kee myths, history, and medical formulas.[171] Soon thereafter, he heard from John Ax and Swimmer the narrative of the origin of fire, the story of the power of weavers to provide for their people.

Anthropologists were fascinated by old customs and tended to see innovations as dilutions of strength and corruptions of purity. By the time Mooney began field-work, reservation trade stores carried a product that revolutionized basketry and unmistakably divided old traditions from new. The product was aniline dye, an ac-cidental creation of English chemist William Perkins (1838–1907). Attempting to make quinine from aniline in 1864, Perkins produced purple dye instead. A number of companies began to package dried aniline, which could produce a range of bright colors in a matter of minutes. In 1886, Joe Singleton exchanged his labor for a package of Diamond Dye at Joseph Cathey's store, the first sale of commercial dye in Qualla trade store records.[172] Basketweavers soon expanded their color reper-toire to include bright purple, blue, gold, pink, green, and orange.

When Mooney bought three baskets in 1888, his commitment to custom col-ored his attitude toward the innovative work of weavers. He described a white oak pack basket as "a poor specimen, the work not having been honestly done." Its red dye, he explained, "is obtained from aniline."[173] He considered an unusual red and green rib basket "an imitation of civilized patterns" that "tho quite pretty repre-sents no Indian idea." And yet, the pedestal base, attached lid, and application of dye represented distinctly Cherokee innovations in rib basketry. The single lid at-tached on the side is unique. Rather than representing "no Indian idea," the con-tainer is like *Ko-hi's* basket—Cherokee and white, conventional and innovative, a collective and an individual expression. It is a piece of woven history that illumi-nates a rapidly changing world, a text of creativity and assertiveness.

In 1887 and 1900, Mooney bought examples of the oldest of basketry tradi-tions: two rivercane doubleweave storage baskets, "yellow and brown with Indian dyes."[174] Although he does not identify the weaver, the ethnologist recorded in his comprehensive history that *Wadi-yahi*, who died in a grippe epidemic in 1897, was "the last old woman who preserved the art of making double-walled baskets."[175] Perhaps she wove the containers Mooney purchased, but she was neither the last nor the only maker of doubleweave baskets. Mooney's was the first of repeated re-ports of the demise of doubleweave basketry among Cherokees.

Although he was mistaken about the disappearance of the doubleweave tech-nique, Mooney was right about another traditional form. From his 1889 field sea-son he acquired one white oak pack basket (*iti*), made to order. "This basket was

White oak rib basket with attached lid and rib pedestal, dyed with red and green aniline (ca. 1888) [l: 14 cm, w: 7.6 cm, h: 16.5 cm up to lid]. Rib baskety inspired a florescence of colors and styles among Cherokee weavers. Catalog No. 130476, Department of Anthropology, Smithsonian Institution.

Rivercane doubleweave storage basket, dyed with bloodroot (ca. 1887)
[l: 14 cm, w: 14 cm, h: 14 cm]. As some weavers innovated with new forms and materials,
others continued to make the difficult and time-consuming rivercane doubleweaves.
Catalog No. 133023, Department of Anthropology, Smithsonian Institution.

formerly used by the women," he recorded, "for carrying corn, chestnuts, etc." He noted that "only two or three badly damaged specimens" could be found among the Eastern Band.[176] The disappearance of the pack basket from the experience and finally from the collective memory of Cherokees signals the end of a way of life based on the matrilineage.

The loss of a form that was once essential signifies different lifeways; and the complete incorporation of a new material documents transformations in concepts, values, and needs, in knowledge, experience, and environments. An 1890 census

White oak pack basket, three bushel capacity, dyed with walnut and bloodroot (ca. 1889). Catalog No. 135178, Department of Anthropology, Smithsonian Institution.

taker reported that "baskets are also made from oak splints and the cane for household and farm uses." In the half century after removal, weavers had fully adopted white oak basketry and commonly made white oak containers for domestic tasks and trade. White oak basketry, shared by men and women, expressed change among Cherokees; rivercane basketry documented persistence, the resilience of women's culture and values. Weaving—the common ground between the two materials—continued to be the conceptual province of women. Two Big Cove women, eighty-year-old *Olt-kinne*, and her neighbor, seventy-year-old *I-bun-li*, identified themselves as basketweavers to the 1890 census taker.[177] No men identified themselves as such. They may have made the baskets, but the trade and the identity still belonged to the women.

Those who came to see "the remnant of the once powerful tribe of Cherokees," as nostalgic reformers called them, might have found that news of their arrival preceded them and that expectations of trade met them at the door. "Basket-making is a universal art," claimed journalist Virginia Young after her Qualla trip in 1892, and well she might have thought so. When she arrived at the home of Chief Nimrod Jarrett Smith (*Tsa-ladi-hi*: Jarrett), women carrying "babies at their backs, in regular papoose fashion," appeared immediately and at least one among them came to trade. A "very aged woman, named Catalsta," Young wrote, "carried a large net fastened around her head in which were a quantity of baskets."[178]

"Everything Changes"

In the final decades of the century, little cash circulated among Cherokees, and they continued to live primarily by farming. To plow the steep hillsides that characterized farmsites, Cherokees who could afford them relied on steers, whose short legs accommodated the mountainous terrain. "The women and children work out in the fields the same as men," and the work of the farm was the responsibility of the entire family, according to a federal agent.[179] Corn remained central to subsistence, and in 1890, farmers cultivated fourteen times more corn than any other crop. They raised virtually no surplus. Those who worked as laborers for whites took their pay in "meat or clothing, or some other commodity." As the century ended the "wealth of the band" was an average of $217.25 per capita.[180]

Visitors commented on the "quantities of wild fruits" that supplemented the Cherokee diet. In addition to "strawberry, blackberry, and grapes" on summer vines, women gathered "chestnuts, butternut, [and] black walnut." They carried corn as well as baskets and herbs "in sacks thrown over their shoulders" into neighboring towns, looking out for trade opportunities. Men might accompany them, but they never carried the corn.[181]

"The Cherokees earn as much and live as well as the white people about them," according to the 1890 census taker. And the number of whites about them was considerable. Surprised by the presence of so many whites on the reservation, federal agents often remarked that they controlled a disproportionately larger amount of

Medicine man and storyteller Swimmer (*Ayun-ini*) stands behind a woman pounding corn in a wooden mortar. A large, dyed rivercane storage basket sits on the cabin roof, and a fish basket hangs from the eaves (ca. 1888). National Anthropological Archives, Smithsonian Institution.

arable land. In 1890, fifty-six white families were "unlawfully upon the tract, occupying and farming 6,000 acres, most of it good land." Cherokees farmed less than half as much land on their own reservation. The census officer reported that 1,520 Cherokees tilled only 2,400 acres.[182]

In these last decades, the state of North Carolina prohibited marriage between Indians and whites and refused to recognize Cherokee marriages. Racism, however, was not limited to whites. Some said "the Indians have a great aversion to any intimate intercourse with the negro race."[183] In contrast to the increasing numbers of whites, few blacks remained among Cherokees, and fascination with blood purity separated all whose ancestry was mixed.

Near the old Cheoah settlements, the county of Graham was organized in 1872 and whites established the hamlet of Robbinsville. Fewer than 200 Cherokees

Women and children dammed the creeks and scattered crushed buckeyes on the water to stun the fish. Wading into the water, they scooped up fish in baskets (ca. 1888). National Anthropological Archives, Smithsonian Institution.

remained scattered along Cheoah tributaries, trading at the King and Cooper store that had replaced Thomas's Ft. Montgomery trading post. Some became Christians and organized the Buffalo Baptist Church, where Young Wolf became pastor.[184] Whites outnumbered Cheoah Cherokees by many hundreds. About the same time, Swain County was carved out of Jackson and Macon Counties, where Qualla lay, and the community of Charleston adjacent to Bird Town became the county seat. The new rail line reached Charleston in 1884, and soon thereafter the town was renamed Bryson City. The county population of whites doubled after the arrival of the railroad.[185]

Cherokees continued to speak their own language, which surprised many whites and offended a few. "One of the most curious facts about this particular people," wrote jurist David Schenck in 1882, "is that they will not learn the English language." Refusal to speak English was perhaps the least subtle resistance to psycho-

Women crossing the river in a dugout canoe with a man poling. Courtesy of the National Museum of the American Indian, Smithsonian Intitution, no. 26838.

logical encroachment. They also continued to build town or council houses, hold dances, and play ball games. They elected councils and chiefs. They planted seven grains of corn in each depression in the soil and sang the *Selu* hymn to insure that new corn rose up to the sun.[186] Women pounded corn into flour with the heavy mortar and pestle that stood beside each of their cabins and made parched corn-meal for journeys. They dried greens and herbs and roots in baskets placed on cabin roofs. They hiked up their long, full skirts to wade into dammed streams to catch stunned fish in big winnowing baskets. Conjurors assisted with medical problems, droughts, prophecy, and love, and elders recounted creation stories that grew briefer each generation. On Sundays, women and men attended Christian churches where conjurors often presided.

As Posey and Bessie Long remarked quietly from their home on Long Branch, "everything changes." In the final decades of the century, the federal government turned once again to bring civilization to the Cherokees. The new federal policy combined education and industrial training, aiming for land allotment and assimilation. At the same time, investors from Northeastern states, having depleted their own woodlands, developed technology to tame the mountains of western North Carolina and embarked on a frenzy of forest destruction that lasted nearly a half century. Roads and railroads finally came to Quallatown and Graham County, and wage work for men rode in on them. As the century of successive crises ended, North Carolina Cherokees were going down a number of different roads, most of them leading away from home.

CHAPTER 3

Honeysuckle

❖ ❖ ❖

Webs of Dawn

A weaver's sister told this story: When they were very young, her sister (*e-do*) wanted to learn how to make baskets. It was their grandmother (*o-gili-si*) who told her what to do. To be a good weaver, the grandmother said, a woman must go outside early in the morning and find certain kinds of spiderwebs, those woven by spiders in the darkness before dawn breaks, the webs that glisten with morning dew. When the woman finds the strong and shimmering webs, the grandmother continued, she must rub them on her hands. Then she would be able to make beautiful, durable baskets. As the weaver's sister told the story thirty years later, she wondered if perhaps their grandmother's advice is what made her sister one of the best honeysuckle basketweavers among contemporary Cherokees.[1]

Honeysuckle baskets differ profoundly from those of rivercane and white oak in material, form, and function. In contrast to the rivercane and white oak that once surrounded Cherokee settlements, honeysuckle came from the other side of the world. It made no contribution to medicine, food, housing, utensils, or dyes. It was not used in ceremonies nor alluded to in myth or story. Honeysuckle is not indicative of fertile soil or deciduous forests; it represents changing landscapes and disrupted ecosystems.

With the incorporation of vine basketry, the ancient, sometimes sacred, and always functional basket became an artful item made for someone other than the weaver. From the start, the light and delicate honeysuckle baskets were made for one purpose—to be sold. Whereas rivercane and white oak made ceremonial, gathering, harvesting, processing, storing, and serving vessels, honeysuckle baskets were primarily decorative containers. No heavy burdens were associated with them, nor were subsistence tasks in fields or forests or gardens or homes. The vines became baskets for household interiors, for artificial flowers, pens and pencils, small

Honeysuckle sewing basket with lid, dyed with walnut, made by Nancy Conseen (1991) [d: 22 cm, h: 13.5 cm]. Private collection. Photograph by William F. Hull.

sewing items, soiled clothes, and paper refuse. They were containers for people who spent more time inside than out, who wanted to beautify their homes. Honeysuckle baskets were made for a market more focused on ornamentation than survival.

"A Pernicious and Dangerous Weed"

There are more than 400 species of honeysuckle in North America, and at least one of them was very familiar to Cherokees and European visitors in the eighteenth and early nineteenth centuries. In 1775, as he slowly rode from Keowee toward the Middle Towns, William Bartram was fascinated by the "delightful landscape" around him. On "the grassy bases of the rising hills" he spotted "the remains of the towns of the ancients," easily identified by the "tumuli, terraces, posts or pillars" that marked deserted Cherokee buildings and homes. Growing in wild abandon, "old Peach and Plumb orchards" silently testified to the Cherokees' absorption of European customs and to their transformation of the land.[2]

Ascending the "more lofty ridges of hills" rising toward the Oconee Mountains, Bartram relished the Carolina spring. "Odiferous groves" of sweet shrub banked the rivers. Dense blossoms hung from rhododendron, stewartia, azalea, silverbells, and dogwood. Vegetation everywhere was "decorated with the sweet roving climbers," yellow jessamine, trumpet creeper, and *Lonicera sempivirens*, or, honeysuckle.[3]

Bartram's "sweet roving climber" is known commonly as trumpet honeysuckle, an indigenous evergreen vine with red and yellow trumpet-shaped flowers that bloom from April to August. Cherokees call it *gvna lun-gi* or *gvna giski* (turkey beard) for the blossom's resemblance to the red beard of the wild turkey. Widely distributed in the North and Southeast as well as parts of the Southwest, trumpet honeysuckle was one of thousands of floral and faunal specimens sent to England by William Bartram's father, English botanist John Bartram. European scientists considered the vine uncommonly beautiful.[4]

Discoveries of new species excited naturalists on both sides of the Atlantic. Initiating a botanical revolution, they loaded ships with everything from ants and eggs to nests and mosses. Crossing paths on the seas by day and night, ships carried an immense variety of trees, vines, shrubs, and flowers from one continent and island to another. European naturalists, botanists, gardeners, and farmers were eager to try new varieties from America, just as American settlers clamored for European samples. Some of the introduced specimens integrated successfully into native flora and fauna. Some did not survive. And a few, like Japanese honeysuckle, initially appeared to be beneficial but ultimately had an irreversible, devastating impact on native vegetation.

The introduction of Japanese plants to American landscapes followed the 1854 opening of diplomacy and trade between the two nations. In March of 1862, George Rogers Hall, resident of Rhode Island, graduate of Harvard Medical School, and successful agent in the Asian trade, offered his collection of Japanese botanical specimens to the Parsons Nursery of Flushing, New York. The nursery owners rejoiced in their good fortune. In the eight years since Japan had reopened its ports to Western trade, botanists had discovered surprising similarities between plants of Japan and eastern North America. From his research laboratory at Harvard, Asa Gray theorized a common origin for the flora separated by half a world.[5]

A common origin for Japanese and American flora meant that each might prosper on the other's soil. With a near certainty of successful propagation and growing enthusiasm for Asian plants, the nursery staff eagerly accepted Hall's offer. Shortly thereafter, six glass cases arrived in the Long Island office. Nurserymen gently extracted from them live specimens of star magnolia, umbrella pine, Japanese maple, wisteria, several kinds of cypresses, and the vine that became known as Japanese honeysuckle, initially called Hall's honeysuckle in honor of the donor.[6]

Following its introduction to American landscapes, Japanese honeysuckle escaped the gardens it had been brought to beautify and spread rapidly across the Northeastern states, down through the Piedmont and over the Coastal Plain. By the 1890s, it appeared throughout the Carolinas and West Virginia, reaching Florida and Texas in the early 1900s. Briefly touted as forage for cattle and a remedy for erosion, Japanese honeysuckle trailed and climbed its way into every part of North Carolina, spreading over trees and bushes to overwhelm indigenous vegetation and reshape ecosystems. It grew along fences and roadways, at woodland edges and in thickets, up trees, across limbs, and over native plants. By the twentieth century, American botanists classified the honeysuckle as a "most pernicious and dangerous weed," encouraged only by "those who do not value the rapidly destroyed indigenous vegetation." With vines that grow as much as thirty feet in one year, Japanese honeysuckle requires little other than an opportunity.[7] Given that, it is nearly impossible to eliminate.

Cut Out and Get Out: Logging the Southern Appalachians

Honeysuckle's invasion coincided with intensive exploitation of Southeastern forests by the timber industry and massive disruption of local landscapes. The great stands of Northeastern forests were depleted by the last quarter of the nineteenth century, and Northern timber interests turned southward for new resources. From New Jersey, Ohio, Maine, Michigan, Pennsylvania, Maryland, New York, and even Europe, men came in search of virgin woods. They sought vast forests in proximity to water and rail lines for the fastest possible extraction of timber. In the Southern Appalachians they found abundant forests and waterways and built their own railroad lines to expand into remote areas.

In 1888, C. F. Buffum and L. C. Cummings of Portland, Maine, acquired the timber rights to 150 miles of the Tuckasegee valley and established the Blue Ridge Lumber Company. In the next two decades, W. E. Heyser from Michigan, W. M. Ritter and the Champion Fibre Company of Ohio, Taylor and Crate of New York, Bemis Hardware of Massachusetts, and the Scottish Carolina Timber and Land Company of Glasgow purchased the rights to hundreds of thousands of acres of Appalachian forests along the Little Tennessee, Cheoah, and Pigeon Rivers.[8] Some operators, like G. V. Litchfield, constructed mills and contracted with local suppliers for lumber. Others, like W. B. Townsend, bought enormous tracts of woodlands, put up logging camps and mill towns for workers, and constructed rail lines to carry timber to the growing number of mills.[9]

In addition to Northern industry, local and regional entrepreneurs established their own lumber companies, mills, and manufacturing plants. The Kitchen Lumber Company of Kentucky built a steamboat of native balsam and white oak to carry logs up the Little Tennessee to the Southern Railroad line at the new lumber town of Fontana. Whiting Lumbering and Manufacturing began grading roads around Cheoah to connect to tram lines. New industries emerged based on timber by-products such as pulp, paper, cardboard, and tannin, which were produced in one plant by burning fifty carloads of wood, six of chemicals, and hundreds of tons of coal every day.[10] The Southern Appalachians provided utility poles and cross ties for national industrialization, boxes and bags for merchandisers, paper for magazines and books, and furniture and flooring for the expanding housing industry.

In the early days of Southern Appalachian logging, men harvested selectively with crosscut saws and concentrated on stands of black walnut, ash, cherry, poplar, and oak. Independent operators snaked logs downhill behind ox or mule teams. On particularly steep slopes, teams dragged trees to the tops of ridges where loggers "ballhooted" them downhill—peeled and rounded the ends, hooked them together, and shoved them over the slope. "Wood hicks," as the lumbermen called themselves, quickly cleared vegetation to create wide lanes for ballhooting, or they built log slides that ran down slopes for as far as two miles. When rain was plentiful and water was high, timber branded with company logos floated swiftly downstream to mill sites, guided and prodded by lumber-herders who leaped from log to log breaking up jams. To speed the water passage, they blasted rocks and boulders out of mountain rivers and streams with dynamite. Some companies constructed enormous splash dams to impound water and then periodically opened the gates to release torrents that rushed logs as far as twenty miles down river. Where water levels were low, companies built wooden flumes down the middle of streams, with side flumes capturing creek water to funnel into the flow.[11]

By the end of the nineteenth century, the Tennessee side of the Smokies was stripped of cherry and walnut, except for scattered stands that could be found only "by going far back in the mountains."[12] In the early twentieth century, mechanical logging with overhead skidders became widespread and forests were stripped cove by cove. The objective of the timber companies was to cut out and get out. Mills, roads, bridges, tramways, camps, and villages were built to last only until timber was removed. Abandoned, they fell quickly to ruin on barren land.

If heavy rains or melting snow elevated water to flood levels, thousands of logs might be hurled downstream and over banks, smashing and crushing everything in their paths. As water subsided, oxen dragged stray logs back to the rivers. Deep gullies made by ballhooting and log snaking channeled the barren slopes. Cleared of rocks, waterways expanded and banks eroded. On high summits, trees stripped of their bark for tannin mills invited disease as they slowly decayed. Abandoned brush contributed to raging forest fires, and soil cleared of surface vegetation leached and dried out, eliminating surface nutrients and subsurface water storage. Without natural vegetation to absorb and contain water, dry and wet seasons as well as natural and human-set fires caused far greater damage.[13] A century later, the scars of the destruction remain. The impact on faunal life was devastating.

In 1887, the Cherokee Council agreed to sell D. L. Boyd the timber rights to 30,000 acres of the Cathcart Survey at Qualla, a tract crossing most of Wolf Town and part of Big Cove.[14] The price was fifty cents an acre. Three years later, the council began negotiations for the sale of the 33,000 acres called the Love Speculation, which extended north from Big Cove to the Tennessee line. When the contract was signed in 1906, the West Virginia purchasers agreed to construct a rail line from the Love tract to the nearest railroad spur. Tracks were laid along the Oconaluftee and Tuckasegee, and trains ultimately ran from Bird Town and Yellow Hill to Big Cove. A flume was built from the head of Soco Creek to the Oconaluftee as far as Ela, just beyond Bird Town. By 1904, at least four sawmills, all owned by whites, operated on the reservation.[15]

Raven's and Straight Forks, the upper tributaries of the Oconaluftee, were logged until the 1930s. While the timber industry flourished, lumbermen, bosses, oxen, logging camps, sawmills, mill towns, commissaries, tram roads, and lumber trains became part of rapidly changing Cherokee landscapes. Men found day work as loggers or rail layers, and women as cooks and washwomen at the Ravensford, Smokemont, and Fontana mills. A limited cash economy developed alongside the bartering that had characterized the nineteenth century.

As woodlands lured industry to the Southern Appalachians, companies dammed rivers to construct power plants for mills, businesses, schools, and towns. The French Broad, Pigeon, New, and Broad Rivers were dammed by 1910. In the same period, the Tallassee Power Company, a subsidiary of the Aluminum Company of America, built the Cheoah and Santeetlah dams to provide power for Tennessee.[16] Like lumber towns, dam villages consisting of tents, barracks, or cabins sprang up on riverbanks. The dams, villages, and roads also provided occasional jobs for Cherokee women and men, expanding their economies and markets while permanently transforming the land and waterways.

Such was the environment that proved so hospitable to Japanese honeysuckle, the alien, opportunistic vine that prospers on massively disrupted landscapes. While industry recast Southern Appalachian earth, water, air, and vegetation, the lifeways and worldviews of all who lived there changed as well and encouraged the development of a new basketry tradition. Honeysuckle basketry grew out of and expressed changes in social and economic systems as well as in ecology. Like the vines themselves, the custom of making light and fanciful containers came from worlds that lay well beyond settlements of western North Carolina. The custom, and those worlds, drew closer with each new road, dam, or village, with every white tourist, educator, and reformer, with government programs, buildings, or policies, and with each opportunity for work in an economy that was chronically depressed. Honeysuckle baskets signify change.

Lucy Nola and the New Material

As the nineteenth century gave way to the twentieth, marketing became increasingly important. While many weavers continued to rely on cane and white oak basketry, some experimented with honeysuckle vines in hope of finding new markets. Perhaps the most successful innovator was Lucy Nola. Born November 17, 1897, in Bird Town, Lucy Nola did not learn basketweaving from her mother, Rebecca Taylor, or from her father, George Squirrel. As she said later, "I realized there were no teachers available and that I would have to learn on my own."[17]

Lucy George was an adult when she learned to make baskets from Japanese honeysuckle. The vines grew long and straight on a bank behind her Bird Town home. From time to time, according to the late Rebecca Grant, friends came through Bird Town to gather the vines for weaving baskets. Appreciative of the free source of material, they finally showed Lucy George how to prepare and weave honeysuckle.[18] No one remembers who those friends were or how they might have learned vine basketry. What remains evident is that neither family nor clan taught George how to weave. Her own memory was that she had to learn by herself.[19]

Just as the inclusion of Japanese honeysuckle for basketry marks important changes in concepts, markets, and ecosystems, the absence of basketry instruction in Lucy Nola's household documents a decline in traditional systems of learning. At one time, clan relationships and family ties might have assured training in weaving, carving, dancing, beading, pottery making, storytelling, or medicinal work. Young women might have assumed they would learn basketry from clan mothers or sisters. By the twentieth century, changing family structures, education, roles, and responsibilities transformed earlier conventions of learning. Neighbors, friends, and, finally, schools became alternative sources for instruction.

Whether she taught herself or learned from grateful friends, during the barren years of the depression, when logging declined and nothing replaced it, Lucy

Lucy Nola George weaving a honeysuckle basket. Still Picture Branch,
National Archives.

George became a weaver of honeysuckle baskets. Her decision was based solely on economics. "It was necessary that I find a way to supplement my family's income," she later said. George knew that many women provided for their children, and often their husbands, "by weaving baskets to sell or trade at the general store." [20] Basketry was a way to acquire food and clothing. It was a means of survival. And making baskets did not interfere with other responsibilities that shaped the days of women. Weavers could prepare material and make baskets in their homes, day or night, winter or summer, in any weather, surrounded by children or working in solitude. With few jobs available for men, the task of providing for families often fell to women. "If it hadn't been for my baskets," remarked one contemporary weaver, "I don't know what we would have done."[21] She could be speaking for them all.

Knowing that most weavers used cane or white oak, Lucy George decided to specialize in honeysuckle. "I knew of only one woman who used the honeysuckle vines as a basketweaving material," she later commented. "I felt that my chances of helping provide for my family's needs would be better if I worked with this material."[22] She did not learn to make baskets for ceremonies, or for use in her home, garden, or field; she wove containers she could barter with or sell. Rather than selecting a material steeped in tradition, like rivercane, or one grounded in utility, like white oak, George chose the material that gave her the best chance of making a living in a depressed economy and uncertain market. The new material lay close and abundantly at hand. Some even said it was simpler and faster to weave.

Cooking Vines and Building Baskets

Honeysuckle grows fastest in its first season, as much as fifteen to thirty feet over the summer months. The youngest vines are easily recognized by their soft, narrow, leafy stems extending along the ground searching for light. As the vine grows, its nearly purple tip, which is covered with leaves, gradually becomes brown and smooth. Vines stop growing during the winter but retain their leaves except in the coldest periods. Leafing again in early spring, they begin photosynthesis as much as two months before competing vegetation does. They hold berries through the winter, and birds that prefer brushy areas—bluebirds, robins, juncos, and bobwhites—eat and disperse their seeds into other open areas. Japanese honeysuckle adapts well to shrubby clearings where vines can twine around saplings and grow quickly to their tops, absorbing and blocking all light.[23]

In the second spring, new vines branch from old tips and the original vines grow tough and dark. Extending along the ground, each vine sinks clusters of roots into moist soil. Nodules develop where roots cluster, creating nodes that weavers must trim as they prepare material for baskets. Subsurface roots can spread laterally, reproducing additional vines. Even when vines are cut or burned, their roots resprout rapidly.[24]

Although honeysuckle weavers can gather their materials any time of year, they prefer fall and winter mornings, when the chill reduces the danger from snakes. They look for vines that grow long and unimpeded along the surface of the ground, rejecting those that are "all curled up and twist around, and they won't straighten up."[25] They choose material that is about two years old and is strong but not yet "brickly." Pulling up extended vines, weavers wind them into continuous coils six to eight feet long. From three or four coils, they can make two medium-sized baskets.[26] The width of the vines does not matter, although most weavers prefer the appearance of baskets made with vines that are relatively uniform.

Soon after the material is collected, it must be prepared so that it will not dry out and become brittle. "The beginning is cleaning the vines," one weaver says as she describes the process of "cooking" the coils in a pot in her yard. Cooking time varies from three to six hours, enough to loosen the thin brown bark and its slick inner sheath. Then the weaver "skins the vines" with her fingers. "It's best to skin them when they're warm," she advises, in order to slip all the bark off.[27] The goal is to begin a basket with vines that are smooth, shiny, and white. Some weavers will even bleach and dry them in the sun.

For most honeysuckle weavers, the next step is to prepare white oak splits for the foundations. There is a practical explanation: white oak foundations add strength and weight to honeysuckle baskets. The combination of materials is unusual, however. With honeysuckle basketry, the weavers of the Eastern Band created a distinctive tradition that included a familiar one. Like strands in the fabric of society, custom and innovation intertwined. Dyes for honeysuckle baskets also represent tradition and change. Weavers choose from the same color repertoire and vegetable sources as did their grandmothers—bloodroot for orange-reds and walnut for dark brown or black. But aniline dyes also proved popular with honeysuckle weavers, and honeysuckle baskets from the early decades of the twentieth century often show signs of bright pink, blue, green, red, purple, and gold dyes.

When they incorporated honeysuckle in their basketry traditions, weavers began to make containers for entirely different functions, such as dresser trays, vases, pencil holders, wastebaskets, and Easter baskets. Yet, old forms lay embedded in the new shapes. Sifters and strainers became trays for crackers or bread. Fish baskets were reduced and reproduced as vases or pencil holders. Wastebaskets derived from the *i-ti* so closely associated with women of the preceding centuries and gathering baskets in diminishing sizes became small containers for children's Easter eggs. Old and new, convention and innovation, past and present were interwoven even in containers made of Asian vines. Women continued to express a distinctive Cherokee identity in basketry.

There are few possible antecedents for the honeysuckle baskets of the twentieth century. They somewhat resemble the Springplace Mission vine baskets of the early 1800s attributed to Peggy Scott. Like the mission baskets, honeysuckle containers are light and delicate, made more for ornamentation than for labor, and they represent trade rather than service. Moreover, like the mission baskets, they indicate changing worlds—new markets, contacts, and influences from beyond the boundaries of Cherokee settlements. The vine baskets from Springplace, however,

Honeysuckle vase (ca. 1930s) [h: 34.3 cm]. Courtesy of The Museum of Appalachia, Norris, Tennessee. Photograph by Roddy Moore.

Honeysuckle vase, dyed with walnut, made by Emily Smith (1990) [d: 22 cm, h: 23 cm].
Private collection. Photograph by William F. Hull.

Honeysuckle button basket with lid made by Lucy Nola George.
Qualla Arts and Crafts Cooperative. Photograph by Ron Ruehl.

remained unique among preremoval containers, and no Southeastern tradition developed from them for a century.

One other fragment of evidence suggests earlier Cherokee vine basketry. In 1839, Chief Yonaguska recounted a vision from his deathbed. He saw, his brother *Willnotah* later recorded, "a great many angels" who showed him his heavenly dwelling place. When Yonaguska asked them how to get there, "the lord had a handsome Basket made of grape vines" to transport the chief and his children "to a better world."[28] The vision became legendary among Cherokees and whites. Unique in written and woven records, the grapevine basket serves as a reminder that weavers of the past undoubtedly made containers of many kinds of materials. The visionary container partakes of the long association of baskets with essential life processes, carrying life and light, connecting sacred and secular worlds. Only with the

Honeysuckle Easter basket, dyed with pink, yellow, and blue aniline,
made by Martha Wachacha (1991) [c: 35 cm, h: 8.4 cm], and honeysuckle earring
dyed with walnut, made by Eva Bigwitch (1989) [c: 4.2 cm, h: 8.4 mm].
Both in private collections. Photograph by William F. Hull.

incorporation of Japanese honeysuckle, however, did weavers develop a full tradition of vine weaving, a tradition that included many individuals, different kinds of
containers, and varied markets. Honeysuckle baskets asserted Cherokee identity
in a new way.

Solving the "Indian Problem": Government Boarding Schools

Native Americans of other tribes may have contributed to the development of vine
basketry among Cherokees. When the federal government brought together Indi-

Honeysuckle vase and lid, dyed with bloodroot and red aniline,
made by Frances Cucumber (1993) [d: 14.5 cm, h: 18 cm].
Private collection. Photograph by William F. Hull.

ans from all over the country to be educated in boarding schools, students became
familiar with customs of other tribal groups, including traditions of basketry. After
1900, Cherokee students who attended boarding schools away from their own communities took classes in basketry and learned different weaving techniques, designs, and forms, and how to work with different materials. In the early years of the
boarding schools, however, learning about native customs was the last thing the
schools had in mind for Indian students.

Initiated by the federal government in 1868 as a way to solve "the Indian problem," boarding schools ultimately appeared in every region of the country. They
resumed the civilization program that was born at the end of the eighteenth century and nourished by missionaries throughout the nineteenth, emphasizing Christianity, agricultural and industrial training, and individual self-sufficiency. Implic-
itly and explicitly, the programs aimed for the complete assimilation of Indians
into white culture, "to eliminate Indianism and supplant it with civilization."[29]
Following the 1887 passage of the Dawes Severalty Act, which provided for individual allotment of tribal lands, the pressure for assimilation greatly intensified.

Reformers, educators, politicians, philanthropists, and scientists anticipated the disappearance of Indian lifeways. Boarding schools became centers to train Indians to live like, or as, whites.

The model for government boarding schools became the Carlisle Indian Industrial School, established in 1879 at an abandoned army barracks in Carlisle, Pennsylvania. Brigadier General Richard Henry Pratt, the ardent assimilationist who founded Carlisle as a laboratory and training ground, believed "the Indians were entitled to a full, fair chance for development in every way" so that they could become "independent, useful American citizens." Their only hope, he asserted, lay in overcoming home influences by severing all tribal relationships. Free from the bonds of "tribal cohesion," Pratt believed Indians would develop the competitive spirit essential to assimilation. The keen sense of individualism that was fundamental to Pratt's notion of American character diverged sharply from what he disparaged as "tribal and race clannishness."[30]

Armed with support from the secretaries of War and Interior and endowed with congressional authorization for Indian education, Pratt personally brought to Carlisle children from dozens of different tribes. Uncompromising in his commitment to assimilation, he abhorred the reservation system and reservation schools, insisting that a tribal environment could produce only material for Wild West shows.[31] In 1900, more than 1,000 students from 79 different tribes attended Carlisle. Although the school usually enrolled about twice as many boys as girls, the imbalance among Cherokees was even greater. Between the time Carlisle was founded in 1879 and its closing in 1918, 274 Eastern Cherokees boarded in the school barracks. Eighty-six were girls.[32]

Indian boarding schools opened elsewhere, and by the 1890s, young Cherokees left home to spend a few months or years, depending on their stamina and success, at the Haskell Institute in Kansas, the Carlisle School in Pennsylvania, and the Chilocco Indian Industrial School in Oklahoma, where they lived, studied, and worked with Native Americans from virtually every geographic area of North America including Canada and Alaska. In the history of American education, no other institutions brought together children of so many different cultures for such extended periods of time. It was a bold and cruel experiment.

In addition to attending Indian boarding schools established specifically to eliminate their cultures, over 1,300 Indians from 65 different tribes enrolled at the Hampton Institute in Virginia, a school founded for freed slaves in 1868 by General Samuel A. Armstrong. Armstrong's goals for African American students were "elementary and industrial teaching . . . and training the hand, head, and heart." Whereas Pratt concentrated on industrial training and individualism, Armstrong proposed a curriculum based on labor, learning, and Christianity. He believed that character developed through work and that true Christianity inevitably followed. Manual training "will make them men and women as nothing else will," he wrote. "It is the only way to make them good Christians."[33] Hampton gradually expanded its program to include 136 Native Americans each year, approximately one-fifth of the total number of boarding students. Native Americans would be "a big card" for the school, Armstrong wrote his wife. "There's money in them I tell you." The federal government appropriated $167 for each Indian student, and private donors contributed scholarships and sponsored individuals. The remaining students worked their way through school.[34]

In 1895, Cherokees comprised the second largest group of Hampton School Indians. Those who attended Hampton—and the other boarding schools beyond the reservation—were handpicked by the Indian agent as promising students who already spoke English. Initially, Indian commissioner E. A. Hayt refused to fund female students because "the education of Indian girls had been a failure." Armstrong disagreed strongly. Convinced that "there is no civilization without educated women," Armstrong persuaded Hayt to relent. Nonetheless, boys usually outnumbered girls at Hampton three to two. In 1895, of the sixty-one Eastern Cherokees who attended Armstrong's school, twenty were girls.[35]

Like earlier programs of civilization, assimilation included Christianity. Boarding schools immersed students in doctrine and values. Faculty members taught Sunday school, and students were required to attend chapel and church. Worship services took up most of every Sunday, and hard work and daily prayer shaped school days as surely as classes in cooking, reading, laundry, or penmanship. "I pray every day and hoe onions," Indian student Kobe wrote home from Hampton.[36]

The goal of assimilation also determined the curriculum of schools on the Cherokee reservation. In 1883, the Society of Friends contracted with the federal government to open the first Cherokee boarding school, which accommodated twenty girls. The following year a separate facility opened for twenty boys. Using funds allocated by the Cherokee Council, Quakers also built day schools in Bird Town, Soco, Big Cove, and Snowbird (Cheoah). Under their management, white males taught in the day schools and white females in the boarding school.

The Cherokee Boarding School emphasized industrial training that would lead to certain kinds of low-wage employment. Girls learned "all branches of domestic industry," including "needlework . . . cutting and making." According to the annual Quaker report, the girls were happy workers who "often adapt their work to some quick Sabbath tune which lightens their labor."[37] When the Quaker contract expired in 1892, the federal government assumed control of the school system and

Cherokee students upon arrival at Hampton (ca. 1895). National Anthropological Archives, Smithsonian Institution.

expanded the industrial training program.[38] Girls were instructed in "cooking, sewing, dress-making, laundry and all the kinds of house work so that they can be fitted for the duties that await them in the future." In 1894, Cherokee superintendent and agent Thomas Potter identified industrial work as the primary goal of education. "It is better to make good laborers, farmers, and mechanics out of the Indians," he wrote, "than to give them the idea that they all must be lawyers, preachers, clerks, or teachers." That year, the Cherokee Boarding School enrolled 135 pupils and Potter sent an additional 45 to Hampton and Carlisle.[39]

A day school on the Qualla Boundary (ca. 1900). Courtesy of the National Museum of the American Indian, Smithsonian Institution, no. 26894.

By 1916, few differences distinguished Indian boarding schools across the nation. Similar programs from Pennsylvania to Oregon facilitated placing students as spaces became available and relocating teachers as needs became apparent. Students entered the Cherokee boarding or day schools at the age of six or seven, and the most promising girls and boys became eligible for further schooling between the ages of twelve and twenty. Lizzie Taylor, for example, arrived at Hampton in May of 1896 after two years of day school and four years at the Cherokee Boarding School. She stayed at Hampton three years, leaving when she was eighteen.[40]

Taylor's mobility was representative of the experiences of boarding school students. Many attended more than one boarding school, moving from Cherokee to Carlisle, Carlisle to Hampton, and Haskell to Chilocco. "I only came to Hampton last October," wrote Stella Blythe to her school sponsors. "I graduated from the Carlisle Indian School last March, then went home. I wished for more education and as there was nothing I could do at home, I came here." She was twenty years old when she arrived at Hampton, and she stayed three years.[41]

Cherokee Boarding School (1893). By the 1890s, more than 150 children boarded and worked at the school. Museum of the Cherokee Indian, Cherokee, N.C.

Not all students went as willingly to school as Stella Blythe. Until 1896, the abduction of children to fill government schools occurred often enough to create administrative problems. Betty Welch, for example, was "dragged out" of the Cherokee Boarding School by former school superintendent H. W. Spray and taken by force on the train to Carlisle. Agent Thomas Potter wrote the commissioner of Indian Affairs that "the girl cried unmercifully," arousing "the indignation of all who saw" the scene. Welch's aunt went to the Cherokee Indian Agency to protest "most bitterly" and demand the child's return, but Betty remained at Carlisle.[42]

Children, parents, and other relatives often resisted such coercion in the name of civilization. "Always after a party has been sent away," wrote Agent Spray in 1901, "the parents of the children who have not gone" kept them at home from "fear that their children might be sent off" next.[43] Defiant parents and frightened children led to a change in school policies that ensured more consistent enrollment. Beginning in 1896, students boarded at schools off their reservations only with the consent of their parents.

Assimilationists wanted children to remain in school as long as possible to break the bonds that connected them to home. "In order to avoid complications," directed a 1902 circular from the Office of Indian Affairs to all agents, "no superintendent of a non-reservation school shall enroll pupils for less than three years term." Even longer terms were preferred. "You will, if possible," the memo continued, "enroll the pupils for periods of four to five years." At Carlisle, Pratt insisted on five-year terms.[44]

Over the long winters and summers of the three-, four-, or five-year school terms, no pupil could return home without special permission from the Office of Indian Affairs. Indian agents and school superintendents assumed authority for deciding when students could return home. "I wish to go home for the summer," Morgan French wrote to the Cherokee agent from Haskell in 1920. "I went home from Carlisle in nineteen hundred seventeen, but for a very short time." Agent James Henderson denied his request. Likewise, David Thompson wrote to his father that he wanted to come home from Carlisle for a visit, "but they say I came in two days to [sic] late" and so would have to wait another year.[45] Agents assumed immense authority over students and, by extension, over their parents.

Agents threatened parents with warrants for failure to send their children to school or to make them return after a visit home. By 1920, Swain and Jackson County ordinances required Indians to "keep their children between the ages of 7 and 19 years in school 9 months each year."[46] Parents and children in every township in Qualla were affected by the laws, and Agent Henderson hoped to get similar legislation passed in Graham County for Cheoah Cherokees. Even though resistance to school diminished every year, some continued to distrust a system that taught children to disparage the customs of their parents and grandparents. Others needed their children to help on their farms. And some simply did not value the training offered by the schools.

School officials drove across the reservation and picked up children in a wagon to take them to boarding school. "You know, they didn't speak kindly to us," Mary Sneed (b. 1915) recalled. "They just said, get in the wagon. You're old enough to go to school." Seventy years later, her memory remained fresh of that frightening first day and night and of her worry about her mother. "I cried myself to sleep," she recalled, "and worried—is Mom still over the mountain? How did she know where we were?" Whipped for getting sick at dinner, Sneed learned quickly where the "crying tree" was, the place children went after being disciplined with rulers.[47]

Although parents might bring their children to the agency, wagon, train depot, or school building, they could not necessarily convince them to stay in school. Runaways were caught and brought back again and again by men hired as truant officers. One tracked a child to a cave and retrieved him from his hiding place behind a pile of rocks, and another lost a captive who leapt from the horse they were riding, "rolled a dozen yards or so down the steep incline, and escaped through the underbrush of the woods."[48] In 1902, three girls drowned in the Oconaluftee as they tried to escape from the boarding school. One was buried on the grounds of the school before her parents received notice that she had died. At the beginning of the following term, Agent Spray reported that parents all over the reservation were using the drownings as an excuse for keeping their daughters at home.[49] Hardly anyone other than Spray could have blamed the frightened parents for holding tightly to their children.

To prepare them for citizenship, schools drilled students in the value of ambition, thrift, and industry while teaching them trades and skills for low-wage employment away from the reservation. Girls learned "domestic arts" including "sewing, kitchen, laundry, and general dormitory work," which meant every possible kind of cleaning, and boys studied "carpentry, shoe and harness making, farming, gardening, and plumbing."[50]

Students provided the labor to run the schools. They raised the food, then processed, cooked, and served it; they cleared and washed the dishes; built and repaired and painted buildings; fed and milked the cows; swept and scrubbed the floors; made, washed, ironed, and mended clothes and school linens; and shod horses, repaired wagons, built fences, made harnesses, and fed livestock, all under the careful supervision of instructors, supervisors, and matrons. "Right after breakfast we had laundry, kitchen," recalled Richard Crowe. "We then went to school about three or four hours till noon. Then in the afternoon, we had some more work detail."[51]

Complete assimilation was the goal of American Indian policy. Annihilation was the alternative, which public officials discussed sarcastically. In 1909, Commissioner of Indian Affairs Robert G. Valentine stated that "it is possible to do only two things with the Indians." The options were "to exterminate them, or to make them into citizens. Whichever we choose should be done in the most business-like manner. If we choose extermination, we should do it suddenly, painlessly and completely." Valentine believed that assimilation aimed to civilize rather than eliminate Native Americans. "Instead of frankly engaging in" annihilation, he explained, "the country has set itself to make the Indians into citizens."[52] The commissioner's speech appeared in "The Red Man," the monthly publication of the Carlisle School.

Such appallingly commonplace rhetoric simplified the issue. Eliminate Native Americans or absorb them. Either way, they disappeared. Nonreservation boarding schools published photographs to document the important first step of assimilation, the physical transformation of students. In monthly journals, photographs of arriving students in native dress with long hair, moccasins, and beads appeared opposite photographs of the same students a few months later, unrecognizable in black Victorian clothing, clipped and coiffed hair, and high-buttoned shoes. Male students wore military uniforms while females adopted the high-necked, long-sleeved, ankle-length dresses of Victorian ladies.

Assembly speeches exhorted students to become accomplished, industrious, and influential. Assailing reservation life because it "engenders shiftlessness and immorality," public officials extolled boarding schools as places to train "splendid types of American citizens."[53] Following their school training, students were admonished to "measure up to your high calling, to the leadership of your people in a higher, nobler and greater life." White civilization drew its net around Indian students and demanded proof "that the money spent by the Government on you has not been wasted." With the transforming experience of boarding school, students were expected "to become leaders, to bring your people out and up to a greater, higher and nobler life than ever has been conceived of before." Graduating students were celebrated as "young missionaries" prepared to convert their own families when they returned home.[54]

To foster suitable attitudes for American citizenship, schools relied on discipline from teachers, obedience from students, and silence from parents. Discipline derived from military drills, and supervisors often came from the ranks of the U.S. Army. Divided into companies, students marched to class, to work, to meals, and to bed, beginning their day at five A.M., with one hour in the afternoon designated for play. The drills punctuate the Cherokee Boarding School memories of John Henry Crowe: "We marched to the dining room. We marched to the boys dorm. We marched to the dining room. We marched to the boy's dorm. We marched to church."[55]

The number of hours spent on manual training exceeded hours in the classroom, for schools emphasized social and industrial training rather than academic instruction. "I believe," wrote Hampton founder Armstrong, "in Labor as a Moral force."[56] At times, the work was so burdensome it compromised the health of the students. In 1926, the Cherokee Boarding School superintendent requested several assistants to help in the girls' school "in order that the girls may be saved of much of the

Cherokee students at Hampton (ca. 1895). National Anthropological Archives, Smithsonian Institution.

slavish work that tends to break down their health." Graded on their labor, students earned credits to purchase clothing supplied by the school. "Sometimes," recalled Richard Crowe, "we ended up owing money, owing credit hours towards our clothes."[57]

The government's most confounding aspect of "the Indian problem" was the great diversity of Native American languages. In 1868, the Indian Peace Commission reported that the variety of tribal languages impeded the reformation of western tribes and declared that only "uniformity of language" could "fuse them into one homogeneous mass." In 1877, native speech was prohibited in all Indian schools because it was "detrimental to the cause of their education and civilization." Hampton students were permitted to "talk Indian" only in special student performances. At Carlisle, any students who lapsed into their own languages during the day came before the entire school assembly in the evening to confess.[58]

The same rules applied in the Cherokee Boarding School. "Will you please state specifically, in writing, what methods and all the means you are using," wrote Agent Spray to one of the teachers, "to stop or control Cherokee talk among the boys under your charge."[59] In their still-fresh memories of the harsh interdiction, Cherokees recall being disciplined severely for speaking their own language. The prohibition nearly destroyed their language in the Southeast, and its damage to the culture is inestimable. When Commissioner Valentine indicated that the government aimed to assimilate rather than annihilate Native Americans, he obscured the fact that prohibiting native speech was a harshly effective form of cultural annihilation.

To facilitate assimilation, both Hampton and Carlisle included in their curriculum an outing system, which placed students in the homes of "the best white families of the East."[60] During outings, students attended classes at local schools and worked as wage servants for their hosts, "paid from seventy-five cents to two dollars per week." The money went directly to the schools and was kept in accounts released only when students graduated. Reporting on a successful summer outing, the Hampton magazine pointed out the diverse jobs available for students. "Some do general house work, some are waiters, and some are nursery maids."[61] Outings prepared students for future domestic work, and wages taught them thrift and responsibility. But more important than either training or pay was constant exposure to the values and attitudes of white society. The purpose of the outing system was to provide an opportunity for Indians "to imbibe the best of civilization." Living in the homes of white families and earning wages for domestic labor helped them "learn to skillfully perform."[62] As they learned to perform in the world of successful white people and absorbed the values of their employers, the influence of their own families diminished and finally, if the schools succeeded, completely disappeared.

Proponents of the outing system recognized that only by separating children from their parents could they eradicate traditions.[63] When Nancy Coleman enrolled at Carlisle, she spent four years with a family in West Chester, Pennsylvania, earning about three dollars a week. She then transferred to Hampton for two years and worked eight months of them in Cornwall, Connecticut. Lizzie Taylor spent eight months of her last year at Hampton working for Mrs. Cleaveland, in West Boxford, Massachusetts. Nearly two of Taylor's three Hampton years were spent in outings.[64]

Although outings were not part of the Cherokee Boarding School program, the curriculum followed the same principles as off-reservation schools; the goal was to train girls for domestic work. The wife of the first school superintendent found jobs for female students in the homes of neighboring whites. "The girls trained by Mrs. Spray have a reputation for skill and housewifery," wrote one admirer in 1894, "and are much sought after in the neighboring towns."[65] Many women who attended the Cherokee Boarding School in the early twentieth century became domestic servants in the homes of teachers and other school personnel during school terms and after they had completed their schooling. The industrial training provided in government boarding schools prepared them well for work as servants.

"Wanders" and Weavers

At the age of eighty, Aggie Ross Lossiah (1880–1966) recalled her Cherokee Boarding School experience in terms of work rather than education. "I use to work at school," she wrote. "I use to mop the hall and the stairs and the palor floor." She was six years old when she arrived at the boarding school in 1886. Her labor was not confined to mopping stairs and halls but extended to the personal requirements of the "Superintends wife." Young Aggie "use to comb her hair in the after noons when she would lie down to rest."[66]

Aggie Ross remained at boarding school until 1890, and during that time she "never saw my grand ma any more for four years." Though she wept profusely when her grandmother first brought her to school, Aggie Ross did not want to leave four years later. The influence of the school was so profound that she "didnt wont to go home." Leaving behind the school family that had enveloped her for four formative years bereaved the ten-year-old child. "I got so lonesome before we got home," she remembered seventy years later. "I use to cry."[67]

For the next several years, Aggie Ross lived with eight different white families, some more than once, for whom she milked cows, carried water, cared for children, ironed, cooked, picked fruit, washed clothes, and sat with the sick and dying. For her work she was given "a bed and what I eat" and from twenty-five to thirty-five cents a week. One generous employer paid Aggie "one dallor a week" to cook for the family, care for the baby, churn butter, and milk cows. In 1903, Aggie Ross moved with her grandparents, Sela and Jessie Techeskee, to Whittier, the town where Josiah Axe found *Ko-hi* and her unusual white oak basket twenty years earlier. At the age of twenty-four, Aggie Ross married Henry Lossiah and started keeping her own home.[68]

No bitterness tinges the memoir written by Aggie Ross. She expressed no regret about boarding school nor about the servant work she undertook as a child as she moved from home to home and from one white employer to another. "She was a good woman," she said of the school matron who supervised her mopping, and Mrs. Henry, who hired Aggie to "help her girl pick blackberries," was "a fine lady to live with." Mrs. Smith, who "was always glad to see me," filled a special role in the child's life. "It was home at Mrs. Smiths house," Aggie Ross remembered. "She was so good to me when I was with her."[69] She also could recall the exact amount of pay she received for each job she had seventy years earlier, when money was scarce and working in the homes and fields of white neighbors was commonplace.

While Aggie Ross tended children, livestock, and dying relatives for white employers, her grandparents also found work for whites in a number of different places. For a time, "Grand pa tended a little grist mill" at the foot of the mountains

Aggie Ross Lossiah (1880–1966) on her front porch with corn, beans, and a basket sifter for making bean bread (1951). Museum of the Cherokee Indian, Cherokee, N.C.

in Tennessee, and "they would come to the mill because grandpa would grind just to please them." The mill did not belong to Jessie Techeskee, nor did much else, for Aggie recalled "we didnt own anything we were just wanders."[70] Crisscrossing the mountains, living sometimes in an abandoned hut, other times in a log cabin, occasionally with relatives, and once in a shelter made of cane splits, Aggie and her grandparents "seemed to get along good." A white woman who lived down the creek "hired grand ma to wash for her," and once "she ask grand ma to split shucks for her to put in bed ticks." Whether their work was grinding corn or stuffing bed ticks, pay was nearly always in the form of food, "some thing to eat meat or flour."[71] While her family lived at Henry Harrison's place on Tallassee Creek, Aggie Ross learned from her grandmother how to weave baskets. "When my grand ma was making baskets," she later recalled, "she showed me how to make them."[72] And once she learned how to weave, Aggie Ross learned how to peddle.

> And when she got her a load of baskets made we went to peddle. And my grand pa made some chairs and he would take his chairs to sell—and so here we would go—we went to Maryville Tenn.—it was alittle town then—that was as far as the train came then and that is where we went to peddle baskets—and I took my few baskets that I had made and I had enough to buy me a cotton dress and a few other little things at the store—that was the first time I bought myself some thing my selfe by selling baskets that I made my self—it took us all day to walk to Maryville from where we lived.[73]

The "selfe" that emerged in young Aggie Ross was deeply grounded in her relationship to her grandparents and in her experience of weaving baskets and selling them for money. Whether living in the forests of Tennessee, as Aggie Ross did, or in white communities like Whittier, or on reservation lands scattered through western North Carolina, women walked many miles with sheets of baskets to sell and barter. "I well remember seeing the Indian women as they came into town," recalled a Bryson City resident, "carrying their brilliantly colored hand-made baskets tied in a sheet on their backs."[74]

Native American Handcrafts: "A Joyous Source of Self-Support"

In 1901, Estelle Reel, federal superintendent of Indian Schools, drew up a new course of study that emphasized practical industrial education. Subsequently, many Indian boarding schools began to offer courses in basketry. Instruction in handcrafts offered a way to develop useful trades while enhancing white ideals of domesticity. Native industries like basketry could cultivate "a taste for what is really artistic in itself," claimed a reformer, and at the same time be profitable enough to help "make the home comfortable and attractive."[75]

Enthusiasm for traditional basketry began in the very institutions designed to eradicate native culture. Inspired by the opportunity to "give to future generations a saner and more attractive view of certain phases of the Indian character," the Carlisle School established a department of Native Indian art in 1906 to "instruct and preserve" selected traditions of Native Americans. They obtained examples of Indian work from the Bureau of American Ethnology at the Smithsonian.[76]

In 1900, Hampton began instruction in raffia basketry using the light and delicate vinelike fiber derived from Madagascar palm leaves. In the school's Normal Department, kindergarten classes of children from the surrounding community learned to weave airy raffia baskets with scalloped rims. Hampton's monthly publication, *The Southern Workman*, featured items produced in manual training classes, including raffia baskets and placemats. The following year, older students in the Domestic Science Department took basketry as part of sewing instruction, and they also learned to weave with raffia.[77]

Instruction specifically in Indian basketry, however, appealed to the Hampton administration. By 1902, *The Southern Workman* embraced the philosophy of an energetic New England reformer, Neltje Doubleday, who saw in Indian handcrafts a chance to solve more than one problem. Native basketry, she reasoned, could replace Japanese and German imports. Leave to whites the trades in which they "naturally excel," she pleaded, and develop among Indians those industries "which were as natural to him as his bronze skin."[78] Another advantage to the development of native basketry was that if philanthropists sponsored Indian industries, they might put influential traders out of business. In place of the trader "who does not allow his victims a living wage," Doubleday called for "teachers, missionaries and the various philanthropic associations" to revive native basketry and create a "new and enlightened policy in the Anglo-Saxon's dealings with subject races."[79] The policy she had in mind for the "subject races" was instruction in certain kinds of weaving.

"Basketry is the most characteristic, most varied, most generally practiced," Doubleday wrote, "most interesting, decorative, and valuable" of Indian work. Scorning innovations, the reformer emphasized the oldest customs of basketry, "not the little aniline-dyed, sweet-grass affairs we are wont to associate with the little half-breeds in the East."[80] Such combinations of nostalgia for past conventions and condescension for contemporary expressions profoundly undercut assimilation policies. Nonetheless, the disparate approaches ultimately became part of school curricula and government strategies for solving the "Indian problem."

Rachel Tyner, absentee Shawnee, making a reed or raffia basket at Hampton
(ca. early 1900s). Courtesy of Hampton University Archives.

Inspired by Doubleday and supported by government funds, Hampton introduced a new basketry course to African American and Native American students. "Basketry," reported *The Southern Workman*, "is not only recognized as a valuable exercise in manual training, but is believed to have possibilities as a profitable industry."[81] The relationship between the creation of a basket and the rewards of the market was integral to the new educational policy.

Along with basketry, Hampton began instruction in lace making and "the hand weaving of the mountain whites." Carlisle included bookbinding and wood burning in its Indian Art classes.[82] To social reformers, all handwork contributed to the goal of manual training. Native American traditions of basketry served the educational process as sources of industry and commerce. Alternative crafts like raffia weaving, bookbinding, wood burning, New England lace making, and Appalachian loom weaving appealed equally to educators because they fit the same model of disciplined work and monetary gain. Imported crafts thus became part of Native American course work.

The Cherokee Boarding School acceded to the Indian Office's new program in a small way. A year after Estelle Reel proposed a curriculum that included native handwork, Agent Spray ordered from the Milton Bradley Company a supply of round reed and raffia and an instructional booklet on raffia and reed weaving. The supplies were designated for the kindergarten class, the entry grade for new students of any age. A few months later, Reel requested that Spray send her office "one or two photographs showing old Indian basket makers at work" as well as "pupils making baskets at school."[83] No records remain to tell us whether Agent Spray complied, but if he did, it must have been with considerable reluctance. "Those of them who make baskets," he reported, "have no market for them except as they travell to sell them which developes a vagabond life not in keeping with the best interests of their crops and home life."[84] Both men and women went on the trading trails, as Aggie Ross remembered, and the autonomy inherent in basket peddling did not suit the agent.

Like a mirror of larger processes, the school programs reflect Indian policy in all its contradictions. What was forbidden to one generation was required of the next. Dedicated to the elimination of the native way of life, schools attempted to erase tribal language, clothing, appearance, customs, values, and beliefs. At the same time, they established programs to maintain selected traditions. Native American art, they reasoned, was "of vital interest and value in art development in general in this country."[85] Basketry, by the turn of the century, was considered art worth preserving.

Reformers like Doubleday admired Native American crafts for their "positive artistic value," which made them marketable commodities and "a joyous source of self-support." For Indian students educated in government boarding schools, Doubleday saw an important role in the development of commercial markets. The "bright young Indians in the institutes," she suggested, formed "the natural connecting link between their people's industries and the Eastern market." Schooled in the advantages of a market economy and its "power of uplift," students could return to their reservations prepared to revive traditional industries and compete with Canadians in canoe building, with Germans in rug weaving, and with Japanese and Germans in basketry.[86]

'Zona

Inspired by Doubleday, in 1902, Hampton hired a young Cherokee woman to teach basketry. 'Zona, as she was called, was born on May 13, 1875, in Big Cove. At the time Arizona Nick was born, the Cove community had spread across the northern section of Raven's Fork, an upper tributary of the Oconaluftee. When the census was taken in 1880, Arizona Nick was five years old. She lived with her twenty-two-year-old mother, Laura Nick, whose second child was a one-year-old son named Lorenzo. Another member of the household was a white farm laborer from Flagpond, Tennessee, named John Swayney, who was thirty-eight years old and divorced. The head of the household, according to the census, was Laura Nick's twenty-five-year-old brother, John Nick, a farmer.[87] Presumably, John Swayney was a laborer for John Nick or a boarder in his home. He spoke Cherokee fluently. By 1900, Laura Nick of Big Cove was married to John "Swinnie." The census that year lists Laura Swayney, age forty-two, as the mother of fourteen children, six of whom were living. The son "Loranza," twenty-one by then, was the oldest of the six identified children. His sister Arizona was not listed on the census. That was the year she became a basketmaker.[88]

In February of 1896, Arizona Swayney left the Cherokee Boarding School and went to Hampton for five years. She did not participate in outings but instead returned home during the summers. On one homecoming, she found her mother extremely ill. "'Zona rejoices that she is there rather than earning money in the North," reported *The Southern Workman*, "for she hopes to be able to give her mother a summer of rest and relief."[89] By fall, her mother regained her health and Swayney returned to Hampton.

Swayney graduated from the Hampton Normal School in 1901. Following Neltje Doubleday's visit to Hampton, where she "encouraged our basketmakers here,"

Photograph 1895

Two Cherokee Maiden

Arizona Swayney (*left*) in 1895.
Swayney family photograph.

Arizona Swayney returned to the reservation to learn "from some of the old women of the tribe the secret of the 'double weave' used in the beautiful Cherokee baskets."[90] In the kind of irony that repeats itself throughout Cherokee history, it seems that when Arizona Swayney went to boarding school, where the goal was to "eliminate Indianism," she decided to learn and teach the basketry of her ancestors.

Like Lucy George, Arizona Swayney did not learn traditional handwork from her mother. And, like Lucy George, she did not record who her teachers were. "There is only one old woman at home who makes real nice baskets," she wrote in the Hampton newspaper, "and only one old woman and one old man who can do the double weave."[91] From these unnamed teachers, female and male, Swayney learned the oldest traditions of rivercane basketry, doubleweaving and the special

After returning home to learn how to weave, Arizona Swayney began teaching basketry at Hampton in 1902. Courtesy of Hampton University Archives.

patterns it produces. "In learning basketry I seem to have attracted the attention of a great many people," Swayney wrote in 1902. "They couldn't understand why I spent so much time on basketry after spending so many years in school to get an education." American education was perceived by whites and Cherokees as the antithesis to all native customs. Cherokees expected their educated sisters and brothers to disdain their own conventions and were amused when they did not. "They laughed at me because I wanted to learn," according to Swayney, "but after seeing a very pretty basket which I had made . . . they were quite anxious to learn basketry too."[92]

Arizona Swayney taught basketweaving at Hampton until 1906. The school was enthusiastic about the potential of the Native American craft, and the *Southern Workman* reported that under Arizona's influence "it is expected that there will eventually be developed here a special pattern to be known as the Hampton basket."[93] Ironically, a modern institution dedicated to the transformation of Native Americans sought, as clans and families once did, to express a particular identity in the subtle patterns of a rivercane basket.

In the summer of 1902, Swayney attended the Mohonk Annual Conference of the Friends of the Indian, "where she represented the Indian" and exhibited a collection of baskets made at Hampton. The conference was an immersion in the rhetoric and policy of assimilation. In addition to showcasing various school industries, participants discussed the allotment of Indian lands. And they also debated the desirability of denying government rations—those insufficient distributions of army surplus foods—to "all able-bodied men" confined to reservations. At the conclusion of the meeting, the Friends of the Indian voted in favor of continuing land allotment and withholding rations. Such steps, they reasoned, were "the best thing for their good."[94] Swayney then returned to Hampton to resume instruction in native industries.

In the summer of 1905, she moved to Summerville, South Carolina, to teach in a tea plantation mission school. To the "very poorest class" of black and white children, Swayney taught a variety of handwork including basketry, lace making, beadwork, chair caning, and rug weaving. Parents initially objected to "any form of industrial training" and complained that "the basketry and rug weaving were not at all acceptable." But when "each child carried home the money for which her basket had sold," reported Swayney, "the parents were very much pleased, and the mothers immediately became anxious to learn also."[95] From the mountains to the coast, among Native Americans, whites, and blacks, basketry held a promise of economic relief for women.

Around 1909, Arizona Swayney married Abe T. Blankenship, a white Tennessean who worked as a logging contractor. They lived with their infant daughter,

In a Hampton basketry class female students learned to make rivercane doubleweave
baskets (ca. early 1900s). Courtesy of Hampton University Archives.

Lillian, on fifty acres of land in Big Cove adjacent to the house of Laura Swayney, Arizona's mother. In addition to the twenty-five acres she farmed, Arizona Blankenship kept a garden close to the house. She raised chickens, cattle, horses, and steers. The Blankenships added a room onto their house for a combination store and post office, called Swayney. For many years Arizona Blankenship served as postmistress.[96]

Throughout her life, Blankenship maintained an interest in education. She sent all her children to the Big Cove Day School and the Cherokee Boarding School and then on to schools beyond the reservation. When the day school teacher needed a place to live, Blankenship rented a room to her for fifteen dollars a month. She also taught periodically and in 1929 substituted at the day school for three months until a replacement could be hired. In 1935, Arizona Nick Swayney Blankenship died at the age of fifty-nine.[97]

Helen Houser, the youngest of Blankenship's five children, remembers her mother as an industrious woman who provided everything the family needed. Like so many women in the Southern Appalachians, she made patchwork quilts by suspending a quilting frame from the ceiling. Relying on catalogs that came in the mail from Sears Roebuck and Montgomery Ward, she ordered furniture that was delivered to the Swayney post office. Baskets remained her specialty. "Yes," Houser recalls, "I remember her gathering the vines and the dyes and boiling them. We carried our lunches to school in baskets she made, little ones with attached lids."[98]

When Arizona Swayney introduced cane basketry to her Hampton classes in the early days of the revival of Indian handwork, she received praise and publicity and was immortalized in Hampton publications. While she was a student at Hampton, she undoubtedly learned raffia or vine basketry and may even have taught it as part of her basketry classes. In 1943, eight years after she died, a basket collector from Oklahoma claimed that honeysuckle basketry "was introduced by a Cherokee woman named Arizona Blankenship who had been educated at the Hampton Institute, Virginia."[99] Blankenship may have been the unidentified friend that collected vines behind Lucy George's house in Bird Town and finally taught George to weave honeysuckle baskets.

Reviving Arts and Crafts

Neltje Doubleday was just one of many whites committed to the revival of Native American arts at the turn of the century. The American era of progressivism and social reform shaped and was shaped by women and men who founded organizations like the Mohonk Conference (1882), the Indian Rights Association (1882), the Women's National Indian Association (1883), the Indian Industries League

(1895), the Sequoyah League (1902), and the American Indian League (1910) in order to heighten awareness of native conditions and press for specific reforms in American Indian policy.[100] Their common goal was assimilation of Native Americans into an American melting pot stocked with Christianity, individualism, private property, and hard work. Through their organizations, Indian reformers made speeches, wrote papers, held conferences, compiled publications, and raised funds to influence public policy and mold private convictions. Their zeal was evangelical and promoting markets for native industries became one outlet for their energies.

In 1901, the Industrial Department of the Women's National Indian Association opened "an Indian department in the most popular department store in New York City" and purchased directly from native workers $5,000 worth of stock for the salesroom.[101] Selling native work linked Indian reformers to the American Arts and Crafts movement, which formed an important part of the market for Indian baskets. Inspired in part by the English social gospel movement of Thomas Carlyle, John Ruskin, and William Morris, the American Arts and Crafts movement flourished between the 1880s and 1930s, emphasizing designs, forms, materials, goods, and colors of the preindustrial past.[102] Native American handiwork seemed a perfect answer to the yearnings expressed in the movement.

The burgeoning enthusiasm for places and people who appeared to retain a sense of tradition led popular magazines to feature Indian wares and advertise excursions to reservations to see native artisans at work. Indian artifacts became objects of fashion as publications successfully promoted home furnishings and decorations made by hand rather than machine. An 1891 California newspaper article that heralded "The Latest Fad Among Artistic People" recommended baskets made by Native Americans as "attractive ornaments for library and parlor."[103] As the Arts and Crafts movement enhanced the market for basketry, it inspired new forms that were ornamental and decorative.

In the early 1900s, collector George Wharton James formed the Basket Fraternity and for a brief period published *The Basket*, a journal for "lovers of the Indian basket and other good things." The quarterly was filled with articles about native societies and baskets and included photographs and detailed instructions for weaving. Subscribers could learn to make a Havasupai plaque, "suitable for card tray or wall decoration," or a Hoopa carrying basket, "suitable for waste basket, potted palm, etc." Companies advertised supplies of raffia, reed, sweet grass, and palm leaf, and weavers from California to Vermont submitted photographs of their carefully copied Indian baskets as well as fanciful containers covered with embellishments.[104] The Arts and Crafts movement swept the country and expressed a deep longing for something its proponents could not even identify.

Motivated by an impulse to offer social redemption to the impoverished, New England reformers came into the Southern Appalachians to open settlement houses, schools, and institutes dedicated to social uplift. Arts and crafts were central to the success of these enterprises. Like the supervisors of Indian schools and the crusading friends of the Indian, social reformers believed in the moral power of industry and handwork and the social benefits of market success. In 1890, Frances Louisa Goodrich established the first of several mission schools nine miles from Asheville. In the next decade, similar centers were established, including Allanstand Cottage Industries and the Biltmore Estates Industries in Asheville, the Fireside Industries in Berea, Kentucky, and the Pi Beta Phi Settlement School in Gatlinburg, Tennessee, just across the mountain from Cherokee communities.[105] Appalachia became a mission field, and the new century brought more reformers and revivals, including the Tryon Toy Makers and Wood Carvers in 1915, the Penland Weavers and Potters in 1923, and the John C. Campbell Folk School in 1925.

Redeeming people and saving traditions were the intertwined goals of social reformers. Their organizations encouraged and marketed the crafts of the Southern Appalachians, bringing satisfaction to the craft revivalists and some benefit to the artisans. With zealous dedication, craft revivalists determined to rescue "the old arts," offer "paying work to women," and inject "interest into their lives" by encouraging them to make "useful and beautiful things." The most profound effect of the craft revival, they believed, was the elevation of Appalachian character. "The question of character is so much involved in this matter of handiwork and the thrift it encourages," wrote Goodrich, "that we feel the key to many of our problems lies in these cottage industries that have been started around our day-schools."[106]

Basketry was not a dying art in the Appalachians. At the turn of the century, Cherokees and whites regularly made and used baskets. In this work, however, the strands of disparate movements overlapped. Basketry was a traditional handwork with economic potential and therefore useful to revivalists, social reformers, and friends of the Indian. While Estelle Reel promoted basketweaving in Indian schools, George Wharton James in publications, and Neltje Doubleday on reservations, craft revivalists encouraged it among white neighbors of the Cherokees. The heightened interest in basketry contributed to the development of new markets and different basket forms.

Goodrich recalled an occasion when a man brought her "our first boat or canoe basket, copied from the Indians." The boat or canoe was a rib basket, a European form that had been so fully incorporated by Cherokee weavers that Goodrich attributed it to them. From the Indian canoe basket, according to Goodrich, a weaver developed another form called a picking basket. "As the years went on," she wrote, "other basket-makers came our way, a few other shapes were discovered and others evolved to make the great variety sold today."[107] Some weavers in Goodrich's cottage industries made baskets of willow "wrought only into light baskets, for sewing, for carrying eggs and other light stuff to market." Light baskets of willow led to those of vine. "Soon after we had a salesroom in Asheville and a manager," reported Goodrich. "She experimented with the honeysuckle vine which grows luxuriantly over the country side, for she had seen some notice of it in a government bulletin." The manager shared her work with another basketweaver "living not far from town," and a new tradition of basketry developed among white Appalachians. The tradition was based on honeysuckle and appealed to the growing market looking for "charming work baskets."[108]

Organizations as varied as women's clubs, church missionary circles, Indian reform organizations, and arts and crafts societies helped develop a cash market for native crafts that influenced early-twentieth-century traditions of basketry. As basketweavers increasingly regarded their work as a means to earn money, the market affected more profoundly each weaver's choice of form, design, color, size, material, and function.

A "Mania" for Collecting

Just as craft revivalists and Indian reformers glorified the handwork of the past, a growing number of antiquarians and collectors sought out older traditions. Traveling directly to reservations to gather artifacts from cultures they assumed were vanishing, collectors searched for handcrafted goods and designs that were unaffected by commerce and industry. They disregarded the fact that pristine, unadulterated forms had never existed in the rich mix of cultures that preceded white encroachment.

In 1882, North Carolina jurist David Schenck disparaged the "mania among Northern tourists in this region for collecting ancient relics of the Cherokees." The interest in Cherokee antiquities was not limited to Northern tourists, however. Schenck found that museums also "have their local agents gathering and forwarding these remnants."[109] The judge may have had a few particular visitors in mind, for that year the Valentine brothers of Virginia arrived to excavate burial mounds and enhance their father's antiquities museum in Richmond. They employed Cherokees to assist them as they gathered human skeletons and grave goods, and before returning to Richmond, they hired local Indian agents to collect any additional artifacts that appeared. The Valentines must have been dismayed to learn later that they inspired a few people in the Carolinas to manufacture artifacts and "give them the appearance of age." Several individuals willingly acknowledged that "they had made some articles for Mr. Valentine."[110] Whether as a form of resistance to grave plundering or eagerness to earn money, Indians were marketing bogus antiquities alongside authentic goods. Both markets thrived on the interest in Indian cultures. Both contributed to museum collections. Both generated cash.

In the summer of 1908, a professional ethnologist, M. R. Harrington of Covert and Harrington Commercial Ethnologists in New York, made his way to the reservation to purchase artifacts and take photographs. Harrington, however, made a singular contribution to Cherokee history. He recorded the names of everyone who sold him baskets and identified the containers with Cherokee terms. From *Ayasta* he bought a cane storage basket (*egwa talu-tsa*) and a white oak carrying basket with a handle (*talu-tsa kabinusti*). Nancy Saunooke, who had attended Hampton, sold him a large cane storage basket and a round covered basket (*aboyali talu-tsa*). Arizona Swayney's niece Lucina provided "a fine sieve used for catching fish after poisoning the water."[111] And one unidentified woman, although she might have thought his request was odd, agreed to demonstrate the sequence of corn processing for Harrington. Together they left an invaluable record. Since the pack basket was obsolete by the end of the nineteenth century, she drew from memory the way her grandmothers suspended baskets on their backs to gather corn from the fields. The winnower, sifter, and sieve were easier to demonstrate, for women continued to use them every day, and perhaps she posed with her own. The mortar she sat beside while winnowing was also commonplace. In fact, another white visitor to the reservation that year reported that in every yard "there is quite sure to be an old fashioned mortar, three feet high, and a pestle, for beating corn."[112]

In addition to Northeastern ethnologists, local and regional collectors also photographed, studied, and purchased baskets. In 1908, historian Fred Olds and an Asheville photographer spent a week on the Qualla Boundary to prepare a series of articles for the *Raleigh Observer* and collect artifacts for the North Carolina Hall of History.[113] Like most white visitors, Olds began by contacting the agent and school superintendent. And, like many who came before and after, Olds ended up at the cabin of *Ayasta*'s son, Hampton graduate Will West Long.

While women and children looked on silently and the photographer immortalized the moment, Olds and Will West Long examined baskets. In one photograph, Olds holds a white oak handle basket that has two broad chain designs encircling the body. A bright and fanciful basket, it was obviously made for the market. Nearby, a Cherokee holds an undyed vine basket with a scalloped rim, virtually identical to baskets made in the Hampton and Carlisle boarding schools. A light and delicate basket, it also was certainly made for the market. Did Olds purchase

In the early 1900s a woman demonstrated the use of a pack basket to gather corn.
By then, the pack basket was nearly obsolete. Photograph by M. R. Harrington (1908).
Courtesy of the National Museum of the American Indian,
Smithsonian Institution, no. 2736.

A woman uses a basket sieve to demonstrate rinsing off the skin from boiled corn before pounding the kernels into flour. Photograph by M. R. Harrington (1908). Courtesy of the National Museum of the American Indian, Smithsonian Institution, no. 2734.

the white oak basket and sell the vine basket, or did he buy both? We can never know, for there are no written records of the transaction. The photograph, however, provides the earliest illustration of vine baskets on the Qualla Boundary.

The photograph also illustrates the primacy of baskets in homes. Well-worn baskets hang from the walls and timbers of the cabin and lie scattered about the yard. The worn and plain appearance of the storage and winnowing baskets, both

In the early 1900s women continued to winnow corn or beans in large, shallow baskets with tightly woven bases and convex sides. Photograph by M. R. Harrington (1908). Courtesy of the National Museum of the American Indian, Smithsonian Institution, no. 2731.

After boiling and rinsing the corn, women pounded it in a wooden mortar to make flour.
Photograph by M. R. Harrington (1908). Courtesy of the National Museum
of the American Indian, Smithsonian Institution, no. 2724.

Women sifted the pounded corn until it was sufficiently fine to make bread. Photograph by M. R. Harrington (1908). Courtesy of the National Museum of the American Indian, Smithsonian Institution, no. 2735.

Women molded flour into "wheels" of bread. The wheels were wrapped in corn blades or hickory leaves and immersed in boiling water. Photograph by M. R. Harrington (1908). Courtesy of the National Museum of the American Indian, Smithsonian Institution, no. 2732.

In 1908 Colonel Fred Olds visited Will West Long and purchased baskets for the new North Carolina Hall of History in Raleigh. N.C. Museum of History.

of white oak, contrasts with the new baskets made for the market. The assemblage represents the divergent paths that were available for basketweavers. In the early twentieth century, women continued to manufacture baskets for their own use and in their own way. At the same time, they responded to and helped develop markets for baskets that were less utilitarian and more decorative. The photograph captures both a moment and an era when old and new patterns, represented by baskets, intertwined in the hands of women and men.

Olds had enlisted the aid of the agent for his visit, requesting to see "one or two typical Indian houses, the oldest men and women . . . and pictures of any of their people in special costumes."[114] He did not record the name of the woman who

Unidentified woman and child, 1908. N.C. Museum of History.

posed for him in front of her home with "her papoose" on her back. He did, however, identify Jim Tail, the fisherman standing in front of a massive chestnut tree with a cane fish basket and bait of wasp grubs.

Olds took a particular interest in baskets. Over the next fifteen years he corresponded with the Cherokee agent, acquiring various kinds of objects for the Hall of History and baskets for his personal collection. In 1917, he even undertook to replenish some of the basketry materials that were steadily dwindling on the

THESE PHOTOGRAPHS, MADE FOR FRED A. OLDS
IN 1908 BY BROCK OF ASHEVILLE, ILLUSTRATE
THE LIFE OF THE EASTERN BAND OF CHEROKEE
INDIANS ON THEIR RESERVATION OF 63,000
ACRES, WHICH IS IN SWAIN AND JACKSON
COUNTIES.

JIM TAIL, FISHERMAN, FISHING POLE, FISH BASKET AND BAIT OF WASP GRUBS.

Jim Tail with a rivercane fish basket, bait of wasp grubs, and a cane fishing pole (1908).
N.C. Museum of History.

Ayasta, wife and mother of medicine men, a basketweaver, and an informant for James Mooney (1888). From the Bureau of American Ethnology Nineteenth Annual Report, Plate 14, p. 273.

Qualla Boundary. He offered Agent Henderson a supply of willow slips and bamboo shoots to provide for future weavers. Although Henderson seemed especially committed to acquiring the bamboo, no written records remain to indicate if and where he planted the invasive Asian relative of rivercane.[115]

Intervention in Cherokee landscapes and lifeways came in different guises and for varying reasons. At about the same time Olds and Henderson exchanged letters, including some expressing concern about the amount of alcohol consumed at Indian ball games, ethnologist Mooney returned to the reservation. He collected a few more baskets in the summers of 1911–14, but he recorded the name of only one weaver, *Ayasta*. More than two decades had passed since she had recounted for Mooney her version of how the world was made, the story of the first brother and sister and their wonderful procreation. Nearly seventy-eight years old, *Ayasta* was considered by Mooney as "one of the best traditionalists in the tribe."[116] Born before removal, a weaver of stories and baskets, and widow of one medicine man and mother of another, *Ayasta* embodied the capacity of women to embrace tradition while adopting change.

As "the only woman privileged to speak in council," she drew on the special legacy of the previous centuries' beloved women. As a weaver, she represented the oldest of women's traditions. Her baskets, however, reveal that she was not confined to convention. She sold Mooney a rivercane storage basket and a white oak pack basket similar to containers of an earlier era. But she also sold him rib baskets so small he called them toys. They were brightly colored with red, yellow, blue, purple, gold, and green commercial dyes. In 1914, when she was eighty, *Ayasta* sold Mooney his last, and perhaps her last, woven container, a model of the old pack basket, the customary container of women in fertile fields.[117]

In the winter of 1913, anthropologist Frank Speck traveled from the University of Pennsylvania to spend "a few weeks" on the reservation. While "investigating decorative arts," he acquired "a small ethnological collection comprising cane basketry, pottery, pipes, blow guns, etc." and archaeological material from the base of a mound near the Cherokee Boarding School. Speck prepared his classic monograph, *Decorative Art and Basketry of the Cherokee*, based on his collections and subsequent research. After lengthy negotiations, he sold the assemblage and monograph to the Milwaukee Public Museum for $125.[118]

According to Speck, "the principle material used in basketry here is cane. . . . The other principle basket materials are white oak (*Quercus alba*) and Basket Oak (*Q. Michauxi*)." Like other ethnographers, Speck made no mention of honeysuckle or vine basketry, and he subsequently reported that "honeysuckle basket weaving was not an original Cherokee Indian art." He later declared that it was "a new technique introduced among the Eastern Cherokee about 1915." In 1914, however, Agent Henderson wrote to the commissioner of Indian Affairs that "the Indians make their baskets of bamboo cane, oak splints and willow twigs."[119] Although ethnologists and collectors might have disregarded their innovations, weavers were experimenting with new kinds of material, such as vines and willow.

Speck also sold some of his Cherokee baskets, including one allegedly made in 1880 by Mary George, to Oklahoma collector Clarke Field. Like the Springplace mission baskets and Yonaguska's legendary grapevine basket, Mary George's 1880 basket is anomalous in form, function, and material. Someone—perhaps Speck or Field—identified the material as honeysuckle, but it has none of the telltale knots or joints that unfailingly appear on honeysuckle baskets. Moreover, honeysuckle did not arrive in the Carolinas until the 1890s. The material looks like peeled willow, or even raffia.[120] The container's form is identical to those made of vine, reed, and raffia in basket classes at Carlisle and Hampton. It is shaped like the container in the photograph of Fred Olds and Will West Long, and its faded red and blue

Rivercane basket, dyed with walnut and red aniline, made by *Ayasta* (ca. 1913)
[l: 35.5 cm, w: 30.5 cm, h: 16.5 cm]. Catalog No. E281403,
Department of Anthropology, Smithsonian Institution.

suggest aniline dyes that became popular in the 1880s. The earliest documented example of vine basketry by Cherokee weavers of the Eastern Band after removal, it foreshadows the popularity of light and airy vine containers made for a new market.

Milestones of Indian Progress: Expositions and Fairs

Anticipating the assimilation of Native Americans and the disappearance of their lifeways, anthropologists and ethnologists gathered everything from household goods to ceremonial feathers for research. They also collected a variety of Indian artifacts to display at national and international expositions and fairs. Popular from the county to the international level, fairs provided opportunities for the entertainment and education of every person who came through the turnstiles. Orga-

White oak model of a pack basket, one quarter the size of a typical pack basket,
dyed with walnut, made by *Ayasta* (1914) [l: 20.3 cm, w: 20.3 cm, h: 33 cm].
Catalog No. E286033, Department of Anthropology, Smithsonian Institution.

nizers made a profit and sponsors got valuable exposure. For a number of years and
a number of expositions, science joined business to promote the accomplishments
of civilization, urbanization, industrialization, and commerce.

In 1890, Chicago won a heated competition to host the World's Columbian Exposition, a national celebration of the four-hundredth anniversary of the voyages

White oak toy rib basket with double lid, dyed with aniline purple, red, and gold,
made by *Ayasta* (1912) [l: 6.4 cm, w: 5 cm, h: 4.5 cm]. Catalog No. 272978,
Department of Anthropology, Smithsonian Institution.

of Columbus. City planners prepared eagerly, contacting representatives of states
and nations, industry and science, medicine and commerce. Exhibits came from all
over the world, and buildings were constructed with America's past and Chicago's
future in mind.

More than fifteen buildings were erected for the fair, including a building of anthropology called "Man and His Works" that housed archaeological and ethnological material from all over the world. The displays extended beyond the walls to
include exhibits of "many interesting tribes of living Indians who are quartered
near the building."[121] Inaugurated by the nationwide celebration of the arrival of
Columbus in a world so new to Europeans, the era of exhibiting Native Americans
as they (supposedly) had lived in the past got well underway.

The display from the state of North Carolina included samples of timber, which
was considered its most marketable resource. Forester Gifford Pinchot obtained

White oak toy rib basket with double lid, dyed with walnut and aniline red, gold, orange, and green, made by *Ayasta* (1913) [l: 12 cm, w: 10.2 cm, h: 6.4 cm]. Catalog No. 281405, Department of Anthropology, Smithsonian Institution.

permission from the Cherokee Council to cut specimen trees from the Cathcart tract to display. "In view of the fact that this timber is in the market," wrote Agent Spencer, "I deem it good policy for the gift to be made." The dimensions and kinds of trees Pinchot took suggest how landscapes must have appeared before the timber boom of the early twentieth century. Pinchot cut a water oak with a circumference of more than seventeen feet, a black walnut with a circumference greater than ten feet, and a chestnut with a circumference larger than twenty-four feet.[122]

Timber was not the only material that came from the reservation to the exposition. In conjunction with the show, University of Chicago anthropologist Frederick Starr assembled a collection of Cherokee material. Thirteen baskets, along with blowguns, thistled darts, ceremonial scratchers, bows and arrows, a medicinal cupping tool, fingerprints, and photographs ended up in Starr's collection. No records indicate whether they became part of the thousands of "curios-

White oak toy rib basket with double lid, dyed with walnut and aniline red, orange, green, and gold, made by *Ayasta* (1913) [l: 12.7 cm, w: 11.5 cm, h: 6.4 cm]. Catalog No. E281406, Department of Anthropology, Smithsonian Institution.

ities and relics" on display, but at the conclusion of the exposition, much of the ethnological material, including the Cherokee baskets, formed the nucleus of the new Field Museum of Natural History.[123] Through the activities of anthropologists, community leaders, and antiquarians, women extended their markets far beyond the boundaries of their reservation.

The scientific community's enthusiasm for Indian exhibitions stirred the anger of assimilationists, who wanted no reminders of tribal customs. From his command post at Carlisle, General Pratt was furious that the Indian commissioner and ethnologists had joined forces to present "an elaborate Indian show." To counteract the lingering impression of "the old Indian camp life," Pratt produced a Carlisle School display in the educational division of the Liberal Arts Building.[124] Visitors could then choose which American concept of Indians they preferred.

Like Pratt, Indian agents often elected to publicize their pupils' progress toward assimilation, and fairs provided likely arenas. In 1895, Agent Potter contacted

Vine or raffia basket, tinted with aniline, made by Mary George (ca. 1880) [d: 28 cm, h: 15.3 cm]. The Philbrook Museum of Art, Tulsa, Oklahoma.

Charles A. Collier, director of the Atlanta Cotton States Exposition, to offer the "4th Regiment Band of this State, composed of twenty full blood Cherokee Indian boys, pupils of this school" for one month of the Atlanta fair. Like Pratt, Potter wanted his students to attend fairs so "that they may see and learn a great deal." The possibility of raising funds for special projects at the same time was an added incentive. The students, he wrote, might "earn a little money to assist in purchasing new instruments." To encourage Collier's interest, Potter pointed out that the boys were "a great curiosity even in their own section" and "would be a greater curiosity in Atlanta." Whether Collier accepted the offer is not recorded. Potter reported later, however, that the boarding school girls were pleased to be able to contribute samples of their work "for the Atlanta Exposition."[125] And in the next generation, Collier's son John reshaped the fairs and affairs of all Native Americans when he became Indian commissioner.

The 1915 Panama Pacific Exposition in San Francisco continued the jingoistic spirit of the Columbian Exposition by commemorating the completion of the Panama Canal and the so-called winning of the West. Interested in seeing Native Americans represented at the celebration, Indian commissioner Cato Sells requested reservation agents to provide examples of items that had competed suc-

Rivercane storage basket with lug handles, dyed with walnut and bloodroot (ca. 1890–1905). The lid to this unusual basket was sent to the Marshall Field department store for sale in the Indian Department. [l: 46.5 cm, w: 29.2 cm, h: 25.4 cm]. Courtesy, The Field Museum, neg. no. A111987.3, Chicago.

cessfully with goods produced by whites. He specifically asked Cherokee agent Henderson to supply a "representative collection of Cherokee baskets" for the Indian exhibit at the fair.[126]

The eight baskets Henderson sent came from his wife's private collection. They included a grain storage basket, a clothes basket, and a general purpose basket made of cane, all so large they had to be shipped by freight rather than mail. He also sent a white oak fish basket and some smaller, general-purpose baskets, explaining that "Cherokees make all of their baskets for service." All the containers, he wrote, "were made by old Cherokee women," but he "was unable to get the names of the makers."[127] Such persistent neglect in recording the names of weavers must be counted as a loss to history as well as to the weavers' descendants.

While national and international expositions created specialized markets for traditional work among antiquarians and ethnologists, local fairs cultivated buyers who would be close at hand and interested in the latest fashions. The early twentieth century was an era of shows, exhibits, and midways that expanded every kind of basket market. Cherokees took advantage of opportunities to display their wares at regional, state, and county festivals—and, starting in 1914, at their own fair. The Office of Indian Affairs promoted Native American fairs as opportunities to educate Indians about American values central to assimilation programs. "I want these fairs so conducted," wrote Commissioner Sells in 1914, "as to open to the Indians the vision of the industrial achievement to which they should aspire." Sells directed agents to encourage Indian fairs and also to establish long-range goals for them. Each fair, he said, could serve as a "milestone fixing the stages of the Indian's progress" toward "self support and independence."[128]

When James Henderson came from the Carlisle school in 1913 to take his post at the Cherokee Agency, he quickly initiated discussion about an agricultural fair. The farm clubs in Big Cove and Bird Town agreed to organize the event. The fair committee selected a site on agency property near the Appalachian Railroad station. Henderson prodded the Cherokee Council, township farm clubs, and a few local merchants to donate exhibit prizes; and the fair committee set the dates for October 13–15. Although the federal Indian commissioner discouraged any form of entertainment, Henderson boldly ordered a merry-go-round from Waynesville.[129]

As the date approached, Henderson wrote local newspapers to publicize the attractions, claiming that "entries already made have exceeded our greatest expectations." Emphasizing the exhibits of "baskets, beadwork, and pottery," he reported that the Cherokee Fair had obtained "perhaps one of the finest collections of native Indian handicraft ever exhibited in the state." An impressive array of handwork came from other Native American tribes, but Henderson thought "the most gratifying feature" was the participation by Cherokees. "Many of the old non-English-speaking Indians," wrote the agent, "have brought in exhibits of their farm products and baskets."[130] Elderly weavers produced between fifty and sixty baskets for the first Cherokee Fair. Henderson was so impressed with their work that he included a photograph of the exhibit in his annual report to the commissioner.

In a room filled with samples of sewing, quilting, and pottery at the fair, weavers exhibited baskets of rivercane and white oak, including split and rib baskets. Large, jar-shaped cane singleweave baskets stood on top of each other, their surfaces covered with patterns in use for two centuries. Rib baskets hung from nails on posts and lined the table and window ledge, crowding white oak split baskets in various sizes, all with handles. A few weavers, like Charlotte Hornbuckle Chiltoskey, demonstrated basketry techniques as part of the exhibition.[131]

For this first fair, weavers made no plain, undecorated, or undyed baskets. They exhibited patterned, ornamented, and fanciful containers wholly different from the utilitarian containers in their homes. When Henderson claimed Cherokees

The basket display at the first Cherokee Fair, October 13–16, 1914.
Cherokee Indian School Annual Report, 1915, National Archives.

only made baskets for service ("and therefore they take less pains in making baskets"), he disregarded the evidence in his agency's front yard.[132] Some white oak
split baskets even boasted fanciful decorations called curls. Like vine basketry,
curls may have come to the reservation in the memories of students who attended
off-reservation boarding schools, for they are variations of a decoration used by
New England tribes.[133] They appeared on many baskets shown in *The Basket*,
George Wharton James's early-twentieth-century publication. By 1908, when
M. R. Harrington bought Margaret Saunooke's white oak handle basket dyed with
aniline and embellished with curls, the custom was widespread and well known,
though few Cherokee weavers had adopted it.

White oak handle basket with curls and crosses, dyed with red and green aniline. Purchased in 1908 from Margaret Saunooke, the basket anticipates by a half century the widespread use of decorated surfaces. [l: 17.8 cm, h: 14 cm]. Courtesy of the National Museum of the American Indian, Smithsonian Institution, no. 1/9186. Photograph by Pamela Dewey.

The first Cherokee Fair made an impression on nearly everyone who saw it. "I remember that the first Cherokee Indian fair was held on the Cherokee Agency Grounds in the fall of 1914," reminisced Frell Owl. He was on his way to Hampton that day, walking from his home on Rattlesnake Mountain to the train station. The strange structure that he saw near the agency was called an ice-cream stand. "I wondered what in the world 'ice cream' could be but the train was soon due and I had to go on."[134] Years later, Dinah Calhoun Welch gave credit for the initiation of the fair to the people of Big Cove, who "brought the resolution to have the 1914 fair at Cherokee to the Tribal Council." Her father, Morgan Calhoun, was a council member who "was proud of the people of his township for taking this important first step." It was a time of first and final steps. As the Big Cove and Bird Town farm clubs developed plans for the fair, Mooney returned home from his last season of Cherokee work with a basket purchased from Morgan Calhoun's mother, *Ayasta*.[135]

The fair was a great success. Displays of handwork, agricultural produce, and canned foods filled the chapel of the boarding school. Henderson thought "the agricultural exhibit was better than at the neighboring county fair."[136] While the farm exhibits may have surpassed those of neighboring whites and gratified the agent, it was the handwork of weavers that made the fair unique. Their names were never recorded, although it seems likely that women of Big Cove like Arizona Swayney Blankenship and *Ayasta* sent baskets, since the Big Cove Farm Club was a sponsor.

The following year, the fair was extended to four days, and Henderson invited Cherokees who had attended nonreservation boarding schools to participate in a special "Returned Students Day." Arizona Blankenship was one of the sixty-six former students who accepted the invitation. Henry Bradley, who had returned from Carlisle, led one of the singing groups that entertained the crowds.[137] His wife, Nancy George Bradley, may have taken advantage of the occasion to sell some of her rivercane baskets, for she had already begun to develop her reputation as a superb weaver.

The 1916 fair was "very much better in every respect" than previous ones. Henderson took several of the baskets displayed for the occasion to the state fair in Raleigh, where Jennie Fodderstack won first prize for her "reed basket" in a competition with weavers from all over the state.[138] Her work had been highly regarded for nearly a decade. Eight years earlier, she had attracted the attention of Harrington when she and her daughter arrived at the Cherokee Boarding School with rib baskets that they likely wanted to sell.[139]

In 1917, the North Carolina State Fair included honeysuckle baskets for the first time, along with baskets made of pine needles, willow, and "oak slips."[140] As a basket material, honeysuckle had officially arrived among whites as well as Cherokees about two decades after trailing and climbing its way into North Carolina's disrupted landscapes.

The participation of weavers in their own fair and those beyond the boundaries of the reservation expanded basket markets. By 1921, Henderson reported that "every available basket" was sold at the fair and "there was a riot when the selling began." Six years later, the Asheville *Sunday Citizen* claimed that "baskets by the thousands are made" for the fair, "but so far the supply has never met the demand."[141] The reporter certainly overstated the number of baskets but perhaps not their marketability. Older weavers recall that "in the old days" they sold all they could bring to the festivals. In a sense, October replaced November as *Nu Da Na Egwa*, the month of Great Trade. The days and nights before mid-October must have been busy for those who gathered and prepared materials, carved handles, checked dye pots, and wove baskets.

After fair season, patrons continued ordering baskets. Agent Henderson became a middleman, taking orders for baskets, purchasing them from local trade stores, mailing them to customers, and, on at least one occasion, supplying basketry

For the 1915 Cherokee Fair, forty-four former Carlisle students accepted
Superintendent Henderson's invitation to participate in "Returned Students Day."
The Red Man 8, no. 5 (Jan. 5, 1916).

materials to a weaver who could not get her own. Visitors gravitated to the agency
grounds, which occupied a large tract of land on the road leading from the train
station. Since the agent also served as school superintendent, he knew all the local
merchants as well as the weavers who frequented the grounds when they had baskets to sell. Men like Henderson were the most accessible and visible contact for
visitors and Cherokees. All inquiries about Cherokees and numerous orders for
their baskets came to the agent. "I am unable to address myself to anyone else,"
apologized one patron, "since I know nobody else in Cherokee."[142]

Following the first fair, requests came steadily and increased with every tourist
season. "Could you get one of the baskets like you were using as a waste basket in
your living room?" queried Lucretia Kinsey. And some time later she wrote again,
"I am going to ask you to buy 1 small hamper and 2 magazine baskets, one with a
good deal of green in it."[143] From all over the state and region, interested buyers
sent for hampers, magazine baskets, wastebaskets, wall pockets, plant holders, and

Jennie Fodderstack, or Jennie Brown, and her daughter with rib baskets to sell at the Cherokee Boarding School and Agency. Courtesy of the National Museum of the American Indian, Smithsonian Institution, no. 26825.

flower holders. They liked baskets with bright colors and often specifically requested green. The forms and functions of these baskets testify powerfully to the changes that took place in twentieth-century basketry. Buyers were interested in baskets for household decoration and interior spaces rather than for agricultural processes and the natural world. The light, airy, and delicate honeysuckle baskets perfectly accommodated such changes in basket use.

Changing markets influenced materials, colors, shapes, names, and functions. "I would like four of the porch vases," wrote Laura S. Walker in 1923, "at least I use the one I have for a porch vase. It has a handle on each side and looks like a vase." As more roads were built, automobiles became more common and "automobile lunch baskets" became popular. From her palatial home at the Biltmore Estates in Asheville, Mrs. George Vanderbilt came to the reservation and "purchased such a basket for her automobile."[144]

Weavers responded to and helped shape changes in basket markets, for they inevitably wove something of their personal tastes, preferences, and styles into their work. Whether in shape, size, color, material, or careful details of manufacture, baskets continued to express the individuality of each weaver. Henderson could not provide exact duplicates of baskets even to the most hopeful or consistent purchasers. He explained to Fred Olds that weavers believed "they should never make two things alike." For buyers who expected perfection, he responded that weavers would not even try to make a perfect basket because if they succeeded, "the Great Spirit would never allow them to make another."[145] Each basket was unique. It carried and conveyed the personal beliefs of the weaver. Whether as forms of resistance or expressions of autonomy, women interwove practicality and spirituality in every basket.

"Good Prices in the Market"

The number of weavers, buyers, and local traders increased in the second decade of the twentieth century, and each influenced the others. Baskets became a regular part of the inventory of most local stores, and merchants opened shops where weavers and buyers could get to them readily. D. K. (Kimsey) Collins's store on the lot near the corner of the Boarding School "kept a good assortment of baskets" most of the year. J. H. Tahquette's store was close to the train station, and Sampson Owl's was across the river. John Tatham's, W. H. Cooper's, and C. Y. Dunlap's Bird Town stores were near the railroad line and the road to Bryson City. Across from the train station in Whittier, R. J. Roan kept a supply of Cherokee baskets. Superintendents referred many buyers to the stores that "always carry a quantity of Indian baskets in stock."[146]

Over the years, as the markets expanded, an increasing number of women began making tourist baskets. In 1910 Agent Henderson had reported that weavers "occupied their leisure time" making pottery, beadwork, and baskets, but the "output of such articles is not large because the demand is rather limited." Apparently unaware of any irony, he claimed that "the principal new industry" was merchandising. At least eleven trade stores operated on the reservation that year, catering to and increasingly dependent upon tourism. The following year, Henderson had written that most native industries had disappeared, although "a few of them still weave baskets." Just seven years later, his reports acknowledged that "there is a great demand for these baskets in this locality at all times and more especially in the summer time."[147]

Between 1922 and 1923, Henderson made an industrial survey of the reservation that revealed the importance of basketry to family economy. At the home of Epps Welch, he found that Welch's "wife is an industrious woman and makes very good baskets which nets a handsome little income during the year." Similarly, Henderson stated that the wife of Nick Toineeta "had been using her spare time making baskets for sale."[148] The agent reported comparable activity at nearly every home. Elizabeth George and her daughter made baskets "which brings in quite a bit of revenue in the course of a year," and Tuskeegee Allen's wife "was making baskets of excellent design and workmanship." John Long's wife, Lowen Standingdeer's wife and mother, Kimsey Squirrel's wife, Will Allen's wife and daughter, and Adam Long's wife and daughter all made baskets that were "handsome" and "would command good prices in the market."[149]

When he surveyed Cheoah households, Henderson photographed Tom Kaloniskee with his wife and children sitting in a field with a basket of fruit. Whether in one-room log cabins or three-room frame houses "painted and well kept," women identified only as wife, daughter, old mother, or female relative impressed Henderson with their basketry. In 1926, he wrote to the Indian commissioner that "basket weaving has become an important industry among them, and there is evidence of a larger number making them all the time."[150]

By 1930, honeysuckle baskets were "in great demand by tourists as they are small and easily carried."[151] But for their own household containers, women and men continued to rely primarily on white oak. Rowena Bradley's mother, Nancy, usually made "a big old white oak basket, like in the summertime of the year, have a garden, she'd go down and gather onions and cabbage and beans, you know, potatoes. A big oak basket, that's what she'd put them in. And my dad usually carried one. He carried stove wood in it, you know."[152] Since cane had become the most difficult material to procure, rivercane basketry gradually became the specialty of a relatively small number of women. "My mother made baskets day in and day out, except on Sunday," recalls Bradley. "It wasn't many that made rivercane baskets, but I know she made them. She never quit making them until she got old and she couldn't see too good. And I don't think she'd been quit a year whenever she died."[153] Those who could get cane marketed their baskets at reservation trade stores, in surrounding white communities, and among collectors.

While weavers succeeded in winning prizes and expanding markets, however, they barely increased their earnings. In July and August of 1908, Harrington purchased seventy-one items for a total of $75. The twenty-one baskets he bought came from fifteen individuals. Cherokees received an average of less than a dollar per basket. For an old rivercane doubleweave with three intricate patterns, Harrington paid Ettie Hill twenty-five cents. Some baskets commanded as little as five or ten cents. The highest price Harrington paid for any basket was $1.25, for a rivercane trunk basket from John Long.[154] That intricate and difficult basketry techniques survived under such circumstances is a miracle.

Following the inception of the Cherokee Fair, with its notable basket exhibit, prices for small baskets remained nearly fixed. When Mrs. C. J. Thompson wrote to Agent Henderson wanting to buy baskets and pottery to sell at the North Carolina State Fair in 1916, she suggested forty cents or less as tolerable prices. Henderson replied that he could make "a nice collection available" for her price.[155] Three years later, Mr. A. Vermont was so delighted with the baskets he purchased at a reservation trade store that he asked for "an other dozen of them." They cost "about fifty cents each, including five cents postage." In 1923, two splint baskets "by one of our best basket makers" cost Henderson "50 cents each at John Tahquette's store." Baskets shaped like vases and boats cost less than a dollar, and the popular auto lunch baskets commanded only $1.25.[156]

Prices on larger baskets were hardly better. In the summer of 1916, Henderson billed Lucretia Kinsey $3.00 for a hamper and $1.50 for a magazine basket. The following year, the agent wrote a prospective buyer that a large hamper "would be worth about $3.50." Henderson may have thought the additional half-dollar excessive, for he added, "if this is too much, let me know." Even though the prices remained nearly static, Henderson claimed four years later that "baskets like everything else have advanced in price."[157] In the 1924 annual report, he estimated that over the course of the year, 100 Cherokees had made 5,000 baskets for $5,000, or an average of a dollar per basket.[158] Low prices ensured marketability. As long as there was a market, weavers continued their difficult and time-consuming work. There was almost no other way for them to make money.

Although vine baskets were exceptional in the nineteenth century, they became commonplace in the early twentieth. They appealed to buyers who were interested in handmade, inexpensive containers that ornamented their homes. Honeysuckle baskets were the first containers that Cherokees wove but did not use in their own households. They were the first baskets made for display rather than subsistence or ceremonial tasks and the first woven from a material that was not indigenous to local landscapes or even to the North American continent. They represent a turning point in basketry traditions—and culture itself. With the incorporation of honeysuckle, baskets that once represented women's sacred association with agriculture

In 1908, M. R. Harrington purchased this "ancient cane double basket" from Ettie Hill for twenty-five cents. [l: 47 cm, h: 22 cm]. Photograph by M. R. Harrington. Courtesy of the National Museum of the American Indian, Smithsonian Institution.

and generativity became most important as a market commodity. The tradition of weaving with honeysuckle grew out of an economic need, an altered landscape, and an effort to attract buyers with special interests and different attitudes toward baskets. The beautiful, light, and colorful honeysuckle baskets express the complexities and contradictions of Cherokee life in the early twentieth century.

In succeeding years, the pace of change accelerated. The cruel and arrogant policy of assimilation came to an end after a half century of the repression of speech and division of families. The lumber companies retreated, leaving scarred landscapes, empty camps, and jobless men behind. After Carlisle closed and the government stopped subsidizing Native Americans at Hampton, the experiment in education ended. Thereafter, few students left the reservation to attend boarding schools, and outings ceased. It became increasingly evident that the day of the Indian was not spent after all. The Arts and Crafts movement intensified, and Indian reformers of a different sort assumed positions of power. In 1934, the first year that Lucy Nola George won a prize at the Cherokee Fair for a honeysuckle basket, the federal government and John Collier undertook a New Deal for Native Americans.

CHAPTER **4**

Red Maple

"Blooming Red All Over"

One spring day in the 1940s, Betty Long Lossiah (b. 1903) set out from her Paint-town home to find white oak saplings for a basket. The task was not easy. Good basket oak had become increasingly scarce as Cherokees cleared land for timber and housing, roads, or commerce. The expanding population depleted forest re-sources, which were "the main source of wealth" for individuals and the Eastern Band.[1] The removal of each white oak to make a few dollars, or a clearing for a home, road, or government right-of-way eliminated one particular tree and all those it might have produced. As removal exceeded regeneration, oak weavers joined cane weavers in a continuing struggle to find good material.

Diminishing white oak affected weavers in every part of the reservation. When Bessie Catolster Long (b. 1917) grew up in Wolftown, she readily got white oak "just around on our property up there." But the once abundant material began to dwindle. "Now, everything's gone," Long commented. "You have to go way up high in the mountains." Similarly, Emma Squirrel Taylor remembered "a long time ago, when I was coming up" in Birdtown, "people just went into the woods and cut a tree down." Those days were long gone. By the late twentieth century, white oak comprised less than 10 percent of reservation forests and could seldom be found near homes. "There aren't many white oaks around here to be cut down," said Taylor. "They go way up in the mountains now to get it."[2]

As weavers found it increasingly difficult to find white oak near their own home-sites, they began cutting from stands in different communities. "A while back," re-called Emma Taylor, "they was going to close that down, pass a law about going on other people's land." Everyone searched for white oak for housing, furniture, fire-wood, timber sales, or basketry, and "so they cut that out." Restrictions on cutting wood from "other people's land" led many weavers to depend on suppliers, men who could find and cut white oak to sell for "fifteen and twenty dollars a bundle."[3]

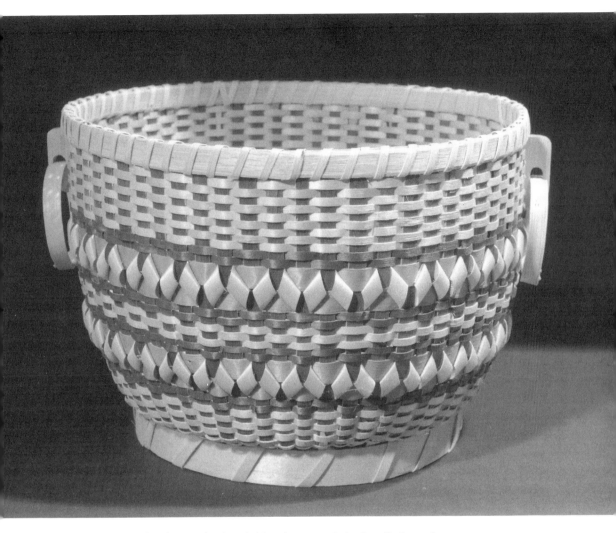

Red maple planter, dyed with bloodroot, made by Lucille Lossiah
(1989) [d: 24 cm, h: 19 cm]. Private collection.
Photograph by William F. Hull.

Buying and selling basket material mark important changes in concepts and economies. A weaver's autonomy, once inextricably bound to her familiarity with surrounding landscapes and her ability to find good materials, diminished as she depended on outside sources. At the same time, the emergence of local markets for white oak and cane enabled older weavers to continue producing baskets even after they no longer could procure their own materials.

Betty Lossiah, who was born on Jenkins Creek in Wolftown, had been making baskets most of her life when the scarcity of white oak became serious. The difficulty of acquiring material permeates her memory of that spring day when she "couldn't find no white oak." Discouraged, she "just sat down and gave up." Her predicament seemed permanent, her memory of it like a refrain. "I can't find no white oak to make baskets." Sitting on a bank "by my husband's mama's house," Lossiah noticed the stand of trees in front of her, a "big bunch of maple about this size, all the straight ones." The straight and slender saplings were "blooming red all over." Lossiah "got up and cut that split" and carried them home. "I make the basket up and then everybody learn," she laughs.[4] Cherokee weavers slowly began a new tradition based on red maple (*Acer rubrum*), a material that had long been part of their landscapes.

There are 125 species of maple in the United States. Thirteen of them, including red maple, are indigenous to this country. One of the great trees of eastern North America, red maple can attain a height of 120 feet. It may grow as much as a foot in the first year, then about two feet a year for seventy to eighty years. Radial growth starts relatively late each season but then proceeds very rapidly. Red maples can begin producing seeds at the age of four, continuing until they die at an average age of 150 years.[5]

In the early spring, the tree produces boldly conspicuous clusters of red flowers. Bright yellow stamens contrast strongly with red petals on male trees, while female trees flower with intense red blooms succeeded by bright red fruits. Female flowers are no more than an eighth of an inch long and hang in clusters, where they cast a red glow on budding leaves. The slightly larger yellow and red male flowers are three-quarters of an inch long. After the flowers are spent in late spring, the fruit appears as inch-long red, nearly translucent keys that look like wings. Each key contains seeds. A healthy maple may produce as many as 91,000 seeds a year, dispersing them in a one- or two-week period between April and July. A high percentage of seeds germinates almost immediately, but those that remain can germinate later with enhanced sources of light. Following any kind of clearing, for example, residual seeds will begin to sprout.[6] During the spring and summer, the leaves grow to two to four inches long, and in the autumn, well ahead of other trees, they turn a brilliant red. In two seasons of the year, as Betty Lossiah observed, the tree appears to be "blooming dark red."

Tolerant of shade and a prolific sprouter, red maple is one of the most abundant and widespread trees of eastern North America. It thrives in mixed hardwood forests and flourishes in wet or moist soils of stream banks, in valleys, swamps, and uplands, and also on dry ridges up to an elevation of 6,000 feet. Growing fast, it pioneers disturbed, burned, or cutover areas, and abandoned fields, barren ridges, and forests. Red maple is a dominant species in hemlock forests of the higher elevations as well as in the oak-pine forests that occur in lower elevations.[7] Although it is susceptible to defects caused by fire injury, red maple sprouts vigorously from stumps after a fire or cut. Too light and soft for furniture and housing, it generally did not appeal to the lumber industry. And by the end of the twentieth century, Cherokee foresters considered it undesirable on reservation lands, a "disturbance-type species."[8] But in the 1940s, its wide distribution and prolific growing habit made red maple an abundant resource for weavers who could no longer find white oak.

As white oak became hard to find, some weavers turned to red maple to develop a kind of basketry that differs in important ways from previous traditions. Light, delicate, and fragile, maple baskets signify continuing changes in life and work. They represent ecological changes that took place as land clearing accelerated. The airy containers signal the disappearance of utilitarian baskets among women, the end of an economy based on barter, and an increasing influence of the cash market on traditions. Maple basketry also signifies the development of tourism as a primary industry, the beginning of the marketing of Cherokee heritage and customs, and the transformation of the oldest surviving mother-to-daughter tradition into a commodity.

Maple baskets appeal to buyers because they tend to be brightly colored and unusually rich in ornamental detail. Weavers, still preferring shades of red, yellow, brown, and black, discovered that on maple splits the colors shine with greater brightness and boldness. Maple has a natural sheen that is almost luminous, a radiance that derives from the quality of the material. The peeled, undyed splits look like satin and are smooth, almost slippery, to the touch. When they are dyed, splits become even more lustrous. The colors that are soft and subdued in rivercane, white oak, and honeysuckle baskets become glossy and polished in maple. The completed maple basket looks as though it is made of bands of satin. "Maple makes a pretty basket—shiny and white," one weaver claims, "and when you color them maples, they look like ribbons."[9] In maple basketry, weavers simultaneously embrace traditional colors made from vegetable dyes and the vibrant hues of commercial dyes.

With the development of maple basketry, weavers began to innovate with designs. The basic checkerwork weave on a maple basket makes a linear design of dark and light blocks. Maple weavers often embellish the surfaces of baskets by adding an overlay of curls or crosses that breaks up the linear design. The overlays fragment the surface with broken angles, and as they twist in and out, they create an illusion of movement across the flat, smooth face of the basket.

Although the application of curls on Native American baskets is at least a century old, Cherokee weavers did not fully incorporate the practice until they began

Red maple planter, dyed with walnut and bloodroot, made by Helen Bradley Smith
(1995) [l: 21.5 cm, w: 21.5 cm, h: 17.5 cm]. Private collection.
Photograph by William F. Hull.

making maple baskets in the middle of the twentieth century.[10] Betty Lossiah does
not recall how or why, but she believes she was "the first one to make cross on the
basket" and also "the first one to make curls." Her contribution is confirmed by
others. "It was Betty Lossiah" who started adding curls to baskets, according to
Martha Ross. "She's the one that started those."[11]

When weavers began to create patterns by superimposing elements onto the
baskets, they literally and figuratively broke apart conventional ones, demonstrating a completely different conceptualization of basketry. Whereas patterns once

White oak basket with curls, dyed with walnut and bloodroot, made by Dinah George (1990) [d: 21 cm, h: 12 cm]. Private collection. Photograph by William F. Hull.

Decorative curlicues on a honeysuckle basket made by Lucy Nola George. Qualla Arts and Crafts Cooperative. Photograph by Ron Ruehl.

had been woven into cane baskets and deeply embedded in memory as associated with family, clan, or village, they became fanciful decorations attached to the surface in maple baskets. In rivercane basketry, patterns appeared as a continuous field of design woven into the container. In maple basketry, elaborate patterns are applied to the basket exterior.

After Lossiah's introduction of overlays on maple baskets, white oak weavers fully incorporated them into their techniques. The new technique of decorating the surface appealed to honeysuckle weavers as well, and they also began to add rows of decorative curlicues to basket surfaces. "Everybody's working like that now," laughs Betty Lossiah.[12] Whereas at one time, innovations and patterns remained within the province of the family that created them, twentieth-century weaving techniques quickly became common property.

Along with curls and crosses, weavers began using other decorative elements. The addition of rings began in the 1950s when white trader William H. Duncan asked Dinah George to copy a basket. "A lot of Indians sold to Mr. Duncan, Mr. Duncan down at Cherokee," George recalled. One day, "they showed me a basket, and it was round. And it had little old ears on it, little old round rings."[13] George carved narrow, thin loops to add to the sides of her baskets like modified handles. Derived from a feature that was once highly functional, stable, and fixed, rings became subtle reminders of the time when handles were essential parts of work baskets. They document changing functions as baskets moved from utilitarian and serviceable containers to ornamented and decorative objects.

When a technique or design increases marketability, weavers know that "people are going to pick it up."[14] Buyers often ask weavers to copy whole baskets or certain patterns, colors, and attributes of baskets. Dinah George's rings became popular, just as Betty Lossiah's crosses and curls did. The ornamentation increased baskets' marketability, and became a part of the long process of converting baskets to market commodities.

To many weavers, the light, colorful, and ornate maple containers contravene essential concepts about basketry, which have to do with strength and permanence. "Maple baskets are pretty," acknowledges Shirley Taylor, "but they don't hold up as good. They're not as sturdy." When Myrtle Jenkins compares maple with other kinds of baskets, she says that "while they're not near so durable, they are pretty."[15] The fragility of maple baskets derives from the nature of the material. The rapid radial growth of the red maple produces such close-grained wood that the splits are extremely thin and brittle. Working with them requires care and caution because they break easily during every stage of the process—the preparation, dying, and weaving. The finished product is also fragile. Many weavers won't work with maple because the splits are so breakable. But they readily acknowledge the

Ornamental rings on a red maple planter made by Lucille Lossiah (1989).
Private collection. Photograph by William F. Hull.

skills of those who can manage the fragile material. "Maple splits are weak," one points out. "They're not as tough as white oak." Some refuse even to add maple curls because they can easily be broken off the basket surface. The lack of durability seems to strike deeply the sensibilities of weavers who shun maple and curls. It makes no sense to them to make baskets that will not last.

The primary purpose of maple baskets is to appeal to the eye. "Well, the ones that make them [use them] just for displays," explains a weaver. "I guess they don't really use them."[16] Although weavers recognize the demands of the market, many do not consider display to be a viable function. The new tradition in maple moved baskets from the world of women's labor and ceremony to a place of ornamentation in household interiors of a consumer culture.

"A Woman Never Got to Stop": Cherokee Life in the 1930s

The tradition of maple basketry grew out of, expressed, and accompanied changes in every part of reservation life. In 1930, the Cherokee population of 3,194 lived in six townships and several separate settlements. The five Qualla townships—Yellow Hill, Birdtown, Painttown, Wolftown, and Big Cove—lay on contiguous lands comprising about 43,000 acres on the Oconaluftee River and its tributaries. Fifty miles west, the Snowbird community consisted of more than 2,000 acres in 23 land parcels in the mountains of Graham County. Adjacent to Graham County, the reservation included more than 5,000 acres scattered among 29 small land parcels in Cherokee County on Grape, Hanging Dog, Vengeance, Graybeard, Hyatt, Colvard, and Will Scott Creeks.

The nearly 4,000-acre township of Yellow Hill, called Cherokee, was the heart of the reservation, the location of the council house, agency headquarters, and the fifty-year-old Cherokee Boarding School. The thirty-eight buildings comprising the school spread across ten acres on the southeast side of the Oconaluftee. One building was a twenty-two-bed hospital, which the 1934 agent considered "quite inadequate in every way." The agency's "fine frame buildings" were maintained by the government and were the only buildings on the reservation with electric lights. Nearly 400 students were enrolled in the nine grades of the boarding school.[17]

The government complex was a focal point for Cherokees and whites, residents and visitors. Next to the council house, Emma Taylor remembers, "there was just rocks" where Cherokees gathered to visit. "The people would just sit there, take in the sun, and enjoy themselves all through the sun, and so they called it the buzzard roost." On Saturdays, men drove wagons, rode horseback, or walked into town to share news and swap stories. "These men would gather at Cherokee,"

Dinah George recalls. "They'd sit down there and talk, . . . these men would talk. They'd buy apples to eat, sit there peeling apples and talking."[18]

The agency and school grounds provided another kind of gathering place for whites and Cherokees. The state improved the road to the agency in 1929, making it possible "for thousands of tourists to visit the reservation." They came each fall for the Cherokee Fair. During the remainder of the year, according to one enthusiastic agent, there were "hundreds of tourists from practically every state in the union driving over our campus every day."[19] The proposed development of a national park in the Great Smoky Mountains drew attention to the reservation and promised an influx of tourists that excited every agent. Tourism meant jobs, roads, and commerce—and changing the face of the reservation and the lives of the Cherokees.

About an eighth of a mile from the agency and school, a second cluster of buildings included "three fairly large stores, a small store, a ware house, a small dilapidated station," and two Cherokee homes. Chief John Tahquette owned the larger store, which also housed the Cherokee post office.[20] Weavers traded baskets at Tahquette's for groceries and other necessities. "There was one little store, one store in Cherokee that sold groceries. That's where she'd take them and trade them for groceries," Rowena Bradley recalls her childhood, remembering the connection between baskets and food, her mother's work and something to eat. "It was a man by the name of John Tahquette. He had a store in Cherokee." Carrying baskets to trade, Nancy Bradley walked from Painttown to Tahquette's store on Soco Creek. Like other weavers, she could only trade as many as she could carry and could only bargain for what she was able to walk back home with.[21]

The "small dilapidated station" was the Cherokee stop for the Appalachian Railroad. The train ran from Ela to Birdtown and Yellow Hill, then followed the Oconaluftee for about ten miles to the lumber villages of Ravensford and Smokemont. In 1928, the two lumber mills closed "on account of the proposed establishment of the Great Smoky Mountains National Park." Cherokees who had worked as loggers or contractors, truck drivers or rail layers, washwomen or cooks, were thrown back to subsistence farming. The end of commercial logging on the reservation meant that Cherokees had "no place near home where they can go to earn a dollar."[22] No other industry existed. As the mills closed and jobs vanished, basket-weavers felt a greater need to help provide for their families. Meanwhile, scarred landscapes began to sprout new vegetation. Red maple began to proliferate in abandoned clearings.

Across the Oconaluftee from Tahquette's, a third cluster of buildings included a store owned by a white man named Mac Jenkins, a "craft and curio store" run by former chief Sampson Owl, a "lunch stand," and the homes of two white families.[23]

Nancy George Bradley, rivercane weaver from Painttown, with baskets
to sell or trade (early 1940s). Courtesy of the National Museum
of the American Indian, Smithsonian Institution, no. 38043.

A swinging bridge spanned the river. On the north side of the Oconaluftee stood the ancient *Nununyi* mound excavated in 1883 by the Valentine brothers.

In 1930, whites came again to explore the mound. Anticipating the establishment on the reservation of a Great Smoky Mountains National Park museum, historians gathered fragments of the past from the base of the mound. Collecting curios stopped in 1935 when it became obvious that the park museum would not be built on the reservation after all and Cherokees balked at turning over materials to a museum beyond their access and control. "The Cherokee Indians have lost much of the ancient artifacts they use to have," reported Superintendent Harold Foght, "and would resent very much giving the little that is left to be removed entirely from the reservation, and for this I cannot blame them."[24]

Beyond the Yellow Hill stores and government buildings, houses were clustered along streams and creeks feeding into Oconaluftee tributaries. Perched on the steep slopes of high and rugged hills, these log homes had greater access to one another than to the commercial buildings in the heart of the township. The shape of the land in Yellow Hill determined much of the business and social life of the residents. On one side of the Oconaluftee, Spray Ridge rises 2,600 feet, and across the river Mt. Noble soars steeply to 3,600 feet. Other than the river valley, little bottomland exists in Yellow Hill. Those who lived along the river fared better than those on steep slopes, where farming was both more difficult and limited.

The remaining Qualla townships were self-contained social and cultural units with their own labor groups (*gadugi*) and often their own ball teams.[25] Approximately three miles southwest of the agency and school, Birdtown spread across bottomlands on both sides of the Oconaluftee and its tributaries, including Nick Bottom, and Cooper, Goose, and Adams Creeks. With more gently rolling terrain than many parts of the reservation, the nearly 3,000 Birdtown acres included some of the better farmland, and, accordingly, a higher population of whites.[26]

The Birdtown mound stood in mute testimony to the antiquity of the settlement, the destructive forces of war, and the restless curiosity of whites. The village associated with the mound had been leveled by Colonel William Moore in 1776, at the same time he destroyed the town of *Nununyi*. In 1882–83, the Valentine brothers nearly obliterated the Birdtown mound in their search for antiquities for their own museum.[27]

Between the Birdtown mound and the Oconaluftee, the state built Highway 107. By 1930 it was a "well developed road" five miles long that led from Ela through Birdtown to the agency at Yellow Hill. The road passed the Birdtown Day School, one of the original schools established by Quakers in the 1880s. Like the other day schools, Birdtown Day School closed intermittently because of the difficulty of keeping teachers and pupils. In 1930, the two-room school of four grades was open, with an average daily attendance of thirty-five students.[28]

Fires, lumbering, and disease had decimated Birdtown forests, and the 1932 agent pronounced the remnant timberlands "unproductive and unsightly." The "danger of overcutting," he reported, "is very clearly demonstrated" in Birdtown.[29] Common timber included chestnut, oak, poplar, and pine, but much had been removed, killed, or injured. Each spring, Cherokees and whites "set the mountain on fire and let it burn" to improve pasturage for cattle.[30] Throughout the year, the Appalachian Railroad trains showered sparks on brush piles, causing them to burst into flame. Summer droughts of 1925–26 weakened hardwoods that gradually died over the next three years but remained standing like scarecrows until they were blown over or burned down.[31] In the scarred forests of Birdtown, Japanese honeysuckle and red maple found abundant opportunities to stake their claims.

By the early 1930s, the chestnut blight was spreading through all the forests of the reservation, virtually eliminating a dominant species of the Southern Appalachians. Discovered in New York in 1904 on Asian chestnut trees that had been introduced several years earlier, the blight was caused by *Endothia parasitica*, a fungus that had spread past control by the time it was identified. Lethal spores traveled on breezes or were transported by birds, insects, and animals. Germinating in wounded bark, the fungus girdled tree trunks and produced more spores that drifted into nearby forests. Trees died slowly, over a period of two to ten years. In the openings created by disappearing chestnut canopies, greater proportions of red maple seedlings survived to form dense stands of saplings.[32]

In 1932, Superintendent Stanion reported that "something like a blight" had already "ruined a great deal" of chestnut. Cherokees believed that trees were dying because the government prohibited their custom of firing woods in the fall to clear brush and facilitate gathering. Once common above 2,000 feet, a source of food for humans and animals, and perhaps the most marketable Cherokee timber, chestnut all but disappeared from their landscapes by the end of the 1930s. Families who once spent evenings telling stories while "sitting around the fireplace hulling chestnuts" lost more than a source of food to the blight.[33]

When the mills closed and farming again became the primary means of subsistence, individuals continued to sell dead chestnut trees for the manufacture of telephone poles or to make tannin in the numerous "tanning plants in this section." The superintendent discouraged the "wholesale indiscriminate taking out of forest products," particularly as prices dropped in the early thirties. He preferred that Cherokees "depend more on their farm products and lessen the sale of forest products for a living."[34] Family farms and gardens color the memories of many who grew up in the thirties. "All the people raised corn back then," Emma Taylor recalls of her Birdtown childhood. Farming shaped different landscapes from those of modern times where "you don't see hardly any cornfields." Virtually everyone maintained a garden, enclosing it with pickets to protect their crops from roving cattle and hogs. In 1930, bean crops were "cut off by the ravages of a pest commonly known as the bean beetle," so farmers substituted cabbage and potatoes in gardens and fields.[35]

Farming and gardening created a special need for women's basketry and a ready market for their wares. With an eye toward the commonplace "big patches of corn," Lydia Ann Thompson Squirrel "made market baskets, [baskets] for work—pick corn, potatoes, anything." Like other weavers, Squirrel sold baskets mostly "to white people, that was our living." Her daughter Emma sold the first basket she made to a white woman from Ela. The memorable sale occurred in 1927, when Squirrel was seven years old. "She wanted willow baskets about this high," she gestures, "and round and big as a pie. And I wondered how I was going to do it." The memory concludes with satisfaction. "She bought the basket."[36]

While Squirrel and her daughter worked on Cooper Creek to make baskets for white farmers and gardeners, Lucy Nola George pulled honeysuckle from the banks of the Oconaluftee behind her home to weave fancy vine baskets for white conventioneers in neighboring Bryson City. No weaver had far to look for customers. Whites always lived among Cherokees, and both white and Cherokee retailers stocked baskets in Birdtown stores they opened near the railroad or highway.[37]

East of Yellow Hill, Painttown covered nearly 3,000 acres in Soco valley. Along Swimmer Branch and Soco, Bigwitch, and Wright's Creeks, Cherokees lived in log houses that usually consisted of one or two rooms. In many homes, the interiors and exteriors were sealed with clapboard, and newspapers and magazines papered the walls.[38] While a few families owned cook stoves, most continued to rely on the fireplace for heat and light. "We had a fireplace, you know, cooked on the fireplace" and "had our eating table in the corner." Bean, chestnut, and sweet potato bread, "all of that, we call it the Indian cooking," was common fare.[39] Although sacks of flour could be purchased at stores, corn pounders and mortars were still found outside many homes.

One family of six children living in Painttown "had two beds and mama had made a mattress, she put it down on the floor, somebody'd sleep on the floor, and that's the way we was raised." Mattresses were stuffed with "pressed straw from these people that raised wheat," and beds were spread with "a big old tick" filled with feathers plucked from ducks or chickens who roosted in trees and nested under cabin floors. "The sheet we would have was probably made from flour sacks" and used as often to carry babies as to cover beds.[40]

In 1930, springs and creeks provided water for most households. On Wright's Creek the Coopers "had a big old garden," and a "big bold spring" ran "right through the middle of the garden." Stacy Cooper kept mutton and other foods fresh by storing them in jugs in the spring. Myrtle Cooper Jenkins (b. 1902) remembers her mother "putting up canned tomatoes" in syrup buckets with lids. "She took a wax cloth, a cloth that was dipped in bees wax," pressed the cloth down, "and she sealed them tomatoes with it." Thirsty children picked sassafras sticks from riverside trees to make tea, and most families bought "big old what we called towsack bags" of green coffee beans, roasted the beans in ovens in the fire, and ground them for coffee made from spring water.[41]

Wash day occupied the time and energy of mothers and daughters. To clean clothes, women set up cast-iron wash pots on rocks beside the running water. On Mink Branch "up in the holler," Lula Owl's mother built a fire under the pot and created a lifetime of memories for her daughter: "I see mother's big old wash pot, where she washed, built a fire, how she used to boil the clothes," Owl recalled. In Nancy Bradley's household on Swimmer Branch, Reva (b. 1918) took charge of washing when she was ten years old, using a five-cent bar of Octagon soap on the clothes. "I'd put that bar of soap and put them on the rub board and rubbed them. Then we boiled them." A second and perhaps a third pot was used for rinse water before women and their daughters from Bigwitch Creek to Stillwell Branch hung their clothes to dry on lines or "on the garden fence made from chicken wire."[42]

There was always plenty to do in a day. On Swimmer Branch, Aggie Wilnoty George gave her children their choice of household chores. "If she was in the field," Dinah George recalls, "she'd say, 'what you'uns want to do, you'uns want to cook or take the field?'" George (b. 1922) laughs as she remembers that "I'd take cooking." Girls shared the work of their mothers even when they were very young. "She expected us to clean the house and cook," one recalls, "and do the washing, you know."[43] Girls often also took charge of their younger siblings.

As in Birdtown, fields surrounded every Painttown house. "Big fields," according to George, "like you see today where all these trees are growing up, all this place here was nothing but a corn field."[44] Every flat of land in Painttown must have held a field or garden, and women are nearly always credited with raising the garden truck. It included "cucumbers, tomatoes, cabbage, onions, beans, peas, radishes, and lettuce," remembers one woman; another says her mother "made the big garden, there were six of us, she had to raise six kids."[45]

Children in Painttown and Wolftown attended the Soco Day School when it was open, walking from their homes in the hills, hollows, and coves to the one-teacher, two-room building on the north side of Soco Creek. The day school regimen differed from the boarding school program. At day school they "didn't have meal cooking, they didn't have laundry, and stuff like they did at the boarding school." In 1932, Soco Day School closed again, and Painttown children returned to the Cherokee Boarding School.[46]

With children to rear, gardens to tend, households to manage, and food to prepare, many Painttown women somehow still found time to weave baskets. "Well, my mother made white oak baskets, she made honeysuckle baskets, you know, at times she couldn't get cane and she'd make honeysuckle and white oak baskets." Nancy George Bradley's basketry winds in and out of her daughter's memories. For gardens or markets, for carrying or sifting or winnowing or gathering, for work or exchange, her mother wove baskets of whatever material was available. "Then she did a direct trade. She wouldn't sell them for money."[47]

Like Rowena Bradley, Dinah George remembers her mother's baskets made for household work as well as those for trade or sale. "She made three kinds of baskets, rivercane, white oak, and then she'd make a rib basket. . . . Oh, mom could make a doubleweave, too." When Aggie George finished a load of baskets, she and her husband would "tie them together, put them on, and take off."[48] They went to trade at Duncan's or Tahquette's in Yellow Hill, and "sometimes they'd take them over to what they call Shoal Creek, over in there" to white communities. In the fall, the Cherokee Fair provided a brief but good market for baskets. "If you made a lot of them," Dinah George recalls, "you could sell all of them."[49]

Next to Painttown, Wolftown spread over a mountainous area descending from Soco Gap, whose elevation surpasses 4,300 feet. The more than 16,000 acres of Wolftown lay on Soco, Washington, Pheasant, Jenkins, Shut-In, Wright's, Black Rock, and Bigwitch Creeks, and on Pipe and Laurel Branches. More creeks coursed through Wolftown than through any other township, supplying water for drinking, bathing, cleaning, and cooking. On Wright's Creek in Painttown and Wolftown, children fished with cane poles or seined with tow sacks to catch "whatever, crawfish, all kinds of fish, mumble heads, knotty heads, and sometimes we'd scoop up some of them native trout fish."[50] In nearly every household, children helped find and bring in greens or berries, fish or roots.

The changing forests and forest edges continued to supply Cherokees with foods, dyes, and medicines. Beginning in late January and continuing until fall, women gathered wild greens. Ramps came from "so far in the woods, uh huh, up the hill and sometimes you have to go down the hill and come back with a load of ramps."

From their log cabin on Long Branch, Dora Bigmeat's mother "used to take a big sack" to carry home the foods. "She used to take that and she wore apron, and big apron, and then she used to go pick some sweet weeds . . . and jellico." Sarah George went "way in the woods" collecting wild plants in her apron, "and then when it gets too heavy for her, then she'll put it in a sack . . . and then she'd go pick some more." Bigmeat (b. 1912) does not romanticize the labor of her mother, who scoured the woods for food for her family. "Yes, she had a hard time, I think. Uh huh, yeah."[51]

Like many families, Bigmeat's parents sold wood they cut, and women shared the burden of the exhausting work. "My mother, she'd be out in the woods getting some . . . pole, they call it pole. . . . And then, we'd go up there with a team of horses and snake them down, down the level place. . . . And then we used the hand-saw." Dora and her mother cut the timber into five-foot lengths, "then we'd bust them in half." While the women worked in the woods, Dora's father would be working "in the fields for some people" as a laborer, "just to here and there, just whoever hired him."[52]

When Superintendent Page tried to discourage Cherokees from "getting out and selling forest products for a living" it must have seemed a nearly hopeless task. Money was scarce and jobs rare, and everyone could make a few dollars selling wood or wood products. Independent wood contractors still operated, and sixty miles away, Canton's Champion Fiber, the "largest paper mill in the United States," provided "an excellent market for pulp wood, such as pine and poplar."[53] The Business Committee of the Cherokee Council met monthly to issue permits for Cherokees to sell wood even from their own landholdings. As a member of the committee, the superintendent attempted to persuade "the Indians" to "cut and sell chestnut and refrain from cutting other species that have future values." In 1933, he reported "unusual conditions of helplessness and poverty" among Cherokees, which led to greater exploitation of the woodlands.[54]

In 1929, to encourage agriculture, the council allocated $5,000 a year for five years to help families buy seed, equipment, and livestock, and the federal farm agent offered "proper instruction and proper leadership in this industry." The superintendent believed Cherokees were "much better off" when they depended entirely on agriculture rather than selling wood products. Since "farming is about the only feasible means of making a living," he reported, "it is very important that their attention be turned to this industry." Hogs, milk cows, and steers were included in the new agricultural initiative.[55]

Since women began to vote for the first time in the 1930 tribal elections, they exercised direct influence on the council and the expenditure of tribal funds for agriculture.[56] They may have considered the money well spent since agriculture was a way of life they knew well. Older women, however, must also have remembered that even before lumber jobs had come and gone, crops and gardens did not provide enough margin for them to rest easy. Their mothers, and theirs before them, had walked too many trails with baskets to trade for what they lacked. The best of times in western North Carolina was often not good enough. "We didn't have no jobs, nothing," remembers the son of a weaver. "All they had to do was make the baskets, go up the mountain. Menfolks would go get the bark and sell it. That's just about all." As the memories come, they take on a joyless rhythm. "Women make baskets, sell it, they need something to eat, go down to the store, take another basket, sell it for groceries."[57] A weaver's sense of comfort that her family could get something to eat when she made a basket must have been offset by an acute awareness of what happened when she made no baskets.

Women took baskets of cane, white oak, or honeysuckle and "sold them to the white people for meat and things they wanted to get." The train was a help to some, extending their markets to more distant customers. "Sometimes we would catch a train," remembers Dora Bigmeat, "and go over to Waynesville to sell baskets."[58] Cash seldom entered into the system, and weavers' children remember that "they weren't no cash to be paid." The names of whites whose homes they frequented have vanished. "We used to carry to, to white people's, and carry to houses and sell them for anything." Better remembered are the names of local store owners like Sampson Owl, who "was buying baskets, not all the time, just sometimes," or John Tahquette, who owned "the grocery store."[59] White traders like Duncan and Jenkins, long established at Yellow Hill, remain familiar figures to weavers' children.

Women sometimes traded baskets for coats or shoes, but most stores in Yellow Hill "didn't sell no dresses or ready-made blouses, something like that. . . . They just had material." Few women retained the spinning wheels their mothers once used to make wool into yarn for stockings or sweaters or gloves, but in the early 1930s, mothers continued to assume the responsibility of making the family clothing. "Mama used to as long as she was living," Bessie Long remembers from her childhood, "and then we had to do it ourselves whenever she died." A growing girl might require two school dresses a year and one extra for Sunday, made either from trade store material or from durable and familiar flour sacks. Aggie George used bags from Nation's Best Flour "to make our underclothes . . . and made baby diapers out of them, and made sheets out of them."[60] Little was wasted when there was little to spare.

In the early 1930s, women's work in the township of Big Cove mirrored the patterns and rhythms of that in Wolftown, Painttown, Yellow Hill, and Birdtown. Big Cove was comprised of more than 13,000 acres that stretched up into the ribs of the Balsam Mountains. Homes in the Cove clustered along Raven's and Straight Forks, and Toe String, Mingo, Pigeon, Bunches, Tooni, Indian, Stilwell, and Galimore Creeks.

A "pretty fair mountain road" led from the agency and boarding school alongside the Oconaluftee to the one-teacher, three-grade day school at Big Cove, one of the original Quaker schools.[61] Like the Soco and Birdtown day schools, the school at Big Cove closed sporadically, and children moved from the boarding school to the day school and back again. Except for those who lived nearby, the distance and terrain discouraged many young Cherokees from attending school. "I didn't go every day," one acknowledges a half century later. "I'd go two days or three days a week. It's too far to walk. Three miles to walk. Every morning." Others shake their heads with the memories of long distances and early mornings, rough trails and rainy weather when "the walk was too much for me."[62]

When the Smokemont and Ravensford mills operated, children occasionally caught rides on the logging train, but most felt that "you're not going to catch a train, they don't run but certain times." Even though the Appalachian Railroad Company had agreed to operate a common carrier, the 1933 superintendent complained that the company had "steadily and continuously violated the terms of their deed" regarding passenger service.[63] Catching a ride to the Big Cove Day School was simply not possible. Children and adults more often used the railway and right-of-way clearings as shortcuts into town. Some were killed by trains on the tracks, and others were frightened by men getting off the train and offering money "if you will go a little way down the road with me."[64] When the lumber mills closed, the trains stopped running past Ravensford.

The Big Cove Day School accommodated thirty pupils, but when Arizona Swayney Blankenship temporarily replaced John Edmonds as teacher in the fall of 1929, the average daily attendance was fifteen, with five girls and ten boys. Following government regulations, teachers served the children a midday meal, usually potatoes and beans. The schoolhouse included a second room for the teacher's housing, and Blankenship cooked with equipment supplied by the Bureau of Indian Affairs for the teacher's quarters.[65] When an unmarried man taught the day school, he hired a young girl to cook and clean. If a married man served as teacher, his wife prepared the students' midday meal.

A lack of roads isolated Big Cove during winter months, or any time the creeks and rivers rose after heavy rains. Two river fords in the area became impassable in high water, and the superintendent reported in 1928 that on a recent trip to the Big Cove Day School, his automobile had to be "hauled out of the river with the car hitched to an ox." Strongly committed to road building, Superintendent Spalsbury proposed improving the existing road to "benefit the few white people in the upper end of the reservation" as well as the "Indians of that section" who would gain "closer contact with civilization." The following year, the agency oversaw the construction of a new road into the Cove. The plea for more money to connect Big Cove Cherokees with civilization continued for the next five years, straight into the commencement of tourism as the major industry.[66]

Those who remember Big Cove in the twenties and early thirties recall that there were "fields all over the place" planted in corn and potatoes. "All the trees growed up there," covering traces of landscapes that wind through memories. "They got big trees where there used to be corn." Chickens, pigs, an occasional cow, steers for plowing or lumber hauling, ducks, sheep, and even turkeys added to the sounds and sights and scents of the lives of Big Cove Cherokees. Children who came back to the Cove from boarding school outings carefully instructed their mothers in new techniques of canning and preserving, but many still dried foods by spreading them on the roofs of their cabins.

Cove Cherokees walked ten to fifteen miles down to Yellow Hill for exchanges with larger trade stores. Ravensford and Smokemont both had commissaries, and J. R. Hall ran a general store at Swayney specializing in dry goods, notions, and country produce. Later, Oscar McDonald, who owned the Ravensford store and was "well liked by the Indians and thoroughly reliable," applied for a permit to trade in Big Cove. Superintendent Foght endorsed the application, speculating that McDonald's store might serve as "an outlet for craftwork in that section of the Reservation."[67]

Big Cove stores served as more than places to obtain food and notions, however. Charlotte Welch Lossiah took in washing and ironing for "the people that were on the mountains logging," and "she had to go to that store to pick up her money." Like women of other townships, Lossiah washed with a "tub and a washboard" and "some kind of paddle. . . . She'd beat those work clothes . . . get them all done and hang them out and then she'd press the shirts, and all the good shirts." Lossiah washed for Cherokees as well as whites and picked up her pay at the store "at the mouth of Straight Fork."[68] She made "very little amount of money," though, which made her basketry even more important.

On weekends, Lossiah went with her husband "over the mountains" to gather white oak. Her daughter gestures to her own stack of wood as she recalls the "big piles like that, in bunches."[69] Like the Birdtown forests, the Big Cove woods had been completely reshaped by lumbering. Sparks from logging trains started fires that burned for days, since little effort was made to control them. In 1921, day school teacher Sarah Hacklander complained to Superintendent Henderson that the most recent fire started by the logging train "stretches over three peaks in sight." She pointed out that if such fire did not kill old trees, "it surely does all young growth."[70] Hacklander was right. The entire ecology of an area changes after fire clears both underbrush and overstory. Red maple and Japanese honeysuckle found ample opportunities to put down roots, sprouting and spreading on burned or barren hillsides from Bunches Creek to Little Snowbird.

In mountainous Graham County, the Snowbird community of Cheoah was the smallest of the townships. In 1930, Snowbird Cherokees lived along the Cheoah and Snowbird Rivers and their tributaries, Buffalo, Mouse, Santeetlah, Panther, and Little Snowbird Creeks. Interspersed among the homes of whites, the one- or two-room log houses of Cherokees lay outside the small town of Robbinsville.

With a subsidy provided by the federal government, Graham County built a new day school for Snowbird Cherokees in 1930, replacing the disgracefully inadequate facilities that had attracted few children and discouraged numerous teachers. Bessie Jumper (b. 1915) was one of many who simply quit the old Snowbird Day School at Zion Hill Baptist Church, where "we had the same book every year. We'd go back to school in the fall, and we still had the same book—nothing improved."[71] The condition of the county school building scarcely bettered the situation. It "was never finished on the inside or outside," and it stood on locust posts "two or three feet off the ground."[72] Handicapped by the lack of books, no midday meal, a drafty building, no sanitary facilities, and hard benches without backs, the Snowbird Day School closed sporadically, leaving parents with the choice of sending their children to boarding school or keeping them home to help with endless chores.

Although the mountainous terrain of Graham County limited the amount of arable land, Cherokees farmed and gardened wherever the ground would hold a crop. They raised corn and beans in fields and gardens and gathered wild greens, mushrooms, fruit, and nuts from the surrounding forests. In preparation for winter, women dried as much food as they could. "Sochan and polk salad—all that there is that's edible, my grandmother dried them," remembers Callie Wachacha (b. 1922). Like their mothers and grandmothers before them, Snowbird women spread food out on a sheet on the roof of the cabin, and "when they dried out we put them in paper bags" and "put them away by hanging them here and there."[73] Strings of beans—called leather britches—and bags of food hung from rafters and walls, visual reminders of the work of the previous season and the promise of the next.

Outside, pigs, cows, sheep, ducks, and chickens roamed free until "this *dis-so-ya-gis-di* happened," the law that "you had to fence in your stock." Most Snowbird Cherokees put fences around their homes and gardens to protect them not only from their own stock animals but also from those that had roamed free until they became wild, or nearly so. Until the blight decimated the chestnut trees in the Southern Appalachians, "pigs and hogs were so fat. There were plenty of chestnuts back then. That's what they lived on." The loss of chestnuts meant, finally, the decline of swine husbandry among Cherokees. Maggie Axe Wachacha (1892–1993) noticed that "now you don't see any pigs."[74] Cattle husbandry declined as well when the fence law prohibited free ranging.

On Sundays, many Snowbird Cherokees attended services at the Buffalo Baptist or Zion Hill Baptist churches, where native elders preached in the Cherokee language. "There used to be a lot of people in church back then," recalls Martha Welch Wachacha (b. 1910). "We were always crowded." Using old songbooks printed in the Cherokee syllabary, which had been treasured by their families for nearly a century, they sang "Guide Me, Jehovah" and "Amazing Grace," hymns they knew by heart. "The eldest people didn't know how to sing in English," Solomon Bird (b. 1902) remembers; but "the elders knew how to sing the Cherokee hymns."[75]

During the week, Snowbird men found jobs doing road, railroad, or timber work, while women looked for employment cooking, cleaning, or taking in wash. All tended their own fields and gardens and, sometimes, those of others. Ella Long Jackson (b. 1919) remembers that when she was thirteen, she worked hoeing corn with her mother and sister for the man she later married. "We left early in the morning to get over there," she recalls. "I got paid fifty cents, and my mother got paid seventy-five cents for all day work." Following their work in Ed Jackson's fields, they went on to those of Henson Rattler, who "had a much bigger cornfield, his went almost to the top of the mountain." And they "hoed for the white people, too."[76]

They were more fortunate than many, for in 1932, few people in western North Carolina could find wage work. "For something to eat we made it good," remembers Game Walker (b. 1907), "but the clothes wore out—no money. You just had to patch them. . . . Everybody was needy; half of them didn't have shoes."[77] Even though he was "young and stout," Walker couldn't find work from Snowbird to South Carolina. As a last resort, he "started making liquor. I had to have some money." He sold "about ten gallons a week" in Bryson City or to "a tourist outfit" on Cowee Mountain. His pay was "two dollars a gallon to deliver."[78] The need for money drove more than one man on the reservation to the moonshine business—to the great dismay of government agents.

Although his own responsibilities seemed more than burdensome, Game Walker remembers clearly the pace of women's days. "You take people back then, they used to eat three times a day. A woman never got to stop. Got up early every morning to cook breakfast. When she got that done and the house cleaned up, it was dinnertime. When she got through with that, it was suppertime. It continued from the time she got up until the time she went to bed."[79] In addition to the meal preparation that Walker remembered so well, women also washed, ironed, made and mended clothes, churned butter, made soap, pieced quilts, planted gardens, wove chair seats, gathered medicines, milked cows, birthed babies, told stories, nursed children, slaughtered animals, and sat with the sick and dying.

And yet, because there was seldom enough of anything, neither food, nor cash, nor clothes, Snowbird women also made baskets and walked long distances to trade them. Bessie Jumper went with her mother to Andrews, which is due south across the Snowbird Mountains. "We'd leave here at five o'clock in the morning," she remembers. "It's a long way. When you get to the top of the mountain, then you go down a long way." They based their prices on what they needed and were able to carry back with them. "Sometimes we sold them for different prices, and sometimes we traded them for groceries. . . . But we always got just what we could carry back." Having left at dawn, the mother and child returned "somewhere around seven or eight at night."[80]

Great Smoky Mountains National Park

One of the obstacles to expanding basket trade in the early thirties was the lack of roads on the reservation. Travel was slow and, occasionally, not even possible. Nearly every superintendent complained about road conditions and requested road money to improve transportation and communication. Education usually absorbed the budget, however, and neither the counties nor the state seemed inclined to spend road money on the reservation. Substantial road paving finally began in conjunction with the proposed Great Smoky Mountains National Park.

Interest in developing a Southern Appalachians park started as early as 1899 with the organization of the Appalachian National Park Association at Asheville. In 1900, the ANPA and the Appalachian Mountain Club of New England sent memorials to Congress urging preservation of the Appalachian forests through the establishment of a national park. In 1901, Secretary of Agriculture James B. Wilson presented a comprehensive report on the extent and condition of the Southern Appalachians. Although he considered them "unique" and "the greatest physiographic feature in the eastern half of the continent," Wilson recommended the creation of a national forest rather than a park. A national forest, he pointed out, would be self-supporting from timber sales.[81] For the time being, nothing came of the memorials or Wilson's recommendation and private lumber interests continued their sweep through the woodlands.

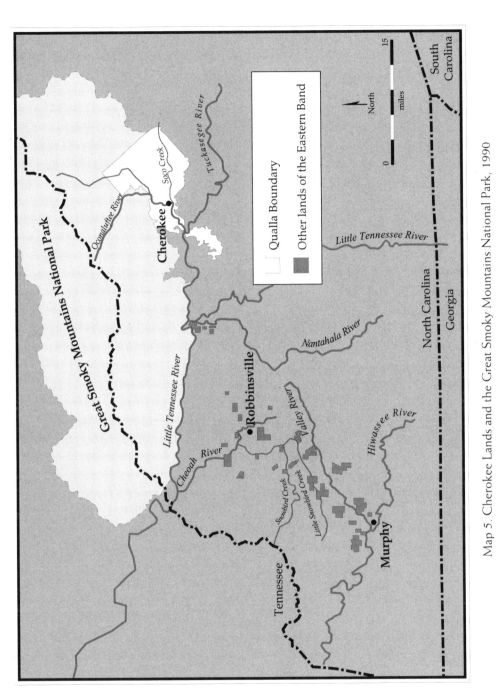

Map 5. Cherokee Lands and the Great Smoky Mountains National Park, 1990

In 1923, a group of Knoxville businessmen organized an effort to build a road across the Smokies to provide eastern Tennessee with ready access to Carolina markets. The businessmen had long considered the mountain range "a despised barrier between Knoxville and western North Carolina."[82] In addition to building the road, some wanted to set aside a portion of the Smokies as a national park. The Knoxville Chamber of Commerce took an interest in the business potential and appointed a park committee to work with the local automobile club. In 1924, the two groups succeeded in gaining federal endorsement of a national park. With an eye toward the development of tourism to boost regional economies, the legislatures of North Carolina and Tennessee voted to award condemnation rights to park commissions of each state, and land purchase began.[83] From its inception, Great Smoky Mountains National Park was more a business venture than a conservation effort, a commodity more than a sanctuary.

For the next decade, park boosters in Tennessee and North Carolina worked to raise money to acquire more than 700,000 acres of land. Unlike conditions that preceded the establishment of other national parks, much of the Smokies was privately owned. Lumber and pulp companies owned 85 percent of the proposed park lands. The remainder belonged to individuals. The endeavor to acquire land was not easy. To create the park, the organizers arranged to condemn land, initiate and settle lawsuits, tear up rail lines, develop campgrounds, destroy stills, build trails, raze buildings, collect artifacts, expel settlers, burn houses, erect facilities, and construct roads.[84] The complications were nearly endless, and many displaced residents were furious.

"Let no one think I did not enjoy life," Edna Maney Wikle wrote of her childhood along the Oconaluftee. When "our homes were confiscated," she recalled, "politicians decided what remuneration we would receive." Was it enough? Was it fair? Memories of displacement intertwined, for some lost not only their homes but the money given for them as well. They placed their money "in banks that went broke during the Depression." Wikle spoke for many when she explained the reason she lost her home. It was "all in the name of progress! All so that a neighboring City and State can reap the financial reward." Gatlinburg and Knoxville would become entryways for tourists. Wikle forfeited her home for "a few hardy backpackers to enjoy the Great North Carolina Wilderness area."[85] Throughout the process of development, extensive publicity reminded residents of both states of the tourist bonanza that would follow.

In the summer of 1932, the "Across the Smokies Highway" was completed from Gatlinburg, Tennessee, across Newfound Gap to Smokemont, approximately five miles north of the reservation. When more than a thousand cars crossed the gap in

Annie Standingdeer and her daughter, Ollie Tooni, were photographed making baskets to advertise the Cherokee reservation and the Great Smoky Mountains National Park (ca. 1936). Courtesy of the National Museum of the American Indian, Smithsonian Institution, no. 38042.

a single day, it appeared that boosters had correctly estimated interest in a park. From the Cherokee reservation, a hopeful superintendent predicted that the new highway "will bring a very large number of tourists through here." Cherokees would benefit, he felt sure, because tourism "will afford a ready market for a great deal of their products."[86] Increased tourism had greater implications than a ready market. Following the opening of the highway and the park, Cherokees looked to tourism as their primary industry.

563—Cherokee Indian Squaw and Papoose, Cherokee Indian Reservation

Adjoining Great Smoky Mountains National Park

Tourist postcards (1930–50)

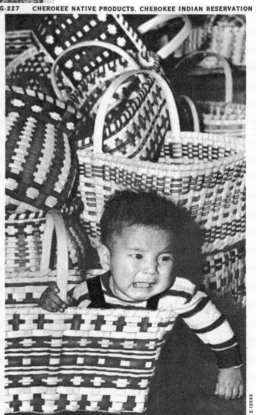

G-227   CHEROKEE NATIVE PRODUCTS, CHEROKEE INDIAN RESERVATION

ADJOINING GREAT SMOKY MOUNTAINS NATIONAL PARK

C-7—Indian Basket Makers, Cherokee, N. C.

9A-H2100

H & CO., INC.

532—Chief Standing Deer, Cherokee Indian Reservation

Ꭰ ᎣᎦᎥᎦ

© CURT TEICH & CO., INC.

OB-H2337

Adjoining Great Smoky Mountains National Park

In 1934, the state of North Carolina completed Highway 441, which ran past the agency and boarding school to Smokemont, where it connected with the Across the Smokies Highway.[87] By then, "the most important source of cash income" for Cherokees was "the sale of handicraft and farm products to the tourist trade." The superintendent was particularly gratified that the director of the National Park Service agreed "to allow only the handicraft products of the mountain people and the Cherokee Indians to be sold in the park."[88] The strands binding women's basketry to tourism wound tighter.

Initially, the park service hoped to use Cherokees as tourist attractions, a notion undoubtedly shared by park boosters. "Several young men attached to the Park Service have dropped in on us," reported the superintendent in 1935, and they "have painted pictures of what is going to be done for the tourists at Smokemont and elsewhere, stressing the Indian feature always." Drawing inspiration from national park programs at Glacier and Yosemite, where Native Americans went periodically to dance and weave baskets, the park service agents hoped to persuade Cherokees to engage in similar enterprises. Superintendent Foght turned them down. "Ours are a different type of Indian," he explained, "who would not wish to lend themselves—at least most of them would not—to exploitation of this kind."[89] It was a position on which Foght contradicted himself many times. Ironically, what he considered to be exploitation of the reservation did not appear as such when it occurred on Cherokee land. He did not want Cherokees to entertain tourists at Smokemont because "it would be setting up competition of [sic] what we are planning to do throughout the summer with pageantry, Indian games, dances, etc." on the reservation.[90] Foght's goal was to bring tourists to Cherokees rather than the reverse.

As the state worked to complete Highway 19 through Birdtown, the number of craft shops on the reservation doubled and baskets and basketweavers became subjects for tourist postcards. With more paved roads and a new park, Cherokee seclusion ended. The number of cars entering the park doubled each year from the time of its opening, in 1934, until 1941. By the 1950s, an estimated 2 million cars passed annually through Qualla on the way to Great Smoky Mountains National Park.[91]

The advance of roads and tourism was always accompanied by predictions of benefits to Cherokees. In 1940, when the Cherokee Council authorized a right-of-way for a highway to the park, the *Asheville Citizen* claimed the road "will be of great economic benefit to the Indians of the Reservation." Parkways and the "thousands of tourists passing over them each year" would stimulate "the production and sale of Indian arts and crafts on the Reservation," helping Cherokees "in their struggle for economic independence." In exchange for the right-of-way, the state agreed to

pave Highway 19 through Painttown and Wolftown "for the benefit of the Cherokee Indians."[92]

In 1935, however, the government's promise of a Soco road remained long over-
due, prompting Superintendent Foght to write Indian commissioner Collier an im-
passioned letter about the road. "The Cherokees have tried to get this road approved for fifteen years," he reported, but money was repeatedly diverted to
roadways outside the reservation. The North Carolina legislature had set aside
money for its construction in 1933, but the Federal Bureau of Roads withheld ap-
proval "pending Parkway location," and the money once again went elsewhere. By
1935, the long-awaited park to park highway was rerouted around the reservation,
to the great disappointment of those who looked forward to tourist bonanzas.
Cherokees had earlier given the Soco right-of-way to the state and were eager for
construction jobs. They "need assistance very badly," explained the superintendent.[93] All along the Soco valley, weavers like Betty Lossiah waited again for the
roads and tourists and economic relief.

"Retaining the Art of Basketry"

While Cherokees of the early thirties struggled to survive by farming and gardening, working at odd jobs and trading baskets, various superintendents tried to for-
mulate new approaches to old problems. As always, schools were the laboratories
to test programs. Changes that were implemented in the school agenda at that time
reveal the attitudes of government employees and point to important shifts in federal Indian policy.

The long-cherished goal of assimilation was not officially abandoned, but increasing emphasis on tourism undercut the very concept. New federal policies extended educational work beyond the schools and specifically into the homes.
Adult training in native industries became widely available in community clubs,
while academic courses for schoolchildren became circumscribed. In order to
strengthen their appeal to the tourist market, Native Americans were encouraged
to remain on reservations, improve their handwork, and learn to sell themselves as
well as their crafts. Native industries had been spurned, then endorsed as art, and
later encouraged for their economic potential. By the 1930s, indigenous handcrafts
had become firmly established as marketable commodities for curious consumers.
And as before, "native" industries included a few imports.

Edna Groves, supervisor of home economics for the Bureau of Indian Affairs,
notified Superintendent Page in 1930 that she had appointed a "Berea-trained
weaver" to the Cherokee Agency. The appointee, loom weaver Ethel Garnett,
according to Groves, was "to devote half time to school and half time to the

reservation." What girls might learn about loom weaving in school, their mothers could learn at home or in community clubs. Highly popular with craft revivalists who worked with white Appalachians, loom weaving was not indigenous to Cherokees. Yet Groves intended for it to become a native industry—and one aimed at the anticipated tourist market. "With the coming of Smokey [sic] Mountain National Park," Groves wrote, "there should be no question about disposing of all native handicraft."[94]

Although she was particularly committed to Garnett's work as a loom weaver, Groves had in mind for her a few additional responsibilities. The young Berea graduate, suggested Groves, "can help in retaining the art of basketry, and in persuading the women to use native dyes." On October 1, 1930, Ethel Garnett was employed as a loom weaver on a temporary basis, and the following February she became a full-time employee of both the agency and the Cherokee School, paid from both funds.[95] Using looms made at Berea, Garnett taught small groups of girls in the boarding and day schools and also visited women in their homes and community clubs to teach them textile weaving.

The educational programs developed at the Cherokee schools during the early thirties explicitly included transforming home and work life. Whereas earlier educational policies endeavored to change families through the influence of students who returned from boarding schools, the later programs aimed to affect directly every aspect of Cherokee life. "Our program of education will be wider than the classroom," wrote Superintendent Spalsbury in 1934. "It will take in the homes, the fields, the forests, the churches, the tribal organization, and every individual entitled to participate in the tribe." Such breathtaking presumption aspired "to improve the economic, social, sanitary and spiritual condition of these people."[96]

Adjustments in the school curriculum included increased emphasis on industries, such as Garnett's loom weaving, and diminished work in academics, such as algebra, which was said to have "no application, especially with the girls." The earlier determination to assimilate Native Americans into white society disappeared, replaced by an intent to prepare them "for life among their people in their own home." Spalsbury felt confident that students "will not require foreign language or higher mathematics to live a good life here." And in what must have seemed a cruel irony to older Cherokees who had suffered through years of boarding school punishment and humiliation, he planned "to offer two years study of the Cherokee language both spoken and written, during the 11th and 12th years of school."[97]

To coordinate the training of girls in the schools and women in their homes, Gertrude Flanagan was transferred from her position as home economics teacher at the Haskell Indian School in Kansas to become Cherokee home economics supervisor. In addition to overseeing domestic science at the boarding school and all the day schools, Flanagan was authorized to "direct the reorganization of home making in every part of the agency."[98] She took charge of women's clubs in each community, directed adult summer work in home economics, and trained all women who worked in the school system. Flanagan swiftly reorganized the school program on the assumption that "the Cherokee youth will become a subsistence farmer who will wish to supplement his livelihood by the practice of crafts" and that "the young women will become the wives and helpmates of these youths." She recommended revising the academic curriculum to emphasize "vocational work" beginning with the fifth grade. She proposed teaching boys various crafts, including reed and cane weaving. The schedule for girls included "three hours of home economics every other day" and residence in a "practice cottage" for six weeks, where they cared for a "garden, chickens, and a cow."[99]

While many of Flanagan's "liberal, not to say radical" suggestions were ignored, others had long-lasting influence. Under her direction, classes began in pottery and basketry, and Cherokee potter Maude Welch was employed as a part-time instructor. Welch's appointment marks a singularly important development in Cherokee education. She was the first native artisan hired to teach in the reservation schools. The conditions were not the best—there was neither kiln nor any other kind of oven, and the girls simply modeled clay. Still, until then, virtually no Cherokees had taught in their own schools, even after completing Normal School training in boarding schools. While Welch taught classes in pottery, basketry remained the province of Gertrude Flanagan and Ethel Garnett for the next few years.[100]

Following up on the federal directive issued by Edna Groves, the home economics supervisor, Flanagan promptly set about to persuade basketweavers to return to the use of vegetable dyes. Sixty years later, some still recall her influence. "This dye now, it just started maybe about twenty-five or thirty years ago." The passage of time has clouded Emma Taylor's recollection of the precise number of years but not the memory of the personalities involved. "A woman connected to that Co-op there, when she first came in, her name was Miss Flanagan," Taylor reminisces. "She started back on the natural colors. So ever since, that's what I've been using."[101] Taylor was not alone. Flanagan succeeded in convincing many weavers to forgo the use of commercial dyes. Much later, when the Cherokees established their co-op and Flanagan was "connected" to it, her influence was even greater.

A New Deal for Native Americans

While some of the changes in the agency and schools followed earlier initiatives, others developed in the highly charged arena of national politics and Indian policy reform. On April 21, 1933, John Collier became commissioner of Indian Affairs and introduced a New Deal for Native Americans. Collier brought to the appointment a professional background in social work and adult education and an intense personal commitment to the reformation of American society through the restoration of community.[102]

As an adult, Collier came to believe that Indian societies retained the sense of community lost to the industrialized world. Tribal groups, he thought, preserved "what the world has lost" and "what the world must have again, lest it die." He attributed to Native Americans a "power for living," which made them "the bearer of one great message to the world." As Indian commissioner, Collier was determined to lift the "sentences of death from these all but invisible Indian societies" and to preserve the society of Indians for the sake of the society of whites.[103]

Born into a prominent Atlanta family in 1884, Collier moved to New York in 1907 and entered settlement house work. For twelve years he worked for the People's Institute of New York and became director of the National Training School for Community Workers. When he left New York in 1919, Collier moved to California to become state director of Community Organization. In nearly constant conflict with state officials, he eventually was accused of communism, and he resigned his position. Jobless and disheartened, Collier accepted Mabel Dodge Luhan's invitation to join her in Taos, New Mexico, where she had established a colony of artists and writers. After the Collier family arrived in 1920 to share the heady atmosphere of reform and protest with assorted New England intellectuals, they made numerous idyllic visits to the Taos Pueblo. The "Taos experience," Collier later wrote, "changed my life plan."[104]

Collier believed he found in the lives of Taos Indians "secrets desperately needed by the white world."[105] In contrast to the fragmentation that characterized white communities, the Indian "way of life" recognized "the individual and his society as wholly reciprocal." Inspired by the "spiritual possessions" of Native Americans, Collier attributed their resilience to "institutionalized and symbol-invested belief." As he watched the Red Deer Dance at Taos Pueblo, he felt the ceremony "enter into myself and each one in my family as a new direction of life—a new, and even wildly new, hope for the Race of Man."[106] In his thirty-eighth year, Collier determined to devote the remainder of his life to preserving "the whole social institution of the tribe and of the race" as a "gift for us all."[107]

Collier was familiar with Native Americans well before his pilgrimage to Taos Pueblo. As an adventurous young man in the South, he often hiked and camped in the mountainous regions where Cherokees made history. His memories echoed with the "sweet speech" of Cherokees who named the "Valley of Nacoochee, Tellico Plains, Nantahala River, Toccoa Falls, Junaluska Creek, Wayah Bald, Tusquit-tee Bald, Hiawassee River," and many more features of the landscape. A memorable hike into the Unicoi Mountains with a young Cherokee guide named Robert took him to the cold and quick waters of Snowbird Creek, where Robert's laughter played "like a song flung into the night." A longer trek one late September ended on the grounds of the Cherokee Boarding School. There, Collier met the superin-tendent, who wore "a uniform of the Army" and a demeanor so intimidating "the little boy inmates could not or would not talk English to each other, and they dared not talk in Cherokee." On such visits to the reservation, Collier witnessed the "self-righteous middle years" of federal Indian policy. He was appalled.[108]

Despite his familiarity with Cherokees and his indignation over their superin-tendent, Collier apparently needed the Taos experience to mobilize his consider-able energies for the fight for Indian rights. When he left New Mexico in 1922, he organized the American Indian Defense Association (AIDA) to protest discrimina-tion, promote reforms, and litigate Indian cases.[109] As executive secretary of the AIDA, Collier excoriated virtually every aspect of Indian policy and every depart-ment of the Bureau of Indian Affairs. His relentless criticism proved highly effec-tive. In 1926, Secretary of the Interior Hubert Work asked the Brookings Institute for Government Research to undertake a thorough study of the "economic and so-cial conditions of the American Indian" and "indicate what remains to be done to adjust the Indians to prevailing civilization." Just two years earlier, Native Ameri-cans had been granted U.S. citizenship.[110]

Under the direction of Brookings staff member Lewis Meriam, the results of the study were published in a 1928 volume entitled *The Problem of Indian Administration*, commonly called the Meriam report. As secretary of the influential AIDA, Collier met periodically with Meriam's special researchers, introduced them to tribal offi-cials, and assisted them in several aspects of the project.[111] When he attained his goal of becoming commissioner of Indian Affairs in 1933, Collier implemented many of the suggestions contained in the Meriam report, including those regard-ing women's basketry.

"Baskets of distinctive character are made by the women of tribes in every sec-tion of the United States," the report acknowledged. "It is doubtful whether any people in the world make baskets of finer workmanship than do some of the Indi-ans." In a lengthy section on economic conditions, the document stated that Na-tive American "prosperity depends upon family earning power rather than upon the ability of the father alone." The promise of "prosperity" rested with women be-cause they "are able to follow at home traditional arts highly respected by discrim-inating white customers."[112]

The pitfalls of dependence on the discrimination of white customers did not trouble Meriam's specialists. Their greater concern was identifying an achievable means of economic relief for Indian families. Since industries such as basketry utilized raw materials obtained from local landscapes, income derived from handwork was "clear gain" for the maker. The report stated flatly that unless the government encouraged native industries, "it is difficult to see how some Indians are ever to achieve a reasonably satisfactory standard of living in their present locations."[113]

Where "economic needs are great," which was on every reservation in the country, the researchers decried the "marked tendency for the native handicrafts to disappear or to degenerate." Assuming a place in the long tradition of social intervenors, the specialists complained that "some basket weavers and many textile weavers now resort to the convenient use of the vivid commercial dyes instead of the more lasting and beautiful vegetable dyes of former times." Although Miriam's researchers commended some innovations, they disparaged experimentation with any commercial material as "marked degeneration."[114]

The committee recognized that much of the religious and social significance of basketry and other industries had disappeared, but they praised the "recreational and artistic aspects" of handwork. Moreover, they believed endeavors like basketry could contribute to the growth of "social amenities" among Native Americans and improve "inter-racial relations" as whites came to appreciate the "distinctive contribution" Indians made to society. The committee concluded that the "Indian Office should include in its program the development of Indian handicrafts." It specifically recommended that the government create a market for Indian goods and standardize Indian handwork for the market.[115] As Indian commissioner, Collier established an agency to accomplish both.

Marketing Native American handwork had long been one of Collier's goals. When he assumed office, he began to establish a federal agency responsible for various industries that were increasingly lumped together as Indian arts and crafts. In that strange mix of preservation and change that characterized federal policy, Collier aimed to improve economic conditions on reservations by maintaining certain native customs while shaping them to appeal to markets. Even though he generally endorsed the Meriam report, Collier asked James Young to chair another committee to "study and make recommendations concerning the whole problem of Indian arts and crafts, in their relation to the economic and cultural welfare of the American Indian."[116]

Following closely the suggestions advanced by Meriam's staff, the Committee on Indian Arts and Crafts reported in September 1934 that "these products" were part of "Indian culture as a whole" and "part of the art heritage of the American people as well as of the Indian." The "real heart of the problem," however, was economic. A great difference existed between the "present and potential source of income" generated by Indian arts and crafts.[117] On one hand, craft work, according to the committee, seemed compatible with an economy "rooted in the land," which had always been the "economic stronghold" of Native American society. On the other hand, Indians were pulled away from their homelands to different locales where they could earn money. Arts and crafts "developed in connection with his basic land economy" could be a source of revenue. The committee surmised that arts and crafts had not retained any religious, ceremonial, or utilitarian value. They were made only to be sold, and if they could not be marketed, "they will cease to be produced." The committee saw merchandising as the only viable means of preserving "these products as expressions of Indian life, or as art."[118] Such expressions of life and art, however, would have to accommodate the market.

Young and his committee members recognized the connection between craft work and poverty. "A good job," they noted with no apparent sense of irony, "will tend to stop craft production." And no good jobs existed on reservations. Two divergent conditions—a need for ready cash and the possibility of selling items for higher prices—led to craftwork. Since prices remained low, the production of handwork was only "a spare time operation." As a result, Native Americans had "no organization of production" and they lacked "production standards or supervision."[119] The role the federal government would play began to take shape.

The committee acknowledged that any government intervention in Native American handwork "involves risks to Indian art and ways of life." Programs needed to proceed "slowly and experimentally, in cooperation with the Indians." Ultimately, however, the government would have to become involved with production and standards as well as marketing and supervision. The question the committee faced was "how can the economic welfare of the Indians be advanced by the Government in cooperation with the Indians through arts and crafts?" The report recommended the formation of a federal agency to address the problems of "production processes," the need for "better products," and "better adaptation of products to American usage."[120] Thus was born the Indian Arts and Crafts Board.

Composed of five members appointed by the secretary of interior, the Arts and Crafts Board was authorized to research markets, advise tribes, establish standards, coordinate agencies, and create government trademarks of authenticity.[121] The goal was to improve the market for Indian crafts and improve Indian crafts for the market. On the Cherokee reservation, another agency was already involved in precisely the same endeavor, the Southern Highland Handicraft Guild.

The Southern Highland Handicraft Guild was formally established in 1930 at the annual meeting of the Conference of Southern Mountain Workers. Composed of the most active and energetic craft revivalists in the Southern Appalachians, the conference included North Carolina activists Olive Dame Campbell of the John C. Campbell Folk School in Brasstown, Frances Goodrich from Allanstand in Asheville, Mary Sloop of Crossnore, and Lucy Morgan of the Appalachian School in Penland. The president of Kentucky's Berea College represented the Fireside Industries, and Evelyn Bishop came from the Pi Beta Phi Settlement School in Gatlinburg, Tennessee. Allen Eaton, from New York's Russell Sage Foundation, joined the conference when he moved to the Southern Appalachians. Eaton became a founder and indefatigable supporter of the guild.[122]

The purpose of the guild was to survey, preserve, and promote the handicrafts of Appalachia by coordinating the efforts of the regional craft revivalists. About twenty-five producing craft centers became organizational members, and the guild became responsible for four craft shops that featured their products. In 1934, the work of the guild became more overtly political when the U.S. Department of Agriculture and the Tennessee Valley Authority both sent representatives to the annual meeting to ask for support of their regional craft programming. With guild assistance, TVA initiated and funded a marketing program called Southern Highlanders, which opened salesrooms in Chattanooga and New York and craft shops at TVA dam sites in Norris and Chickamauga, Tennessee. Clem Douglas, a founder and director of the guild, became the director of Southern Highlanders.[123]

The guild enthusiastically supported the establishment of the Great Smoky Mountains National Park. Members even agreed to lend their personal collections of artifacts and craftwork for exhibit in the proposed park museums. Anticipating the influx of tourists who represented expanding markets, the guild also endorsed the park service plan of "utilizing handicrafts in the Great Smoky Mountains and Shenandoah National Parks as part of their educational program." The proposed sale of authentic Appalachian crafts in park shops gratified guild founders, who believed the policy indicated a growing appreciation at the highest political level for the handcrafts of the Southern Appalachians.[124] With political connections, an admissions committee, restricted membership, craft standards, and the ability to organize and sponsor exhibits, the Southern Highland Handicraft Guild exercised considerable influence on artisans and on the attitudes of the buying public. It did little, however, to raise the prices of the crafts made by its members.

When guild organizers expressed an interest in Cherokee membership in 1932, Superintendent Spalsbury and "several members of the School and Agency" attended the annual meeting in Gatlinburg. Filled with enthusiasm, Spalsbury promptly started work on "the problem of organizing a Hand Craft guild among the Indians" to expand their markets through "the Guild stores, as well as through our own local guild." The Cherokee Council authorized the expenditure of tribal funds "to finance the local unit of the Southern Mountain Handicraft Guild" and agreed to set aside a craft room in the new council house.[125]

Spalsbury sympathized with the guild's policy of remaining exclusive. He expressed his intention to organize a "small charter membership consisting of the best craftsmen on the reservation." Other artisans could join "when they improve their work to such a point that it meets with the standard set up by the organization itself." The superintendent recognized that one purpose of the guild was to raise "the standards of workmanship," and he apparently had no problem with the imposition of standards from beyond the reservation.[126] Such intervention was in keeping with traditional federal policy.

By the spring of 1933, two representatives from each Qualla township belonged to the local guild. Arizona Blankenship and Pearl Toineeta represented Big Cove, Mary Owle and Frankie Fisher came from Birdtown, honeysuckle weaver Carolyn Conseen represented the 3200 Acre Tract, Betty Smith and potter Maude Welch represented Painttown, basketweaver Nannie Youngbird and Nan Smith spoke for Yellow Hill, and Jarrett Smith and Mrs. Ned Stamper represented Wolftown. The next year, 129 Cherokees belonged to the guild. Snowbird, the smallest of the townships, led the guild membership of Cherokees with 44 members.[127]

The guild paid cash for members' work and, through regional and national exhibits, geographically expanded their markets. The first year Cherokees belonged, the guild organized an exhibit that traveled to art galleries from Nebraska to Wisconsin. At the Corcoran Gallery in Washington, fifty dollars worth of Cherokee baskets was sold, and the superintendent reported that subsequent orders came in "faster than we have been able to fill them." In 1934, the guild purchased nine Cherokee baskets for Chicago's Century of Progress Exposition. Payment for the baskets amounted to an appallingly low $9.50. That year, the Southern Highland Handicraft Guild distributed nearly $500 to its Cherokee members, an average of less than four dollars each.[128]

As supervisor of home economics on the reservation, Gertrude Flanagan quickly became active in the Southern Highland Handicraft Guild and served on the board of directors. Flanagan and "a number from this school always attend the annual and other special meetings of the organization," which included craft fairs where guild centers operated. The popular fairs provided the guild with marketing opportunities, and artisan members attended to demonstrate their work.

Fair and Unfair Representation

During the thirties, fairs continued to be a source of cash for basketweavers. In addition to guild fairs, Cherokees attended county and regional fairs where they could demonstrate and sell their work. Whites enjoyed seeing weavers making baskets, never knowing how many hours of preparation—gathering, splitting, trimming, cleaning, dyeing—preceded their appearance at demonstration tables. An uninformed public shared a general curiosity about Native Americans as exotic novelties. Cherokees found themselves to be considered a special kind of entertainment and received numerous requests to appear in festivals, fairs, parades, and shows. The 1934 Southeastern Fair in Atlanta was such an occasion.

To accommodate Commissioner John Collier's suggestion that Cherokees participate in the Indian Exposition at the Southeastern Fair, the council voted to change the opening of their own fair so that fifty Cherokees could spend the first week in October "camped at Lakewood Park" in Atlanta with twenty Seminoles and an equal number of Navajos and Pueblos. "This is in no sense of the word a 'side show,'" reported Harold Hemrick in the *Atlanta Journal*. (Above his article, a bold headline read "Indians *Invade* Atlanta.") Instead, he claimed that "Atlanta's first American Indian Exposition has been broadly conceived and developed with the purpose of education as its only motive." [129]

For the week of the fair, according to newspapers, Cherokees lived in "small villages which are exact replications of their native homes." Although the Lakewood Fairgrounds little resembled western North Carolina or the regions of the other Native American participants, the press pledged that during the fair Indians "will live as they do on their reservations." Regardless of reporters' assurances that fairgoers would see them in realistic settings, Cherokees stayed in "six large wigwams" that were "nearly exact copies of their former dwellings" of the eighteenth century, painstakingly constructed under the supervision of an archaeologist. Moreover, the men wore feathered headdresses, carried tomahawks for newspaper photographs, and participated in archery and blowgun contests, wrestling matches, and ball games. The press reported that the Cherokee competitions were the "biggest feature" of the exposition and recommended the ball game as "probably the roughest game in America" and "more entertaining" than any other activity. [130]

Cherokee exhibit at the 1934 Southeastern Fair in Atlanta. 1934 Annual Report
of Extension Workers, National Archives.

While the men performed rituals from the past for the edification of fairgoers,
a display of basketry "furnished through the courtesy of the Indian Bureau under the
direction of John Collier" quietly revealed how women continued to weave new
worlds.[131] Rivercane, white oak, and honeysuckle baskets in rib, single, and doubleweave techniques, with old and new patterns in old and new forms, lined the display table in the fair's replica of a trading store. The proliferation of forms and patterns in the twenty years between the first Cherokee Fair in 1914 and the 1934
Southeastern Fair indicates the effect that basket markets in and beyond the reservation had on the art of basketry. At the same time, the exhibit testifies to the creativity of weavers as they responded to changing conditions of basket production.

Oddly, Superintendent Harold Foght thought that it was difficult to get much
craftwork "that is truly worthwhile" to send to the fair. "Few of the women are

working at the craft," he claimed, "due largely to the employment of the men on Government projects." His suggestion that women worked less because men earned money on public relief projects seems ironic at best. In his annual report the next year, Foght stated that the limited relief money necessitated "staggering the employment—that is, giving two weeks per man per month." Anyone who applied for public work was required first "to plant and maintain such crops as their holdings will permit."[132] On a reservation in a destitute area of an impoverished region during the depression, the work of women and men overlapped more than ever. Relief work provided desperately needed jobs. At the same time, it left some weavers with no one or no way to procure basketry materials. Others found themselves with additional home responsibilities, such as maintaining the required crops, that precluded weaving.

Regardless of Foght's concerns, federal home economics supervisor Edna Groves organized the basket exhibit and accompanied the Cherokees to Atlanta. Repeating the periodic forecast of the disappearance of doubleweave basketry, Groves reported that "there are only two women able to make double baskets." She did not provide their names but instead suggested a link between their ancestry and skills. The two women "are a full blood mother and her daughter, who live at Cherokee, North Carolina." To draw attention to other basketry features, Groves praised the handles that interlocked under the basket bases and boasted that "the handles of these baskets never pull out as do the handles of the modern basket made by the white man."[133] She did not add, and perhaps did not realize, that the Cherokee handles and baskets were also modern.

On the second day of the fair, John Collier returned to his city of birth to "inspect the American Indian Exposition." Collier's support of such expositions grew out of a century of contradictions in federal Indian policy. The tension between Indian performance as entertainment and as education, like the conflict between progress and preservation, compromised all public edification. Dependence on tourism, encouraged by the New Deal for Native Americans, exacerbated the tension.

The year following the Cherokee appearance in Atlanta, Superintendent Foght flatly rejected an invitation for "a troop of Indians to put on programs," claiming that "the United States Government is frankly not interested in having the reservation Indians become public performers."[134] That same season, however, he arranged for a group of "our Cherokee Indians" to dance at the National Folk Festival in Chattanooga, persuaded "22 younger Indian ball players [to] take part in the Dogwood Festival at the State University of North Carolina," and sent "100 Indians to Asheville to take part in the Annual Rhododendron Show." While protesting the exploitation of Indians as performers, Foght directed the ballplayers to "do what the Navajos and others do, paint up the naked part of the body in fantastic colors." Navajo body paint, he thought, would "add to the spectacle."[135]

The "spectacles" were indeed successful. Planning for the Rhododendron Festival the following year, the chairman of the Indian Committee for the Asheville Chamber of Commerce felt free to complain that men who "wore collars and ties with their costumes" ruined the effect of the parade. For the "make-believe show," he wanted their appearance to be "exciting and spectacular."[136] Men accustomed to wearing collars and ties for festive occasions did not meet the public's expectations. The efforts to preserve native customs in order to educate white audiences thus slid hopelessly and inevitably into an endeavor to entertain.

The end of the thirties brought a different superintendent and another performance policy. Incoming Superintendent C. M. Blair informed festival promoters that "in the future our policy should be to confine this type of program to the environs of Cherokee." The superintendent claimed that the decision to circumscribe native performance was in part "sentimental," but it also "would result in increased financial returns to the Indians."[137] In 1939, the tourism generated by the Great Smoky Mountains National Park held great promise for economic relief. It was a promise that tantalized the economically depressed communities of western North Carolina for the remainder of the century.

Although they were paid for their work as entertainers at other expositions, the fair most Cherokees preferred was their own. From 1914 until 1942, when World War II stopped most commercial activity on the reservation, the Cherokee Fair provided an annual opportunity for artisans to market their products for cash. Held at the Cherokee Boarding School, the fair lasted three to six days, and from its earliest days included basket exhibits and demonstrations. The exhibitions were also places for competitions, and teachers from the boarding school served as judges. During the mid-1930s, as federal policies and craft revivalists focused on basketry, categories in the basket display became more explicit and also more varied. The 1931 fair offered one dollar premiums simply for the "best cane basket" and "best splint basket." Six years later, after Gertrude Flanagan had taken over the home economics program for the reservation, $2.50 premiums were offered for seven different types of cane and white oak baskets and three types of honeysuckle baskets.

As the craft revival movement peaked in 1938, fair programs included a notice that "the use of commercial dyes will disqualify any item from competing."[138] Dyes from roots and hulls or berries and bark fit better with the nostalgia for forms untainted by industrial progress. The elimination of commercial dyes was one aspect of the basket standardization that craft revivalists considered so important. For nearly fifty years, weavers had applied commercial dyes to every kind of basket they made. Red, purple, pink, blue, gold, and orange shades of varying intensity appeared on fish baskets, storage baskets, strainers, sifters, sieves, and gathering, trinket, and all-purpose baskets made of rivercane, white oak, and honeysuckle. Singleweave and doubleweave alike took on bright hues, and weavers readily combined commercial with vegetable dyes on the same baskets. They could get Diamond or Rit dye readily and cheaply and produce a variety of colors in a fraction of the time it took to make natural dyes. Bloodroot, walnut, poke, or sumac had to be located, sometimes on a seasonal basis, then dug up or stripped off, cleaned, pounded or crushed, then simmered over a fire in a pot filled with spring water for twelve to twenty-four hours. Commercial dyes must have seemed like a godsend to weavers, especially older ones for whom gathering materials for and preparing natural dyes grew increasingly difficult.

The color revolution had run unchecked until craft revivalists like Flanagan pressured and persuaded weavers to return to natural dyes since they were more traditional and lasted longer. Bright and varied colors had been popular for fifty years. Martha Lossiah recalls that her mother used them "for the stores downtown, because that's what they wanted."[139] The market had sustained and reinforced the weavers' choices. John Collier, Gertrude Flanagan, and the craft revivalists represented a different market, one that valued preindustrial traditions. By the 1940s, the custom of commercial dyes faded as surely as their florid colors as craft revivalists decided which traditions were most authentic.

Changes in the 1935 Cherokee Fair attractions indicate the influence the craft revival had on the agency. Superintendent Foght reported that he hoped "to be able to change our annual fair to make it truly worthwhile," which meant "doing away with the old ballyhoo of noise and sideshows." In place of earlier forms of entertainment, he planned "an all-Indian pageant entitled the 'Spirit of the Great Smokies.'" He invited Margaret Speelman, the girls advisor at the Haskell Indian School, "to help us whip the pageant into shape"; and Vivian Hayman planned "to bring her Indian Dramatics Club from Chillocco to add color and finish" to the effort.[140]

Foght drew his inspiration from the folk pageants in Europe so admired by the founders of settlement and folk schools in the Southern Appalachians. The first year the pageant was presented on the reservation, the Cherokee Fair took on a new name: the Cherokee Indian Folk Festival. That there was resistance to the name change is evident in the compromise name that appeared the next year: the Cherokee Fair and Folk Festival. "People in this section," Foght had claimed "are enthu-

Throughout the 1930s the annual Cherokee Fair brought together people
from surrounding communities for entertainment, agricultural and craft exhibits,
and trade. Ferrell Collection. N.C. Museum of History.

siastically in favor of the new type of festival to supplant the old." He may have
been right, but in two years' time, the name reverted to its original and the pageant
was rescheduled for weekly performances during the summer.[141] By decade's end,
pageantry stopped on the reservation. The Folk Festival was once again the Cherokee Fair.

Teacher of Weavers: Lottie Queen Stamper

While the superintendents negotiated the challenges of festivals and fairs, another
initiative began that profoundly affected the course of Cherokee basketry. On a
warm spring day in 1937, Gertrude Flanagan accompanied boarding school principal Sam Gilliam to the Painttown home of basketweaver Lottie Queen Stamper
and asked her to teach basketry at the school. Stamper knew Gilliam and Flanagan,
for she had already earned a reputation as a basketweaver. "Different ones would
come to see me working at home," Stamper later wrote, "and I got acquainted."
Those who came to call usually intended to "buy some of my baskets." Gilliam and

Flanagan had undoubtedly been among her customers, but their motive for visiting that spring day was different. They intended to fulfill a longstanding pledge to hire a Cherokee weaver to teach classes in basketry. For several years, the Cherokee Agency's annual reports to the Bureau of Indian Affairs had included proposals to hire a Cherokee weaver. Gilliam and Flanagan finally acted on the proposal. "The High School Principal, Sam Gilliam along with a Home Economics Teacher Gertrude Flanagan ask me if I'd try," Stamper wrote. In June, she assumed the position of Indian Assistant, and for slightly over $1,000 a year, she began to teach cane, white oak, and honeysuckle basketry.[142]

Lottie Queen was born in 1906 "on a little farm" in Soco. She was the fifth of six children and the fourth of five daughters born to Levi and Mary Queen. Her father farmed, she remembered, "and on bad days he helped my mother with baskets for extra income." They "use to go to the hills" to get white oak saplings for baskets. It was a seasonal task, timed with the rhythms of planting and undertaken only "after the cultivation of the fields and gardens" was finished. As a child, she learned from her father "how the log was to be split," and then "my mother took over and showed me how to make splits." All six children in the family "learned basketweaving from my mother." Specializing in white oak basketry, Mary Queen "did not use vegetable dyes." Stamper acknowledged that learning to weave was difficult. "At times I did it with tears," she recalled, "until my mother approved my work." When Lottie's work was finally good enough to sell, she used the money she earned for her "new clothes and shoes to wear back to school each fall."[143]

After she married, Stamper learned from her mother-in-law how to weave with rivercane. Both joined the Southern Highland Handicraft Guild, and Lottie Stamper became a regular demonstrator at their fairs. As she learned the oldest weaving traditions, she began to use vegetable dyes. Bill Stamper's mother "made the dyes herself from the roots of the butternut tree and the roots of the bloodroot." Lottie Stamper found the different dyeing techniques "more interesting as time went by."[144] By the time she agreed to teach, Stamper was accomplished in different kinds of weaving and accustomed to using natural dyes.

Stamper's school courses were an instant success. "The teaching of basketry has taken surprisingly well," reported Superintendent Foght, "and quite a group of girls are planning to make this their major craft activity."[145] That first year, and many thereafter, Stamper taught throughout the summer and winter. In the meantime, Gertrude Flanagan maintained a great interest in basketry. She kept on a shelf in her school office "some real old doublewoven baskets" that were made by "old lady Mrs. Toineeta" on Swimmer Branch. Committed to preserving the oldest basketry traditions, Flanagan agreed to pay Stamper to learn the doubleweave tech-

Lottie Stamper's 1947 reproduction of the rivercane doubleweave basket and lid carried to London in 1725 by Governor Francis Nicholson [l: 26.3 cm, w: 14.5 cm, h: 15 cm]. University of Pennsylvania Museum, neg. no. T35–2007.

nique from Toineeta. Stamper wrote later that Toineeta "didn't much want" to teach her, but "she showed me and told me a little bit about it." When it was time "to go work in the corn," she dismissed Stamper. After a few lessons, Toineeta told her "not to come back for help any more."[146] Lottie Stamper eventually learned to doubleweave.

Stamper's contribution to Cherokee basketry is immeasurable. For more than thirty years, she taught both young girls and grown women. She worked in the Cherokee Boarding School until it closed in the early fifties, then taught high school classes and adult extension courses. Her name is inseparable from those of two generations of weavers in every township. Her baskets are in museum collections all over the country, and her photograph appears in virtually every book and scrapbook about twentieth-century Cherokee basketry. For nearly thirty years, anyone who visited the reservation with an interest in baskets ended up talking to Lottie Stamper.

In the late 1930s, someone sent her a photograph of the two rivercane doubleweave baskets Governor Nicholson had carried with him from Charleston back to London in 1725. Stamper painstakingly wove a smaller version of each container, using more than 500 splits of cane. The patterns in the baskets were not familiar to her and she had to recreate the designs on paper. "It took me two and one half days to work out the pattern," she later acknowledged.[147] Her effort is dramatic testimony to the intricacies of Cherokee basketweaving.

Stamper's successful recapture of traditional designs and her ability to weave the long and narrow forms led to a widespread misconception that she reintroduced the doubleweave technique to Cherokee weavers. But other women, including Nancy George Bradley, her daughter Rowena, Arizona Swayney Blankenship, Aggie Wilnoty George, and "old lady Mrs. Toineeta," were making doubleweaves at the time. And some of them were teaching others. The reproductions of the Nicholson baskets, however, attracted considerable attention and enhanced the reputation of the doubleweave technique and of Cherokee basketry. Stamper's work in the schools teaching younger women to doubleweave contributed to the vitality of the old tradition. Lottie Stamper did not reintroduce the doubleweave technique; rather, she powerfully and publicly reinforced it.

Through school classes, Stamper and Flanagan cooperated to revive another disappearing form, the burden or pack basket that once had been so common among women. According to Agnes Welch, Gertrude Flanagan lent her a burden basket and instructed her to duplicate it. Welch's teacher was Lottie Stamper. "I learned at school," Welch nods, "Lottie Stamper." Pointing to an example of the basket that became her specialty, Welch relates that "Miss Flanagan gave me a basket like that a long time ago for me to learn on. They didn't have designs like this. I did this myself. When I learned, they were just plain. And no dye."[148]

In 1937, the same year Stamper introduced basketry classes, twelve-year-old Welch attended school for just nine months. At the conclusion of the school term she was told that she was too old to continue. During the nine months Agnes Welch had attended school, she took two hours of basketry every day. She learned to weave rivercane patterns and white oak burden baskets. In her hands, the burden basket became highly stylized, heavily patterned, and richly colored with vegetable dyes. Her daughters learned from her, and the new tradition of old burden baskets was established, conveyed from one generation of women to another.

School classes in basketry mark a profound change in the way traditions were passed on. With the introduction of Lottie Stamper's basketweaving classes, a tradition of teaching and learning moved from the household province of mothers and daughters to the public sphere of the government school, where all students gained exposure to the same techniques. Stamper collected old patterns, copied them in a notebook, and reproduced them on graph paper. Drawings of rivercane patterns hung on the walls of her classroom, and her students practiced reproducing them on graph paper in order to learn the numerical combinations for each de-

Agnes Welch of Big Cove making a white oak burden basket (1955).
North Carolina Collection, University of North Carolina
Library at Chapel Hill.

sign. Patterns that once belonged to families became common property. And patterns that once belonged only to rivercane were shared with white oak.

Copying the work of others became commonplace, but public dissemination of family traditions contravened customs of knowledge and training. Patterns of basketry—and life—were undoubtedly lost in the process. The old rivercane

Lottie Stamper's basketry class (1940s). Reproductions of rivercane patterns hung on the walls of the classroom where Stamper taught weaving. Museum of the Cherokee Indian, Cherokee, N. C.

designs hanging on the classroom walls represented a great deal more than weaving techniques. They were strands that connected family members, expressed identity, documented concepts shared through time, preserved knowledge and experience, and interwove past and present. Patterns were forms of communication and assertions of self. "Some people say if you copied their baskets," one weaver remarks quietly, "they say you're taking their patterns away."[149] The implications are profound.

As family patterns moved into public arenas, they took on new names. Most weavers recall that the names of basket patterns came from Gertrude Flanagan and Edna Groves. The names, like "Flowing Water" and "Chief's Daughter," tended toward nostalgia. Many say that such names have no meaning to them and that their mothers and grandmothers did not identify patterns by name. Others, however, fully adopted the custom and participated in the new practice of naming designs and patterns. After Stamper replicated the Nicholson basket, she claimed that "we basket makers named the bottom part 'The Pine Tree' and the top 'The Casket.'"[150]

Tourism: "The One Great Opportunity"

As Lottie Stamper taught more and more students to make baskets and Ethel Garnett taught their mothers to loom weave, the need for a sales outlet increased. Ethel Garnett set up a small sales area in a corner of the school reception room. By 1938, craft classes were so busy with Christmas requests that they had to "bring in adult basketmakers to fill the orders." But, even with more orders, more tourists, greater exposure, and federal intervention, the prices of baskets remained relatively low. The cost of rivercane baskets ranged from $1.25 for a small wastebasket to $2.25 for a market basket. Flanagan sent two white oak baskets to the 1938 San Francisco Fair for two dollars each.[151]

Tourism, road building, marketing, teaching, fairs, revivals, and federal policies converged to encourage more basketry, and increasing numbers of Cherokees turned to craft production. In the context of the promise of ready cash, even in such small amounts, Betty Lossiah decided to try to make baskets with maple when she could no longer find white oak. As the 1940s began, tourism remained the only hope of financial relief for Cherokees. And tourists continued to show interest in buying handwoven, root-dyed, inexpensive Cherokee baskets.

The Second World War temporarily ended tourism and greatly reduced craftwork. At the same time, the war effort provided jobs and regular incomes to several hundred Cherokee families. More than 250 men and women enlisted in the armed forces, and their dependents received monthly pay from the government. More than 200 men worked on the construction of TVA's Fontana Dam on the Little Tennessee River, receiving regular paychecks for their labor. Prices for timber increased during the war, and Cherokees cut more than five million board feet from their forests in 1943. Although the Indian Agency's annual report of 1944 identified agriculture as "the most important phase of the economy," the amount of cash circulating on the reservation had never been as great.[152]

At the end of the war, attention turned again to the reformation of Indian life and the enhancement of Indian economies. John Collier's brother, Charles A. Collier, vice president of the Georgia Power Company, surveyed the reservation for the federal government's Office of Indian Rehabilitation. He was accompanied and assisted by Principal Sam Gilliam, the new superintendent Joe Jennings, craft instructor Ethel Garnett, and home economics supervisor Gertrude Flanagan. Collier prepared a detailed report "setting forth some of the problems and opportunities" he found on the reservation. There were only two craft shops, nine restaurants, and a total of seven "rooming houses" available for tourists. Few of the establishments, according to Collier, would appeal to the "better class of tourist trade." All local jobs, including those related to the timber industry, the Fontana Dam, and local businesses, were "wholly insufficient to insure anything like an average, decent standard of living." With no industry, diminishing forests, a decreasing land base, and no ready market for crafts or agricultural produce, he anticipated serious "post-war problems."[153]

Collier proposed a solution whose antecedents wound back several decades. The development of tourism, he wrote, offered *"the one great opportunity"* for economic vitality. To attract tourists, he recommended improving the appearance of the reservation, opening facilities for lodging and eating, and creating recreational outlets. He specifically proposed the establishment of a "high-class museum" and the construction of a "building to house the arts and crafts salesroom." Crafts, he believed, "open up an almost unlimited market."[154] It was a familiar refrain that dated back to the Arts and Crafts revival at the turn of the century.

The following year, Superintendent Jennings and about sixty craftworkers formed the Qualla Arts and Crafts Cooperative and Jennings suggested moving the salesroom from the school to the agency. The establishment of the co-op in a building separate from the school meant that for the first time artisans had a sales outlet that remained open during summer months, the period of greatest tourism. Two years later, the co-op moved from the agency to its own building. Jennings provided business guidelines recommended by the Indian Arts and Crafts Board, and he assigned "responsibility for all purchases" to Gertrude Flanagan "in order to have uniformity" of marketable items.[155]

In 1951, the Indian Arts and Crafts Board hired Gertrude Flanagan as Arts and Crafts Specialist for the Southeastern region. In her new role, she assumed responsibility for encouraging and directing craftwork among Choctaws, Seminoles, and Catawbas, as well as Cherokees. Maintaining her office in the co-op, Flanagan influenced policy as well as purchasing. She instructed weavers about shapes, forms, materials, and dyes. "When we joined the Qualla Arts and Crafts Mutual," one weaver recalls, "we weren't allowed to use store bought dyes." Flanagan also set prices.[156] The board of the Cherokee co-op included Cherokees only, and it hired Cherokee managers, but Flanagan's control of membership standards, purchases, and prices left little room for discussion. Women's baskets themselves, however, reveal a continuing assertion of individual identity within the constraints of the market.

Weavers continued to experiment with forms, just as Betty Lossiah did with materials. Since trade baskets were almost wholly associated with household interiors and decorative functions rather than subsistence tasks, weavers made them smaller and lighter "for just decoration in the home."[157] Smaller baskets required less support, and handles diminished in size and strength. In contrast to the powerful

Drop handles on a white oak purse basket made by Emily Smith (1986).
Private collection. Photograph by William F. Hull.

White oak basket trays dyed with walnut, made by Elsie Watty (1991)
[*left*, l: 22.5 cm, w: 7.5 cm, h: 4.7 cm; *right*, l: 17 cm, w: 17 cm, h: 5.8 cm].
By the second half of the twentieth century, some weavers fashioned very narrow splits
for their baskets as a special design technique. Private collection.
Photograph by William F. Hull.

White oak rib toy cradle, dyed
with walnut and bloodroot,
made by Dinah Wolfe (1991)
[l: 21 cm, w: 11 cm, h: 13 cm].
Toys and miniatures became
increasingly popular
with tourists in the second half
of the twentieth century.
Private collection.
Photograph by William F. Hull.

White oak wastebasket
with elaborated base and rim
bindings dyed with walnut and
bloodroot, made by Emma Taylor
(1989) [d: 21.5 cm, h: 24 cm].
Private collection.
Photograph by William F. Hull.

White oak burden basket with rivercane patterns, dyed with walnut and bloodroot, made by Agnes Welch (1987) [base: 16 cm × 16 cm, h: 32.5 cm]. Private collection. Photograph by William F. Hull.

White oak wastebasket with rivercane patterns, dyed with walnut and bloodroot, made by Carol Welch (1995) [d: 27 cm, h: 33.7 cm]. Private collection. Photograph by William F. Hull.

interlock handles that Edna Groves boasted about at the 1934 Southeastern Fair, light and graceful drop handles did not support the basket or bear much weight. As weavers sought new markets, they elaborated their baskets from top to bottom. They expanded the amount of surface decoration and the number of patterns. They made white oak baskets with increasingly narrow splits and added rims to the bases of maple baskets. They reduced the thickness of rims, doubled them, and embellished bindings. And they began to combine techniques from different traditions. Rivercane patterns appeared on white oak baskets. White oak rimmed baskets of cane and honeysuckle. Maple curled in and out of white oak surfaces. The advent of tourism brought an explosion of forms, designs, decorations, and embellishments in baskets made as "just souvenirs." Weavers and buyers shaped new traditions based on appearance. Just as the ceremonial use of baskets disappeared in the nineteenth century, their utilitarian purpose vanished in the twentieth. As Bessie Long says, "there's nowhere you can use it now."[158] Baskets had no function other than ornamentation, so weavers developed ornamental forms for every basket feature. The price was the only aspect of basketry that scarcely changed.

When Flanagan retired from her job as crafts specialist in 1973, schoolteacher Steve Richmond succeeded her and promptly moved the regional office out of the co-op building. Before leaving her office for the last time, Flanagan told the new manager, Betty Craig DuPree, that craft prices were as high as they could go.[159] DuPree, however, knew something about the difficulty of weaving and dyeing, of finding material, and of making a living from craftwork. She was an enrolled member of the Eastern Band who grew up on the reservation, attended the Cherokee Boarding School, and took basketry classes from Lottie Stamper. She immediately began to raise prices of all crafts sold in the co-op. As members got more money for their work, prices began to rise in shops all across the reservation.

Nonetheless, weavers could not earn a living from basketry. Basketweaving continued to provide an identity but not a means to economic independence. Craft income depends on constant production, marketing, and a steady supply of material. And the number of hours necessary to prepare and weave baskets never diminishes. As tourism increased on the reservation, weavers turned to seasonal low-wage jobs. They became waitresses, cooks, and maids in reservation motels and restaurants, or salespersons in the craft shops. The jobs lasted from late spring through fall. From November through April, almost every enterprise on the reservation closed. During the cold and quiet winter months, only the co-op remained open and continued to purchase crafts. The "promise of prosperity" envisioned by the Meriam report, the potential that could be fulfilled by women who followed "traditional arts highly respected by white customers," remained a mere promise and a fading hope.[160]

"They Forgot It All": History and Tourism in the 1950s

In 1946, Joe Jennings met with a group of businessmen from the eleven counties in western North Carolina to organize the Western North Carolina Associated Communities. To encourage tourism in their impoverished region, they agreed to develop a drama similar to the *Lost Colony*, an outdoor historical play produced in Manteo, North Carolina. The counties contributed funds for an annual production portraying Cherokee history, staged on the reservation, which was the most likely tourist attraction in the mountain counties. As plans got underway, the group incorporated the Cherokee Historical Association (CHA) to produce and manage the show.[161]

Written by a graduate student at the University of North Carolina named Kermit Hunter, *Unto These Hills* held its first performance in the summer of 1950 and was an instant success, setting a record for attendance at outdoor dramas. Since its first production in 1950, more than 4.8 million people have seen the show. It is credited with bringing more tourists into the area than any other attraction. The play recreates the history of the Eastern Band from the time of contact with Spanish conquistadors to the 1842 return of Chief Junaluska to North Carolina. It focuses on removal and concludes on a positive and optimistic note. The crises of the Civil War, the massive destruction of landscapes, and the cruelties of the assimilation program do not fit into the play's chronology or its themes.[162]

While tourists, mostly white, watched a version of Cherokee history unfold on stage in the Yellow Hill amphitheater, another kind of history was being made nearby. Two years after the drama opened, the Nantahala Power Company brought electricity to Big Cove. Eighty-three families in the Big Cove were the last on the reservation to get electricity. Arizona Swayney's son, Roy Blankenship, who was president of the Big Cove Community Club at the time, worked with Joe Jennings to arrange a compromise with the power company, which had resisted for years to bring power to the area because it "could not afford the expense of clearing a right-of-way." They persuaded the Tribal Council to purchase the poles and the community Free Labor crew (*gadugi*) to clear the land. Men worked every Friday to create a path twenty-three miles long and forty feet wide. At midday, they "sat on nearby logs to eat lunches brought from home in paper pokes."[163] As they completed the job, memories of lunch baskets woven by wives and mothers faded along with the darkness.

The year after lights went on in Big Cove, the Cherokee Historical Association opened a second tourist attraction, the Oconaluftee Indian Village. Based on research by the anthropology departments of the Universities of Tennessee, Geor-

Oconaluftee Indian Village basket station (1956). A re-creation of a 1750 Cherokee settlement, the village features stations where Cherokee employees demonstrate skills, arts, and crafts. Courtesy of the Cherokee Historical Association, Cherokee, N.C.

gia, and North Carolina, the village is a "living museum" that depicts an imaginary 1750 Cherokee town. Cherokees who work in the village wear period costumes to perform tasks, such as basketweaving, wood carving, cooking, and pottery making, at different stations. From May through October they patiently respond to a wide range of questions from tourists who follow an interpretive tour from one work station to another.

Like the drama *Unto These Hills*, the village presents only an impression of Cherokee life. At the basket station, women sit together weaving containers of rivercane, white oak, honeysuckle, and maple. They trim their splits with pocket knives, add twentieth-century curls, curlicues, and rings, and attach drop handles carved by men at the woodworking station. In the village, life and work appear serene and easy. But neither the village nor the drama can convey the complex, densely woven history of women and basketry, ecosystems and economies, oppression and resistance. Neither can approximate the extraordinary changes the Cherokees have participated in, responded to, and helped shape. Both leave the visitors lost in nostalgia and the Cherokees lost in an imaginary antiquity.

Cherokees like Emma Taylor who work at the village talk about the past. "Sometimes we talk, the basketweavers you know, we're all about the same age, we tell one another, we say 'Wonder what the Indians did, really did, way back then.'" Wearing nearly identical calico skirts and blouses, they ask each other "where did they get their cloth to make their clothes?" Emma Taylor shakes her head and smiles. "But nobody knows. They forgot it all."[164]

While employees of the village muse about what really happened in the past, an irony of history threads through the workstations, for the village has become the new training ground for weaving. Younger weavers learn from older ones how to work with different materials. Copies of old rivercane patterns on graph paper are stored in a nearby locker. The Cherokee Historical Association pays someone to gather and prepare the basketry material, and weavers have access to ready-made handles, rims, and rings produced by men in the wood carving station. They do not keep the baskets they make but are paid for making them in public. And in the meantime, younger weavers are learning by watching and listening. Since Lottie Stamper's death, basket classes have been offered only sporadically on the reservation and the village has come to serve as a teacher of weavers.

One other source of history, education, and entertainment developed following the recommendations of Charles Collier. For more than a half century, collectors had been paying meager amounts of money for Cherokee antiquities. When history teacher Louvica Wyman began collecting artifacts from the families of her students to display at the fair in 1933, she hoped to "preserve the Cherokee arts of long ago" by persuading people to give "their relics to the museum" rather than selling them "to tourists at a price below their values." While one teacher attempted to gather a collection for the school, the park service and Indian Office discussed their own ideas for developing a museum on the reservation. For a time, they planned to establish one near the *Nununyi* mound but abandoned construction because of the war.[165] Charles Collier's recommendation to develop a museum on the Qualla Boundary grew out of the hopes and schemes of many who had come before him. In the 1950s, the Cherokee Historical Association purchased a private collection of artifacts that formed the basis for the present-day Museum of the

Cherokee Indian. The collection belonged to a wealthy businessman from Asheville who had been instrumental in creating the Great Smoky Mountains National Park and who had often discussed the possibility of building a park museum on the reservation.

In 1976, the CHA turned the museum over to the Eastern Band. When the museum moved into a new building, Ellen Johnson Merwin of Knoxville, Tennessee, donated a rivercane doubleweave basket that had been purchased by her great-grandmother from a Cherokee neighbor about the time of removal. It is one of the oldest Cherokee baskets in the world.

The drama, the village, and the museum are three centers that provide a sense of history to late-twentieth-century visitors to the reservation—and to Cherokees as well. All three ventures developed in the 1950s as part of the Cherokee Historical Association's goal to "perpetuate the history and traditions of the Cherokee people."[166] Their ability to succeed depends on tourism, which undercuts both history and tradition in the interest of making them marketable. And yet, without them, little on the reservation would tell the story of Cherokee persistence in the face of nearly impossible odds.

Old and new, custom and change constantly interweave in processes of transformation. After the Second World War, Cherokees looked for different ways to attract the long-promised tourists and develop a healthier economy. Baskets had always been the source of food and heat and light, and women had always been providers, using what they had to make what they needed. Reshaping customs to create and sustain different markets, basketweavers turned to a fourth material, red maple, developing another tradition of basketry. The material was indigenous but the tradition was entirely new. Women had once again begun to weave new worlds.

Epilogue

❖ ❖ ❖

The Legacy of Legend and History: The Meaning of Weaving

Baskets serve as a metaphor for history. Among Cherokees, women have been the primary weavers and users of baskets, and so baskets serve particularly as metaphors for the history of Cherokee women. Over the course of several centuries, women have woven with materials gathered from local landscapes. Baskets thus also serve as metaphors for an ecological history, for ways women and men live in, shape, and are influenced by their environments. Every basket reveals something about the social conditions of production, how weavers live, and why they weave. Changes in baskets—in material, form, and function—document changes in ways weavers experience, participate in, and respond to the world around them. Every basket is a hybrid that weaves together past and present experiences, interlacing historical processes and individual concepts. Every basket is both a collective and an individual text of the past and present.

Baskets carry many levels of meaning. They evoke the primeval era, mythological time, and the genesis of the world and the people themselves. They recall the original weaver, *Kanane-ski Amai-yehi* (Spider Dwelling in the Water), who was, by her very name as well as her habitation and manner of living, literally connected to water. Universally identified as female, the first weaver associated women with water, an association that was born out in the early Cherokee division of labor that gave women the responsibility for carrying water.

The brief narrative of the First Fire identifies certain characteristics of the weaver. "She can run on top of the water or dive down to the bottom," Swimmer and John Ax explained to James Mooney.[1] The legendary weaver crosses boundaries between worlds, moving from the surface to the depth, from land to water, from water to fire, and finally, for the sake of the people, from darkness to light and from cold to heat. Crossing and connecting worlds, she posits a relationship between two places, elements, and conditions. As a female, as a being connected to water, and as one who moves from one world to another, she evokes women's ability to be simultaneously one person and two, an individual and also a woman carrying an infant in a sac of water in her belly. She embraces change and brings new traditions and customs to her people. The female creature spins out material from her abdomen to weave a container. In a replication of giving birth, *Kanane-ski Amai-yehi* creates a container that ensures future life. Weaving thus becomes a part of women and their generative power. Weaving is unambiguously acknowledged as essential, for without it the people would perish in the cold darkness.

The myth of the First Fire celebrates the weaver, the act of weaving, and, finally, the container itself. The container carries fire, the earthly representation of the sun, who was also female in the early Cherokee pantheon. *Kanane-ski Amai-yehi's* container of fire parallels early Cherokee households that had central hearths where women maintained fires. Homes and the fires in them belonged to women in the matrilineal, matrilocal systems that characterized their society before removal.

In surviving myth fragments, baskets carry elements of sacred power even in their most commonplace usage. The first woman, *Selu*, takes a basket with her when she goes into the seclusion of the corn house. There, "leaning over the basket," she gives metaphorical birth to corn by rubbing her belly, and to beans by rubbing her sides.[2] The sacred story associates baskets with women, women with food, and food with baskets, all the while interweaving reminders of women's generative power. *Selu* repeatedly gives birth to corn and beans, not only in the myth but also in every agricultural season. Just as *Kanane-ski Amai-yehi's* container holds fire, *Selu's* belly and basket hold food. The basket corresponds to the belly, the source of nourishment that preserves life and carries the children that guarantee the future of the society. Moreover, the story of *Selu* represents change—from one kind of food production to another, from one way of life to another. By understanding the necessity for change, *Selu* guarantees the future of the Cherokee people.

Another myth fragment affirms the importance of weaving and celebrates women as the source of life and society. In the story of How the World Was Made, Swimmer and John Ax described the earth as "a great island floating in a sea of water, and suspended at each of the four cardinal points by a cord hanging down from the sky vault."[3] Weaving, the narrative suggests, literally holds the world in place. *Ayasta's* brief addition to the story celebrates woman as life bringer and head of the matrilineage. Concerned for resources, she spaces out the birth of her children and thus protects the very society she is creating. Concerned for her children, she changes herself.

The stories of the First Fire, *Selu*, and How the World was Made are like double-woven baskets, multilayered and densely textured. They are expressions of the customs, behaviors, and beliefs of women and assert a culture and identity of women that is specifically Cherokee. Together, the three fragments establish the significance of basketry and connect baskets with women, fertility, life, and sustenance. This complex of memory and meaning is the legacy of Cherokee women, the legacy of weavers.

Early accounts consistently identify women with weaving and the use of baskets in work and ceremonies. The association of women with basketry has persisted to the present, even though men may be involved in some or perhaps all aspects of basket production.[4] In 1926, Ben Dixon MacNeil wrote in the *Raleigh News and Observer* that "no amount of civilization seems to have been able to interfere with . . . the women in the weaving of baskets."[5] The inability of "civilization" to interfere with their weaving testifies to the significance of women's legacy. Among a people whose survival was threatened, whose families were displaced, whose language was forbidden, and whose beliefs were prohibited, the ability to say "I learned by watching my mother," or grandmother, or another Cherokee woman, can be a powerful wellspring.

Weavers have not simply replicated the work of their predecessors. Basketry has been a living tradition that has changed over time. The most significant changes have occurred in the selection of material. Over a period of several hundred years, Cherokees developed four major basketry traditions based on weaving materials. Each new material, and its associated forms, has been added to earlier conventions rather than supplanting them. The development of only four basketry traditions, three of them in the last 150 years, among a people who used containers continuously in ceremonies, trade, and work, a people who knew and utilized literally thousands of plants and trees in their lives, indicates the extraordinarily conservative nature of their basketry in terms of material. New materials and forms have been adopted only when they proved useful and could be integrated into social and economic systems.

Weavers have had access to many possible materials. Even with such a variety of resources, they emphasized rivercane above all others for hundreds of years. It was a logical choice. The material was abundant and it was durable. Yet, there was more to the choice than practicality. Their preference for rivercane accompanied a spiritual association with flowing water. Flourishing in dense stands along waterways near their settlements, rivercane was the margin, boundary, and bridge between Cherokees and the Long Person. "Every important ceremony," wrote Mooney, "contains a prayer to the 'Long Person.'"[6] Cherokees lived by the water spiritually, psychologically, and physically. The historical period when rivercane was their primary basket material correlates with an elaborate ceremonial life that continuously connected them to water.

In the period of rivercane, Cherokees occupied three physiographic regions—the Piedmont, Ridge and Valley, and Blue Ridge Mountain provinces. Transforming landscapes around them, they exploited a great variety of resources for food, clothing, shelter, and trade. Women were responsible for agriculture and households, for gathering wild foods, for the production of clothing, and for weaving baskets for ceremony, utility, and trade. Rivercane baskets of the period were smooth and seamless, with subtle and intricate designs woven into them. Their surfaces were continuous fields of cane. Their rims, bases, and lids were cane, and they were dyed with roots, bark, and hulls.

Following a series of wars in the eighteenth century, Cherokees forfeited their Piedmont lands. Their brilliant efforts to retain their remaining lands and avoid removal included the adoption of various aspects of the so-called civilization program, such as animal husbandry and different farming techniques, residential patterns, and gender roles. Ecosystems changed as indigenous species vanished and imported ones took hold. Rivercane began to diminish, literally and metaphorically.

Following removal, Southeastern Cherokees were restricted to the mountains of North Carolina and surrounded by white settlers. Weavers adopted materials traditionally used by whites, and their willingness to do so indicates profound change. The full incorporation of white oak occurred in a century marked by a series of disasters, including removal, repeated challenges to the right of Cherokees to remain in North Carolina, the loss of health and life during the Civil War period, and the threatened loss of land following the insanity, bankruptcy, and death of the white agent, William H. Thomas. The inclusion of white oak into the essentially conservative tradition of rivercane basketry indicates the depth and breadth of change and loss.

Although Cherokees adopted various customs of surrounding whites they continued some of their own conventions. These different strands are represented and evoked by the coexistence and intermixing of rivercane and white oak basketry. New customs and patterns emerged as social systems and basket production changed. Gender roles blurred as men adopted farming and became weavers of baskets. Necessity shaped the manufacture of white oak containers, and utility governed form. Rib baskets, closely associated with small farms and male weavers in white communities, became commonplace. Gardening and basket trade remained women's work, and bartering became increasingly important in domestic economies. Women and children walked trails and rode trains to neighboring communities of white people to obtain clothes and food in exchange for baskets.

The development of Cherokee white oak basketry accompanied a growing forest emphasis, a gradual distancing from their spiritually integrated world, an increasing proximity to white culture, and the transformation of established social systems. No evidence indicates the use of white oak baskets as ceremonial or ritual objects. Rather, the incorporation of white oak marks the disappearance of the basket as an explicitly ritual article. Baskets remained essential in subsistence. Contemporary Cherokees do not romanticize earlier dependence on woven containers. "You used them just as necessity," one remembered. Baskets were necessary, said another, because "that's all we had to use. We didn't have nothing else to use."[7]

As the nineteenth century gave way to the twentieth, regional forests became the focus of Northeastern lumbering interests. Timber companies purchased watersheds and stripped forests of hardwoods, taking white oak trees for barrel staves, house lumber, and furniture and bark for tannic acid used to process leather. Mill villages sprang up, and logging trains penetrated Cherokee forests. Trains showered sparks into logging residues, and fires leapt across mountain slopes, removing humus and topsoil from fragile ecosystems. Stream life choked on sawdust and debris. Nesting sites vanished along with vegetation. In addition, the invasion of lumber companies initiated familiar conflicts of interests between land and money. "They do not despise the money that comes into the country," commented a 1916 traveler, "but they deplore the slaughter of the forests."[8] As Cherokees moved closer to a market economy, forests emerged as their only source of collective or individual wealth. The reservation was devoid of employment, but Cherokees retained control of one resource the nation wanted.

In the same period, basketweavers added a third material to their basket inventory. The adoption of honeysuckle, the alien vine that prospers in massively disrupted landscapes, represents women's exploitation of recovering fields and forest edges where opportunistic vegetation thrives. Honeysuckle basketry grew out of changes in the social conditions of basket production and use, for the light and delicate honeysuckle containers are more ornamental than utilitarian, more decorative than durable. They represent and accompanied changing markets, concepts, and lifeways.

Honeysuckle basketry developed in a period of extraordinary discrepancy between the rhetoric of American liberty and the reality of Indian policy. On the reservation and well beyond it, government schools undertook to "civilize" Cherokees for assimilation into white culture. Children left their homes and entered strict military regimens in schools where native speech was prohibited and regard for family customs was undermined. Government schools provided marginal education and emphasized skills appropriate for low-wage work. Female students learned vine and raffia weaving as part of training in domestic arts. The Arts and Crafts movement encouraged the preservation of native crafts while the near-genocide of western Native Americans accompanied the development of American anthropology and the promotion of expositions celebrating American progress.

Contradictory forces of assimilation, annihilation, and preservation brought whites to the reservation and sent Cherokees from their homes. Men found sporadic wage work with lumber and railroad companies, and women developed different venues of trade for baskets. Local and regional fairs brought weavers into direct contact with wider markets, and national and international expositions exhibited Indians as relics and their handwork as art. Decorative containers sold for cash alongside domestic work baskets bartered for food and clothing. Men continued to make white oak baskets for daily tasks on small farms, but the increasingly ornamented rivercane, white oak, and honeysuckle baskets remained the province of women. The availability of commercial dyes led to a florescence of color on baskets of all three materials.

In the 1940s, weavers added a fourth material, the indigenous red maple that grows fast in forest clearings. The addition of maple occurred as other basket materials dwindled in changing landscapes. The chestnut blight and widespread logging had permanently altered forest composition. Conditions of basket production changed as new federal policies encouraged native handwork in conjunction with developing tourism. The Great Smoky Mountains National Park opened amid animated discussions about constructing reservation roads, tourist lodges, restaurants, shops, and local museums.

Paved roads and tourism brought new ideas, contacts, and relationships. To romantics who thought of Native Americans only as a part of the landscape, paved roads despoiled an area of great beauty. A 1916 visitor described the remoteness of "a pitching, stony road" that passed "filmy waterfalls" and led him "through roaring Soco again and again on rock slants that made our horses tremble, and into a wild and winding valley, the first of the Indian lands."[9] He could easily idealize a place in which he did not live. Older Cherokees remember well that there were no roads when they were growing up, but the absence holds little charm for them. The lack of roads meant limited access to education, medical assistance, and commerce.

In contrast to the 1916 description of lyrical beauty, a 1990 newspaper article described the main road through Qualla as "a grand strand, . . . [a] rusted neon glitz above warmweather stopoffs."[10] Many arrogant visitors have condemned the kind of development they see on the reservation, but the strand has been built to appeal to tourists coming to Great Smoky Mountains National Park. The opening of the park altered local economies as cash became the basis for exchange and wage labor replaced the barter of goods and services. Dependence on tourism is the final and complete inversion of early Cherokee resistance to white encroachment.

As part of the effort to cultivate tourism, institutions replaced traditional social relationships of exchange and education—and even of basketry training itself. In the government school, Lottie Stamper began to teach basketweaving and collect old patterns for students to copy. Traditions of basketry that had once belonged to clans or families became part of institutional learning. All across the country, Native Americans began literally to capitalize on tribal tradition and heritage. On the Cherokee reservation, history was carefully packaged for tourists, and entrepreneurs began marketing pseudo-Indian products to a public hungry for nostalgic images of a fictional past. Craft shops and motels sprang up as whites leased land from Cherokees who could not acquire enough capital to develop small businesses of their own. New kinds of wares replaced utilitarian containers, and baskets became ornaments to decorate homes. For the consumer society, the value of baskets became their appearance. For weavers, the value of baskets became their marketability. As marketability was becoming a basket's most important characteristic, the Qualla Arts and Crafts Cooperative was established to ensure a place for year-round sales. Basket prices began to increase. Yet, the co-op remains the exclusive domain of those who can meet the strict admissions standards: membership hovers around 300—out of a total population of more than 10,000. While the co-op attracts a tourist market, contributes to the community, and subsidizes its members, it cannot solve the deep economic problems of reservation life.

As the twentieth century draws to a close, weavers rely on all four materials. Most specialize in one. Baskets and conditions of basket production have continued to change in the face of diminishing resources. Property laws and a shrinking land base have separated cane and oak weavers from their sources of material. They can occasionally buy oak or bloodroot from itinerant salesmen. As basket materials are harder to acquire, contemporary weavers identify baskets by the number of splits they need to make them. "I know the size before I start," Emma Taylor explains. "It's just the count. It's got nine splits in each side, so eighteen splits altogether." Another recognizes a basket she wove several years earlier. "Twenty-one splits—total, forty-two."[11] The number of splits and the size and kind of basket are conceptually interwoven.

Changes in form are expressions of societal as well as ecological changes. Handles have become part of basket ornamentation, and a specialization has developed for handle carvers. At one time, baskets were literally woven around handles. Integral to the basket's function, the handle actually identifies the basket in one weaver's memory: "They had—well, they call them, you know, these handles, these interlock handles, they call those market baskets."[12] In the present, however, drop handles lie outside the basket, attached by narrow hooks that slide into the sides. On light and ornamental contemporary baskets, "a lot of them want these drop handles."[13]

Smaller baskets also have lighter, thinner rims. The density of the rim, according to Shirley Taylor, "depends on the type of basket that you make. Like if it's a big basket you've got to have a thicker rim. If it's a small basket you can have a thinner rim on the outside."[14] Rims bound with hickory, a feature Frank Speck called "an almost infallible characteristic," once identified Cherokee baskets. Other studies concur with Speck's analysis.[15] By the mid-twentieth century, however, weavers also bound rims with white oak, and in the last half of the century they began to elaborate the binding to make it more decorative.

Surface decoration has increased until it covers almost the entire basket. Once devoid of surface ornamentation, contemporary baskets may be covered with segments of color and elements of form that leap from the surface. Curls, rings, curlicues, ears, crosses, and elaborate bindings decorate fanciful, colorful containers. What had once appeared as a continuous field that was internally constructed in rivercane gradually became an elaborate design that was externally applied in white oak, honeysuckle, and maple.

Contemporary baskets are decorative items rather than ceremonial or work objects. "Today you don't see hardly any cornfields," Emma Taylor reflects, "and that's how come today we only make baskets for just decoration in the home. Unless somebody uses it. . . . Today they just buy small baskets. . . . We just make small baskets. Unless somebody speaks for a big basket."[16] Miniature baskets are suitable for household interiors and are marketable because they are relatively inexpensive. Baskets have become "just souvenirs," says Bessie Long, because "there's nowhere you can use it now." Such souvenirs seldom decorate the homes of weavers, however, but only those of tourists.[17]

The ceremonial use of baskets disappeared in the nineteenth century, and domestic functions waned in the twentieth. As the twentieth century draws to a close, weavers produce complex, beautiful baskets in order to pay bills. Basketry gives women a degree of control over certain resources and a measure of pride. Louise Goings suggests that "what I make with my hands, that's my money. It's a different type of money than what you make working your regular job and taking care of things that way."[18] This feeling is another legacy of Cherokee women and of weavers.

A Reason for Weaving

In Cherokee basketry there is both meaning and reason. Cherokees continue to weave and sell baskets primarily because they depend on income from basket sales. Tourism has not provided enough regular employment to provide a margin of safety, and the reservation has attracted little other industry. In the 1970s four manufacturing plants operated in the area, providing work. Three of them subsequently closed, leaving their deserted buildings as part of the landscape.

Many weavers have worked intermittently for various manufacturers who have opened and closed plants, and they have also worked seasonally in local motels and restaurants. When Bessie Long recalls her work experience, for example, she begins, "Well, I worked at the Vassar Company, Vassar. I worked there ten years. And then I went to Pancake House and then Kentucky Fried Chicken three years, and then went to Holiday Inn." The cadence produces a narrative of economic struggle. "I worked in the laundry three years, and then they let me off one fall. . . . But I needed to work a job, and then I went on to Heritage. . . . It's gone. It didn't last long, it just got bankrupt or something, it just went out."[19] Annie French has had similar experiences, working at "Vassar, this Barclay, Harn, and White Shield." She does not think she would be able to get factory employment now because "some factories won't hire any just—they have to be younger." Louise Goings "worked at . . . a factory for hair accessories for about seven months. Seven or eight months, I guess. And then, the following spring, I guess, after I got laid off at the factory, I got hired at the school."[20]

The 1980 census reported that 34 percent of Cherokees on the reservation earned less than $3,000 per year. In 1994, the director of the tribal office of tourism claimed that more than 50 percent of Cherokees lived below the national poverty level. Median family income on the reservation is less than half that of families in the surrounding counties.[21] Tourism is seasonal. Of the fifty-eight motels on the reservation, only a half dozen remain open in the winter. Unemployment reaches 45 percent in winter months. In the remainder of Swain and Jackson Counties, where most of the reservation lies, winter unemployment rates are 18 and approximately 9 percent respectively. During tourist season, unemployment rates may drop to less than 5 percent. Jobs from April through October include domestic work in motels and restaurants, domestic and sales work in craft shops, and work in the village and drama. In 1990, most seasonal jobs paid minimum wage—$3.85 per hour.[22] Seasonal employment is not guaranteed, so if tourism declines, an employee is likely to be laid off. Moreover, seasonal employment increases only on the Qualla Boundary. Communities that have not turned to tourism, such as Snowbird, where approximately 400 Cherokees live, experience no change in unemployment rates during the tourist season.[23] Unemployment is chronic year-round in Snowbird.

Seasonal tourism is unpredictable and adversely affected by a wide range of factors including weather, fuel prices, competition, and local and national economies. In 1982, the Cherokee BIA reported that "all business income from the Cherokee area was off drastically this year." The proximity of the World's Fair in Knoxville less than three hours from the reservation hurt rather than helped business. The 1996 Summer Olympics in Atlanta also adversely affected Cherokee tourism as visitors either concentrated in Georgia or avoided the region altogether. Motels reported fewer customers,[24] and reduced motel occupancy means decreased business for restaurants, craft shops, and recreational venues. In 1994, Chief Jonathan L. Taylor stated flatly that "tourism is not as good as it used to be."[25]

Dependence on tourists who are in town an average of one day per visit contributes to a proliferation of gimmicks to attract their business. "Grasshopper chiefs," who work in the summer, wear, as one of them says, "ten thousand feathers" made into Plains Indian headdresses. They stand beside wooden tepees near craft shops to lure in visitors. They pose for photographs, often with children. They talk to tourists, who frequently ask "if I'm a real Indian."[26] The question reveals the extent to which the flamboyant roadside displays undercut potential understanding of Cherokee culture. During tourist season, Cherokees who come into the most public areas of the reservation may be asked where their tepees, beads, and tomahawks are. They are greeted with "Ugh" and "How." The tension between entertaining and educating tourists, between appealing to and enlightening them, has persisted throughout the twentieth century. Tourism is an economic strategy, but it can also be a cultural thief.

There is another aspect to the tourist business, for those who consider themselves enlightened carry with them to the reservation a preconception of appropriate Cherokee appearance and behavior. Cherokees have thus found themselves dependent on the unreliable industry that continually judges them if they do not act, look, or sound as expected, and then condemns their community for the way it has developed. "The Cherokee strip," according to a 1995 news article, "is one of those artificial tourist destinations left like sticky fingerprints on the majestic Smokies." The journalist continued his assessment that "the face that Cherokees offer to the world often seems a cheap caricature of Native Americans." Such judgment is but another incarnation of the attitudes brought to Native Americans by agents of Christianization, civilization, and assimilation. Throughout history

Cherokees have encountered those who presume to know what is best for Native American people.[27]

In the 1980s, Cherokees began offering high stakes bingo on the Qualla Boundary, which brings in approximately $600,000 a year. In 1990, they added a weekly Lotto game, which became even more profitable, and they subsequently began negotiating with the state to allow the establishment of casino gambling.[28] Profits from the games are used for community services and for individual disbursements. With the advent of gambling, the basis of tourism shifts from family to adult entertainment. Those who come for games arrive in buses that wait in parking lots with their engines idling. When the games end, players depart. They seldom tour the reservation or express interest in crafts or history. Furthermore, states all across the country are challenging the right of Native Americans to establish gaming centers on their reservations. If states begin to compete with reservations, Native Americans may once again lose.

The unpredictability of tourism and the lack of alternative employment has long meant that Cherokees must create their own source of income, which has, in the past, been some kind of marketable craftwork. "When you've got a family to support," says Dinah George, "you're going to have to go to work." Yet, with so few steady jobs available, as Bessie Long observes, "everybody's got some extra to do."[29] Making baskets for the tourist market has become an important way women provide "some extra" for their families. When a productive weaver like Agnes Welch is asked what she does with all the baskets she makes, she laughs and says, "sell them all."[30]

"We supported ourselves," one weaver recalls of a childhood filled with dyes and splits, weaving and bartering. Reliance on basketry has continued into her middle years. "If I have to pay my telephone bill or some appliance bills, I get on my own to make a basket."[31] And basket prices have increased steadily since they were first marketed for cash. Weavers often comment on the differences between current prices and those of the past. Bessie Long says that in the late 1930s and early 1940s, wastebaskets cost twenty-five cents. Martha Ross remembers her mother's big market baskets that sold for $2.50 each in the late 1940s. Her mother walked into town to "a two-story building there and there was a man from out of Georgia running that shop, and he bought baskets for seventy-five or twenty-five cents." The little square cracker baskets Louise Goings made in the 1950s cost about twenty-five cents.[32] Tourists in every decade have counted on paying as little as possible for the work of Cherokee artisans and are offended by current prices. By the end of the 1990s, prices ranged from twenty-five dollars for the simplest honeysuckle vase to more than a thousand for the complex and intricate rivercane doubleweaves.

While talking to weavers about basket prices and learning about the intricate, difficult, and time-consuming processes involved in basketry, I thought often of the legend of the First Fire, of *Kanane-ski Amai-yehi*, who spun a thread right out of her body to provide heat and light for her people, and of *Selu*, who carried a basket with her every day, filling it with corn and beans that poured from her body to feed her children. For centuries, women have walked the mountains, pulled vines, dug roots, collected hulls, barked trees, hewed wood, busted sticks, scraped splits, banked fires, stirred pots, and sat for hours deep into the night to weave containers in order to provide for their families. They have walked untold miles to find someone to buy a basket or accept one in exchange for food or clothing. They have carried with them the knowledge of their mothers and grandmothers or of any older women who had the skill and patience and knowledge of weaving. The amount of history, labor, time, and skill invested in one basket is incomprehensible to many people who visit the Cherokee reservation.

One cool fall morning as I stood studying a basket display in the co-op, an indignant white woman stalked up, grasping tightly in her hand a medium-sized white oak wastebasket. The basket was dyed with bloodroot and walnut hulls and woven with splits that had been peeled, scraped, cut, and trimmed to three different sizes. Its smooth, narrow base and double rim were hand carved from white oak; two rows of luminous maple curls twisted uniformly on and off the surface. She shook the basket angrily and exclaimed, "Have you seen the prices on these baskets? Don't they know we're tourists? I wish I had bought those baskets on the South Carolina coast!" There was no adequate response. My surprise has never been what baskets cost in the present, but rather, what they cost in the past. "Yes," I replied to the visitor to the Cherokee reservation, "Yes, I feel sure they know we're tourists."

Notes

Abbreviations Used in Notes

ABCFM	Papers of the American Board of Commissioners for Foreign Missions, Shorter College, Rome, Ga.
APS	American Philosophical Society, Philadelphia
BM	British Museum, London
BPRO	British Public Records Office
CA	Cherokee Agency
CIA	Commissioner of Indian Affairs
CSAR	Cherokee School Annual Report
DU	Special Collections Library, Duke University, Durham, N.C.
EU	Special Collections, Woodruff Library, Emory University, Atlanta, Ga.
FRCEP	U.S. Federal Records Center, East Point, Ga.
HSP	Historical Society of Pennsylvania, Philadelphia
HU	University Archives, Huntington Library, Hampton University, Hampton, Va.
LCN	Laws of the Cherokee Nation
LOC	Library of Congress, Washington, D.C.
MAS	Moravian Archives, Salem, N.C.
MCI	Museum of the Cherokee Indian, Cherokee, N.C.
MPM	Milwaukee Public Museum, Milwaukee, Wis.
NA	National Archives, Washington, D.C.
NAA	National Anthropological Archives, Smithsonian Institution, Washington, D.C.
NCC	North Carolina Collection, University of North Carolina, Chapel Hill
NCDAH	North Carolina Department of Archives and History, Raleigh, N.C.
NL	Ayer Collection, Newberry Library, Chicago
NMAI	National Museum of the American Indian, New York
NYPL	New York Public Library
QACM	Qualla Arts and Crafts Mutual, Inc., Cherokee, N.C.
SHC	Southern Historical Collection, University of North Carolina
SI	Smithsonian Institution, Washington, D.C.
TGI	Thomas Gilcrease Institute of American History and Art, Tulsa, Okla.
TSLA	Tennessee State Library and Archives, Nashville, Tenn.
UP	University of Pennsylvania, Philadelphia
WCU	Special Collections, Western North Carolina University, Cullowhee, N.C.
WLCUM	William L. Clements Library, University of Michigan

Introduction

1. The Qualla Boundary is the largest of several tracts of land comprising what is now called the Cherokee Indian reservation.

2. Author interview with Rowena Bradley, Jan. 11, 1989.

3. Ibid.

4. Ibid.

5. Ibid.

6. See, for example, McLoughlin and Conser, "Cherokees in Transition," 678–703.

7. Speck, "Decorative Art and Basketry," 57.

8. Author interview with Louise Goings, May 4, 1989.

9. Author interview with source requesting anonymity.

10. Author interview with Agnes Welch, May 8, 1989.

Prologue

1. The fragment of the Cherokee origin myth was told to James Mooney by Cherokee elders between 1887 and 1890 (see Mooney, *Myths of the Cherokee*, 239). The first field-trained American anthropologist, Mooney began his long and distinguished career working with Southeastern Cherokees. He published their history, myths, and medico-religious formulas in the Nineteenth and Seventh Annual Reports of the Bureau of American Ethnology in 1897 and 1898, which were subsequently combined and reproduced by Charles and Randy Elder, Booksellers, Nashville, 1982.

2. Mooney interprets *Yunwi Gunahita* as the Long Person and also as the Long Man; for Person see *Myths of the Cherokee*, 341; for Man see ibid., 547, and Mooney, "The Cherokee River Cult." I have followed the first convention as less burdened by gender associations.

3. Mooney, *Myths of the Cherokee*, 240.

4. For discussion of Cherokee beliefs about water see Hudson, *Southeastern Indians*, 122–28.

5. Payne MSS 4:27, quotation on 72, NL; Samuel Williams, *Memoirs of Timberlake*, 90. Poet and journalist John Howard Payne (1791–1852) visited the Cherokees in the 1830s to compile information on their traditions. One of his primary sources was missionary Daniel S. Butrick, who had worked among them since 1818. Henry Timberlake volunteered to accept an invitation for an English officer to visit the Overhills following the Cherokee wars of 1760–61. He subsequently conducted two delegations of Cherokees to England, where he died in 1765.

6. Variations abound in the names of Southern Appalachian ranges. Although it is continuous, the western segment changes names from one geographic area to another. Between the Doe and Nolichucky Rivers the name "Unaka" applies. From the Nolichucky to the Big Pigeon the range is called the "Bald," and from the Big Pigeon to the Little Tennessee it is known as the "Great Smokies." The southern terminus of the Unakas is called the "Unicoi," a word that is itself a corruption of the word "Unaka." These names were standardized in 1932 by the U.S. Geographic Board (see *Guide to the Appalachian Trail*, 6-2).

7. Frome, *Strangers in High Places*, 14–18; *North Carolina: WPA Guide*, 10.

8. Samuel Williams, *Adair's History*, 238; Keel, *Cherokee Archaeology*, 6; *North Carolina: WPA Guide*, 11; Murlless and Stallings, *Hiker's Guide*, 20; Sutton and Sutton, *Eastern Forests*, 86.

9. Van Doren, *Travels of William Bartram*, 275–76, 294.

10. Mooney, *Myths of the Cherokee*, 319–20. The *ani-dawehi* (pl.) were the most knowledgeable and skilled of all magico-medical practitioners, familiar with witchcraft as well as healing, and identified with the sacred. See Lee Irwin, "Cherokee Healing," 237–57.

11. Mooney, *Myths of the Cherokee*, 316–19. *U-tlun-ta* was one of the most feared of the mythological characters. The ability to change forms identified an individual as a witch, one to be greatly feared but also acknowledged as a part of the natural order.

12. Ibid., 317.

13. White, "Our Eastern Highlands," 7; Gilbert, "Eastern Cherokees," 183; Chapman, *Tellico Archaeology*, 22; *North Carolina: WPA Guide*, 11; Sutton and Sutton, *Eastern Forests*, 86; Murlless and Stallings, *Hiker's Guide*, 21. In 1901, the secretary of agriculture estimated the annual rainfall in the Southern Appalachians to range from 60 to 71 inches a year but pointed out that in 1898 the annual precipitation in western North Carolina was 105.24 inches (see *Report of the Secretary of Agriculture*, 31, 34).

14. Royce, *Cherokee Nation of Indians*, 11–13; Mooney, *Myths of the Cherokee*, 14. Royce points out that the Six Nations, the Shawnee, and the Delaware also claimed the vast hunting territory included in the Great Kanawha and Ohio River valleys, areas in the present states of West Virginia and Kentucky.

15. De Vorsey, *DeBrahm's Report*, 105.

16. White, "Smoky Mountain Flora," 20; Callaway, Clebsch, and White, "Multivariate Analysis," 116–19; Peattie, "Men, Mountains, and Trees," 156; Ogburn, *Southern Appalachians*, 159; Sutton and Sutton, *Eastern Forests*, 81.

17. Odum, *Ecology and Our Endangered Life Support Systems*, 187–89.

18. Van Doren, *Travels of William Bartram*, 288; Payne MSS 4:196, NL; Samuel Williams, *Adair's History*, 387; Halls, "Common Persimmon," 294–98; Edwin Lawson, "Eastern Redcedar," 131–39.

19. Varner and Grier, *Florida of the Inca*, 296; Van Doren, *Travels of William Bartram*, 49–50.

20. Lamson, "Red Mulberry," 654–57; Crane, *Southern Frontier*, 103 n. 101; Hatley, *Dividing Paths*, 9.

21. Samuel Williams, *Adair's History*, 453–54.

22. Butrick to Payne, July 25, 1837, Payne MSS 4:265, NL.

23. Catesby to Sloane, Nov. 27, 1724, Sloane MSS 4047, fol. 290, BM.

24. Hammett, "Ethnohistory of Aboriginal Landscapes," 24–27; Rink, "Butternut," 386–89; Robert Williams, "Black Walnut," 391–99.

25. "Narrative of the Expedition of Hernando de Soto," 178; Van Doren, *Travels of William Bartram*, 38.

26. "William Bartram's Observations," 152; Samuel Williams, *Adair's History*, 439; Van Doren, *Travels of William Bartram*, 57; see also Payne MSS 4:196, 199–200, 201, and "Cherokee History and Habits and Language," 155a, both in NL. For archaeological evidence see Hammett, "Ethnohistory of Aboriginal Landscapes," 24, Runquist, *Analysis of the Flora and Faunal Remains*, 284, 308–11, Chapman, *Tellico Archaeology*, 45, and Harrington, *Cherokee and Earlier Remains*, 220–21.

27. Graney, "Shagbark Hickory," 219–25.

28. Payne MSS 4:2, 73, 200, 202, NL; Harrington, *Cherokee and Earlier Remains*, 220–21; Hill, "Basket of History"; Richard Foreman, *Cherokee Physician*, 188–89; Hamel and Chiltoskey, *Cherokee Plants*, 61; Witthoft, "Early Cherokee Ethnobotanical Note," 74.

29. Schafale and Weakley, *Classification of Natural Communities*, 62–64; Hawkins, *Sketch and Letters*, 18.

30. Robert Rogers, "White Oak," 605–13; Silver, *New Face on the Countryside*, 19–21; Ogburn, *Southern Appalachians*, 159–60; Sutton and Sutton, *Eastern Forests*, 83; Peattie, "Men, Mountains, and Trees," 164–67; Shelford, *Ecology of North America*, 32.

31. Payne MSS 4:2, 196, NL; "William Bartram's Observations," 152.

32. Chapman, *Tellico Archaeology*, 22; *Audubon Society Field Guide to Trees*, 286–99; White, "Smoky Mountain Flora," 20; Ogburn, *Southern Appalachians*, 156; Peattie, "Men, Mountains, and Trees," 168; Sutton and Sutton, *Eastern Forests*, 28, 59, 83.

33. Goodman and Lancaster, "Eastern Hemlock," 609; Ogburn, *Southern Appalachians*, 165; Sutton and Sutton, *Eastern Forests*, 84.

34. Ogburn, *Southern Appalachians*, 165; Silver, *New Face on the Countryside*, 23; Sutton and Sutton, *Eastern Forests*, 85; Peattie, "Men, Mountains, and Trees," 159–62.

35. White, "Our Eastern Highlands," 8–9; Sutton and Sutton, *Eastern Forests*, 35–36, 86; Ogburn, *Southern Appalachians*, 153–54. Eighteenth- and nineteenth-century botanists were well aware of the common occurrence of northern plants in the Southern Appalachians. From the summit of the Oconee Mountains, William Bartram observed "many plants common in Pennsylvania, New-York and even Canada" (Van Doren, *Travels of William Bartram*, 275).

36. Mooney, *Myths of the Cherokee*, 240, 430.

37. Payne MSS 1:45, NL.

38. Ibid.

39. Longe, "Small Postscript," 4, LOC; Payne MSS 1:20–21, NL. Alexander Longe was a British trader who lived in exile with Cherokees from 1714 to 1724. Following a repatriation visit to Charles Town in 1725, he wrote "A Small Postscript," which is apparently an addendum to a longer manuscript, now missing, prepared for the English Society for the Propagation of the Gospel in Foreign Parts. A remarkable ethnographic document, the postscript also reveals the arrogance with which the British met American Indians. It contains frequent references to "foolish beliefs" and to purported eagerness for enlightenment by missionaries. Longe, and many others after him, misinterpreted Cherokee rhetoric as subservience to assumed English superiority.

40. Payne MSS 1:56–69, NL.

41. Ibid., 58–60; see also 3:26. Another version lists as sacred firewood black jack oak, post oak, red oak, locust, red bud, and plum (see 4:241). In the late nineteenth and early twentieth centuries, sacred woods included beech, birch, hickory, locust, maple, oak, and sourwood. Some Cherokees substituted ash for sourwood, depending on the availability and appearance of the trees (see Hamel and Chiltoskey, *Cherokee Plants*, 11).

42. Mooney, *Myths of the Cherokee*, 252.

43. Van Doren, *Travels of William Bartram*, 291; Samuel Williams, *Adair's History*, 186n, 246–48, 388–89, quotation on 246; Witthoft, "Early Cherokee Ethnobotanical Note," 73–74; Mooney, *Myths of the Cherokee*, 339; Fogelson, "Conjuror in Eastern Cherokee Society,"

60–87. For additional references to ginseng among Cherokees see Samuel Williams, *Memoirs of Timberlake*, 70; "William Bartram's Observations," 165.

44. See Fogelson, "On the Petticoat Government."

45. Payne MSS 4:119, NL.

46. Ibid., 1:86 and 3:107; "Journal of the Mission at Brainerd," 416; Gilbert, "Eastern Cherokees," 327.

47. Payne MSS 1:94–96, NL; Gilbert, "Eastern Cherokees," 327.

48. Justice and Bell, *Wildflowers of North Carolina*; Duncan and Duncan, *Trees of the Southeastern United States*; Gupton and Swope, *Fall Wildflowers of the Blue Ridge*; Duncan and Foote, *Wildflowers of the Southeastern United States*; Hamel and Chiltoskey, *Cherokee Plants*; Sutton and Sutton, *Eastern Forests*, 84.

49. Witthoft, "Early Cherokee Ethnobotanical Note," 73–75, "Cherokee Indian Use of Potherbs," 250–55, and "Cherokee Economic Botany," 24–38, APS.

50. Payne MSS 4:201, NL; "William Bartram's Observations," 165; Van Doren, *Travels of William Bartram*, 89–90.

51. Mooney, *Myths of the Cherokee*, 259; Butrick, *Antiquities of the Cherokee*, 16, NL; Samuel Williams, *Adair's History*, 439.

52. Van Doren, *Travels of William Bartram*, 289–90. Such association of women's sexuality and their basketry threads through other European accounts. See, for example, Boyd, ed., *Byrd's Dividing Line Histories*, 122.

53. "William Bartram's Observations," 151.

54. Hill, "Basket of History," 13–14.

55. Van Doren, *Travels of William Bartram*, 274.

56. Spongberg, *Reunion of Trees*, 143–45; Ogburn, *Southern Appalachians*, 152–56. The similarity of Asian and eastern North American forms was apparent to numerous nineteenth-century botanists. Asa Gray first proposed the reasons for the similarities in his 1859 paper "Diagnostic characters of new species of . . . plants."

57. Boyd, ed., *Byrd's Dividing Line Histories*, 218; De Vorsey, *DeBrahm's Report*, 9; Mooney, *Myths of the Cherokee*, 470 n. 71. Byrd claimed the fires were caused by unextinguished campfires left carelessly by retreating war parties. If they did so, they unwisely alerted enemies to their presence.

58. Samuel Williams, *Memoirs of Timberlake*, 71. For a thorough discussion of animals among the Cherokees, see Fradkin, *Cherokee Folk Zoology*.

59. Payne MSS 3:44–47 and 4:29–31, NL; Norton, *Norton's Journal*, 23; Hudson, *Southeastern Indians*, 266–67.

60. Stuart to Board of Trade, Mar. 9, 1764, 24, BPRO.

61. Samuel Williams, *Adair's History*, 171–75; Payne MSS 3:63 and 4:29, 31, 80, 83, NL. Similar prohibitions regarding women applied to the ball game, which Cherokees called *a ne tsa*, the "Little Brother to War" (Payne MSS 4:62–63, NL; Fogelson, *Cherokee Ball Game*).

62. Mooney, *Myths of the Cherokee*, 250–52.

63. Samuel Williams, *Adair's History*, 8, 178, 452; Payne MSS 3:69 and 4:57, 74, NL; Mooney, *Myths of the Cherokee*, 410; Longe, "Small Postscript," 15, LOC; see also Speck and Broom, *Cherokee Dance and Drama*.

64. Stevens, "How the Wolf is Being Heard."

65. Samuel Williams, *Adair's History*, 101; see also ibid., 7–9, 124, 447; "William Bartram's Observations," 164; Fyffe, "Letter to Brother John," 5, TGI; Samuel Williams, *Memoirs of Timberlake*, 43, 55–56, 61.

66. Payne MSS 3:18–23 and 4:28, 267, NL; Fradkin, *Cherokee Folk Zoology*, 265–66.

67. Longe, "Small Postscript," 4, LOC.

68. Samuel Williams, *Adair's History*, 330.

69. Shelford, *North American Ecology*, 29; Sutton and Sutton, *Eastern Forests*, 604.

70. Mooney, *Myths of the Cherokee*, 264, 472–74.

71. Boyd, ed., *Byrd's Dividing Line Histories*, 196.

72. Samuel Williams, *Adair's History*, 446.

73. Payne MSS 4:202, NL; Samuel Williams, *Adair's History*, 101, 115, 129, 437.

74. Payne MSS 4:25–28, 202, NL; Mooney, *Myths of the Cherokee*, 261–80; Samuel Williams, *Memoirs of Timberlake*, 75–76; Speck and Broom, *Cherokee Dance and Drama*, 69–79; Fradkin, *Cherokee Folk Zoology*, 354–92.

75. Samuel Williams, *Adair's History*, 28, and *Memoirs of Timberlake*, 71; "Brother Martin Schneider's Report," 263.

76. Boyd, ed., *Byrd's Dividing Line Histories*, 216; see also John Lawson, *New Voyage to Carolina*, 50–51.

77. Sutton and Sutton, *Eastern Forests*, 438–40, 443–46, 451–54; Godfrey, *Sierra Club Guide*, 52–55.

78. Samuel Williams, *Adair's History*, 28, 90, 91.

79. Longe, "Small Postscript," 12, LOC.

80. Samuel Williams, *Memoirs of Timberlake*, 100. Timberlake explained that "old warriors, likewise, or war-women, who can no longer go to war, but have distinguished themselves in their younger days, have the title of Beloved" (94). Butrick reported that during the Festival of Propitiation, the priest "took the wing of a perfectly white heron and waved it four times over the cauldron, so as to waft the steam in every direction and prayed again to himself." This part of the ceremony was to implore that the people be cleansed from all impurities of the preceding year (Payne MSS 1:62 and 4:203, NL).

81. Payne MSS 1:14 and 4:203, NL; Samuel Williams, *Memoirs of Timberlake*, 103.

82. Samuel Williams, *Adair's History*, 137.

83. Ibid., 28, and Samuel Williams, *Memoirs of Timberlake*, 71–72; Payne MSS 4:48, NL.

84. Samuel Williams, *Adair's History*, 387; Shelford, *Ecology of North America*, 59.

85. Longe, "Small Postscript," 14, LOC; Payne MSS 4:26, 264, NL.

86. Samuel Williams, *Memoirs of Timberlake*, 63, 94, 103, 107; Gideon Blackburn to Dr. Morse, Feb. 8, 1808, *Missionary Herald* 3 (May 1808): 567, and Payne MSS 6:220, both in NL.

87. Samuel Williams, *Memoirs of Timberlake*, 52.

88. Samuel Williams, *Adair's History*, 432–34, and *Memoirs of Timberlake*, 69.

89. Sutton and Sutton, *Eastern Forests*, 90.

90. Mooney, *Myths of the Cherokee*, 360.

91. Sturtevant, "Louis-Philippe on Cherokee Architecture," 200.

92. Samuel Williams, *Memoirs of Timberlake*, 73–74.

93. Samuel Williams, *Adair's History*, 250.

94. Mooney, *Myths of the Cherokee*, 297, 252–54; Hudson, "The Uktena," 62–73.

95. Mooney, *Myths of the Cherokee*, 298–300.

96. Ibid., 250.

97. Ibid., 240.

98. Gambolds to the Rev. John Herbst, Nov. 10, 1810, MAS. The number of clans varied from one era to the next, falling and rising with population fluctuations. John Stuart identified nine, "each distinguished by some bird or beast." In the early 1800s, Agent Return J. Meigs named "8 families or clans," with "Paint family" the most numerous and "Thorn Bush" the least. In 1821, Anna and John Gambold claimed "12 clans among the Cherokees." The *Cherokee Phoenix* reported "seven clans, such as Wolf, Deer, Paint, etc." William Martin acknowledged in 1842 "a tradition that there were formerly twelve." Through most of the nineteenth and twentieth centuries, the number of clans is cited as seven, a number that recurs in myth and medicine as sacred and powerful (Stuart to Board of Trade, Mar. 9, 1764, BPRO; Gambold to Salem, Feb. 19, 1821, MAS; Meigs Family Papers, 17,052, LOC; Martin to Lyman Draper, July 7, 1842, Draper Collection, 14DD, 113, EU).

99. Samuel Williams, *Adair's History*, 18–19; Gambolds to the Rev. John Herbst, Nov. 10, 1810, MAS. In 1805, John and Anna Gambold came from Salem, North Carolina, to take charge of the Moravian Springplace mission to the Cherokees, which had been established in 1801. Anna died there in 1821, and John then organized a second mission at Oochgelogy, where he died in 1827.

100. Gambolds to the Rev. John Herbst, Nov. 10, 1810, MAS.

101. John Gambold to Charles Gottlieb Reichel, May 22, 1809, MAS; McLoughlin, *Cherokees and Missionaries*, 65.

102. J. P. Evans, "National Characteristics of the Cherokees," in Payne MSS 6:202, NL; Mooney, "Upper and Middle Cherokee (*Tsalaki*)," Bureau of American Ethnology Cherokee Collection, NAA; John Brown, *Old Frontiers*, 527. Mooney points out that the distinct names for the mother's (as opposed to the father's) parents show "the greater importance attached to the female line" ("Upper and Middle Cherokee [*Tsalaki*]," 135).

103. Kilpatrick, "*Wahnenauhi* Manuscript," 185; Fyffe, "Letter to Brother John," 18, TGI.

104. Samuel Williams, *Adair's History*, 454.

105. Stuart to Board of Trade, Mar. 9, 1764, BPRO; Fyffe, "Letter to Brother John," 12–13, TGI; Samuel Williams, *Adair's History*, 418–20. Adair points out that "the spirits of those who are killed by the enemy, without equal revenge of blood, find no rest, and at night haunt the houses of the tribe [clan] to which they belong" (158).

106. Stuart to Board of Trade, Mar. 9, 1764, BPRO; Payne MSS 1:14, NL.

107. Samuel Williams, *Memoirs of Timberlake*, 93–94. In January 1716 the Charles Town government collected presents for nine women who agreed to "follow their Warrier's Camp" in battle against the Yamasees (McDowell, *Colonial Records of S.C.: Journals of the Commissioners of the Indian Trade*, 155). See also De Vorsey, *DeBrahm's Report*, 109; "William Bartram's Observations," 153; Stuart to Lyttleton, Oct. 6, 1759, Lyttleton Papers, and Stuart to Gage, Apr. 24, 1779, Gage Papers, both in WLCUM; and *New American State Papers*, vol. 1 (Treaty of Hopewell, Nov. 23, 1785), 41.

108. Mooney, *Myths of the Cherokee*, 384–85, 395; McClary, "Nancy Ward," 352–61; Carolyn Foreman, *Indian Women Chiefs*, 72–86; Kilpatrick, "*Wahnenauhi* Manuscript," 185.

Daughter of Wolf Clan member Tame Doe and a Delaware chief, *Nane-hi* (ca. 1737–1822) was the niece of Old Hop and sister of *Ata-gulkalu* (Atakullakulla, Little Carpenter), prominent Cherokee leaders. She later married Irish trader Bryant Ward and became wealthy as owner of an inn on Womankiller Ford on the Ocoee River.

109. Fyffe, "Letter to Brother John," 12, 13, TGI; Menzies, "A true Relation," 197; Payne MSS 4:31, 335, NL; Perdue, *Slavery and the Evolution of Cherokee Society*, 9, 38. Tom Hatley assigns the Menzies account to the popular literary genre of captivity narratives, significant here as a hostile commentary on native women (*Dividing Paths*, 150–51).

110. Longe, "Small Postscript," 24, LOC; see also Samuel Williams, *Adair's History*, 452. In an illuminating article on Cherokee women before removal, Raymond D. Fogelson discusses the psychological component of the mother-child relationship (see "On the Petticoat Government," 161–81).

111. Longe, "Small Postscript," 3, 10, LOC; Payne MSS 1:14, NL; Kilpatrick and Kilpatrick, *Walk in Your Soul*, 19. Among contemporary Cherokees, some associate *Ani-sahoni* (Blue Holly Clan) with expertise in the arts and *Ani-wadi* (Paint Clan) with sacred prayers.

112. Longe, "Small Postscript," 32, LOC; see also Samuel Williams, *Adair's History*, 199. Marriage restrictions extended also to members of the father's clan. The most acceptable alliances, encouraged by nearly every aspect of the social system, were with members of the grandfather's clan.

113. Longe, "Small Postscript," 22, LOC. The ceremony varied, but throughout the eighteenth century, it centered on food.

114. Ibid.

115. Samuel Williams, *Adair's History*, 113, 244; Longe, "Small Postscript," 7, LOC.

116. Van Doren, *Travels of William Bartram*, 289. For a notable example of the role of older women as arbiters of behavior, see Hatley, *Dividing Paths*, 55–56.

117. Bleeding men, such as injured warriors, were also isolated in small dwellings removed from the general population (Samuel Williams, *Adair's History*, 129–31; Fyffe, "Letter to Brother John," 19, TGI; Payne MSS 4:91, NL). Fogelson offers valuable insights into Cherokee attitudes toward menstrual and postpartum blood, identifies menstrual blood as *wo-di*, and suggests a parallel between warriors and menstruating women ("On the Petticoat Government," 172–76).

118. Samuel Williams, *Adair's History*, 133, 152–53, 174; see also Longe, "Small Postscript," 30, LOC, Samuel Williams, *Memoirs of Timberlake*, 89, Fyffe, "Letter to Brother John," 17, TGI, Hatley, *Dividing Paths*, 52–56, 148, 151–52, and Fogelson, "On the Petticoat Government," 164–65, 169–70.

119. Stuart to Board of Trade, Mar. 9, 1764, BPRO; "William Bartram's Observations," 158; Samuel Williams, *Memoirs of Timberlake*, 92.

120. McDowell, *Colonial Records of S.C.: Journals of the Commissioners of the Indian Trade*, Nov. 16 and 24, 1716. It is likely that her brother gave Peggy the French man to compensate for a family loss. She may have used the Board of Trade to enhance the compensation since she requested payment in men's goods.

121. Samuel Williams, *Memoirs of Timberlake*, 89–90; see also Fyffe, "Letter to Brother John," 4, TGI, Norton, *Norton's Journal*, 137, and Hatley, *Dividing Paths*, 148.

122. Samuel Williams, *Adair's History*, 199; Gambold to Reichel, May 22, 1809, MAS; Fogelson, "On the Petticoat Government," 171–72.

123. Samuel Williams, *Memoirs of Timberlake*, 90. In contrast to many similar observations, Longe reported in 1725 that fathers took male children and mothers took the females ("Small Postscript," 22, LOC).

124. Longe, "Small Postscript," 22, LOC.

Chapter 1

1. Mooney, *Myths of the Cherokee*, 240–42.

2. Samuel Williams, *Adair's History*, 454.

3. "Letter of Abraham Wood," 26; "Narrative of Father Marquette," 43.

4. Boyd, ed., *Byrd's Dividing Line Histories*, 192.

5. Van Doren, *Travels of William Bartram*, 198.

6. "François André Michaux's Travels," 231; "Account of Father James Gravier," 68.

7. Boyd, ed., *Byrd's Dividing Line Histories*, 194; "François André Michaux's Travels," 94–95.

8. Catesby, *Natural History of Carolina*, 11; Frick and Sterns, *Mark Catesby*, 24–29; Hawkins, *Sketch and Letters*, Nov. 25, 27, and 28, Dec. 4, 1796, Mar. 25, 26, and 29, 1797.

9. Payne MSS 3:46 and 4:196, NL.

10. Varner and Grier, *Florida of the Inca*, 315–16.

11. See Mooney, *Myths of the Cherokee*, 490.

12. In her list of plants used by Cherokees near the Springplace Moravian Mission, Anna R. Gambold wrote that the root of *Sanguinaria canadensis* (bloodroot) "is used for the red dye in basket making" (Witthoft, "Early Cherokee Ethnobotanical Note," 75). Butrick mentions bloodroot as well as black walnut, butternut, and sourwood as dyes (Payne MSS 4:202, 204, NL).

13. Ludovic Grant to Gov. Glen, July 22, 1754, McDowell, *Colonial Records of S.C., 1750–1754*, 19.

14. Komarek, "Fire Ecology," 184.

15. Ibid.

16. See Duggan and Riggs, *Studies in Cherokee Basketry*, 24.

17. Payne MSS 4:37, NL.

18. Ibid., 3:20.

19. James Mooney identified this kind of container as a "trinket basket" or "woman's work basket" ("Upper and Middle Cherokee Vocabulary," Bureau of American Ethnology Cherokee Collection, NAA).

20. Payne MSS 1:58, 60–69, 94–95, and 3:20, NL.

21. Ibid., 3:26–29, 114, and 4:186, 240, 242; quotation on 1:60, 62.

22. Samuel Williams, *Adair's History*, 106.

23. Ibid., 111–12. See also Payne MSS 1:49–53, 76–85, and 4:225–30, NL, Gilbert, "Eastern Cherokees," 329–30, and Wetmore, "Green Corn Ceremony," 46–54.

24. See Longe, "Small Postscript," 6–18, LOC, Samuel Williams, *Adair's History*, 99–121, and *Memoirs of Timberlake*, 88–89, and Van Doren, *Travels of William Bartram*, 399.

25. Samuel Williams, *Adair's History*, 104.

26. Payne MSS 3 : 100, NL.

27. Mooney, *Myths of the Cherokee*, 364.

28. Author interview with Alice Walkingstick, Mar. 23, 1989.

29. Samuel Williams, *Adair's History*, 95.

30. "Brother Martin Schneider's Report," 257; Ulmer and Beck, *Cherokee Cooklore*.

31. See Witthoft, "Cherokee Economic Botany," 103–5, APS.

32. Payne MSS 4 : 73, NL.

33. Samuel Williams, *Adair's History*, 437–38.

34. "Brother Martin Schneider's Report," 257; for discussion of vegetable preparation among Southeastern Indians see Swanton, *Indians of the Southeastern United States*, 351–68; on food preparation among nineteenth-century Cherokees see Payne MSS 4 : 28–29, NL; on food preparation among modern Cherokees see Ulmer and Beck, *Cherokee Cooklore*.

35. Witthoft, "Cherokee Economic Botany," 106, APS.

36. Payne MSS 4 : 74, NL; Samuel Williams, *Adair's History*, 439.

37. Swanton, *Indians of the Southeastern United States*, 604; Samuel Williams, *Memoirs of Timberlake*, 61.

38. John Lawson, *New Voyage to Carolina*, 195.

39. Brickell, *Natural History of North Carolina*, 349.

40. Among numerous discussions of the deerskin trade see Crane, *Southern Frontier*, 108–12, and Hudson, *Southeastern Indians*, 436. Like other Southeastern natives, Cherokees supplied a staggering number of deer and other animal skins to the English. On Oct. 10, 1716, for example, Cherokee trader Theophilus Hastings sent 2,087 "drest Skins," 89 "raw skins," and 36 "Bever's" to Charles Town (McDowell, *Colonial Records of S.C.: Journals of the Commissioners of the Indian Trade*).

41. McDowell, *Colonial Records of S.C.: Journals of the Commissioners of the Indian Trade*, Nov. 1 and 16, 1716.

42. Ibid., Nov. 16, 1716.

43. Ibid.

44. Ibid., Nov. 23, 1716, Jan. 23, 1717, Feb. 5, 1717. For discussion of Charles Town trade in the public monopoly see Crane, *Southern Frontier*, 187–205.

45. McDowell, *Colonial Records of S.C.: Journals of the Commissioners of the Indian Trade*, Jan. 23 and 25, 1716/17.

46. Catesby, *Natural History of Carolina*, 21.

47. Samuel Williams, *Adair's History*, 456.

48. Nicholson (1655–1728) previously served as lieutenant governor of the Dominion of New England, New York, and Virginia, lieutenant governor, then governor of Maryland, and governor of Virginia. Recalled to London in 1704, he became consultant to the Board of Trade, a member of the Society for the Propagation of the Gospel in Foreign Parts, and a member of the Royal Society of London. He returned to America as lieutenant general, and subsequently became governor of governors and major general. On Sept. 25, 1720, he was appointed the first Royal Governor of South Carolina, his final colonial office, retained even after his return to London (McCully, "Governor Francis Nicholson"; Noble, *Life of Francis Nicholson*; Webb, "The Strange Career of Francis Nicholson").

49. Apparently, the first attribution of the basket to the Cherokees was made by David I. Bushnell Jr. In a 1907 article, Bushnell stated that "this basket is of the type described by Adair as being used in Carolina about the middle of the eighteenth-century. The description as given by him applies perfectly to the British Museum specimen." Adair's description is of Cherokee rivercane hampers. See Bushnell, "Sloane Collection," 678–79, and Samuel Williams, *Adair's History*, 456.

50. Dr. F. R. Barrie of the British Museum (Natural History) graciously identified the botanical name based on Robert Morison's 1699 publication, *Plantarum historiae universalis Oxoniensis, pars tertia* (522). According to Barrie, Sir Hans Sloane, in his 1607 book on the natural history of Jamaica, referred to *Solanum Virginianum rubrum* and *solanum racemosum Americanum* synonymously: "It is used by the Indians in New England to dye their skins and the Barks where with they make their Baskets. English people in Virginia call it Red Weed" (Sloane, *Voyage to the Islands*, 199–200). Sloane apparently relied on Parkinson, *Theatricum Botanicum*, 347–48.

51. Hill, "Basket of History," 12–15. The red is considerably deeper than that usually imparted by pokeweed.

52. The year following his report, Atkin was named superintendent of Southern Indians. Jacobs, *Appalachian Indian Frontier*, 49; Paul Demere to Lyttleton, May 2, 1759, in McDowell, *Colonial Records of S.C., 1754–1765*.

53. Heckewelder, *Narrative of the Mission of the United Brethren*, 203; Hatley, *Dividing Paths*, 220.

54. Hitchcock, *Manual of the Grasses*, 27–30; Alan Weakley, botanist, North Carolina Natural Heritage Program, personal communication. I am grateful to Alan Weakley for discussions of rivercane, butternut, and poke in western North Carolina.

55. Hughes, "Fire Ecology of Canebrakes," 150; Hatley, "Eighteenth-Century Tallapoosa Landscape," 86–89.

56. Catesby, *Natural History of Carolina*, 14. Variables affecting the rate of regrowth include soil fertility, drainage, and the season of disturbance. Documentation of fire-disturbed cane far surpasses that of flood-disturbed stands. Generally, cane grows fastest the first two years after fire, reaches its maximum foliage production in two to four years, and begins to decline ten years following fire (see Hughes, "Fire Ecology of Canebrakes," 155–57).

57. Hughes, "Fire Ecology of Canebrakes," 154–56.

58. Hatley, "Eighteenth-Century Tallapoosa Landscape," 86.

59. Examples of cane beyond the settlements come from soldiers' accounts. In the 1776 destruction of the Lower Towns, for example, Col. Neel's army burned Estatoe, Qualhatchie, and Toxaway and then "scouted the cane brakes along the river to Toxaway"; in Williamson's parallel campaign, the soldiers at Chota "were passing through a thick cane break near dusk" when Captain Elliott was shot (Draper MSS 3VV, 74, 146, EU). See also John Brown, *Old Frontiers*, 94, 173, 199–200.

60. Samuel Williams, *Adair's History*, 239.

61. Longe, "Small Postscript," 31, LOC; Komarek, "Fire Ecology," 169–97, 181–83.

62. Goodwin, *Cherokees in Transition*, 26; Van Doren, *Travels of William Bartram*, 267, 280, 279.

63. "Report of Steiner and de Schweinitz," 478. For communal hunting with fire see Boyd, ed., *Byrd's Dividing Line Histories*, 284–86, Corkran, *Cherokee Frontier*, 9, and Schwarze, *History of the Moravian Missions*, 174. For forest firing see Goodwin, *Cherokees in Transition*, 63–65, and

Samuel Williams, *Adair's History*, 248. Compare Van Doren, *Travels of William Bartram*, 107, 149, 154; for fire ecology see Komarek, "Fire Ecology," 188–89.

64. Hatley, "Eighteenth-Century Tallapoosa Landscape," 86–88; Wright and Bailey, *Fire Ecology*, 377–78; Dahlgren, Clifford, and Yeo, *Families of the Monocotyledons*, 419–40. Hatley points out that the optimal interval for burning to maintain the vitality of cane stands is three years and that cane and other clonal vegetation can recolonize an abandoned site in fifty years.

65. Longe, "Small Postscript," 20–21, LOC.

66. Ibid., 12–13; Norton, *Norton's Journal*, 80.

67. See "Narrative of the Expedition of Hernando de Soto," Varner and Grier, *Florida of the Inca*, and Hudson, *Juan Pardo Expeditions*.

68. "Narrative of the Expedition of Hernando de Soto," 173; Rangel, "Account of the Northern Conquest," 254, 259; Robertson, "Account of the Gentleman of Elvas," 138.

69. Among the many discussions of the impact of foreign disease on native populations see Crosby, *Columbian Exchange*, Dobyns, *Their Numbers Become Thinned*, Marvin Smith, *Archaeology of Aboriginal Culture Change*, Ramenofsky, *Vectors of Death*, and Blakely and Detweiler-Blakely, "Impact of European Diseases."

70. "Narrative of the Expedition of Hernando de Soto," 176.

71. Ibid., 176–78, quotation from 178. The Spanish narratives are filled with exaggerations of every sort, which reach their zenith with allusions to the affection the Southeastern natives expressed for the invaders.

72. Ibid., 178.

73. Ibid., 177.

74. Hudson, *Juan Pardo Expeditions*, 94–100, 265–67.

75. Ibid., 302–3.

76. Ibid., 267.

77. Archaeological evidence indicates that the ancestral Cherokees settled along virtually every Southern Appalachian river and its tributaries. For discussion of archaeological sites see Dickens, *Cherokee Prehistory*, and Keel, *Cherokee Archaeology*; see also Mooney, *Myths of the Cherokee*, 21.

78. "Gov. Johnson to the Council of Trade and Plantations," Jan. 12, 1715, *Calendar of State Papers* 31, 301, 302; Crane, *Southern Frontier*, 131; Varnod, "A true and exact account," HSP; Thornton, *The Cherokees*, 5–30. British estimates of "Middle Settlements" combined Middle and Valley Towns, giving no estimates for Valley Towns. Estimations for the Middle Settlements are roughly twice that of the Lower and Upper Settlements. Problems identifying Cherokee towns from eighteenth-century accounts derive from variations in spelling, inaccuracies of early maps, and periodic abandonment of towns as a result of warfare or contagion. For excellent discussion and synthesis see Betty Smith, "Distribution of Eighteenth-Century Cherokee Settlements," 46–60.

79. Wood, "Changing Population," 63, 38.

80. Samuel Williams, *Adair's History*, 450.

81. Ibid., 443, and Samuel Williams, *Memoirs of Timberlake*, 84; Van Doren, *Travels of William Bartram*, 296.

82. Samuel Williams, *Memoirs of Timberlake*, 84; Cochrane to Gage, Jan. 4, 1765, Gage Papers, WLCUM; De Vorsey, *DeBrahm's Report*, 110.

83. Van Doren, *Travels of William Bartram*, 296.

84. Samuel Williams, *Memoirs of Timberlake*, 84.

85. Samuel Williams, *Adair's History*, 448.

86. De Vorsey, *DeBrahm's Report*, 110. Adair claimed Cherokees called their corn houses *watohre*, the same word used "for the penis of any creature" (Samuel Williams, *Adair's History*, 78).

87. Samuel Williams, *Adair's History*, 452; Van Doren, *Travels of William Bartram*, 285.

88. Samuel Williams, *Memoirs of Timberlake*, 85.

89. Samuel Williams, *Adair's History*, 450–51.

90. Ibid., 453, and Samuel Williams, *Memoirs of Timberlake*, 61–62. See also Richardson, "An Account of my Proceedings," Dec. 18, 1758, Wilburforce Eames Collection, NYPL.

91. Samuel Williams, *Adair's History*, 451–52.

92. Samuel Williams, *Memoirs of Timberlake*, 59. See also Longe, "Small Postscript," 4, LOC, Van Doren, *Travels of William Bartram*, 297, "Report of Steiner and de Schweinitz," 445–525, 479, and Richardson, "An Account of my Proceedings," Dec. 28, 1759, Wilburforce Eames Collection, NYPL.

93. Van Doren, *Travels of William Bartram*, 297–98. According to Gerald Schroedl, the construction of the Cowee Town House differed from those in the lower Little Tennessee River valley (see Schroedl, "Louis-Philippe's Journal").

94. Samuel Williams, *Memoirs of Timberlake*, 64.

95. Van Doren, *Travels of William Bartram*, 296–98. For cane benches or mats see Richardson, "An Account of my Proceedings," Dec. 29, 1758, Wilburforce Eames Collection, NYPL, French, "Journal of an Expedition," 284, Samuel Williams, *Memoirs of Timberlake*, 59, and Sturtevant, "Louis-Philippe on Cherokee Architecture," 200. For a description of a later Town House and changing ceremonials see Norton, *Norton's Journal*, 54.

96. Richardson, "An Account of my Proceedings," Dec. 28, 1759, Wilburforce Eames Collection, NYPL. Timberlake also saw part of a physic ceremony (see Samuel Williams, *Memoirs of Timberlake*, 100–102).

97. Samuel Williams, *Adair's History*, 84.

98. Payne MSS 1:49, 60, NL.

99. Fyffe, "Letter to Brother John," 6, TGI.

100. Chicken, "Journal," Aug. 12, 1725, Grant Foreman Papers, TGI. For prohibition of weapons in town houses see Ludovic Grant, "Historical Relation of Facts," 54.

101. "Letter of Abraham Wood," 28.

102. Chicken, "Journal of the Commissioner of Indian Affairs," July 25, Sept. 25, Oct. 9, 1725, Grant Foreman Papers, TGI. Since the English sought to transform Indian war customs and to initiate conflict, Chicken also advised Cherokees to preempt attacks by sending out an army (see "Journal of the Commissioner of Indian Affairs," Sept. 14, 1725).

103. Rich Dudgeon to Gen. Amherst, Aug. 16, 1760, CO5/59, 193937, BPRO; Samuel Williams, *Memoirs of Timberlake*, 80.

104. "William Bartram's Observations," 152.

105. Royce, *Cherokee Nation of Indians*, 256; Wood, "Changing Population," 38, 63–65; Goodwin, *Cherokees in Transition*, 103; Hatley, *Dividing Paths*, 146.

106. French, "Journal of an Expedition," 281, 284, 288.

107. Ibid., 275–96; "Diary of Alexander Monypenny," 320–31; Hatley, *Dividing Paths*, 119–40.

108. Mooney, *Myths of the Cherokee*, 45–53; Royce, *Cherokee Nation of Indians*, 2–3, 17–23, 256; Milling, *Red Carolinians*, 319–20; Hatley, *Dividing Paths*, 119–226.

109. "Brother Martin Schneider's Report," 256.

110. Mooney, *Myths of the Cherokee*, 242–49. See also Payne MSS 1:26–28 and 2:51–56, NL.

111. Mooney, *Myths of the Cherokee*, 229. All the myths appearing in the Prologue and first chapter were considered sacred.

112. Ibid., 244.

113. Ibid.

114. See Fogelson, "Analysis of Cherokee Sorcery."

115. Mooney, *Myths of the Cherokee*, 244.

116. Ibid.

117. Payne MSS 1:24, 102, NL.

118. Ibid.

119. Samuel Williams, *Adair's History*, 435; "William Bartram's Observations," 160.

120. Samuel Williams, *Adair's History*, 439. Adair states that they placed "five or six grains in one hole." Mooney found North Carolina Cherokees planting seven grains, corresponding with the clans and the sacred number seven. Adair's uncharacteristic impreciseness may derive from the varying number of clans that existed prior to removal.

121. Samuel Williams, *Memoirs of Timberlake*, 68–69.

122. See Hatley, "Cherokee Women Farmers." Hatley points out that other complementary attributes induced a balance of insect species (40).

123. Samuel Williams, *Adair's History*, 438–39. In contrast to Adair, Bartram found the fields "kept clean of weeds" (Van Doren, *Travels of William Bartram*, 287).

124. Gremillion, "Adoption of Old World Crops," 17; Longe, "Small Postscript," 21, LOC.

125. Raymond Demere to Lyttleton, Oct. 13, 1756, in McDowell, *Colonial Records of S.C., 1754–1765*, 214; "William Bartram's Observations," 165; Hatley, "Cherokee Women Farmers," 37–51, and *Dividing Paths*, 93–94. Hatley's meticulous analysis explains the welcome that was accorded English garrisons by Cherokees seeking peace and a balance among competing interests.

126. "William Bartram's Observations," 165, 236 n. 27; see also Hawkes, *The Potato*, 18, 32, and Hatley, "Cherokee Women Farmers," 42. White and sweet potatoes belong to different families.

127. Brief comments on the sweet potato appear in Foster and Cordell, eds., *From Chilies to Chocolate*, xii, xiv, 11. See also Waselkov and Braund, *William Bartram on the Southeastern Indians*, 235–39 n. 27.

128. "Journal of Antoine Bonnefoy," 153. See also Savage and Savage, *André and François André Michaux*, 94–95.

129. Gremillion, "Adoption of Old World Crops," 15–16, and "Late Prehistoric and

Historic Paleoethnobotany"; Chapman and Shea, "Archaeobotanical Record"; Samuel Williams, *Memoirs of Timberlake*, 70; "William Bartram's Observations," 165; Payne MSS 4:196, NL; Samuel Williams, *Adair's History*, 437; "Brother Martin Schneider's Report," 257.

130. Van Doren, *Travels of William Bartram*, 284.

131. Samuel Williams, *Adair's History*, 438. Frank Speck identified "pompions" as crookneck squash (*Gourds of the Southeastern Indians*, 19).

132. Samuel Williams, *Adair's History*, 436–37; Hatley, "Cherokee Women Farmers," 39–41.

133. Samuel Williams, *Adair's History*, 436–37; "Brother Martin Schneider's Report," 261; Fyffe, "Letter to Brother John," 6, 7, TGI; Stuart to Board of Trade, Mar. 9, 1764, BPRO; Louis-Philippe, *Diary of My Travels*, 73; *Missionary Herald* 14, no. 9 (Sept. 1818): 415, NL. Europeans' perception that Cherokee women had no choice in the sexual division of labor reveals more about their own society than that of Cherokees. By insisting that native women were enslaved by their agricultural system and native men were indolent and lazy, Europeans justified their appropriation of native land.

134. Longe, "Small Postscript," 16, LOC. See also Fyffe, "Letter to Brother John," 18, TGI.

135. "William Bartram's Observations," 159–60.

136. John Stuart to Board of Trade, Mar. 9, 1764, BPRO.

137. Van Doren, *Travels of William Bartram*, 286.

138. Norton, *Norton's Journal*, 125–26.

139. McDowell, *Colonial Records of S.C., 1750–1754*, Nov. 20, 1751, and July 6, 1753; for 1755 famine see Corkran, *Cherokee Frontier*, 72; for 1759 famine see *South Carolina Gazette*, Sept. 29, 1759; for 1760 famine see Samuel Williams, *Memoirs of Timberlake*, 67; for 1804 famine see Doublehead to Return Meigs, Mar. 27, 1804, RG 75, *Records of the Cherokee Indian Agency in Tennessee*, M-208, FRCEP; for 1824 famine see McLoughlin, *Cherokees and Missionaries*, 201; for 1811 famine see Samuel Williams, *Early Travels in the Tennessee Country*, 453n; for 1821 flood see *Missionary Herald* (Oct. 1821): 39, NL; for 1825 drought see Evan Jones, "Cherokee Indian Mission," Sept. 23, 1826, ABCFM.

140. Payne MSS 1:27, 102–4, and 2:54, NL; Swanton, *Indians of the Southeastern United States*, 770; Longe, "Small Postscript," 6, LOC.

141. Chicken, "Journal of the Commissioner of Indian Affairs," Sept. 30 and Oct. 10, 1725. To the south, seventeenth-century Creeks and Seminoles owned horses supposedly descended from the Spanish Andalusian breed, and Catawbas and other Carolina Indians owned horses as early as 1670 (Braund, *Deerskins and Duffels*, 76); William Owen to Lord Ashley, Sept. 15, 1670, in Cheeves, "Shaftsbury Papers," 201.

142. Samuel Williams, *Adair's History*, 242, 436.

143. Ibid., 242.

144. McDowell, *Colonial Records of S.C.: Journals of the Commissioners of the Indian Trade*, 14–15, 264; Samuel Williams, *Memoirs of Timberlake*, 72; Fyffe, "Letter to Brother John," 19, TGI.

145. Samuel Williams, *Adair's History*, 435, 242, 436.

146. Raymond Demere to Lyttelton, July 19, 1756, and Paul Demere to Lyttelton, Aug. 18, 1757, in McDowell, *Colonial Records of S.C., 1754–1765*.

147. Raymond Demere to Lyttelton, June 23, 1756, in ibid.

148. Raymond Demere to Lyttelton, Oct. 13, 1756, Jan. 2 and 6, 1757, in ibid.

149. Mante, *History of the Late War*, 289.

150. James Grant to William Bull, letter reprinted in *South Carolina Gazette*, June 7–16, 1760; King, "Powder Horn," 25; Hatley, "Three Lives of Keowee," 223–48, and *Dividing Paths*, 119–40.

151. French, "Journal of an Expedition," 283–85.

152. Diary of Arthur Faerie, Draper MSS 3VV, 33, 56, 172, EU; Rockwell, "Parallel and Combined Expeditions," 212–20; see also Hatley, *Dividing Paths*, 179–203, 226–28.

153. "Report on the Proceedings, 26 Feb. 1781," Greene Papers, LOC.

154. *New American State Papers*, 2:41.

155. *Katteuka* to Franklin, Sept. 8, 1787, in Hazard, *Original Documents*, 181; Dickson, "Judicial History of the Cherokee Nation," 67.

156. *Pennsylvania Packett and Daily Advertiser*, Aug. 25, 1789, MSS 87-54, MCI.

157. "Report of Proceedings of a Commission . . . to Conduct Talks with the Cherokees," July 26–Aug. 2, 1781, Greene Papers, LOC; *Katteuka* to Franklin, Sept. 8, 1787, in Hazard, *Original Documents*; Beloved Woman, Aug. 25, 1789, quoted in *Pennsylvania Packett and Daily Advertiser*, MSS 87–54, MCI.

158. Kappler, *Indian Affairs Laws and Treaties*, 2:29–32. The Nov. 28, 1785, Treaty of Hopewell was the first treaty between the two nations. It included articles placing Cherokees under the protection of the United States, prohibiting "punishment of the innocent under the idea of retaliation," and granting the federal government the right to regulate and manage Indian trade and affairs. An important aspect of the treaty removed from individual states the right to negotiate with Indians for their property. In general, the states ignored the treaty. When the Constitution replaced the Articles of Confederation, it gave Congress and the president authority over Indians, facilitating the establishment of a single Indian policy.

159. Thomas Jefferson to William Henry Harrison in Prucha, ed., *Documents of United States Indian Policy*, 21–22.

160. "Report of Steiner and de Schweinitz," 478–80.

161. Arthur Faerie's Journal, 1776, Draper MSS 2VV, 198, EU; "Report of Steiner and de Schweinitz," 472.

162. Norton, *Norton's Journal*, 70.

163. Catesby, *Natural History of the Carolinas*, 14; Samuel Williams, *Adair's History*, 241.

164. "François André Michaux's Travels," 257; Boyd, ed., *Byrd's Dividing Line Histories*, 108; William Rogers, "Life in East Tennessee," 35.

165. "François André Michaux's Travels," 33. See also Catesby, *Natural History of the Carolinas*, 12.

166. Hughes, "Fire Ecology of Canebrakes," 154, 156.

167. Samuel Williams, *Adair's History*, 445.

168. "Journey of D'Artaguette," 79–80.

169. Van Doren, *Travels of William Bartram*, 62; Horan, "Ghost Prairies of the East."

170. Van Doren, *Travels of William Bartram*, 77; Shackford, *David Crockett*, 77.

171. Henning, *Statutes at Large* 2:274–75; Clark, *State Records of North Carolina*, 23:288; Fries, *Records of the Moravians* 5, 2140; Shackford, *David Crockett*, 59.

172. Samuel Williams, *Memoirs of Timberlake*, 94, 103; Witthoft, "Bird Lore of the Eastern

Cherokee," 376; Speck and Broom, *Cherokee Dance and Drama*, 41–42; Mooney, *Myths of the Cherokee*, 281–83; Payne MSS 6:220, NL.

173. Payne MSS 1:24, NL; William Martin to Lyman Draper, 1842, Draper MSS, 14 DD, 113, EU; Speck and Broom, *Cherokee Dance and Drama*, 7–8; Wetmore, "Green Corn Ceremony"; Gilbert, "Eastern Cherokees," 327.

174. Norton, *Norton's Journal*, 79, 80. Butrick wrote later, however, that information about belief systems was difficult to learn, "most expressly" if "sought for any white person, all of whom are supposed to feel a contempt for such forms and faith, which the Indian cannot brook" (Payne MSS 1:41, NL).

175. Norton attended several Green Corn dances but apparently never witnessed the kindling of a new fire (Norton, *Norton's Journal*, 70, 73, 79–80); Payne MSS 1:13–18, and 4:112, 211, 240–41, NL; *Missionary Herald* 14, no. 9 (Sept. 1818): 416, NL.

176. Kentucky gained independence from Virginia and was admitted to statehood in 1792. Tennessee became a state in 1796, when its population exceeded 60,000 (Meinig, *Shaping of America*, 348–49, 351).

177. McLoughlin and Conser, "Cherokees in Transition," 681, 693–94. The Cherokee census of 1825 enumerates 13,583 Cherokees, 147 white men married to Cherokees, 73 white women married to Cherokees, 1,277 African slaves, and 400 North Carolina Cherokees "not included in the census and who have since merged among us" (John Ridge to Albert Gallatin, Feb. 27, 1826, Payne MSS 9:103, NL).

178. See Perdue, *Slavery and the Evolution of Cherokee Society*, 50–69, and "Cherokee Planters," 110–28, and McLoughlin and Conser, "Cherokee Censuses," 215–50. With the establishment of a national and centralized government, the Cherokee nation became, officially, the Nation.

179. Steiner to Heckewelder, Mar. 6, 1820, Vaux Papers, HSP.

180. *Missionary Herald* 25, no. 4 (Apr. 1829): 132, NL; Strickland, *Fire and the Spirits*; LCN in ibid., resolutions 3–4, 11–12. Codification of laws was an aspect of changes in the Cherokee Nation. It is difficult to assess the effect on those who lived in the Nation's hinterlands; Cherokees beyond the Nation's boundaries may have been largely untouched by the adoption of the civilization program.

181. *Missionary Herald* 25, no. 4 (Apr. 1829): 132, NL; Strickland, *Fire and the Spirits*, esp. 81–102, LCN in ibid., resolutions 1, 2, 11, 20; Hawkins to James McHenry, May 4, 1797 in Hawkins, *Sketch and Letters*. The Lighthorse was established in 1808, clan revenge was abolished in 1810, and courts and judges were appointed in 1820. Hawkins claimed Cherokees asked to abandon blood revenge in cases of accidental deaths.

182. Jefferson, *Writings*, 561.

183. Strickland, *Fire and the Spirits*, 98.

184. LCN, resolution 57, in ibid., 217–18. The Cherokee National Council and courts arbitrated numerous inheritance disputes. See Payne MSS 7:57–61, NL; Gambolds to the Rev. John Herbst, Nov. 10, 1810, MAS.

185. Ridge to Gallatin, Feb. 27, 1826, Payne MSS 9:109, NL; see also Springplace Diary, May 22, 1809, MAS. Ridge's letter is reproduced in Perdue and Green, *Cherokee Removal*, 34–45. John Ridge, son of Cherokee chief Major Ridge and his "mixed-blood" wife Susie Wickett, attended the mission school at Brainerd, then went on to Cornwall Academy in

Connecticut. After marrying the white daughter of a local innkeeper, he returned to the Cherokee nation and assumed a position of leadership and influence. By 1832, he led a group of dissidents, known as the Ridge or Treaty Party, to conspire to accept the federal government's terms of removal. In 1835, Ridge violated the Cherokee law prohibiting land sales and signed the Treaty of New Echota ceding all remaining Cherokee land in the Southeast. Following removal, Ridge and two other leaders of the Treaty Party were executed by Cherokees.

186. Ridge to Gallatin, Feb. 27, 1826, Payne MSS 9:111, NL; Fogelson, "On the Petticoat Government," 171; Evan Jones to Dr. Bolles, Jan. 20, 1830, ABCFM, 18.3.1, vol. 2; McLoughlin, *Cherokees and Missionaries*, 77, 204–5, 217.

187. Norton, *Norton's Journal*, 77–78. For examples of other marriage laws see LCN, resolutions 38, 57, in Strickland, *Fire and the Spirits*.

188. The Gambolds to Rev. Charles Gottlieb Reichel, Sept. 15, 1810, 3, M412, Folder 1, MAS.

189. "Brother Martin Schneider's Report," 262; Gilbert, "Eastern Cherokees," 318–21.

190. Gambold to the Rev. John Herbst, Nov. 10, 1810, 2, MAS; *Missionary Herald* 25, no. 4 (Apr. 1829): 132, NL.

191. Fyffe, "Letter to Brother John," 19, TGI.

192. "William Bartram's Observations," 152; Longe, "Small Postscript," 22, LOC. Hatley, in *Dividing Paths*, examines changing European attitudes toward native women in the eighteenth century. Fogelson relates changes in women's status to "local ecology, economics, social structure, and political organization" ("On the Petticoat Government," 170).

193. Jefferson, *Writings*, 1117, 1118.

194. Louis-Philippe, *Diary of My Travels*, 75, 81–83; "Report of Steiner and de Schweinitz," 464; "François André Michaux's Travels," 264. See Peake, *History of the United States Indian Factory System*, 13.

195. Hawkins, *Sketch and Letters*, Nov. 28, 1796.

196. Ibid., Nov. 28, Dec. 2 and 3, 1796, Jan. 26, 1797.

197. Ibid., Nov. 30, 1796.

198. Jacob Wohlfarht to Rev. Charles Gotthold Reichel, Feb. 13, 1803, 15, M411, Folder 3, MAS; John Gambold to Rev. Christian Lewis Benzien, Dec. 7, 1806, 24, M411, Folder 5, MAS. For Moravian work among the Cherokees see Fries, *Records of the Moravians*, Walker, *Torchlight to the Cherokees*, Henry W. Malone, *American Indians and Christian Missions*, McLoughlin, *Cherokees and Missionaries*, and Ruff, "To Ascertain the Mind."

199. According to the Meigs 1809 Cherokee census (in MAS), Vann was one of the wealthiest Cherokees in the Nation and one of the richest men in the Southeast. By the time of his death in 1809, he owned a ferry on the Chattahoochee River, 115 black slaves, 250 horses, 1,000 cattle, 150 hogs, and 9 sheep.

200. Gambolds to Rev. Charles Gottlieb Reichel, Sept. 15, 1810, 30, M412, Folder 1, MAS; John Gambold to a friend in Salem, Nov. 14, 1810, 1, M420:b1, MAS.

201. In 1955 the director of the Moravian Historical Society in Bethlehem, Pennsylvania, donated the baskets to the Peabody Museum of Natural History at Yale University and identified them as having come from the Springplace Mission (William Sturtevant, personal communication, 1991).

202. "Report of Steiner and de Schweinitz," 488, 485.

203. Hawkins, *Sketch and Letters*, Nov. 30 and Dec. 1, 1796; Return J. Meigs's "Journal of Occurrences," Feb. 13, 1805, Records of Cherokee Indian Agency in Tenn., 1801–1835, RG 75, M208, Roll 6, FRCEP; McLoughlin, "Cherokee Anomie," 138–39.

204. Norton, *Norton's Journal*, 71, 125, 132.

205. Meigs, Census of Cherokees, 1809, MAS; *Cherokee Phoenix* June 18, 1828, EU; McLoughlin and Conser, "Cherokees in Transition," 682. See also Perdue, "Southern Indians and the Cult of True Womanhood," 38–40.

206. James Wilkinson, Benjamin Hawkins, and Andrew Pickens to Henry Dearborn, Sept. 6, 1801, in Hawkins, *Sketch and Letters*.

207. Longe, "Small Postscript," 19.

208. Newman, "Acceptance of European Domestic Animals"; Meigs, Census of Cherokees, 1809, MAS; *Cherokee Phoenix*, June 18, 1828, EU. For earlier references to Cherokee adoption of livestock see Samuel Williams, *Memoirs of Timberlake*, 67, and *Adair's History*, 242, "Report of Steiner and de Schweinitz," 479, 492, and Fyffe, "Letter to Brother John," 5, TGI; see also McLoughlin and Conser, "Cherokees in Transition," 681, and Hatley, "Cherokee Women Farmers," 43–44.

209. Hawkins, *Sketch and Letters*, Dec. 2, 1796; Norton, *Norton's Journal*, 70, 120; Meigs, Census of Cherokees, 1809, MAS; *Cherokee Phoenix*, June 18, 1828, EU. In the 1835 census no record was made of the number of cattle owned by Cherokees.

210. Norton, *Norton's Journal*, 72.

211. *Missionary Herald* 14, no. 2 (Feb. 1818): 67, NL.

212. Evans, "Jedediah Morse's Report," 62 n. 10. In 1820, Rev. Dr. Jedediah Morse, educator and geographer, undertook a two-year journey to various Indian tribes to gather information for the federal government regarding the success of the civilization program. Much of Morse's data on the Cherokees was supplied by Cherokee leader Charles Hicks, an educated and wealthy convert to Christianity. Elias Boudinot, graduate of the Springplace Mission school and Cornwall Academy, became translator for the American Board of Missions, editor of the *Cherokee Phoenix*, and lecturer on Cherokee progress toward civilization. Instrumental in the establishment of the Cherokee Nation and its republican form of government, Boudinot subsequently signed the Treaty of New Echota, a capital offense for which he was assassinated by fellow Cherokees.

213. Ridge to Gallatin, Feb. 27, 1826, Payne MSS 8 : 104, NL; Abraham Steiner to John Heckewelder, Mar. 6, 1820, Vaux Papers, HSP.

214. Pillsbury, "Europeanization of the Cherokee Settlement Landscape," 68.

215. "Brother Martin Schneider's Report," 260; "Report of Steiner and de Schweinitz," 485, 490. Betsy Martin was the daughter of Nancy Ward and the wife of Gen. Joseph Martin.

216. "Cherokee History and Habits and Language," 5–6, NL; *Cherokee Phoenix*, May 8, 1830, EU.

217. "Report of Steiner and de Schweinitz," 485, 490, 492; Norton, *Norton's Journal*, 58, 120.

218. Hawkins, *Sketch and Letters*, Dec. 1, 1796; Norton, *Norton's Journal*, 141. For an earlier report see "Brother Martin Schneider's Report," 260–61.

219. In *Missionary Herald* 15, no. 4 (April 1818): 171–72, NL.

220. Royce, *Cherokee Nation of Indians*, 260; Ward's speech appears in several places: Cherokee Council for Cherokee Women, May 2, 1817, Andrew Jackson Papers, vol. 14, 6452–53, LOC, Henry T. Malone, *Cherokees of the Old South*, 82, and Jensen, *With These Hands*, 28.

221. Cherokee Council for Cherokee Women, May 2, 1817, Andrew Jackson Papers, vol. 14, 6452, LOC.

Chapter 2

1. Author interview with Bessie and Posey Long, Oct. 4, 1989. Josiah Axe later added the surname Long.

2. Ibid.

3. Santa Claus Land is a tourist development built in 1966 on the reservation. Advertised as a place where you can have Christmas all year round, it is owned by whites who lease the property from a member of the Eastern Band.

4. The best analysis of the game is Fogelson, *Cherokee Ball Game*; see also Mooney, "Cherokee Ball Play."

5. Stephenson, *Basketry of the Appalachian Mountains*, 13, 14, 22, 28; Eaton, *Handicrafts of the Southern Highlands*, 50, 153, 168, 203; Goodrich, *Mountain Homespun*, 17; Law and Taylor, *Appalachian White Oak Basketmaking*, 3–4; John Irwin, *Baskets and Basket Makers*, 77; Silver, *New Face on the Countryside*, 118–19.

6. See John Irwin, *Baskets and Basket Makers*.

7. Samuel Williams, *Adair's History*, 449.

8. Van Doren, *Travels of William Bartram*, 298.

9. See Catesby to Sloane, Nov. 27, 1724, Sloane MSS 4047, fol. 290, BM, Samuel Williams, *Adair's History*, 106, 456, and *Memoirs of Timberlake*, 61, "Brother Martin Schneider's Report," 260, 262, "Report of Steiner and de Schweinitz," 471, 479, and Payne MSS 3:18, 26, 114, and 4:29, NL.

10. Among the many examples see Cherokee Claims for Property Valuations and Spoilations, 1838–42, Cherokee Nation East, Box 6, Book E, Claims 10, 106, and Book F, Part 2, Claims 700, 710, 716, 730, and 749, all in Allen Collection, TSLA.

11. Cherokee Claims for Property Valuations and Spoilations, 1838–42, Cherokee Nation East, Box 5, Book 3-C, Claims 12, 129, Box 3, Book F, Claim 532, and Box 6, Book E, Claim 106, all in Allen Collection, TSLA. See also Duggan and Riggs, *Studies in Cherokee Basketry*, 27. The claims vary greatly in detail but include many hundreds of baskets.

12. Sutton and Sutton, *Eastern Forests*, 382–83; Duncan and Duncan, *Trees of the Southeastern United States*, 412; Robert Rogers, "White Oak," 605–13.

13. Abrahms, "Fire and the Development of Oak Forests," 346–53; Robert Rogers, "White Oak," 609.

14. Van Doren, *Travels of William Bartram*, 273, 293; Michaux, *North American Sylva*, 23; "Survey from Fort Butler towards Fort Delaney and from Fort Delaney to Fort Lindsay," 6:C35, "Reconnocsance of a Route Commencing . . . about Delaney to Fort Lindsay," 6:C35, "Reconnocsance of a Route 3 miles above Hiwassee Gap," 3:A7, A9, A12, and

"Survey from Fort Butler to the Boundary Line," 4:7, 12, 41, all in Field Notes of Reconnaissances and Surveys, RG 49, NA; Gray, "Notes of a Botanical Excursion," 25.

15. Robert Rogers, "White Oak," 608.

16. Gremillion, "Late Historic and Prehistoric Period Paleoethnobotany," 244–49; Payne MSS 4:196, NL; Witthoft, *Cherokee Economic Botany*, 46, APS.

17. Author interview with Emma Taylor, Dec. 14, 1988. For an excellent description of wood and the splitting process, see Law and Taylor, *Appalachian White Oak Basketmaking*, 38–42.

18. Author interview with source requesting anonymity.

19. Author interview with Bessie and Posey Long, Oct. 4, 1989.

20. Author interview with Emma Taylor, Dec. 14, 1988.

21. Author interview with Bessie and Posey Long, Oct 4, 1989.

22. Author interview with Shirley Taylor, Jan. 4, 1989.

23. Author interview with Emma Taylor, Dec 14, 1988.

24. Author interview with Shirley Taylor, Jan 4, 1989.

25. Author interview with Louise Goings, May 4, 1989.

26. Ibid.

27. Author interview with Bessie and Posey Long, Oct 4, 1989.

28. Author interview with Louise Goings, May 4, 1989; author interview with Bessie and Posey Long, Oct. 4, 1989.

29. Author interview with Louise Goings, May 4, 1989.

30. Author interview with source requesting anonymity.

31. Author interview with Shirley Taylor, Jan. 4, 1989.

32. Author interview with Dinah George, May 5, 1989.

33. Author interview with Bessie and Posey Long, Oct. 4, 1989; author interview with Alice Walkingstick, March 23, 1989.

34. Author interview with Bessie and Posey Long, Oct. 4, 1989.

35. Author interview with Alice Walkingstick, March 23, 1989.

36. Author interview with Bessie and Posey Long, Oct. 4, 1989.

37. Royce, *Cherokee Nation of Indians*, 83–100; Blethen and Wood, "Pioneer Experience," 72; Arthur, *Western North Carolina*, 141–42; Finger, *Eastern Band*, 10–11.

38. Blethen and Wood, "Pioneer Experience," 71–78; Mooney, *Myths of the Cherokee*, 477.

39. *New American State Papers*, 12:316; Mooney, *Myths of the Cherokee*, 106, 164; Royce, *Cherokee Nation of Indians*, 85, 93–96; Finger, *Eastern Band*, 10. The exact number who emigrated to the Arkansas River area was a source of dispute. Since a higher number of emigrants meant a greater cession of Cherokee land, the government intensely pressured Cherokees to emigrate and may have exaggerated the number who chose to do so. Tennessee governor McMinn reported to the federal government that 5,291 Cherokees had already removed or agreed to remove. In contrast, Southeastern Cherokees insisted that the number who had removed to the Arkansas, or who planned to do so, did not total more than 3,500.

40. Hampton, *Cherokee Reservees*, 1–15; King, "Origin of the Eastern Cherokees," 164–80, 166–67; Finger, *Eastern Band*, 10–11; McLoughlin, "Experiment in Cherokee Citizenship,"

153–91; Peters, *Case of the Cherokee Nation*, 268, 270, NL; "Memorial of Tickoneeska," *Indian Documents*, vol. 2, NL. Life-estate reserves were granted to 311 heads of families with the stipulation that they could not sell the estates during their lifetime. Fee-simple reserves were awarded to an additional 31 heads of families who were deemed capable of managing their own property. No restrictions were placed on the fee-simple reserves.

41. "Memorial and Argument of Nancy Reed," Mar. 18, 1847, *Indian Documents*, vol. 6, NL. Also see affidavit of Preston Starritt accompanying W. H. Thomas's argument on behalf of Nancy Reed.

42. Ibid.

43. Evan Jones, May 5, 1837, Rev. Evan Jones Journal 3, Cherokee Indian Mission, Valley Towns Mission, 1836–37, Unit 6, Reel 737, ABCFM. I am grateful to Robert Garner for making this reel available to me.

44. See *Egwanulti* in Mooney, *Myths of the Cherokee*, 517.

45. Evan Jones, Dec. 20, 1829, Rev. Evan Jones Journal 2, Cherokee Indian Mission, Valley Towns Missions, Unit 6, Reel 737, ABCFM.

46. McLoughlin and Conser, "Cherokees in Transition," 687–91, and "Cherokee Censuses"; Finger, *Eastern Band*, 15–16; Wilms, "Cherokee Land Use."

47. Tyner, *Those Who Cried*, 154.

48. See Wilms, "Cherokee Land Use," 15–17.

49. McLoughlin and Conser, "Cherokees in Transition," 685, 688, 689, and "Cherokee Censuses," 232–37. See also Perdue, *Slavery and the Evolution of Cherokee Society*, 50–69.

50. Georgia objected immediately to the life-estate provisions on the basis of the 1802 compact by which the federal government agreed to extinguish all Indian title in the state as "early as the same can be peaceably obtained on reasonable terms" (Articles of Agreement and Cession, Apr. 24, 1802, *New American State Papers*). For discussion of events in this very complex and dark chapter of Georgia history see Mooney, *Myths of the Cherokee*, 114–25, Perdue, *Slavery and the Evolution of Cherokee Society*, 60–67, and "Conflict Within," 55–74, and McLoughlin, "Experiment in Cherokee Citizenship," 153–91.

51. *New American State Papers*, 12:312; McLoughlin, "Experiment in Cherokee Citizenship," 161–79.

52. *New American State Papers*, 12:312; Finger, *Eastern Band*, 14–18. For examples of unrecorded deeds see "List of Deeds and grants for Lands in Indian boundary for which no deed to Thomas appears," in Undated Letters and Papers, Thomas Collection, DU. Judge A. S. Clayton of Georgia also ruled that the federal treaty with the Cherokees took precedence over the state lottery law, but the antagonism of Georgia citizens was so great that Congress passed an appropriation to enable the state to extinguish all Indian titles (McLoughlin, "Experiment in Cherokee Citizenship," 165).

53. *North Carolina Supreme Court*, 155–61; Bridgers, "Legal Digest," 21–42, 22; Thomas to Graham, Oct. 15, 1838, in Wheeler, *Historical Sketches of North Carolina*, 205; *New American State Papers*, 12:3.

54. "Scott to War Department," 216–17, quote on 216; "Williams's Memoir Relating to Cherokee Nation," 209, RG 77, NA; Mooney, *Myths of the Cherokee*, 159; King, "Origin of the Eastern Cherokees," 166; Godbold and Russell, *Life of William Holland Thomas*, 12; Finger, *Eastern Band*, 10–11.

55. Tyner, *Those Who Cried*, 154.

56. U.S. Congress, Senate *Document 120*, 535, 620.

57. "Williams's Memoir Relating to Cherokee Nation," 209, RG 77, NA. In 1829, sixty "citizen Indians" put their marks on a paper designating John L. Dillard as their attorney, stating that they were "often imposed on, cheated and defrauded by some of the people of this country" (see King, "Origin of the Eastern Cherokees," 166, Finger, *Eastern Band*, 10, 11, and Godbold and Russell, *Life of William Holland Thomas*, 21–24).

58. Arthur, *Western North Carolina*, 569–70, 580–81; King, "Powder Horn," 23–40; French, "Journal of an Expedition," 275–96; Mooney, *Myths of the Cherokee*, 533.

59. Godbold and Russell, *Life of William Holland Thomas*, 13. In addition to Godbold and Russell's volume, the story of Thomas appears notably in: Mooney, *Myths of the Cherokee*, 158–62, 168–74, Finger, *Eastern Band*, and Iobst, "William Holland Thomas."

60. Godbold and Russell, *Life of William Holland Thomas*, 9.

61. Although no account books are available for the Felix Walker store, records from all other stores of the period indicate frequent exchanges with Cherokees (see Thomas and King, *Account Book, 1836–1841*, and *Day Book, Indian Town, 1837*, both in Thomas Collection, DU). In an 1876 letter to the commissioner of Indian Affairs, Thomas claimed that Yona-guska "adopted me as one of the clan to which he belonged . . . without my knowledge or consent." With no explanation, he added that the adoption "in all probability saved my life" ("Letter to the Commissioner," NL, and Godbold and Russell, *Life of William Holland Thomas*, 29).

62. Thomas was usually identified as the agent or business agent for the Cherokees. For some of the many examples of powers of attorney, see "List of Cherokees East from whom I received power of attorney," in Undated Letters and Papers, Thomas Collection, DU.

63. Godbold and Russell, *Life of William Holland Thomas*, 67–77, 90–128; Arthur, *Western North Carolina*, 241, 580–81, 584–86; "Census of 1860," 556–61. See also Crow, *Storm in the Mountains*.

64. See *Indian Book, 1837*, and *Day Book, 1832–43*, both in Thomas Collection, DU. Cherokee names appear scattered throughout most of the account books, but several contain separate sections marked "Indian Accounts" or "Indian Debts."

65. Rebecca Davis, "Qualla," 582.

66. Finger, *Eastern Band*, 97; Rozema, *Footsteps of the Cherokees*, 207–8.

67. Mooney, *Myths of the Cherokee*, 164, 165. Junaluska was among those exiled west, but he walked from the Indian Territory back to Cheoah. The state subsequently awarded him a tract of land in recognition of his service to America in the war against the Creek Red Sticks.

68. Mooney, *Myths of the Cherokee*, 405; McRorie, "Formation of Counties and Towns," 101, 114–16; Arthur, *Western North Carolina*, 192–94.

69. Mooney, *Myths of the Cherokee*, 330–31, 474–75, 535; Rossman, *Where Legends Live*, 26, 29.

70. Mooney, *Myths of the Cherokee*, 329–32, 474–75; Godbold and Thomas, *Life of William Holland Thomas*, 17–18, 28–31; Iobst, "William Holland Thomas," 183; Arthur, *Western North Carolina*, 188, 581; "Indian Census, 1835."

71. See Fogelson, *Cherokee Ball Game*.

72. *Missionary Herald* 20, no. 1 (Jan. 1824): 10, NL; Godbold and Russell, *Life of William Holland Thomas*, 28; *Graham County Centennial*, 8. I am indebted to Gary J. Pressley, librarian at Graham County Public Library, for sending me the *Centennial*.

73. Indian Census, 1835; *Missionary Herald* 20, no. 1 (Jan. 1824): 10, NL; Mooney, *Myths of the Cherokee*, 405, 531; Rossman, *Where Legends Live*, 24.

74. Godbold and Russell, *Life of William Holland Thomas*, 28; Indian Census, 1835.

75. Mooney, *Myths of the Cherokee*, 407; Rozema, *Footsteps of the Cherokees*, 256–57; Rossman, *Where Legends Live*, 41.

76. "Williams's Memoir Relating to Cherokee Nation," 203, RG 77, NA.

77. Ibid., 207. The text reproduced in the *Journal of Cherokee Studies* 4, no. 4 (Fall 1979), reads "the Indians have *resided* all inroad." The original, however, clearly reads "the Indians have *resisted* . . ." (see "Williams's Memoir Relating to Cherokee Nation," 9, RG 77, NA).

78. "Williams's Memoir Relating to Cherokee Nation," 205, RG 77, NA.

79. *Missionary Herald* 20, no. 1 (Jan. 1824): 9, NL.

80. "Smoky Mountain Turnpike," 1836, and Collins, *Roadbook*, both in MCI; "Smoky Mountain Turnpike," 1840, in Undated Letters and Papers, and *Day Book, Quallatown, 1855–56*, both in Thomas Collection, DU. See also Allen, *Annals of Haywood County*, 453–54, and Frome, *Strangers in High Places*, 79.

81. Blethen and Wood, "Pioneer Experience," 71–75; Bell, "Economic Development," 192–93. See also Wilburn, "Indian Gap Trail," 6, 10, 12, 13, 19, NCC, Godbold and Russell, *Life of William Holland Thomas*, 12, 28–29, Arthur, *Western North Carolina*, 26–28, 235–36, 241–43, 285–87, and Blackmun, *Western North Carolina*, 176–78, 214–21.

82. "Williams's Memoir Relating to Cherokee Nation," 206, RG 77, NA.

83. Tyner, *Those Who Cried*, 134, 127.

84. Ibid., 119–27.

85. U.S. Congress, Senate *Document 408*, 11.

86. Arthur, *Western North Carolina*, 185–88.

87. "Cherokees in North Carolina and Tennessee," in Undated Letters and Papers, Thomas Collection, DU.

88. "Williams's Memoir Relating to Cherokee Nation," 208, RG 77, NA.

89. U.S. Congress, Senate *Document 408*, 22; Harmon, "North Carolina Cherokees," 251; Andrew Jackson Papers, vol. 14, 6452–55, LOC.

90. This episode is extremely significant in the history of the Eastern Band. The story provides a legendary hero, *Tsali*, who gave himself up for execution by United States soldiers in 1838 in exchange for a promise that his people could remain in their homeland. Historical records suggest that *Tsali* was hunted, captured, and executed by Cherokees cooperating with removal forces. Oconaluftee citizen Cherokees and Cherokees from the Nantahala River, under the direction of Thomas, located *Tsali*.

The legend of *Tsali*'s martyrdom grew from an 1849 narrative by journalist Charles Lanman, who visited Quallatown and presumably heard the story from his host, William Thomas. In 1890, Mooney recorded the legend based on "conversations with Colonel Thomas and with *Wasituna* [*Tsali*'s son] and other old Indians." Mooney describes Lanman's account as "ornate but somewhat inaccurate." For discussions of the legend and revision see Mooney, *Myths of the Cherokee*, 157–58, Finger, *Eastern Band*, 22–28, King, "Origin of the

Eastern Cherokees," 165–66, 170–76, King and Evans, "Tsali," Godbold and Russell, *Life of William Holland Thomas*, 37–40, and Arthur, *Western North Carolina*, 577–80.

91. "Cherokees in North Carolina and Tennessee," in Undated Letters and Papers, Thomas Collection, DU; "1835 Residences of Cherokees," 240; Finger, *Eastern Band*, 29.

92. In 1817, Jacob Siler and William Britton came to Cartoogechaye, "spent the night with a friendly Indian, and next morning bargained with him for his home." In 1819, they sold out to William Siler and moved farther down the creek, where Jacob "bought a farm from an old Indian named Wallace" (Allen, *Annals of Haywood County*, 435). See also Mooney, *Myths of the Cherokee*, 49, 411, and Alexis, "Visit to the Cartoogechaye Indians," 118.

93. Margaret Siler, *Cherokee Indian Lore*, 13–14.

94. Ibid.; Alexis, "Visit to the Cartoogechaye Indians," 116–17. For the 1851 census of Sand Town Cherokees see David Siler, *Eastern Cherokee*, 62–65; see also Finger, *Eastern Band*, 71. For store records see *Ledger, 1839–45, Day Book, Ft. Montgomery, 1852–54*, and *Day Book, Ft. Montgomery, 1854–57*, all in Thomas Collection, DU.

95. Alexis, "Visit to the Cartoogechaye Indians," 116.

96. Ibid.

97. Ibid. Margaret Siler, *Cherokee Indian Lore*, 20–21.

98. Macon County Deed Book m201, in Margaret Siler, *Cherokee Indian Lore*, 13–14, 20–21, 108–9 nn. 2, 7; Morgan, *History of St. John's*, 2–3. Woodpecker's property deed was not recorded until 1871, at which time the land was seized by the state and sold to A. S. Bryson. The Woodpecker sons continued to live on the property until the 1880s.

99. "List of Claims for Pre-emptions in Buffalo," in Undated Letters and Papers, Thomas Collection, DU; "Reconnaisence from Nantayale to Little Tennessee," 10:E16, and "Commencement of a Survey from Ft. Butler Towards Ft. Delaney," 12:B4, both in Field Notes of Reconnaissances and Surveys, RG 49, NA; Arthur, *Western North Carolina*, 211–12. Siler's 1851 census shows Buffalo Town with 68 families of 267 individuals (David Siler, *Eastern Cherokee*, 40–51). See also Finger, in *Eastern Band*, 71, who counts 168 individuals at Buffalo.

100. Armstrong, *Diary: 1842–1848*, MCI (original in the McClung Historical Collection, Lawson McGhee Library, Knoxville, Tennessee).

101. Among many examples of slave purchases see *Day Book, Ft. Montgomery, 1852–1854*, 13, 18, 39, 54, 56, 57, 70, 99, 116, 126, Thomas Collection, DU; for a record of the purchases of Adams, Hyde, and Deaver see ibid., 8, 12, 13, 30, 41, 44, 50, 60, 61.

102. Ibid. Among the numerous examples see 8, 23, 27, 39, 42, 44, 45, 46, 47.

103. Ibid. See 13, 23, 52, 58, 64, 65, 79, 92, 99, 100, 178. Purchases in 1852 also reflect the federal disbursement of approximately fifty dollars to each Cherokee.

104. Ibid. See 18, 22, 27, 32, 102, 110, 130, 131.

105. Ibid., 67, 94, 99, 103, 114, 119, 125.

106. Ibid., 4, 11; *Day Book, Ft. Montgomery, 1854–1857*, 47, Thomas Collection, DU. For Junaluska see *Graham County Centennial*, 15–16.

107. For reference to "the farm" see *Day Book, Ft. Montgomery, 1852–1854*, Mar. 18, 1853, Thomas Collection, DU; for reference to Welch and anonymous Indians see *Day Book, Ft. Montgomery, 1854–1857*, 47, 98, 113, Thomas Collection, DU; for *Tiyohih* see *Day Book, Ft. Montgomery, 1854–1857*, Nov. 29, 1856, n.p., Thomas Collection, DU.

108. David Siler, *Eastern Cherokee*, 45, 51–55, 55–61.

109. Ten families remained at Alarka and seven at Stecoa. Tomatla Cherokees were included among those enumerated in the Murphy or Valley area ("Cherokees in North Carolina and Tennessee," Undated Letters and Papers, Thomas Collection, DU); Van Doren, *Travels of William Bartram*, 289–90.

110. Wheeler, *Historical Sketches of North Carolina*, 204; Kilpatrick and Kilpatrick, "Chronicles of Wolftown," 19.

111. According to the 1851 Siler Roll, 86 families with a total of 350 members lived in the Soco valley in Paint Town, along Swimmer Branch, Soco Creek, and Wright's Creek. Immediately west and extending to the end of the valley, Wolf Town had 61 families with 266 total members scattered on Big Witch Creek and the northeastern stem of Wright's Creek (David Siler, *Eastern Cherokee*, 1–26). For figures on white settlement see Arthur, *Western North Carolina*, 192, Blethen and Wood, "Pioneer Experience," 69, 81, "List of Names, residences, and amount due" and "Amount of B-, Dec. 31, 183-," in Undated Letters and Papers and "An Estimate of the Cost of Land Purchased Lying on the Waters of Soco Creek," *Account Book, Haywood County, 1838–1841*, all in Thomas Collection, DU. For more on Saunders see "Census of the Cherokees Under the Act of July 29, 1848," in Undated Letters and Papers, 13, Thomas Collection, DU.

112. Thomas also owned a slave named Cudjo, whose name appears on numerous accounts from Quallatown to Ft. Montgomery (see "List of the Names of Cherokees who made payments to Asaph and Abraham Enloe for Land," in Undated Letters and Papers, Thomas Collection, DU). References to persons like "Nickajack's girl" and "Yonaguska's girl" may indicate more slaves (*Ledger and Indian Accounts, Quallatown, Haywood County, 1840–1858*, 70, Thomas Collection, DU). The record covers only 1840. I am grateful to the staff of the Perkins Library for microfilming the ledger and making it available to me.

113. Price, *Holston Methodism*, 252–54; Highfill, "Ulrich Keener Log Parsonage"; Kilpatrick and Kilpatrick, "Wolftown Chronicles," 33–47, membership totals on 42. Fifty-seven were from Raven, forty-four from Wolf Town, and sixty-one from Paint Town.

114. Siler expressed concern about enrolling offspring of mixed marriages, and the Indian Office directed him to leave the decision to local councils. His census records a Bird Town population of 72 families with 267 members. A. H. H. Stuart to Siler, Apr. 25, 1851, from Indian Division Letters Sent, no. 1, 88, and Lea to Siler, Aug. 20, 1851, from OIA Letterbook, no. 45, 81, both in Litton, "Enrollment Records," 210–12; see also David Siler, *Eastern Cherokee*, 27–39, and Mooney, *Myths of the Cherokee*, 162, 525.

115. Bush, *Ocona Lufta Baptist Church*, 36–37.

116. "List of the Names of Cherokees and the Clans to Which They Belong," in Undated Letters and Papers, Thomas Collection, DU. Gilbert claimed that Deer Town was part of Paint Town ("Eastern Cherokees," 204).

117. No census refers to Yellow Hill or Big Cove until 1880. The Wolf Town council records mention Raven in 1858 and Yellow Hill in 1859. Based on conversations with Thomas, Mooney claimed Thomas "laid off" land in five towns "which he named Bird town, Paint town, Wolf town, Yellow Hill, and Big Cove." He acknowledged that "there was also, for a time, a Pretty Woman town." Neither Big Cove nor Yellow Hill is mentioned in Thomas's census data or the 1851 Siler census. It is unlikely that Thomas laid them out or named them. See Mooney, *Myths of the Cherokee*, 161 and n. 1, and Kilpatrick and Kilpatrick,

"Wolftown Chronicles," 34, 67; I am grateful to Mary U. Chiltoskey for the information about the Lufty family's assistance.

118. Bush, *Ocona Lufta Baptist Church*, 11, 13, 57.

119. "Early Land Grants"; Arthur, *Western North Carolina*, 140–41.

120. *Ledger and Indian Accounts, 1840–1858*, Quallatown, Thomas Collection, DU.

121. Ibid., 45, 55, 61, 73, 101; *Indian Book, Haywood County General Accounts, 1837*, n.p., Thomas Collection, DU.

122. *Ledger and Indian Accounts, 1840–1858*, 25, 36, 38, 44, Thomas Collection, DU.

123. Ibid. For examples of old clothes see ibid., 3, 6, 14, 35, 46; for new clothes see ibid., 2, 4, 5, 11; for shoes see ibid., 22, 42, 46, 49; for combs or beads see ibid., 41, 42, 43, 44, 46, 48, 49, 53, 58.

124. Mooney verifies the use of material as payment for medicine (*Myths of the Cherokee*, 337).

125. *Account Book, Haywood County, 1838–1841*, n.p., and *Day Book, Quallatown, Haywood County, 1853–1854*, inside cover, both in Thomas Collection, DU; Kilpatrick and Kilpatrick, "Chronicles of Wolftown," 10.

126. *Day Book, Quallatown*, Haywood County, *1840–1841*, Dec. 10, 12, and 22, n.p., and ibid., *1848–1850*, 243, 549, 561, 562, 564, 598, both in Thomas Collection, DU.

127. Swanton, *Indians of the Southeastern United States*, 104–5; Hudson, *Catawba Nation*, 65–66; Merrell, *Indians' New World*, 250–57; Finger, *Eastern Band*, 43; Mooney, *Myths of the Cherokee*, 165.

128. Blumer, "Catawba Influences," 165–67; Mooney, *Myths of the Cherokee*, 165; Merrell, *Indians' New World*, 265; Finger, *Eastern Band*, 43. In 1907, anthropologist M. R. Harrington purchased a doubleweave from Polly Sanders, who was listed on the 1900 census as a Catawba (*Twelfth U.S. Census*, Schedule 1, RG 29, FRCEP).

129. Sherrill, *Account Book*, Thomas Collection, DU; Branson, *North Carolina Business Directory*, 386; *Southern Business Directory*, 214, 398–400; *Graham County Centennial*, 9.

130. Litton, "Enrollment Records," 207–8.

131. Mullay to Medill, Dec. 14, 1848, from OIA Cherokee, M-285, in Litton, "Enrollment Records," 208.

132. Ibid., 208; Lanman, "Letters from the Alleghany Mountains," in Mooney, *Myths of the Cherokee*, 166.

133. Harmon, "North Carolina Cherokees," 251; Thomas, "Letter to the Commissioner of Indian Affairs," 11, NL.

134. In 1850, approximately 700 Qualla Cherokees owned 516 hogs, 416 sheep, 105 cows, 45 oxen, 135 "other cattle," and 93 horses. In 1860, they owned 829 "swine," 121 sheep, 107 "milch cows," 17 "working oxen," 45 "other cattle," and 159 horses (*Productions of Agriculture, Seventh U.S. Census*, and *Productions of Agriculture, Eighth U.S. Census*, North Carolina State Archives, Raleigh). See also Alexis, "Visit to the Cartoogechaye Indians," 116, and Finger, *Eastern Band*, 70.

135. *Productions of Agriculture, Eighth U.S. Census*, North Carolina State Archives, Raleigh.

136. Lanman, "Cherokee Customs," in *Adventures in the Wilds*, MS 4146, doc. 1, 5, Bureau of American Ethnology Cherokee Collection, NAA; Alexis, "Visit to the Cartoogechaye Indians," 116–17. Siler's census also indicates nuclear households (*Eastern Cherokees*).

137. Mooney, *Myths of the Cherokee*, 163; "Cherokees in North Carolina and Tennessee, 1840," in Undated Letters and Papers, Thomas Collection, DU; Sloane to Simpson, MCI.

138. Kilpatrick and Kilpatrick, "Chronicles of Wolftown," 59–60.

139. Ibid.

140. Mooney, "Notes on clans," Bureau of American Ethnology Cherokee Collection, n.p., NAA.

141. Mooney, *Myths of the Cherokee*, 252–54, 256–57, 259, 273, 290–93, 310–11, 323–24, 337–41, 345–47, 349–50, 456.

142. Witthoft, "Will West Long," 357.

143. Lanman, "Cherokee Customs," in *Adventures in the Wilds*, MS 4146, doc. 1, 5, Bureau of American Ethnology Cherokee Collection, NAA.

144. Ibid., 4–5. See Speck and Broom, *Cherokee Dance and Drama*, 3, 25–39, Fogelson, "Conjuror in Eastern Cherokee Society," 63, and Fogelson and Walker, "Self and Other," 88–100.

145. Lanman, "Cherokee Customs," in *Adventures in the Wilds*, MS 4146, doc. 1, 1–3, Bureau of American Ethnology Cherokee Collection, NAA; Mooney, "Cherokee Ball Play," 105–32.

146. Barnard to Dudley, Governors' Papers 91, NCDAH; also in Finger, *Eastern Band*, 68, Lanman, "Cherokee Customs," MS 4146, doc. 1, 1, Bureau of American Ethnology Cherokee Collection, NAA, and *Day Book, Quallatown, Haywood County, 1858–63*, 228, Thomas Collection, DU. Thomas paid $15 to an unknown number of ballplayers in August 1859.

147. *Tse-ghisini* to *I-noli*, July 8 and 20, 1862, in Kilpatrick and Kilpatrick, *Shadow of Sequoyah*, 6, 7.

148. Love to Vance, May 10, 1864, Governor's Papers 177, NCDAH. See also Thomas to Vance, May 13, 1864, Governor's Papers 177, NCDAH, Finger, *Eastern Band*, 82–100, Crow, *Storm in the Mountains*, Kilpatrick and Kilpatrick, *Shadow of Sequoyah*, 3–15, and Godbold and Russell, *Life of William Holland Thomas*, 90–128.

149. Kilpatrick and Kilpatrick, "Record of a North Carolina Cherokee Township Trial," 22–23.

150. Kilpatrick and Kilpatrick, *Shadow of Sequoyah*, 15–16; Mooney, *Myths of the Cherokee*, 171–72; Finger, *Eastern Band*, 100; Godbold and Russell, *Life of William Holland Thomas*, 131; F. B. Sherrill to Evans (?), June 9, 1866, NAA. I am indebted to Joan Greene, MCI archivist, for pointing out this document to me.

151. Mooney, *Myths of the Cherokee*, 172; Godbold and Russell, *Life of William Holland Thomas*, 129–40, 149; Finger, *Eastern Band*, 101, 105, 119–25, quotation on 112.

152. Simpson, "William Brewster's Exploration," 52.

153. Ibid., 55–57, 59, 61.

154. Ibid., 61, and note.

155. Ibid., 63.

156. Ibid., 64.

157. Ibid., 73.

158. Mooney to Henshaw, Series 15, Bureau of American Ethnology Cherokee Collection, NAA; Zeigler and Grosscup, *Heart of the Alleghanies*, 36; Witthoft, "Bird Lore of the Eastern Cherokee," 376; Beattie, "Passenger Pigeon Parable."

159. Rebecca Davis, "Qualla," 579–80.

160. Ibid., 583; Zeigler and Grosscup, *Heart of the Alleghanies*, 36.

161. Rebecca Davis, "Qualla," 583, 585.

162. Ibid., 583–84.

163. Ibid., 584.

164. Ibid., 585.

165. Schenck, "Cherokees in North Carolina," 325; Rebecca Davis, "Qualla," 581; Roy Cantrell, *My Friends the Cherokee*, 10.

166. Rebecca Davis, "By-Paths in the Mountains," 534.

167. Mooney, *Myths of the Cherokee*, 181.

168. Dippie, *Vanishing American*, 167–71; Duggan and Riggs, *Studies in Cherokee Basketry*, 33; Moses, *Indian Man*, 13, 16–17.

169. Bureau of American Ethnology, *3rd Annual Report*, Dept. of Anthropology, SI.

170. Olds, "Cherokee Indian School," pt. 2, 130.

171. Moses, *Indian Man*, 12–16.

172. James Mitchell, *Random House Encyclopedia*, 1, 560; Cathey, *Day Book* and *Account Book, 1875–1890*, SHC. Cherokee weavers could have obtained aniline dyes off the reservation well before the 1880s, but museum collections of Cherokee baskets confirm the relatively late (1880s) appearance of commercially dyed baskets.

173. Mooney Catalogue Notes, cat. no. 130475, Dept. of Anthropology, SI.

174. Ibid., cat. no. 133023.

175. Mooney, *Myths of the Cherokee*, 179.

176. Mooney Catalogue Notes, cat. no. 135178, Dept. of Anthropology, SI.

177. *Population Schedules of the Tenth U.S. Census*, Microcopy 969, RG 29, FRCEP.

178. Virginia Young, "Sketch of the Cherokee People," 169, 170, 173. *I-wi Ka-tal-sta*, daughter of Yonaguska, lived in the same township as Smith in the 1890s, but there is no way to verify who came to the chief's house with a load of baskets to sell.

179. Churchill Collection, Box 33, Folder 5, NMAI.

180. Carrington, "Eastern Band of Cherokees," 501–2; Churchill Collection, Box 33, Folder 5, NMAI.

181. Carrington, "Eastern Band of Cherokees," 502–3; U.S. Bureau of the Census, *Ninth Census*, 1870, Jackson County, Qualla Town; Schenck, "Cherokees in North Carolina," 325.

182. Carrington, "Eastern Band of Cherokees," 501.

183. According to the 1870 census, 68 African Americans and 13 Cherokees lived in Valley Town, 35 African Americans lived in Quallatown, and nearly 200 "colored" who were not Indian lived at Cheoah. Examples of census data from Qualla include Nick Woodfin, a forty-year-old Indian farmer married to a black forty-year-old, Lucy, who kept house; and the household of a white man, Scroop Enloe, which included a twenty-five-year-old black man, Hugh Hardy, who worked on the farm, and his twenty-five-year-old wife, Ancondis, who worked in the house (*Population Schedules of the Ninth U.S. Census*, Microcopy 1130, Microcopy 1146, and Microcopy 1144, FRCEP; Schenck, "Cherokees in North Carolina," 324–25).

184. Arthur, *Western North Carolina*, 210–12; *Graham County Centennial*, 8, 16; Van Noppen and Van Noppen, *Western North Carolina*, 56–57; Finger, *Eastern Band*, 140; "Tennessee River Baptist Association, North Carolina," 40–46.

185. Van Noppen and Van Noppen, *Western North Carolina*, 3, 57; *Heritage of Swain County*, 9, 19–20.

186. Thomas, *Indian Book 1857*, Thomas Collection, DU.

Chapter 3

1. The sister told me this family story in a parking lot near the motel where both women worked as maids. She preferred to remain anonymous.

2. Van Doren, *Travels of William Bartram*, 272. See also Hatley, "Three Lives of Keowee," 223–48.

3. Van Doren, *Travels of William Bartram*, 273.

4. *Audubon Society Field Guide to North American Wildflowers*, 446; Darlington, *Memorials of John Bartram*, 182, 86.

5. Spongberg, *Reunion of Trees*, 138–55, 143–45. Gray's theory of the common origin of Japanese and American flora supported Darwin's unpublished theory of adaptation, evolution, and natural selection, which he had described to Gray in correspondence.

6. Ibid., 150–53.

7. Patterson, "History and Distribution of Five Exotic Weeds," 177–81, 41, 177; Lindsey Thomas, *Impact of Three Exotic Plant Species*, 56; *Audubon Society Field Guide to North American Wildflowers*, 446; *Gray's Manual of Botany*, 1334; Hardt, "Japanese Honeysuckle," 28.

8. Bell, "Economic Development," 159–63; Robert Lambert, "Logging the Great Smokies," 350–54; Oliver, *Hazel Creek*, 55–70.

9. Bell, "Economic Development," 159–63; Robert Lambert, "Logging the Great Smokies," 351–52; Oliver, *Hazel Creek*, 55–70; Weals, *Last Train to Elkmont*, 1–8.

10. Boyden, *Village of Five Lives*, 18–20; "Champion Fibre Company," 18. See also Bartlett, *Troubled Waters*.

11. Robert Lambert, "Logging the Great Smokies," 352–53; Weals, *Last Train to Elkmont*, 1–3; Oliver, *Hazel Creek*, 55–57.

12. Robert Lambert, "Logging the Great Smokies," 352.

13. *Report of the Secretary of Agriculture*, 25–26.

14. The sale did not actually occur until 1893, when the council, frustrated by restrictions placed on them by the federal government, sold the tract to two different buyers. Legal issues related to Cherokee status and the viability of the contractors held up the sale until 1897 (see Finger, *Eastern Band*, 169–76).

15. Boyd later sold out to the Mason and Dixon Lumber Company. C. F. Nesler to SI, Aug. 3, 1904, M-1059, 7:793, DeWitt Harris to C.I.A., Oct. 4, 1906, and Harris to Gryson and Black, Nov. 20, 1906, all in RG 75, CA, Series 1, Box 5, FRCEP; Supt. to C.I.A., Mar. 5, 1908, Churchill Papers, DU; Carl Lambert, "Many Moons Ago," 24; Finger, *Cherokee Americans*, 17–18.

16. Boyden, *Village of Five Lives*, 21; Van Noppen and Van Noppen, *Western North Carolina*, 354–55.

17. "Basketry of Lucy George," 6.

18. Mary Chiltoskey, personal communication.

19. "Basketry of Lucy George," 6.

20. Ibid.

21. Author interview with Shirley Taylor, Jan. 4, 1989.

22. "Basketry of Lucy George," 6.

23. Hardt, "Japanese Honeysuckle," 30.

24. Leftwich, "Making Honeysuckle Baskets," 27–29; Hardt, "Japanese Honeysuckle," 30. Leftwich states that hollow cores of honeysuckle vines expand with age and collapse when woven, which creates problems of brittleness and breakage. Contemporary weavers I interviewed are not familiar with this problem.

25. Author interview with Lucy Ben George, Nov. 28, 1990.

26. Stephenson, *Basketry of the Appalachian Mountains*, 36.

27. Author interview with Lucy Ben George, Nov. 28, 1990.

28. *Willnotah*, "Life and Memory and Death," 15–16.

29. *The Red Man* 4, no. 1 (Sept. 1911), 39. See also Armstrong, *Twenty-Two Years' Work*, 9, Dippie, *Vanishing American*, 111–21, Peabody, *Education for Life*, 145–207, and Pratt, *Indian Industrial School*.

30. Pratt, *Indian Industrial School*, 10, 25, 32. A career army officer, Pratt (1840–1924) led a detachment of black enlisted men and Cherokee scouts in the Indian Territory. He developed his theories of Indian education while supervising seventy-two Indian prisoners of war jailed at Ft. Marion in St. Augustine, Florida. Assisted by interested citizens, Pratt drilled his prisoners in English language, military discipline, and industrial and agricultural work. His commitment to educating Native Americans away from reservations was reinforced at the end of three years when twenty-two younger prisoners asked to continue their training in eastern schools rather than return home.

31. In Prucha, *Great Father*, 697. See also Pratt, *Battlefield and Classroom*, and Ryan, "Carlisle Indian Industrial School."

32. Enrollment Records of the Carlisle Indian Industrial School, RG 75, Series 1330, NA.

33. Armstrong, *Twenty-Two Years' Work*, 2, 6. Armstrong (1839–93) commanded the United States Colored Troops in the Civil War and worked for the Freedmen's Bureau in Virginia for two years before appealing to the American Missionary Association to establish a school for freed women and men. In 1870, the school was incorporated, financially supported by missionary societies, philanthropists, and endowment funds (see Peabody, *Education for Life*, 55–126, 360–61).

34. Armstrong, *Twenty-Two Years' Work*, 7, 9; *To Lead and to Serve*, 18; Peabody, *Education for Life*, 154–55. See also Tingey, "Indians and Blacks Together," and Lindsey, *Indians at Hampton Institute*.

35. Armstrong, *Twenty-Two Years' Work*, 314. The Hampton experiment in Indian education ceased when the federal government withdrew its funding for Native American students in response to charges that "educating them in the same school with negro children" humiliated and degraded "the red race" (see Rep. John Hall Stephens, Chairman of the House Committee on Indian Affairs, in *To Lead and to Serve*, 51–52).

36. Armstrong, *Twenty-Two Years' Work*, 313; *To Lead and to Serve*, 31–32; Peabody, *Education for Life*, 152.

37. Neely, "Role of Formal Education," 25.

38. For a brief period, Cherokee education came under state jurisdiction (see John Pool

to the Commissioner of Indian Affairs, Aug. 26, 1876, Superintendent of Public Instruction Papers, NCDAH, Neely, "Quaker Era," 314–22, 316, and Orr, "Civilize the Indian," 27–39). See also Donaldson, "Statistics of Indians," 502.

39. Annual Report, June 6, 1894, Potter to Superintendent of Indian Schools, Feb. 6, 1894, and Potter to Sarhawk, Sept. 29, 1894, all in RG 75, CA, Series 1, Box 1, FRCEP.

40. Hampton School Student Records Collection, HU. I am indebted to Fritz J. Malval and the staff of the university archives for making these records available to me.

41. Stella Blythe to Friends, Jan. 23, 1906, Hampton School Student Records Collection, HU.

42. Potter to CIA, Sept. 15, 1894, RG 75, CA, Series 1, Box 1, FRCEP.

43. Spray to CIA, Nov. 12, 1901, RG 75, CA, Series 1, Box 1, FRCEP.

44. Education Circular No. 83, Oct. 15, 1902, RG 75, CA, Series 5, Box 3, FRCEP; Ryan, "Carlisle Indian Industrial School," 136.

45. French to Henderson, 1920, and Thompson to father, Mar. 30, 1916, both in RG 75, CA, Series 5, Box 16, FRCEP.

46. Of the many examples see Supt. to Ned Stamper, Mar. 9, 1915, Box 11, Supt. to Coolarche Watty, Nov. 19, 1918, Box 5, and Supt. to CIA, May 7, 1925, Box 5, all in RG 75, CA, Series 5, FRCEP.

47. Fisher, "Interview with Mary Sneed, Part 2."

48. Owl, "Eastern Band of Cherokee Indians," 159–60. Owl's mother was Nettie Harris, one of the great Catawba potters who moved to the Cherokee reservation in 1884 and married Lloyd Owl (see Blumer, "Catawba Influences," 153–73).

49. Spray to CIA, May 5 and Oct. 24, 1902, RG 75, CA, Series 1, Box 1, FRCEP.

50. CSAR, July 31, 1911, RG 75, CA, Series 6, Box 24, FRCEP.

51. Friedman, "Annual Report of the Carlisle Indian School," 1; Fisher, "Interview with Richard 'Geet' Crowe, Part 2." In 1900, the Office of Indian Affairs required that a half day be devoted to "the literary department" and the other half to industrial training (Education Circular 43, Sept. 19, 1900, RG 75, CA, Series 5, Box 5, FRCEP).

52. Valentine, "Making Citizens," 13.

53. McClung, "Indian of the East," 71.

54. Richard Young, "Solving the Indian Problem," 393; Ryan, "Carlisle Indian Industrial School," 126.

55. See, for example, Spencer to Spec. Agent Cooper, 1892, RG 75, CA, Series 1, Box 1, FRCEP; Fisher, "Interview with John Henry Crowe."

56. Peabody, *Education for Life*, 201.

57. CSAR, 1926, RG 75, CA, Series 6, Box 25, FRCEP; Fisher, "Interview with Richard 'Geet' Crowe."

58. Prucha, *Great Father*, 690, and *Documents of United States Indian Policy*, 175–76; Orr, "Civilize the Indians," 30–31; *Southern Workman* 28, no. 5 (May 1899): 189; Ryan, "Carlisle Indian Industrial School," 50; Pratt, *Indian Industrial School*, 32.

59. Spray to Rudolf C. Baird, June 9, 1902, RG 75, CA, Series 1, Box 1, FRCEP.

60. *Indian Craftsman* 1, no. 1 (1909): inside back cover, n.p.

61. *Southern Workman* 26, no. 8 (Aug. 1897): 156.

62. *Indian Craftsman* 1, no. 1 (1909): inside back cover, n.p.; Friedman, "Annual Report of the Carlisle Indian School," 122.

63. In 1880, Commissioner Ezra A. Hayt called for year-round boarding schools because "the home influence brought to bear upon the Indian children will neutralize in (2) two months, the good work of the other (10) ten" (from Finger, *Eastern Band*, 135).

64. Hampton School Student Records Collection, HU.

65. Virginia Young, "Sketch of the Cherokee People," 174.

66. Lossiah, "Story of My Life," 89–99, 89.

67. Ibid., 92.

68. Ibid., 96; 89–99.

69. Ibid., 92, 94, 95.

70. Ibid., 93, 97.

71. Ibid., 89, 91, 92, 96.

72. Ibid., 90.

73. Ibid.

74. Gibson, "Pioneer Days," 19. Mrs. Gibson had moved to Charleston (later named Bryson City) in 1878.

75. Course of Study for Indian Schools, 54–61; Richards, "Training of the Indian Girl," 510. Traditional arts such as basketry were viewed as benign. See Moorehead, "Indian Arts and Industries," 9.

76. Friedman, "Annual Report of the Carlisle Indian School," 122; Ryan, "Carlisle Indian Industrial School," 137.

77. *Southern Workman* 29, no. 6 (June 1900): 344, and 30, no. 5 (May 1901): 202.

78. Ibid., 31, no. 2 (Feb. 1902): 55; Doubleday, "Aboriginal Industries," 81–85, 83.

79. Doubleday, "Aboriginal Industries," 83.

80. Ibid., 84–85; Doubleday, "Indian Industrial Problems," 55.

81. "Hampton Incidents," *Southern Workman* 29, no. 12 (Dec. 1900): 729.

82. Ibid.; Ryan, "Carlisle Indian Industrial School," 137.

83. Spray to Milton Bradley, Oct. 30, 1902, Box 4, and Reel to Spray, Mar. 25, 1903, Box 1, both in RG 75, CA, Series 1, FRCEP.

84. Spray to Estelle Reel, July 29, 1902, RG 75, CA, Series 1, Box 4, FRCEP.

85. Friedman, "Annual Report of the Carlisle Indian School," 122.

86. Doubleday, "Aboriginal Industries," 82–84.

87. *Population Schedules of the Tenth U.S. Census*, Roll 963, RG 29, FRCEP.

88. *Population Schedules of the Twelfth U.S. Census*, Microcopy 623, Roll 1201, RG 29, FRCEP. I am grateful to the Swayney's grandchildren who recalled John Swayney's proficiency in Cherokee.

89. *Southern Workman* 27, no. 7 (July 1898): 139.

90. Ibid., 31, no. 2 (Feb. 1902): 55, and no. 5 (May 1902): 278.

91. Ibid. (June 1902): n.p., HU.

92. Untitled news article, HU.

93. *Southern Workman* 31, no. 3 (1902): 165.

94. "The Mohonk Conference," *The Indian Friend*, Nov. 1902, HU.

95. Arizona Swayney, Nov. 1906, notes, HU.

96. *Population Schedules of the Thirteenth U.S. Census*, Indian Population, Microcopy 624, Rolls 1123 and 1116, RG 19, FRCEP; Information Regarding Returned Students, RG 75, CA, Series 5, Box 16, FRCEP.

97. Mrs. A. T. Blankenship to Henderson, Sept. 12, 1917, RG 75, CA, Series 5, Box 3, and Temporary Employment Contract, Arizona Blankenship, Sept. 14, 1929, RG 75, CA, Series 6, Box 27, both in FRCEP.

98. Helen Blankenship Houser, personal communication.

99. Field, "Fine Root Runner Basketry." Newsman and traveling salesman Clarke Field was born Jan. 6, 1882. In 1918 he started collecting baskets and amassed one of the largest collections in America. After donating over 1,000 baskets to the Philbrook Art Center in Tulsa, Oklahoma, Field wrote an exhibition catalog wherein he attributed Cherokee honeysuckle basketry to Arizona Blankenship. His source was likely Frank Speck, from whom he purchased several Cherokee baskets.

100. See *Southern Workman* 31, no. 4 (Apr. 1902): 102.

101. Doubleday, "Indian Industrial Problems," 102.

102. Morris, "Revival of Handicrafts," 331–41; Triggs, *Chapters in the History*, 62–129; Eaton, *Handicrafts of the Southern Highlands*, 291–92; Whisnant, *All That Is Native and Fine*, 58–61; Boris, *Art and Labor*.

103. Linn, "In Search of the Natural," 126–32, 128–29. Of the many publications that emphasized crafted goods, *The Craftsman*, begun in 1901 by furniture maker Gustav Stickley, became the most influential.

104. James, *The Basket*, vols. 2, 3, 4.

105. Susan Chester founded the Log Cabin Settlement in the midnineties, Mrs. Frances Goodrich opened the Allanstand shop in 1895, Mrs. George Vanderbilt started the Biltmore Industries in 1901, and the Pi Beta Phi school opened in 1912. See Whisnant, *All That Is Native and Fine*, for a penetrating critique of the cultural intervention of the Arts and Crafts movement in the Southern Appalachians.

106. Quoted in Goodrich, *Mountain Homespun*, 28. For discussions of the craft revival movement in the Southern Appalachians, see Eaton, *Handicrafts of the Southern Highlands*, Barker, *Handcraft Revival*, and Whisnant, *All That Is Native and Fine*.

107. Goodrich, *Mountain Homespun*, 27.

108. Ibid., 18, 28.

109. Schenck, "Cherokees in North Carolina" 329.

110. In addition to the Bird Town and Yellow Hill mounds, the Valentines opened a mound in Murphy, one at Charleston (later named Bryson City), one on Galbraith's Creek, and one on Will Thomas's farm. Edward Pleasants Valentine to Mann Satterwhite Valentine, July 17, 1883, Archives, Valentine Museum, Richmond, Virginia; Bureau of American Ethnology, *12th Annual Report*, SI, 347.

111. Harrington Collection, Archives Box 116, NMAI.

112. Olds, "Cherokee Indian School," pt. 2, 130.

113. *The Red Man* 9, nos. 3, 4, 5 (1915).

114. Fred Olds to DeWitt Harris, Aug. 5, 1908, RG 75, CA, Series 3, Box 1, FRCEP.

115. Olds to Henderson, Aug. 15, 16, and 28, 1917, and Henderson to Olds, Nov. 19, 1917, RG 75, CA, Series 5, Box 13, FRCEP. Olds and Henderson may have been responsible for the healthy stand of bamboo growing on an island in the Oconaluftee across from the agency. No one weaves with it.

116. Mooney, "Collections made on Cherokee trip," June–Sept. 1911, NAA. Mooney

purchased from *Ayasta* the formula book that belonged to her late husband, *Gahuni*. The price was a half-dollar, divided among *Ayasta* and her three sons (Mooney, *Myths of the Cherokee*, 313–14).

117. Mooney, *Myths of the Cherokee*, 237, 313–14.

118. Speck to Barrett, Mar. 18, 1913, and "Notes Concerning a Collection of Ethnological and Archaeological Specimens From the Eastern Cherokee Indians, Swain County, N.C.," Acc. 3717, in Speck Collection, MPM. Speck's ethnographic collections included 26 "old, typical baskets," 200 potsherds, 2 blowguns with darts, carved wooden spoons and ladles, pottery vessels currently in use, 4 stone pipes, 1 pair of moccasins, 1 pair of ball sticks, and a dugout canoe 28 feet long.

119. Speck, "Decorative Art and Basketry," 59; Speck Catalogue Notes, 46-6-65, University Museum of Archaeology and Anthropology, UP; Henderson to CIA, Nov. 5, 1914, RG 75, CA, Series 5, Box 3, FRCEP. For references to early Cherokee honeysuckle or willow basketry see John Irwin, *Baskets and Basket Makers*, 85, and Stephenson, *Basketry of the Appalachian Mountains*, 36.

120. Accession records, Philbrook Museum of Art, Tulsa; Speck and Broom, *Cherokee Dance and Drama*, 21–22; Duggan and Riggs, *Studies in Cherokee Basketry*, 1–4.

121. Truman, *History of the World's Fair*, 255–62, quotation on 262; *Report of the President to the Board*. Nine world's fairs were held in America between 1893 and World War I.

122. Andrew Spencer to CIA, Jan. 31, 1893, RG 75, CA, Series 1, Box 1, FRCEP.

123. In 1905 the Field Museum purchased Starr's "material collected in 1892 at Cherokee, Swain County." I am indebted to Jan Klein, Field Museum registrar, for making the accession notes available to me.

124. Pratt, *Indian Industrial School*, 34–35.

125. Potter to Charles A. Collier, June 20, 1895, and Annual Report, June 30, 1895, RG 75, CA, Series 1, Box 2, FRCEP. Boarding school girls sent "sewing, fancy work, etc."

126. Cato Sells to Superintendents, Jan. 25, 1915, and Henderson to CIA, Dec. 31, 1914, RG 75, CA, Series 5, Box 1, FRCEP.

127. Henderson to CIA, Dec. 31, 1914, and Henderson to Edgar K. Miller, Jan. 15, 1915, RG 75, CA, Series 5, Box 1, FRCEP.

128. Circular Letter 896, Sept. 2, 1914, RG 75, CA, Series 5, Box 3, FRCEP.

129. CSAR, 1911, CSAR, 1915, RG 75, CA, Series 6, Box 24, FRCEP; Chiltoskey, *Cherokee Fair and Festival*, 5–8; *Asheville Citizen*, Oct. 12, 1926, in Horace Kephardt Collection, Journal 3, 1057, WCU; Henderson to Johnson Owl, Sept. 18, 1914, and Henderson to Sentell, Oct. 6, 1914, RG 75, CA, Series 5, Box 1, FRCEP.

130. Henderson to *The Asheville Citizen*, Oct. 12, 1914, RG 75, CA, Series 5, Box 1, FRCEP.

131. Goingback and Mary Ulmer Chiltoskey, personal communication.

132. Henderson to Edgar K. Miller, Jan. 15, 1915, RG 75, CA, Series 5, Box 1, FRCEP.

133. Mason, *American Indian Basketry*, 271; Turnbaugh and Turnbaugh, *Indian Baskets*, 18, 20, 83, 115; Law and Taylor, *Appalachian White Oak Basketmaking*, 139, 142, 183.

134. Chiltoskey, *Cherokee Fair and Festival*, 7.

135. Ibid.; Mooney Catalogue Notes, cat. no. 286033, Dept. of Anthropology, SI.

136. CSAR, 1915, RG 75, CA, Series 6, Box 24, FRCEP. Cherokees remember several kinds of entertainment as well (see Chiltoskey, *Cherokee Fair and Festival*, 6–7).

137. Henderson to Henry Bradley, Sept. 21, 1915, Henderson to William Hornbuckle, Sept. 21, 1915, and Mrs. A. T. Blankenship to Henderson, Oct. 4, 1915, RG 75, CA, Series 5, Box 1, FRCEP.

138. Henderson to CIA, Oct. 30, 1916, RG 75, CA, Series 5, Box 1, FRCEP.

139. When Frank Churchill and his wife came to the reservation in 1907 to complete another roll for the government, they noted that Jennie Fodder, or Jennie Brown, "is one of the best basket makers" (Churchill Collection, Box 33, No. 5, NMAI).

140. North Carolina Extension Service Third Annual report, 44, NCDAH.

141. Henderson to Nellie R. Denny, Sept. 30, 1921, RG 75, CA, Series 5, Box 14, FRCEP; *Asheville Citizen*, Apr. 10, 1927.

142. Henderson to CIA, May 31, 1916, RG 75, CA, Series 5, Box 3, and A. Vermont to Henderson, Nov. 26, 1919, RG 75, CA, Series 5, Box 14, both in FRCEP.

143. Kinsey to Henderson, June 2 and Oct. 7, 1916, RG 75, CA, Series 5, Box 14, FRCEP.

144. Laura S. Walker to Henderson, Nov. 14, 1923, and Henderson to Walker, Dec. 5, 1923, RG 75 CA, Series 5, Box 15, FRCEP.

145. Henderson to Olds, Dec. 14, 1923, RG 75, CA, Series 5, Box 14, FRCEP.

146. Supt. to Mrs. M. R. Richardson, May 22, 1919, RG 75, CA, Series 5, Box 14, FRCEP.

147. CSAR, 1910, and CSAR, 1911, RG 75, CA, Series 6, Box 24, and Henderson to S. J. Allen, Dec. 19, 1918, RG 75, CA, Series 5, Box 14, all in FRCEP.

148. CSAR, Industrial Survey 1922, 1923, RG 75, CA, Series 6, Box 25, FRCEP.

149. Ibid.

150. CSAR, 1926, RG 75, CA, Series 6, Box 25, FRCEP.

151. Harold Foght to Mrs. S. A. Carnes, May 9, 1936, RG 75, CA, Series 6, Box 88, FRCEP.

152. Author interview with Rowena Bradley, Jan. 11, 1989.

153. Ibid.

154. Harrington Collection, Box 116, NMAI.

155. Henderson to Thompson, Sept. 1916, RG 75, CA, Series 5, Box 1, FRCEP.

156. A. Vermont to Henderson, Nov. 26, 1919, and Henderson to Olds, Dec. 14, 1923, RG 75, CA, Series 5, Box 14, and Henderson to Mrs. J. L. Walker, Dec. 14, 1923, RG 75, CA, Series 5, Box 15, all in FRCEP.

157. Henderson to Kinsey, July 20, 1916, RG 75, CA, Series 5, Box 14, Henderson to W. H. Ferguson, Nov. 19, 1917, RG 75, CA, Series 5, Box 13, and Henderson to W. T. Oestmann, Sept. 1921, RG 75, CA, Series 5, Box 14, all in FRCEP.

158. CSAR 1924, RG 75, CA, Series 6, Box 25, FRCEP. Henderson's report of the number of weavers and baskets was an estimate. He was much more likely to know the basket prices since he purchased them regularly. In 1928 the agent estimated that 30 Cherokees made 2,850 baskets for a total of $5,700, or an average of 95 baskets each for $2 apiece.

Chapter 4

1. CSAR, 1932, RG 75, CA, Series 6, Box 25, FRCEP. In 1935 Superintendent Harold Foght claimed that "deliberate plundering of these resources by unscrupulous Indians" depleted the forests (Foght to John Collier, Jan. 10, 1935, RG 75, CA, Series 6, Box 9,

FRCEP). In 1934 Superintendent Spalsbury reported that "their timber resources have been stolen from time immemorial" (Spalsbury to CIA, Jan. 15, 1934, RG 75, CA, Series 6, Box 8, FRCEP).

2. Author interview with Bessie Long, Oct 4, 1989; author interview with Emma Taylor, Dec 14, 1988; Zane Bowman, forester, Bureau of Indian Affairs, Cherokee, North Carolina, personal communication.

3. Author interview with Emma Taylor, Dec 14, 1988.

4. Author interview with Betty Lossiah, May 9, 1989.

5. Walters and Yawney, "Red Maple," 61–63; *Audubon Society Field Guide to Trees*, 570.

6. Walters and Yawney, "Red Maple," 62.

7. Sutton and Sutton, *Eastern Forests*, 418–19; *Audubon Society Field Guide to Trees*, 577–78.

8. Zane Bowman, personal communication.

9. Author interview with Dora Bigmeat, May 2, 1989.

10. Curls appear on Iroquoian and Seneca baskets as early as the 1880s (Mason, *American Indian Basketry*, 271; Turnbaugh and Turnbaugh, *Indian Baskets*, 18, 20, 246–47).

11. Author interview with Betty Lossiah, May 9, 1989; author interview with Martha Lossiah Ross, May 2, 1989.

12. Author interview with Betty Lossiah, May 9, 1989.

13. Author interview with Dinah George, May 5, 1989. As early as 1933, trader William H. Duncan leased his building from a Cherokee. He specialized in hardware, "with a little flour and feed," as well as "Indian handcrafts" (see Spalsbury to CIA, Apr. 5, 1933, and July 20, 1933, RG 75, CA, Series 6, Box 8, FRCEP).

14. Author interview with Dinah George, May 5, 1989.

15. Author interview with Shirley Taylor, Jan 4, 1989; author interview with Myrtle Jenkins, Feb. 8, 1989.

16. Author interview with source requesting anonymity.

17. CSAR, 1935, RG 75, CA, Series 6, Box 25, FRCEP, 7; Owl, "Eastern Band of Cherokee Indians," 133, 158.

18. Author interview with Emma Taylor, Dec. 14, 1988; author interview with Dinah George, May 5, 1989.

19. Ralph Stanion to CIA, Feb. 13, 1929, Circular 2542, Box 7, and CSAR, 1929, Box 25, both in RG 75, CA, Series 6, FRCEP.

20. Owl, "Eastern Band of Cherokee Indians," 133. In 1933, in addition to Duncan, a white man named Freeman ran a general store that sold groceries and "Indian handcraft": see Spalsbury to CIA, Aug. 5, 1933, RG 75, CA, Series 6, Box 8, FRCEP. In 1934, a white man named R. L. McLean ran a "rather extensive general store and trading post" on a privately owned tract of land at the entrance to the agency grounds (see Spalsbury to CIA, Apr. 4, 1934, RG 75, CA, Series 6, Box 9, FRCEP).

21. Author interview with Rowena Bradley, Jan 11, 1989.

22. Stanion to CIA, Feb. 21, 1929, RG 75, CA, Series 6, Box 7, and CSAR, 1930, and CSAR, 1932, RG 75, CA, Series 6, Box 25, all in FRCEP.

23. Myrtle Jenkins, personal communication; Blumer, "Catawba Influences," 158; Owl, "Eastern Band of Cherokee Indians," 133. In 1933, applications to run trade stores were required for the first time. At that time, Cherokee W. R. McCoy ran "a small restaurant" with

slot machines in Cherokee (see Spalsbury to CIA, July 27, 1934, RG 75, CA, Series 6, Box 9, FRCEP).

24. See Wilburn, "*Nununyi*," RG 75, CA, Series 6, Box 27, FRCEP; Great Smoky Mountains National Park Museum Committee, June 2, 1934, and Harold W. Foght to George McCoy, Nov. 14, 1935, both in RG 75, CA, Series 6, Box 87, FRCEP.

25. See Fogelson and Kutsche, "Cherokee Economic Cooperatives," 322–44.

26. Thomas, "Culture History of the Eastern Cherokee," 13, typescript, and Hood, "Brief Study of Birdtown," 4, typescript, both in NCC.

27. Wilburn, "*Nununyi*," 5–13, RG 75, CA, Series 6, Box 27, FRCEP.

28. Owl, "Eastern Band of Cherokees," 156; Fisher, "Interview with Sam Owl."

29. CSAR, 1932, RG 75, CA, Series 6, Box 25, FRCEP.

30. Fisher, "Interview with Louise Maney."

31. CSAR, May 15, 1932, RG 75, CA, Series 6, Box 8, FRCEP; Henderson to CIA, Mar. 16, 1928, RG 75, CA, Series 6, Box 7, FRCEP.

32. Woods and Shanks, "Natural Replacement of Chestnut," 358.

33. CSAR, 1932, RG 75, CA, Series 6, Box 8, FRCEP; Ashe and Ayres, "Trees of the Southern Appalachians," 97; Fisher, "Interview with Emmaline Cucumber."

34. CSAR, Mar. 15, 1932, RG 75, CA, Series 6, Box 8, FRCEP.

35. Author interview with Emma Taylor, Dec. 14, 1988; CSAR, Mar. 15, 1932, RG 75, CA, Series 6, Box 8, FRCEP.

36. Author interview with Emma Taylor, Dec. 14, 1988.

37. Peggy Lambert, personal communication. In 1918, W. H. Cooper ran a general store in Birdtown (see Cooper to Henderson, Oct. 8, 1918, RG 75, CA, Series 5, Box 11, FRCEP).

38. CSAR, 1932, RG 75, CA, Series 6, Box 8, FRCEP.

39. Author interview with Dinah George, May 5, 1989.

40. Ibid.

41. Author interview with Myrtle Jenkins, May 3, 1989.

42. Fisher, "Interview with Lula Owl," "Old Houses Around Cherokee," and "Interview with Reva Bradley, Part 2."

43. Author interview with Dinah George, May 5, 1989.

44. Ibid.

45. Ibid.; Fisher, "Interview with Reva Bradley, Part 2."

46. Author interview with Dinah George, May 5, 1989; CSAR, 1932, RG 75, CA, Series 6, Box 8, FRCEP.

47. Author interview with Rowena Bradley, Jan. 11, 1989.

48. Author interview with Dinah George, May 5, 1989.

49. Ibid.

50. Fisher, "Interview with Reva Bradley, Part 1."

51. Author interview with Dora Bigmeat, May 2, 1989.

52. Ibid.

53. In 1927 Superintendent Henderson permitted Dr. W. P. McGuire of Sylva to place a sawmill on Pheasant Creek where the Mason Lumber mill once stood and to transport his logs over the old Mason logging roads (Henderson to McGuire, Dec. 8, 1927, RG 75, CA, Series 6, Box 7, and CSAR, 1932, RG 75, CA, Series 6, Box 8, both in FRCEP).

54. CSAR, 1932, and Spalsbury to CIA, May 8 and Apr. 27, 1933, both in RG 75, CA, Series 6, Box 8, FRCEP.

55. CSAR, 1932, RG 75, CA, Series 6, Box 8, FRCEP.

56. See A. M. Adams to Paul Lambert, Jan. 26, 1939, RG 75, CA, Series 6, Box 87, FRCEP.

57. Author interview with Bessie and Posey Long, Oct. 4, 1989.

58. Author interview with Myrtle Jenkins, Feb. 8, 1989; author interview with Dora Bigmeat, May 2, 1989.

59. Author interview with Dora Bigmeat, May 2, 1989; author interview with Bessie and Posey Long, Oct. 4, 1989.

60. Author interview with Bessie and Posey Long, Oct. 4, 1989; author interview with Dinah George, May 5, 1989.

61. Superintendent to CIA, July 28, 1930, RG 75, CA, Series 6, Box 7, FRCEP; Spalsbury to CIA, Dec. 15, 1932, and CSAR, 1932, both in RG 75, CA, Series 6, Box 8, FRCEP.

62. Author interview with source requesting anonymity.

63. Spalsbury to CIA, Oct. 24, 1933, RG 75, CA, Series 6, Box 8, FRCEP.

64. "Camel Toe is Killed by Train Thursday, February 24, 1933," 10–11; Deposition of Minda Hill, Mar. 14, 1919, RG 75, CA, Series 5, Box 11, FRCEP.

65. Arizona Blankenship to Roy Adams, Sept. 16, 1929, and Arizona Blankenship, Temporary Employment for Emergency Work in the Field, Sept. 14, 1929, both in RG 75, CA, Series 6, Box 27 (but marked 161), FRCEP; September 1929 Report, Big Cove Day School, RG 75, CA, Series 6, Box 9, FRCEP.

66. Spalsbury to CIA, May 18, 1928, and Superintendent to CIA, July 28, 1930, both in RG 75, CA, Series 6, Box 7, FRCEP; Spalsbury to CIA, Nov. 10, 1933, RG 75, CA, Series 6, Box 8, FRCEP.

67. See Ralph Stanion to CIA, Oct. 12, 1928, RG 75, CA, Series 6, Box 7, and Harold Foght to CIA, May 27, 1937, RG 75, CA, Series 6, Box 10, both in FRCEP.

68. Author interview with Martha Lossiah Ross, May 2, 1989.

69. Ibid.

70. Hacklander to Henderson, Mar. 9, 1921, RG 75, CA, Series 5, Box 3, FRCEP.

71. "Bessie Jumper Interview," 29. See Finger, *Cherokee Americans*, 62, and L. W. Page to CIA, Oct. 3, 1929, and Dec. 8, 1930, RG 75, CA, Series 6, Box 7, FRCEP.

72. Spalsbury to CIA, Aug. 28, 1933, RG 75, CA, Series 6, Box 8, FRCEP.

73. "Mose and Callie Wachacha Interview," 59–60.

74. "Maggie Wachacha Interview," 50.

75. "Martha Wachacha Interview," 56; "Solomon Bird Interview," 14.

76. "Ed and Ella Jackson Interview," 22–23, 21.

77. "Game and Bessie Walker Interview," 63–64.

78. Ibid.

79. Ibid., 65–66.

80. "Bessie Jumper Interview," 30–31.

81. *Report of the Secretary of Agriculture*, 38–40, 160. The creation of the U.S. Forest Service in 1911 stimulated interest in acquiring woodlands in the Smokies and led ultimately to the establishment of large tracts of forest reserves in the Southern Appalachians.

82. Campbell, *Birth of a National Park*, 13, 17, 71–72.

83. Ibid., 15–17, 19–28.

84. Martini, *Inside the Smokies*, 18–20. For a thorough study of human displacement for park building, see Dunn, *Cade's Cove*.

85. "Maney Family," 222.

86. Martini, *Inside the Smokies*, 57; Spalsbury to CIA, Apr. 28, 1932, RG 75, CA, Series 6, Box 8, FRCEP.

87. I am indebted to Jan Tripp, Department of Planning and Environment, Department of Transportation, North Carolina, for her assistance in verifying the dates for road completions in the area of the Smokies.

88. Annual Extension Report, Dec. 1, 1933–Dec. 31, 1934, RG 75, CA, Entry 789, NA.

89. Foght to George McCoy, Nov. 21, 1935, RG 75, CA, Series 6, Box 87, FRCEP.

90. Ibid.

91. C. M. Blair to Louis West, May 5, 1937, RG 75, CA, Series 6, Box 87, FRCEP; Gulick, *Cherokees at the Crossroads*, 1; Cherokee Indian Agency, 1944, RG 75, CA, Series 6, Box 32, FRCEP. Although the basketweavers on the postcards were not identified by name, Dinah George states that they are Annie Standingdeer and her daughter, Ollie Tooni.

92. *Asheville Citizen*, Mar. 5, 1940.

93. Foght to CIA, July 13, 1935, RG 75, CA, Series 6, Box 9, FRCEP.

94. Groves to Page, Sept. 17, 1930, RG 75, CA, Series 6, Box 7, FRCEP. Groves was Supervisor of Home Economics for the Indian School Service from 1922 to 1936. She transferred to the Cherokee Agency at the end of 1936, remaining until she requested a transfer to the west coast in 1939 (see Peairs to Superintendent, Dec. 9, 1922, Series 5, Box 5, Zimmerman to the Secretary, Jan. 16, 1937, Series 6, Box 45, and Willard Beatty to C. M. Blair, Oct. 16, 1939, Series 6, Box 48, all in RG 75, CA, FRCEP).

95. Groves to Page, Sept. 17, 1930, Box 7, and Ethel Garnett Efficiency Report, Apr. 1, 1931, Box 48, both in RG 75, CA, Series 6, FRCEP.

96. Spalsbury to CIA, May 18, 1934, RG 75, CA, Series 6, Box 9, FRCEP.

97. Superintendent to CIA, Jan. 19, 1930, Box 7, Spalsbury to CIA, July 8, 1933, Box 8, and Spalsbury to CIA, May 18, 1934, Box 9, all in RG 75, CA, Series 6, FRCEP. At the time, the school extended only to the tenth grade, although an eleventh grade was planned.

98. Foght to CIA, Oct. 16, 1934, RG 75, CA, Series 6, Box 9, FRCEP.

99. Gertrude Flanagan and C. D. Stevens to Harold W. Foght, Nov. 7, 1934, RG 75, CA, Series 6, Box 85, FRCEP.

100. Ibid. For earlier recommendations regarding native arts in the schools, see Stanion to CIA, July 30, 1928, Box 7, Jessie Minns, Maria Sanders, and Viola Adams to Roy Adams, Feb. 8, 1932, 3, Box 2, "Memorandum Left with Superintendent Ross L. Spalsbury and Mr. Kirk . . . by Miss Cleora C. Hebling," Feb. 9, 1933, Box 85, and Efficiency Report on Ethel Garnett, Apr. 1, 1933, Box 49, all in RG 75, CA, Series 6, FRCEP.

101. Author interview with Emma Taylor, Dec 14, 1988.

102. Educated at Columbia University and the College of France, Collier became a staff member of the Peoples Institute in New York and president of the National Community Center Association. From 1915 to 1919, he directed the national training school for community centers.

103. Collier, *Indians of the Americas*, 15, 28. See also ibid., *From Every Zenith*.

104. Philp, *John Collier's Crusade*, 1; Kelly, *Assault on Assimilation*, 103–12; Collier, *Indians of the Americas*, 20.

105. Philp, *John Collier's Crusade*, 2.

106. Collier, *Indians of the Americas*, 21; Kelly, *Assault on Assimilation*, 119.

107. Collier, *Indians of the Americas*, 22.

108. Collier, untitled article in *Indians at Work*, 3.

109. The AIDA called on the Indian Office to encourage rather than suppress Native American commitment to "group loyalties and communal responsibilities," encourage the development of native arts and crafts as well as agriculture and industry, enhance medical support on reservations, give Native Americans full religious and social freedom (that did not contravene "public morals"), and stop interference with dance traditions (Kelly, *Assault on Assimilation*, 272).

110. [Meriam] Institute for Government Research, *Problem of Indian Administration*, viii; see Finger, *Cherokee Americans*, for discussion of the complications of the citizenship act for the Eastern Band of Cherokees.

111. [Meriam] Institute for Government Research, *Problem of Indian Administration*, 77.

112. Ibid., 532–33.

113. Ibid., 533.

114. Ibid., 647. The report endorsed the Paiute innovation of covering split baskets with beads, stating that the "designs are characteristically Indian, the color combinations fairly good, and the ingenuity and workmanship remarkable, especially in the adaptation of the woven design to spherical surfaces" (647–48).

115. Ibid., 651.

116. In Prucha, *Great Father*, 974.

117. James Young, "Report of the Committee on Indian Arts and Crafts," Sept. 1934, 1–2, RG 75, CA, Series 6, Box 87, FRCEP.

118. Ibid.

119. Ibid., 3.

120. Ibid., 3–4, 11–12. Most of the recommendations of the Young committee had been suggested earlier by the Eastern Association of Indian Affairs in an undated paper entitled "Service of Indian Applied Arts," NAA.

121. Qualla Arts and Crafts Mutual, Inc., *Contemporary Artists and Craftsmen*, v; Prucha, *Great Father*, 975–76; Schrader, *Indian Arts and Crafts Board*.

122. See Eaton, *Handicrafts of the Southern Highlands*, 237–54, Barker, *Handcraft Revival*, 17–19, and Whisnant, *All That Is Native and Fine*, 161–64.

123. Eaton, *Handicrafts of the Southern Highlands*, 251–52, 295; Whisnant, *All That Is Native and Fine*, 162–63; Barker, *Handicraft Revival*, 14–25.

124. Eaton, *Handicrafts of the Southern Highlands*, 252, 261, 296.

125. Spalsbury to CIA, Apr. 28, 1932, and Dec. 21, 1932, Box 8, and Spalsbury to CIA, June 6, 1933, Box 29, both in RG 75, CA, Series 6, FRCEP.

126. Spalsbury to CIA, Apr. 26 and Dec. 21, 1932, RG 75, CA, Series 6, Box 8, FRCEP.

127. It seems likely that the guild membership was actually made up of the community clubs. In addition to the 44 members from Snowbird, there were 21 from the Big Cove

Community Club, 26 from Birdtown, 12 from Yellow Hill, 17 from Wright's Creek in Soco, and 9 from the 3200 Acre Tract (*Asheville Citizen*, May 30, 1933; CSAR, 1934, RG 75, CA, Series 6, Box 25, FRCEP).

128. *Smoky Mountain Indian Trail*, Dec. 14, 1933, 1; CSAR, 1933, and CSAR, 1934, both in RG 75, CA, Series 6, Box 25, FRCEP. The exhibit also went to the Brooklyn Museum, the Milwaukee Arts Institute, Joslyn Memorial in Omaha, the Norfolk Art Institute, museums in Decatur, Ill., Scranton, Pa., and the National Folk Festival in St. Louis. An indication of the influence of the Southern Highland Handicraft Guild comes from the prominence of the exhibit sponsors: Mrs. Herbert Hoover, Mrs. Calvin Coolidge, and Mrs. Franklin Roosevelt (Eaton, *Handicrafts of the Southern Highlands*, 253–54; Barker, *Handicraft Revival*, 13–25; and Whisnant, *All That Is Native and Fine*, 161–62).

129. "Southeastern Fair Opens Sunday," and Hemrick, "Indians *Invade* Atlanta," in *Atlanta Journal*, Sept. 30, 1934.

130. Hemrick, "Indians *Invade* Atlanta," in *Atlanta Journal*, Sept. 30, 1934.

131. "Southeastern Fair Opens Sunday," in *Atlanta Journal*, Sept. 30, 1934.

132. Foght to CIA, Sept. 13, 1934, and Oct. 19, 1935, RG 75, CA, Series 6, Box 9, FRCEP.

133. "Southeastern Fair Opens Sunday," *Atlanta Journal*, Sept. 30, 1934.

134. "John Collier Due in Monday," *Atlanta Journal*, Sept. 30, 1934; Foght to Mrs. H. C. Allen, Feb. 2, 1935, RG 75, CA, Series 6, Box 16, FRCEP.

135. Foght to CIA, May 21, 1935, RG 75, CA, Series 6, Box 9, and Foght to Standingdeer, Apr. 19, 1935, RG 75, CA, Series 5, Box 31, both in FRCEP.

136. Holmes Bryson to Foght, May 29, 1936, RG 75, CA, Series 5, Box 31, FRCEP.

137. Blair to L. M. Glenn, Aug. 15, 1939, RG 75, CA, Series 5, Box 31, FRCEP.

138. Cherokee Indian Fair programs for 1931–41, quote on page 19 of 1938 program, RG 75, CA, Series 6, Box 24, FRCEP.

139. Author interview with Martha Lossiah Ross, May 2, 1989.

140. Foght to CIA, July 17, 1935, RG 75, CA, Series 6, Box 9, FRCEP.

141. Foght to CIA, Mar. 16 and July 17, 1935, Box 9, and Foght to CIA, May 3, 1937, Box 10, both in RG 75, CA, Series 6, FRCEP; see also Finger, *Cherokee Americans*, 99–100. In addition to the pageant, Foght arranged for the construction of a village "along the lines of the one at the Southeastern Fair in Atlanta" that would feature "Indian activities"; he also planned for all of the popular Indian athletics to take place on an athletic field. A group of Hopi Indians, "more or less professional," also expected to attend and set up "a Hopi Indian Village" (Foght to Groves, Sept. 11, 1935, RG 75, CA, Series 6, Box 85, FRCEP).

142. Stamper, *Biographical Manuscript 1*, QACM; Foght to CIA, June 17, 1937, RG 75, CA, Series 6, Box 10, FRCEP. I am indebted to Betty DuPree, manager of the Qualla Arts and Crafts Mutual, Inc., for providing me with a copy of Stamper's manuscript.

143. Stamper, *Biographical Manuscript 1*, QACM.

144. Ibid.

145. Foght to CIA, June 17, 1937, RG 75, CA, Series 6, Box 10, FRCEP.

146. Stamper, *Biographical Manuscript 1*, QACM.

147. Ibid.

148. Author interview with Agnes Welch, May 8, 1989.

149. Author interview with source requesting anonymity.

150. Stamper, *Biographical Manuscript 1*, QACM.

151. Author interview with Mollie Blankenship, Nov. 27, 1990; Dec. 1938, RG 75, CA File, Entry 791, Division of Extension and Industry, NA; Gertrude Flanagan to C. M. Blair, Aug. 27, 1938, RG 75, CA, Series 6, Box 87, FRCEP; Ethel Petty to Rene d'Harnoncourt, July 30, 1938, RG 435, Box 11, 023, NA.

152. Cherokee Indian Agency Report, 1944, RG 75, CA, Series 6, Box 32, FRCEP.

153. "Rehabilitation of the Eastern Band of Cherokee Indians," RG 75, CA, File 36822, NA.

154. Ibid.

155. Author interview with Mollie Blankenship, Nov. 27, 1990; Leftwich, *Arts and Crafts*, 3; Jennings to LaVatta, June 7, 1946, Box 23, and Jennings to Flanagan, May 31, 1946, Box 87, both in RG 75, CA, Series 6, FRCEP.

156. Jennings to Mr. Beatty, June 21, 1951, RG 75, CA, Series 6, Box 88, FRCEP; Steve Richmond, personal communication.

157. Author interview with Emma Taylor, Dec. 14, 1988.

158. Author interview with Bessie and Posey Long, Oct. 4, 1989.

159. Steve Richmond, personal communication; author interview with Betty DuPree, Nov. 27, 1990. Richmond concentrated on developing one-person or one-family shows for co-op members and photographing them and their work. After he retired, the Arts and Crafts Board did not hire another fieldworker.

160. [Meriam] Institute for Government Research, *Problem of Indian Administration*, 532–33.

161. Author interview with Mollie Blankenship, Nov. 27, 1990; Glassberg, *American Historical Pageantry*, 275; *Asheville Citizen*, Dec. 5, 1990. The CHA awards $2,500 per year to craft exhibitors at the Cherokee Fall Festival; pays approximately $20,000 per year to sponsor woodcarving and wood sculpture classes at the Cherokee School; awards ten $500 scholarships annually; contributes approximately $4,000 per year to local causes; and manages an annual payroll of $900,000 ($524,835 of which went to "non-Indians" and $309,000 went to "Indians" in 1990). In addition, the CHA paid a tribal levy (the reservation equivalent of local taxes) of $96,908 in 1987. The Historical Association "was chartered as a non-profit corporation . . . with a board of twenty-one trustees including the governor, Mr. [Samuel] Selden, representatives from the Cherokee Tribal Council, and citizens from several western counties" (Stephens, "Beginnings of the Historical Drama," 214).

162. *Unto These Hills* program notes, 1990, 3; Bob Scott, "Unto These Hills," *Asheville Citizen*, Dec. 5, 1990.

163. Aubry Jennings, "Two Years Hard Work Nets People of Big Cove Electricity for Homes," *Asheville Citizen*, Aug. 16, 1952.

164. Author interview with Emma Taylor, Dec. 14, 1988.

165. "Tribal Antiquities Will Be Preserved and Put On Display," *Asheville Citizen-Times*, Oct. 8, 1933; Charles Collier to C. M. Blair, Oct. 13, 1941, John Collier to Blair, Oct. 13, 1941, Blair to John Collier, Oct. 20, 1941, Blair to Charles Collier, Mar. 2, 1942, Charles Collier to Blair, Mar. 4, 1942, D'Arcy McNickle to Blair, Apr. 8, 1942, Blair to McNickle,

Apr. 20, 1942, Blair to Charles Collier, June 20, 1942, all in RG 75, CA, Series 6, Box 23, FRCEP.

166. *Unto These Hills* program notes, 1990, 1.

Epilogue

1. Mooney, *Myths of the Cherokee*, 241.

2. Ibid., 244.

3. Ibid., 239.

4. Among Native Americans the association of women with basketry is so widespread as to be almost universal (see Mason, *American Indian Basketry*, and Turnbaugh and Turnbaugh, *Indian Baskets*). In contrast, among European Americans and African Americans, women and men are associated with basketry.

5. Ben Dixon MacNeil, *The Raleigh News and Observer*, Jan. 3, 1926, NCC.

6. Mooney, *Myths of the Cherokee*, 341.

7. Author interview with Myrtle Jenkins, Feb. 8, May 3, 1989; author interview with Alice Walkingstick, May 23, 1989.

8. Canby, "Top o' Smoky," 581.

9. Ibid., 578–80.

10. *Asheville Citizen*, Dec. 5, 1990.

11. Author interview with Emma Taylor, Dec. 14, 1988; author interview with Agnes Welch, May 8, 1989.

12. Author interview with Dinah George, May 5, 1989.

13. Ibid.

14. Author interview with Shirley Taylor, Jan. 4, 1989.

15. Speck, "Decorative Art and Basketry," 60–61; Gettys, *Basketry of the Southeastern United States*, 27. In his 1954 article on white oak basketry, Leftwich noted that either hickory or white oak was used to bind basket rims ("Cherokee White Oak Basketry," 26).

16. Author interview with Emma Taylor, Dec. 14, 1988.

17. Author interview with Bessie and Posey Long, Oct. 4, 1989.

18. Author interview with Louise Goings, May 4, 1989.

19. Author interview with Bessie and Posey Long, Oct. 4, 1989.

20. Author interview with Annie French, May 5, 1989; author interview with Louise Goings, May 4, 1989.

21. *Asheville Citizen*, Dec. 5, 1990; *Asheville Citizen-Times*, Nov. 27, 1994.

22. *Asheville Citizen*, Dec. 5, 1990.

23. Ibid., Dec. 4, 1990.

24. Cherokee 1982 Bureau of Indian Affairs Annual Report; Betty DuPree, personal communication. I am grateful to Superintendent Wilbur Paul for making the reports available to me.

25. Clarke Morrison and Bob Scott, "Tribe's Gambling Expansion Proposed," *Asheville Citizen-Times*, Apr. 23, 1994, reprinted in *The Cherokee One Feather*, Apr. 27, 1994.

26. *Asheville Citizen*, Dec. 5, 1990.

27. *Atlanta Journal Constitution*, Jan. 19, 1995.

28. In 1993, the tribe made $500,000 from its Cherokee bingo, $599,000 from its Tribal bingo, and $822,000 from Lotto (Tribal Budget Committee, July 30, 1993).

29. Author interview with Dinah George, May 5, 1989; author interview with Bessie and Posey Long, Oct. 4, 1989.

30. Author interview with Agnes Welch, May 8, 1989.

31. Author interview with source requesting anonymity.

32. Author interview with Bessie and Posey Long, Oct. 4, 1989; author interview with Martha Lossiah Ross, May 2, 1989; author interview with Louise Goings, May 4, 1989.

Bibliography

Manuscript Collections

Ann Arbor, Mich.
  William L. Clements Library, University of Michigan
    Gage Papers. American Series. Vol. 29.
    Lyttleton Papers.
Atlanta, Ga.
  Georgia Department of Archives
    Moravian Mission Diaries, Springplace. Vol. 1. 1800–1818.
      Translated by Dr. Carl Maelshagaen. TS.
    Selected Letters from New Echota, 1824–1837. By Samuel A. Worchester, Isaac Proctor,
      William Chamberlain, Ellsworth, John Ridge, Elias Boudinot. American Board of
      Commissioners for Foreign Missions. Microfilm.
  Woodruff Library, Emory University
    Francis Lyman Draper Collection. Microfilm.
    The Cherokee Phoenix. Microfilm.
  Special Collections, Woodruff Library, Emory University
    Dorris, James. *Store Record Books, 1827–1844*. 2 vols.
Chapel Hill, N.C.
  Southern Historical Collection
    Cathey, Joseph. *Day Book* and *Account Book, 1875–1890*. 2 vols. Group 3430.
    Lenoir Family Papers. 13 vols. Thomas Lenoir Diary 1832–49. Group 426.
  University of North Carolina
  North Carolina Collection
    Batts, Richard D. Letter to the Commissioner of Indian Affairs. 1958.
    Cashion, Jerry C. "Fort Butler and Cherokee Indian Removal: Draft Report Pre-
      pared for Historical Sites Division and State Department of Archives and His-
      tory." 1970. MS.
    Hood, Flora. "A Brief Study of the Birdtown Community, Cherokee Indian Reser-
      vation, North Carolina." 1958. MS.
    Kutsche, Paul. "The Decline of the Importance of Clan Among the Eastern Chero-
      kee." Paper presented at the 56th Annual Meeting of the American Anthropo-
      logical Association, Chicago, Dec. 1957. TS.
    Lenoir, William. "An Account of the Expedition Against the Cherokee Indians in
      1776, Under General Griffith Rutherford." TS.

Thomas, Robert K. 5 TSS. 1958. Institute for Research in Social Science, University of North Carolina.

"Cherokee Values and World View."

"Culture History of the Eastern Cherokee."

"Eastern Cherokee Acculturation."

"The Present 'Problem' of the Eastern Cherokee."

"Report on Cherokee Social and Community Organization."

Wilburn, Hiram C. "The Indian Gap Trail: Great Smoky Mountains National Park Historical Paper No. 5." 1940. TS. U.S. Department of the Interior, National Park Service.

Cherokee, N.C.

Church of the Latter Day Saints

Indian Census, 1835. Index C. Genealogy Library.

Museum of the Cherokee Indian

Armstrong, Drury P. *Diary: 1842–1849.* TVA Archaeological Bibliography note.

Collins, Robert. *Roadbook.* MS 159.45.

Davis, Hester. "A Survey of a Cherokee Indian Community: Cherokee, North Carolina." May 14, 1955. TS.

The Pennsylvania Packett and Daily Advertiser, Aug. 25, 1789. MSS 87-54.

Sloane, William, to Richard Simpson, Dec. 28, 1843. MS 87-52.

"Smoky Mountain Turnpike." 1836. MS 159.44.

Qualla Arts and Crafts Mutual, Inc.

Stamper, Lottie. *Biographical manuscripts, 1 and 2.* TSS.

Qualla Public Library

Gibson, Mrs. J. L. "Pioneer Days in Bryson City, North Carolina." TS.

Chicago, Ill.

Newberry Library

Ayer Collection of Americana

Butrick, Daniel S. *Antiquities of the Cherokee Indians.*

"Cherokee History and Habits and Language."

Cherokee Indians of North Carolina. 251 C2165 T4A.

Indian Documents. Cherokee Claims and Memorials.

"Memorial and Argument of Nancy Reed," March 18, 1847.

"Memorial of Tickoneeska to the Hon. Edward Hardin and Benjamin H. Brewster."

Missionary Herald. 25 vols.

Payne, John Howard. MSS. 10 vols.

Peters, Richard. *The Case of the Cherokee Nation,* Philadelphia: N.p., 1831.

Thomas, William Holland. "Letter to the Commissioner of Indian Affairs Relative to Claims of the North Carolina Cherokees from Wm. H. Thomas, 1876."

Cullowhee, N.C.

Special Collections, Western North Carolina University

Comprehensive Plan: Eastern Band of Cherokee Indians. 4 vols. Raleigh, N.C.: North Carolina Dept. of Natural and Economic Resources, 1974.

Horace Kephardt Collection.

William Holland Thomas Papers.

Durham, N.C.

Special Collections Library, Duke University

Frank Churchill Papers.

H. P. King, *Miscellaneous Memoranda, 1842–1843, Quallatown, North Carolina.*

North Carolina Business Directory.

Samuel P. Sherrill, *Account Book, 1845–1847, Quallatown, N.C.*

William Holland Thomas Collection.

Account Book, 1834–1836, Scott's Creek, Haywood Co., N.C.

Account Book, 1849–1850, Scott's Creek, Haywood County, N.C.

Account Book, Haywood County, 1838–1841.

Accounts, 1837–1838, Scott's Creek, Haywood County, N.C.

Accounts, 1845–1849, Day Book, 1850–1851, Quallatown, Haywood County, N.C.

Accounts, Record of Indebtedness and Inventory of Goods, 1836–1853, Scott's Creek, Haywood Co., N.C.

Accounts of Indebtedness, 1839–1842, Murphy, Cherokee County, N.C.

Day Book, 1832–1843, Scott's Creek, Haywood County, N.C.

Day Book, Indian Town, 1837.

Day Books, Ft. Montgomery, 1852–1854, 1854–1857.

Day Books, Quallatown, Haywood County, N.C., 1840, 1840–1841, 1848–1850, 1853–1854, 1854–1855, 1855–1856, 1856–1857, 1858–1863. 9 vols.

Indian Book, 1857, Quallatown, Haywood Co., N.C.

Indian Book, Haywood County General Accounts, 1837.

Journal and Day Book, 1840–1844, Quallatown, Haywood Co., N.C.

Ledger, 1839–1845, Cherokee Co., N.C.

Ledger and Indian Accounts, 1840–1858, Quallatown, Haywood Co., N.C.

William Holland Thomas and J. W. King, *Account Book, 1836–1841, Indiantown, Haywood Co., N.C.*

Day Book, 1836–1845, Murphy, Cherokee Co., N.C.

Day Book, 1841–1842, Murphy, Cherokee Co., N.C.

Undated Letters and Papers.

East Point, Ga.

U.S. Federal Records Center

Cherokee Indian Fair. Programs, 1931–41.

Record Group 29. Records of the Bureau of the Census.

Population Schedules of the Ninth U.S. Census, 1870.

Microcopy 593. North Carolina, Roll 1130, Cherokee, Chowan, Clay Counties; Roll 1146, Lincoln, Macon Counties; Roll 1144, Iredell, Jackson Counties.

Population Schedules of the Tenth U.S. Census, 1880.

Microcopy 9. North Carolina, Roll 969, Iredell, Jackson, Johnston Counties; Roll 971, Jones, Lenoir, Lincoln, McDowell, Macon Counties; Roll 983, Surrey, Swain, Transylvania, Tyrrell, Union Counties.

Population Schedules of the Twelfth U.S. Census, 1900.
    Microcopy 623. North Carolina, Roll 1201, Jackson County.
Population Schedules of the Thirteenth U.S. Census, 1910. Indian Population.
    Microcopy 624. North Carolina, Roll 1116, Jackson County; Roll 1123, Swain
    County.
Record Group 75. Records of the Bureau of Indian Affairs.
    Cherokee Agency. Series 1, Superintendent's Letterbooks, 1892–1914. 9 Boxes.
    Cherokee Agency. Series 5, Subject-Numeric Correspondence, 1914–26. 18 Boxes.
    Cherokee Agency. Series 6, General Correspondence, 1926–44. 89 Boxes.
    Records of the Cherokee Indian Agency for 1886–1952.
    Records of the Cherokee Indian Agency in Tennessee. 1801–1835. Microcopy 208.
    Records Relating to Enrollment of the Eastern Cherokee by Guion Miller. 1908–1910. Micro-
      copy 685. Roll 12.
    Selected Letters Received by the Office of Indian Affairs Relating to the Cherokee of North Carolina.
      1851–1907. Microcopy 1059.
    Superintendent's Annual Narrative and Statistical Reports. 1907–1938. Microcopy 1011.
Hampton, Va.
  University Archives, Huntington Library, Hampton University
    Hampton School Student Records Collection, 1878–1923.
London
  British Museum
    Sloane, Sir Hans. 1723–24. MSS 4047. Fols. 90, 147, 212, 290, 307.
  British Public Records Office
    Dudgeon, Rich, to Gen. Amherst, Aug. 16, 1760. CO 5/59, 193937.
    Stuart, John. To the Board of Trade. March 9, 1764. MS CO 323/17, XC 194020.
Milwaukee, Wis.
  Milwaukee Public Museum
    Frank Speck Collection.
Nashville, Tenn.
  Tennessee State Library and Archives
    Penelope Allen Collection of Cherokee Manuscripts.
New York
  National Museum of the American Indian
    Frank C. Churchill Collection. Boxes 33 and 37.
    M. R. Harrington Collection.
  New York Public Library
    Wilburforce Eames Collection.
    Richardson, William. "An Account of my Proceedings since I accepted the Indian
      Mission in October 2nd, 1758, to go and exercise my office as a Minister among
      the Cherokees or any other Indian Nation that would allow me to preach to
      them," Dec. 18, 1758.
Oklahoma City, Okla.
  Oklahoma Historical Society
    Grant Foreman Collection.
    Indian Pioneer History.

Philadelphia, Pa.
American Philosophical Society
Witthoft, John. "A Cherokee Economic Botany from Western North Carolina: Man and Nature in the Southern Appalachians," 1960.
Historical Society of Pennsylvania
Varnod, Francis. "A true and exact account of the Numbers and Names of all the Towns belonging to the Cherrikee Nation, 1721."
Vaux Papers.
University Museum of Archaeology and Anthropology, University of Pennsylvania
Frank Speck Catalogue Notes.
Raleigh, N.C.
North Carolina Department of Archives and History
Governors' Papers 91.
Barnard, Andrew, to Gov. Edward Dudley, Apr. 6, 1840.
Governors' Papers 177.
Love, Margaret E., to Governor Vance, May 10, 1864.
Thomas, William Holland, to Governor Vance, May 13, 1864.
Superintendent of Public Instruction Papers. Box 475.
North Carolina State Archives
North Carolina Extension Service Third *Annual Report*, 44.
Productions of Agriculture, Seventh U.S. Census, 1850. Haywood County, North Carolina.
Productions of Agriculture, Eighth U.S. Census, 1860. Jackson County, North Carolina.
Rome, Ga.
Shorter College
Papers of the American Board of Commissioners for Foreign Missions. Microfilm.
Salem, N.C.
Moravian Archives
John and Anna Gambold Diaries and Correspondence. Cherokee Missions.
Meigs, Return Jonathan. Census of Cherokees, 1809.
Springplace and Oothcaloga Missions Diaries and Letters.
Tulsa, Okla.
Thomas Gilcrease Institute of American History and Art
Grant Foreman Papers.
Chicken, Col. George. "Journal of the Commissioner of Indian Affairs on his journey to the Cherokees and his Proceedings there. Aug. 12, 1725."
Fyffe, William. "Letter to Brother John, Feb. 1, 1761."
Washington, D.C.
Library of Congress
Nathanael Greene Papers.
Andrew Jackson Papers.
Longe, Alexander. "A Small Postscript of the ways and maners of the Indians Called Charikees." Copy of (lost) MS. Box 5536. Great Britain Society for the Propagation of the Gospel in Foreign Parts. South Carolina, 1715–1851.
Meigs Family Papers, 1772–1862.
National Archives, Washington, D.C.

Record Group 49. General Land Office.

Field Notes of Reconnaissances and Surveys Made in the Cherokee Nation in North Carolina and extending Over the Border, 1837–38. F83. 13 Notebooks.

Record Group 75. Records of the Bureau of Indian Affairs.

Cherokee Agency. Entry 785. Annual Reports of the Director of Extension, 1932–39.

Cherokee Agency. Entry 789. Annual Reports of Extension Workers, 1934–43.

Cherokee Agency. Entry 791. Division of Extension and Industry. Dec. 1938.

Cherokee Agency. "Rehabilitation of the Eastern Band of Cherokee Indians." Cherokee File 36822: 1945. Acc. 61A-182. Cherokee 259.

Enrollment Records of Students of the Carlisle Indian Industrial School. Series 1330.

Record Group 77. Civil Works. Map File.

"Capt. W. G. Williams's Memoir Relating to Cherokee Nation within the Limits of North Carolina and its Immediate Vicinity, Feb., 1838." U.S. 125-4.

Record Group 435. Records Relating to Exhibits and Expositions 1939–41: Box 3 "Cherokee Products."

Smithsonian Institution

Dept. of Anthropology

Bureau of American Ethnology, *3rd Annual Report (1881–1882)*. Washington, D.C.: Government Printing Office, 1884.

Bureau of American Ethnology, *12th Annual Report (1892–1893)*. Washington, D.C.: Government Printing Office, 1894.

James Mooney Catalogue Notes.

Edward Palmer Catalogue Notes.

National Anthropological Archives

Bureau of American Ethnology Cherokee Collection.

"Cherokee Missionary Reports, 1818–25." MS 3153.

Evarts, Jeremiah. Diary. 1822. MS 3153.

Gatschet, Albert S. "Eastern Cherokee vocabulary. Quallatown, N.C. May, 1855." Notebook. MS 390.

Hawkins, Benjamin. "Excerpts from letters." MS 4146.

Lanman, Charles. "Excerpts from *Adventures in the Wilds*." MS 4146.

Mooney, James.

"Collections made on Cherokee trip, 1911." MS 3629.

"Material on Cherokee botany, 1887." 4 Notebooks. MS 1894.

"Miscellaneous Notes, 1911." MS 3443.

"Notes on clans." MS 3965.

"Upper and Middle Cherokee Vocabulary and 5 kinship charts, 1885–1887." Notebook. 1885, 1886, and Aug.–Nov. 1887. MS 351, Schedule 17.

Olbrechts, Franz. "Miscellaneous ethnography, 1926–31." MS 4600.

"Service of Indian Applied Arts." MSS 4525, Box 1.

Sherrill, F. B., to K. J. Evans (?), June 9, 1866. MS 2241-a.

Valentine, E. P. "Life Among the Cherokees." Clipping from *Richmond Daily Dispatch*, August 1883. MS 3326.
Bureau of American Ethnology Records.
Mooney to Henshaw, Aug. 7, 1888. Series 15.

Newspapers

Asheville [N.C.] Citizen, 1914, 1926–27, 1933, 1940, 1952, 1990.
Asheville Citizen-Times, 1994.
Asheville Sunday Citizen, 1927.
Atlanta Journal, 1893–95, 1934.
Charlotte Observer, 1926, 1929.
Cherokee [N.C.] One Feather, 1988–93.
Cherokee Phoenix and Indians' Advocate, 1828–34.
New York Times, 1995.
Raleigh [N.C.] Register, 1799–1822.
Richmond Daily Dispatch, 1883.
Smoky Mountain Indian Trail, 1933.
South Carolina Gazette, 1732–45, 1759–60.

Government Documents

A Report of the Secretary of Agriculture in Relation to the Forests, Rivers, and Mountains of the Southern Appalachian Region. Washington, D.C.: Government Printing Office, 1902.
U.S. Bureau of the Census. *Compendium of the Tenth Census, Part 1. The Statistics of the Population of the United States*. Washington, D.C., 1885.
————. *Extra Census Bulletin: Indians: Eastern Band of the Cherokee in North Carolina. Eleventh Census of the United States*. Washington, D.C., 1892.
————. *Ninth Census: The Statistics of the Population of the United States*. Washington, D.C., 1872.
————. *Report of the Population of the United States at the Eleventh Census: 1890*. Washington, D.C., 1895.
————. *Tenth Census: The Statistics of the Population of the United States*. Washington, D.C., 1883.
U.S. Congress. Senate. *Document 120*. 25th Cong., 2nd sess., Washington, D.C.: Government Printing Office.
U.S. Congress. Senate. *Document 408*. "Cherokee Indians Residing in North Carolina." 29th Cong., 1st sess., Washington, D.C.: Government Printing Office, 1845.
U.S. Department of Agriculture Report of Cooperative Extension Work in Agriculture and Home Economics, 1918. Washington, D.C.: Government Printing Office, 1919.
U.S. Department of Agriculture Report of Cooperative Extension Work in Agriculture and Home Economics, 1929. Washington, D.C.: Government Printing Office, 1931.
U.S. Department of Agriculture Report of Cooperative Extension Work in Agriculture and Home Economics, 1931. Washington, D.C.: Government Printing Office, 1932.

Books

Allen, W. C. *The Annals of Haywood County, North Carolina.* Spartanburg, S.C.: The Reprint Company, Publishers, 1977.

Anderson, William L., ed. *Cherokee Removal, Before and After.* Athens: University of Georgia Press, 1991.

Armstrong, S. C. *Twenty-Two Years' Work of the Hampton Normal and Agricultural Institute.* Hampton, Va: Normal School Press, 1893.

Armstrong League of Hampton Workers. *Memories of Old Hampton.* Hampton, Va.: The Institute Press, 1909.

Art and Romance of Indian Basketry. Tulsa, Okla.: Philbrook Art Center, n.d.

Arthur, John Preston. *Western North Carolina, A History From 1730–1913.* Raleigh: Edwards and Broughton Printing Co., 1914.

Audubon Society Field Guide to North American Trees. New York: Alfred A. Knopf, 1980.

Audubon Society Field Guide to North American Wildflowers, Eastern Region. New York: Alfred A. Knopf, 1979.

Barker, Garry G. *The Handcraft Revival in Southern Appalachia, 1930–1990.* Knoxville: University of Tennessee Press, 1991.

Bartlett, Richard A. *Troubled Waters: Champion International and the Pigeon River Controversy.* Knoxville: University of Tennessee Press, 1995.

Blackmun, Ora. *Western North Carolina: Its Mountains and Its People to 1880.* Boone: Appalachian Consortium Press, 1977.

Boris, Eileen. *Art and Labor: Ruskin, Morris, and the Craftsman Ideal in America.* Philadelphia: Temple University Press, 1986.

Bourne, Edward Gaylord, ed. *Narratives of the Career of Hernando de Soto.* 2 vols. New York: N.p., 1922.

Boyd, William K., ed. *William Byrd's Dividing Line Histories.* Raleigh: North Carolina Historical Commission, 1929.

Boyden, Lucille Kirby. *The Village of Five Lives: The Fontana of the Great Smoky Mountains.* Washington, D.C.: Government Services, 1964.

Branson, Levi, ed. *North Carolina Business Directory for 1884.* Raleigh: Levi Branson, 1884.

Braund, Kathryn E. Holland. *Deerskins and Duffels.* Lincoln: University of Nebraska Press, 1993.

Brewer, Alberta, and Carson Brewer. *Valley So Wild: A Folk History.* Knoxville: East Tennessee Historical Society, 1975.

Brewer, Carson. *Just Over the Next Ridge.* Knoxville: The Knoxville News-Sentinel, 1987.

Brickell, John. *The Natural History of North Carolina.* James Carson, 1737. Reprint, New York: Johnson Reprint Corporation, 1969.

Brown, Catharine. *Memoir of Catharine Brown, Christian Indian of the Cherokee Nation.* Transcribed by Rufus Anderson. Glasgow: Chalmers and Collins, 1825; Philadelphia: American Sunday School Union, 1831.

Brown, John. *Old Frontiers.* Kingsport, Tenn.: Southern Publishers, Inc., 1938.

Burt, Larry W. *Tribalism in Crisis: Federal Indian Policy, 1953–1961.* Albuquerque: University of New Mexico Press, 1982.

Bush, Florence Cope. *Ocona Lufta Baptist Church: Pioneer Church of the Smokies, 1836–1939*. Concord, Tenn.: Misty Cove Press, 1990.

Bushman, Richard, Neil Harris, David Rothman, Barbara Miller Solomon, and Stephen Thernstrom, eds. *Uprooted Americans*. Boston: Little, Brown, and Co., 1979.

Butrick, Daniel S. *Journal, 1819–1845*. American Board of Commissioners for Foreign Missions. Georgia Department of Archives, Atlanta. Microfilm.

Calendar of State Papers. Colonial Series. British Public Records Office. London.

Campbell, Carlos C. *Birth of a National Park*. Knoxville: University of Tennessee Press, 1960.

Candler, Allen Daniel. *The Colonial Records of Georgia*. Atlanta: Franklin-Turner Co. and Charles P. Byrd, State Printer, 1904–1916.

Cantrell, Roy. *My Friends the Cherokee*. Cherokee, N.C.: Howineetah Publications, 1973.

Carroll, Bartholomew Rivers. *Historical Collections of South Carolina*. New York: Harper and Bros., 1836.

Catesby, Mark. *The Natural History of Carolina, Florida and the Bahama Islands*. Savannah, Ga.: The Beehive Press, 1974.

Chapin, Walter. *The Missionary Gazetteer*. Woodstock: David Watson, 1825.

Chapman, Jefferson. *Tellico Archaeology*. Knoxville: Tennessee Valley Authority, 1985.

Cheeves, Langdon. *Year Book of the City of Charleston 1894*. Charleston, S.C.

Chiltoskey, Mary Ulmer. *Cherokee Fair and Festival: A History through 1978*. Asheville, N.C.: Gilbert Printing Co., 1979.

Clark, Walter, ed. *State Records of North Carolina*. Goldsboro, N.C.: Nash Bros. Book and Job Printers, 1904.

Clark Field American Indian Pottery and Basket Collections. Tulsa, Okla.: Philbrook Art Center, 1952.

Collier, John. *From Every Zenith*. Denver: Sage Books, 1963.

———. *The Indians of the Americas*. New York: W. W. Norton and Co., 1947.

Conner, R. W. D. *History of North Carolina, Vol. 1*. New York: Lewis Publishing Co., 1919; Spartanburg, S.C.: The Reprint Co., 1973.

Corkran, David H. *The Cherokee Frontier, Conflict and Survival, 1740–62*. Norman: University of Oklahoma Press, 1962.

Corn, James Franklin. *Red Clay and Rattlesnake Springs: A History of the Cherokee Indian of Bradley County, Tennessee*. Cleveland, Tenn.: Walsworth Publishing Co., 1959.

Cotterill, R. S. *The Southern Indians: The Story of the Civilized Tribes Before Removal*. Norman: University of Oklahoma Press, 1954.

Course of Study for the Indian Schools of the United States. Washington, D.C.: Government Printing Office, 1901.

Crane, Verner. *The Southern Frontier 1670–1732*. Durham: Duke University Press, 1928.

Cronon, William. *Changes in the Land*. New York: Hill and Wang, 1983.

Crosby, Alfred W., Jr. *The Columbian Exchange: Biological and Cultural Consequences of 1492*. Westport, Conn.: Greenwood Press, 1972.

Crow, Vernon. *Storm in the Mountains*. Cherokee, N.C.: Museum of the Cherokee Indian, 1982.

Cumming, William P., ed. *The Southeast in Early Maps*. Princeton: Princeton University Press, 1958.

Dahlgren, R. M. T., H. T. Clifford, and P. F. Yeo. *The Families of the Monocotyledons*. New York: Springer-Verlag, 1985.

Darlington, William. *Memorials of John Bartram and Humphrey Marshall*. Philadelphia: Lindsay and Blakeston, 1849.

Davis, Richard C., ed. *Encyclopedia of American Forest and Conservation History*. Vol. 1. New York: Macmillan Publishing, 1983.

The De Soto Chronicles. 2 Vols. Edited by Lawrence A. Clayton, Vernon James Knight Jr., and Edward C. Moore. Tuscaloosa: University of Alabama Press, 1993.

De Vorsey, Louis, Jr., ed. *DeBrahm's Report of the General Survey in the Southern District of North America*. Columbia: University of South Carolina Press, 1971.

————. *The Indian Boundary in the Southern Colonies, 1763–1775*. Chapel Hill: University of North Carolina Press, 1966.

Dickens, Roy S., Jr. *Cherokee Prehistory: The Pisgah Phase in the Appalachian Summit*. Knoxville: University of Tennessee Press, 1976.

Dippie, Brian. *The Vanishing American*. Middletown, Conn.: Wesleyan University Press, 1982.

Dirr, Michael A. *Manual of Woody Landscape Plants*. Champaign, Ill.: Stipes Publishing, 1975.

Dobyns, Henry F. *Their Numbers Become Thinned: Native American Population Dynamics in Eastern North America*. Knoxville: University of Tennessee Press, 1983.

Duggan, Betty J., and Brett H. Riggs. *Studies in Cherokee Basketry Occasional Paper No. 9*. Knoxville: The Frank H. McClung Museum, University of Tennessee, 1991.

Duncan, Wilbur F., and Marion B. Duncan. *Trees of the Southeastern United States*. Athens: University of Georgia Press, 1988.

Duncan, Wilbur H., and Leonard E. Foote. *Wildflowers of the Southeastern United States*. Athens: University of Georgia Press, 1975.

Dunn, Durwood. *Cade's Cove*. Knoxville: University of Tennessee Press, 1988.

DuPuy, Edward L., and Emma Weaver. *Artisans of the Appalachians*. Asheville: The Miller Printing Company, 1967.

The Eastern Cherokees and How They Live Today. Knoxville: J. L. Caton, 1937.

Eaton, Allen H. *Handicrafts of the Southern Highlands*. Russell Sage Foundation, 1937. Reprint, New York: Dover Publications, 1973.

Eggan, Fred, ed. *Social Anthropology of the North American Tribes*. Chicago: University of Chicago Press, 1937.

Field, Clark. "Fine Root Runner Basketry Among the Oklahoma Cherokee Indian." Philbrook Art Center *Bulletin Number 1*, 1943.

Finger, John. *Cherokee Americans: The Eastern Band of Cherokees in the Twentieth Century*. Lincoln: University of Nebraska Press, 1991.

————. *The Eastern Band of Cherokees, 1819–1900*. Knoxville: University of Tennessee Press, 1984.

Fixico, Donald L. *Termination and Relocation: Federal Indian Policy, 1945–1960*. Albuquerque: University of New Mexico Press, 1986.

Fleming, Robert. *Sketch of the Life of Elder Humphrey Posey*. Philadelphia: King and Bond Printers, 1852.

Fogelson, Raymond D. *The Cherokee Ball Game: A Study in Southeastern Ethnology*. Ann Arbor: University Microfilms, 1962.

Foreman, Carolyn Thomas. *Cherokee Weaving and Basketry*. Muskogee, Okla.: The Star Printery, 1948.

———. *Indian Women Chiefs*. Muskogee, Okla.: The Star Printery, 1954.

Foreman, Richard. *The Cherokee Physician or the Indian Guide to Health*. New York: James M. Edney, 1857. Reprint, Norman, Okla.: Chi-ga-u, 1988.

Foster, Nelson, and Linda S. Cordell, eds. *From Chilies to Chocolate*. Tucson: University of Arizona Press, 1992.

Fradkin, Arlene. *Cherokee Folk Zoology: The Animal World of a Native American People, 1700–1838*. New York: Garland Publishing, 1990.

Frick, George Frederick, and Raymond Phineas Sterns. *Mark Catesby: The Colonial Audubon*. Urbana: University of Illinois Press, 1961.

Fries, Adelaide L., ed. *Records of the Moravians in North Carolina*. Vol. 5 (1784–92). Raleigh: State Dept. of Archives and History, 1968.

Frome, Michael. *Strangers in High Places: The Story of the Great Smoky Mountains*. Knoxville: University of Tennessee Press, 1966.

Fundaburk, Emma Lila, and Mary Douglas Fundaburk Foreman. *Sun Circles and Human Hands, the Southeastern Indians Art and Industries*. Luverne, Ala.: Emma Lila Fundaburk, 1957.

Galloway, Mary R. U., ed. and comp. *Aunt Mary, Tell me a Story: A Collection of Cherokee Legends and Tales. As told by Mary U. Chiltoskey*. Cherokee, N.C.: Cherokee Communications, 1990.

Gaynes, David. *Artisans, Appalachia, USA*. Boone, N.C.: Appalachian Consortium Press, 1977.

Gettys, Marshall, ed. *Basketry of the Southeastern United States*. Idabel, Okla.: Museum of the Red River, 1984.

Glassberg, David. *American Historical Pageantry*. Chapel Hill: University of North Carolina Press, 1990.

Godbold, E. Stanley, Jr., and Mattie U. Russell. *The Life of William Holland Thomas, Confederate Colonel and Cherokee Chief*. Knoxville: University of Tennessee Press, 1990.

Godfrey, Michael A. *Introduction to Wild Southlands*. Charlottesville: Thomasson-Grant, 1990.

———. *A Sierra Club Naturalists' Guide to the Piedmont*. San Francisco: Sierra Club Books, 1980.

Godfrey, Robert K., and Jean W. Wooten. *Aquatic and Wetland Plants of the Southeastern United States*. Athens: University of Georgia Press, 1979.

Goodrich, Frances Louisa. *Mountain Homespun*. New Haven: Yale University Press, 1931.

Goodwin, Gary. *Cherokees in Transition: Changing Culture Prior to 1778*. Chicago: University of Chicago Department of Geography, 1977.

Graham County Centennial. Graham County Public Library, Robbinsville, N.C.

Gray's Manual of Botany. Eighth (Centennial) Edition. Rewritten and expanded by Merritt Lyndon Fernold. New York: American Book Company, 1950.

Gross, Emma R. *Contemporary Federal Policy Towards American Indians*. New York: Greenwood Press, 1989.

Guide to the Appalachian Trail in Tennessee and North Carolina: Cherokee, Pisgah, and Great Smokies. Harpers Ferry, W.Va.: Appalachian Trail Conference, 1973.

Gulick, John. *Cherokees at the Crossroads.* Rev. ed. Chapel Hill: Institute for Research in Social Science, University of North Carolina, 1973.

Gupton, Oscar W., and Fred C. Swope. *Fall Wildflowers of the Blue Ridge and Great Smoky Mountains.* Charlottesville: University Press of Virginia, 1987.

Hamel, Paul B., and Mary U. Chiltoskey. *Cherokee Plants—Their Uses—A 400 Year History.* Sylva, N.C.: Herald Publishing, 1975.

Hampton, David Keith, comp. *Cherokee Reservees.* Oklahoma City: Baker Publishing, 1979.

Harrington, M. R. *Cherokee and Earlier Remains on the Upper Tennessee River.* New York: Museum of the American Indian, Heye Foundation, 1922.

Hatley, M. Thomas. *The Dividing Paths: Cherokees and South Carolinians Through the Era of Revolution.* New York: Oxford University Press, 1993.

Hawkes, J. G. *The Potato.* Washington, D.C.: Smithsonian Institution Press, 1990.

Hawkins, Benjamin. *A Sketch of the Creek Country in the Years 1798 and 1799 and Letters of Benjamin Hawkins, 1796–1806.* Spartanburg, S.C.: The Reprint Co., 1974.

Haywood, Judge John. *The Natural and Aboriginal History of Tennessee, 1823.* Edited by Mary U. Rothrock. Jackson, Tenn.: McCowat-Mercer Press; Kingsport, Tenn.: F. M. Hill-Brooks, 1973.

Hazard, Samuel, ed. *Original Documents.* Vol. 11, 1st ser. Pa. Archives. Philadelphia: Joseph Severns and Co., 1852–56.

Heckewelder, John G. E. *A Narrative of the Mission of the United Brethren Among the Delaware and Mohegan Indians.* Philadelphia: McCarty & Davis, 1820.

Henning, William W. *The Statutes at Large: Being a Collection of All Laws of Virginia from the First Session of the Legislature in the Year 1619.* Vol. 2. Richmond: Samuel Pleasants, 1809–23.

Henri, Florette. *The Southern Indians and Benjamin Hawkins, 1796–1816.* Norman: University of Oklahoma Press, 1986.

Heritage of Swain County, North Carolina. Winston-Salem, N.C.: Hunter Publishing, 1987.

Hifler, Joyce Sequichie. *A Cherokee Feast of Days.* Tulsa, Okla.: Council Oak Books, 1992.

Hinsley, Curtis. *The Smithsonian and the American Indian: Making a Moral Anthropology in Victorian America.* Washington, D.C.: Smithsonian Institution Press, 1981.

Hitchcock, A. S. *Manual of the Grasses of the United States.* Rev. ed. New York: Dover Publications, 1971.

Holt, Mrs. Russell. *Life With the Cherokees.* Cherokee, N.C.: Museum of the Cherokee Indians, n.d.

Hudson, Charles. *The Catawba Nation.* Athens: University of Georgia Press, 1970.

———. *The Juan Pardo Expeditions.* Washington, D.C.: Smithsonian Institution Press, 1990.

———. *The Southeastern Indians.* Knoxville: University of Tennessee Press, 1976.

———, ed. *Four Centuries of Southern Indians.* Athens: University of Georgia Press, 1975.

The Indian Craftsman. Vols. 1 and 2. Carlisle, Pa.: U.S. Indian School, 1909–10.

In the Smokies: Handbook 125. Washington, D.C.: National Park Service Division of Publications, n.d.

Irwin, John Rice. *Baskets and Basket Makers in Southern Appalachia.* Exton, Pa.: Schiffer Publishing, 1982.

Jackson, Curtis E., and Marcia Galli. *A History of the Bureau of Indian Affairs and Its Activities Among Indians*. San Francisco: R & E Research Associates, 1977.

Jacobs, Wilbur R., ed. *The Appalachian Indian Frontier: The Edmund Atkin Report and Plan of 1755*. Columbia: University of South Carolina Press, 1954.

Jameson, J. Franklin, ed. *Spanish Explorers in the Southern United States, 1528–1543*. New York: Charles Scribner's Sons, 1907.

Jefferson, Thomas. *Notes on the State of Virginia, 1788*. Edited by Merrill D. Peterson. Viking Press, 1975; New York: Penguin Books, 1977.

———. *Writings*. New York: Library of America, 1984.

Jensen, Joan M. *With These Hands*. New York: The McGraw-Hill Book Company, 1981.

Jorden, David J., and Marc J. Schwartz, eds. *Personality and the Cultural Construction of Society: Papers in Honor of Melvin E. Spiro*. Tuscaloosa: University of Alabama Press, 1990.

Justice, William S., and C. Ritchie Bell. *Wildflowers of North Carolina*. Chapel Hill: University of North Carolina Press, 1968.

Kappler, Charles J., comp. and ed. *Indian Affairs Laws and Treaties* Vol. 2. Washington, D.C.: Government Printing Office, 1904.

Keel, Bennie C. *Cherokee Archaeology: A Study of the Appalachian Summit*. Knoxville: University of Tennessee Press, 1976.

Kellett, Alexander. *A Pocket of Prose and Verse*. Bath: R. Cruttwell, 1778. Reprint, Greenwood, Conn.: Garland Publishing, 1975.

Kelly, Lawrence C. *The Assault on Assimilation*. Albuquerque: University of New Mexico Press, 1983.

Kilpatrick, Jack Frederick, and Anna Gritts Kilpatrick. *The Shadow of Sequoyah: Social Documents of the Cherokees, 1862–1964*. Norman: University of Oklahoma Press, 1965.

———. *Walk in Your Soul: Love Incantations of the Oklahoma Cherokees*. Dallas: Southern Methodist University Press, 1965.

———, eds. *New Echota Letters: Contributions of Samuel A. Worcester to the Cherokee Phoenix*. Dallas: Southern Methodist University Press, 1968.

King, Duane, ed. *The Cherokee Indian Nation: A Troubled History*. Knoxville: University of Tennessee Press, 1979.

Krochmal, Arnold, Russell J. Walters, and Richard M. Doughty. *A Guide to Medicinal Plants of Appalachia: Agricultural Handbook No. 400, Forest Service, USDA*. 1969. Reprint, Washington: Government Printing Office, 1971.

Kvasnicka, Robert M., and Herman J. Viola, eds. *The Commissioners of Indian Affairs, 1824–1977*. Lincoln: University of Nebraska Press, 1979.

Law, Rachel Nash, and Cynthia W. Taylor. *Appalachian White Oak Basketmaking: Handing Down the Basket*. Knoxville: University of Tennessee Press, 1991.

Lawson, John. *A New Voyage to Carolina, 1709*. Edited by Hugh Talmage Lefler. Chapel Hill: University of North Carolina Press, 1967.

Leary, Helen F. M., and Maurice Stirewalt, eds. *North Carolina Research Genealogy and Local History*. Saline, Mich.: McNaughton and Gunn, 1980.

Leftwich, Rodney L. *Arts and Crafts of the Cherokee*. Cherokee, N.C.: Cherokee Publications, 1970.

Lindsey, Donal F. *Indians at Hampton Institute, 1877–1923.* Urbana: University of Illinois Press, 1995.

Louis-Phillipe. *Diary of My Travels in America.* Translated by Stephen Becker. New York: Delacorte Press, 1977.

McCall, William A. *Cherokees and Pioneers.* Asheville, N.C.: The Stephens Press, 1952.

McDowell, William L., Jr., ed. *Colonial Records of South Carolina: Documents Relating to Indian Affairs, May 21, 1750–August 7, 1754.* Columbia: University of South Carolina Press, 1958.

———. *Colonial Records of South Carolina: Documents Relating to Indian Affairs, 1754–1765.* Columbia: University of South Carolina Press, 1970.

———. *Colonial Records of South Carolina: Journals of the Commissioners of the Indian Trade, September 20, 1710–August 29, 1718.* Columbia: University of South Carolina Press, 1955.

McLoughlin, William G. *The Cherokee Ghost Dance.* Macon, Ga.: Mercer University Press, 1984.

———. *Cherokee Renascence in the New Republic.* Princeton: Princeton University Press, 1986.

———. *Cherokees and Christianity, 1794–1870.* Edited by Walter H. Conser Jr. Athens: University of Georgia Press, 1994.

———. *Cherokees and Missionaries, 1789–1839.* New Haven: Yale University Press, 1984.

McMullen, Ann, and Russell G. Handsman, eds. *A Key Into the Language of Wood Splint Baskets.* Washington, Conn.: American Indian Archaeological Institute, 1987.

Malone, Henry Thompson. *Cherokees of the Old South: A People in Transition.* Athens: University of Georgia Press, 1956.

Malone, Henry W. *American Indians and Christian Missions.* Chicago: University of Chicago Press, 1981.

Mante, Thomas. *History of the Late War in America.* London, 1772. Reprint, New York: Arno Press, 1970.

Martini, Don. *Inside the Smokies.* Sevierville, Tenn.: Nandel Publishing Co., 1989.

Mason, Otis Tufton. *American Indian Basketry.* Doubleday, Page, and Co., 1904. Reprint, New York: Dover Publications, 1988.

Mason, Robert Lindsay. *The Lure of the Great Smokies.* Boston: Houghton Mifflin Co., 1927.

Meinig, D. W. *The Shaping of America Vol. 1, Atlantic America, 1492– 1800.* New Haven: Yale University Press, 1986.

Mereness, Newton D., ed. *Travels in the American Colonies.* New York: The MacMillan Company, 1916.

[Meriam] Institute for Government Research. *The Problem of Indian Administration.* Baltimore: The Johns Hopkins Press, 1928.

Meriwether, Robert L. *The Expansion of South Carolina, 1729–1765.* Kingsport, Tenn.: Southern Publishers, 1940.

Merrell, James H. *The Indians' New World: Catawbas and Their Neighbors From European Contact Through the Era of Removal.* Chapel Hill: University of North Carolina Press, 1989.

Merrens, H. Roy, ed. *The Colonial South Carolina Scene.* Columbia: University of South Carolina Press, 1977.

Michaux, François André. *The North American Sylva.* Translated by J. Jay Smith. Philadelphia: D. Rice and A. N. Hart, 1857.

Milling, Chapman J. *Red Carolinians.* Chapel Hill: University of North Carolina Press, 1940.

Mitchell, James, ed. *The Random House Encyclopedia.* New York: Random House, 1972.

Mitchell, Robert D., ed. *Appalachian Frontiers Settlement: Society and Development in the Preindustrial Era*. Lexington: University Press of Kentucky, 1991.

Mooney, James. *Historical Sketch of the Cherokee*. Chicago: Aldine Publishing Co., 1975.

———. *Myths of the Cherokee and Sacred Formulas of the Cherokee: From 19th and 7th Annual Reports B.A.E., 1900 and 1891*. Nashville: Charles and Randy Elder Booksellers, 1982.

Morgan, A. Rufus. *History of St. John's Episcopal Church*. Franklin, N.C.: Nonah Foundation, 1974.

Morris, William. *The Collected Works of William Morris*. With an introduction by May Morris. London: Longmans, 1910–15.

Moses, L. G. *The Indian Man: A Biography of James Mooney*. Chicago: University of Illinois Press, 1984.

Murlless, Dick, and Constance Stallings. *Hiker's Guide to the Smokies*. San Francisco: Sierra Club Books, 1973.

Neely, Sharlotte. *Snowbird Cherokees: People of Persistence*. Athens: University of Georgia Press, 1991.

New American State Papers: Indian Affairs. 13 volumes. Wilmington, Del.: Scholarly Resources, 1972.

North Carolina: The WPA Guide to the Old North State. Chapel Hill: University of North Carolina Press, 1939. Reprint, Columbia: University of South Carolina Press, 1988.

North Carolina and Its Resources: State Board of Agriculture, Raleigh. Winston-Salem: M. I. and J. C. Stewart, Public Printers and Binders, 1896.

North Carolina Reports. Vol. 10 (1824). Raleigh: Edwards and Broughton Printing Co., 1917.

Norton, Major John. *The Journal of Major John Norton, 1816*. Edited by Carl F. Klinck and James J. Talman. Toronto: The Champlain Society, 1970.

Nuttall, Thomas. *A Journal of Travels into the Arkansas Territory During the Year 1819*. Philadelphia: Thomas H. Palmer, 1821. Reprinted as vol. 8 of *Early Western Travels, 1748–1846*. Edited by Reuben Gold Thwaites. Cleveland: The Arthur H. Clark Co., 1905.

Odum, Eugene P. *Ecology and Our Endangered Life Support Systems*. 2nd ed. Sunderland, Mass.: Sinnauer Asso., Inc., 1993.

Ogburn, Charlton. *The Southern Appalachians*. New York: William Morrow, 1975.

Oliver, Duane. *Hazel Creek From Then Till Now*. Maryville, Tenn.: Stinnett Printing Co., 1989.

Owen, Narcissa. *Memoir of Narcissa Owen, 1831–1907*. Owensboro, Kentucky. Reprint, Siloam Springs, Ark.: Siloam Springs Museum, 1980.

Painter, C. C. *The Eastern Cherokees. A Report*. Philadelphia: Indian Rights Association, 1888.

Parkinson, John. *Theatricum Botanicum*. London: N.p., 1640.

Pascoe, C. T. *Two Hundred Years of the S.P.G., 1701–1900*. London: Society for the Propagation of the Gospel Office, 1901.

Payne, John Howard. *John Howard Payne to His Countrymen*. Edited by Clemens de Baillou. Athens: University of Georgia Press, 1961.

Peabody, Francis Greenwood. *Education for Life: The Story of Hampton Institute*. College Park, Md.: McGrath Publishing, 1969.

Peake, Ora Brooks. *A History of the United States Indian Factory System, 1795–1822*. Denver: Sage Books, 1954.

Perdue, Theda. *Nations Remembered: An Oral History of the Five Civilized Tribes, 1865–1907*. Westport, Conn.: Greenwood Press, 1980.

————. *Slavery and the Evolution of Cherokee Society, 1540–1866*. Knoxville: University of Tennessee Press, 1979.

Perdue, Theda, and Michael D. Green, eds. *The Cherokee Removal: A Brief History with Documents*. Boston: Bedford Books of St. Martin's Press, 1995.

Peters, Richard. *The Case of the Cherokee Nation*. Philadelphia: N.p., 1831.

Philp, Kenneth R. *John Collier's Crusade for Indian Reform, 1920–1954*. Tucson: University of Arizona Press, 1977.

Porter, Frank W., III. *The Art of Native American Basketry*. New York: Greenwood Press, 1990.

Powell, William. *North Carolina: A History*. Chapel Hill: University of North Carolina Press, 1977.

Pratt, Richard Henry. *Battlefield and Classroom: Four Decades with the American Indian, 1867–1904*. Edited by Robert M. Utley. Lincoln: University of Nebraska Press, 1964.

————. *The Indian Industrial School, Carlisle, Pennsylvania*. 1908. Reprint, Carlisle, Pa.: Cumberland County Historical Society Publications 10, no. 3, 1979.

Price, R. N. *Holston Methodism: Vol. III, 1824–1844*. Nashville: Publishing House of the M. E. Church, South, 1908.

Prucha, Francis Paul. *The Great Father*. 2 vols. Lincoln: University of Nebraska Press, 1984.

————, ed. *Documents of United States Indian Policy*. 1975. Reprint, Lincoln: University of Nebraska Press, 1990.

Qualla Arts and Crafts Mutual, Inc., comp. *Contemporary Artists and Craftsmen of the Eastern Band of Cherokee Indians: Promotional Exhibitions, 1969–1985*. Cherokee, N.C.: Qualla Arts and Crafts Mutual, 1987.

Radford, Albert C., Harry Ahles, and C. Ritchie Bell. *Atlas of the Vascular Flora of the Carolinas: UNC Dept. of Botany Tech. Bull. #16*. March, 1965.

Ramenofsky, Ann F. *Vectors of Death: The Archaeology of European Contact*. Albuquerque: University of New Mexico Press, 1987.

Ramsey, J. G. M. *The Annals of Tennessee to the End of the Eighteenth Century*. 1853. Reprint, Knoxville: East Tennessee Historical Society, 1967.

Randolph, J. Ralph. *British Travelers Among the Southern Indians, 1660–1763*. Norman: University of Oklahoma Press, 1973.

The Red Man. Vols. 2–9. Carlisle, Pa.: U.S. Indian School, 1910–1917.

Reid, John Phillip. *A Better Kind of Hatchet*. University Park: Pennsylvania State University Press, 1976.

Report of the President to the Board of Directors of the World's Columbian Exposition. Chicago: Rand, McNally, 1898.

Rights, Douglas L. *The American Indian in North Carolina*. Winston-Salem: John F. Blair, Publisher, 1957.

Rosengarten, Dale. *Row Upon Row: Sea Grass Baskets of the South Carolina Lowcountry*. Columbia: McKissick Museum, University of South Carolina, 1986.

Rossman, Douglas A. *Where Legends Live*. Cherokee, N.C.: Cherokee Publications, 1988.

Royce, Charles C. *The Cherokee Nation of Indians*. Chicago: Aldine Publishing Co., 1975.

Rozema, Vicki. *Footsteps of the Cherokees.* Winston-Salem, N.C.: John F. Blair, Publisher, 1995.

Runquist, Jeanette. *Analysis of the Flora and Faunal Remains from Proto-Historic North Carolina Cherokee Indian Sites.* Ann Arbor: University Microfilms, 1994.

Salley, A. S., ed. *Hunter's Map of the Cherokee Country and the Path Thereto in 1730.* Columbia: South Carolina Historical Commission, 1917.

————. *Journal of the Commissioner of the Indian Trade of South Carolina, September 20, 1710– April 12, 1715.* Columbia: South Carolina Historical Commission, 1926.

Satz, Ronald N. *Tennessee's Indian Peoples.* Knoxville: University of Tennessee Press, 1979.

Saunders, William L., ed. *The Colonial Records of North Carolina.* 10 vols. Raleigh: Josephus Daniels, 1886–1907.

Savage, Henry, Jr., and Elizabeth J. Savage. *André and François André Michaux.* Charlottesville: University Press of Virginia, 1987.

Schafale, Michael P., and Alan S. Weakley. *Classification of the Natural Communities of North Carolina, Third Approximation.* Raleigh: North Carolina Natural Heritage Program, 1990.

Schiffer, Nancy. *Baskets.* Exton, Pa.: Schiffer Publishing, Ltd., 1984.

Schrader, Robert Fay. *The Indian Arts and Crafts Board: An Aspect of the New Deal Indian Policy.* Albuquerque: University of New Mexico Press, 1983.

Schwarze, Edmund. *History of the Moravian Missions Among Southern Indian Tribes of the United States. Transactions of the Moravian Historical Society Special Series.* Vol. 1. Bethlehem, Pa.: Times Publishing Company, 1923.

Shackford, John B. *David Crockett: The Man and the Legend.* 1956. Reprint, Chapel Hill: University of North Carolina Press, 1986.

Shelford, Victor E. *The Ecology of North America.* Urbana: University of Illinois Press, 1978.

Siler, David W. *The Eastern Cherokee: A Census of the Cherokee Nation in North Carolina, Tennessee, Alabama, and Georgia in 1851.* Cottonport, La.: Polyanthos Inc., 1972.

Siler, Margaret R. *Cherokee Indian Lore and Smoky Mountain Stories.* Reissued by heirs of Margaret Siler, 1993.

Silver, Timothy. *A New Face on the Countryside.* Cambridge: Cambridge University Press, 1990.

Silvics of North America. USDA Forest Service Agriculture Handbook 654. 2 vols. Washington, D.C.: Government Printing Office, 1990.

Sloane, Sir Hans. *A Voyage to the Islands of Madras, Barbados, Nieves, S. Christopher, and Jamaica . . . .* Vol. 1. London: Privately published, n.d.

Small, John Kunkel. *Manual of the Southeastern Flora.* New York: Published by the author, 1933.

Smith, Marvin Thomas. *Archaeology of Aboriginal Culture Change in the Interior Southeast: Depopulation During the Early Historic Period.* Gainesville: University Presses of Florida, 1987.

————. *Depopulation and Culture Change in the Early Historic Period Interior Southeast.* Ann Arbor: University Microfilms, 1984.

Smith, Dr. W. R. L. *The Story of the Cherokees.* Cleveland, Tenn.: The Church of God Publishing House, 1928.

The Southern Business Directory and General Commercial Advertiser. Charleston, S.C.: Steam Power Press, 1854.

The Southern Workman. Vols. 24–36. Hampton, Va.: Hampton Institute, 1896–1923.

Speck, Frank. *Gourds of the Southeastern Indians*. Boston: New England Gourd Society, 1941.

Speck, Frank, and Leonard Broom, and Will West Long. *Cherokee Dance and Drama*. Norman: University of Oklahoma Press, 1983.

Spongberg, Stephen A. *A Reunion of Trees*. Cambridge: Harvard University Press, 1990.

Starr, Emmet. *History of the Cherokee Indians*. Muskogee, Okla.: Hoffman Printing Co., 1984.

Stephenson, Sue. *Basketry of the Appalachian Mountains*. New York: Prentice Hall Press, 1977.

Strickland, Rennard. *Fire and the Spirits: Cherokee Law From Clan to Court*. Norman: University of Oklahoma Press, 1975.

Stuart, Paul. *The Indian Office*. Ann Arbor: University Microfilms, 1978.

Summers, Thomas Osmund, ed. *Joseph Brown or the Young Tennessean: An Indian Tale*. Nashville: E. Stevenson & J. E. Evans, Agents for the Methodist Episcopal Church, South, 1856. Reprint, New York: Garland Publishing, 1977.

Sutton, Ann, and Myron Sutton. *Eastern Forests: The Audubon Society Nature Guides*. New York: Alfred A. Knopf, 1985.

Swanton, John R. *Indians of the Southeastern United States*. 1946. Reprint, Washington, D.C.: Smithsonian Institution Press, 1979.

Tax, Sol, ed. *World Anthropology. American Economic Development*. Paris: Mouton Publishers, The Hague, 1978; distributed in U.S. by Aldine Publishing, Chicago.

Thomas, Cyrus. *The Cherokees in Pre-Columbian Times*. New York: N. D. C. Hodges, 1890.

Thomas, Lindsey Kay, Jr. *The Impact of Three Exotic Plant Species on a Potomac Island*. National Park Service Scientific Monograph Series. No. 13. Washington, D.C.: U.S. Department of the Interior, 1980. Microfiche.

Thornton, Russell. *The Cherokees: A Population History*. Lincoln: University of Nebraska Press, 1990.

Thwaites, Reuben Gold, ed. *Early Western Travels, 1748–1846*. Vol. 3. Cleveland: The Arthur H. Clark Company, 1904.

To Lead and To Serve: American Indian Education at Hampton Institute 1878–1923. Catalogue essay and chronology by Mary Lou Hultgren and Paulette F. Molin. Virginia Beach: Virginia Foundation for the Humanities and Public Policy in cooperation with Hampton Institute, 1989.

Triggs, Oscar Lovell. *Chapters in the History of the Arts and Crafts Movement*. Chicago: Bohemian Guild of the Industrial Arts League, 1902.

Truman, Benjamin C. *History of the World's Fair*. New York: Arno Press, 1976.

Turnbaugh, Sarah Peabody, and William A. Turnbaugh. *Indian Baskets*. West Chester, Pa.: Schiffer Publishing, 1986.

Tyner, James W., comp. *Those Who Cried: A Record of the Individual Cherokees Listed in the United States Official Census of the Cherokee Nation Conducted in 1835*. Norman, Okla.: Chi-ga-u, 1974.

Ulmer, Mary, and Samuel Beck, eds. *Cherokee Cooklore*. Cherokee, N.C.: Museum of the Cherokee Indian, 1951.

Unto These Hills: The Drama of the Cherokee Indian. Program and playbill. Cherokee, N.C.: The Cherokee Historical Association, 1990.

Van Doren, Mark, ed. *The Travels of William Bartram*. 1791. Reprint, New York: Dover Publications, 1955.

Van Noppen, Ina, and John J. Van Noppen. *Western North Carolina Since the Civil War.* Boone, N.C.: Appalachian Consortium Press, 1973.

Varner, John Grier, and Jeannette Johnson Grier, trans. and eds. *The Florida of the Inca: A History of the Adelantado, Hernando de Soto . . . written by the Inca, Garcilaso de la Vega.* Austin: University of Texas Press, 1962.

Wakelyn, J. L., and R. F. Sauders, eds. *The Web of Southern Social Relation: Essays on Family Life, Education, and Women.* Athens: University of Georgia Press, 1985.

Walker, Robert S. *Torchlight to the Cherokees.* New York: Macmillan and Co., 1931.

Waselkov, Gregory A., and Kathryn E. Holland Braund, eds., *William Bartram on the Southeastern Indians.* Lincoln: University of Nebraska Press, 1995.

Washburn, Cephas. *Reminiscences of the Indians: With a Biography of the Author by Rev. J. W. Moore.* Richmond, Va.: Presbyterian Committee of Publication, 1869; New York: Johnson Reprint Co., 1971.

Wax, Murray L., and Robert W. Buchanan, eds. *Solving the Indian Problem: The White Man's Burdensome Business.* New York: New Viewpoints, New York Times Company, 1975.

Weals, Vic. *Last Train to Elkmont.* Knoxville: Olden Press, 1991.

Wetmore, Ruth Y. *First on the Land: The North Carolina Indians.* Winston-Salem, N.C.: John F. Blair, Publisher, 1975.

Wheeler, John H. *Historical Sketches of North Carolina from 1584 to 1851.* Philadelphia: Lippincott, Grambo and Co., 1851.

Whisnant, David E. *All That Is Native and Fine.* Chapel Hill: University of North Carolina Press, 1983.

Wilburn, Hiram C. *Cherokee Landmarks Around the Great Smokies.* Asheville: The Stephens Press, 1966.

Williams, Max R., ed. *The History of Jackson County.* Sylva, N.C.: The Jackson County Historical Association, 1987.

Williams, Samuel Cole, ed. *Adair's History of the American Indians.* 1775. Reprint, New York: Promontory Press, 1930.

———, ed. *Early Travels in the Tennessee Country, 1540–1800.* Johnson City, Tenn.: The Watauga Press, 1927.

———. *The Memoirs of Lieut. Henry Timberlake, 1756–1765.* 1765. Reprint, Marietta, Ga.: Continental Book Co., 1948.

Williams, Walter L., ed. *Southeastern Indians Since the Removal.* Athens: University of Georgia Press, 1979.

Willis, William Shedrick. *Colonial Conflict and the Cherokee Indians.* Ann Arbor: University Microfilms, 1975.

Wilms, Douglas C. *Cherokee Land Use in Georgia.* Ann Arbor: University Microfilms, 1979.

Wood, Peter H., Gregory A. Waselkov, and M. Thomas Hatley, eds. *Powhatan's Mantle.* Lincoln: University of Nebraska Press, 1989.

Woodward, Grace Steele. *The Cherokees.* Norman: University of Oklahoma Press, 1963.

Wright, Henry A., and Arthur W. Bailey. *Fire Ecology.* New York: John Wiley and Sons, 1982.

Zeigler, Wilbur G., and Ben J. Grosscup. *The Heart of the Alleghanies.* Raleigh: Alfred Williams & Co., 1883.

Articles

Abrahms, Marc D. "Fire and the Development of Oak Forests." *Bioscience* 42, no. 5 (May 1992): 346–53.

"Account of Father James Gravier." In *Early Travels in the Tennessee Country*, edited by Samuel Cole Williams, 67–69. Johnson City, Tenn.: The Watauga Press, 1928.

Alexis. "A Visit to the Cartoogechaye Indians." *North Carolina University Magazine* 1, no. 3 (April 1852): 116–18.

Ashe, W. W., and H. B. Ayres. "Trees of the Southern Appalachians." In *A Report of the Secretary of Agriculture in Relation to the Forests, Rivers, and Mountains of the Southern Appalachian Region*, 93–106. Washington, D.C.: Government Printing Office, 1902.

"William Bartram's Observations on the Creek and Cherokee Indians." In *William Bartram on the Southeastern Indians*, edited by Gregory A. Waselkov and Kathryn E. Holland Braund, 133–91. Lincoln: University of Nebraska Press, 1995.

"Basketry of Lucy George." Exhibition Catalogue. Qualla Arts and Crafts Cooperative, 1970.

Beattie, Kirk A. "A Passenger Pigeon Parable." *Wildlife North Carolina* 41, no. 3, 14–16.

Bell, John L. "Economic Development." In *The History of Jackson County*, edited by Max R. Williams, 187–218. Sylva, N.C.: The Jackson County Historical Association, 1987.

"Solomon Bird Interview." *Journal of Cherokee Studies* 14 (1989): 10–16.

Blakely, Robert L. and Bettina Detweiler-Blakely. "The Impact of European Diseases in the Sixteenth-Century Southeast: A Case Study." *Mid-Continental Journal of Archaeology* 14 (1989): 62–89.

Blethen, H. Tyler and Curtis W. Wood. "The Pioneer Experience to 1851." In *The History of Jackson County*, edited by Max R. Williams, 67–96. Sylva, N.C.: The Jackson County Historical Association, 1987.

Blumer, Thomas J. "Catawba Influences on the Modern Cherokee Pottery Tradition." *Appalachian Journal* 14, no. 2 (1987): 153–73.

Bockoff, Esther. "Cherokee Basketmakers, the Old Tradition." *The Explorer* 19, no. 4 (1977): 10–15.

BonneFoy, Antoine. "Journal of Antoine BonneFoy's Captivity Among the Cherokee, 1741–1742." In *Travels in the American Colonies*, edited by Newton D. Mereness, 239–58. New York: The MacMillan Co., 1916.

Bridgers, Ben Oshel. "A Legal Digest of the North Carolina Cherokees." *Journal of Cherokee Studies* 4, no. 1 (1979): 21–43.

"Brother Martin Schneider's Report of His Journey to the Upper Cherokee Towns (1783–1784)." In *Early Travels in the Tennessee Country, 1540–1800*, edited by Samuel Cole Williams, 245–65. Johnson City, Tenn.: The Watauga Press, 1927.

Brown, James A. "The Artifact." *Spiro Studies*. Vol. 4. Tulsa: University of Oklahoma, University of Oklahoma Research Institute, 1976.

Bryson, Anne D. "Last Cherokees of East Cling to Savage Beliefs in Spite of Education." *Asheville Sunday Citizen* 8 (April 10, 1927): 6.

Bushnell, David I. "The Sloane Collection in the British Museum." *American Anthropologist New Series* 8 (1906): 671–85.

Callaway, Ragan N., Edward E. C. Clebsch, and Peter S. White, "A Multivariate Analysis of Forest Communities in the Western Great Smoky Mountains National Park." *The American Midland Naturalist* 118, no. 1 (July 1987): 116–19.

"Camel Toe is Killed by Train Thursday, February 24, 1933." *The Bone Rattler* 11, no. 2 (1995): 10–11.

Canby, Henry Seidel. "Top o' Smoky." *Harper's Magazine* 132, no. 790 (March 1916): 573–83.

Carrington, Henry B. "Eastern Band of Cherokees of North Carolina." In *Extra Census Bulletin. Indians: Eleventh Census of the United States*. By Thomas Donaldson. Washington, D.C.: U.S. Census Printing Office, 1892, 11–21.

"Census of 1860." In *The History of Jackson County*, edited by Max R. Williams, 524–61. Sylva, N.C.: The Jackson County Historical Assoc., 1987.

"The Champion Fibre Company of Canton." *The Carolina Mountaineer* 3, no. 6 (Dec. 21, 1916): 18.

Chapman, Jefferson, and Andrea B. Shea. "The Archaeobotanical Record: Early Archaic Period to Contact in the Little Tennessee River Valley." *Tennessee Anthropologist* 6 (1981): 61–84.

Cheeves, Langdon, ed. "The Shaftsbury Papers and Other Records Relating to Carolina and the First Settlement of Ashley River Prior to the Year 1676." South Carolina Historical Society *Collections* 5. Charleston, S.C., 1897.

Chicken, Col. George. "Journal of the March of the Carolinians into the Cherokee Mountains, 1715–1716." In *Year Book of the City of Charleston 1894*, by Langdon Cheeves, 324–52. Charleston, S.C.: N.p, n.d.

Collier, John. [Untitled]. In *Indians at Work: A News Sheet for Indians and the Indian Service* 9, no. 1 (September 1941): 1–8.

Davis, Rebecca Harding. "By-Paths in the Mountains." *Harpers New Monthly Magazine* 1 (1880): 533–36.

―――. "Qualla." *Lippincott's* (Nov. 1875): 576–85.

De Filippis, M., ed. "An Italian Account of Cherokee Uprisings at Fort Loudon and Fort Prince George, 1760–1761." *The North Carolina Historical Review* 2 (1943): 247–59.

"Diary of Alexander Monypenny." *Journal of Cherokee Studies* 2, no. 3 (1977): 320–31.

Dickens, Roy S. "The Origins and Development of Cherokee Culture." In *The Cherokee Indian Nation: A Troubled History*, edited by Duane King, 3–33. Knoxville: University of Tennessee Press, 1979.

Dickerman, Henry. "Secrets of Indian Basketry." *The Red Man* 7, no. 5 (Jan. 1915): 176–82.

Donaldson, Thomas. "Statistics of Indians." *Extra Census Bulletin. Indians: Eastern Band of the Cherokee in North Carolina. Eleventh Census of the United States*. Washington, D.C.: U.S. Census Printing Office, 1892, 7–9.

Doubleday, Neltie de G. "Aboriginal Industries." *The Southern Workman* 30, no. 2 (February 1901): 81–85.

―――. "Indian Industrial Problems." *Southern Workman* 31, no. 2 (Feb. 1902): 55–56.

"Early Land Grants." *The Bone Rattler* 8, no. 2 (1991): n.p.; no. 3 (1992): n.p.

"1835 Residences of Cherokees Who Avoided Removal." *Journal of Cherokee Studies* 4, no. 4 (Fall 1979): 240.

Evans, E. Raymond. "Jeddiah Morse's Report to the Secretary of War on Cherokee Indian Affairs in 1822." *Journal of Cherokee Studies* 6, no. 2 (1981): 60–78.

Faulkner, Charles H. "Origin and Evolution of the Cherokee Winter House." *Journal of Cherokee Studies* 3, no. 2 (1978): 87–93.

Fenton, William N., and John Gulick, eds. "Symposium on Cherokee and Iroquois Culture." *Bureau of American Ethnology Bulletin* 180 (1961): 87–123.

Finger, John R. "Conscription, Citizenship, and 'Civilization': World War I and the Eastern Band of Cherokee." *North Carolina Historical Review* 63, no. 3 (1986): 283–308.

———. "The Saga of Tsali: Legend Versus Reality." *North Carolina Historical Review* 56, no. 1 (1979): 1–18.

Fisher, Eunice. "An Interview with Mary Sneed, Part 2," *Cherokee One Feather*, Feb. 17, 1993.

———. "An Interview with Sam Owl." *Cherokee One Feather*, March 24, 1993.

———. "An Interview with Louise Maney." *Cherokee One Feather*, Mar. 31, 1993.

———. "An Interview with Reva Bradley, Part 1." *Cherokee One Feather*, May 12, 1993.

———. "An Interview with Reva Bradley, Part 2." *Cherokee One Feather*, May 19, 1993.

———. "An Interview with Richard 'Geet' Crowe, Part 1." *Cherokee One Feather*, May 27, 1993.

———. "An Interview with Richard 'Geet' Crowe, Part 2." *Cherokee One Feather*, June 2, 1993.

———. "An Interview with John Henry Crowe." *Cherokee One Feather*, July 11, 1993.

———. "An Interview with Lula Owl." *Cherokee One Feather*, August 18, 1993.

———. "An Interview with Emmaline Cucumber." *Cherokee One Feather*, Oct. 1, 1993.

———. "Old Houses Around Cherokee." *Cherokee One Feather*, Sept. 22, 1993.

Fleming, William. "Col. William Fleming's Journal in Kentucky From Nov. 10, 1779, to May 27th, 1780." In *Travels in the American Colonies*, edited by Newton D. Mereness, 617–58. New York: The MacMillan Company, 1916.

Fogelson, Raymond D. "An Analysis of Cherokee Sorcery and Witchcraft." In *Four Centuries of Southern Indians*, edited by Charles M. Hudson, 113–31. Athens: University of Georgia Press, 1975.

———. "Cherokee Notions of Power." In *The Anthropology of Power*, edited by R. D. Fogelson and R. N. Adams, 185–94. New York: Academic Press, 1977.

———. "The Conjuror in Eastern Cherokee Society." *Journal of Cherokee Studies* 5, no. 2 (1980): 60–87.

———. "Major John Norton as Ethno-ethnologist." *Journal of Cherokee Studies* 3, no. 4 (1978): 250–55.

———. "On the Petticoat Government of the Eighteenth-Century Cherokee." In *Personality and the Cultural Construction of Society: Papers in Honor of Melvin E. Spiro*, edited by David K. Jorden and Marc J. Schwartz, 161–81. Tuscaloosa: University of Alabama Press, 1990.

Fogelson, Raymond D., and Paul Kutsche. "Cherokee Economic Cooperatives: The Gadugi." In "Symposium on Cherokee and Iroquois Culture," edited by William N. Fenton and John Gulick, 87–123. *Bureau of American Ethnology Bulletin* 180 (1961).

Fogelson, Raymond D., and Amelia B. Walker. "Self and Other in Cherokee Booger Masks." *Journal of Cherokee Studies* 5, no. 2 (1980): 88–100.

Freeman-Witthoft, Bonita. "Cherokee Craftswomen and the Economy of Basketry." *Expedition* 19, no. 3 (Spring 1977): 17–27.

French, Captain Christopher. "Journal of an Expedition to South Carolina." *Journal of Cherokee Studies* 2, no. 3 (Summer 1977): 275–302.

Friedman, M. "Annual Report of the Carlisle Indian School." *The Red Man* 3, no. 2 (Oct. 1910): 47–70.

———. "The Carlisle Indian School; Its Foundation and Work." *The Red Man* 3, no. 3 (Nov. 1910): 117–23.

Fries, Adelaide, "Report of the Brethren Abraham Steiner and Freidrich Christian von Schweinitz of Their Journey into the Cherokee Nation." *North Carolina Historical Review* 21, no. 4 (1944): 330–76.

Frizzell, George. "The Politics of Cherokee Citizenship, 1898–1930." *North Carolina Historical Review* 61, no. 2 (1984): 205–30.

Gearing, Fred. "Priests and Warriors: Social Structure for Cherokee Politics in the 18th Century." Memoir 93. *American Anthropological Association* 64, no. 5 (October 1962): 1–124.

———. "The Structural Poses of 18th Century Cherokee Villages." *American Anthropologist* 60, no. 6 (Dec. 1958): 1148–57.

Gibson, J. L. "Pioneer Days in Bryson City, North Carolina." In *The Heritage of Swain County, North Carolina, 1988*, 19–20. Winston-Salem, N.C.: Swain County Genealogical and Historical Society, 1988.

Gilbert, William Harlen, Jr. "The Eastern Cherokees." *Bureau of American Ethnology Bulletin 133* (1943): 169–413.

———. "Eastern Cherokee Social Organization." In *Social Anthropology of the North American Tribes*, edited by Fred Eggan, 285–338. Chicago: University of Chicago Press, 1937.

Gillespie, John D. "Some Cherokee Dances Today." *Southern Indian Studies* 13 (1961): 29–43.

Goodman, R. M., and Kenneth Lancaster. "*Tsuga canadensis* Eastern Hemlock." In *Silvics of North America*. Vol. 1. USDA Forest Service *Agriculture Handbook 654*, 604–12. Washington, D.C.: Government Printing Office, 1990.

Graney, David L. "*Carya ovata* Shagbark Hickory." In *Silvics of North America*. Vol. 2. USDA Forest Service *Agriculture Handbook 654*, 219–25. Washington, D.C.: Government Printing Office, 1990.

Grant, Ludovic. "Historical Relation of Facts, Delivered by Ludovic Grant, Indian Trader, to His Excellency the Governor of South Carolina." *South Carolina Historical and Geneological Magazine* 10 (Jan. 1909): 54.

Gray, Asa. "Diagnostic characters of new species of phaenogamous plants, collected in Japan by Charles Wright . . . With observations upon the relations of the Japanese flora to that of North America, and other parts of the Northern Temperate Zone." *Memoirs of the American Academy of Arts and Sciences* 2 6: 377–452.

———. "Notes of a Botanical Excursion to the Mountains of North Carolina." *American Journal of Science and Arts* 42, no. 1 (1842): 1–49.

Green, Rayna. "Kill the Indian and Save the Man." In *To Lead and To Serve, American Indian Education at Hampton Institute 1878–1923*, 9–13. Virginia Beach: Virginia Foundation for the Humanities and Public Policy, in cooperation with Hampton Institute, 1989.

Gremillion, Kristen J. "Adoption of Old World Crops and Processes of Cultural Change in the Historic Southeast." *Southeastern Archaeology* 12, no. 1 (Summer 1993): 15–21.

Halls, Lowell K. "*Diospyros virginiana* Common Persimmon." In *Silvics of North America*. Vol. 2. USDA Forest Service *Agriculture Handbook 654*, 294–98. Washington, D.C.: Government Printing Office, 1990.

Hamilton, Henry W. "The Spiro Mound." *The Missouri Archaeologist* 14 (1952).

Hammett, Julia E. "Ethnohistory of Aboriginal Landscapes in the Southeastern United States." *Southern Indian Studies* 41 (Oct. 1992): 24–27.

Hardt, Richard A. "Japanese Honeysuckle: From 'One of the Best' to Ruthless Pest." *Arnoldia* 46, no. 2 (Spring 1986): 27–34.

Harmon, George D. "The North Carolina Cherokees and the New Echota Treaty of 1835." *North Carolina Historical Review* 2 (1929): 237–53.

Hatley, M. Thomas. "Cherokee Women Farmers Hold Their Ground." In *Appalachian Frontiers Settlement, Society and Development in the Preindustrial Era*, edited by Robert D. Mitchell, 37–51. Lexington: University Press of Kentucky, 1991.

————. "The Eighteenth-Century Tallapoosa Landscape Revisited." In *Archaeological Excavations at the Early Historic Creek Indian Town of Fusihatchee, Phase I, 1988–1989*. Report to the National Science Foundation by University of South Carolina, Auburn University-Auburn, and Auburn University-Montgomery, edited by Gregory A. Waselkov, John W. Cottier, and Craig T. Sheldon Jr., 77–109. N.p., 1990.

————. "The Three Lives of Keowee: Loss and Recovery in Eighteenth-Century Cherokee Villages." In *Powhatan's Mantle*, edited by Peter H. Wood, Gregory A. Waselkov, and M. Thomas Hatley, 223–48. Lincoln: University of Nebraska Press, 1989.

Hawkins, Benjamin. "Indians." *The Raleigh Register*, January, 1802.

"Haywood County." Bureau of American Ethnology *12th Annual Report*. Washington, D.C.: Government Printing Office, 1894.

Hicks, Charles. "Manners and Customs of the Cherokee Indians." *The Raleigh Register*, November, 1818.

Highfill, Connaree K. "Ulrich Keener Log Parsonage History." In *Holston Methodism, Vol. 3, 1824–1844*, 1–4. Nashville: Publishing House of the M. E. Church, South, 1908.

Hill, Sarah H. "Weaving History: Cherokee Baskets From the Springplace Mission." *William and Mary Quarterly*, 3d ser., 53, no. 1 (Jan. 1996): 115–35.

Holt, Albert C. "The Economies and Social Beginnings of Tennessee." *The Tennessee Historical Quarterly* 7, no. 3 (Oct. 1921): 194–230.

Horan, Jack. "Ghost Prairies of the East." *Nature Conservancy* 45, no. 4 (July–Aug. 1995): 8–9.

Hudson, Charles. "The Uktena: A Cherokee Anomalous Monster." *Journal of Cherokee Studies* 3, no. 2 (Spring 1978): 62–73.

Hughes, Ralph H. "Fire Ecology of Canebrakes." In Fifth Annual Tall Timbers Fire Ecology Conference *Proceedings*, 149–58. Tallahassee: Tall Timbers Research Station, 1966.

Iobst, Richard W. "William Holland Thomas and the Cherokee Claims." In *The Cherokee Indian Nation: A Troubled History*, edited by Duane King, 181–201. Knoxville: University of Tennessee Press, 1979.

Irwin, Lee. "Cherokee Healing: Myths, Dreams, and Medicine." *American Indian Quarterly* 16, no. 2 (1992): 237–57.

Jackson County Census of 1860. In *The History of Jackson County*, edited by Max R. Williams, 524–61. Sylva, N.C.: The Jackson County Historical Association, 1987.

"Jackson, Ed and Ella, Interview." *Journal of Cherokee Studies* 14 (1989): 17–23.

James, George Wharton, ed. *The Basket: The Journal of the Basket Fraternity or Lovers of the Indian*

Basket and Other Good Things. Vol. 2, nos. 2, 3, 4. Pasadena, Calif.: The Basket Fraternity, 1904.

"John Ridge on Cherokee Civilization in 1826," edited by William C. Sturtevant. *Journal of Cherokee Studies* 6, no. 2 (Fall 1981): 79–91.

Johnson, Robert. "A Governor Answers a Questionnaire, 1719–1720." In *The Colonial South Carolina Scene*, edited by H. Roy Merrens, 56–66. Columbia: University of South Carolina Press, 1977.

"Journal of Antoine Bonnefoy (1741–1742)." In *Early Travels to the Tennessee Country*, edited by Samuel Cole Williams, 147–65. Johnson City, Tenn.: The Watauga Press, 1927.

"Journal of the Mission at Brainerd," *Missionary Herald* 14, no. 9 (Sept. 1818): 413–16.

"Journey of D'Artaguette (1723)." In *Early Travels to the Tennessee Country*, edited by Samuel Cole Williams, 74–82. Johnson City, Tenn.: The Watauga Press, 1927.

"Jumper, Bessie, Interview." *Journal of Cherokee Studies* 14 (1989): 24–35.

Kilpatrick, Jack Frederick. "The *Wahnenauhi* Manuscript: Historical Sketches of the Cherokee." *Bureau of American Ethnology Bulletin 196* (1966): 175–213.

Kilpatrick, Jack Frederick, and Anna Gritts Kilpatrick. "Cherokee Ritual Pertaining to Medicinal Roots." *Southern Indian Studies* 16 (1964): 24–28.

———. "Chronicles of Wolftown: Social Documents of the North Carolina Cherokees, 1850–1862." *Bureau of American Ethnology Bulletin 196* (1966): 5–111.

———. "Record of a North Carolina Cherokee Township Trial (1862)." *Southern Indian Studies* 16 (1964): 21–23.

King, Duane. "The Origin of the Eastern Cherokees as a Social and Political Entity." In *The Cherokee Indian Nation: A Troubled History*, edited by Duane King, 164–81. Knoxville: University of Tennessee Press, 1979.

———. "A Powder Horn Commemorating the Grant Expedition Against the Cherokees." *Journal of Cherokee Studies* 1, no. 1 (Summer 1976): 23–40.

King, Duane, and E. Raymond Evans. "Tsali, the Man Behind the Legend." *Journal of Cherokee Studies*, no. 4 (1979): 184–201.

Komarek, E. V., Sr. "Fire Ecology—Grasslands and Man." In Fourth Annual Tall Timbers Fire Ecology Conference *Proceedings*, 169–98. Tallahassee: Tall Timbers Research Station, 1965.

Kupferer, Harriet. "'The Principal People,' 1960: A Study of Cultural and Social Groups of the Eastern Cherokees." *Bureau of American Ethnology Bulletin 196* (1966): 217–321.

Lambert, Carl G. "Many Moons Ago." *The Bone Rattler* 11, no. 4 (1995): 22–30.

Lambert, Robert S. "Logging the Great Smokies, 1880–1930." *Tennessee Historical Quarterly* 20, no. 4 (Dec. 1961): 350–63.

Lamson, Neil I. "*Morus rubra* Red Mulberry." In *Silvics of North America*. Vol. 2. USDA Forest Service *Agriculture Handbook 654*, 654–57. Washington, D.C.: Government Printing Office, 1990.

Lawson, Edwin R. "*Juniperus virginiana* Eastern Redcedar." In *Silvics of North America*. Vol. 1. USDA Forest Service *Agriculture Handbook 654*, 131–39. Washington, D.C.: Government Printing Office, 1990.

Leftwich, Rodney. "Cherokee White Oak Basketry." *School Arts* 54, no. 1 (Sept. 1954): 28–36.

————. "Making Honeysuckle Baskets." *School Arts* 55, no. 6 (Feb. 1956): 27–29.

"Letter of Abraham Wood Describing Needham's Journey (1673)." In *Early Travels to the Tennessee Country*, edited by Samuel Cole Williams, 17–38. Johnson City, Tenn.: The Watauga Press, 1927.

Linn, Natalie Fay. "In Search of the Natural." *Antiques and Fine Art* 8, no. 1 (Nov.–Dec. 1990): 126–32.

Litton, Gaston. "Enrollment Records of the Eastern Band of the Cherokee Indians." *North Carolina Historical Review* 17, no. 3 (1940): 199–231.

Lossiah, Aggie Ross. "The Story of My Life as Far Back As I Can Remember." Edited by Joan Greene. *Journal of Cherokee Studies* 9, no. 2 (Fall 1984): 89–99.

McClary, Ben Harris. "Nancy Ward: The Last Beloved Woman of the Cherokees." *Tennessee Historical Quarterly* 21, no. 4 (1962): 352–61.

McClung, Littel. "The Indian of the East." *The Red Man* 3, no. 2 (Oct. 1910): 70–74.

McCully, Bruce T. "Governor Francis Nicholson, Patron *Par Excellence* of Religion and Learning in Colonial America." *William and Mary Quarterly*, 3rd ser., 34, no. 2 (April 1982): 310–33.

McIlwain, Charles Howard. Introduction to *An Abridgement of the Indian Affairs*, by Peter Wraxall. Edited by Charles Howard McIlwain, 1915.

McLoughlin, William G. "Cherokee Anomie, 1794–1809." In *Uprooted Americans*, edited by Richard Bushman, Neil Harris, David Rothman, Barbara Miller, Solomon Thernstrom, and Stephen Thernstrom, 27–160. Boston: Little, Brown, and Co., 1979.

————. "Cherokee Anti-Mission Sentiment, 1824–1828." *Ethnohistory* 21 (1974): 361–70.

————. "Experiment in Cherokee Citizenship, 1817–1829." In *The Cherokee Ghost Dance*, by William C. McLoughlin, 153–91. Macon, Ga.: Mercer University Press, 1984.

McLoughlin, William C., and Walter H. Conser Jr. "The Cherokee Censuses of 1809, 1825, and 1835." In *The Cherokee Ghost Dance*, by William C. McLoughlin, 215–50. Macon, Ga.: Mercer University Press, 1984.

————. "The Cherokees in Transition: A Statistical Analysis of the Federal Cherokee Census of 1835." *Journal of American History* 64, no. 3 (Dec. 1977): 678–703.

McRorie, J. D. "Formation of Counties and Towns." In *The History of Jackson County*, edited by Max R. Williams, 101–41. Sylva, N.C.: The Jackson County Historical Association, 1987.

"The Maney Family." In *The Heritage of Swain County, North Carolina, 1988*, 222. Winston-Salem, N.C.: Swain County Genealogical and Historical Society, 1988.

Menzies, David. "A true Relation of unheard of Sufferings of DAVID MENZIES, Surgeon, among the CHEROKEES, and of his surprizing Deliverance." In Alexander Kellett, *A Pocket of Prose and Verse*. 1778. Reprint, Greenwood, Conn.: Garland Publishing, 1975.

"André Michaux's Travels into Kentucky, 1793–1796." In *Early Western Travels, 1748–1846*, vol. 3, edited by Reuben Gold Thwaites. Cleveland: The Arthur H. Clark Co., 1904.

"François André Michaux's Travels West of Alleghany Mountains, 1802." In *Early Western Travels, 1748–1846*, vol 3., edited by Reuben Gold Thwaites. Cleveland: The Arthur H. Clark Co., 1904.

Mooney, James. "The Cherokee Ball Play." *American Anthropologist*, o.s., no. 3 (1890): 105–32.

———. "The Cherokee River Cult." *Journal of American Folk-Lore* 12, no. 48 (Jan.–Mar. 1900): 1–10.

Moorehead, Warren K. "Indian Arts and Industries." *The Red Man* 2, no. 5 (Jan. 1910): 9–16.

Morris, William. "The Revival of Handicrafts." In *The Collected Works of William Morris*, edited by May Morris. London: Longmans, 1910–15.

Morrison, A. J. "The Virginia Indian Trade to 1673." *William and Mary Quarterly* 1, no. 4 (1921): 217–36.

"Narrative of Father Marquette (1673)." In *Early Travels to the Tennessee Country*, edited by Samuel Cole Williams, 41–45. Johnson City, Tenn.: The Watauga Press, 1927.

"Narrative of the Expedition of Hernando de Soto By the Gentleman of Elvas," ed. Theodore H. Lewis. In *Spanish Explorers in the southern United States, 1528–1543*, edited by Frederick W. Hodge and Theodore H. Lewis. 1907. Reprint, Austin: The Texas State Historical Association, 1990.

Neely, Sharlotte. "Acculturation and Persistence among North Carolina's Eastern Band of Cherokee Indians." In *Southeastern Indians Since the Removal Era*, edited by Walter L. Williams, 154–74. Athens: University of Georgia Press, 1979.

———. "The Quaker Era of Cherokee Indian Education, 1880–1892." *Appalachian Journal* 2, no. 4 (1975): 314–22.

Newman, Robert D. "The Acceptance of European Domestic Animals by the Eighteenth Century Cherokee." *Tennessee Anthropologist* 4, no. 1 (Spring 1979): 102–5.

North Carolina State Board of Public Welfare: Report of a Social Study of the Eastern Band of Cherokee Indians. Raleigh: North Carolina State Board of Public Welfare, 1952.

Olds, Fred A. "The Cherokee Indian School." Parts 1–3. *The Red Man* 9, nos. 2, 4, 6 (1917).

Orr, Joan Greene. "Civilize the Indian: Government Policies, Quakers, and Cherokee Education." *The Southern Friend, Journal of the North Carolina Friends Historical Society* 10, no. 2 (Autumn 1988): 27–39.

Patterson, David T. "The History and Distribution of Five Exotic Weeds in North Carolina." *Castanea, The Journal of the Southern Appalachian Botanical Club* 41 (1976): 177–81.

Peattie, Donald Culross. "Men, Mountains, and Trees." In *The Great Smokies*, edited by Roderick Peattie. New York: Vanguard Press, 1943.

Perdue, Theda. "Cherokee Planters: The Development of Plantation Slavery Before Removal." In *The Cherokee Indian Nation: A Troubled History*, edited by Duane King, 110–28. Knoxville: University of Tennessee Press, 1979.

———. "The Conflict Within: Cherokees and Removal." In *Cherokee Removal: Before and After*, edited by William L. Anderson, 55–74. Athens: University of Georgia Press, 1991.

———. "Remembering Removal: Interview with Cornelia C. Chandler." *Journal of Cherokee Studies* 2, no. 2 (Fall 1982): 70–72.

———. "Southern Indians and the Cult of True Womanhood." In *The Web of Southern Social Relations: Essays on Family Life, Education, and Women*, edited by J. L. Wakelyn and R. F. Saunders. Athens: University of Georgia Press, 1985.

Persico, J. Richard Jr. "Early Nineteenth-Century Cherokee Political Organization." In *The Cherokee Indian Nation: A Troubled History*, edited by Duane King, 92–110. Knoxville: University of Tennessee Press, 1979.

Philp, Kenneth R. "John Collier, 1933–45." In *The Commissioners of Indian Affairs, 1824– 1977*, edited by Robert M. Kvasnicka and Herman J. Viola, 273–76. Lincoln: University of Nebraska Press, 1979.

Pillsbury, Richard. "The Europeanization of the Cherokee Settlement Landscape Prior to Removal: a Georgia Case Study." *Geoscience and Man* 23 (1983): 59–69.

Rangel, Rodrigo. "Account of the Northern Conquest and Discovery of Hernando de Soto." Translated and edited by John E. Worth. In *The De Soto Chronicles*. Vol. 1, edited by Lawrence A. Clayton, Vernon James Knight Jr., and Edward C. Moore, 247–306. Tuscaloosa: University of Alabama Press, 1993.

"Report of the Journey of the Brethren Abraham Steiner and Frederick C. de Schweinitz to the Cherokee and the Cumberland Settlements (1799)." In *Early Travels in the Tennessee Country*, edited by Samuel Cole Williams, 448–525. Johnson City, Tenn.: The Watauga Press, 1927.

Richards, Josephine E. "The Training of the Indian Girl as the Uplifter of the Home." *The Southern Workman* 29, no. 9 (September 1900): 507–10.

Rink, George. "*Juglans cinerea* Butternut." In *Silvics of North America*. Vol. 2. USDA Forest Service *Agriculture Handbook 654*, 386–90. Washington, D.C.: Government Printing Office, 1990.

Robertson, James Alexander. "The Account of the Gentleman of Elvas." In *The De Soto Chronicles*, edited by Lawrence A. Clayton, Vernon James Knight Jr., and Edward C. Moore. Tuscaloosa: University of Alabama Press, 1993.

Rockwell, E. F., ed. "Parallel and Combined Expeditions against the Cherokee Indians in South and North Carolina in 1776." *Historical Magazine and Notes and Queries*, n.s., 2 (Oct. 1867): 212–20.

Rogers, Robert. "*Quercus alba* White Oak," *Silvics of North America*. Vol. 2. USDA Forest Service *Agriculture Handbook 654*, 605–13. Washington, D.C.: Government Printing Office, 1990.

Rogers, William Flinn. "Life in East Tennessee Near End of Eighteenth Century." *East Tennessee Historical Society's Publications* 1 (1929): 27–42.

Rothrock, Mary. "The Carolina Traders Among the Overhill Cherokees, 1690–1760." *East Tennessee Historical Society's Publications* 1 (1929): 3–18.

Schenck, David. "The Cherokees in North Carolina." *At Home and Abroad* 2, no. 5 (Feb. 1882): 321–31.

Schroedl, Gerald. "Louis-Philippe's Journal and Archaeological Investigations at the Overhill Cherokee Town of Toqua." *Journal of Cherokee Studies* 3, no. 4 (1978): 206–20.

"Scott, Maj. Gen. Winfield, to War Department, Nov. 6, 1838." *Journal of Cherokee Studies* 4, no. 4 (Fall 1979): 216–17.

Simpson, Marcus B., Jr. "William Brewster's Exploration of the Southern Appalachian Mountains: The Journal of 1885." *North Carolina Historical Review* 57, no. 1 (1980): 43–77.

Smith, Betty Anderson. "Distribution of Eighteenth-Century Cherokee Settlements." In *The Cherokee Indian Nation: A Troubled History*, edited by Duane King, 46–60. Knoxville: University of Tennessee Press, 1979.

Snell, William R. "The Councils at Red Clay Council Ground, Bradley County, Tennessee, 1832–1837." *Journal of Cherokee Studies* 2, no. 4 (Fall 1977): 344–56.

Speck, Frank G. "Decorative Art and Basketry of the Cherokee." *Bulletin of the Public Museum of the City of Milwaukee* 2, no. 2 (July 1920): 53–86.

———. "The Question of Matrilineal Descent in the Southeastern Siouan Area." *American Anthropologist* 40, no. 1 (1938): 1–13.

Stephens, George Myers. "The Beginnings of the Historical Drama 'Unto These Hills.'" *North Carolina Historical Review* 28, no. 2 (Apr. 1951): 212–18.

Stevens, William K. "How the Wolf is Being Heard Again in Old Haunts," *The New York Times*, Jan. 31, 1995.

Stringfield, William W. "North Carolina Cherokee Indians." *North Carolina Booklet* 3 (1903): 5–24. In *Annals of Haywood County*. Raleigh, N.C.: E. M. Uzell and Co., 1903.

Sturtevant, William C. "Louis-Philippe on Cherokee Architecture and Clothing in 1797." *Journal of Cherokee Studies* 3, no. 4 (1978): 198–205.

Swain, D. L. "Historical Sketch of the Indian War of 1776." *Historical Magazine* 2 (November 1867): 273–75.

Swayney, Arizona. "Basketmaking." 1902. Clipping. *Hampton Student Records Collection*, Hampton University Archives, Hampton, Va.

"Tennessee River Baptist Association, North Carolina." *The Bone Rattler* 6, no. 1 (Summer 1989): 40–46.

Thomas, Lindsay K., Jr. "The Impact of Three Exotic Plant Species on a Potomas Island." In *National Park Service Scientific Monograph Series, No. 13*. Washington, D.C.: U.S. Department of the Interior, 1980. Microfiche.

Thomas, William Holland. "Letter to Governor James Graham, Oct. 15, 1838." In *Historical Sketches of North Carolina from 1584 to 1851*, edited by John H. Wheeler, 205–6. Philadelphia: Lippincott, Grambo and Co., 1851.

Tobler, John. "John Tobler's Description of South Carolina," edited and translated by Walter C. Robbins. *South Carolina Historical Magazine* 71 (October 1970): 143–61.

Valentine, R. G. "Making Citizens of the Indians." *The Indian Craftsman* 1, no. 8 (Sept. 1909): 9–14.

"Wachacha, Maggie, Interview." *Journal of Cherokee Studies* 14 (1989): 46–50.

"Wachacha, Martha, Interview." *Journal of Cherokee Studies* 14 (1989): 51–57.

"Wachacha, Mose and Callie, Interview." *Journal of Cherokee Studies* 14 (1989): 58–62.

Waddell, Maude. "Horace Kephart." *Charlotte Observer*, October 1928.

Wahrhaftig, Albert L. "Making Do with the Dark Meat: A Report on the Cherokee Indians in Oklahoma." In *World Anthropology. American Economic Development*, edited by Sol Tax, 409–510. Paris: Mouton Publishers, The Hague, 1978. Distributed in U.S. by Aldine Publishing, Chicago.

———. "We Who Act Right: The Persistent Identity of Cherokee Indians." *Currents in Anthropology* (1979): 40–53.

"Walker, Game and Bessie, Interview." *Journal of Cherokee Studies* 14 (1989): 63–67.

Walters, Russell S., and Harry W. Yawney, "*Acer rubrum L.* Red Maple." In *Silvics of North America*. Vol. 2. USDA Forest Service *Agriculture Handbook 654*, 61–63. Washington, D.C.: Government Printing Office, 1990.

Webb, Stephen Saunders. "The Strange Career of Francis Nicholson." *William and Mary Quarterly*, 3rd ser., 23, no. 4 (October 1966): 513–48.

Wedgewood, Josiah. "An Expedition in Search of Cherokee Clay, 1767–68." In *The Colonial South Carolina Scene*, edited by Roy H. Merrens, 234–47. Columbia: University of South Carolina Press, 1977.

Wetmore, Ruth Y. "The Green Corn Ceremony of the Eastern Cherokees." *Journal of Cherokee Studies* 8, no. 1 (Spring 1983): 46–57.

White, Peter S. "Our Eastern Highlands." *The Nature Conservancy Magazine* 38, no. 2 (Mar./Apr. 1988): 7.

———. "Smoky Mountain Flora, Diversity in a Protected Landscape." In *Great Smoky Mountains National Park Official Golden Anniversary Book*. Gatlinburg, Tenn.: Oakley Enterprises, 1984.

Williams, Robert D. "*Juglans nigra* Black Walnut." In *Silvics of North America*. Vol. 2. USDA Forest Service *Agriculture Handbook 654*, 391–99. Washington, D.C.: Government Printing Office, 1990.

Williams, Samuel Cole. "An Account of the Presbyterian Mission to the Cherokees, 1751–1759." *Tennessee Historical Magazine* 1 (January 1931): 125–29.

Williams, Capt. W. G. "Military Intelligence Report on North Carolina Cherokees in 1838." *Journal of Cherokee Studies* 4, no. 4 (Fall 1979): 202–12.

Williams, Walter L. "The Merger of Apaches with Eastern Cherokees: Qualla in 1893." *Journal of Cherokee Studies* 2, no. 2 (Spring 1977): 240–46.

———. "Patterns in the History of the Remaining Southeastern Indians, 1840–1975." In *Southeastern Indians Since the Removal Era*, edited by Walter L. Williams, 193–211. Athens: University of Georgia Press, 1979.

Willnotah. "The Life and Memory and Death of My Brother *Yonah Gus Kah*. Feb. 21, 1844." *The Bone Rattler* 11, no. 2 (1995): 15–16.

Wilms, Douglas C. "Cherokee Land Use in Georgia." In *Cherokee Removal: Before and After*, edited by William Anderson, 1–28. Athens: University of Georgia Press, 1991.

Witthoft, John. "Bird Lore of the Eastern Cherokee." *Journal of the Washington Academy of Science* 36, no. 11 (1946): 372–84.

———. "Cherokee Indian Use of Potherbs." *Journal of Cherokee Studies* 2, no. 2 (Spring 1977): 250–55.

———. "An Early Cherokee Ethnobotanical Note." *Journal of the Washington Academy of Sciences* 37, no. 3 (1947): 73–75.

———. "Eastern Woodlands Community Topology and Acculturation." *Bureau of American Ethnology Bulletin 180* (1961): 67–76.

———. "Will West Long, Cherokee Informant." *American Anthropologist* 50 (1948): 355–59.

Wood, Peter. "The Changing Population of the Colonial South: An Overview by Race and Region, 1685–1790." In *Powhatan's Mantle*, edited by Peter Wood, Gregory A. Waselkov, and M. Thomas Hatley, 35–103. Lincoln: University of Nebraska Press, 1989.

Woods, Frank W., and Royal E. Shanks. "Natural Replacement of Chestnut by Other Species in the Great Smoky Mountains National Park." *Ecology* 40, no. 3 (July 1959): 349–61.

Young, Richard. "Solving the Indian Problem." *The Red Man* 3, no. 9 (May 1911): 392–94.

Young, Virginia D. "A Sketch of the Cherokee People on the Indian Reservation of North Carolina." *Woman's Progress* (Jan. 1984): 169–74.

Unpublished Works

Arnold, Dorothy. "Some Recent Contributions of the Cherokee Indians of North Carolina to the Crafts of the Southern Highlands." Master's thesis, University of Tennessee, 1981.

Banks, William A. "Ethnobotany of the Cherokee Indians." Master's thesis, University of Tennessee, 1953.

Bookout, Timmy Joe. "Traditional Basketmakers in the Southeastern and South Central United States." Ph.D. diss., Florida State University, 1987.

Cook, William Hinton. "A Grammar of North Carolina Cherokee." Ph.D. diss., Yale University, 1979.

Dickson, John Lois. "The Judicial History of the Cherokee Nation From 1721 to 1835." Ph.D. diss., University of Oklahoma, 1964.

Gearing, Frederick O. "Cherokee Political Organizations, 1730–1775." Ph.D. diss., University of Chicago, 1956.

Grant, John. "Behavioral Premises in the Culture of Conservative Eastern Cherokee Indians." Ph.D. diss., University of North Carolina, Chapel Hill, 1957.

Greene, Joan. "Federal Policies in the Schools of the Eastern Cherokees, 1892–1932." Master's thesis, Western Carolina University, 1986.

Gremillion, Kristen J. "Late Prehistoric and Historic Period Paleoethnobotany of the North Carolina Piedmont." Ph.D. diss., University of Tennessee, 1989.

Hill, Sarah H. "A Basket of History." Paper delivered at the Symposium on Cherokee History, Tahlequah, Okla., Sept. 1–3, 1993.

Horton, Wade Alston. "Protestant Missionary Women as Agents of Cultural Transition Among Cherokee Women, 1801–1839." Ph.D. diss., Southern Baptist Theological Seminary, 1992.

Jackson, Louise M. "Basketworks: Continuing Traditions in North America Traditional and Non-Traditional Basketry." Master's thesis, University of Michigan, 1982.

King, Duane Harold. "A Grammar and Dictionary of the Cherokee Language." Ph.D. diss., University of Georgia, 1975.

Marsh, Daniel Lee. "The Taxonomy and Ecology of Cane, Arundinaria Gigantea (Walter Muhlenberg)." Ph.D. diss., University of Arkansas, 1977.

Monteith, Carmaleta Littlejohn. "The Role of the Scribe in Eastern Cherokee Society, 1821–1985." Ph.D. diss., Emory University, 1985.

Neely, Sharlotte. "The Role of Formal Education Among the Eastern Cherokees, 1880–1971." Master's thesis, University of North Carolina, Chapel Hill, 1971.

Noble, Dorothy Louise. "Life of Francis Nicholson." Ph.D. diss., Columbia University, 1958.

Owl, Frell. "The Eastern Band of Cherokee Indians Before and After Removal." Ph.D. diss., University of North Carolina, 1929.

Ruff, Rowena McClinton. "To Ascertain the Mind and Circumstance of the Cherokee Nation, Springplace, Georgia, 1805–1821." Master's thesis, Western Carolina University, 1992.

Russell, Mattie. "William Holland Thomas, White Chief of the North Carolina Cherokee." Ph.D. diss., Duke University, 1956.

Ryan, Carmalita S. "The Carlisle Indian Industrial School." Ph.D. diss., Georgetown University, 1962.

Shearin, Marjorie. "A Study of Craft Programs in North Carolina Art Museum, Colleges and Universities, Craft Organizations, and Regional Craft Centers." Master's thesis, University of Tennessee, 1965.

Thomas, Robert K. "The Origin and Development of the Redbird Smith Movement." Ph.D. diss., University of Arizona, 1953.

Tingey, Joseph Willard. "Indians and Blacks Together: An Experiment in Biracial Education at Hampton Institute (1878–1923)." Ph.D. diss., Columbia Teacher's College, 1978.

Waselkov, Gregory A., John W. Cottier, and Craig T. Sheldon Jr., *Archaeological Excavations at the Early Historic Creek Indian Town of Fusihatchee, Phase I, 1988–1989*. Report to the National Science Foundation by University of South Carolina, Auburn University–Auburn, and Auburn University–Montgomery, 1990.

Index

Acorns, 10, 11, 20, 21, 23, 117, 118
Across the Smokies Highway, 278–79, 282
Adair, James: on fruits and nuts, 8, 10, 14, 82;
    on mat weaving, 9; on herbal medicine, 13;
    on vegetation growths, 15, 91; on Cherokee
    women, 18; on animal populations, 19–20,
    21–23, 24; on Cherokee clans, 28; on
    Cherokee marriage, 32, 33; on women's
    basketry, 54, 58, 59; on physical geography,
    61; on Cherokee houses, 69, 70; on
    Cherokee farming, 80, 82, 85
Adultery, 31, 32, 97
Agriculture, 160–61, 180–81; corn growing,
    61, 82, 180; *Selu* legend of, 79; women and,
    80–81, 82, 83, 84, 105, 168, 270–71, 341
    (n. 133); gardens, 80–82, 267; fields, 82–84;
    civilization program and, 89, 105, 317;
    cotton raising, 105; European practices,
    106–7; subsistence, 135, 180, 266–67;
    Cherokee Council and, 270–71
Ah-nee-cheh (Aroneach), 154, 161
A-lee, 148, 149
Alexis, 148, 149, 161
Allen, Tuskeegee, 251
Allen, Will, 251
American Indian Defense Association (AIDA),
    287, 367 (n. 109)
Aniline dye, 176, 194, 236–37, 355 (n. 172)
Animals, 1, 16–21, 25, 76–78, 106; scarcity of,
    91–93, 166–67. *See also* Livestock raising
Anjelica leaves, 42
Annihilation proposals, 206–7, 209
Anthropologists, xxi, 169–70, 176, 237
Appalachian Mountains, 2, 4, 5, 7, 8, 11, 16, 19,
    64, 92, 113, 118, 165, 166, 167, 188, 189,
    190, 221, 223, 266, 275, 276, 290, 296
Appalachian Railroad, 263, 266, 272
Apple trees, 81, 90
Armstrong, Drury, 151
Armstrong, Samuel A., 200–201, 207, 357
    (n. 33)
Artifact collecting, xxi, 169–70, 224–25, 237,
    265, 312–13

Arts and Crafts movement, xviii, 222, 253, 318
Asheville Rhododendron Show, 294, 295
Assimilation, 105, 237, 241–42; government
    policy and, xviii, 184, 199–200, 206–7, 209,
    253; schools and, 200, 201, 205, 207, 209,
    318; reform organizations and, 222; tourism
    and, 283
Atkin, Edmund, 59
Atlanta Cotton States Exposition (1895),
    241–42
Automobile lunch baskets, 249–50, 252
Ax, John, 2, 36, 76, 108, 163, 176, 314, 315
Axe, Josiah, 110, 111, 113, 137, 166
Ayasta (Spoiler), 154, 163, 169, 235–36; telling
    of creation story, 25, 26, 235, 315; baskets
    woven by, 130, 225, 236, 237, 238, 239,
    240, 241, 246, 247

Back basket. *See* Pack baskets
Ball game, 112, 141, 164, 235, 292, 331 (n. 61)
Bamboo baskets, xv, 236
Bartram, William, xx; on physical geography,
    5–6, 61; on berries and nuts, 9, 10, 14–15,
    153–54; on Cherokee women, 31, 74, 97;
    on vegetation growths, 39, 118, 186–87; on
    Cherokee houses, 71, 72, 114; on gardens
    and fields, 82, 83; on animal populations, 92
Basketry, xxi–xxii; scarcity of materials for, xv,
    254–56, 319, 320; materials used for, xvii,
    xviii, 41, 236, 316; and Cherokee history,
    xvii–xix; women and, xix–xx, xxi, 37–38,
    314, 315–16; classes in, 212–16, 285, 298,
    300, 312, 319
Basket trade. *See* Trade baskets
Bear, black, 8, 10, 11, 16, 19–20, 22, 23, 55, 60,
    71, 81, 92
Bear Paw, Tom, 149
Berry baskets, 170–71
Big Cove, 156, 190, 262, 271–73, 310
Big Cove Day School, 201, 272
Big Cove Farm Club, 244, 247
Bigmeat, Dora, 270, 271
Big Tellico, 90

Bigwitch, Eva, 198
Bingo games, 323, 370 (n. 28)
Bird, Solomon, 275
Birds, 15, 21–23, 166
Bird Town (Birdtown), 155, 244, 262, 265, 266, 352 (n. 114)
Birdtown Day School, 201, 265–66
Blacks, 162–63, 181, 355 (n. 183)
Blair, C. M., 295
Blankenship, Abe T., 219
Blankenship, Arizona Swayney, 216–21, 247, 272, 291, 300
Blankenship, Lillian, 221
Blankenship, Roy, 310
Blood, 13, 22, 25, 26, 27, 32, 33, 77, 79, 80, 94, 95, 160, 181, 334 (n. 117)
Bloodroot dye, 42, 43, 62, 126, 194
Blue Ridge Mountains, 4, 5, 316
Blythe, Stella, 203
Boarding schools, 198–209, 359 (n. 63); basketry courses, 212–16
Boudinot, Elias, 107, 345 (n. 212)
Boyd, D. L., 190
Bradley, Eva, 119
Bradley, George, xvi
Bradley, Helen, 125
Bradley, Henry, xvi, 123, 247
Bradley, Mary, xvi, xvii
Bradley, Nancy George, xv, xvi, 247, 251, 263, 264, 268, 269, 300
Bradley, Reva, 268
Bradley, Rowena, xv–xvi, xvii, 45, 251, 263, 269, 300
Bradley, Savetta Rowena, xvi, xvii
Bread making, 51–52, 230–31
Brewster, William, 165–67
Bryson City, N.C., 182. See also Charles Town
Buffalo, 16, 18, 20, 22, 39, 55, 63, 71, 81, 85, 91–92
Buffalo Baptist Church, 182, 275
Buffalo Town (Yunsa-i), 142, 153
Bullet, Nancy, 149
Burden basket. See Pack baskets
Bureau of Indian Affairs, 272, 287, 298
Burning Town, 87
Bushnell, David I., Jr., 337 (n. 49)
Butrick, Daniel S., 46, 51, 141, 142, 328 (n. 5), 332 (n. 80)
Butternut trees, 9; dye from, 42, 62, 296
Byrd, William, 16, 21, 39, 91

Cacica of Cofitachequi, 66
Calhoun, Morgan, 246
Campbell, Olive Dame, 290
Canoe basket, 223
Carlisle Indian Industrial School, 241, 253;

establishment of, 200; and Indian assimilation, 200, 205, 208, 209; student "outings" with white families, 209; native art classes, 213, 215
Carrying baskets, 127, 129. See also Pack baskets
Cartoogechaye Creek, 147–48
Catawba Indians, 158
Catesby, Mark, xx, 9, 39, 54–55, 58, 60, 91
Cathcart Survey, 156, 190
Cathey, Joseph, 176
Catolster, Eve, 112
Catolster, Sally Ann Saddle, 111, 112, 166
Cattle raising, 85, 91, 106, 275
Ceremonial basketry: rivercane, 45–49, 73; disappearance of, 151, 309, 317–18, 321
Charles Town (Charleston), 56, 67, 155, 165, 182. See also Bryson City, N.C.
Charlotta, 152, 153
Cheoah River, 141, 143, 145, 188
Cheoah township, 149, 274, 355 (n. 183)
Cheoah valley settlements, 149–52
Cherokee, N.C., 156, 262–63
Cherokee Boarding School, 262, 269, 299; establishment of, 201; curriculum, 201–2, 209, 215; students' labor at, 207–8, 210; and eradication of Cherokee language, 208–9, 287
Cherokee Council, 244, 291; and timber rights, 190, 270; school funding, 201; and road construction, 282
Cherokee County, N.C., 145–46, 262
Cherokee Fair, 246–47, 263, 296–97; establishment of, 244; basketry exhibits, 244–45, 247, 252, 269, 295
Cherokee Historical Association (CHA), 310, 311, 312, 313, 369 (n. 161)
Cherokee language, 27, 182; dialects, 67; Sequoyan syllabary, 139, 163, 168; attempts to eradicate, 208–9
Cherokee National Council: establishment of, 94; patrilineal inheritance, 96; and land cessions, 109, 146
Cherokee reservation: whites living on, 180–81; schools, 201–2, 284; stores, 250, 282, 303–4, 309, 320; population, 262; roads and, 276, 278–79, 282–83; tourist attractions, 310–13, 319, 320; unemployment on, 318, 322
Cherokees, 343 (n. 177); basketry tradition, xvii–xviii, 37–38, 44, 114; dependence on tourism, xix, 250, 263, 282, 294, 303, 313, 319, 322–23; interaction with whites and, xx, 65, 66, 67, 107; North Carolina population, xxi, 135, 147; anthropological studies of, xxi, 169–70, 176, 225; creation legends, 1–2, 3, 25–27; and water, 3, 4; settlements in

Southern Appalachians, 4–5, 7, 64, 67, 134; and mountains, 6; and forests, 8, 12; and fire, 12–13, 36–37, 61; and medicine, 13–14, 18; and animals, 17–18, 22; clans, 27, 28, 30, 95; marriage regulations, 30–31, 96–97, 162–63; trade with Europeans, 56–57, 59; wars with Europeans, 59, 74–75, 86–87; migration legend, 63–64; town construction, 69, 73–74; land cessions, 74, 75, 76, 94, 108–9, 132–33, 137; and farming, 79, 80–84, 106–7, 135, 160–61, 168, 180, 266–67, 270–71; livestock raising, 84–85, 106, 161; treaties with United States, 87–88, 89, 109, 137; civilization program and, 89–90, 95, 105–7, 109, 134–35, 184; intermarriage, 94, 153, 162–63, 181; adoption of laws and government, 95–96, 343 (n. 178); removal from Southeastern lands, 114–15, 132, 135–36, 137, 142, 144–48, 159–60, 347 (n. 39); state citizenship and life estates, 133–34, 136–37, 147; and Christianity, 134, 155; land ownership, 135, 136, 181; government surveys of, 136, 142, 144–45, 159–60; Civil War and, 164–65; education and, 168, 199, 200, 201, 208–9, 219, 284–85, 318; scarcity of employment for, 263, 303–4, 309, 318–19, 321–22, 324; income, 282, 322, 323

Chestnut trees, 10, 266, 270; blight, 266, 275, 319

Chicago World's Columbian Exposition (1893), 238–41

Children: clan system and, 26, 27, 30; women's responsibilities to, 29–30, 33, 34; inheritance rights, 96; schooling and, 200, 201–2, 204–6, 207–9, 269, 272, 318

Chiltoskey, Charlotte Hornbuckle, 244

Chota town, 90

Christianity, 89–90, 134, 155, 163, 201

Chu-tah-so-tih (James Woodpecker), 149

Citizenship: state, 133, 136–37, 147; American, 206, 207, 287

Civilization program, 89–90, 147; and agriculture, 89, 105, 317; and land cession, 89, 105–6, 109, 134–35; and clan revenge, 95; and private property, 95–96, 105; and cotton spinning and weaving, 105; and breakup of settlements, 107; boarding schools and, 199

Civil War, 164–65, 317

Clans, 22, 27, 28, 333 (n. 98); revenge responsibility, 28, 33, 95, 333 (n. 105); specializations, 30; and marriage restrictions, 30–31, 97, 163, 334 (n. 112); intermarriage and, 94

Clothes making, 9, 157, 161, 271

Clothes washing, 268

Cochran, Katy, 52

Coleman, Nancy, 209

Collier, Charles A., 241–42

Collier, Charles A., Jr., 303–4, 312–13

Collier, John, 283; and New Deal for Native Americans, xix, 253, 286, 294; appointed as Indian commissioner, 242, 286; background, 286–87, 366 (n. 102); promotion of native handicrafts, 288, 292, 296

Collins, D. K., 250

Collins, Robert, 143, 156

Committee on Indian Arts and Crafts, 288–89

Conot, Tom, 156

Conseen, Carolyn, 291

Conseen, Nancy, 186

Cooper, Stacy, 268

Cooper, W. H., 250

Corn, 79–80; festivals honoring, 31, 48, 64, 80, 84, 93; farming, 61, 82, 180

Corn cribs, 70

Cornmeal, 50–51, 52

Cotton production, 105

Cowee Middle Town, 72, 114

Craft revival movement, xviii, 290, 295–96

Craft shops, 282, 290, 303, 304, 309, 320

Creation legend, 1–2, 25

Creek Indians, 29, 75, 97; Red Stick revolt, 140

Crockett, David, 92–93

Crowe, John Henry, 207

Crowe, Richard, 206, 208

Cucumber, Emmaline, 110

Cucumber, Frances, 199

Cuhtahlatah, 29

Culsatehee, 115

Curls, 245, 257–58

Cut-clo-clena, 152

Davis, Rebecca Harding, 167–69

Dawes Severalty Act (1887), 199

DeBrahm, William, 7–8, 16, 69, 70

Decoration: on basket surfaces, 245, 257–60, 309, 321; as function of baskets, 249, 260–62, 304–9, 319, 320, 321

Deer, white-tail, 8, 10, 16, 19, 20, 22, 71, 92

Deerskin trade, 56, 64, 84

Deer Town, 155

Demere, Paul, 59

Demere, Raymond, 81, 85–86

Disease: plant medicines for, 13, 18, 93; origins of, 18, 25; white settlement and, 65, 67; smallpox epidemics, 67, 74, 165; Civil War and, 165

Dobson, Joseph, 156

Dobson, Mary, xv, xvi

Domestic baskets, 113, 269, 321; rivercane, 49–55; white oak, 114, 129, 131, 227–32
Doubleday, Neltje, 213, 216, 221, 223
Doubleweave technique, 44, 99, 176, 217–19, 294, 300
Douglas, Clem, 290
Drought, 83, 84, 341 (n. 139)
Dudgeon, Rich, 74
Duncan, William H., 260, 363 (n. 13)
Dunlap, C. Y., 250
DuPree, Betty Craig, 309
Dyeing: vegetable dyes, 42, 62, 124–26, 298; colors, 42, 126–27, 176, 257, 296, 319; mordants, 42–43, 126; in white oak, 124; in clothes making, 157; aniline dye, 176, 194, 236–37, 355 (n. 172); in honeysuckle, 194; in red maple, 257; commercial versus vegetable, 285, 288, 295–96, 319

Eagles, 23, 93, 167
Eagle Tail Dance, 23
Eastern Band of Cherokees, xxi, 134, 165, 178, 194, 237, 309, 310, 313
Eaton, Allen, 290
Echota Methodist Church, 155
Echoy Middle Town, 75
Education, 168, 219; clan responsibility for, 30; federal policies, 184, 253, 357 (n. 35); boarding schools, 198–209, 212, 216; and assimilation, 200, 201, 205, 207, 209, 318; industrial training and home economics, 201–2, 206, 209, 212, 284–85, 318; basketry courses, 212–16, 285, 298, 300, 312, 319; day schools, 269, 284–85
Egwanee town, 134
Elk, 91, 92
Employment, 153, 158; road construction, 143–44; school training and, 201–2, 206, 209; logging, 263, 303; tourism and, 263, 303–4, 309, 319, 321, 322; scarcity of, 275, 289, 304, 318–19, 321–22, 324; public relief work, 294; World War II and, 303
Enloe, Abraham and Asaph, 154
Ethnologists, xxi, 169–70, 225, 237
Etowah town, 106, 108
Euchella v. Welch (1824), 136
European settlers, xviii, 106–7; and forest resources, 7–8; and Cherokee women, 31, 66, 341 (n. 133); and deerskin trade, 56; and Cherokee basket trade, 56, 57, 58, 59; wars with Cherokees, 59, 74–75, 86–87; diseases from, 65, 67; and horses, 84; firing of vegetation, 91; and hunting, 92; patriarchal authority, 97; basketry traditions, 113–14, 118, 127

Fairs, 244, 292, 319; North Carolina State Fair, 247, 252; Atlanta Southeastern Fair (1934), 292–94; Cherokee Fair and Folk Festival, 296; San Francisco Fair (1938), 303. *See also* Cherokee Fair
Famine, 31, 40, 83, 341 (n. 139)
Feathers, 6, 22, 23, 35, 47, 93, 114, 268, 323
Festivals, 12–13, 22, 37, 47, 48, 73, 93; corn, 31, 48, 64, 80, 84, 93
Field, Clarke, 236, 360 (n. 99)
Fields, 82–84, 268
Fire: ritual, 12–13, 36–37; and vegetation growth, 16, 60, 61, 91, 117–18; First Fire legend, 35–37, 61, 314–15, 324; lightning and, 61; in houses, 70, 71–72, 315; forest destruction, 190, 273–74, 318
"First Fire, The," 35–37, 61, 314–15, 324
First New Moon of Spring festival, 12, 19, 37
Fish, Nathaniel, 115
Fisher, Frankie, 291
Fishing, 23–24, 182; baskets for, 24, 171, 174
Flanagan, Gertrude, 284–85, 291–92, 302; and basketry classes, 285, 297–98, 301; and basket prices, 295, 303, 304, 309; and natural dyes, 296, 304
Floods, 60, 61
Fodderstack, Jennie, 247, 249
Foght, Harold W., 265, 273, 282, 283, 293–95, 296–97, 298, 362–63 (n. 1)
Food: gathered from forests, 8–9, 10, 65–66; women's responsibility for, 10, 22, 54, 78, 79, 85, 269–70, 275–76, 315; baskets for, 48, 49–55, 61–62, 170–71, 315
Forests, 7–12, 15–16, 66, 144–45, 166; foods gathered from, 8–9, 10, 65–66; fires and, 16, 61, 190, 273–74, 318; destruction of, 184, 189–90, 254, 318; logging industry and, 188–90, 318, 319; economic dependence on, 266–67, 270
French, Annie, 322
French, Christopher, 75–76, 86–87
French, Morgan, 205
Fyffe, William, 28, 29, 73, 97

Gambling, 323–24
Gambold, John, and Anna R., 97, 99, 333 (n. 99)
Gardens, 80–82, 149, 268
Garnett, Ethel, 283–84, 303
Gender roles, xviii, 90, 120, 131, 317, 341 (n. 133)
George, Aggie Wilnoty, 268, 269, 271, 300
George, Dinah, 259, 260, 262–63, 268, 269, 324
George, Elizabeth, 251
George, Lucy Nola, 191–92, 193, 197, 217, 221, 253, 259, 267
George, Mary, 236, 242
George, Sarah, 270

Georgia, 108–9, 132, 135–36, 137, 348 (nn. 50, 52)
Gilliam, Sam, 297–98, 303
Girls, 29–30, 34, 268; boarding schools and, 201, 202, 206, 209
Goings, Louise, xxii, 124–26, 321, 322, 324
Gold prospecting, 137, 139, 145
Goodrich, Frances Louisa, 223–24, 290
Graham County, N.C., 181, 184, 205, 262, 274
Grant, James, 76, 86, 137
Grant, Rebecca, 191
Grapes, wild, 14
Grapevine baskets, 197
"Grasshopper chiefs," 323
Gray, Asa, 118, 187
Great New Moon of Autumn Feast, 14, 37
Great Smoky Mountains, 4, 189, 278–79, 328 (n. 6)
Great Smoky Mountains National Park, xix; establishment of, 263, 265, 276, 278, 290; and tourism, 263, 278, 282, 295, 319; and road construction, 276; commercialism of, 278, 290, 319
Green Corn Festival, 22, 31, 64, 73, 84, 93
Groves, Edna, 283–84, 285, 294, 302, 309, 366 (n. 94)

Hacklander, Sarah, 273–74 .
Hall, George Rogers, 187
Hampton Institute, 200–201, 253, 357 (n. 35); and assimilation of Native Americans, 201, 208, 209; basketry classes, 213, 215, 216, 219, 220, 221
Handles, basket, 43, 127–29, 172, 294, 309, 320
Harrington, M. R., 51, 52, 54, 225, 245, 251–52, 253
Haskell Institute, 200
Hastings, Theophilus, 57, 336 (n. 40)
Hawkins, Benjamin, 39, 98, 105, 108
Hayman, Vivian, 296
Hayt, Ezra A., 201, 359 (n. 63)
Henderson, James, 205, 235; on Cherokee basketry, 236, 244–45, 247–48, 250–51, 252, 362 (n. 158); and fair exhibits, 243, 244, 246, 247
Henessa, David, 153
Hickory nuts, 9, 10
Hicks, Charles, 93, 345 (n. 212)
Highway 19, 282–83
Highway 441, 282
Hill, Ettie, 112, 252, 253
Hiwassee River, 5, 64, 118, 145
Hiwassee Town, 90, 106
Hog raising, 65, 85, 91, 106, 161, 275
Home economics classes, 284–85
Honeysuckle, 186–87; Japanese, xviii, 187–88, 190, 193, 266; trumpet, 187; and ecological disruption, 188, 190–91, 266, 318
Honeysuckle basketry, 224, 236, 247; adoption of, xviii–xix, 191–93, 194–98, 221, 318; decorative and trade function of, 185–86, 192–93, 194, 249, 251, 252–53; gathering and preparation of materials, 193–94; dyeing, 194; surface decorations, 260; prices for, 324
Hopewell, Treaty of (1785), 342 (n. 158)
Hornbuckle, Charley, 154
Hornbuckle, Jefferson, 154, 161
Hornbuckle, Lucy, 54
Horses, 65, 84, 91, 106
Hot houses, 70–72, 108
Household furnishings, 70, 108
Houser, Helen, 221
Houses, 69–70, 107–8, 148, 267; summer, 69; winter, 70–72, 108
"How They Came on This Maine," 62–63
"How the World Was Made," 1, 25, 315
Humans, origin of, 25–26
Hunter, Kermit: *Unto These Hills*, 310
Hunting, 17, 92

I-hun-li, 180
Incest, 26, 30
Indian Arts and Crafts Board, 289, 304
"Indian Peggy," 32–33
Indian Removal Act (1830), 134
Inheritance rights, 95–96, 162
Ino-li (Blackfox), 155, 161, 162, 168
Intermarriage, 94, 153, 162–63, 181

Jackson, Andrew, 134, 140
Jackson, Ed, 275
Jackson, Ella Long, 275
Jackson County, N.C., 141, 205, 322
James, George Wharton, 222, 223, 245
Jefferson, Thomas, 95–96, 98, 108–9
Jenkins, Mac, 263
Jenkins, Myrtle Cooper, 260, 268
Jennings, Joe, 303, 304, 310
Jones, Evan, 134
Jones, John, 57–58
Jumper, Bessie, 274, 276
Junaluska (*Tsunu-lahunski*), 140, 349 (n. 67)

Kaloniskee, Tom, 251
Kanane-ski Amai-yehi, 36, 48, 49, 314, 315, 324
Kana-ti, 76, 77
Katal-sta, 139
Katteuka, 88
Keener, Rev. Ulrich B., 154–55
Keowee River, 4
Keowee town, 9, 86
Kingfisher, 29
Kinsey, Lucretia, 248, 252

Kitchen Lumber Company, 189
Kitu-hwa (Kittuwah) town, 5, 76, 155
Ko-hi, 110, 127, 129, 131, 145
Kul-lo-nos-kih, 155
Kulsathee, 105, 107, 108
Kwa-li, 134

Land auctions, 133
Land cessions, 74, 75, 76, 94, 108–9, 132–33,
    137, 147; civilization program and, 89,
    105–6, 109, 134–35; government trade
    policy and, 98
Land clearing, 76
Land grants, 94, 156
Land ownership, 33–34, 89–90, 136, 162
Lanman, Charles, 161, 164, 350 (n. 90)
Lan-zi, 168
Laurel Branch, 110
Laws, 95–96, 135–36
Lids, basket, 43, 129, 131, 176
Life estates, 133–34, 136, 347–48 (n. 40)
Lightning, 35, 61
Little Tennessee River, 5, 64, 76, 188, 303
Livestock raising, 84–85, 90–91, 105, 106,
    153, 161, 274–75
Logging, xviii, 188–89, 253; and environmental
    destruction, 189–90, 318, 319; and forest
    fires, 190, 273–74, 318; and Cherokee
    employment, 263, 303
Log houses, 107, 108, 148, 267
Long, Adam, 251
Long, Bessie Catolster, 110, 111–13, 184;
    on basket trade, 111, 309, 321, 324; on
    basketweaving methods, 112, 122, 124, 126,
    129, 131, 254; on clothes making, 271; on
    jobs, 322, 324
Long, John, 251, 252
Long, Posey, 110, 112–13, 184
Long, Will West, 163, 169, 225
Long Blanket, 154
Longe, Alexander, 61, 63, 83, 330 (n. 39);
    on Cherokee rituals, 12, 18, 19, 84; on
    Cherokees and animals, 18, 19, 106; on
    Cherokee women and marriage, 29–30, 31,
    34, 97; on Cherokees and foods, 67, 81
Long Island, Treaty of (1781), 87
Long Person, 3, 316
Loom weaving, 284
Lossiah, Aggie Ross, 210–12, 215
Lossiah, Betty Long, 254, 255–56, 258, 260,
    283, 303, 304
Lossiah, Charlotte Welch, 273
Lossiah, Henry, 210
Lossiah, Lucille, 255, 261
Loudon, Fort, 33, 59, 76, 86
Louis-Philippe (king of France), 24, 98
Love, Margaret, 165
Lowen, 149

Lower Towns, 4, 67, 69, 84; land cession from,
    76; British burning of, 86
Lufty Indians, 134
Lyttleton, William Henry, 59, 86

Mammals, 16–17, 20, 166–67
Maple trees, 256; sugar, 11; red, 256–57, 263,
    266. *See also* Red maple basketry
Market baskets, 320
Marriage: clan restrictions on, 30–31, 97,
    163, 334 (n. 112); women's autonomy in,
    31, 32, 97, 163; polygyny, 33, 96–97, 162;
    intermarriage, 94, 153, 162–63, 181
Martin, Betsy, 107, 108
Matrilineage, 163; and clan identity, 27; incest
    and, 30; and women's economic security, 32,
    33; matrilineal ownership and inheritance,
    33–34, 95–96, 162; intermarriage and, 94,
    96; clan revenge and, 95
Matrilocal residence, 34, 161
Mat weaving, 9, 40, 71, 72–73
Medicine, 48; from plants, 10, 13, 18, 93;
    women and, 10, 13–14, 93; origin of, 25
Meigs, Return J., 105, 106
Men, 3, 4; and farming, xviii, 105, 317; and
    basketweaving, xviii, 120, 122, 317, 319;
    warfare and hunting, 17; and children's
    education, 30
Menstruation, 32, 334 (n. 117)
Meriam report (*Problem of Indian Administration*),
    287–88, 309–10
Michaux, André, xx
Michaux, François André, xx, 39, 91, 118
Middle Towns, 5, 67, 75, 76, 338 (n. 78); British
    burning of, 86–87, 133, 137; land cessions
    in, 132, 133
Missionaries, xx, 89, 99, 134; and Cherokee
    clan relations, 27; and Cherokee marriages,
    96, 97; and Cherokee ball games, 164
Missionary Herald, 97
Mohonk Annual Conference of the Friends of
    the Indian, 219, 221
Montgomery, Archibald, 86
Montgomery, Fort, 141, 151–52
Mooney, James, xxi, 169, 328 (n. 1); records of
    Cherokee legends, 2, 25, 36, 77, 108, 176,
    235, 314, 316; collection of Cherokee
    baskets, 176–78, 235, 236, 246
Moore, William, 265
Moravian missionaries, 97
Mordants, 42–43, 126
Mulberries, 8–9
Mullay, John C., 159–61
Murphy, N.C., 141, 165
Museum of the Cherokee Indian, 313

Na-kih, 155
Nane-hi (Nancy), 29

Nantahala River, 118, 143
National Park Service, 282
Native Americans: assimilation policies and, xviii, 199–200, 201, 205, 206–7, 209, 222, 237; tourist promotion and, xix, 283, 323; ethnological interest in, xxi, 170, 237; trade with white settlers, 56, 98; European diseases and, 67; land cessions, 98; boarding schools for, 198–209, 357 (n. 35); native languages prohibited, 208–9; handicraft arts, 215–16, 221, 222, 283, 288–89, 318, 319; social reform movement and, 221–22, 223; sense of community, 286; U.S. citizenship, 287; Meriam report on, 287–88; gambling businesses, 323–24
Ned, Susan, 169
New Deal for Native Americans, xix, 253, 286, 294
New Echota, Treaty of (1836), 114–15, 135, 137, 141, 159, 343–44 (n. 185)
Nicea, 161
Nicholson, Sir Francis, 336 (n. 48); Cherokee basket collection, 38, 58, 59, 99, 299, 302
Nick, John, 216
Nick, Laura, 216
Nick, Lorenzo, 216
Nikwasi mound, 133
North Carolina, 239; Cherokee population, xxi, 135, 147; eradication of wolves, 92; Cherokee land cessions to, 132–33, 136; state citizenship for Indians, 133, 136–37, 147; land sales to white settlers, 133, 144; removal of Cherokees, 135, 136, 137, 145–46, 317; prohibition of intermarriage, 181; and Great Smoky Mountains Park, 278
North Carolina General Assembly, 144, 145–46, 283
North Carolina Hall of History, 225, 233
Norton, John, 90, 93, 97, 105, 106, 108
Nottely town, 141
Nunnehi, 133, 142
Nununyi town, 265
Nun-yunu-wi. See Stone Man
Nut trees, 9–10, 11

Oak trees, 8; white, 11, 113–14, 117–18; acorns from, 11, 117, 118; dye from, 42; white, scarcity of, 254, 255–56, 257
Oconaluftee Indian Village, 311–12
Oconaluftee River, 132–33, 134, 136, 190
Oconee Mountains, 5, 118
Old Estatoe Middle Town, 74
Old Grass, 153
Olds, Fred, 225–27, 232–35, 250
Olt-kinne, 180
Oos-kel-lo-kih (Hogbite), 148
Oostanaula town, 106
Oo-tla-no-teh, 168

"Origin of Game and Corn, The," 76–80
Overhill Towns, 5, 67, 69, 80; British burning of, 87; land cessions from, 132, 133
Owl, Frell, 246
Owl, Lula, 268
Owl, Sampson, 250, 263, 271
Owle, Mary, 291

Pack, Sophia Moody, 101, 151
Pack baskets, 49, 128, 176–78, 179, 225, 226, 238, 300, 307
Paint Town (Painttown), 154, 262, 267, 268, 269, 352 (n. 111)
Palisades, 73–74
Palmer, Edward, 170, 171–72
Pardo, Juan, 66–67
Patterns, weaving, 300–302, 309, 312; rivercane, 43–44, 59, 99, 101, 127, 260, 317; white oak, 127, 309; red maple, 258–60
Payne, John Howard, 71, 79–80, 328 (n. 5)
Peach trees, 81–82
Perkins, William, 176
Persimmons, 8
Pestle and mortar, 51, 53, 225, 229
Phillips, Ruth, 133–34
Picking basket, 223
Piedmont Plateau, 4, 94, 316, 317
Pigeons, passenger, 21, 167
Pigs. *See* Hog raising
Pilgrim Dance, 164
Pine Log village, 98, 105
Pine trees, 8, 10–11
Plants, 14–16, 25; medicine from, 10, 13, 18, 93
Pokeweed, 15; dye from, 42, 59, 62
Polygamy, 96–97, 162
Polygyny, 33, 96–97, 162
Potter, Thomas, 202, 204, 241–42
Pottery classes, 285
Poverty, 270, 289
Pratt, Richard Henry, 200, 205, 241, 357 (n. 30)
Pretty Woman Town, 155
Prices, basket, 252, 303, 309, 320, 324, 362 (n. 158)
Priesthood, 30, 46–47
Prince George, Fort, 85–86
Property rights, 32, 95–96, 136
Propitiation and Purification Festival (*Ah-tawh-hung-nah*), 12–13, 14, 47–48, 73, 332 (n. 80)
Purse baskets, 172, 305

Quakers, 201, 265
Qualla Arts and Crafts Cooperative, 304, 320
Qualla Boundary, xxi, 225, 227, 328 (n. 1); townships in, 262, 265; employment in, 322; gambling business, 323–24
Quallatown, 134, 146, 147, 154; citizen Indians in, 136; roads to, 143, 167, 184, 319;

livestock raising in, 161; ball games at, 164; sale of timber rights, 190; blacks in, 355 (n. 183)
Quallatown Store, 140; records of Cherokee trade at, 156–59
Queen, Levi, 298
Queen, Mary, 298

Racism, 162, 181
Raffia basketry, 213
Railroads, 182, 271, 318
Ramps, 269
Rattler, Henson, 275
Raven town, 155–56
Red maple basketry, xix, 257–62, 309, 319
Reel, Estelle, 212, 215, 223
Removal, 132, 135–36, 137, 142, 144–48, 159–60
Reservations, xix, xxi, 207
Revenge, clan, 28, 33, 95, 333 (n. 105)
Rib basketry, 129–31, 176, 177, 317
Richardson, William, 73
Richmond, Steve, 309
Ridge, John, 96, 107, 343–44 (n. 185)
Rims, basket, 43, 172, 309, 320–21
Rivercane, 37–40, 60–62; destruction of, 90–91
Rivercane basketry, xviii, 40–41, 99–105, 114–15, 131, 151, 179–80, 316; gathering and preparation of materials, 41–42, 60, 61–62; dyeing, 42–43, 62; lids, 43; handles, 43, 172; rims, 43, 172; weaving patterns, 43–44, 59, 99, 101, 127, 260, 317; doubleweaving, 44, 99; strength and durability of, 44–45, 58; ceremonial baskets, 45–49, 73; domestic baskets, 49–55; trade baskets, 55, 56, 57–60, 98, 99; scarcity of materials for, 251, 317; prices for, 303, 324
Rivercane mats, 40, 47–48
Road construction, 142, 272–73, 276; Cherokee employment on, 143–44; and tourism, 278–79, 282–83
Robbinsville, N.C., 181
Ross, John, 137
Ross, Martha Lossiah, 127, 258, 296, 324
Running Wolf, 115

Salo-la, 154
Sanders, Polly, 159
Sand Town Cherokees, 148, 161
San Francisco Panama Pacific Exposition (1915), 242–43
Saunooke, Margaret, 245, 246
Saunooke, Nancy, 225
Schenck, David, 182, 224
Schneider, Martin, 21, 52, 76, 97

Schweinitz, Frederic de, 90, 98, 108
Scott, Peggy, 99, 109, 194
Sells, Cato, 242–43, 244
Selu, 76, 77, 78–79, 80, 315, 324
Sequoyah, Mollie Runningwolfe, 53
Sequoyan syllabary, 139, 163, 168
Serving baskets, 54–55
Sexual freedom, 31–32, 163
Sherrill, Samuel P., 152, 153, 158
Sieves, 52–54, 170, 227
Sikwa-yi (Sequoyah), 139
Siler, William, 147–48, 351 (n. 92)
Slave ownership, 135
Sloane, Sir Hans, 9, 58, 59
Smallpox, 67, 74, 165
Smith, Betty, 291
Smith, Emily, 196, 305
Smith, Helen Bradley, 258
Smith, Jarrett, 291
Smith, Nan, 291
Smith, Nathaniel, 136
Smith, Nimrod Jarrett, 180
Smithsonian Institution, 170, 176, 213
Smoky Mountain Turnpike, 143
Snakes, 24–25
Sneed, Mary, 205–6
Snowbird Cherokees, 262, 274–75, 276, 322
Snowbird Day School, 201, 274
Snowbird Mountains, 142
Society of Friends, 201
Soco Creek, 110, 139
Soco Day School, 201, 269
Soco valley, 154, 167, 352 (n. 111)
Southern Highland Handicraft Guild, 289–92, 298, 367–68 (n. 127)
Southern Workman, 213, 215, 219
Sowenosgeh, 168
Spalsbury, Ross L., 272–73, 284, 291, 362–63 (n. 1)
Spanish invaders, 64–68, 81
Speck, Frank, xxi, 236, 321, 361 (n. 118); Decorative Art and Basketry of the Cherokee, 236
Spencer, Andrew, 240
Spinning wheels, 105
Spray, H. W., 204–5, 206, 208–9, 215
Springplace Mission, 99, 103–5, 194, 344 (n. 201)
Squirrel, George, 191
Squirrel, Kimsey, 251
Squirrel, Lydia Ann Thompson, 267
Stamper, Bill, 298
Stamper, Lottie Queen, 297–300, 302–3, 312, 319
Stamper, Mrs. Ned, 291
Standingdeer, Annie, 279
Standingdeer, Lowen, 251

Stanion, Ralph, 266
Starr, Frederick, 240
Stecoa town, 86–87, 137–39
Steiner, Abraham, 90, 95, 98, 108
Stone Man (*Nun-yunu-wi*), 6, 13
Storage baskets, 50, 61–62, 171, 173
Storehouses, 70
Strawberries, 14–15
Stuart, John, 17, 28
Sumac, 15, 42
Swain County, N.C., 182, 205, 322
Swayney, Arizona. *See* Blankenship, Arizona
    Swayney
Swayney, John, 216
Swayney, Lucina, 51
Sweet potatoes, 81
Swimmer (*Ayun-ini*), 2, 36, 76, 154, 176, 181,
    314, 315

Tahquette, John H., 250, 252, 263, 271
Tail, Jim, 233, 234
Taylor, Emma Squirrel, 121, 262, 267, 306, 312;
    on basketweaving methods, 120, 122, 254,
    285, 320, 321
Taylor, Jonathan L., 323
Taylor, Lizzie, 203, 209
Taylor, Rebecca, 191
Taylor, Shirley, 122, 124, 127, 260, 320
Techeskee, Jessie, 210–12
Techeskee, Sela, 210
Tellico town, 98
Tel-tlua-gih, 149
Tennessee, 135, 136, 278; Cherokee land
    cessions to, 94, 132; removal of Cherokees,
    137
Tennessee River, 4–5, 23, 46, 87
Tennessee Valley Authority (TVA), 290, 303
Teyoet-lih, 149
Thomas, William H., 145, 161, 349 (n. 61);
    stores owned by, xxi, 140, 141, 142, 151–52,
    156–58; as Indian agent, 137, 139, 140, 147,
    159; landholdings, 137–39; in Civil War,
    139–40; demise of, 140, 165, 317; and road
    construction, 142, 143, 144; employment of
    Cherokees, 143, 153; land purchases for
    Cherokees, 147, 154, 162; and ball games,
    164
Timber industry, xviii, 188–89, 253; and
    environmental destruction, 189–90, 318,
    319; and forest fires, 190, 273–74, 318; and
    Cherokee employment, 263, 303
Timberlake, Henry, 328 (n. 5); on animal
    populations, 16–17, 21, 23, 24; on Cherokee
    women, 29, 32, 33, 71, 74, 332 (n. 80); on
    Cherokee baskets, 55; on Cherokee houses,
    70, 71, 72; on Cherokee farming, 80, 85

Tiyohib, 153
Tlanusi-yi (Leech Place), 141
Toineeta, Nick, 251
Toineeta, Pearl, 291, 298–99, 300
Tools, 6–7, 152, 157
Tooni, Ollie, 279
Tourism: economic dependence on, xix, 250,
    282, 294, 303, 319, 322–23; and basket
    trade, 249–51, 257, 309, 320, 324, 325;
    Cherokee Fair and, 263; Great Smoky
    Mountains Park and, 263, 278, 282, 295,
    319; and employment, 263, 303–4, 309, 319,
    321, 322; road construction and, 278–79,
    282–83; tourist postcards, 280–81, 282;
    and native handicraft production, 282, 283,
    303, 304, 309–10, 319, 324; and Indian
    assimilation, 283; historical attractions,
    310–13, 319–20
Town houses, 12, 72–73, 93, 149, 163–64
Towns, 69, 74, 107, 338 (n. 78); British
    destruction of, 76, 86–87
Trade, 56–57, 273; store accounts, xxi, 151–53,
    156–59; women and, 32–33, 56, 85–86, 98;
    federal policy and, 98; missionaries and,
    99
Trade baskets, 103; rivercane, 55, 56, 57–60,
    98, 99; white oak, 111, 169, 317; importance
    in family economy, 151, 192–93, 251, 263,
    271, 276, 317, 321; honeysuckle, 185–86,
    192–93, 194, 249, 251, 252–53; fairs and,
    247–49, 269, 319; tourism and, 249–51,
    257, 309, 320, 324, 325; prices for, 251–52,
    320, 324; red maple, 260, 262; ornamentation
    of, 260, 304–9, 320
Treaties, 87, 89, 109, 131–32
Treaty of 1817, 109, 132
Trees, 7–13, 61, 69, 240
Tsali, legend of, 350 (n. 90)
Tse-ghisini, 165
Tsunu-lahunski. See Junaluska, 140, 349 (n. 67)
Tuckasegee River, 5, 76, 132–33
Tuckasegee valley, 188
Tumplines, 49, 127, 128
Turkey, wild, 22–23
Twill weave, 43, 103, 127, 172
Tyner, Rachel, 214

Uk-tena, 25
Ulunsu-ti, 46
Unaka Mountains, 4, 142, 328 (n. 6)
Underwood, Tom, 44
Unemployment, 322
United States: treaties with Cherokees, 87–88,
    89, 109, 137; population growth, 94;
    Congress, 136, 159, 348 (n. 52); Department
    of Agriculture, 290

Utensils, 70
U-tlun-ta, 6, 329 (n. 11)

Valentine, Robert G., 206–7, 209
Valentine brothers, 224–25, 265
Valley River, 5, 141, 142, 143, 145, 160
Valley Town, 142, 355 (n. 183)
Valley Towns, 5, 76, 87, 107, 338 (n. 78)
Vann, James, 99, 108, 344 (n. 199)
Vine baskets, 103–4, 185–86, 191, 194–98, 225–27, 236–37, 252
Voting rights, 270

Wachacha, Callie, 274
Wachacha, Maggie Axe, 275
Wachacha, Martha Welch, 198, 275
Wadi-yahi, 176
Walker, Felix, 139, 140, 156
Walker, Game, 275–76
Walkingstick, Alice, 49, 131
Walnuts, 10
Walnut trees, 9; dyes from, 42, 43, 62, 124, 194; scarcity of, 189
Ward, Nancy, 29, 87, 88, 109, 146
Warfare, 17, 28–29, 74–75
Washington, George, 88–89
Water, 1, 2–4, 314, 316
Watermelons, 81
Watty, Elsie, 305
Waya Gap, 148
Waynesville, N.C., 133, 271
Weaving, 2, 37, 38, 315
Webster, N.C., 133, 140–41, 144
Welch, Agnes, xxii, 126, 300, 307, 324
Welch, Andrew, 156
Welch, Betty, 204
Welch, Carol, 308
Welch, Dinah Calhoun, 246
Welch, Edward, 153
Welch, Epps, 251
Welch, Maude, 285, 291
White oak basketry, 303, 319; European influence, xviii, 113, 114, 118, 127; functions of, 111, 114, 169, 171–72, 179, 251, 317–18; gathering and preparation of materials, 120–24; dyeing, 124–27; weaving patterns, 127, 309; handles, 127–29; rib baskets, 129–31; in honeysuckle baskets, 194; scarcity of materials for, 254, 255–56, 257; surface decorations, 260, 309

Whiteside Mountain, 6, 166
Whittier, N.C., 137
Williams, W. G., 142–43, 144–45, 146
Willinawaw, 33
Willnota, 197
Willow baskets, 224, 236
Wilowisteh, 168
Winnowing baskets, 24, 50, 51, 228
Witchcraft, 78–79
Witthoft, John, xxi
Woleyohah, 152
Wolfe, Dinah, 306
Wolf Town (Wolftown), 154, 190, 262, 269, 352 (n. 111)
Wolves, 18–19, 92–93
Women, xviii, 9; and basketry, xix–xx, xxi, 37–38, 314, 315–16; and water, 3, 4; and medicine, 10, 13–14, 93; responsibility for food, 10, 22, 54, 78, 79, 85, 269–70, 275–76, 315; and animals, 17, 24; authority of, 22, 66, 88, 97, 163; in creation legend, 25, 26–27; and clan relations, 27, 28; as warriors, 29; responsibilities to children, 29–30, 33, 34; autonomy of, 31, 32, 34; sexual freedom, 31–32, 97, 163; and marriage, 32, 33, 97; property ownership, 32, 33–34, 96; and trade, 32–33, 56, 85–86, 98; and fire, 37, 70, 315; domestic responsibilities, 49, 70, 275–76; and agriculture, 80–81, 82, 83, 84, 105, 168, 270–71, 341 (n. 133); intermarriage, 94, 162–63; civilization program and, 105; and gender roles, 120; removal deaths, 146; voting rights, 270
Wood, Abraham, 38
Worcester, Samuel, 108
Work, Hubert, 287
World War II, 295, 303
Wright's Creek, 269
Wyman, Louvica, 312

Yellow Hill, 155, 156, 262, 265, 271
Yellowroot dye, 42, 124–26
Yonaguska, 139, 154, 197, 349 (n. 61)
Yonah-cunna-heet (Long Bear), 148, 149
Young, Virginia, 180
Youngbird, Nannie, 291
Young Wolf, 182
Yunsa-i. See Buffalo Town